Lecture Notes in Computer Science

Edited by G. Goos and J. Hartmanis

202

Rewriting Techniques and Applications

Dijon, France, May 20–22, 1985

Edited by Jean-Pierre Jouannaud

Springer-Verlag
Berlin Heidelberg New York Tokyo

Editor

Jean-Pierre Jouannaud
CRIN, Centre de Recherche en Informatique de Nancy
Boite postale 239, 54506 Vandoeuvre-les-Nancy cedex, France

CR Subject Classification (1985): F 4, I 1, I 2.2, I 2.3

ISBN 3-540-15976-2 Springer-Verlag Berlin Heidelberg New York Tokyo
ISBN 0-387-15976-2 Springer-Verlag New York Heidelberg Berlin Tokyo

Library of Congress Cataloging-in-Publication Data. Main entry under title: Rewriting techniques and applications. (Lecture notes in computer science; 202) 1. Electronic digital computers–Programming–Congresses. 2. Algorithms–Congresses. I. Jouannaud, Jean-Pierre. II. International Conference on Rewriting Techniques and Applications (1st: 1985: Dijon, France) III. Series.
QA76.6.R464 1985 005 85-22164
ISBN 0-387-15976-2 (U.S.)

Printed in Germany

Printing and binding: Beltz Offsetdruck, Hemsbach/Bergstr.
2145/3140-543210

Foreword

This *First International Conference on Rewriting Techniques and Applications,* held in Dijon, Burgundy, France, May 20-22, 1985, was preceded by an earlier workshop at Schenectady, New York, USA. This first Worshop was organized as an answer to the surge of interest in term rewriting techniques. This surge has been sparked both by significant progress in understanding the theorical aspects of rewriting systems and by the development of important new applications to these systems.

While the progress of research into rewriting systems has been significant, it has been impeded by the inordinate difficulty of implementing and using the increasingly complex algorithms prevalent in state-of-the-art term rewriting research. The main purpose of the first workshop was to offer to a wide community an easy access to sophisticated softwares.

Today, those software are used by a very large community and support many applications, some of them being described in these proceedings. Our goal now is to provide a regular forum for people working in the field of term rewriting or using term rewriting techniques in other fields of computer science. This conference proves the need of such a forum, both by focusing on new important advances in term rewriting technologies, and on new applications. I hope that this is a good start towards a regular international conference.

To emphasize the success of the conference, the committee decided to award Kathy Yelick, for her paper *Combining unification algorithms for confined regular equational theories.* The reasons are the following:
- Unification is a main topic in term rewriting techniques, and we are pleased to recognize a significant contribution in this area.
- Kathy Yelick is currently completing her master's degree at MIT, and we are pleased to recognize a major advance in this field by a young student.
- Yelick's paper solves a problem left open for many years: how to obtain a complete unification algorithm for a combination of theories that individually have a complete unification algorithm. More precisely, she shows how to lift a complete unification algorithm for the variable only case of each individual theory to a complete unification algorithm for the whole theory, under two basic assumptions on individual theories: they must be *confined* (i.e., involve different sets of symbols); they must be *regular* (i.e., the axioms must have exactly the same variables on their left and right hand sides, and a variable cannot be a left or right hand side of an axiom).

As a particular consequence, she obtains a completeness proof for Stickel's famous associative-commutative unification algorithm. As she points out, lifting the variable only case was the main difficulty of this algorithm, whose termination was only recently proved by François Fages in a paper published in the proceedings of CADE, 1984.

A few others should be mentioned, because they have made similar or related progress in this area: Claude Kirchner from Nancy, recently addressed the same problem, independently from Kathy Yelick. Based on a different approach, his algorithm is able to handle erasing axioms. However, theories are also assumed to be permutative, i.e., have finite congruence classes. Although they are different, both algorithms use complexity measures in order to prove termination. Not surprisingly, both complexity measures are variations around Fages's complexity measure used for proving termination of Stickel's algorithm. Fages's work should therefore also be recognized as a major step towards these new advances.

I finally want to thank many people for their help:

John Guttag, David Musser and Pierre Lescanne, for the help they gave me when pushing this project from nil to the top of the stack;

SRI and CRIN, for providing me with staff support when needed;

The sponsors, NSF, CNRS, ADI, and Bull, for their financial help;

Ravi Sethi for his invaluable experience in committee meetings;

The referees, whose work was sometimes heavy. Their names are listed below;

Jean-Jacques Chabrier and Jean-Marc Pallo for the local organization;

The University of Dijon, who provided us with a conference room inside the historic center of the City.

Jean-Pierre Jouannaud

Program Committee
Jan Bergstra, Amsterdam
Joseph Goguen, SRI-International
John Guttag, MIT
Jean-Pierre Jouannaud, Nancy (co-chairman)
Pierre Lescanne, CRIN
David Musser, General Electric Labs (co-chairman)
Peter Padawitz, Passau
David Plaisted, Chapel Hill
Ravi Sethi, Bell Labs
David Turner, Kent

List of Referees: Bergstra J., Bibel W., Bloniarz P., Bougé L., Courcelles B., Dershowitz N., Gallier J., Gaudel M.C., Goguen J., Guessarian I., Guttag J. , Hsiang J., Huet G., Jouannaud J.P., Kaplan S., Kapur D., Kirchner C., Kirchner H., Lescanne P., Levy J.J., MacNaughton R., MacQueen D., Meseguer J., Meyer A., Mitchell J., Musser D., Narendran P., O'Donnel M., Padawitz P., Plaisted D., Puel L., Sethi R., Siekman J., Stickel M., Turner D., and Winkler F..

CONTENTS

-=-=-=-=-=-=-

Basic Features and Development of the Critical-Pair/Completion Procedure

Bruno Buchberger
Johannes Kepler University
A4040 Linz, Austria (Europe)

Table of Contents

INTRODUCTION

The critical-pair/completion (CPC) approach is an algorithmic problem solving strategy that combines two key ideas:
completion and
the formation of critical pairs.

The CPC technique was independently initiated by three papers in the mid sixties in three seemingly far apart areas:
automated theorem proving
polynomial ideal theory and
solution of word problems in universal algebras.
In retrospect, however, it turns out that the key ideas of the CPC approach implicitly were already around in early forerunners.

In the twenty years since 1965 the CPC approach has found more and more useful applications in various areas of algorithmic problem solving. In the most recent years research on applications of the CPC technique has been particularly intensive and successful.

Various technical questions for improving and analyzing CPC algorithms and for broadening the scope of applicability of the CPC approach have been and are studied by an increasing research community: termination, strategies for selecting critical pairs, criteria for omitting certain critical pairs, complexity of CPC computations. Various implementations of CPC algorithms have been described in the literature, starting from the early implementations in the mid sixties and proceeding to sophisticated implementations as parts of software systems for symbolic computation.

The main goal of this paper is to elaborate the basic ideas and major advances in CPC research by pointing to some key papers. We hope this will contribute to a further cross-fertilization between the different areas involved in CPC research and applications. Elaborating the basic ideas of the class of CPC algorithms may serve also as a case study for the more general objective of establishing certain basic algorithm types in computer science as a natural supplement to the study of data types, which is one of the author's secondary hobbies, see (Buchberger 84).

I apologize that my presentation is biased towards polynomial ideal theory both in the application section and in the technical section. This is certainly due to my own involvement in this root of CPC research and also due to my lack of expertise in the other branches. However, this paper addresses the participants of a rewrite rules conference. I therefore hope that polynomial ideal theory is that branch of CPC research that may provide some information supplementary to the ordinary background of researchers working in rewrite rule techniques and, hence, may be of some interest to the audience of this conference.

Most probably the readers will not be satisfied with my tracing back the historical roots of the CPC approach either: only during writing this survey I detected how difficult it is to give fair and complete credit to the work of all the people who have been involved in CPC research. Fortunately, there is a "bottom element" to the historical priority graph in CPC research: it is well known that Euclid's algorithm for polynomials is (an instance of a) CPC algorithm. Recently, as a curiosity, it has been shown also that Euclid's algorithm for integers may be viewed as an instance of CPC algorithms, see (Loos 1981) and (Buchberger 1983). Thus, Euclid spares me the trouble of tracing priorities too pedantically.

KEY IDEAS AND BASIC STRUCTURE OF THE CPC APPROACH

Typically, the CPC approach can be applied when one has

> a set T of (linguistic, algebraic, symbolic) objects
> together with a binary "reduction" relation $\rightarrow$ on T that is generated by a
>   set F of (finitely) many "patterns" F
> and one wants to solve "word problems" of the kind
>   "for $s,t \in T$:
>   is (s,t) in the reflexive, symmetric, transitive closure of $\rightarrow$?"
>   or problems that can be reduced to such problems.

Sets of objects

Typical sets of objects are

the set of clauses over an alphabet of function and predicate symbols,
the set of polynomials over a coefficient ring,
the set of equations between terms over an alphabet of function symbols,
the set of words over a finite alphabet of constants.

Reduction relations generated by patterns

For generating "reduction" relations $\rightarrow$ from patterns one starts from a set F of finitely many "patterns" ("basic reductions" or "rules") $(s,t) \in T \times T$ of reductions that, by definition, are assumed to be in $\rightarrow$, i.e. one stipulates:

for all $s,t \in T$: if $(s,t) \in F$ then $s \rightarrow t$. (pattern rule)

(We write $s \rightarrow t$ instead of $(s,t) \in \rightarrow$. For s and t in a pattern $(s,t) \in F$ we sometimes say "left-hand side" and "right-hand side of the pattern" respectively.)

In addition, one has an (infinite) set Σ of "multipliers" ("substitutions", "operators") that can be applied to objects of T and yield objects in T. (We write σs for the application of the substitution σ to the object s). Now, for the application of substitutions to both sides of patterns one stipulates:

for all $s,t \in T$, $\sigma \in \Sigma$: if $(s,t) \in F$ then $\sigma s \rightarrow \sigma t$. (multiplier rule)

Thus, by applying all substitutions σ, each of the patterns $s \rightarrow t$ in F generates a whole "spectrum" $\{ \sigma s \rightarrow \sigma t : \sigma \in \Sigma \}$ of reductions.

Finally, in the cases amenable to the CPC approach, one has a concept of "places" in the objects of T and, correspondingly, a concept of "replacement" in objects. Let P be the set of possible places in objects, let us write r/u for "the object located at place u in the object r" and let us write $r[u \leftarrow t]$ for "the object resulting from replacing the subobject located at place u in r by the object t". Then one stipulates

for all $r,s,t \in T$, $\sigma \in \Sigma$, $u \in P$:
if $(s,t) \in F$ and $r/u = \sigma s$ then $r \rightarrow r[u \leftarrow \sigma t]$. (replacement rule)

(This means that objects r can be reduced by replacing a subobject "of the form σs" by σt whenever $s \rightarrow t$ is a pattern in F.)

The relation $\rightarrow$ generated from a set F of patterns in the way described above, i.e. by applying the pattern rule, substitution rule and replacement rule, will be called "the reduction relation generated by F" (denoted by $\rightarrow_F$). This notion is not meant to be a serious mathematical "definition" on which the rest of the paper could be based in a closed deductive presentation. The description given here, rather, is an attempt to extract as many common features as possible from the various situations in which CPC algorithms have been applied successfully. An axiomatic approach to CPC algorithms exclusively based on the above three notions of patterns, multipliers and replacements seems to be promising. However, this has not yet been achieved satisfactorily although much progress has been made in general formulations of the CPC approach (see the section on unifying approaches).

Word problems

In situations where one has a reduction relation $\rightarrow_F$ generated by patterns, typically, many algorithmic problems can be reduced to the following problem (the uniform word problem for reductions relations generated by patterns in T):

for arbitrary $s,t \in T$ and (finite) $F \subset T \times T$ decide whether $s \leftrightarrow_F^* t$.

($\leftrightarrow^*$ denotes the reflexive, symmetric, transitive closure of the binary relation $\rightarrow$.)

Examples of such problems are:

the problem of deciding whether the empty clause can be derived from a set of clauses,

the problem of constructing a vector space basis for the residue ring modulo a multivariate polynomial ideal,

the problem of deciding whether a given equation can be derived from the axioms of a given equational theory,

the reachability problem for reversible Petri nets,

the problem of constructing direct implementations for abstract data types,

the problem of finding a generating set for the module of all syzygies of a polynomial ideal,

the problem of solving algebraic systems of equations,

and many others (see the section on applications).

Finite termination

So far we have not yet motivated why we spoke about "reductions" when we introduced the concept of relations generated by patterns. Actually, in algorithmic problem solving one is only interested in those situations where by one "step" $s \rightarrow_F t$ the "complexity" or "size" of s is "reduced". Whatever the notion of complexity is, one of course would not like to admit that the complexity can be reduced infinitely often. This means that one normally is interested only in noetherian relations $\rightarrow_F$ (A binary relation $\rightarrow$ on T is called noetherian iff there is no infinite chain $t_1 \rightarrow t_2 \rightarrow t_3 \rightarrow \ldots$. Sometimes these relations are also said to have the finite termination property.) Thus, normally, when speaking about a reduction relation generated by F we presuppose that the relation, in addition to being generated by the process described above, is noetherian. On the other hand, it may sometimes be reasonable to disregard the question of finite termination and still try to apply the CPC approach.

Solving word problems: Church-Rosser property and confluence

Given a (reduction) relation $\rightarrow$ on T, it is clear that if s and t have "a common successor" then $s \leftrightarrow^* t$. In general, the converse does not hold. Noetherian relations $\rightarrow$ for which the converse does hold have a decidable word problem. We state these well known and easy facts more formally. (For proof details see, for example, (Buchberger, Loos 1982), pp. 27.)

Let $\rightarrow$ be a binary relation on T. As usual, the inverse and the transitive closure of $\rightarrow$ are denoted by $\leftarrow$ and $\rightarrow^*$ respectively. Furthermore, for $s,t \in T$:

$s \downarrow t$ (s and t have a common successor) $:\Longleftrightarrow (\exists r)(\, s \rightarrow^* r \leftarrow^* t \,)$,

$\underline{s}$ (s is in normal form) $:\Longleftrightarrow$ not $(\exists t)(\, s \rightarrow t)$.

Definition: $\rightarrow$ has the Church-Rosser property iff $(\forall s,t)(\, s \leftrightarrow^* t \Longrightarrow s \downarrow t)$.

Lemma (Decidability of Church-Rosser relations): If $\rightarrow$ is noetherian and has the Church-Rosser property then $\leftrightarrow^*$ is decidable.

Proof (Sketch): The following function S is a canonical simplifier for $\leftrightarrow^*$:

S(s) := if s is in normal form then s else S(Sel(s)),

where Sel is a "selector" function for $\rightarrow$. Hence, we have the following decision algorithm:

$s \leftrightarrow^* t$ iff $S(s) = S(t)$.

(A function S defined by a recursion of the above type is called a normal form algorithm.

A computable function Sel:T-->T is called a selector function for $\rightarrow$ iff for all $s \in T$ that are not in normal form: $s \rightarrow Sel(s)$.

A computable function S: T-->T is called a canonical simplifier for an equivalence relation $\sim$ on T iff for all $s,t \in T$:

$S(s) \sim s$, (closure)

if $s \sim t$ then $S(s) = S(t)$ (uniqueness).

Note that in the above proof we need the existence of a computable selector function and the decidability of the predicate "is in normal form". We do not explicitly mention these assumptions in the lemma in order not to distract the attention from the crucial points. Actually, in the practically interesting cases the validity of these two assumptions is no problem.)

The proof tells us that, in the case of noetherian Church-Rosser relations $\rightarrow$, for deciding $s \leftrightarrow^* t$ we only need to reduce s and t iteratively by "applying" $\rightarrow$ until we arrive at normal forms s' and t'. Then $s \leftrightarrow^* t$ iff s'=t'.

Of course, in general, it is not easily possible to determine whether a given relation $\rightarrow$ has the Church-Rosser property since the condition in the definiens in general involves tests for infinitely many pairs (s,t) each of which may give rise to infinitely many attempts to find common succesors for s and t. The following lemma gives an equivalent formulation that presents an "easier" but still non-constructive test.

Definition: $\rightarrow$ is confluent iff $(\forall r,t,s \in T)(s \leftarrow^* r \rightarrow^* t \implies s \downarrow t)$.

Lemma (Reduction of the Church-Rosser property to confluence): $\rightarrow$ has the Church-Rosser property iff $\rightarrow$ is confluent.

Lemma (Alternative formulation of confluence): $\rightarrow$ is confluent iff $(\forall r,s,t \in T)(\underline{s} \leftarrow^* r \rightarrow^* \underline{t} \implies s=t)$.

Solving the word problem: the idea of completion

Stated in the context of confluence the idea of completion is straightforward:

- Given a set F of patterns we try to find a set G such that

  $\leftrightarrow_F^* = \leftrightarrow_G^*$ and
  $\rightarrow_G$ has the Church-Rosser property.
  (By the lemma on the decidability of Church-Rosser relations, we then have a decision algorithm for $\leftrightarrow_F^*$.)

  (A set of patterns having the property that $\rightarrow_G$ has the Church-Rosser property will be called a completed set.)

- The lemma on the reduction of the Church-Rosser property to confluence (using the alternative formulation for confluence) suggests the following procedure for finding a suitable set G:

<u>"Algorithm"</u> (Completion of a set of patterns):

G:= F

B:= $\{ (s,t) : (\exists r)(\underline{s} \leftarrow_F^* r \rightarrow_F^* \underline{t}) \}$.

<u>while</u> B $\neq \emptyset$ <u>do</u>

(s,t) := an element in B
B := B - $\{(s,t)\}$

<u>if</u> $s \neq t$ <u>then</u>
analyze (s,t)
G:= G $\cup$ $\{(s,t)\}$.

The completion proceeds by locating all situations (r,s,t) in which confluence is injured. In these situations, as a remedy, $s \rightarrow t$ (or $t \rightarrow s$) is adjoined to the set of "patterns" (dependent on the analysis whether adjoining $s \rightarrow t$ or $t \rightarrow s$ leaves the finite termination property untouched. If both possibilities destroy the finite termination property then this procedure must be terminated "with failure".) It should be clear that adjoining these $s \rightarrow t$ as patterns preserves the condition $\leftrightarrow_F^* = \leftrightarrow_G^*$ and, if the algorithm terminated, $\rightarrow_G$ would have the confluence (and, hence, the Church-Rosser) property (G has been <u>"completed"</u>). However, in general, B is an infinite set and, hence, the above construction is not algorithmic.

The above completion procedure can be slightly improved by using Newman's lemma on <u>local confluence</u>.

<u>Definition</u>: $\rightarrow$ is <u>locally confluent</u> iff $(\forall r,s,t \in T)(s \leftarrow r \rightarrow t \implies s \downarrow t)$.

<u>Lemma</u> (Reduction of confluence to local confluence; (Newman 1942)): Let $\rightarrow$ be noetherian. Then $\rightarrow$ is confluent iff $\rightarrow$ is locally confluent.

<u>Proof</u>: By noetherian induction. The lemma is due to (Newman 1942). In its full generality it has been proven in (Huet 1977). The proof may also be found, for example, in (Buchberger, Loos 1982).

<u>Lemma</u> (Alternative formulation of Newman's lemma): Let $\rightarrow$ be noetherian and S be a normal form algorithm for $\rightarrow$. Then
$\rightarrow$ is confluent iff $(\forall r,s,t \in T)(s \leftarrow r \rightarrow t \implies S(s) = S(t))$.

Using the alternative formulation of Newman's lemma it is clear that in the above completion procedure the second statement can be replaced by

B := $\{ (s,t) : (\exists r,s',t') (s' \leftarrow_F r \rightarrow_F t', s=S(s'), t=S(t')) \}$.

Intuitively, using this B, "fewer" situations have to be checked than in the first formulation of the completion procedure. However, in general, B is still an infinite set.

A further improvement of the completion construction is suggested by taking into account that the reduction relations $\rightarrow_F$ "generated by patterns F" are built by substitutions and then replacements. Intuitively, one may expect that a sound notion of replacement has the following compatibility property with respect to reduction:

$$(\forall r,s,t \in T,\ u \in P)\ (\ s \to t \implies r[u \leftarrow s] \to r[u \leftarrow t]\ ). \qquad \text{(compatibility)}$$

(In fact, in some important cases, compatibility in this strong form is not available. This raises technical difficulties!) In case compatibility holds it is clear that it suffices to consider confluence on the "spectra" of the patterns rather than general confluence, i.e. in the completion procedure the second statement can be replaced by

$$B := \{\ (s,t)\ :\ (\exists r \in \text{spectrum}(F), s', t')\ (\ s' \leftarrow_F r \to_F t',\ s = S(s'),\ t = S(t')\ )\ \},$$

$$\text{where spectrum}(F) := \{\ \sigma s\ :\ (\exists t)((s,t) \in F),\ \sigma \in \Sigma\ \}.$$

Again, this definition of B is a step towards turning the completion procedure into a real algorithm. It even gives us some hint how to exhaust B by generating finite subsets of B: in one step one could consider those r in the spectrum(F) that are generated by a fixed substituion σ from the left-hand sides of patterns in F. (The expert reader will note that in this introduction we oversimplify the situation for the sake of bringing to light the key ideas at the cost of details: actually one often has to consider $r \in$spectrum(F) that are subobjects in other $r' \in$spectrum(F).)

Solving the word problem: the idea of critical pairs

The analysis given so far shows us that for completing F (and, hence, solving the word problem for $\to_F$) we should look at the "spectra" of the patterns $s \to t$ in F

$s \to t$

$\sigma_1 s \to \sigma_1 t$

$\sigma_2 s \to \sigma_2 t$

....

....

....

and locate objects r that can be conceived as the left-hand sides $\sigma_i s = \tau_j p$ of reductions in two different spectra:

$s \to t$ $\qquad\qquad\qquad\qquad$ $p \to q$

$\sigma_1 s \to \sigma_1 t$ $\qquad\qquad\qquad$ $\tau_1 p \to \tau_1 q$

$\sigma_2 s \to \sigma_2 t$ $\qquad\qquad$ $\tau_2 p \to \tau_2 q$

....

....

....

$\sigma_i s \to \sigma_i t$ $\qquad\qquad\qquad\qquad$ (superposition diagram)

$\tau_j p \to \tau_j q$

....

....

....

....

In such situations we have for $r := \sigma_i s = \tau_j p$

$\sigma_i t \leftarrow r \to \tau_j q$

and we only need to check whether $S(\sigma_i t) = S(\tau_j q)$. From the suggestive superposition diagram above the idea of critical pairs may come naturally to one's mind:

> Instead of considering the (infinitely) many objects r that can be conceived as the left-hand sides of reductions in two different spectra, does it suffice to consider the "first possible" situations in which a "superposition" happens and to remove a possible injury of local confluence in these situations? These situations are called the "critical situations" and the pairs $(\sigma_i t, \tau_j q)$ are called the "critical pairs".
>
> Differently stated: the idea of critical pairs is the desire to "come as quickly as possible to a situation where something interesting can happen by the interaction (interference, superposition) of two patterns".

In fact, it turned out that this idea works in many interesting examples. From the superpositon diagram it should be clear that, as minimal requirements, for the idea to work one needs

> a notion of "the first possible superposition situation" for two patterns, i.e. a superposition situation from which all other superposition situations for these two patterns can be generated by application of multipliers (substitutions).

More formally (but, again, not meant as a "definition"): given two "patterns" $s \to t$ and $p \to q$ the two objects x, y form a critical pair for the two patterns if

there exist two substitutions σ and τ such that
- $\sigma s = \tau p$,
- for all substitutions σ', τ' for which $\sigma' s = \tau' p$
  - there exists a substitution χ such that $\sigma' s = \chi \sigma s$,
- and $x = \sigma t$, $y = \tau q$

(i.e. x and y result from applying the patterns $s \to t$ and $p \to q$ to a "first possible superposition" of s and p.)

In more general situations, where we consider objects σs that are subobjects of τp or where the set of all superposition situations of two patterns are generated by more than one generating situation, more than one critical pair can correspond to two patterns.

Combining the idea of completion with the idea of critical pairs, finally, leads to the following CPC algorithm schema.

<u>Algorithm</u> (Structure of critical-pair/completion algorithms):

G:= F

B:= $\bigcup_{f,g \in G}$ set of critical pairs of f and g

<u>while</u> B ≠ ∅ <u>do</u>

(s,t) := an element in B
B := B - {(s,t)}
(s,t) := (S(s),S(t))

<u>if</u> s≠t <u>then</u>

analyze (s,t)

B:= B ∪ $\bigcup_{(p,q) \in G}$ set of critical pairs of (s,t) and (p,q)

G:= G ∪ {(s,t)}.

Introducing critical pairs was the crucial advance in the development of the CPC approach because in many typical application areas the sets of critical pairs (for the finitely many f,g ∈G) are finite and, hence, the completion construction has a chance to become a real algorithm. Still the termination of CPC algorithms may remain a difficult problem for three reasons. First, in the particular context where one wants to apply the CPC approach it may be difficult to establish a Noetherian ordering on the objects that is compatible with reduction. Second, when analyzing (s,t) it may turn out that the finite termination property can not be guaranteed after augmenting G by (s,t). And third, in the while-loop, B will be diminished and increased iteratively and it is by no means trivial that it ever becomes empty.

Note that the above structure of CPC algorithms does not reflect any of the more subtle details of the approach, for example the strategy of keeping patterns in G reduced with respect to all other patterns in G, see the section on strategies.

THREE CPC ALGORITHMS IN THE MID SIXTIES

The CPC approach was introduced in three papers in the mid sixties in three different areas that, at first sight, seem to be far apart:

universal theorem proving
polynomial ideal theory
word problems in universal algebras.

These three papers contained complete correctness proofs for the respective algorithms and described computer implementations of the algorithms. We give a short review of these three algorithms.

The resolution procedure (Robinson 1963, 1965)

The original problem:

Given F, a set of clauses in first-order predicate logic.
Semi-decide whether F is unsatisfiable.

Robinson's resolution algorithm needs some distortion in order that it can be viewed as a CPC algorithm. However, it surely shows the two key ideas of the CPC approach: completion and critical pairs.

Objects: The set T of clauses.

Patterns: The clauses in F. Each clause $\{L_1,\ldots,L_i,M_1,\ldots,M_j\}$, however, can be viewed in several ways as a "pattern" (s,t) depending on which of the positive literals $L_1,\ldots,L_i$ or negative literals $M_1,\ldots,M_j$ is taken as the "left-hand side" s. Note that, in the context of the resolution algorithm, clauses are the objects and the rules. We will have a similar situation also in the context of polynomials (and general rings, see the section on generalizations.)

Multipliers: The substitutions σ of first-order predicate logic can be viewed as the multipliers. Each clause C=(s,t) generates a whole "spectrum" of clauses σC.

Replacements: A special case of resolution may be viewed as a replacement: $C \to C[u \leftarrow \sigma t]$, if the literal L at "place" u is the negation of σs, where (s,t) is a clause in F, conceived as a "pattern".

Critical pairs: By formal distortion, one basic step in the resolution algorithm can be viewed as forming a critical pair: for two clauses (s,t) and (-p,q) in F (where the minus sign stands for "not"), conceived as patterns, "most general unifiers" σ and τ are determined such that $\sigma s=\tau p$. From σs, in one reduction, one obtains σt and $-\tau q$. $(\sigma t,-\tau q)$ could be added to F now. (No simplification by a "normal form algorithm" S is foreseen in the resolution procedure!) Instead, $(\sigma t+\tau q)$ is added to F, where the plus sign stands for "or". ($(\sigma t,-\tau q)$, formally, would not be a clause!). The notion of a most general unifier and the unification algorithm that determines the most general unifier for two expressions (if it exists), introduced in (Robinson 1965) is an important concept that has motivated a whole stream of research in symbolic computation.

Completion: Adding $(\sigma t+\tau q)$ to F is the completion step in the resolution procedure.

Completed sets: They do not play an explicit role in the context of resolution because in the successful cases the procedure stops when the empty clause is generated and the set of clauses G, generated until then, is not used further.

Remarks: It is interesting to note that, disregarding formal details, the key idea of critical pairs seems to have been very clear in the intention of J. A. Robinson because in (Robinson 1979, p. 292) he writes: "The idea that, instead of trying all instantiations over the Herbrand Universe, one might predict which ones would produce a 'winning combination' by using what we have called the Unification Algorithm, ...". In a colloquium lecture at ETH (Zürich, 1978) we proposed to consider the resolution procedure as a CPC algorithm using the sketch given above. Meanwhile the conception of the resolution procedure as a CPC algorithm has been worked out much more specifically by J. Hsiang and others based on the Peterson-Stickel version of the Knuth-Bendix algorithm, see the section on unifying approaches. We still think it would be worthwhile to look for a unifying approach that it based on an axiomatization of "multipliers" and "replacement". Also including "simplification by resolution" into the resolution procedure seems to be promising (for simplification only matching, not unification is necessary; see also the concept of "narrowing" in a later section). Of course, it also should be mentioned that some details of the resolution procedure in its original form are far apart from the general structure of CPC algorithms sketched in the preceding section. For example, termination of the reduction process, orientation of rules, the Church-Rosser property and local confluence do not play any explicit role in the original resolution context. Also, at first sight, the problem solved by the resolution procedure is not a word problem. (However, note that F is insatisfiable iff "the empty clause is reachable from F by resolution steps").

Introductory reading: (Robinson 1979) is the authoritative presentation of the resolution method.

An algorithm for polynomial ideals (Buchberger 1965)

The original problem:

Given F, a finite set of multivariate polynomials over a field K.
Find a linearly independent basis A and the multiplication table M for the associative algebra $K[x_1,...,x_n]/\mathrm{Ideal}(F)$, where Ideal(F) is the ideal generated by F.

The algorithm presented in (Buchberger 1965) has all the structural characteristics of a CPC algorithm. Using this algorithm the above problem can be solved as follows:

1. Construct a completed set G using the algorithm.
2. A:= the set of (the residue classes of) all power products that are not multiples of leading power products of polynomials in G.
3. The linear representation of the products u.v ($u,v \in B$) can be obtained by reducing u.v to normal form using $\to_G$.

Objects: $T := K[x_1,...,x_n]$, the set of polynomials over the field K.

Patterns: The polynomials in F. In order to conceive a polynomial f as a "pattern" we present it in the form $f = s - t$, where s is the "leading power product" in f with respect to a given linear ordering of the power products and t comprises the remaining monomials in f. (Without loss of generality we may assume that the coefficient of this power product is 1. In the original paper we always took the "lexicographical ordering graded by degrees" as a fixed ordering for the power products. Later it turned out that the algorithm can be carried through for a whole class of orderings that can be characterized by two easy and natural axioms.)

Multipliers: The monomials (coefficients times power products) serve as "multi-liers". The "application" σs of a multiplier σ to a polynomial s is just the product of σ and s.

Replacements: The "places" of a polynomial are the power products. $r[u \leftarrow t]$ must be interpreted as "the polynomial that results from replacing the monomial at place u in r by the polynomial t". r/u must be interpreted as "the monomial at place u in r". The general reductions generated by a set F of patterns, then, are reductions of the following form:

$$r \rightarrow r[u \leftarrow \sigma t], \quad \text{if } (s,t) \varepsilon F \text{ and } r/u = \sigma s.$$

(A careful definition of the notion of a "polynomial" is crucial in this context. The concept of a polynomial must not be confused with the concept of an arithmetical term. For an exact definition see, for example (Buchberger, Loos 1982, p. 16). As one of the isomorphic models of the set of polynomials $K[x_1,\ldots,x_n]$ one can take the set { s : s is a function from $\mathbf{N}_0{}^n$ in K such that s is zero for almost all arguments }. In this model the "places", then, are just the tupels u in $\mathbf{N}_0{}^n$. We wish to emphasize these well known distinctions because they sometimes still cause some confusion and wrong "proofs" in papers on CPC algorithms and simplification modulo ideals in polynomial rings.)

Critical pairs: With the above interpretation of "application of multipliers" and "replacement" the definition of a critical pair can now be literally taken from the section on the key ideas: Given (s,t) and (p,q) ε F the two polynomials x, y form a critical pair for the two patterns if

there exist two multipliers σ and τ such that
$\sigma s = \tau p$,
for all multipliers σ', τ' for which $\sigma' s = \tau' p$
there exists a multiplier χ such that $\sigma' s = \chi \sigma s$
and $x = \sigma t$, $y = \tau q$.

More explicitly, in order to find σ and τ, we only have to compute the least common multiple m of s and p. σ and τ, then, are just the monomials that satisfy $\sigma s = m$ and $\tau t = m$.

Completion: With the interpretations described above, the algorithm developed in (Buchberger 1965) introduced exactly the structure of the CPC algorithm schema shown in the section on the key ideas. In the context of polynomials, adjoining (s,t) to G must be realized by adjoining r:= s-t to G. As a "pattern", r then splits into its leading power product and the remaining monomials. The step "analyze" is not necessary in the context of polynomials because $\rightarrow_G$ is noetherian for every G. The termination of the algorithm in the general case has been shown in (Buchberger 70) by rediscovering Dickson's lemma (Dickson 1913). The original correctness proof of the algorithm was inductive in nature but not based on Newman's lemma. It can be based on Newman's lemma, see (Bachmair, Buchberger 1980) for absorbing the set theoretical part of the underlying induction. However, the crucial part of the proof, which consists in exploiting the power of the critical pair construction, goes beyond Newman's lemma and must also cope with certain technical difficulties concerning the reduction process for polynomials.

Completed sets: The notion of a set G completed by the CPC algorithm was explicitly introduced in (Buchberger 1965) by stating its ideal theoretically characteristic property: all polynomials in G can be reduced to zero by iteratively applying the reduction $\rightarrow_G$. Later, in (Buchberger 1976), we called these sets Gröbner bases (for historical reasons, see the section on early forerunners.)

Remarks: We derived the crucial intuition behind our 1965 algorithm from drawing pictures showing the "spectra" of the leading power products of the polynomials in F in the way shown in the section on the key ideas and analyzing the "first points where something interesting can happen". These points are the least common multiples of the leading power products. It is interesting to compare this with the intuition described by Robinson for his resolution procedure. Instead of reducing both polynomials x and y in a critical pair to normal form, in our algorithm, we reduce the difference x-y. If h:= S(x-y) is not equal to zero then h is adjoined to G. Computationally, this is slightly better because we need only one reduction to normal form instead of two. Logically, in the context of polynomials over K, these two procedures are equivalent. In (Buchberger 1965) the difference x-y of the components x and y of the critical pair corresponding to the polynomals p and q is called called the "S-polynomial" of s and p.

Introductory reading: (Buchberger 1983c) gives an easy introduction to the algorithm for computing Gröbner bases and its many applications.

An algorithm for word problems in universal algebras (Knuth-Bendix 1967)

The original problem (the word problem in universal algebras):
Given F, a finite set of identities described by pairs of first-order terms and two terms s and t.
Decide whether the identity "s=t" can be derived from the identities in F.

Again, the algorithm presented in (Knuth-Bendix 1967) for the solution of this problem has all the structural characteristics of a CPC algorithm. Using this algorithm the above problem can be solved as follows:

1. Construct a completed set G using the algorithm.
2. (If the algorithm terminated successfully:)
   "s=t" is derivable from F (iff "s=t" derivable from G) iff
   S(s) is identical to S(t), where S is a normal form algorithm for the reduction $\rightarrow_G$.

Objects: T := the set of first-order terms over a given alphabet of function symbols.

Patterns: Pairs (s,t) of terms ("identities"), where s>t in some noetherian ordering > of the terms. Term orderings suitable in this context must satisfy certain basic properties. (Essentially, if a term p reduces to a term q, then q must be smaller than p in the ordering.)

Multipliers: As in the resolution algorithm, the substitutions of terms for variables serve as the "multipliers".

Replacements: The "places" in a term are the places where the subterms occur. $r[u\leftarrow t]$ must be interpreted as "the term that results from replacing the subterm at place u in r by the term t". r/u must be interpreted as "the term at place u in r". The general reductions generated by a set F of patterns, then, are reductions of the following form:

$$r \to r[u\leftarrow \sigma t], \text{ if } (s,t)\in F \text{ and } r/u = \sigma s.$$

Critical pairs: With the above interpretation of "application of multipliers" and "replacement" the definition of a critical pair could now be taken literally from the section on the key ideas. However, in the context of first-order terms, one has to consider also "superpositions" between terms and subterms of other terms and not only between terms and other terms. Given two patterns (s,t) and $(p,q) \in F$, the two terms x, y form a critical pair for the two patterns if

there exist two substitutions σ and τ and a place u such that
$\sigma(s/u) = \tau p$,
for all substitutions σ',τ' for which $\sigma'(s/u) = \tau' p$
there exists a substitution χ such that $\sigma' = \chi\sigma$
(and some technical conditions on variables hold),
and $x = \sigma t$, $y = \sigma s[u\leftarrow \tau q]$.

The substitutions σ and τ form a most general unifier exactly in the same sense as in the resolution algorithm. Actually, the same unification algorithm as in (Robinson 65) was also proposed in (Knuth, Bendix 1967).

Completion: With the interpretations described above, the algorithm introduced in (Knuth, Bendix 1967) has exactly the structure of the CPC algorithm schema shown in the section on the key ideas. The step "analyze" is crucial in the context of rewriting terms: before adjoining (s,t) to G it must be analyzed whether s>t or t>s or s is incomparable with t. In the first two cases, (s,t) or (t,s) is adjoined respectively. In the third case the algorithm must be terminated "with failure". In general, nothing interesting can be said in this case. Termination of this algorithm can not be guaranteed in general. In the cases when it terminates the resulting set G of identities has the property that $\to_G^*$ is Church-Rosser. The original correctness proof of the algorithm was already based on a version of Newman's lemma. Again, the crucial part of the proof, which concerns the power contained in the concept of critical pairs, goes beyond Newman's lemma and must also take account of the technicalities pertinent to first-order terms.

Completed sets: The notion of a "complete set" is explicitly introduced in (Knuth, Bendix 1967) by essentially defining: G is complete iff $\to_G$ has the Church-Rosser property.

Remarks: The algorithm and the correctness proof presented in (Knuth, Bendix 1967), actually, is due to Knuth alone, whereas Bendix, a student of Knuth, did the implementation as has been pointed out to me by D. Lankford. From the point of view of heuristics, it is interesting to see that, in the original paper (Knuth, Bendix 1967), the authors do not mention the intuition of locating "the first possible superposition situation" as the view underlying the notion of a critical pair. However, they apparently arrived at the notion of a critical pair by a careful analysis of how local confluence can be injured, i.e. in which cases it is possible that, in a situation $s \leftarrow_G r \to_G t$, s and t have no common successor. It turns out that only one "critical case" remains, namely just the case of a general superposition of "spectra", which they found can be reduced to the case of a "most general superposition".

Introductory reading: Most probably, Huet (1977) contains the best presentation of the Knuth-Bendix algorithm.

EARLY FORERUNNERS

The three papers mentioned in the preceding section had a number of early forerunners that contained, more or less explicitly, the two key ideas of the CPC approach. In retrospect, by the recent increased interest in the CPC method, more and more of these forerunners are discovered. Of course, (Newman 1942) is a basis for all considerations on establishing the Church-Rosser property. However, in this section, I would like to concentrate on forerunners that showed versions or initial ideas of the critical-pair concept which, personally, I consider as the crucial part of the CPC approach. (Newman's lemma does not turn the infinite completion procedure into a finite algorithm. Rather, it only may help to nicely organize correctness proofs. In fact, only one of the correctness proofs of the three papers discussed in the last section, namely (Knuth, Bendix 1967) was based on Newman's lemma. Also, the idea of critical pairs may be useful in situations where the Church-Rosser property is not the main concern.)

Forerunners of the resolution procedure

J. A. Robinson himself traces the idea of his resolution algorithm back to (Prawitz 1960). In (Robinson 1979, p. 292) he writes: "The idea that, instead of trying all instantiations over the Herbrand Universe, one might predict which ones would produce a 'winning combination' by using what we have called the Unification Algorithm, turns out to have been sitting there all these years, unnoticed, in Herbrand's doctoral thesis (Herbrand 1930). (Prawitz 1960), following ideas of (Kanger 1957), was, as far as the present author is aware, the first to describe this idea at length in print." At a different place, (Robinson 1967), he writes: "The unification algorithm is essentially a cleaned-up and simplified version of the process described somewhat obscurely in (Prawitz 1960). Recently it came to my attention that essentially the same procedure was found by the late Emil Post and called by him the 'L.C.M.' process, but was never published. (See Davis 1965)." For me this latter reference is particularly thrilling because in my own algorithm I compute an LCM (without quotation marks) for obtaining a critical pair. Unification, of course, is a crucial ingredient in the first-order resolution algorithm. However, I think, it is the combination of unification (looking for the "first possible", the "most general" interesting situation) and (propositional) resolution (reduction by cutting away the unified parts) that makes Robinson's algorithm a "critical pair" algorithm.

Forerunners of the polynomial ideal algorithm

My own research on the polynomial ideal algorithm was stimulated by my thesis advisor, Prof. W. Gröbner (1899-1980). He encouraged me to work on the problem described in the preceding section (finding multiplication tables for residue class rings), which he presented in a seminar 1964 together with his own ideas how to attack the problem. In the terminology of the section on key ideas, his approach was as follows: Consider all power products r and reduce them to normal form (i.e. compute s and t such that $\underline{s} \leftarrow_G^* r \rightarrow_G^* \underline{t}$) in all possible ways using the polynomials in G. If $s \neq t$ then adjoin s-t to G. Thus, he proposed a completion procedure. However, he did not yet see that we can directly move to the "first possible" power products, where distinct reductions can occur, i.e. to the least common multiplies of leading power products, and that it suffices to consider only these particular power products. Also, he did not really present a general correctness proof for his procedure. Still, he showed extremely sound intuition because he recommended starting systematically from low power products in terms of degree. Thus, he was very close to critical pairs.

In (Buchberger 1970) I quoted Gröbner's ideas as an "oral communication". Strangely enough, Gröbner never told me that he had published his ideas already in 1950 in (Gröbner 1950) with the following additional remark: "I have used this method for approximately 17 years in various cases including complicated ones and ...". Only by chance, in 1984, during a stay in Halle (GDR) I learned from B. Renschuch, who had written a book in the spirit of W. Gröbner's ideal theoretical approach to commutative algebra (Renschuch 1976), about the existence of (Gröbner 1950). When I resumed work on the subject of constructive methods for polynomial ideals in (Buchberger 1976), in order to underline Gröbner's crucial contribution to my 1965 algorithm, I called the completed sets obtained by application of the algorithm "Gröbner bases" and gave various characterizations for them.

In fact, as pointed out in (Buchberger 1965, 1970), in the case of univariate polynomials and in the case of linear multivariate polynomials my 1965 algorithm specializes to Euclid's algorithm and Gauss' algorithm respectively. Hence, these two algorithms may be viewed as very early forerunners.

Recently some authors, for example (Bayer 1982), have also pointed out that essentially the same notion as "Gröbner bases" (i.e. the notion of bases with respect to which all elements in an ideal can be reduced to zero), in the context of formal power series, had already been introduced in Hironaka's famous paper (Hironaka 1964). Hironaka calls these ideal bases "standard bases" and calls the corresponding reduction process "division algorithm". He proves that for every ideal basis F there exists a corresponding standard basis. However, the proof is not constructive (it is essentially done by the "Schreier-construction", see (Bauer 1981, p.18)), i. e. it does not give an algorithm how to obtain the standard basis corresponding to a given arbitrary basis F. In particular, there is no indication of the idea of critical pairs in Hironaka's paper. A short version of such an inconstructive existence proof for Gröbner bases, from which Hilbert's basis theorem can be obtained as a corollary, is also presented in (Buchberger 1982).

Forerunners of the Knuth-Bendix algorithm

In (Knuth, Bendix 1965), both very general and very special credit is given to forerunners: "The formal development of this paper is primarily a precise statement of what hundreds of mathematicians have been doing for many decades, so no great claims of originality are intended for most of the concepts or methods used. ... . The main new contribution of this paper is intended to be an extension of some methods used by Trevor Evans, (Evans 1951). We allow operators of arbitrary degree, and we make use of a well-ordering of words which allows us to treat axioms such as the associative law." Consulting (Evans 1951) one sees that the core of the method to which Knuth alludes seems to be a procedure described in (Evans 1951a, p.69) by which a "closed" set of relations is produced from generators and relations of certain finitely generated algebras in the presence of equational axioms. When preparing this lecture, in an admittedly superficial reading, I tried to find out whether the procedure described in (Evans 1951a), which surely has the character of a "completion" procedure, also contains the concept of "critical pairs". Frankly, I was not able to decide this question and I think that, in any case, Knuth showed a lot of non-straightforward ingenuity when deriving the very general and clearly formulated procedure in (Knuth, Bendix 1967) from (Evans 1951 or 1951a). See, however, the preface of (Lankford 1975) and (Lankford, Butler 1984) for an appreciation of Evans' work as a forerunner of (Knuth, Bendix 1967).

Other forerunners

In retrospect, it seems that several of the early algebraic algorithms had some flavor of the CPC method, see, for example (Dehn 1911), (Greenlinger 1960), and also Gauss' algorithm for presenting a symmetrical polynomial in terms of the elementary symmetrical polynomials, as has been pointed out by (Loos 1981).

GENERALIZATIONS, INDEPENDENT DEVELOPMENTS AND UNIFYING APPROACHES

Generalizations of the resolution principle

It cannot be the objective of this paper to review how the resolution method developed since its invention in 1965. (For the various refinements of the method see the textbooks on automated theorem proving, for example, (Chang, Lee 1973), (Loveland 1978), (Robinson 1979)). Here, we are exclusively interested in the CPC aspect of the resolution method. In this respect, paramodulation as introduced by (Robinson, Wos 1969) can be viewed as a further inclusion of CPC ideas in resolution: for treating the equality sign, instead of resolvents, paramodulants can be taken from two clauses. Roughly, paramodulation can be viewed as allowing resolution and forming critical pairs in the style of the Knuth-Bendix procedure at the same time. A step further in this direction was the introduction of "narrowing" in (Fay 1979). One narrowing step transforming term t into term t' consists of three substeps:

- a subterm of t is singled out that can be unified by a most general unifier σ with the left-hand side of a rule,
- in $\sigma(t)$ the subterm is replaced by the right-hand side of the rule (after application of σ),
- the resulting term is reduced to normal form using the rules of the rule system.

An overview on narrowing with applications is contained in (Rety et al. 1985).

A more intimate amalgamation of the resolution method with the Knuth-Bendix completion procedure was introduced by (Lankford 1975, 1975a), inspired by (Slagle 1974) who considered term simplifiers without referring to the

Knuth-Bendix procedure. Lankford proposed using the Knuth-Bendix procedure in connection with the resoluton method in order to complete the sets of equalities used in the resolution method. In (Lankford, Ballantyne 1979) it is shown that this leads to a refutation complete proof procedure that goes beyond paramodulation. The ideas developed in this approach also led to a recent interaction between resolution theorem proving and the Knuth-Bendix type completion procedure developed by J. Hsiang and others, see the section on the generalizations of the Knuth-Bendix procedure.

Generalizations of the CPC approach for polynomial rings

(Lauer 1976) was the first to modify my 1965 algorithm to treat polynomial ideals with integer coefficients. The case of integer coefficients needs a modification of the reduction relation "$s \to_F t$" because, in one step, one cannot expect to be able to totally cancel a power product in s since, in the multipliers, we only have integer coefficients available. Instead of one type of S-polynomials ("critical pairs"), Lauer had to introduce two different types, "S-polynomials" and "T-polynomials". As the main result he proved that a finite set F of multivariate polynomials with integer coefficients is a Gröbner basis if the S-polynomials and T-polynomials of the elements in F can be reduced to zero modulo F. (I think that Lauer's work is important since being able to construct Gröbner bases for integer polynomial ideals implies that the uniform word problem for finitely generated rings can be solved.)

In this context it should be also mentioned that in 1976, based on the methods of (Szekeres 1952), R. Stokhamer gave an algorithm for constructing "canonical forms" of multivariate integer polynomials modulo a given ideal F, see (Stokhamer 1975, 1976). A polished version of Stokhamer's work is also contained in (Lauer 1976) and, in short version, in (Lauer 1976a). Stokhamer's method is not a CPC method. It is still not sufficiently worked out how his method compares with the CPC methods, see however (Winkler 1983, 1984).

A different generalization of my algorithm was proposed in (Spear 1977) and, independently, in (Trinks 1978). Their approach consists in defining a class of rings that allow an algorithmic solution of the ideal membership and the syzygy problem (construction of generators for the solution set of linear diophantine equations) and in showing that if R belongs to this class then also $R[x_1,...,x_n]$ belongs to that class. The proof is constructive and involves a generalization of my 1965 algorithm. Instead of the original critical pairs, combinations of the multiples of all the elements in F have to be taken whose leading monomials cancel. The approach of (Spear 1977) was fully developed in (Zacharias 1978) and also in (Schaller 1979). In (Schaller 1979) the rings satisfying the above effectiveness conditions are called "simplification rings". Since fields are simplification rings their approach yields my 1965 algorithm as a special case and, since Z is also a simplification ring, they also achieve a constructive method for obtaining Gröbner bases over Z (and, hence, solving the basic algorithmic problems for integer polynomial ideals).

Apparently independently of my own work, (Bergman 1978) rediscovered essentially the same algorithm, however, in a slightly more general form, namely for free associative k-algebras $k\langle X\rangle$, where X is a set (of indeterminates) and k is a commutative, associative ring with 1. These algebras cover an impressively broad range. However the approach is not broad enough to encompass the case of integer polynomial ideals because (Bergman 1978) only admits pure words in X as the left-hand sides of "patterns" in F. A generalization of my algorithm for the case of non-commutative polynomials has been announced in (Mora 1985a).

In an independent effort, also (Ballantyne, Lankford 1981) rediscovered a special case of my algorithm, namely the case when F contains only polynomials of the form p-q, where p and q are power products. These sets of polynomials may be viewed as the relations describing finitely generated abelian semigroups. The algorithm then yields a solution to the uniform word problem for finitely generated abelian semigroups. Although the algorithm in (Ballantyne, Lankford 1981) is a special case of mine, it is interesting because it was the beginning of a merge of the two branches in CPC research stemming from my 1965 algorithm and from the Knuth-Bendix algorithm, see also the next subsection.

Yet another generalization was initiated by (Bayer 1982) and further developed by (Mora, Möller 1983a) who consider $K[x_1,...,x_n]$-modules and ideals in these modules instead of considering simply ideals in $K[x_1,...,x_n]$. Early ideas in this direction were also announced by (Guiver 1982). (Mora 1985), also treats local rings by the same method. These generalizations produce important applications in algebraic geometry. A special algorithm patterned after my 1965 algorithm but with essentially different term ordering was (Mora 1982) for the computation of tangent cones.

Also working independently, Galligo became interested in standard bases for modules over $K[x_1,...,x_n]$. After some earlier work, for example (Galligo 1979), in which he did not consider the construction of standard bases but only the division algorithm with respect to standard bases, in (Galligo 1984) he developed an algorithm for constructing standard bases that, again, could be viewed as a CPC algorithm. The same idea was then used in (Castro 1984) for ideals of differential operators, see also (Galligo 1985).

Recently, I pursued a new axiomatic approach to generalizing the CPC method to general rings, not only polynomial rings, (see Buchberger 1983a). As a byproduct, this approach yields a CPC algorithm for $\mathbb{Z}[x_1,...,x_n]$ whose structure is identical with my original algorithm for the case of field coefficients. It neither needs two different kinds of S-polynomials as in (Lauer 1976) nor does the axiomatization involve the relatively complicated conditions of the above simplification rings. Independently, arriving from studying the interplay between the Knuth-Bendix algorithm and my algorithm (Kandri-Rody, Kapur 1983), in (Kandri-Rody, Kapur 1984) essentially the same algorithm as in (Buchberger 1983a) is developed and immediately generalized to the case of $R[x_1,...,x_n]$ for Euclidean coefficient rings R in (Kandri-Rody, Kapur 1984a).

Generalizations of the Knuth-Bendix algorithm

The main direction in generalizing the Knuth-Bendix algorithm was to establish procedures that can handle the case when some of the axioms in F destroy the finite termination property of the reduction relation. The general approach pursued for resolving this difficulty was to separate the set A of axioms into to groups of axioms, R and E, and to consider the axioms in R as generators of a corresponding reduction relation $\to_R$ whereas the axioms E are considered to generate a congruence relation $\sim_E$ on the set of terms. The problem then is to develop algorithms that, essentially, operate on the congruence classes of terms w.r.t. $\sim_E$ rather than on the set of terms.

On the set theoretical level all these approaches are based on generalizations and refinements of Newman's lemma (Newman 1942), which has been elegantly proven in (Huet 1977) based on earlier work in (Church, Rosser 1936), (Hindley 1969, 1974), (Aho, Sethi, Ullman 1972), (Sethi 1974), (Lankford 1975), (Staples 1975); see (Huet 1977) for a detailed reference to these contributions. Recently, (Coquand, Huet 1985) gave a machine-checked proof of Newman's lemma. In connection with working over equivalence classes, various generalized versions of Newman's lemma have been proven, for example in (Huet 1977). (A generalization of Newman's lemma of a totally different type, with a different purpose, is developed in (Buchberger 1983a)).

In the context of generalizing the Knuth-Bendix method for congruence classes of terms E-unification, the generalization of the original unification problem for E-congruence classes, plays an essential role. (Two terms s and t are E-unifiable iff there exists a substitution σ such that $\sigma s \sim_E \sigma t$.) E-unification was initiated in (Plotkin 1972). A bibliography on E-unification is (Raulefs et al. 1979). Extensive bibliographies are also contained in (Lankford 1980) and (Fages 1983). Most of the work on E-unification for different sets of axioms E, including (Huet 1976), (Livesey, Siekmann 1976), (Makanin 1977), (Siekmann 1978), (Lankford 1979), (Fay 1979) is reviewed in (Huet, Oppen 1980). Some recent papers on E-unification are (Siekmann, Szabo 1982), (Kirchner 1984), (Jouannaud, Kirchner, Kirchner 1983), (Fages, Huet 1983), (Yellick 1985), (Fortenbacher 1985) and (Tiden, Arnborg 1985). Because of its practical importance, the case of E consisting of axioms expressing associativity and commutativity of function symbols was of central interest in E-unification research. (Stickel 1975, 1976, 1981) developed an algorithm for generating a complete set of unifiers for the associative-commutative (AC) case and showed its partial correctness. However, only recently F. Fages (Fages 1983, 1984) was able to show its total correctness by very subtle complexity measures for terms. This was one of the main achievements in unification research. As a subproblem of the AC-unification problem the solution of linear diophantine equations over the natural numbers appears. A crude algorithm for this problem in (Stickel 1975) is improved in (Huet 1978).

For attacking the problem of establishing a generalization of the Knuth-Bendix method for quotient sets of terms modulo $\sim_E$ different approaches have been developed in the literature. For the discussion of these approaches let us define

$$\rightarrow_{R/E} := \sim_E \circ \rightarrow_R \circ \sim_E,$$

i.e. $\rightarrow_{R/E}$ is the reduction relation induced on the congruence classes modulo $\sim_E$.

The first approach is the one developed in (Lankford, Ballantyne 1977a, 1977b). It works with the above induced reduction relation. The original notion of critical pairs of terms is used for the representatives of the classes. This approach works for finite congruence classes only, because in general the induced reduction relation is undecidable for infinite congruence classes. However, the method tends to be quite inefficient also in the limited case of finite congruence classes.

The other approaches may be viewed in one general framework by introducing one more reduction relation R' between $\rightarrow_R$ and $\rightarrow_{R/E}$:

$$\rightarrow_R \subset R' \subset \rightarrow_{R/E}.$$

This general view has been worked out in (Jouannaud, Kirchner 1984). R' gives one more degree of freedom in executing reductions and establishing Church-Rosser theorems. Using R', the following notions may be distinguished (recall $A=E \cup R$):

$\rightarrow_R$ is R'-Church-Rosser (modulo E) iff
    $t1 \sim_A t2$ implies
    $t1 \rightarrow_{R'}^{*} t1'$, $t2 \rightarrow_{R'}^{*} t2'$ and $t1' \sim_E t2'$ (for some t1', t2'),

$\rightarrow_{R'}$ is confluent (modulo E) iff
    $t \rightarrow_{R'}^{*} t1$, $t \rightarrow_{R'}^{*} t2$ implies
    $t1 \rightarrow_{R'}^{*} t1'$, $t2 \rightarrow_{R'}^{*} t2'$, $t1' \sim_E t2'$ (for some t1', t2'),

$\rightarrow_R$ is R'-local-confluent (modulo E) iff
    $t \rightarrow_{R'} t1$, $t \rightarrow_R t2$ implies
    $t1 \rightarrow_{R'}^{*} t1'$, $t2 \rightarrow_{R'}^{*} t2'$, $t1' \sim_E t2'$ (for some t1', t2'),

$\rightarrow_{R'}$ is coherent (modulo E) iff
    $t \rightarrow_{R'}^{+} t1$, $t \sim_E t2$ implies
    $t1 \rightarrow_{R'}^{*} t1'$, $t2 \rightarrow_{R'}^{+} t2'$, $t1' \sim_E t2'$ (for some t1', t2'),

$\rightarrow_{R'}$ is local-coherent (modulo E) iff
    $t \rightarrow_{R'} t1$, $t \sim_E t2$ implies
    $t1 \rightarrow_{R'}^{*} t1'$, $t2 \rightarrow_{R'}^{+} t2'$, $t1' \sim_E t2'$ (for some t1', t2').

Now the most general Church-Rosser result, due to (Jouannaud, Kirchner 1984), can be formulated as follows:

$\rightarrow R$ is R'-local-confluent and $\rightarrow_{R'}$ is local-coherent iff (*)
    $\rightarrow_R$ is R'-Church-Rosser.

The link between $\rightarrow_{R'}$ and $\rightarrow_{R/E}$ is established by the following observation:

If $\rightarrow_{R/E}$ is terminating, $\rightarrow_{R'}$ is confluent and coherent then
    $\rightarrow R'$-normal-forms and $\rightarrow_{R/E}$-normal-forms coincide.

Hence, instead of working witch R/E, one may work with R' on representatives in the E-congruence classes. In retrospect, one now may view the different approaches as having worked with different R':

The approach initiated by (Lankford, Ballantyne 1977c) and, independently, by Peterson and Stickel in a preliminary version of (Peterson, Stickel 1981) uses R' := R,E (i.e. matching modulo E) and a version of (*) that replaces coherence by compatibility (which is stronger). This approach is restricted to linear equations that possess a finite-complete E-unification algorithm. The approach developed in (Huet 1977) uses R':= R. This approach is restricted to left-linear rules. (Pederson 1984, 1985) use $R' := R \circ E$, where E-equalities are allowed only in variable substitutions, but not at internal occurrences of the rule to be applied. This permits to rewrite an instance of a left-hand side with multiple occurrences of a variable having different (but E-equal) values. Based on (*), this approach has no theoretical restrictions. (Jouannaud, Kirchner 1984) use $R' := Rl \cup Rnl,E$, where Rl contains only left-linear rules and Rnl contains the other rules. This approach is restricted to equational theories E with finite congruence classes and finite-complete unification algorithm. In Kirchner's thesis this approach is generalized to using $R' := R_l \cup R_{nl1,E} \cup R_{nl2} \circ E$. In all these approaches, then, it must be shown that the left-hand side of (*) is implied by the confluence of critical pairs.

A CPC algorithm for the associative-commutative case is given in (Peterson, Stickel 1981). This algorithm has been successfully applied to various axiom systems. A drawback of the algorithm is: it may add new rules even when the initial set of rules generates already a Church-Rosser reduction. (Pederson 1984) gives an algorithm based on his approach. However, now proof details are provided. (Huet 1977) gives an algorithm for left-linear rules. It is faster than the others, but may diverge in examples where the Peterson-Stickel algorithm would converge, because R as a rewrite relation is not strong enough in some practical cases. On the other hand, Huet's algorithm is a semi-decision procedure for equality, which is not guaranteed for the Peterson-Stickel algorithm. (Jouannaud, Kirchner 1984) give an algorithm that combines advantages of Huet's and Peterson-Stickel's algorithm.

Other sources for improvements and generalizations of the above approaches (including the case when $\to_{R/E}$ is not terminating) are (Fages 1983), (Padawitz 1983), (Jouannaud, Kirchner, Remy 1983), (Perdrix 1984), (Göbel 1984).

Some research has also been carried out in generalizing the Knuth-Bendix completion procedure to conditional rewrite systems (i.e. equations preceded by conditions as necessary, for example, for formulating certain of the field axioms). This research was initiated by (Lankford 1979a, 1979c), see also (Brand et al. 1978). The first critical-pair result in this area was proved in (Remy 1982). A recent paper is (Kaplan 1984), which contains the references relevant for the Knuth-Bendix approach in conditional rewriting.

Recently, (Lankford, Butler 1984), (Ballantyne, Butler, Lankford 1984) and (Butler, Lankford 1984) seem to develop a different approach to completing systems involving AC-axioms that resumes the early Evans approach of embedding and brings it together with the methods in (Buchberger 1983a) and (Kandri-Rody, Kapur 1984, 1984a) of constructing Gröbner bases for integer polynomial ideals. A complete analysis of the possible interactions between the approaches seems to be one of the most promising future research topics. It is exciting to see that the research activities that started twenty years ago from very different roots, finally, meet and merge; see also the next section.

Theorem proving by equational rewriting and polynomial reduction

The Peterson-Stickel methodology, by which for a wide class of equational theories complete sets of axioms can be derived, gave rise to an interesting connection between resolution theorem proving and the CPC procedures for term rewriting. Whereas in the early approach of (Lankford 1975, 1975a) the completion procedure for equational axioms was embedded as a subalgorithm into the resolution procedure, in the recent approach by (Hsiang 1981, 1982), see also (Hsiang, Dershowitz 1983) the resolution mechanism itself is described as a reduction with respect to an equational axioms system. The same approach has also been considered by (Fages 1983) and, recently, by (Paul 1985, 1985a). At the core of this method are complete axiom systems for boolean algebra. The existence of such systems is by no means trivial since the straightforward approach by prime implicants does not lead to unique normal forms for boolean terms. (Hsiang 1982) arrives at a complete system of axioms for boolean rings by using the "exclusive or" instead of the usual "or". Basically the canonical forms obtained are the the Reed-Muller forms (Reed 1954), (Muller 54), although in these early papers no notion of term rewriting was involved. (Implicitly these forms are also contained in Stone's theorem on the representation of boolean algebras and in the Venn diagrams.) Roughly, the connection between the resolution method and equational rewriting is established by proving theorems of the following type

> A set C of clauses is unsatisfiable iff
> the Peterson-Stickel completion procedure applied to the boolean algebra axiom system together with an equational transcription of the clauses in C yields the equation "1=0".

(Kapur, Narendran 1985) propose a similar approach that use the algorithm developed in (Buchberger 1983a) and (Kandri-Rody, Kapur 1984) for the completion of polynomial ideals over rings instead of the Peterson-Stickel algorithm.

In the above approach, equational rewriting is used for clausal theorem proving. However, it is conjectured to apply to non-clausal theorem proving as well. In this direction the recent work of (Manna, Waldinger 1985) is of particular interest. They provide a class of inference rules for the treatment of special relations in automated deduction that are based on a general notion of polarity. The rules generalize to an arbitrary binary relation the paramodulation and E-resolution rules. I conjecture that the (Manna, Waldinger 1985) approach and the above approach eventually could merge, if one extended the above approach to non-clausal theorem proving and, at the same time, views the rules in (Manna, Waldinger 1985) as a very general critical-pair formation.

Unifying the Knuth-Bendix algorithm with the Gröbner basis approach

Motivated by the structural similarity between the Knuth-Bendix algorithm and my 1965 algorithm for constructing Gröbner bases, a number of people have tried to show that, in fact, my algorithm can be viewed as a special case of the Knuth-Bendix algorithm. Since my algorithm is concerned with operations in commutative fields (or rings) it is near at hand that embedding my algorithm in the Knuth-Bendix methodology can only be achieved by considering the Peterson-Stickel generalization with AC-unification. Still, there is a crucial difficulty in the case of field coefficients because of the fact that the field axioms are not pure equations. Also, there is an essential difference between the variables used in first order term rewriting and the indeterminates in polynomial rings. The latter obstacle can be handled by considering the indeterminates as constants in the corresponding rewrite system. Starting from a rough sketch in (Loos 1981) of how my algorithm could be embedded in the Peterson-Stickel procedure, the following papers were concerned with filling in the details: (Kandri-Rody, Kapur 1983), (LLopis de Trias 1983) and (Le Chenadec 1983). However, none of these papers really could close all the gaps. For an analysis of the subtle deficiencies left open in these papers see (Winkler 1984), who also provided a construction of a completion procedure that incorporates the Peterson-Stickel procedure and my 1965 algorithm as special cases. The construction developed in (Winkler 1984) distinguishes between reduction and simplification steps. This is an idea borrowed from (Kandri-Rody, Kapur 1984).

Although such embeddings do not add to the computational efficiency of the algorithms (the more general an algorithm is the more it must leave out potential knowledge that can speed up the algorithm in the special case), they have some theoretical value for obtaining a clear picture of what is essential in the constructions. For practical purposes, however, it is of course much better to use the "least common multiple" construction of the polynomial ideal algorithms than to use the whole mechanism of AC-unification (and essentially arrive at the same end.) Embeddings, however, can have the practical significance of making flexible implementations possible that follow the software philosophy of polymorphic data types, see for example the new SCRATCHPAD system (Jenks 1984).

Still, I think that a totally different approach based on an axiomatization of the notion of patterns, multipliers and replacements should be tried sometime, not for obtaining good algorithms but out of structural interest. In this respect, (Bauer 1981) is an outstanding paper that developed much of the CPC approach from an axiomatization of the concept of "substitution".

Other CPC approaches

(Loos 1981) gives some examples of algorithms that could be conceived as CPC algorithms, for example, the collection algorithm in computational group theory (McDonald 1976). There is also a major research activity in confluent Thue systems, see (Book 1982, 1982a, 1985). However, it seems that in this context the tool of critical pairs is not in the center of interest, see however (Nivat 1971). Also, the unification algorithm used as a subalgorithm in resolution theorem proving and in the Knuth-Bendix procedure could be viewed as a CPC algorithm.

APPLICATIONS

Applications of the resolution method

Since universal theorem proving, theoretically, provides the mechanization of mathematics, the application of the resolution method would be universal. Practically, however, there are some reservations whether universal theorem proving will ever play an important role in mathematical discovery. Special theorem provers for particular decidable theories, as for example the quantifier elimination method in (Collins 1975) seem to be more promising for eventual impact on mathematical research. Rather, I guess that most people will agree that universal theorem proving has had its biggest practical impact by providing a method for constructing terms that establish answers to existential theorems. Starting from early (1965) efforts using resolution theorem proving in "question answering" and "program deduction" - see (Chang, Lee 1973) for a review - this development now becomes of central importance in the logic programming movement (Kowalski 1979). This field is too big to be included in the present review.

Applications of the Gröbner bases method

A review of applications of the Gröbner basis method is given in (Buchberger 1983b). We summarize the most important achievements.

Applications for properties of ideals

After having transformed an arbitrary polynomial ideal basis F to a corresponding Gröbner basis G, a number of important algorithmic problems can be solved easily: $f \in$ Ideal(F) can be decided by reducing f to normal form modulo G. Actually, the normal form algorithm with respect to G is a canonical simplifier for ideal congruence. As a special case, the uniform word problem for commutative semigroups (reachability problem for reversible Petri nets) can be solved. Furthermore, the structure of the residue class ring modulo Ideal(F) is fully available: a vector space basis and the complete multiplication table for the residue class ring can be found by the method sketched in the section on the mid sixties algorithms. An easy test on the leading power products of the polynomials in the Gröbner basis G shows whether the ideal has (topological) dimension zero or has higher dimension. Inverses of elements in the residue class rings can be calculated if they exist. (This has applications in radical simplification.) Furthermore, it is easy to compute the Hilbert function of an ideal when a Gröbner basis is known. The above application were contained in the original paper (Buchberger 1965). (Schrader 1976) has shown how to apply Gröbner bases for supporting primary decomposition computations for polynomial ideals. (Kandri-Rody 1984) has shown how, for Gröbner bases, the maximality and primality of polynomial ideals can be tested. He also gave a method for determining the radical and the dimension of an ideal. (Gianni, Trager 1985) have given methods for factorization and gcd computations for multivariate polynomials using Gröbner bases. (Mora, Möller 1983) have given a better algorithm for computing the Hilbert-function bases on Gröbner bases. (Mora 1982) gives a CPC algorithm for computing the tangent cone of a polynomial ideal. (Möller 1976) and (Möller, Buchberger 1982) apply Gröbner bases to construct certain desirable auxiliary formulae for designing multivariate numerical integration formulae. (Wolf 1985) shows how systems of differential equations can be transformed algebraically to Gröbner basis form in order to facilitate subsequent numerical solution. (Wu 1978), for geometrical theorem proving, considers polynomial sets that are close to the characteristic sets considered in (Kandri-Rody 1984). Characteristic sets can be obtained easily from Gröbner bases. Geometrical theorem proving using Gröbner bases is considered in (Kutzler, Stifter 1985). (Robbiano, Valla 1983) consider the application of Gröbner bases to the set-theoretic complete intersection problem for curves in P^3.

The algorithm in (Buchberger 1983a) and (Kandri-Rody, Kapur 1984, 1984 a), besides allowing to solve the membership and canonical simplification problem for polynomial ideals over the integers, also yields a solution for the uniform word problem for finitely presented commutative rings. (The defining relations can be viewed as polynomials with integer coefficients.) Since Gröbner bases are unique (Buchberger 1976), (Kandri-Rody, Kapur 1984) one can construct bijective enumerations of all polynomial ideals over $\mathbf{Z}$. This may lead to a classification of all possible residue class rings. A compilation of results on word problems for various finitely presented structures based on the Gröbner bases approach is given in (Kandri-Rody et al. 1985). In this paper also some complexity results for the respective algorithms are given.

Application for the exact solution of polynomial equations

Having a Gröbner basis G corresponding to a set F of multivariate polynomials (equations) one can effectively determine univariate polynomials $p_i(x_i)$ with minimal degree in the ideal such that the set of zeros of G (F) is contained in the combinations of zeros of the p_i (Buchberger 1970). This method has been improved in (Böge, Gebauer, Kredel 1985) by combining it with factorization. A different method based on Gröbner basis has been introduced in (Trinks 1978). Trinks observed that, if Gröbner bases are computed with respect to the "purely lexicographical term ordering" then they automatically turn out to have their variables "separated". Thus, the system of equations can be solved by successive computation of the components of the zeros. Stated differently, a Gröbner bases G w.r.t. the purely lexicographical ordering allows to read of all the elimination ideals directly from the elements in G.

Application for computation of syzygies

(Spear 1977) and (Zacharias 1978) have first observed that the S-polynomials (critical pairs) of the elements of a Gröbner bases essentially form a generating set for the module of all syzygies of a polynomial ideal, i.e. linear diophantine equations with polynomial coefficients can be solved effectively by considering S-polynomials. This method has been greatly extended to compute the whole chain of syzygy modules of a polynomial ideal (the "free resolution") by (Bayer 1982) and (Mora, Möller 1983a). (Möller 1985) has applied the method to Taylor resolution.

Applications of the Knuth-Bendix type algorithms

The original and main application of the Knuth-Bendix algorithm and the algorithms derived from it are the completion of equational axiom systems for solving the word problem for the respective equational theories, i. e. the problem to decide, for given terms s and t, whether "s=t" can be derived in the theory by equational reasoning. (It also should be stated at this place that by the correctness proof for the Knuth-Bendix procedure given in (Huet 1981) the procedure, under certain conditions, yields at least a semidecision procedure for "s=t" even if it does not terminate). Through the years, by the different variants of the procedure, an impressive list of axiom systems have been completed. Such lists have been published several times in the literature. Thus, in the present paper, we only point to these reviews: (Knuth, Bendix 1967), (Lankford 1979b), (Lankford 1980), (Hullot 1980), (Butler, Lankford 1980), (Le Chenadec 1983), (Jouannaud, Kirchner 1984). As pointed out earlier, recently, a particular interest evolved in completing boolean algebra (Hsiang 1982), (Fages 1983), (Paul 1985). For some more examples see (Pederson 1984).

For some important axiom systems - lattices and modular lattices, Heyting algebras, Lie algebras, fields - no complete systems are known.

Special completion methods have been derived for solving word problems for finitely generated groups, see (Bücken 1979, 1979a) and (Richter, Kemmenich 1980) and also (Le Chenadec 1983, 1985). The word problem for a finitely presented group may be solved by deciding whether or not a given word is equal to the unit element. This idea leads to the notion of limited confluence (which is useful also in boolean algebras, see the work of (Paul 1985) on the confluence of valid formulae). Dehn's algorithm (Dehn 1911) for small cancellation groups is a well known algorithm that follows this idea. This algorithm may be viewed as a rewriting system computed by completion limited to superpositions between a finite group presentation and the complete sets of rules for free groups. The connection between Dehn's algorithm and completion algorithms was proved in Bücken's thesis and further analyzed by Le Chenadec. (Bauer 1981) analyzes connections between rewrite rules and standard combinatorial techniques (free, direct, semi-direct and amalgamated products etc.) and gives a complexity hierarchy. Le Chenadec gives complete systems for several families of classical groups (Coxeter, polyhedral, surface groups etc.). See also (Lankford, Butler, Ballantyne 1983) for the case of finitely presented abelian groups.

(Choppy, Johnen 1985) give applications of completed rule sets for deciding properties of Petri nets. (In the case of reversible Petri nets the reachability property is known to be easily decidable using the method of Gröbner bases, see (Buchberger 1983b)).

Particular practical interest in completed axiom systems developed from progress in the use of abstract data types. For practical computation in the direct implementation of algebraically specified abstract data types the decidability of the corresponding word problem for terms is a prerequisite, see for example (Gerhart et al. 1980), (Lichtenberger 1980). The Knuth-Bendix completion method provides a general tool for producing decision algorithms. Research on this application was pursued, for example, by (Musser 1977, 1978, 1978a), (Goguen et al. 1982), (Musser, Kapur 1982), (Jouannaud 1983)

An exciting application was developed by (Musser 1980), (Huet, Hullot 1980), (Goguen 1980) and others: "inductionless induction". The method consists in showing the validity of an equation e in the "initial model" of a set E of equations by applying the Knuth-Bendix completion algorithm to $E \cup \{e\}$. (Under certain conditions) e is valid in the inital model iff the algorithm stops without generating an inconsistency (1=0). Thus, this method allows to automatically prove sentences that normally would require inventing an induction hypothesis for an inductive proof. The original method is due to Musser with extensions by Goguen. They require that the user axiomatizes equality. The method by Huet and Hullot does not require this but presupposes that the set of function symbols is partitioned into constructors (completely free operators) and other operators. An extension of the method that works under very weak assumptions is announced by Jouannaud and Kounalis. Finally, the application of equational completion for simulating clausal theorem proving may be viewed as a step in the same direction but more general in nature. The respective contributions were reviewed in the section on generalizations.

TECHNICALITIES

Termination

Termination of Gröbner bases algorithms

Reduction of polynomials is always noetherian. Thus, the termination problem in Gröbner basis algorithms is mainly the problem of terminating completion. For my 1965 algorithm the termination proof for the general case is given in (Buchberger 1970), where Dickson's lemma has been rediscovered. Essentially Dickson's lemma is also sufficient for showing termination of other Gröbner basis algorithms. A very elegant proof of Dickson's lemma, based on abstract properties of products of ordered set, has recently been given by (Cousineau 1984). A different termination proof for my algorithm can be given by applying Hilbert's basis theorem, see (Bergman 1978). Alternatively, Dickson's lemma and the concept of a Gröbner basis can be taken as primitives and Hilbert's basis theorem, then, is a corollary, see (Buchberger 1982). The equivalence of Dickson's lemma and Hilbert's basis theorem, together with other interesting results, were also proven in (Butler, Lankford 1984). (Kollreider 1978) and (Robbiano 1985) characterized the term orderings that are admissable for the Gröbner basis approach.

Termination of the Knuth-Bendix type algorithms

In this context, the crucial problem is the invention of noetherian term orderings that are compatible with the reduction. Several methods have been developed: well-founded mapping, increasing interpretation, simplification ordering, recursive path ordering, homomorphic interpretation etc. The literature on this topic including (Kruskal 1960), (Nash-Williams 1963), (Manna, Ness 1970), (Dershowitz 1979a, 1979b), (Dershowitz, Manna 1979), (Plaisted 1978, 1978a), (Lankford 1979b), (Kamin, Lévy 1980) and others, is reviewed in (Huet, Oppen 1980). Recent contributions to termination orderings are (Jeanrond 1980), (Lescanne 1981), (Dershowitz 1982), (Jouannaud, Lescanne, Reinig 1982), (Jouannaud, Lescanne 1982), (Munoz 1983), (Plaisted 1983), (Lescanne 1984), (Jouannaud, Munoz, 1984), (Bachmair, Plaisted 1985),

(Huet, Lankford 1978) show that the uniform halting problem for rewrite systems is undecidable.

Strategies

Strategies for the resolution method

The sequence in which resolvents are built and other techniques play a crucial role for improving the efficiency of the resolution method. This was an extensive field for research, see the textbooks on resolution theorem proving mentioned above. The work of Hsiang sketched above may also be seen in this context. His N-strategy can be viewed as a combination of parts of several strategies used in resolution theorem proving. In the context of this paper the strategies used in resolution theorem proving are interesting because, by the similarities between the CPC algorithms, it might be worthwhile to study possibilites for carrying some of the strategies from the resolution method over to, say, the Knuth-Bendix type algorithms. This idea has been pursued to a certain extent in (Küchlin 1982).

Strategies for the Knuth-Bendix and the Gröbner bases algorithms

Already in (Buchberger 1965) and in (Knuth-Bendix 1967) it was suggested to keep the systems of patterns developing in the course of the algorithm mutually reduced. The organization of this strategy is a non-trivial task. (Huet 1981) gave a complete proof for the correctness of the Knuth-Bendix algorithm when incorporating successive reduction of rules. In the case of Gröbner bases algorithms, in addition, it is suggested to consider first critical pairs with overlapping power products of low degree. The reasons for this are explained in some detail in (Buchberger 1979).

Criteria for omitting certain critical pairs

In (Buchberger 1979) it was shown that certain critical pairs need not be considered in the CPC algorithm because it can be predicted that they are reducible to the same normal form. The theoretical reason for this can be based on a generalized Newman lemma that has been formulated in full generality in (Buchberger 1983a). I included its proof in (Winkler, Buchberger 1983). Roughly, the lemma says that for guaranteeing local confluene it suffices that each critical pair can be connected "below" its common ancestor. Recently, it has been shown that essentially the same criterion can be applied to Knuth-Bendix type algorithms (Winkler, Buchberger 1983), (Winkler 1985), (Küchlin 1985). The approach of speeding up CPC algorithms by criteria of the above type is based on additional mathematical insight rather than on heuristics.

Complexity

Relatively little is known on the complexity of CPC algorithms.

Complexity of Gröbner bases algorithms

A first (very coarse) complexity analysis for the case of two variables was already given in (Buchberger 1965). A realistic analysis for this case can be found in (Buchberger 1983) and for the trivariate case in (Winkler 1984, 1984a). In the bivariate case the maximal degree of the Gröbner basis corresponding to a given basis is a linear function of the maximal degree of the input polynomials. A similar bound is derived in (Lazard 1983) and in (Giusti 1985). Lazard showed that a linear bound also holds in the general case of arbitrarily many variables if some special properties of the ideal are presupposed. Similar results are contained in (Bayer 1982). (Möller, Mora 1984) give some more bounds on the degrees. Intrinsically, the problem of computing Gröbner bases is difficult. (Cardoza, Lipton, Meyer 1976) and (Mayr, Meyer 1981) showed that the uniform membership problem for polynomial ideals is essentially exponentially space complete. This is supported by the investigation in (Huynh 1984) for some special classes. The practical relevance of these results is a matter of point of view. (Applications of CPC algorithms often are in the "sweep coherence" (Goad 1980) context). However, practical experiences show that, in fact, Gröbner bases computations are complex. Polynomials in six variables of degree, say, three mark the size of problems that are at the border of practical feasibility.

Complexity of Knuth-Bendix computations

The only complexity result I am aware of is (Bauer, Otto 1984), where it is shown that complete rewrite systems may have an arbitrarily complex word problem.

Implementations

Implementations of the resolution method

A review on such implementations is outside the scope of this paper. See the textbooks on automated theorem proving.

Implementations of Gröbner basis algorithms

Special implementations have been undertaken several times: (Buchberger 1965), (Schrader 1976), (Zacharias 1978), (Winkler 1978), (Schaller 1979). A very flexible and user-friendly implementation is described in (Böge, Gebauer, Kredel 1985). This implementation is in the SAC-2 computer algebra system (Collins, Loos 1980). At present, implementations are also available in all other major computer algebra systems, for example, MACSYMA (Pavelle, Wang 1985), REDUCE (Hearn 1984), NEW SCRATCHPAD (Jenks 1984), muMATH (Stoutemyer 1985).

Implementations of Knuth-Bendix type algorithms

The first implementation was in (Knuth, Bendix 1967). Other implementations in "rewrite rule laboratories" are described in (Hullot 1980), (Stickel 1981), (Küchlin 1982a), (Lescanne 1983), (Kirchner, Kirchner 1983), (Kapur, Sivakumar 1983), (Lescanne 1983), (Le Chenadec 1983), (Forgaard, Guttag 1984), (Thomas 1984), (Dick 1985), (Hussmann 1985), (Musser 1980a) in the framework of AFFIRM, (Futatsugi et al. 1985) in the framework of OBJ. (Fages 1985) is a manual on the (Hullot 1980) completion system developed at INRIA. A symposium on implementations of the Knuth-Bendix algorithm has been held recently (Guttag et al. 1984). Stickel's implementation is now available on LISP machines and seems to be the fastest implementation for full CA. Hullot's system, the KB system, is well documented and easily available (in MacLISP, FranzLISP, ZetaLISP etc.). The REVE system (Lescanne 1983), (Forgaard, Guttag 1984), (Kirchner, Kirchner 1983, 1985) provides semi-automated termination proofs.

ACKNOWLEDGEMENT

J. Dick, F. Fages, J. Hsiang, G. Huet, J.-P. Jouannaud, S. Kaplan, P. Le Chenadec, and D. Musser gave valuable comments to various parts of the paper. J. Dick did a careful proof reading. My best thanks to all of them.

This work was supported by a grant from SIEMENS Munich (Dr. H. Schwärtzel).

REFERENCES

Aho, A., Sethi, R., and Ullman, J.D., 1972:
Code Optimization and finite Church-Rosser theorems.
In: Design and Optimisation of Compilers (ed. by R. Rustin), Prentice Hall, 89-105.

Armbruster, D., 1985:
Bifurcation theory and computer algebra: an initial approach.
Proc. EUROCAL 85, LNCS, Springer,to appear.

Bachmair, L., and Buchberger, B., 1980:
A simplified proof of the characterization theorem for Gröbner bases.
ACM SIGSAM Bull 14/4, 29-34.

Bachmair, L., and Plaisted, D.A., 1985:
Termination orderings for associative commutative rewriting systems.
J. of Symbolic Computation (Academic Press), to appear.

Ballantyne, A.M., and Lankford, D.S., 1981:
New decision algorithms for finitely presented commutative semigroups.
Computers and Maths. with Appls. 7, 159-165; preliminary version: Rep. MTP-4, Louisiana Tech Univ., Dep. of Math. 1979.

Ballantyne, M., Butler, G., and Lankford, D., 1984:
On practical uniform decision algorithms for the uniform word problem in finitely presented commutative rings of characteristics ∞, ..., 3, 2, 1.
Tech. Report, Louisiana Tech Univ., Dep. of Math.

Bauer, G., 1981:
The representation of monoids by confluent rule systems.
Ph.D. thesis, University of Kaiserlautern (FRG), Dept. of Comp. Scie.

Bauer, G., and Otto, F, 1984:
Finite complete rewriting systems and the complexity of the word problem.
Manuscript, Univ. of Kaiserslautern, Dep. Comp. Scie.

Bayer, D., 1982:
The division algorithm and the Hilbert scheme.
Ph.D. thesis, Harvard University, Cambridge, Mass., Math. Dept.

Bergman, G.M., 1978:
The diamond lemma for ring theory.
Advances in Math. 29, 178-218.

Blass, A., and Gurevich, Yu., 1983:
Equivalence relations, invariants, and normal forms.
Proc. Logic and Machines: Decision Problems and Complexity, (ed. by E. Börger, G. Hasenjaeger, D.Rödding), Springer LNCS 171, 24-42.

Böge, W., Gebauer, R., and Kredl, H., 1985:
Gröbner-Bases using SAC2.
Proc. EUROCAL 85, to appear.

Book, R.V., 1982:
Confluent and other types of Thue systems.
J. ACM 29/1, 171-182.

Book, R.V., 1982a:
The power of the Church-Rosser property for string rewriting systems.
Proc. 6th Conference on Automated Deduction, New York, (ed. by D. W. Loveland), Springer LNCS 138, 360-368.

Book, R.V., 1985:
Thue systems as rewriting systems.
These proceedings.

Brandt, D., Darringer, J.A., and Joyner, W.H., 1978:
Completeness of conditional reductions.
IBM Research Center, Yorktown Heights.

Buchberger, B., 1965:
An algorithm for finding a basis for the residue class ring of a zero-dimensional polynomial ideal (German).

Ph.D. thesis, Univ. of Innsbruck (Austria), Math. Inst.
Buchberger, B., 1970:
An algorithmical criterion for the solvability of algebraic systems of equations (German).
Aequationes mathematicae, 4/3, 374-383.
Buchberger, B., 1976:
A theoretical basis for the reduction of polynomials to canonical form.
ACM SIGSAM Bull. 10/3, 19-29 and 10/4, 19-24.
Buchberger, B., 1979:
A criterion for detecting unnecessary reductions in the construction of Gröbner bases.
Proc. EUROSAM 79, Marseille, June 1979, (ed. by W. Ng), Springer LNCS 72, 3-21.
Buchberger, B., 1982:
Miscellaneous Results on Gröbner bases for polynomial ideals II.
Techn. Report CAMP 82-23, Univ. of Linz, Math. Inst.; also Techn. Report 83-1, Univ. of Delaware, Dep. of Comp. and Inform. Scie.
Buchberger, B., 1983:
A note on the complexity of constructing Gröbner bases.
Proc. EUROCAL 83, London, March 1983, (ed. by J. A. van Hulzen), Springer LNCS 162, 137-145.
Buchberger, B., 1983a:
A critical-pair/completion algorithm for finitely generated ideals in rings.
Proc. Logic and Machines: Decision Problems and Complexity, (ed. by E. Börger, G. Hasenjaeger, D.Rödding), Springer LNCS 171, 137-161.
Buchberger, B., 1983b:
Gröbner bases: an algorithmic method in polynomial ideal theory.
Techn. Report CAMP-83.29, Univ. of Linz, Math. Inst.; to appear as Chapter 6 in: Recent Trends in Multidimensional Systems Theory (ed. by. N. K. Bose), Reidel, 1985.
Buchberger, B., 1984:
Mathematics for computer science II - algorithm types and problem solving strategies.
Lecture notes, Univ. of Linz, Math. Institute, CAMP-Nr. 84-4.0.
Buchberger, B., and Loos, R., 1982:
Algebraic simplification.
In: Computer Algebra - Symbolic and Algebraic Computation (ed. by B. Buchberger, G. Collins, R. Loos eds.), Springer, Wien - New York, 11-43.
Bücken, H., 1979:
Reduction systems and word problems (German).
Rep. 3, RWTH, Aachen, FRG, Computer Science Inst.
Bücken, H., 1979:
Reduction systems and small cancellation theory.
Proc. 4th Workshop on Automated Deduction, 53-59.
Butler, G., Lankford, D., 1980:
Experiments with computer implementations of procedures which often derive decision algorithms for the word problem in abstract algebras.
Techn. Rep. MTP-7, Louisiana Tech. Univ., Dep. of Math.
Butler, G., Lankford, D., 1984:
Dickson's lemma, Hilbert's basis theorem, and applications to completion in commutative noetherian rings.
Manuscript, Dept. Math. and Statistics, Louisiana Tech. Univ., Ruston.
Cardoza, E., Lipton, R., and Meyer, A.R., 1976:
Exponential space complete problems for Petri nets and commutative semigroups.
Conf. Record of the 8th Annual ACM Symp. on Theory of Computing, 50-54.
Castro, F., 1984:
Théoreme de division pour les opérateurs differentiels et calcul des multiplicités.
Thèse 3ème cycle, Univ. Paris VII.
Chang, C., and Lee, R.C., 1973:

Symbolic logic and mechanical theorem proving.
Academic Press.
Church, A., Rosser, J.B., 1936:
Some properties of conversion.
Trans. AMS 39, 472-482.
Collins, G., 1975:
Quantifier elimination for real closed fields by cylindrical algebraic decomposition.
Proc. 2nd GI Conf. on Automata Theory and Formal Languages, (ed. by H. Brakhage), Kaiserslautern, Springer LNCS 33, 134-183.
Collins, G.E., and Loos, R.G., 1980:
ALDES and SAC-2 now available.
ACM SIGSAM Bulletin Vol. 14/2, p. 19.
Coquand, T., and Huet, G., 1985:
Constructions: a higher order proof system for mechanizing mathematics.
Invited paper in Proc. EUROCAL 85, Springer LNCS, to appear.
Cousineau, G., 1984:
Preuves de terminaison des systèmes de réécriture.
Notes de cours de DEA, University Paris 7.
Davis, M. (ed.), 1965:
The undecidable: basic papers on undecidable propositions, unvsolvable problems and computable functions.
Raven Press, Hewlett, New York.
Dehn, M., 1911:
On infinte discontinuous groups (German).
Math. Ann. 71, 116-144.
Dershowitz, N., 1979a:
Orderings for term-rewriting systems.
Proc. 20th Symp. on Foundations of Comp. Sci., 123-131.
Dershowitz, N., 1979b:
A note on simplification orderings.
Inf. Process. Lett. 9/5, 212-215.
Dershowitz, N., 1982:
Orderings for term-rewriting systems.
J. of Theoretical Computer Science 17, 279-301.
Dershowitz, N., 1982a:
Applications of the Knuth-Bendix completion procedure.
Prelim. rep., Univ. of Illinois at Urbana-Champaign, Dep. Comp. Scie.
Dershowitz, N., 1985:
Termination issues in term rewriting systems.
These proceedings.
Dershowitz, N., and Manna, Z., 1979:
Proving termination with multiset orderings.
Comm. ACM 22, 465-475.
Dershowitz, N., Hsiang J., Josephson, N.A., and Plaisted, D.A., 1983:
Associative-commutative rewriting.
Proc. 10th IJCAI, Karlsruhe 1983, 990-994.
Detlefs, D., Forgaard, R., 1985:
A procedure for automatically proving the termination of a set of rewrite rules.
These proceedings.
Dick, A.J.J., 1985:
ERIL - Equational reasoning: an interactive laboratory.
Proc. EUROCAL 85, LNCS, Springer, to appear.
Dickson, L.E., 1913:
Finiteness of the odd perfect and primitive abundant numbers with n distinct prime factors.
Am. J. of Math. 35, 413-426.
Evans, T., 1951:
On multiplicative systems defined by generators and relations I; normal form theorems.
Proc. Cambridge Philosophy Soc. 47, 637-649.

Evans, T., 1951a:
The word problem for abstract algebras.
The J. of the London Math. Soc. 26, 64-71.
Evans, T., 1978:
Word problems.
Bull. AMS 84/5, 789-802.
Fages, F., 1983:
Formes canoniques dans les algèbres booléennes et applications à la démonstration automatique en logique de premier ordre.
These 3eme cycle, Universite Paris VI.
Fages, F., 1984:
Associative-commutative unification.
Proc. 7th CADE, (ed. by R. Shostak), Napa Valley, Springer LNCS 170.
Fages, F., 1985:
KB reference manual.
INRIA Rep. no. 368.
Fages, F., and Huet, G., 1983:
Complete sets of unifiers and matchers in equational theories.
Proc. CAAP 83, L' Aqila, (ed. by G. Ausiello, M.Protasi), Springer LNCS 159, 205-220.
Fay, M., 1979:
First order unification in equational theories.
Proc. 4th CADE, Springer LNCS 87, 161-167.
Forgaard, R., and Guttag, J.V., 1984:
REVE: A term rewriting system generator with failure-resistent Knuth-Bendix.
MIT-LCS.
Fortenbacher, A., 1985:
An algebraic approach to unification under associativity and commutativity.
These proceedings.
Futatsugi, K., Goguen, J., Jouannaud, J.P., Mesenguer, J., 1985:
Principles of OBJ2.
Proc. of the 1985 Symp. on Principles of Progr. Lang., to appear.
Galligo, A., 1979:
The division theorem and stability in local analytic geometry (French).
Extrait des Annales de l'Institut Fourier, Univ. of Grenoble, 29/2.
Galligo, A., 1984:
Algorithmes de calcul de base standards.
Manuscript, Univ. of Nice, France.
Galligo, A., 1985:
Some algorithmic questions on ideals of differential operators.
Proc. EUROCAL 85, Springer LNCS, to appear.
Gerhart, S.L., Musser, D.R., Thompson, D.H., Baker, D.A., Bates, R.L., Erickson, R.W., London, R.L., Taylor, D.G., Wile, D.S., 1980:
An overview on AFFIRM: a specification and verification system.
In: Information Processing 80 (ed. by S.H. Lavington), North-Holland, 343-387.
Gianni, P., and Trager, B., 1985:
GCD's and factoring multivariate polynomials using Gröbner bases.
Proc. EUROCAL 85, Springer LNCS, to appear.
Giusti, M., 1984:
Some effectivity problems in polynomial ideal theory.
Proc. EUROSAM 84, Cambridge, (ed. J. Fitch), Springer LNCS 174, 159-172.
Giusti, M., 1985:
A note on the complexity of constructing standard bases.
Proc. EUROCAL 85, Springer LNCS, to appear.
Goad,C.A., 1980:
Proofs of descriptions of computation.
Proc. 5th CADE, Springer LNCS 87, 39-52.
Göbel, R., 1983:
A completion procedure for globally finite term rewriting systems.
Proc. of an NSF Workshop on the Rewrite Rule Laboratory, General Electric,

1983, Schenectady, (ed. by J.V. Guttag, D. Kapur, D.R. Musser), Rep. no. 84GEN008, 155-206.

Goguen, J.A., 1980:
How to prove algebraic inductive hypotheses without induction, with applications to the correctness of data type implementations.
Proc. 5th CADE, (ed. by W.Bibel and R. Kowalski), Springer LNCS 87, 356-373. 222

Goguen, J.A., Meseguer, J., and Plaisted, D., 1982:
Programming with parameterized abstract objects in OBJ.
In: Theory and Practice of Software Technology (ed. by D. Ferrari, M. Bolognani and J. Goguen), North-Holland, 163-193.

Greenlinger, M., 1960:
Dehn's algorithm for the word problem.
Comm. on Pure and Applied Math. 13. 67-83.

Gröbner, W., 1950:
On elimination theory (German).
Monatshefte für Mathematik 54, 71-78.

Guiver, J.P., 1982:
Contributions to two-dimensional systems theory.
Ph. D. thesis, Univ. of Pittsburgh, Math. Dept.

Guttag, J.V., Kapur D., and Musser, D.R., (eds.), 1984:
Proc. of an NSF Workshop on the Rewrite Rule Laboratory, Sept. 6-9, 1983, General Electric, Schenectady, NY, Rep. no. 84GEN008.

Hearn, A.C., 1984:
Reduce user's manual: version 3.1.
The Rand Corporation, Santa Monica, California.

Herbrand, J., 1930:
Researches in the theory of demonstration.
Ph.D. thesis, Univ. of Paris; reprinted in: From Frege to Gödel: A Source Book in Mathematical Logic, (ed. by van J. Heijenoort), Harvard Univ. Press, Cambridge, Mass.

Hermann, G., 1926:
The question of finitely many steps in the theory of polynomial ideals (German).
Math. Ann. 95, 736-788.

Hindley, R., 1969:
An abstract form of the Church-Rosser theorem I.
J. of Symbolic Logic, 34/4, 545-560.

Hindley, R., 1974:
An abstract form of the Church-Rosser theorem II: applications.
J. of Symbolic Logic 39+1, 1-21.

Hironaka, H., 1964:
Resolution of singularities of an algebraic variety over a field of characteristic zero: I, II.
Annals of Math., 79, 109-326.

Hsiang, J., 1981:
Refutational theorem proving using term rewriting systems. AI J. 1985.
Manuscript, Univ. of Illinois at Urbana Champaign, Dep. Comp. Scie.

Hsiang, J., 1982:
Topics in automated theorem proving and program generation. AI J. 1985.
Ph. d. thesis, Univ. of Illinois at Urbana-Champaign, Dept. of Comp. Scie.

Hsiang, J., 1985:
Two results in term rewriting theorem proving.
These proceedings.

Hsiang, J., and Dershowitz, N., 1983:
Rewrite methods for clausal and non-clausal theorem proving.
Proc. ICALP 83, 10th Colloqium, Barcelona, Spain, Springer LNCS 154, 331-346.

Hsiang, J., and Plaisted, D., 1982:
Deductive program generation.
Techn. Rep., Univ. of Illinois at Urbana-Champaign, Comp. Scie. Dept.

Huet, G., 1976:

Résolution d'équation dans des languages d'ordre 1, 2, ..., ω.
Thèse d'etat, Univ. Paris VII.
Huet, G., 1977:
Confluent reductions: abstract properties and applications to term rewriting systems.
J. ACM 27 (1980), 797-821; preprint: 21st FOCS.
Huet, G., 1978:
An algorithm to generate the basis of solutions to homogenous linear diophantine equations.
Information Processing Letters 7/3, 144-147.
Huet, G., 1981:
A complete proof of the Knuth-Bendix completion algorithm.
J. Comp. and System Sci. 23, 11-21.
Huet, G., and Hullot, J.M., 1980:
Proofs by induction in equational theories with constructors.
21st IEEE Symp. on Foundations of Comp. Scie., 96-107; also: J. ACM 25 (1982), 239-266.
Huet, G., and Lankford, D.S., 1978:
On the uniform halting problem for term rewriting systems.
Rapport Laboria 283, INRIA, Rocquencourt, Les Chesnay, France.
Huet, G., and Oppen, D.C., 1980:
Equations and rewrite rules: a survey.
In: Formal Language Theory, Perspectives and Open Problems (ed. by R. V. Book), Academic Press, 349-405.
Hullot, J.M., 1979:
Associative-commutative pattern matching.
5th IJCAI, Tokyo.
Hullot, J.M., 1980:
A catalogue of canonical term rewriting systems.
Techn. Rep. CSL-113, SRI International, Menlo Park, Calif.
Hullot, J.M., 1980a:
Canonical forms and unification.
Proc. 5th CADE, (ed. by W. Bibel and R. Kowalski), Springer LNCS 87, 318-334.
Hullot, J.M., 1980 a:
Compilation de formes canoniques dans les theories équationnelles.
Thèse 3ème cycle, U. Paris Sud.
Hussmann, H., 1985:
Unification in conditional equational theories.
Proc. EUROCAL 85, Springer LNCS, to appear.
Huynh, D.T., 1984:
The complexity of the membership problem for two subclasses of polynomial ideals.
Manuscript, Iowa State Univ., Ames, Comp. Scie. Dep.
Jeanrond, J., 1980:
Deciding unique termination of permutative rewrite systems: choose your term algebra carefully.
Proc. 5th CADE, (ed. by W. Bibel and R. Kowalski), Springer LNCS 87.
Jenks, R.D., 1984:
A primer: 11 keys to NEW SCRATCHPAD.
Proc. EUROSAM 84, Cambridge, England, (ed. by J. Fitch), Springer LNCS 174, 123-147.
Jouannaud, J.P., 1983:
Confluent and coherent equational term rewriting systems.
Proc. CAAP 83, L' Aqila, (ed. by G. Ausiello, M.Protasi), Springer LNCS 159, 269-283.
Jouannaud, J.P., and Kirchner, H., 1984:
Completion of a set of rules modulo a set of equations.
Techn. Rep. SRI International, Menlo Park, Calif.; see also:
Proc. of an NSF Workshop on the Rewrite Rule Raboratory, General Electric, 1983, Schenectady, (ed. by J.V. Guttag, D. Kapur, D.R. Musser), Rep. no. 84GEN008, pp.207-228.

Jouannaud, J.P., Kirchner, C., and Kirchner, H., 1983:
Incremental construction of unification algorithms in equational theories.
Proc. ICALP 83, 10th Colloqium, Barcelona, Spain, Springer LNCS 154, 361-373.
Jouannaud, J.P., Kirchner H., and Remy, J.L., 1983:
Church-Rosser properties of weakly terminating equational term rewriting systems.
Proc. 10th IJCAI, Karlsruhe.
Jouannaud, J.P., Lescanne, P., and Reinig, F., 1982:
Recursive decomposition ordering.
Conf. on Formal Description of Programming Concepts, (D. Bjorner), North Holland.
Jouannaud, J.P., and Lescanne, P., 1982:
On multiset orderings.
Information Processing Letters 15, 57-62.
Jouannaud, J.P., and Munoz, M., 1984:
Termination of a set of rules modulo a set of equations.
Proc. 7th CADE, (ed. by R. Shostak), Springer LNCS 170, 175-193.
Kamin, Lęvy, 1980:
Attempts for generalizing the recursive path ordering.
Unpublished manuscript, Univ. of Paris 7.
Kandri-Rody, A., 1984:
Effective methods in the theory of polynomial ideals.
Ph.D. thesis, Rensselaer Polytechnic Institute, Troy, NY, Math. Dep.
Kandri-Rody, A., and Kapur, D., 1983:
On relationship between Buchberger's Gröbner basis algorithm and the Knuth-Bendix completion procedure.
Rep. no. 83CRD286, General Electric, Schenectady.
Kandri-Rody, A., and Kapur, D., 1984:
Computing the Gröbner basis of an ideal in polynomial rings over the integers.
3rd MACSYMA Userss' Conf., Schenectady, NY, July 1984.
Kandri-Rody, A., and Kapur, D., 1984a:
Algorithms for computing Gröbner bases of polynomial ideals over various Euclidean rings.
Proc. EUROSAM 84, Cambridge, (ed. J. Fitch), Springer LNCS vol. 174, 195-206.
Kandri-Rody, A., Kapur, D., Narendran, P., 1985:
An ideal-theoretic approach to word problems and unification problems over finitely presented commutative algebras.
These proceedings.
Kanger, S., 1957.
Provability in logic.
Stockholm.
Kaplan, S., 1984:
Fair conditional rewriting systems: unification, termination and confluence.
Techn. Rep. No. 194, Lab. de Recherche en Informatique, Orsay, France.
Kapur, D., and Krishnamurthy, B., 1983:
A natural proof system based on rewriting techniques.
Proc. of an NSF Workshop on the Rewrite Rule Laboratory, General Electric, Schenectady, 1983, (ed. by J.V. Guttag, D. Kapur, D.R. Musser), Rep. no. 84GEN008, 337-348.
Kapur, D., and Narendran, P., 1985:
An equational approach to theorem proving in first-order predicate calculus.
Proc. IJCAI 1985, Los Angeles, to appear.
Kapur, D., and Sivakumar, G., 1983:
Architecture of and experiments with RRL, a rewrite rule laboratory.
Proc. of an NSF Workshop on the Rewrite Rule Laboratory, General Electric, Schenectady, (ed. by J. V. Guttag, D. Kapur, D. R. Musser), Rep. no. 84GEN008, 33-56.

Kirchner, C., 1984:
A new equational unification method: a generalization of Martelli-Montanari algorithm.
Proc. 7th CADE, (ed. by R. Shostak), Springer LNCS 170.
Kirchner, C., and Kirchner, H., 1983:
Current implementation of the general E-completion algorithm.
Techn. Rep., Centre de Recherches en Informatique de Nancy.
Kirchner, H., 1984:
A general inductive completion algorithm and application to abstract data types.
Proc. 7th CADE, (ed. by R. Shostak), Springer LNCS 170.
Kirchner, C., and Kirchner, H., 1985:
Implementation of a general completion procedure parameterized by built-in theories and strategies.
Proc. EUROCAL 85, Springer LNCS, to appear.
Knuth, D.E., 1970:
Notes on central groupoids.
J. Comb. Theory 8, 376-390.
Knuth, D.E., and Bendix, P. B., 1967:
Simple word problems in universal algebras.
Proc. of the Conf. on Computational Problems in Abstract Algebra, Oxford, 1967, (ed. by J. Leech), Pergamon Press, Oxford, 1970, 263-298.
Kollreider, C., 1978:
Polynomial reduction: the influence of the ordering of terms on a reduction algorithm.
Techn. Rep. CAMP 78-4, Univ. of Linz, Austria (Europe), Math. Dep.
Kruskal, J.B., 1960:
Well-quasi-ordering, the tree theorem and Vazsonyi's conjecture.
Trans. AMS 95, 210-225.
Küchlin, W., 1982:
A theorem-proving approach to the Knuth-Bendix completion algorithm.
Proc. EUROCAM 82, Marseille, (ed. by J. Calmet), Springer LNCS, 144, 101-108.
Küchlin, W., 1982a:
An implementation and investigation of the Knuth-Bendix completion procedure.
Internal Rep., Comp. Scie. Dept., Univ. of Karlsruhe, FRG.
Küchlin, W., 1985:
A confluence criterion based on the generalized Newman lemma.
Proc. EUROCAL 85, Springer LNCS, to appear.
Kutzler, B., and Stifter, S., 1985:
Geometrical theorem proving: a comparison between Wu's algorithm and the use of Gröbner bases.
Tech. Rep. CAMP 85-17.0, Univ. of Linz, Math. Dept., to appear.
Lankford, D.S., 1975:
Canonical algebraic simplification.
Rep. ATP-25, Univ. of Texas, Austin, Dep. Math. Comp. Sci.
Lankford, D.S., 1975a:
Canonocal inference.
Rep. ATP-32, Univ. of Texas, Austin, Dep. Math. Comp. Sci.
Lankford, D.S, 1979:
A unification algorithm for abelian group theory.
Rep. MTP-1, Louisiana Tech Univ., Math. Dep.
Lankford, D.S., 1979a:
Mechanical theorem proving in field theory.
Rep. MTP-2, Louisiana Tech Univ., Math. Dep.
Lankford, D.S., 1979b:
On proving term rewriting systems are noetherian.
Rep. MTP-3, Louisiana Tech Univ., Math. Dep.
Lankford, D.S., 1979c:
Some new approaches to the theory and applications of conditional term rewriting systems.

Rep. MTP-6, Louisiana Tech Univ., Math. Dep.
Lankford, D.S., 1980:
Research in applied equational logic.
Rep. MTP-15, Louisiana Tech Univ., Ruston, Math. Dep.
Lankford, D.S., 1981:
A simple explanation of inductionless induction.
Rep. MTP-14, Louisiana Tech Univ., Ruston, Math. Dep.
Lankford, D.S., and Ballantyne, A.M., 1977a:
Decision procedures for simple equational theories with commutative axioms: Complete sets of commutative reductions.
Rep. ATP-35, Univ. of Texas, Austin: Dep. Math. Comp. Sci.
Lankford, D.S., and Ballantyne, A.M., 1977b:
Decision procedures for simple equational theories with permutative axioms: Complete sets of permutative reductions.
Rep. ATP-37, Univ. of Texas, Austin: Dep. Math. Compu. Sci.
Lankford, D.S., and Ballantyne, A.M., 1977c:
Decision procedures for simple equational theories with commutative-associative axioms: Complete sets of commutative-associative reductions.
Rep. ATP-39, Univ. of Texas, Austin: Dep. Math. Comp. Sci.
Lankford, D.S., and Ballantyne, A.M., 1979:
The refutation completeness of blocked permutative narrowing and resolution.
4th CADE, Austin, 53-59.
Lankford, D.S., and Butler, G., 1984:
On the foundations of applied equational logic.
Tech. Rep., Louisiana Tech Univ., Dep. of Math.
Lankford, D.S., and Butler, G., 1984:
On faster Smith normal form algorithms.
Manuscript, Louisiana Tech Univ., Dep. of Math.
Lankford, D.S, Butler, G., and Ballantyne, A.M., 1983:
A progress report on new decision algorithms for finitely presented abelian groups.
Proc. of an NSF Workshop on the Rewrite Rule Laboratory, General Electrics Schenectady, 1983, (ed. by J.V. Guttag, D. Kapur, D.R. Musser), Rep. no. 84GEN008, 137-154.
Lauer, M., 1976:
Canonical representatives for residue classes of a polynomial ideal.
Diploma thesis, Univ. of Kaiserslautern, Dep. Math.
Lauer, M., 1976a:
Canonical representatives for residue classes of a polyomial ideal.
Proc. ACM SYMSAC 76, Yorktown Heights, N. Y., (ed. by R. D. Jenks), 339-345.
Lazard, D., 1982:
Commutative algebra and computer algebra.
Proc. EUROCAM 82, Marseille, France, (ed. by J. Calmet), Springer LNCS 144, 40-48.
Lazard, D., 1983:
Gröbner bases, Gaussian elimination and resolution of systems of algebraic equations.
Proc. EUROCAL 83, London, (ed. by J. A. van Hulzen), Springer LNCS 162, 146-156.
Le Chenadec, P., 1983:
Formes canoniques dans les algèbres finiment présentées.
Thèse 3ème cycle, Univ. Paris-Sud, Centre d' Orsay. English version 1984.
Le Cenadec, P., 1985:
A Knuth-Bendix completion of some Coxeter groups.
Proc. EUROCAL 85, Springer LNCS, to appear.
Lescanne, P., 1981:
Decomposition orderings as a tool to prove the termination of rewriting systems.
Proc. 7th IJCAI, Vancouver, Canada, 548-550.
Lescanne, P., 1983:
Computer experiments with the REVE term rewriting system generator.

Proc. 10th POPL conference, Austin, Texas.

Lescanne, P., 1984:
How to prove termination? An approach to the implementation of a new recursive decomposition ordering.
Proc. 6th Conf. on Automata, Algebra and Programming, Bordeaux.

Lichtenberger, F., 1980:
PL/ADT: a system for using algebraically specified abstract data types (German).
Ph.d. thesis, Univ. of Linz, Austria (Europe), Math. Inst.

Lipton, R., and Snyder, L., 1977:
On the halting problem of tree replacement systems.
Conf. on Theoretical Computer Science, U. of Waterloo, 43-46.

Livesey, M., and Siekmann, J., 1976:
Unification of bags and sets.
Techn. Report, Univ. of Karlsruhe, FRG, Comp. Sci. Dep.

Llopis de Trias, R., 1983:
Canonical forms for residue classes of polynomial ideals and term rewriting systems.
Techn. Rep., Univ. Autónoma de Madrid, División de Matemática.

Loos, R., 1981:
Term reduction systems and algebraic algorithms.
Proc. GWAI-81, Bad Honnef, (ed. by J. H. Siekmann), Springer Informatik-Fachberichte 47, 214-234.

Loveland, D.W., 1978:
Automated theorem proving: a logical basis.
North-Holland, Amsterdam - New York - Oxford.

MacDonald, I.D., 1974:
A computer application to finite p-groups.
J. Austral. Math. Soc. 17, 102-112.

Makanin, G. S., 1977:
The problem of solvability of equations in a free semigroup.
Dokl. AN SSSR 233/2.

Manna, Z., and Ness, S., 1970:
On the termination of Markov algorithms.
3rd Hawai Internat. Conf. on System Scie., 789-792.

Manna, Z., Waldinger, R., 1985:
Special relations in automated deduction.
Proc. of the 12th ICALP, Nafplion (Greece), Springer LNCS, to appear.

Mayr, E. W., and Meyer, A. R., 1981:
The complexity of the word problems for commutative semigroups and polynomial ideals.
Report LCS/TM-199, M.I.T., Laboratory of Computer Science.

Metivier, B., 1983:
About the rewriting systems produced by the Knuth-Bendix completion algorithm.
Information Processing Letters 16, 1983.

Möller, H.M., 1976:
Multidimensional Hermite-interpolation and numerical integration.
Math. Z. 148, 107-118.

Möller, H.M., 1985:
A reduction strategy for the Taylor resolution.
Proc. EUROCAL 85, Springer LNCS, to appear.

Möller, H.M., and Buchberger, B., 1982:
The construction of multivariate polynomials with preassigned zeros.
Proc. EUROCAM 82, Marseille, (ed. by J. Calmet), Springer LNCS 144, 24-31.

Möller, H.M., and Mora, F., 1984:
Upper and lower bounds for the degree of Gröbner bases.
Proc. EUROSAM 84, Cambridge, (ed. by J. Fitch), Springer LNCS, 174, 172-183.

Mora, F., 1982:
An algorithm to compute the equations of tangent cones.
Proc. EUROCAM 82, Marseille, (ed. J. Calmet), Springer LNCS 144, 158-165.

Mora, F., 1985:
An algorithmic approach to local rings.
Proc. EUROCAL 85, Springer LNCS, to appear.
Mora, F., 1985a:
Gröbner bases and standard bases for non-commutative polynomial rings.
AAECC-3 conference, Grenoble, July 1985.
Mora, F., and Möller, H. M., 1983:
The computation of the Hilbert function.
Proc. EUROCAL 83, London, (ed. by J. A. van Hulzen), Springer LNCS 162, 157-167.
Mora, F., and Möller, H. M., 1983a:
New constructive methods in classical ideal theory.
Manuscript, Univ. of Genova, Italy, Math. Dept., submitted to publication.
Muller, D.E., 1954:
Application of Boolean algebra to switching circuit design & error detection.
Trans. Inst. of Radio Eng., EC-3, 6-12.
Munoz, M., 1983:
Probleme de terminaison finie des systemes de reecriture equationels.
Thêse 3ême cycle, Univ. Nancy 1.
Musser, D.R., 1977:
A data type verification system based on rewrite rules.
Tech. Rep., USC Information Scie. Inst., Marina del Rey, Calif.
Musser, D.R., 1978:
Convergent sets of rewrite rules for abstract data types.
Tech. Rep., USC Information Scie. Inst., Marina del Rey, Calif.
Musser, D.R., 1978a:
A data type verification system based on rewrite rules.
6th Texas Conf. on Computing Systems.
Musser, D.R., 1980:
On proving inductive properties of abstract data types.
7th ACM Symp. POPL, 154-162.
Musser, D.R., 1980a:
Abstract data type specification in the AFFIRM system.
IEEE Trans. on S.E., Vol. SE-6, No.1.
Musser, D.R., and Kapur, D., 1982:
Rewrite rule theory and abstract data type analysis.
Proc. EUROCAM 82, Marseille, France, (ed. by J. Calmet), Springer LNCS 144, 77-90.
Nash-Williams, C.St.J.A., 1963:
On well-quasi-ordering finite trees.
Proc. Cambridge Phil. Soc. 59, 833-835.
Newman, M.H.A., 1942:
On theories with a combinatorial definition of "equivalence".
Annals of Math., 43/2, 223-243.
Padawitz, P., 1983:
Equational data type specification and recursive program schema.
IFIP Working Conf. on Formal Description of Programming Concepts II, (ed. by D. Bjorner), North-Holland.
Paul, E., 1985:
Equational methods in first order predicate calculus.
J. of Symbolic Computation (Academic Press), Vol. 1/1, to appear.
Paul, E., 1985a:
On solving the equality problem in theories defined by Horn clauses.
Proc. EUROCAL 85, Springer LNCS, to appear.
Pavelle, R., and Wang, P.S., 1985:
MACSYMA from F to G.
J. of Symbolic Computation (Academic Press), Vol. 1/2, to appear.
Pederson, J., 1984:
Confluence methods and the word problem in universal algebra.
Ph.D. thesis, Emory Univ., Dep. Math. and Comp. Scie.
Pederson, J., 1985:

Obtaining complete sets of reductions and equations without using special unification algorithms.
Proc. EUROCAL 85, Springer LNCS, to appear.

Perdrix, H., 1984:
Propriétés Church-Rosser de systèmes de réécriture équationnels ayant la propriété de terminaison faible.
Proc. STACS 84, Paris, (ed. M. Fontet, K. Mehlhorn), Springer LNCS 166, 97-108.

Peterson, G.E., 1983:
A technique for establishing completeness results in theorem proving with equality.
SIAM J. of Computing 12/1, 82-100.

Peterson, G.E., and Stickel, M.E., 1981:
Complete sets of reductions for some equational theories.
J. ACM 28/2, 233-264.

Plaisted, D.A., 1978:
Well-founded orderings for proving termination of systems of rewrite rules.
Rep. 78-932, Univ. of Illinois at Urbana-Champaign, Dept. of Comp. Science.

Plaisted, D.A., 1978a:
A recursively defined ordering for proving termination of term rewriting systems.
Rep. 78-943, Univ. of Illinois at Urbana-Champaign, Dept. of Comp. Science.

Plaisted, D.A., 1983:
An associative path ordering.
Proc. of an NSF Workshop on the Rewrite Rule Laboratory, General Electrics, Schenectady, (ed. by J.V. Guttag, D. Kapur, and D.R. Musser), Rep. no. 84GEN008, 123-136.

Plotkin, G., 1972:
Building-in equational theories.
Machine Intelligence 7, 73-90.

Prawitz, D., 1960:
An improved proof procedure.
Theoria 26, 102-139.

Raulefs, P., Siekmann, J., Szabó, P., Unvericht, E., 1979:
A short survey on the state of the art in matching and unification problems.
ACM SIGSAM Bull. 13/2, 14-20.

Reed, I. S., 1954:
A class of multiple error correcting codes and the decoding scheme.
Trans. Inst. of Radio Eng., IT-4, 38-49.

Remy, J.-L., 1982:
Etude des systemes de recriture conditionnels et applications auy types abstraits algebriques.
These d'etat, Nancy, France.

Renschuch, B., 1976:
Elementary and practical ideal theory (German).
VEB Deutscher Verlag der Wissenschaften, Berlin.

Rety, P., Kirchner, C., Kirchner, H., and Lescanne, P., 1985:
Narrower, a new algorithm for unification and its application to logic programming.
These proceedings.

Richter, M.M., Kemmenich, S.:
Reduction systems and decision procedures (German).
Rep. 4, RWTH, Aachen, FRG, Comp. Sci. Inst.

Robbiano, L., 1985:
Term orderings on the polynomial ring.
Proc. of the EUROCAL 85, Springer LNCS, to appear.

Robbiano, L., Valla, G., 1983:
Some curves in $\mathbf{P}^3$ are set-theoretic complete intersections.
Manuscript, Univ. of Genova, Italy, Dep. Math.

Robinson, G.A., and Wos, L.T., 1969:
Paramodulation and theorem proving in first-order theories with equality.

Machine Intelligence 4, American Elsevier, 135-150.
Robinson, J.A., 1963:
A machine-oriented logic (abstract).
J. Symbolic Logic 28, 302.
Robinson, J.A., 1965:
A machine-oriented logic based on the resolution principle.
J. ACM, 12/1, 23-41.
Robinson, J.A., 1967:
A review of automatic theorem proving.
Proc. Symp. Appl. Math., Am. Math. Soc. 19, 1-18.
Robinson, J.A., 1979:
Logic: form and function. The mechanization of deductive reasoning.
University Press, Edinburgh.
Rosen, B.K., 1971:
Subtree replacement systems.
Ph.D. thesis, Harvard Univ.
Rosen, B.K., 1973:
Tree-manipulation systems and Church-Rosser theorems.
J. ACM 20, 160-187.
Rusinovitch, M., 1985:
Plaisted ordering and recursive decomposition ordering revisited.
These proceedings.
Schaller, S., 1979:
Algorithmic aspects of polynomial residue class rings.
Ph.D. thesis, Techn. Rep. 370, Univ. of Wisconsin-Madison, Comp. Scie. Dept.
Schrader, R., 1976:
Contributions to constructive ideal theory (German).
Diploma thesis, Univ. of Karlsruhe, FRG, Math. Inst.
Sethi, R., 1974:
Testing for the Church-Rosser property.
J. ACM 21/4, 671-679.
Shtokhamer, R., 1975:
Simple ideal theory: some applications to algebraic simplification.
Tech. Rep. UCP-36, Univ. of Utah, Salt Lake City.
Shtokhamer, R., 1976:
A canonical form of polynomials in the presence of side relations.
Tech. Rep., Technion, Haifa, Phys. Dep.
Siekmann, J., 1978:
Unification and matching problems.
Ph.D. thesis, Memo CSM-4-78, University of Essex.
Siekmann, J., and Szabo, P., 1981:
A Noetherian and confluent rewrite system for idempotent semigroups.
SEKI-project memo, Univ. of Karlsruhe, FRG, Dep. Comp. Scie.
Siekmann, J., and Szabo, P., 1982:
Universal unification and classification of equational theories.
Proc. 6th CADE (ed. by D.W. Loveland), Springer LNCS 138.
Slagle, J.R., 1974:
Automated theorem proving for theories with simplifiers, commutativity and associativity.
Smith, D., 1966:
A basis algorithm for finitely generated Abelian groups.
Math. Algorithms 1/1, 13-26.
Spear, D., 1977:
A constructive approach to commutative ring theory.
Proc. MACSYMA Users' Conf., Berkeley, July 1977, (ed. by R. J. Fateman), published by M.I.T., 369-376.
Staples, J., 1975:
Church-Rosser theorms for replacement systems.
In: Algebra and Logic, (ed. by J. Crossley), Springer LN in Math., 291-307.
Stickel, M.E., 1975:
A complete unification algorithm for associative-commutative functions.

Advance papers 4th Int. Joint Conf. on Artificial Intelligence, Tbilisi, USSR, pp. 71-76.

Stickel, M.E., 1977:
Unification algorithms for artificial intelligence languages.
Ph.D. thesis, Carnegie-Mellon Univ.

Stickel, M.E., 1981:
A unification algorithm for associative commutative functions.
J. ACM. 28/3, 423-434; preliminary version: 4th IJCAI, 1975.

Stoutemyer, D.R., 1985:
A preview of the next IBM-PC version of muMATH.
Proc. EUROCAL 85, Springer LNCS, to appear.

Szekeres, G., 1952:
A canonical basis for the ideals of a polynomial domain.
Am. Math. Monthly 59/6, 379-386.

Thomas, C., 1984:
RRLab - Rewrite Rule Labor.
Memo SEKI-84-01, Fachbereich Informatik, Universität Kaiserslautern, Postfach 3049, D6750 Kaiserslautern.

Tiden, E., Arnborg, S., 1985:
Unification problems with one-sided distributivity.
These proceedings.

Trinks, W., 1978:
On B. Buchberger's method for solving systems of algebraic equations (German).
J. Number Theory, 10/4, 475-488.

Winkler, F., 1978:
Implementation of an algorithm for constructing Gröbner bases (German).
Diploma thesis, Univ. of Linz, Austria (Europe), Math. Inst., to appear in ACM TOMS.

Winkler, F., 1983:
An algorithm for constructing detaching bases in the ring of polynomials over a field.
Proc. EUROCAL 83, London, (ed. by J. A. van Hulzen), Springer LNCS 162, 168-179.

Winkler, F., 1984:
The Church-Rosser property in computer algebra and special theorem proving: an investigation of critical-pair/completion algorithms.
Ph.D. thesis, Univ. of Linz, Austria (Europe), Math. Inst.

Winkler, F., 1984a:
On the complexity of the Gröbner-bases algorithm over K[x,y,z].
Proc. EUROSAM 84, Cambridge, (ed. by J. Fitch), Springer LNCS 174, 184-194.

Winkler, F., 1985:
Reducing the complexity of the Knuth-Bendix completion algorithm: a "unification" of different approaches.
Proc. EUROCAL 85, Springer LNCS, to appear.

Winkler, F., Buchberger, B., 1983:
A criterion for eliminating unnecessary reductions in the Knuth-Bendix algorithm.
Proc. of the Coll. on Algebra, Combinatorics and Logic in Comp. Scie., Györ, to appear in Coll. Math. Soc. J. Bolyai, North-Holland.

Wolf, T., 1985:
Analytic decoupling, decision of compatibility and partial integration of systems of nonlinear ordinary and partial differential equations.
Proc. EUROCAL 85, Springer LNCS, to appear.

Wu, W., 1978:
On the decision problem and the mechanization of theorem-proving in elementary geometry.
Scientia Sinica 21/2, 159-172.

Yellick, K., 1985:
Combining unification algorithms for confined equational theories.
These proceedings.

Zacharias, G., 1978:

Generalized Gröbner bases in commutative polynomial rings.
Bachelor Thesis, M.I.T., Dept. Comp. Scie.

CONTEXTUAL REWRITING

Hantao Zhang* and Jean-Luc Remy
Centre de Recherche en Informatique de Nancy
Campus Scientifique BP239
54506 Vandoeuvre France

*** Current address: Department of Computer Science**
Rensselaer Polytechnic Institute
Troy, NY 12181, USA

1. INTRODUCTION

One of the main tools in formal computation is term rewriting, which has been applied to many domains of computer science such as algebraic computation, logical proofs, abstract data type specifications, etc. ([KnB 70], [GHM 78], [Les 83], [Der 84])

Conditional rewriting rules are similar to conditional instructions in programming language and case analysis in proof methods. While much effort is given to purely equational term rewriting systems, not much progress was made concerning conditional term rewriting.

Brand et al [BDJ 78] and Lankford [Lan 79] were the first to study this topic. They showed in particular that different evaluation mechanisms were possible.

Pletat et al [PEE 82], Bergstra et al [BeK 82] and Drosten [Dro 83] have investigated rules satisfying syntactic conditions such as left-linearity, non-overlapping, etc.

Remy ([Rem 82], Rem[83]) considered questions related with confluence and the Knuth-Bendix procedures in a hierarchical framework.

Kaplan [Kap 84] has recently attempted another approach to conditional rewriting and proposed an extension to the Knuth-Bendix procedure. His results are very interesting but they have not yet been implemented.

In this paper, we consider a mechanism called *contextual rewriting* as a way to study conditional term rewriting systems whose rules are of the form:

c :: l -> r

where c is a term of sort **bool**, called *condition* or *premise*; l and r are terms of the same sort. Moreover, the variables of c and r are included in those of l.

Contextual rewriting was first introduced by Brand et al. [BDJ 78]. They defined contextual rewriting on a set of pairs of terms (a term with a context, denoted by c::t in this paper) as: when a term t in the set is reduced by c::l->r to t', we add **not**(c)::t to the set. They also discussed properties of this way of rewriting. But they ignored the property of termination although, as well known, almost all properties of rewriting are undecidable without this condition.

Remy studied contextual rewriting in his "These d'Etat" [Rem 82]. To avoid the termination problem, he considered hierarchical systems. The contextual rewriting is defined on terms: a term t under the context c is reducible by c::l->r if a subterm of t is an instance of l (written $t/u = \sigma(l)$, where σ is a substitution) and c implies $\sigma(c)$. He gives an extension of Knuth-Bendix theorem based on the notion of contextual normal form; however, under a given context, a term, that is irreducible by his definition, may be "reducible" under the normalization. As in [BDJ 78], [Rem 82] did not give sufficient conditions under which contextual rewriting is correct.

The contextual rewriting defined in this paper is different from these of [BDJ 78] and [Rem 82]. Informally, a rule c :: l -> r contextually rewrites a term t, if the unconditional rule l -> r rewrites t then associates an instance of the condition c to the reduced term. In order to give a strict definition, we first extend the concept of a term to a contextual term which is a pair of terms: the first part is of sort bool called *context* and the second one is called *kernel.* Usual properties in classical term rewriting theory are extended in a similar way. By this contextual rewriting, we are able to extend the Knuth-Bendix confluence check to conditional term rewriting systems and also to prove conditional equations in an initial algebra.

The main results of this paper have been implemented in REVEUR 4.

The structure of the paper is as follows: Section 2 presents basic notions and results of the field; In Sections 3, 4 and 5, we introduce the concepts of contextual rewriting, complete set of contextual normal forms (CNF for short) and the relation between two CNFs. Section 6 discusses sufficient conditions under which contextual rewriting is correct; counter-examples are exhibited to illustrate the scope of these conditions. Section 7 gives a method for the conditional rewriting system confluence on ground terms. We define contextual confluence in Section 8 and discuss its properties. In conclusion, we give several perspectives of our research.

2. PRELIMINARIES

We assume that the reader is familiar with the basic notions of many-sorted algebras and term rewriting systems ([GTW 78], [HuO 80]).

Let F be a finite set of function symbols of fixed arity and X be an enumerable set of variables. By T(F,X) we denote both the set of possible terms that can be constructed using F and X and the term algebra. If X is empty, T(F,X), denoted as T(F), is the set of ground terms. We assume that T(F) is not void, that is, there exists at least one constant symbol in F.

For a term t, Var(t) denotes the set of all variables that occur in t, and Occ(t) the set of all occurrences of t. t/u denotes the subterm of t at the occurrence u and t[u <- t'] the term obtained by replacing t/u by t' in t.

A *conditional equation* is a triple of terms <c, l, r> where l and r are the same sort and the sort of c is boolean. In the following, we write it as c :: l = r. If c = **true**, we call it *unconditional equation* and write it by l = r. Both conditional and unconditional equations are called *equations*. When the variables in c and l are included in those of l, we call also <c, l, r> *conditional rule* and write it as c :: l -> r.

c :: l = r is *valid* in an algebra A iff for all morphisms ϕ from T(F,X) to A, ϕ(c) = ϕ(**true**) implies ϕ(l) = ϕ(r).

Given a set of equations E over T(F,X), $=_E$ denotes the smallest congruence relation generated by E over T(F,X), and (F,E)-Alg denotes the equational variety generated by E, which is the class of F-algebras in which all equations of E are valid. By an extension of Birkhoff's theorem, an equation c :: t = t' is valid in (F,E)-Alg iff c $=_E$ **true** implies t $=_E$ t'([Kap 83], [Zha 84]).

The initial algebra of (F,E)-Alg is written as T(F)/$=_E$. An algebra in (F,E)-Alg is called finitely generated if there exists a surjective morphism from T(F)/$=_E$ to that algebra. The class of all finitely generated algebras in (F,E)-Alg is noted by (F,E)-Gen. An equation is valid in (F,E)-Gen iff it is valid in T(F)/$=_E$.

A specification SP = (S,F,E) is composed of a set S of sorts, a finite set F of S-sorted function symbols and a set E of equations.

A specification SP = (S,F,E) is considered as a term rewriting system R if each equation in E is viewed as a rewriting rule. Brand et al and Remy have defined *conditional rewriting relation* as follows: given a term t and a rewriting rule c::l->r, if a subterm t/u of t is an instance of l, that is, there exists a substitution σ, $\sigma(l) = t/u$ and $\sigma(c) =_E$ **true** then t is rewritten (or reduced) to t[u<-σ(r)], noted by t-->$_R$ t[u<-σ(r)].

Let -->$^*_R$ (or -->* simply) denote the reflexive transitive closure of -->$_R$ and <-*->$_R$ the reflexive, symmetric and transitive closure of -->$_R$.

The rewriting relation is *confluent* (on ground terms) iff for all (ground) terms t, t1 and t2, t -->* t1 and t -->* t2, then there exists t' such that t1 -->* t' and t2 -->* t'. The confluence property is also called the Church-Rosser property. If R is confluent and **true** is irreducible by R then t $=_E$ t' iff t-->*t1 and t'-->*t1 for some t1 [Rem 82].

A *hierarchical (or structured) specification* is a finite sequence of specifications (SP_0, SP_1, ..., SP_n) such that for all i in [1..n], SP_{i-1} SP_i (that is, $S_{i-1} \subseteq S_i$, $F_{i-1} \subseteq F_i$ and $E_{i-1} \subseteq E_i$ respectively) and for every c::l->r in $E_i - E_{i-1}$, $l \in T(F_i,x) - T(F_{i-1},X)$ and $c \notin T(F_i,X) - T(F_{i-1},X)$.

Definition 2.1. (sufficient completeness)

A hierarchical specification (SP_0, ..., SP_n) is sufficiently complete iff for each term t in $T(F_i)$, if the sort of t is in S_{i-1}, then there exists a term t' in $T(F_{i-1})$ such that $t =_{Ei} t'$, where i in [i..n].

A sequence of rewriting systems (R_0, ..., R_n) is called *hierarchical rewriting system* if the corresponding specification (SP_0, ..., SP_n) is a hierarchical specification.

In the following, the symbol set F_i is assumed implicitly associated with R_i and the terms in $T(F_0,X)$ are called primitive terms.

By definition, R_0 contains only unconditional equations including the boolean system, for example Hsiang's system (BoolSys for short) [Hsi 83]. The constant **true** is irreducible in R_0.

Definition 2.2 (hierarchical rewriting)

Let R = (R_0, .., R_n) be a hierarchical system.

A term t is hierarchically rewritten to t', noted by t -->$_{H,R}$ t', if there exists a rule c::l->r in Ri, a subterm t/u of t and a substitution σ such that

1) $t/u = \sigma(l)$;
2) $\sigma(c)$ is a term in $T(F_{i-1},X)$;
3) $\sigma(c)$ -->$^*_{H,R}$ **true** and t' = t[u <- σ(r)].

By Condition 2), hierarchical rewriting is a particular case of classical rewritings. In [NaO 84], a sufficient condition is given for the equivalence of those two rewritings.

Proposition 2.3 [NaO 84]

Let R = (R_0, ..., R_n) be sufficiently complete. Then <-*->$_{H,R}$ is equal to <-*->$_R$ on ground terms, where <-*->$_{H,R}$ is the reflexive, symmetric and transitive closure of -->$_{H,R}$ and <-*->$_R$ is defined as above.

This proposition guarantees the completeness of hierarchical rewriting. The restriction on ground terms is due to that the sufficient completeness is defined on ground terms.

In order to be coherent with the following sections, we introduce more conventions and restrictions:

Throughout this paper, we shall use R = (R0, R1) to denote a hierarchical rewriting system of two levels.

By definition, $<\!\!-^{*}\!\!->_R$ equals to $=_E$. We shall use $=_R$ for both $<\!\!-^{*}\!\!->_R$ and $=_E$. In the same way, we use R for E where R is considered as set of equations if no ambiguity arises. For example, we use (F,R)-Alg, (F,R)-Gen instead of (F,E)-Alg, (F,E)-Gen.

3. CONTEXTUAL REWRITING

Contextual rewriting is defined on contextual terms instead of terms. A *contextual term* (c-term for short) is a pair of terms noted c::t, where the *context* c is of sort boolean and t is the *kernel* of c::t. Each term can be viewed as a contextual term with the default context **true**. A context may be enriched by concatenating instances of conditions of rules during contextual rewriting.

Definition 3.1: (contextual rewriting)

Given R = (R0, R1), a rule c :: l -> r in R contextually rewrites (or reduces) c::t to c'::t' if

1. $t/u = \sigma(l)$ where u an occurrence of t and σ: Var(l) -> T(F,X)
2. $\sigma(c)$ is in T(F0, X) (primitive term) such that
   $t' = t[u \leftarrow \sigma(r)]$ and $c' = c \ \& \ \sigma(c)$.

This is noted by (c::t) $-\!\!->_{R,C}$ (c'::t') (or --> if there is no ambiguity)

Remark:

1. By definition, (c' ==> c) $=_R$ **true** since c' = c & σ(c);
2. If the all rules in R are unconditional (c = **true**), contextual rewriting coincides with classical rewriting, which means (**true** :: t) $-\!\!->_{R,C}$ (**true** :: t') iff t $-\!\!->_R$ t'.
3. By the condition 2, a context never contains conditional operators.
4. Hierarchical rewriting is a particular case of contextual rewriting.

Example 3.2:

R = (R0, R1)
R0 = BoolSys + the definition of "<" + { (x < y) & (y < x) -> **false** }
R1 = R0 + { x < y :: inf(x, y) -> x   **not**(x < y) :: inf(x, y) -> y }

Let t = inf(inf(x, y), z), then
(**true** :: t) $-\!\!->_{R,C}$ (x < y :: inf(x, z)) $-\!\!->_{R,C}$ ((x < y) & (x < z) :: x)
Note that we do not allow the following rewriting:
(**true** :: t) $-\!\!->_{R,C}$ (inf(x, y) < z :: inf(x, y))
It is because the context inf(x, y) < z is not a primitive term.

Since a context is itself a term, it can also be reduced by rules in R. For simplicity, such rewritings are also legitimate contextual rewritings on c-terms. In the following, when the context of a c-term is reduced, we say that this c-term is contextually reduced, too.

Proposition 3.3:

1/ If **true** is irreducible by R then (**true** :: t) $-\!\!->^{*}_{R,C}$ (**true** :: t') iff t $-\!\!->^{*}_{H,R}$ t'

2/ If R is sufficiently complete, then for any ground term t, (**true** :: t) $-\!\!->^{*}_{R,C}$ (**true** :: t') iff t $-\!\!->^{*}_R$ t'.

4. CONTEXTUAL NORMAL FORMS

Intuitively, a c-term (c::t) is in normal form under R if c and t are all irreducible by R.

Definition 4.1: (Contextual Normal Form)

A c-term (c::t) is a *contextual normal form* in R iff there does not exists c-term (c'::t') such that (c::t) $\text{-->}_{R,C}$ (c'::t') and c' $\neq$ **false**.

In the example 3.2, (a<b)::inf(a,b) $\text{-->}_{R,C}$ (a<b)::a , the c-term (a<b)::a is a normal form of (a<b)::inf(a,b).

The existence of contextual normal forms for each c-term is guaranteed by the contextual termination.

Definition 4.2: (R,C-noetherian)

A system is *R,C-noetherian* (or *R,C-terminated*) iff there does not exist infinite sequence of c-terms { c_j::t_j } such that

$(c_0::t_0) \text{-->}_{R,C} (c_1::t_1) \text{-->}_{R,C} \cdots \text{-->}_{R,C} (c_i::t_i) \text{-->}_{R,C} \cdots$

Proposition 4.3: [Zha 84]

If for each c::l->r in R, l > r, for some simplification order >, then R is R,C-noetherian.

In the following, we simply say R is noetherian if R is R.C-noetherian.

Unlike the classical case, a c-term can have several normal forms, even if R is confluent. For example, c-term (**true** :: inf(x, y)) can be reduced into two normal forms:

true::inf(x, y) $\text{-->}_{R,C}{}^*$ **not**(x < y)::y and

true::inf(x. y) $\text{-->}_{R,C}{}^*$ (x < y)::x

Therefore we study contextual normal form sets.

Definition 4.4: (complete contextual normal forms (CNF))

A *complete set of contextual normal forms* of c::t, denoted as CNF(c::t), is defined by CNF(c::t) = { c'::t' | c'::t' is a normal form of c::t }

Remark:

1/ If **false** is irreducible by R, by definition, the complete set of contextual normal forms of (**false** :: t) is empty.

2/ This definition is different from that of [Rem 82]. In [Rem 82], a c-terms set M is complete if the disjunction of contexts is equal to **true**.

Example 4.5:

Using the system given in the example 3.2,

CFN((x < z) :: inf(x, inf(y, z))) =

{ 1) (x < z) & (y < z) & (x < y) :: x

2) (x < z) & (y < z) & **not**(x < y) :: y

3) (x < z) & **not**(y < z) :: x }

Theorem 4.6: [Zha 84]

If R = (R0, R1) is R,C-noetherian, CNF(c::t) is computable for each c::t.

An algorithm for computing CNF is implemented in REVEUR4 [Zha 84].

5. RELATION BETWEEN CNFs

In this section, we introduce a binary relation on c-terms called R-coherence and extend it to sets of c-terms. Then we give a sufficient condition under which the R-coherence is an equivalence on sets of c-terms.

Two c-terms c1::t and c2::t are called *identical* since their kernels are identical. Two c-terms c1::t1 and c2::t2 are said to be *disjoint*, if c1 & c2 $=_R$ **false**. We unify these two notions into one:

Definition 5.1: (R-coherence of c-terms)

1. Two c-term c::t and c'::t' are *R-coherent*, noted by c::t <R> c'::t', iff
   a) t = t' or b) c & c' $=_R$ **false**
2. Two sets M1 and M2 of c-terms are *R-coherent* iff for all ci::ti in M1, cj::tj in M2, ci::ti <R> cj::tj. We note this also by M1 <R> M2.

Let M = { c(x) :: a(x), **not**(c(x) :: b(x) }, then M <R> M.
In general, R-coherence on c-term sets is neither transitive nor reflexive, for example, {a::x} <R> {**not**(a)::y} and {**not**(a)::y} <R> {a::z}, but {a::x} and {a::z} are not R-coherent. If M = {a::x, a::z}, it is not the case that M <R> M.
However, R-coherence has the following properties:

Definition 5.2:
A set M of c-terms is *separated* iff for any (c'::t') and (c"::t") of M, t' $\neq$ t" implies c' & c" $=_R$ **false**.

Remark: By definition, a set M of c-terms is separated iff it is R-coherent with itself.

Proposition 5.3:
If M be separated then M1 $\subseteq$ M and M2 $\subseteq$ M implies M1 <R> M2.

Notation 5.4:
Context({cj::tj | j in J}) = V {cj | j in J}, the disjunction of a contexts of c-terms.
For example, Context({p(x)::a, **not**(p(x))::b}) = p(x) V **not**(p(x)) $=_R$ **true**.

Definition 5.5:
A c-term set M is well-covered by a context c iff c $=_R$ Context(M).

Proposition 5.6:
Let M1, M2, M3 be all well-covered by a context c. Then
1. M1 <R> M2 implies M1 and M2 are separated;
2. M1 <R> M2 and M2 <R> M3 implies M1 <R> M3.

Sketch of proof:
1. If M1 is not separated, then there exists c1::t1, c2::t2 in M1 such that t1 $\neq$ t2 and (c1&c2) $\neq_R$ **false**. Since M2 is well-covered by c and (c1 & c2 ==> c) $=_R$ **true**, it can be shown by case analysis that there exists c'::t' in M2 such that (c1 & c2 & c') $\neq_R$ **false**. On the other hand, c1::t1<R>c'::t' and c2::t2 <R> c'::t'. Since (c1 & c') $\neq_R$ **false** and (c2 & c') $\neq_R$ **false**, so t1=t'=t2. This leads to contradiction.
2. Let c1::t1 in M1, c3::t3 in M3, we prove (c1::t1) <R> (c3::t3).
If c1 & c3 $=_R$ **false** then it is true. Else, c1 & c3 $\neq_R$ **false**. Because M2 is well-covered by c and ((c1 & c3) ==> c) $=_R$ **true**, there exists c2::t2 in M2 such that (c1&c3&c2) $\neq_R$ **false**.
By hypothesis, (c1::t1) <R> (c2::t2) and (c2::t2) <R> (c3::t3), so t1 = t2 = t3. []

In general R-coherence is not an equivalence relation on c-term sets. But by the above propositions, we may assert that it is an equivalence relation on separated c-term sets well-covered by the same context.

Corollary 5.7:
R-coherence is an equivalence on separated c-term sets well-covered by the same context.

Proof:
R-coherence is symmetric by definition. Reflexity holds from Proposition 5.3. and transitivity holds from Proposition 5.6.2. []

Example 5.8:
In the system given in Example 3.2, we get (+: **or**-exclusive)

CNF(inf(inf(x, y), z)) =
{ 1. (x < y) & (x < z) :: x
2. (y < z) + (x < y) & (y < z) :: y
3. (x < z) + (x < y) & (x < z) :: z
4. (x < y) + (x < y) & (y < z) :: z }

CNF(inf(x, inf(y, z))) =
{ 1. (x < y) & (y < z) :: x
2. (x < z) + (x < z) & (y < z) :: x
3. (y < z) + (x < y) & (y < z) :: y
4 .**true** + (x < z) + (y < z) + ((x < z) & (y < z)) :: z }

It is easy to prove that these two contextual normal forms sets are R-coherent.

In [Rem 82], an equivalent relation is given on c-term sets in which all c-term kernels are distinct:

Definition 5.9 [Rem 82]:
Two c-term sets M, N are R-equivalent if there exists a bijection π: M -> N such that for each c::t in M, t = π(t) and c $=_R$ π(c). This relation is noted by M $=_{Remy}$ N.

R-coherence does not require the kernels in CNFs to be distinct.

Proposition 5.10:
If M is separated then M $=_{Remy}$ M' implies M <R> M'.

Proof:
Assume c::t in M and c'::t' in M'.
If t = t', then c::t <R> c'::t'. Otherwise, since M $=_{Remy}$ M', there exists c"::t" in M such that t' = t" and (c' $=_R$; c").
On the other hand, (c & c") $=_R$ **false**. Since M is separated, thus (c & c') $=_R$ **false**, that is, c::t <R> c'::t'. []

6. CORRECTION OF CONTEXTUAL REWRITING

The following two properties are easy to show for classical rewriting:
1. t $\rightarrow_R$ t' ==> t $=_R$ t';
2. t$\downarrow$ = t'$\downarrow$ ==> t $=_R$ t' where t$\downarrow$ denotes the normal form of t.

By analogy we ask the following questions about the correction of contextual rewriting:

1. If (c::t) $-->_{R,C}$ (c'::t'), under what conditions and in which class of algebras, is (c&c')::t=t' valid ?
2. If CNF(**true** :: t) $=_R$ CNF(**true** :: t'), does the relation t $=_R$ t' hold?

The following proposition provides an answer to the first question.

Proposition 6.1:
Let c::t $-->_{R.C}$ c'::t', then (F,R)-Alg |= c' :: t = t'.

Proof:
By definition, c' :: t = t' is valid in (F,E)-Alg iff for all A in (F,E)-Alg, for all application ϕ: T(F,X) -> A, ϕ(c') = ϕ(**true**) implies ϕ(t) = ϕ(t').

If the result is false, then there exists an algebra B in (F,E)-Alg and an application ϕ: T(F,X) -> B such that ϕ(c') = ϕ(**true**) and ϕ(t) $\neq$ ϕ(t').

Assume c::t $-->_{R,C}$ c'::t' by a rule p::l->r of R with the substitution s. By definition c' = c & s(p). Since ϕ(c') = ϕ(**true**), so ϕ(s(p)) = ϕ(**true**) by the property of the operator & (**and**) (in usual sense), thus ϕ(s(l)) = ϕ(s(r)). But ϕ(s(l)) = ϕ(s(r)) implies ϕ(t) = ϕ(t'), a contradiction. []

Remark:

1. $-->_{R,C}$ can be replaced by $-->^*_{R,C}$, the reflexive, transitive closure of $-->_{R,C}$.
2. If c' = **true** (so c = **true**), we have t $=_R$ t'.

Before we answer the second question, let us look at an example:

Example 6.2:
Consider the following signature:

F0 = BoolSysF + { 0: -> int, s: int -> int, p: int -> bool }
F1 = F0 + { a: int -> int, b: int -> int }
R0 = BoolSys
R1 = R0 + { p(x) :: a(x) -> s(x)   **not**(p(x)) :: a(x) -> 0
            p(x) :: b(x) -> s(x)   **not**(p(x)) :: b(x) -> 0 }

CNF(**true** :: a(x)) = CNF(**true** :: b(x)) = { p(x) :: s(x), **not**(p(x)) :: 0 }

It is obvious that CNF(**true** :: a(x)) <R> CNF(**true** :: b(x)), however, the equation a(x) = b(x) is neither valid in (F,R)-Alg nor in (F.R)-Gen, since the predicate p is not defined. For example, p(0) is neither **true** nor **false**, a(0) is equivalent neither to 0 nor to s(0), the same thing holds for b(0), so a(0) $\neq$ b(0).

From this example, we require that all predicates to be totally defined, or R to be sufficiently complete. We can also ask that the boolean algebra to contain only two elements true and false. The condition for the existence of such algebra is that R is sufficiently complete and consistent on the primitive boolean specification (containing only the constants **true** and **false**).

Example 6.3:
Take the same signature as in Example 4.

R0 = BoolSys + { p(0) = **false**,   p(s(x)) = **true** }
R1 = R0 + { a(0) = 0,   p(x)::a(x) = x,   b(0) = s(0),   p(x)::b(x) = x }

(R0, R1) is sufficiently complete;

We have

CNF(**true** :: a(x)) = CNF(**true** :: b(x)) = { p(y) :: y }

It is easy to see that CNF(**true** :: a(x)) <R> CNF(**true** :: b(x)). However, a(x) = b(x) is not valid in (F,R)-Alg, indeed, p(x) :: a(x) = b(x) is valid in (F,R)-Alg.

Proposition 6.4:

Assume R noetherian and sufficiently complete and CNF(c::t) <R> CNF(c'::t').

Then Context(CNF(c::t)) & Context(CNF(c'::t')) :: t = t' is valid in (F,R)-Gen.

Proof:

It is sufficient to prove the proposition for the initial algebra A = T(F)/$=_E$.

Let C = Context(CNF(c::t)) and C' = Context(CNF(c'::t')).

For any application ϕ from T(F,X) to A, if ϕ(C & C') = ϕ(**false**), then the proposition is trivially true.

Suppose ϕ(C & C') = ϕ(**true**).

Since C (resp. C') is the disjunction of the contexts in CNF(c::t) (resp. CNF(c'::t')), by the sufficient completeness, there exists c1::t1 in CNF(c::t) and c2::t2 in CNF(c'::t') such that ϕ(c1) = ϕ(c2) = ϕ(**true**).

We can now conclude that c1 & c2 $\neq_R$ **false**.

By hypothesis, CNF(c::t) <R> CNF(c'::t'), so t1 = t2.

By Proposition 6.1, ϕ(t) = ϕ(t1) and ϕ(t') = ϕ(t2), thus ϕ(t) = ϕ(t'), or

A |= (C & C') :: t = t'.

Note that we cannot prove (F,R)-Alg |= (C & C') :: t = t', since in the above proof, we use the sufficient completeness to prove that ϕ(C & C'') = ϕ(**true**) implies ϕ(c1) = ϕ(c2) = ϕ(**true**). []

Corollary 6.5:

Let R be as in Proposition 6.4 and CNF(c::t) <R> CNF(c'::t') and c $=_R$ Context(CNF(c::t)), c' $=_R$ Context(CNF(c'::t')).

Then (F,R)-Gen |= c & c' :: t = t'.

The above corollary allows us to prove conditional equations in the initial algebra. In the following, we look for a sufficient condition under which, for all c-term c::t, c is equal to Context(CNF(c::t). Note that it is inefficient to compute each time the disjunction of contexts in this case.

Notation 6.6:

SUC(c::t) = { c'::t' | c::t $\rightarrow_{R,C}$ c'::t' } all c-terms obtained by applying contextual rewriting one time on c::t;

SUC*(c::t) = { c'::t' | c::t $\rightarrow^*_{R,C}$ c'::t' } all c-terms derived from c::t.

Definition 6.7:

R = (R0, R1) is *well-covered* iff for all c::t, if c::t is not in normal form, then SUC(c::t) is well-covered by c.

Remark:

All unconditional systems are well-covered.

Proposition 6.8:

If R is well-covered, then CNF(c::t) is well-covered by c for all c::t.

Example 6.9:

Take the same signature as Example 6.2 and replace rules a(0) -> 0 and b(0) -> s(0) by **not**(p(x)) :: a(x) -> 0 and **not**(p(x)) :: b(x) -> s(0), then the system becomes well-covered:

R0 = BoolSys + { p(0) -> **false**, p(s(x)) -> **true** }
R1 = R0 + { **not**(p(x)) :: a(x) -> 0, p(x) :: a(x) -> x
not(p(x)) :: b(x) -> s(0) p(x) :: b(x) -> x }
Let c::t = **true** :: a(y).
CNF(c::t) = { **not**(p(y)) :: 0, p(y) :: y }, well-covered by **true**.

Here is a sufficient condition for testing that R is well-covered: the disjunction of the conditions of rules with same left hand sides (after renaming of variables) is equal to **true**.

We now give the main result of this section.

Theorem 6.10:

If R is noetherian, sufficiently complete and well-covered, then CNF(c::t) <R> CNF(c'::t') implies that c & c' :: t = t' is valid in (F,R)-Gen.

Proof:

It is a consequence of Corollary 6.5 and Proposition 6.8 []

For instance, in Example 5.10, we prove that

CNF(**true** :: inf(inf(x, y), z)) <R> CNF(**true** :: inf(x, inf(y, z)))

By the above theorem, we conclude that inf(inf(x, y), z) = inf(x, inf(y, z)) is valid in the initial algebra defined in Example 3.2.

7. CONFLUENCE ON GROUND TERMS

In this section, we prove that the convergence of the contextual critical pairs implies the confluence on ground terms in a noetherian system.

We first give the definition of a contextual critical pair (c-pair for short).

Definition 7.1: (contextual critical pair)

Let c1 :: l1 -> r1, c2 :: l2 -> r2 be two conditional rules such that Var(l1) and Var(l2) are disjoint.

A triple of terms <c, t, t'> is a *contextual critical pair (c-pair)* iff there exists an occurrence u in Occ(l1) and a substitution h: X -> T(F, X) such that

a. l1/u is not a variable;
b. σ is the most general unifier of l1/u and l2;
c. σ(c1 & c2) is a primitive term in T(F0, X),

and c = σ(c1 & c2), t = σ(l1(u <- r2)) and t' = σ(r1).

Example 7.2: (system of integer-set)

F = (F0, F1)
F0 = BoolSysF +
{ 0:->int, s:int->int, eq:int,int->bool, s-empty:->set, +:int,set->set }
F1 = F0 + { isin:int,set->bool }
R = (R0, R1)
R0 = BoolSys +
{ r1) eq(x, x) -> true,
r2) eq(s(x), s(y)) -> eq(x, y) ,

r3) eq(0, s(x)) -> false,
r4) eq(s(x), 0) -> false }

R1 = R0 +
{ r5) eq(v, w) :: (v + (w + u)) -> (w + u),
r6) isin(x, s-empty) -> false,
r7) eq(x, y) :: isin(x, (y + u)) -> true,
r8) not(eq(x, y)) :: isin(x, (y + u)) -> isin(x, u) }

A c-pair between the rules (r5) and (r7) is obtained as follows:

isin(x, (v + (w + u)))
(r5) ↙ ↘ (r7)
eq(v,w) :: isin(x, (w + u)) eq(x,v) :: **true**

<c, t1, t2> = <eq(v,w) & eq(x,v), isin(x, w + u), **true**>
which is often written in equation form:

eq(v,w) & eq(x,v) :: isin(x, w + u) = **true**

Definition 7.3:
A c-pair <c, t1, t2> is *contextually convergent* (in a noetherian system) if CNF(c::t1) <R> CNF(c::t2).

Theorem 7.4: (extension of the Knuth-Bendix theorem)
Let R = (R0, R1) be sufficiently complete, well-covered and noetherian.
If all c-pair <c, t, t'> in R are convergent, then R is confluent on ground terms.

Proof:
Since R is noetherian, by Newman's lemma [Hue 81], it is sufficient to prove that the convergence of c-pairs implies the local confluence on ground terms.
Moreover, since R is sufficiently complete, by Proposition 2.3, it is sufficient to prove that hierarchical rewriting (cf. Definition 2.2) is locally confluent on ground terms.
The following lemmas achieve these proofs.

Lemma 7.5:
Let R as in the main theorem and <c, t1, t2> be a c-pair of R;
Then CNF(c::t1) <R> CNF(c::t2) implies that for all ground substitution σ such that σ(c) is primitive term, if $\sigma(c) =_R$ **true**, then there exists a term t such that
σ(t1) -->* t and σ(t2) -->* t.

Proof:
Because R is sufficiently complete and well-covered, if $\sigma(c) =_R$ **true**, there exist c-terms c_j::t_j in CNF(c::t1) and c_k::t_k in CNF(c::t2) such that $\sigma(cj) =_R \sigma(ck) =_R$ **true**.
Since CNF(c::t1) <R> CNF(c::t2) and cj & ck $\neq$ **false**, we have tj = tk.
Thus we have σ(t1) -->* $\sigma(t_j)$, σ(t2) -->* $\sigma(t_j)$ (= $\sigma(t_k)$) []

Lemma 7.6:
Let R be the same as in Lemma 7.5.
If all c-pairs of R are convergent, then R is locally confluent on ground terms.

Proof:
Let (r1) c_1 :: l_1 -> r_1 and (r2) c_2 :: l_2 -> r_2 reduce a ground term t respectively to t1 and t2 at the occurrence u and w of t. We denote them by
t -->(u. r1) t1 and t -->(v, r2) t2.

We want to prove that t1 -->* t' and t2 -->* t' for some t'. The proof is very similar to Huet's proof of Knuth-Bendix algorithm [Hue 81]. There are three cases:

Case 1: u and w are disjoint, that is, there does not exist an occurrence v such that u = w.v ou w = u.v .

Then t1 can be rewritten by (r2) at the occurrence w and t2 be rewritten by (r1) at the occurrence u to the same term.

Case 2: Assume v is an occurrence such that w = u.v and l_1/v = x (variable). Let t' = t/w, t' is reducible by (r2), we note t' -->(r2) t".

Let m, n be respectively numbers of occurrences of x in l_1, r_1, then the numbers of occurrences of t' in t1 and t2 are respectively at least n and m-1.

We rewrite n times t1 by t' -->(r2) t" and rewrite m-1 times t2 by t' -->(r2) t" (at appropriate occurrences) then rewrite once t2 at the occurrence v by the rule r1), where the variable x in Var(l_1) is replaced by t" instead of t'. We obtain the same term.

Case 3: Only in this case, we involve c-pairs.

Let v be an occurrence such that w = u.v and l_1/v is not a variable. In this case, there exists a contextual critical pair between r1) and r2). Let t/u -->(r1) t1 and t/w -->(r2) t2. Since t/u is a ground instance of l_1 and t/w is a ground instance of l_2, by sufficient completeness, we have that <**true**, t1, t2> is a ground instance of the c-pair between r1) and r2). By Lemma 7.5, t1 and t2 are confluent. []

The above theorem allows us to design an algorithm for testing the confluence of conditional systems on ground terms. It has been implemented on top of the REVE rewriting rule laboratory [FoG 84]. The software implementing the algorithm is called REVEUR 4. A first report is given in [ReZ 84], a detailed description is in [Zha 84].

For the system given in Example 7.2, we can prove that

<c, t1, t2> = <eq(v,w) & eq(x,v), isin(x, w + u), **true**>

is convergent, since

CNF(c::t1) = CNF(c::t2) = { eq(x, v) & eq(v, w)) :: **true** }

Note that unlike the KB-theorem for unconditional rules, the inverse of Theorem 7.4 does not hold. Even in systems confluent on ground terms, non-convergent c-pairs may exist, as illustrated by the following example.

Example 7.7:

Let F0 = { a: -> s, b: -> s, +: s, s -> s, p: s -> bool }

R0 = { b + a -> a + b, p(a) -> **true**,
(x + y) + z -> x + (y + z) p(b) -> **false** }

F1 = { f: s, s -> s }

R1 = { p(x) V p(y) :: f(x, y) -> x + y, **not**(p(x)) :: f(x, y) -> y + x }

R = (R0, R1) is noetherian, sufficient complete and well-covered. The following is a c-pair of R: (p(x) V p(y)) & **not**(p(x)) :: x + y = y + x

Since x + y and y + x are irreducible, so this c-pair is not convergent. However, x + y = y + x is an inductive theorem, that is, for all ground substitution σ, σ(x+y) and σ(y+x) are convergent (see [Zha 84] for details). In fact, R is confluent on ground terms.

8. CONFLUENCE OF CONTEXTUAL REWRITING

In this section, we study the confluence of contextual rewriting. The aim is twofold: we expect that contextual confluence enables us to decide confluence of systems and to prove conditional equality.

Definition 8.1: (c-confluence)

R is contextually confluent (c-confluent) iff for all c-terms c::t, c'::t' c"::t", c::t -->* c'::t' and c::t -->* c"::t", there exist two sets of c-terms M1 and M2 such that

1). M1 $\subseteq$ SUC*((c' & c")::t') and M2 $\subseteq$ SUC*((c' & c")::t");

2). M1 and M2 are well-covered by (c' & c");

3). M1 <R> M2.

Remark:

1. If all equations are unconditional, then all contexts are **true** and R is well-covered. It is sufficient that M1 (resp. M2) contains only one element, which is exactly the classical confluence;

2. We suppose that the empty set is well-covered by the context **false**. If c' & c" $=_R$ **false**, then M1 and M2 can take the empty set and the conditions 1)-3) are satisfied.

Theorem 8.2:

Let R be sufficiently complete, well-covered and noetherian. Then following three propositions are equivalent:

1) R is contextually confluent;

2) CNF(c::t) is separated for all c-term c::t.

3) For all c::t, c'::t', c"::t" such that c::t -->* c'::t' and c::t -->* c"::t",
CNF(c' & c" :: t') <R> CNF(c' & c" :: t")

Sketch of the proof:

1) => 2). If CNF(c::t) is not separated, then there exist c1::t1 and c2::t2 in CNF(c::t) such that t1 $\neq$ t2 and c1 & c2 $\neq_R$ **false**. Since c1::t1 and c2::t2 are derived from c::t and they are all in normal form,

SUC*(c1 & c2 :: t1) = { c1 & c2 :: t1 }
and SUC*(c1 & c2 :: t2) = { c1 & c2 :: t2 }

It can be shown that in this case the three conditions of c-confluence can never be satisfied together. This is a contradiction to 1).

2) => 3). Let c::t -->* c1::t1 and c::t -->* c2::t2.

Since R is noetherian, CNF(c1&c2::t) exists. By hypothesis, CNF(c1&c2::t) is separated. Moreover, CNF(c1&c2::t1) and CNF(c1&c2::t2) are subsets of CNF(c1&c2::t).

By Proposition 5.3, CNF(c1&c2::t1) <R> CNF(c1&c2::t2).

3). => 1). Since CNF(c1&c2::t1) and CNF(c1&c2::t2) satisfy all three conditions in the definition of c-confluence, the proof is evident. []

Now we study the relation between c-confluence and classical confluence. We start from an example:

Example 8.3:

Take the same signature as in Example 6.2 plus (k: int -> int).

R0 = BoolSys + { p(0) -> **true**, p(s(0)) -> **false**, p(s(s(x)) -> x }

R1 = R0 +
{ k(x) -> a(x), k(x) -> b(x),

not(p(x)) :: a(x) -> 0,   p(x) :: a(x) -> x ,
not(p(x)) :: b(x) -> 0,   p(x) :: b(x) -> x   }

It's easy to test that R is c-confluent. For example, the c-pair <**true**, a(x), b(x)> is convergent since

CNF(**true** :: a(x)) <R> CNF(**true** :: b(x))

However, R is not confluent on the three terms k(x), a(x), b(x):

k(x) -> a(x) -> ?
k(x) -> b(x) -> ?

This counter-example illustrates that c-confluence does not imply classical confluence on terms with variables, although it does provide classical confluence on ground terms.

Theorem 8.4:

Let R be sufficiently complete, well-covered.
If R is c-confluent then R is confluent on ground terms.

Proof:

Let t -->* t' and t -->* t" where t, t', t" are ground terms. Then we have **true** :: t $-->^*_{R,C}$ **true**::t' and **true**::t $-->^*_{R,C}$ **true**::t". By c-confluence, there exist c-term sets M' and M" such that

1) M' $\subseteq$ SUC*(**true**::t') and M" $\subseteq$ SUC*(**true**::t"),
2) M' <R> M" and
3) M' and M" are well-covered by **true**.

Moreover, R is sufficient complete, so there exist **true**::t1 in M' and **true**::t2 in M", that is, t' -->* t1 and t" -->* t2. Since **true**::t1 <R> **true**::t2, then t1 = t2. []

By the Knuth-Bendix theorem, in a noetherian unconditional rewriting system, if all the critical pairs are convergent then the system is confluent. We ask then whether a noetherian system is c-confluent if all the c-pairs are convergent.

Unfortunately, the following example gives a negative answer to this question:

Example 8.5:

F0 = { 0: -> int, s: int -> int, zero: int -> bool }
R0 = BoolSys + { zero(0) -> **true**,   zero(s(x)) -> **false** }
F1 = { +: int, int -> int, f: int, int, int -> int }
R1 = R0 + { r1) zero(x) :: x + s(y) -> s(y),
r2) **not**(zero(x)) :: x + s(y) -> s(x + y),
r3) zero(x) :: x + 0 -> 0,
r4) **not**(zero(x)) :: x + 0 -> x,
r5) zero(y) V zero(z) :: f(x, y, z) -> x + s(0),
r6) **not**(zero(z)) :: f(x, y, z) -> s(x + 0)   }

R = (R0, R1) is noetherian, well-covered and sufficiently complete.

It is easy to prove that all c-pairs are convergent. However, the system is not c-confluent on the following c-term:

true :: f(x' + x", y, z)
r3) ↙   ↘ r6)
zero(y) V zero(z) :: (x' + x") + s(0)   **not**(zero(z)) :: s((x' + x") + 0)

(x' + x") + s(0) and s((x' + x")) + 0 are c-irreducible by R,
so R is not c-confluent.

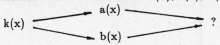

The reason for that is because contextual rewriting forbids that conditional operators appear in contexts (cf. Condition 2 of Definition 3.1). **true** :: x + s(0) is contextually reducible by the rules r1) and r2). On the contrary, **true** :: (x' + x") + s(0) is not reducible by the rules r1) and r2) even if (x' + x") + s(0) is an instance of x + s(0), because the operator "+" cannot appear in contexts.

9. CONCLUSION

We have shown that contextual rewriting is a simple mechanism which can be used to check ground confluence of conditional rewriting systems and to prove conditional equality.

We have now three types of confluence for conditional systems: ground confluence, classical confluence and contextual confluence. As we know, both classical confluence and contextual confluence (under certain conditions) imply ground confluence but the inverse does not hold. We have shown that contextual confluence cannot imply classical confluence, the inverse is not true, either. It remains a field of research that how to check classical confluence and contextual confluence while ground confluence can be checked by the convergence of contextual critical pairs in some cases.

Note that we can only check ground confluence of conditional systems but not complete a system when it is not confluent; that is done in unconditional case by Knuth-Bendix' procedure. We hope that when a c-pair is not convergent, we can add it in the system as a new equation. The main difficulties are as follows:

1. We forbid the rules such as p(x,y) :: a(x) -> b(y) where the variables in the left hand do not contain those of the precondition and of the right hand. If a c-pair is like that equation, we do not know how to do in this case;

2. When a c-pair is not convergent, it is maybe an inductive axiom in the initial algebra. In this case, we shall use inductionless induction method to prove convergence of the c-pair ([Mus 80], [Gog 80]).

3. A boolean system with predicates is in general difficult to make confluent. It is possible that the context of a c-pair is equivalent to **false** but the system cannot reduce it to **false**. To overcome this problem, we can adopt a refutation strategy to prove the equivalence of boolean contexts.

Another drawback of our approach is that we only deal with hierarchical systems. This restriction simplifies largely the context computation and avoids termination problem. We wanted to extend hierarchical concepts to include more complex systems; an attempt to this problem has been done in [Zha 84].

All the algorithms presented here are implemented in REVEUR4. Since theoretical results are rather hard to obtain, we hope that experiments will motivate researches in this important domain.

ACKNOWLEDGEMENTS:

This paper was written with the supports of the education ministry of the People's Republic of China, the GRECO Programmation of the Centre National de la Recherche Scientifique and the Agence de l'Informatique.

During the period the paper was written, the second author visited State University of New York at Stony Brook (N.Y.) (December 1984-April 1985) with the aid of U.S.-French Exchange Program N.S.F. grant no INT 8412371.

We'd like to thank the members of EURECA at CRIN, especially to P. Lescanne, H. & C. Kirchner and E. Kounalis for their helps in doing this work and improving readability of the paper. We own thanks also to D. Kapur, J. Hsiang and S. Kaplan for their good suggestions on the draft of the paper.

10. REFERENCE

[BBTW 81] Bergstra J.A., Broy M., Tucker J.V. and Wirsing M.
On the power of algebraic specifications, 10th MFCS, LNCS 218, Springer Verlag, Berlin, pp 193-202, 1981

[BeK 82] Bergstra J. and Klop J.
Conditional rewrite rules: confluency and termination, Report IW 198/82, Amsterdam, 1982.

[BDJ 78] Brand D., Darringer J.A., Joyner W.H.
Completeness of conditional reductions, Research report RC 7404 IBM, 1978

[Der 84] Dershowvitz N.,
Computing with Rewrite systems, Proc. of NSF, Workshop on the RRL, Report No. 84GENOO8 April 1984.

[Dro 83] Drosten K.
Toward executable specifications unsing conditional axioms, Report 83-01, t.U. Braunschweig, 1983. A.C.M. 29, pp 206-227, 1982

[FoG 84] Forgaard R. and Guttag J.V.
REVE: a term rewriting system generator with failure-resistant knuth-Bendix, Laboratory for computer science MIT 1984.

[GHM 78] Guttag J.V., Horowitz R., Musser D.R.
The design of data type specifications, Current Trends in Programming Methodology, Vol. IV. R. Yeh, (Ed.), Prentice Hall (1978)

[Gog 80] Goguen J.A.
How to prove algebraic inductive hypotheses without induction, with applications to the correctness of data type implementation, Proc. the Workshop on Automated deduction, Les Arcs, 1980

[GTW 78] Goguen J.A., Thatcher J.W. and Wagner E.G.,
An Initial Algebra Approach to the Specification, Correctness, and Implementation of Abstract Data Types, "Current Trends in Programming Methodology", Vol 4. Ed. Yeh R, Prentice-Hall, pp. 80-149, 1978

[Hsi 81] Hsiang J.
Refutational theorem proving using term rewriting systems, Res. Report, Dept of Comp. Sc, U. of Illinois, Urbana, 1981

[Hue 81] Huet G.
A complete proof of correctness of the Knuth-Bendix completion algorithm J.C.S.S. 231 11-21 1981.

[HuO 80] Huet G. and Oppen D.,
Equations and rewrite rules: a survey, in formal languages: perspectives and open problems, Ed. Book R, Academic Press, 1980

[Kap 83] Kaplan S.
Un langage de specification de types abstraits algebrique, These de 3eme cycle, Orsay, 1983.

[Kap 84] Kaplan S.
Fair conditional term rewriting systems: unification, termination and confluence, Manuscript, LRI, Orsay, 1984.

[KnB 70] Knuth D. and Bendix P.
Simple word problems in universal algebras, in computational problems in abstract algebra, Ed. Leech J, Pergamon Press, pp. 263-297, 1970

[Lan 79] Lankford D.S.
Some new approaches to the theory and applications of conditional term rewriting systems, report MTP-6, math. Dept, Lousiana Tech. U, Aug. 1979

[Les 83] Lescanne P.
Computer experiments with the REVE term rewriting system generator, 1983, Proceedings 10th ACM symposium principles of programming languages, Austin (Texas, USA)

[Mus 80] D. L. Musser
On Proving Inductive Properties of Abstract Data Types, Proceedings of the 7th Annual Acm Symposium on Principles of Programming Languages, Las Vegas, P. 154-162, 1980

[NaO 84] Navarro M. and Orejas F.
On the equivalence of hierarchical and non-hierarchical rewriting on conditional term rewriting systems, Eurosam 84, Oxford.

[PEE 82] Pletat U., Engels G., Ehrich H.D.,
Operational semantics of algebraic specifications with conditional equations, 7eme CAAP, (Lille), L.N.C.S. Springer Verlag 1982

[Rem 82] Remy J.L.
Etudes des systemes reecriture conditionnelles et applications aux types abstraits algebriques, These d'etat, Universite NANCY 1, 1982

[Rem 83] Remy J.L.
Proving conditional identities by equational case reasoning rewriting and normalization, 1983, Actes seminaire laboratoire informatique theorique de Paris.

[ReZ 84] Remy J.L., Zhang H.
REVEUR 4: a system for validating conditional algebraic specifications of abstract data types, Proce of 6th ECAI, Pisa, pp. 563-572 (1984)

[Zha 84] Zhang H.,
REVEUR4: L'etude et la mise en oevre de la reecriture conditionnelle." These de 3eme cycle, University of NANCY 1 (1984).

THUE SYSTEMS AS REWRITING SYSTEMS[†]

Ronald V. Book

Department of Mathematics
University of California at Santa Barbara
Santa Barbara, Ca. 93106, USA

Introduction

Replacement systems arise in the study of formula manipulation systems such as theorem provers, program optimizers, and algebraic simplifiers. Such systems may take the form of term rewriting systems, tree manipulating systems, graph grammars, etc. The study of abstract data types is another area where such systems are useful. The principal problem in this context is the word problem: given a system and two objects, are the two objects equivalent? From a slightly different viewpoint the problem can be stated as follows: can one of these objects be transformed into the other by means of a finite number of applications of the rewriting rules in the given system? This leads naturally to the question of the decidability of the word problem for a given class of systems. In general it is desirable to be able to describe canonical representatives or unique normal forms for objects in the domain of the rewriting system. If unique normal forms are guaranteed to exist and there is an algorithm for computing the unique normal form of an object, then the word problem is decidable.

Recently there has been a great increase in interest in rewriting and replacement systems. Part of this increased interest stems from the advances made in symbolic computation in general and also in building systems for automated deduction and for computer algebra. In addition, there have been a number of new results that add to our understanding of the underlying theory and to certain applications,

[†]The preparation of this paper was supported in part by the National Science Foundation under grant DCR-8314977.

e.g., algorithms underlying computer algebra.

If one uses an algorithm to solve some problem, then it is important to consider whether or not the algorithm is efficient. In complexity theory much effort is expended in attempting to determine whether or not specific problems actually have efficient algorithms, that is, whether or not specific problems are tractable or feasible. Sometimes the solution of a problem by use of rewriting systems allows one to determine bounds on the inherent complexity of the problem. Unfortunately it is extremely difficult to obtain results about tractable problems of rewriting systems in general. It appears that such results can only be obtained by restricting attention to specific types of objects. In this paper we consider the rewriting of strings and the inherent computational complexity of problems that arise there.

When one considers strings, then the appropriate notion of replacement system appears to be that of a Thue system, especially in the case that the strings in question are taken from some free monoid on a finite alphabet. Recall that a Thue system is simply a set of ordered pairs (u,v) of strings over the alphabet and that rewriting a given string w is performed by (nondeterministically) replacing some occurrence of string u in w by the string v or by replacing some occurrence of string v in w by the string u. When dealing with Thue systems, there is an advantage that is not always available when dealing with more general types of rewriting systems: the multiplication in a free monoid (that is, concatenation) is associative. Thue was interested in the general problem of rewriting, considering systems of rules for rewriting combinatorial objects such as graphs or trees as well as strings (see [56]) and he studied the word problem in this context. Thue systems have also been studied by computer scientists and by logicians interested in computability theory, and properties of Thue systems often suggest problems and serve as useful examples or counter-examples for the study of other types of rewriting systems.

Viewed as rewriting systems on strings, Thue systems are also of interest to algebraists since they are presentations of monoids. A Thue system induces a congruence on the free monoid generated by the alphabet of the system. The collection of congruence classes forms a quotient monoid under the multiplication obtained by first multiplying (concatenating) strings in the free monoid and then taking the congruence class of the product. Of course, it is possible that this monoid is in fact a group.

In order to study Thue systems to learn more about general rewriting systems, one looks for an ordering on the strings and properties of the rewriting rules that enable unique normal forms to exist. There are many ways to do this and one might hope to find ways such that when a Thue system is both noetherian and confluent, then the word problem is guaranteed to be tractable. Unfortunately, even for objects as conceptually simple as quotient monoids of finitely generated free monoids this is not possible in general. In Section 2 we survey a number of results that show just how badly this notion fails. This leads us to consider one case where a number of positive results are known and where there are results in the complexity theory literature that can be used to determine bounds on the complexity of certain specific problems. In this case the notion of "reduction" in the rewriting process depends on length.

Consider the partial order on free monoids determined by comparing lengths of strings. For a given Thue system T, a string x <u>reduces</u> to a string y if y can be obtained from x by applying a sequence of length-decreasing rules of T. The system T has the <u>Church-Rosser</u> <u>property</u> (or "is Church-Rosser") if for every x and y, x and y are congruent if and only if there exists a z such that both x and y reduce to z. Because the ordering is based on length, it is clear that for every string w there exists an "irreducible" string $\bar{w}$ such that w reduces to $\bar{w}$; when the Thue system is Church-Rosser, the string $\bar{w}$ is unique. In the case of a finite Thue system that is Church-Rosser, there is a linear time algorithm to solve the word problem. Further, there is a polynomial time algorithm to determine whether a Thue system is Church-Rosser.

This approach to the study of Thue systems and Thue congruences was initiated by Maurice Nivat and his colleagues and students in France. The principal contributions of that group were made in the late 1960's and early 1970's. The motivation of Nivat's school was based on the intertwining of algebra and formal language theory that has been characteristic of the achievements made by this school in theoretical computer science. Berstel [8] has written a survey of the main results in this area obtained by that school through the mid-1970's. More recent work, particulary outside of France, has been influenced not only by the work of Nivat's school but also by questions arising in the study of term-rewriting systems, symbolic computation, and computability theory. A variety of proof techniques and combinatorial algorithms has been developed and their applications have produced a number of interesting results and have stimulated some important work.

In Section 2 certain results about string rewriting systems are described. Here the notion of reduction is not based on length; rather, it is assumed that the rewriting system generates a relation that is both noetherian and confluent. Such systems are called complete and have properties that are similar to complete term-rewriting systems. The results show that a system's being complete does not itself guarantee that the word problem will be easy to solve. In Section 3 properties of arbitrary Thue systems and those with the Church-Rosser property are described. The properties that are featured include those that have played the most important role in recent developments. Several new results are described.

In Section 4 an example showing the usefulness of the notion of reduction based on length is developed. This example is from work on a mathematical model for communications protocols for public-key encryption systems.

As noted above a Thue system can be viewed as a presentation of a monoid. The study of properties of the algebraic properties of monoids with presentations as Thue systems that are Church-Rosser has been extremely fruitful. As examples, one might consider Dehn's problems for groups and then study the same problems for monoids. Some of the most interesting results in this area have been develped quite recently; of particular interest are the results by Otto [46]. This is the topic of Section 5. While properties of groups and monoids are not necessarily central to the interests of researchers studying other types of rewriting systems, the results obtained serve to illustrate the power of the underlying notions.

Thue systems with a single rewriting rule ("one-rule systems") yield examples and counter-examples for a number of questions. This was certainly true in the early work of Nivat's school and it is true today. Properties of such systems are surveyed in Section 6.

In the last ten years a wide variety of proof techniques has been applied by those studying problems of Thue systems. The rich collection of results that have been obtained show that this aspect of the theory of rewriting systems is not purely algebra or logic or formal language theory, but techniques from each of those areas are useful in such studies and one can expect to find results about Thue systems that speak to problems in each of these areas. It is hoped that the results obtained in this area, particularly the results concerning the inherent computational complexity of various problems, will lead to similar results in the study of more general types of rewriting systems.

Section 2. Complete Rewriting Systems and the Word Problem

A rewriting system R that is both noetherian and confluent defines a unique normal form for each element of its domain and each maximal R-chain reaches a normal form in finitely many steps. Rewriting systems of this type are called complete. The word problem for a complete rewriting system is decidable since for two objects x, y one computes the normal forms $\bar{x}$, $\bar{y}$ and then compares $\bar{x}$ and $\bar{y}$ to see if they are equal: x and y are "equivalent" if and only if $\bar{x}$ $\bar{y}$ are identical. Many problems arising in automated deduction, computer algebra, and other aspects of symbolic computation can be stated as a combination of one or more word problems; therefore, one attempts to find complete rewriting systems in order to solve these problems, that is, there are problems that "seek a rewriting system" for their solution.

Once one knows that a problem is decidable the next step is to classify its inherent complexity. If a problem is tractable, then a good algorithm exists for its solution, an algorithm that can be guaranteed to perform well when properly implemented. Thus, one would like to know when the existence of a complete rewriting system guarantees that the word problem is tractable.

Unfortunately, many problems are known to be undecidable and so there are cases where the search for a complete rewriting system is hopeless. But when a complete rewriting system exists, does this guarantee that the complexity of the corresponding problems, say the word problem, is sufficiently low? Recent results have shown that this is not the case. Some of these results will be sketched here.

The rewriting of strings appears to be one of the simplest cases of term-rewriting. First, there are no variables. Second, the multiplication in a free monoid, i.e., concatenation, is associative; thus, if one wishes to apply a rewriting rule u v to a string w, one must only find an occurrence of u in w, say by reading w from left-to-right with a "window" of size the length of u until that window is filled by u. But even in this case problems arise. To be able to precisely state the known results and the open problems, let us develop some notation.

A Thue system T over an alphabet Σ defines the monoid $\Sigma^*/\overset{*}{\longleftrightarrow}$ which we will denote more simply by M_T. The pair $[\Sigma; T]$ is a <u>monoid presentation</u> (of M_T). A <u>monoid presentation</u> $[\Sigma; T]$ <u>admits a (finite) complete rewriting system</u> if there exists a (finite) complete rewriting system R over Σ such that the congruences determined by T and R coincide, that is, both $[\Sigma; T]$ and $[\Sigma; R]$ present precisely the same quotient monoid of Σ^*. A <u>monoid</u> M <u>admits a (finite) complete rewriting system</u> if there exists a monoid presentation of M that admits a (finite) complete rewriting system.

Bauer and Otto [7] have noted that a result of O'Dunlaing [39, 41] can be used to obtain the following facts.

<u>Theorem 2.1</u>. The following problems are undecidable:

(a) INSTANCE: a finite monoid presentation $[\Sigma; T]$;
QUESTION: does $[\Sigma; T]$ admit a finite complete rewriting system?

(b) INSTANCE: a finite monoid presentation $[\Sigma; T]$;
QUESTION: does the monoid presented by $[\Sigma; T]$ admit a finite complete rewriting system?

Kapur and Narendran [30] have studied the monid M_T with presentation $[\Sigma; T]$ where $\Sigma = \{a,b\}$ and $T = \{(aba, bab)\}$. Since aba and bab have the same length, the word problem for M_T is decidable nondeterministically using at most linear space and, hence, deterministically in time $O(2^{cn})$ for some $c > 0$. Kapur and Narendran have an interesting result.

<u>Theorem 2.2</u>. There is no finite complete rewriting system R over $\Sigma = \{a,b\}$ that is equivalent to $T = \{(aba, bab)\}$, that is, the monoid presentation $[\Sigma, T]$ does not admit a finite complete rewriting system.

However, Bauer and Otto [7] have found another presentation of the monoid M_T that does admit a finite complete rewriting system; this is done by adding one generator so that the new system presents a quotient monoid on $\{a, b, c\}^*$ and this monoid is isomorphic to M_T. Thus, Bauer and Otto summarize in the following way.

<u>Theorem 2.3</u>. The property of allowing a finite complete rewriting system depends on the specific presentation of the monoid.

Thus, to show that a finitely presented monoid with a decidable word problem does not allow a finite complete rewriting system, it is necessary to show that no finite presentation of this monoid admits such a system. Also, notice that Theorem 2.3 shows that the two parts of Theorem 2.1 are in fact different questions.

We are left with a fundamental question: does every monoid with a decidable word problem admit a finite complete rewriting system? Bauer and Otto state the question in this way but it is well known in more general forms (see [26, 27]). Much recent work in automated deduction has been directed at the corresponding problem for groups and it seems that the question for monoids ought to be closely tied to the question for groups. There is one recent contribution to the question for monoids that must be noted.

A two-level rewriting system R over Σ is a pair $\langle R_1, R_2 \rangle$ where R_1 and R_2 are rewriting systems over Σ with the following rule of application of rewriting rules: the only admissible sequences of applications of rules in R starting from a string $w \in \Sigma^*$ are such that all applications of rules from R_1 come before any application of a rule from R_2.

Bauer [5,6] has studied "n-level" rewriting systems and has established the following result.

Theorem 2.4. Let **M** be a finitely presented monoid. Suppose that the word problem for **M** is decidable. Then there exists a finite 2-level rewriting system R on some finite alphabet Δ such that the monoid with presentation $[\Delta; R]$ is isomorphic to **M** and R is complete. That is, every finitely presented monoid with a decidable word problem admits a finite complete 2-level rewriting system.

Now consider the complexity of the word problem. If a monoid **M** admits a finite complete rewriting system, what can be said about the computational complexity of the word problem for **M**? One way to approach this problem is to consider the derivational complexity of rewriting systems, in particular, of rewriting systems where the word problem is decidable.

Suppose that R is a rewriting system on Σ such that the word problem for the monoid with presentation $[\Sigma; R]$ is decidable. Define a function f as follows: for $x,y \in \Sigma^*$, $f(x,y)$ is the minimum number of steps in a sequence of transformations under R that begin with x and end with y (or vice versa) if such a sequence exists, and is "no" otherwise. The function f is the derivational complexity of the rewriting system R.

One might think that the derivational complexity of a rewriting system defines the computational complexity of the word problem. In fact, this is not the case. Madlener and Otto [33] have considered this situation in the case that the derivational complexity is a primitive recursive function. For each $n > 0$, let E_n be the class of functions in the nth level of the Grzegorczyk hierarchy.

Theorem 2.5. For each $m \geq 4$, there is a finitely presented group $G(m)$ with an E_3-decidable word problem such that $G(m)$ has a presentation with derivational complexity in E_m but no finite group presentation of $G(m)$ has derivational complexity in E_{m-1}.

Bauer and Otto [7] use the techniques of Madlener and Otto [33] to obtain result about the derivational complexity of finite complete rewriting systems.

Threorem 2.6. For each $m \geq 2$, there exists a finite complete rewriting system R_m with the following properties:
(a) there is an algorithm to solve the word problem for R_m that has its running time bounded above by a function in E_1;
(b) the derivational complexity of R_m is in E_m but is not bounded above by any function in E_{m-1}.

Further, the hope that a finite complete rewriting system may be guaranteed to have a word problem that is computationally feasible has been dashed. Bauer and Otto [7] have established the following result.

Theorem 2.7. For every $n \geq 3$, there is a finite complete rewriting system R_n such that the word problem for R_n is decidable by an algorithm whose running time is bounded above by a function in E_n but not by any function in E_{n-1}.

In the remaining sections we consider Thue systems where the notion of reduction is based on length, that is, where reduction depends on applying length-reducing rules. Based on this notion of reduction, we consider Thue systems that are Church-Rosser and develop properties of these systems and the monoids they present. One important theme for future work is to identify those properties that are decidable when reduction is based on length and are still decidable when reduction is based on some other ordering. Another important theme is the study of the complexity of problems of monoids and of Thue systems when reduction is based on length. In particular, we are concerned with properties that are tractable. A number of results have already been obtained in this case and some of them will be surveyed here.

Section 3. Strings and Thue Systems

In this section we provide formal definitions of Thue systems, Thue congruences, etc. We introduce the notion of length as the metric on strings as a basis for the notion of reduction, leading to the notion that reduction is a Noetherian relation. This is the basis for the principal results developed in this and the later sections.

For any set Σ of symbols, Σ^* is the free monoid generated by Σ under the operation of concatenation with the empty word e as identity. If $w \in \Sigma^*$, then the length of w, denoted $|w|$, defined as follows: $|e| = 0$, $|a| = 1$ for $a \in \Sigma$, and $|wa| = |w| + 1$ for $w \in \Sigma^*$ and $a \in \Sigma$. If $A,B \subseteq \Sigma^*$, then the concatenation of A and B, denoted AB, is defined to be $\{xy \mid x \in A, y \in B\}$. If $A \subseteq \Sigma^*$, then define $A^0 = \{e\}$, $A^1 = A$, and $A^{n+1} = A^nA$ for $n \geq 0$. If $A \subseteq \Sigma^*$, then define $A^* = \cup_{i\geq 0}A^i$.

It is clear that if $A \subseteq \Sigma^*$, then A^* is the free submonoid of Σ^* generated by A and $A^* = \{x_1 \ldots x_n \mid n \geq 1, \text{ each } x_i \in A\} \cup \{e\}$. Recall that if Σ is a finite alphabet, then the regular subsets of Σ^* form the smallest class containing the finite subsets and closed under union, concatenation, and $*$.

Let Σ be an alphabet. A Thue system T on Σ is a subset of $\Sigma^* \times \Sigma^*$ and each element (u,v) of T is a rewriting rule. The Thue congruence $\overset{*}{\longleftrightarrow}_{(T)}$ generated by T is the transitive, reflexive closure of the relation $\longleftrightarrow_{(T)}$ defined as follows: for $(u,v) \in T$ and $x,y \in \Sigma^*$, $xuy \longleftrightarrow_{(T)} xvy$ and $xvy \longleftrightarrow_{(T)} xuy$. Two strings $x,y \in \Sigma^*$ are congruent (mod T) if $x \overset{*}{\longleftrightarrow}_{(T)} y$ and the congruence class of w (mod T) for $w \in \Sigma^*$ is $[w]_{(T)} = \{z \in \Sigma^* \; z \overset{*}{\longleftrightarrow}_{(T)} w\}$.

The subscript (T) will be omitted whenever ambiguity is not

We lose no generality by assuming that for every Thue system T, if $(u,v) \in T$, then $|u| \geq |v|$.

If T is a Thue system on alphabet Σ, then the <u>monoid M_T presented by</u> T is defined as follows: (i) the elements are $[x]$, $x \in \Sigma^*$, (ii) the multiplication is $[x]\cdot[y] = [xy]$, $x,y \in \Sigma^*$, and (iii) the identity is $[e]$. If Σ is a finite alphabet, then M_T is <u>finitely-generated</u>, and if both Σ and T are finite, then M_T is <u>finitely presented</u>. We will assume that if T is finite, then the alphabet Σ is also finite.

If T_1 and T_2 are Thue systems on Σ such that for all $x,y \in \Sigma^*$, $x \overset{*}{\longleftrightarrow}_{(T_1)} y$ implies $x \overset{*}{\longleftrightarrow}_{(T_2)} y$, then T_1 <u>refines</u> T_2. If T_1 refines T_2 and T_2 refines T_1, then T_1 and T_2 are <u>equivalent</u>.

The notion of equivalence of Thue systems has to do with the congruence on the free monoid generated by the alphabets of the two systems. The alphabets must be the same and the systems are equivalent if and only if they generate the same congruence on the corresponding free monoid. It is clear that if T_1 and T_2 are equivalent Thue systems, then the monoids M_{T_1} and M_{T_2} are identical and, hence, isomorphic. But two monoids may be isomorphic without being equivalent.

Now we apply the notion of the length of a string to develop restrictions on the rewriting process.

Let Σ be an alphabet and let T be a Thue system on Σ. If $x,y \in \Sigma^*$, $x \overset{*}{\longleftrightarrow} y$, and $|x| > |y|$, then define $x \to y$; this is the <u>reduction</u> relation. Let $\overset{*}{\longrightarrow}$ be the reflexive, transitive closure of the relation $\to$; abusing the terminology, we also call this relation <u>reduction</u>. A string $z \in \Sigma^*$ is <u>irreducible (mod T)</u> if there is no w such that $z \to y$. Let IRR(T) denote the set of all strings that are irreducible (mod T). A string $z \in \Sigma^*$ is <u>minimal with respect to $\overset{*}{\longleftrightarrow}_{(T)}$</u> if there is no y such that $|y| < |z|$ and $y \overset{*}{\longleftrightarrow} z$. If $x \overset{*}{\longrightarrow}_{(T)} y$, then y is a <u>descendant</u> of x and y is an <u>ancestor</u> of y.

The set IRR(T) of irreducible strings with respect to a given Thue system T on alphabet Σ is the complement of an ideal of Σ^* since if y is reducible, then for all x,z, xyz is reducible. Berstel [8] has noted the following useful fact.

Theorem 3.1. Let T be a finite Thue system on finite alphabet Σ. The set IRR(T) is a regular subset of Σ^*. Further, there is an algorithm that on input such a system T will produce a finite-state acceptor (or regular expression) for IRR(T).

It is clear that if T is a finite Thue system on finite alphabet Σ, then the question of whether any given string is irreducible is easily decidable. Now a string that is minimal is also irreducible modulo any Thue system that generates the same congruence as T. Thus, the cardinality of M_T is at most the cardinality of IRR(T). However, for some Thue systems there are irreducible strings that are not minimal so the cardinality of M_T is not necessarily the cardinality of IRR(T). Thus, it would be desirable to have an algorithm for determining when a string is minimal, but this is not the case.

Theorem 3.2. [15]. The following problem is undecidable:

INSTANCE: a finite Thue system T on finite alphabet Σ and a string $w \in \Sigma^*$;

QUESTION: is w minimal with respect to $\overset{*}{\longleftrightarrow}_{(T)}$?

It is clear that if T is a Thue system, then the reduction relation $\overset{*}{\longrightarrow}_{(T)}$ is noetherian and so for every string w there exists an irreducible string z such that $w \overset{*}{\longrightarrow} z$. It is easy to see that one can compute (by exhaustive search) all such z but this is much too costly. Hence it would be desirable to have an efficient algorithm for computing an irreducible descendant of a given string. We have such an algorithm.

Theorem 3.3 [9]. Let T be a finite Thue system on finite alphabet Σ. There is a linear-time algorithm that on input a string $w \in \Sigma^*$ will compute an irreducible string z such that $w \overset{*}{\longrightarrow} z$.

Now we turn to properties of Thue systems that are Church-Rosser where the notion of reduction is based on length of strings. This approach appears to have been pursued for the first time by Nivat. A survey of the work of Nivat and his colleagues and students was presented by Berstel [8].

Let T be a Thue system on alphabet Σ. If for all $x,y \in \Sigma^*$, $x \overset{*}{\longleftrightarrow} y$ implies that for some $z \in \Sigma^*$, $x \overset{*}{\longrightarrow} z$ and $y \overset{*}{\longrightarrow} z$, then

T is <u>Church-Rosser</u>. If for all $w,x,y \in \Sigma^*$, $w \xrightarrow{*} x$ and $w \xrightarrow{*} y$ imply that for some $z \in \Sigma^*$, $x \xrightarrow{*} z$ and $y \xrightarrow{*} z$, then T is <u>confluent</u>.

Thus, if a Thue system is Church-Rosser, then two strings are congruent modulo this system if and only if they have a common descendant. This means that any sequence of applications of the rewriting rules can be replaced by one in which first only length-decreasing rules are applied and then only length-increasing rules are applied.

Thue system that are Church-Rosser have many desirable properties that will be described in this section. The next result provides a characterization of such systems that strengthens a result of Cochet and Nivat [23].

<u>Theorem 3.4</u>. Let T be a Thue system. Every congruence class of $\overset{*}{\longleftrightarrow}$ has a unique irreducible string if and only if T is Church-Rosser.

Combining Theorems 3.3 and 3.4 we have the following fact.

<u>Theorem 3.5</u> [9]. Let T be a finite Thue system. If T is Church-Rosser, then there is a linear-time algorithm to solve the word problem for T.

The word problem for Church-Rosser Thue systems is equivalent to the common descendant problem. However the common ancestor problem is equivalent to the Correspondence Problem of Post and so is undecidable for finite Thue systems [14], even if they are Church-Rosser [37].

The decidability of the word problem for Church-Rosser Thue systems leads to an algorithm for testing the equivalence of finite Church-Rosser systems [15], a question that is undecidable for arbitrary finite Thue systems.

Recall from Theorem 3.1 that if T is finite, then the set IRR(T) of strings that are irreducible (mod T) is regular and can be effectively specified. From Theorem 3.4 we see that if T is Church-Rosser, then a string is irreducible (mod T) if and only if it is minimal with respect to $\overset{*}{\longleftrightarrow}_{(T)}$ so that the cardinality of M_T is precisely the cardinality of IRR(T). Hence, if T is finite and Church-Rosser, then one can effectively determine the cardinality of M_T [15]; this means that it is decidable whether M_T is trivial or is finite, properties that are generally undecidable for finitely presented monoids. This leads us to consider the problem of determining whether a finite Thue system is Church-Rosser.

Theorem 3.6 [16]. There is a polynomial time algorithm to solve the following problem:

INSTANCE: a finite Thue system T;
QUESTION: is T Church-Rosser?

Now suppose that a Thue system T_1 is not Church-Rosser. Does there exist a Thue system T_2 such that T_2 is Church-Rosser and M_{T_2} is isomorphic to M_{T_1}? The answer is always "yes" since one can consider the alphabet $\Delta = \{m \mid m \in M_{T_1}\}$ and the Thue system $T = \{(m_1m_2, m_3) \mid m_1m_2 = m_3 \text{ in } M_{T_1}\}$. The system T is Church-Rosser since multiplication in any monoid is associative so that the rules of T only mimic the multiplication table of M_{T_1}, and the monoid M_T is clearly isomorphic to M_{T_1}. However this situation is not satisfactory since T_1 may be taken over a finite alphabet while if M_{T_1} is infinite, then T is taken over an infinite alphabet. Thus, we restrict attention to Thue systems that are equivalent to T_1, that is, if Σ is the smallest alphabet such that T_1 can be taken over Σ, then we consider only Thue systems T_2 on Σ such that M_{T_2} is precisely equal to M_{T_1}. With this restriction the answer to our question is "no," as was shown by Ó'Dúnlaing [39,41].

Theorem 3.7. The following problem is undecidable:

INSTANCE: a finite Thue system T_1;
QUESTION: does there exist a Thue system T_2 such that T_2 is equivalent to T_1 and T_2 is Church-Rosser?

One motivation for studying Thue system with the Church-Rosser property is the fact that in some cases congruence classes are context-free languages. Nivat and his colleagues initiated research in this area and their choice of topics was influenced by the interface between algebra and formal language theory.

A language L is congruential if there is a finite Thue system T such that L is the union of finitely many of T's congruence classes.

Berstel [8] has shown that the linear context-free language $\{ww^R \mid w \in \Sigma^*\}$ is not congruential.

Some but not all congruential languages are context-free. To see one example of a congruential language that is not context-free, consider $\Sigma = \{a,b,c\}$ and $T = \{(abc,ab), (bbc,cb)\}$. It is clear that T is Church-Rosser. The string abb is irreducible but the congruence class of abb is not context-free since $[abb] \cap \{a\}^*\{b\}^*\{c\}^* = \{ab^{f(n)}c^n \mid n \geq 0,\ f(n) = 2^n + 1\}$ which is not context-free. This leads us to consider certain restrictions.

A Thue system T is monadic if $(u,v) \in T$ implies $|u| > |v|$ and $1 \geq |v|$, and is special if $(u,v) \in T$ implies $v = e$ and $u \neq e$.

Theorem 3.8 [14]. Let T be a finite monadic Thue system on alphabet Σ. For every context-free language $L \subseteq \Sigma^*$, the set of ancestors of strings in L is a context-free language, i.e., $\{y \mid$ for some $x \in L$, y is an ancestor of $x\}$ is context-free. Further, from T and a context-free grammar for L one can construct a context-free grammar that generates the set of ancestors.

Nivat [38] established a weaker version of this result by considering the case when L is a singleton set.

The case for descendants is different. The first result is positive.

Theorem 3.9 [14,17]. Let T be a finite monadic Thue system on Σ. For every regular set $R \subseteq \Sigma^*$, the language $\Delta^*(R) = \{y \mid$ for some $x \in R$, y is a descendant of $x\}$ is again a regular set. Further, from T and a regular expression for R one can construct a regular expression for $\Delta^*(R)$.

The second result is negative.

Theorem 3.10 [14]. Let Σ be a finite alphabet. For every recursively enumerable set $L \subseteq \Sigma^*$, there is a finite special Thue system T and a context-free language C such that T is Church-Rosser and $\Delta^*(C) \cap \Sigma^* = L$. Thus, there exists a finite special Thue system T

and a context-free language C such that $\Delta^*(C)$ is not recursive, let alone context-free.

Now we have one of the strongest results in this area. Cochet and Nivat [23] observed that if T is finite, special, and Church-Rosser, then for every string x, the congruence class of x is an unambiguous context-free language. This result can be greatly strengthened.

<u>Theorem 3.12</u> [9]. Let T be a finite monadic Thue system on alphabet Σ. Suppose that T is Church-Rosser. If $R \subseteq \Sigma^*$ is a regular set, then $[R] = \{y \mid \text{for some } x \in R, x \text{ is congruent to } y\}$ is a deterministic context-free language.

The results on Thue systems and formal languages sketched above are of interest not only due to their importance in formal language theory. Since the theory of regular sets and of context-free languages contains many results about the decidability (and undecidability) of various problems, one can use results such as Theorems 3.8 - 3.12 when attempting to determine whether properties of Thue systems or of the monoids presented by Thue systems are decidable or undecidable. This technique is exploited in a strong way in [12] and some of the results will be sketched in Section 5.

There is a very useful notion that has been introduced recently. A Thue system T on alphabet Σ is <u>reduced</u> if for every rewriting rule $(u,v) \in T$ neither u nor v can be reduced using $T - \{(u,v)\}$. Kapur and Narendran [31,37] have established the following fact.

<u>Theorem 3.13</u>. For any Thue system T_1 that is Church-Rosser, there is a unique reduced Thue system T_2 that is Church-Rosser and equivalent to T_1. Further, if T_1 is finite, then one can effectively construct T_1 from T_2.

Theorem 3.13 is useful in a variety of settings, particularly in showing that certain questions are undecidable. One example of its usefulness is due to Narendran [37]. Consider the Thue system $T_1 = \{(aba,ab)\}$ on $\{a,b\}$. It is easy to see that T_1 is not Church-Rosser since abba is congruent to abb and both of these strings are irreducible. Further, T_1 is not equivalent to any finite Thue

system that is Church-Rosser. But the Thue system $T_2 = \{(ab^na, ab^n) \mid n \geq 1\}$ is equivalent to T_1 and is Church-Rosser. Hence, a given Thue system may not be equivalent to any finite Church-Rosser system while still being equivalent to an infinite Church-Rosser system.

Notice that in this example, both T_1 and T_2 are reduced. Pan [49] has considered Thue systems that are finite and reduced, and has asked whether two such systems can be equivalent (by Theorem 3.13 it cannot be the case that both are Church-Rosser). Pan answered the question in the affirmative and established the following fact.

Theorem 3.14. The following problem is undecidable:

INSTANCE: a reduced finite Thue system T_1;

QUESTION: does there exist a reduced finite Thue system T_2 such that T_2 is both Church-Rosser and equivalent to T_1?

In this section we have sampled only a few of the results about Thue systems with the Church-Rosser property that are of interest. The reader interested in investigating the vast unexplored territory should consult the references.

Section 4. Algebraic Protocols

Recently, some of the results on Thue systems with Church-Rosser properties have been used in the study of mathematical models for communication protocols used in public-key cryptosystems. The basic semantics for such models are briefly described in this section along with the formal connections to Church-Rosser systems.

Public-key encryption as used in network communication has been investigated extensively. The main advantage of the techniques developed in this area is the potential for secure communication. Dolev and Yao [24] have shown how informal arguments about protocols can lead to erroneous conclusions and have developed formal models for two-party cascade protocols and for two-party name-stamp protocols intended to be used for the exchange of plaintext messages. In terms of their model, Dolev and Yao developed an elegant characterization of secure cascade protocols, a characterization with conditions that can be checked by inspection.

Consider a set Γ of functions and a set Δ of symbols such that each function in Γ has the free monoid Δ^* as domain and as co-domain. In an algebraic protocol the set Γ depends on the set of users and is defined as follows:

(a) for each user X, the <u>encryption</u> function E_X and the <u>decryption</u> function D_X are in Γ;

(b) only finitely many users are assumed so that there is a constant $m > 0$ such that every user X has a "name" that is encoded as a string in Δ^* of length m; for any string $w \in \Delta^*$, if $|w| \geq m$, then let $w = \text{head}(w)\,\text{tail}(w)$ where $|\text{tail}(w)| = m$;

(c) for each user X there is a <u>name-appending</u> function i_X where for any $w \in \Delta^*$, $i_X(w) = wX$ (use X for the code of X), and there is a <u>name-matching</u> function d_X in Γ where

$$d_X(w) = \begin{cases} \text{head}(w) & \text{if } \text{tail}(w) = X \\ \text{undefined} & \text{otherwise} \end{cases}$$

(d) there is a <u>deletion</u> function d in Γ where

$$d(w) = \begin{cases} \text{head}(w) & \text{if } |w| \geq m \\ \text{undefined} & \text{otherwise.} \end{cases}$$

One important assumption is that for two different users X and Y, the set $\{E_X, E_Y, D_X, D_Y, i_X, i_Y, d_X, d_Y, d\}$ consists of nine different functions.

The semantics of a protocol is given by a set of "cancellation rules." A set T of <u>cancellation rules</u> on Γ is any subset of the union of all the relations descrived below:

(a) for every user X, D_X composed with E_X is the identity function 1 on Δ^*;

(b) for every user X, E_X composed with D_X is 1;

(c) for every user X, d_X composed with i_X is 1;

(d) for every user X, d composed with i_X is 1.

Consider the composition of function in Γ. Recall that composition is associative, that each function in Γ has Δ^* as both domain and co-domain, and that the identity function 1 is an identity with respect to composition. Thus, if we consider the set of all compositions of functions in Γ, then this set is a free monoid, and from the standpoint of syntax, we can identify this set with Γ^*. This means that syntactically each function in Γ^* has a unique factorization as a composition of functions in Γ.

A set of cancellation rules on Γ can be viewed as a Thue system

T on Γ. Since there are no relations on the functions in Γ^* except those that result from applications of the cancellation rules, the Thue congruence generated by T yields the semantics of the elements in Γ^* when they are used as functions on Δ^*, that is, if γ and δ are two different elements of Γ^*, then $\gamma \overset{*}{\longleftrightarrow} \delta$ if and only if for every $M \in \Delta^*$, $\gamma(M) = \delta(M)$. Hence, if T is Church-Rosser, then for every $\gamma \in \Gamma^*$, there is a unique irreducible $\bar{\gamma} \in \Gamma^*$ such that for all $M \in \Delta^*$, $\bar{\gamma}(M) = \gamma(M)$.

Recall that if two functions are in Γ, then they are indeed different functions on Δ^*, that is, Γ is a set of functions, not a set of names of functions. Thus, if γ and δ are in Γ and $\gamma \neq \delta$, then γ and δ are not congruent with respect to any set of cancellation rules, and every element of Γ is irreducible with respect to every set of cancellation rules.

It is easy to prove the following result.

Theorem 4.1 [17]. If T is a set of cancellation rules on Γ, then T is Church-Rosser.

The reason for introducing the Church-Rosser property when studying the syntax and semantics of protocols is that the order of applications of reductions in reaching an irreducible object is not important since any order will do and hence one can use the most convenient order.

Theorem 4.1 allows the use of Theorem 3.9 when studying a set of cancellation rules. Thus, for any set T of cancellation rules and any regular set $R \subseteq \Gamma^*$, one can obtain a specification of $\Delta^*(R)$ IRR(T) from a specification for R. This fact underlies the work of Dolev and Yao [24] and is used explicitly by Book and Otto [17-19] and by Pan [50].

A set of cancellation rules is an example of a Thue system of a restricted type.

Let T be a Thue system on Σ. If there is an integer $k > 0$ such that $(u,v) \in T$ implies $|u| = k$ and $v = e$, then T is homogeneous of degree k. A Thue system is homogeneous if there exists a $k > 0$ such that it is homogeneous of degree k.

Thus a set of cancellation rules is a Thue system that is homogeneous of degree 2. One might suspect that Theorem 4.1 can be extended to show that every Thue system of degree 2 is Church-Rosser. This is not the case but a slightly weaker result was established in [13].

Section 5. Monoids with Church-Rosser Presentations

Suppose that **M** is a monoid with a finite Church-Rosser presentation. What can be said about the algebraic structure of **M** based on this fact? More specifically, how can one characterize those monoids with finite Church-Rosser presentations? Which algebraic properties are decidable for monoids with finite Church-Rosser presentations? There are a number of results relating to these questions and we will review some of them here.

We must clarify certain notions and introduce some useful notation. Let T be a Thue system on alphabet Σ. We denote by $[\Sigma;T]$ the monoid generated by T, that is, the monoid $\mathbf{M}_T = \Sigma^*/\overset{*}{\longleftrightarrow}_T$. We also view T as a set of relations that presents a group; in this case, we assume for every generator $\sigma \in \Sigma$, the inverse σ^{-1} (which is not in Σ) and the trivial relators $(\sigma\sigma^{-1},e)$ and $(\sigma^{-1}\sigma,e)$. We write $\langle\Sigma;T\rangle$ or $\mathbf{G}_T$ for this group. Another way to present the group $\mathbf{G}_T$ is to let Σ^{-1} be a set that is in one-to-one correspondence with Σ but is disjoint from Σ, say $\Sigma^{-1} = \{\bar{\sigma} \mid \sigma \in \Sigma\}$ where $\Sigma \cap \Sigma^{-1} = \emptyset$, and let $gr(T) = T \cup \{(\sigma\bar{\sigma},e),(\bar{\sigma}\sigma,e) \mid \sigma \in \Sigma\}$. Then the monoid $[\Sigma \cup \Sigma^{-1};\ gr(T)]$ is a group and is isomorphic to $\mathbf{G}_T$, and the pair $(\Sigma \cup \Sigma^{-1}, T \cup T^{-1})$ is a <u>monoid presentation of the group</u>. If $\mathbf{M}_T$ is a group, then $\mathbf{M}_T$ is isomorphic to $\mathbf{G}_T$ (but $\mathbf{G}_T$ is always a group whether or not $\mathbf{M}_T$ is a group.)

Now we consider the question of which monoids have Church-Rosser presentations. The first result is a characterization theorem due to Cochet [22].

<u>Theorem 5.1</u>. Let T be a finite special Church-Rosser Thue system on alphabet Σ. Suppose that $[\Sigma;\ T]$ is a group $\mathbf{G}$. Then $\mathbf{G}$ is the free product of finitely many cyclic groups. Conversely, every group that is the free product of finitely many cyclic groups has a presentation of this type.

Call a Thue system T <u>two-monadic</u> if T is monadic and (u,v) T implies $|u| = 2$. Avenhaus, Madlener, and Otto [4] have characterized those monoids with finite two-monadic presentations that are Church-Rosser.

Theorem 5.2. Let T be a finite 2-monadic Thue system on alphabet Σ. Suppose that T is Church-Rosser and $[T;\Sigma]$ is a group. Then the group $[T;\Sigma]$ is a free product of a finitely generated free group and a finite number of finite groups. Conversely, any group that is a free product of a finitely generated free group and a finite number of finite groups has a presentation of this type.

Gilman [25] has conjectured that a group **G** is a free product of finitely generated free groups and finite groups if and only if there is a monadic Thue system T on a finite alphabet Σ such that the monoid $[\Sigma; T]$ is in fact the group **G**. It is easy to see that any such group has a presentation of this type but the converse has not been established.

Now consider commutative monoids that are presented as quotients of free noncommutative monoids. Avenhaus, Book, and Squier [2] have one result on these monoids.

Theorem 5.3. Let T be a finite Church-Rosser Thue system. Suppose that $\mathbf{M_T}$ is both commutative and infinite. If $\mathbf{M_T}$ is cancellative or T is special, then $\mathbf{M_T}$ is either the free cyclic group or the free cyclic monoid.

Recall that a unit of a monoid is an element that has a two-sided inverse and, further, that the submonoid generated by the set of units is a subgroup of that monoid. Consider a monoid **M** with a finite special Church-Rosser presentation. Squier [53] has shown that the property of being Church-Rosser is inherited by a presentation of the group of units. This strengthens a result of Adjan [1]: from a finite special presentation of a monoid one can construct a presentation of its group of units. By using Theorem 5.1, Squier concludes that the group of units of a monoid with a finite special Church-Rosser presentation is a free product of finitely many cyclic groups.

The more general questions of characterizing the type of monoid or the type of group with a finite Church-Rosser presentation remain open. These questions are very challenging.

Now let us turn to the question of decidability of various algebraic properties. We must separate the notion of "algebraic properties" into different types. First, consider properties of a specific monoid **M**. We have the following examples of problems:

the word problem

INSTANCE: two words $u, v \in \Sigma^*$;

QUESTION: are u and v equal in M?

the power problem

INSTANCE: two words $u, v \in \Sigma^*$;

QUESTION: does there exist an integer $n \geq 0$ such that u and v^n are equal in M?

Second, consider properties of a class C of monoids. We have the following examples of problems:

the uniform word problem

INSTANCE: a finite presentation of a monoid M in C;

QUESTION: is the word problem for M decidable?

the group problem

INSTANCE: a finite presentation of a monoid M in C;

QUESTION: is the monoid M a group?

the freeness problem

INSTANCE: a finite presentation of a monoid M in C;

QUESTION: is M a free monoid?

In general, all of the problems described in the last paragraph are undecidable. However, there are numerous questions that while being undecidable for arbitrary finite Thue systems (or finitely presented monoids) are decidable for Thue systems that are **finite, monadic, and Church-Rosser**. This was explored in [12] where a decision procedure for properties expressible by "linear sentences" was developed. A linear sentence is a quantified formula in prenex form such that (i) there are constants from Σ^* and both existential and universal variables but every variable is bound by a quantifier, (ii) each variable appears at most once in the formula, and (iii) the quantifiers are existential or universal or both but there is at most one alternation between existential and universal or vice versa; for details, see [12]. The technique depends heavily on the notion that if T is a finite, monadic, Church-Rosser Thue system on alphabet Σ and R is a regular subset of Σ^*, then the set $\Delta^*(R)$ of descendants of $R(\text{mod } T)$ is again a regular set.

The properties amenable to attack by the method of linear sentences include the following: the group problem, the power problem, the generalized word problem (for regular set R and string w, is $[w]$ in the submonoid generated by R?), the inclusion problem (for regular sets A and B, is the submonoid generated by A included in the submonoid generated by B?), the ideal problem (for regular set A, is the submonoid generated by A a left, right, or two-sided ideal?), and the independent set problem (for a finite set A, is there no $w \varepsilon A$ such that $[w]$ is in the submonoid generated by $A - \{w\}$?). In addition, it was shown that Green's relations are decidable for monoids presented by finite, monadic, Church-Rosser Thue systems. Otto [42] has explored the limitations of the linear sentences technique and has shown how strongly it depends on the presentation (i.e., the Thue system) being monadic and Church-Rosser.

One benefit of the method of linear sentences is that the complexity of its application is amenable to analysis. If the technique is applied to appropriate questions about the congruence generated by a given finite, monadic, Church-Rosser Thue system T, then one can conclude that the questions are decidable deterministically in polynomial time if the sentence is not in the form $\forall \exists$; in the $\forall \exists$ case it is decidable in polynomial space and the method is applicable to some PSPACE-complete problems.

There are a number of questions that are not known to be amenable to attack by the decision procedure for linear sentences. In particular, the method does not appear to apply to presentations that are not monadic. Recently, Otto [46,47] has developed other techniques and has shown that each of the following problems is decidable when the Thue system T is finite and Church-Rosser:

(i) is M_T free?
(ii) is M_T a group?
(iii) is M_T torsion-free?
(iv) is M_T a free group?

Some of the techniques used by Otto suggest a theme that has been investigated only recently. Consider a Thue system T on alphabet Σ, the monoid $M_T = [\Sigma; T]$, and the group $G_T = \langle \Sigma; T \rangle$. Which properties of G_T are inherited by M_T and vice versa? One example is the following fact due to Perrin and Schupp [51].

Theorem 5.4. Let Σ be a finite alphabet, let $w \varepsilon \Sigma^*$, $w \neq e$, and let $T = \{(w,e)\}$. There exists a string $z \varepsilon \Sigma^*$ such that if $T' = \{(z,e)\}$, then the monoid $M_{T'}$ is isomorphic to the group G_T.

In Theorem 5.4, the string w is said to have positive exponents since only generators from Σ occur in w, that is, none of the inverses of generators occur in w. Thus, Theorem 5.4 says that if a group G has a one-relator presentation that has positive exponents, then there is a relator with positive exponents **on the same set of generators** such that the monoid generated by that single relator is in fact the group G. Wrathall [57] has observed that Theorem 5.4 can be generalized in the following way. Let Σ be a finite alphabet and let T be a Thue system on Σ such that there is at least one rule in T having the form (w,e). Then there exists a Thue system T' on Σ such that the monoid $M_{T'}$ is isomorphic to the group G_T presented by T. (Notice that T' is on the alphabet Σ, not the alphabet $\Sigma \cup \Sigma^{-1}$.)

Another example of properties of M_T that are inherited by G_T is due to Wrathall [57].

Theorem 5.5. Let T be a Thue system on alphabet Σ. If the monoid M_T is free, then the group G_T is also free.

It is an open question whether the converse of Theorem 5.5 holds.

The proofs of these observations depend on the fact that when viewed a set of relations that present a group T, each of the rules in T has positive exponents. This observation leads to the following observation: for a finite Thue system T on finite alphabet Σ, if gr(T) is Church-Rosser (then T is Church-Rosser) and $A \subset \Sigma^*$ is finite, then A is an independent set in the submonoid of G_T generated by the set of words with positive exponents if and only if A is an independent set in the monoid M_T.

Another theme in the investigation of the properties of monoids presented by finite (monadic, special) Church-Rosser Thue systems may be described in the following way. Each free monoid has a presentation (the trivial presentation) as a Church-Rosser Thue system. Many questions about strings and about the regular or context-free subsets of finitely generated free monoids are decidable since one can invoke the techniques of the theory of finite-state acceptors and the theory of context-free grammars (or pushdown store acceptors). These same techniques have been used to establish many of the known results regarding the decidability of properties of monoids presented by finite Church-Rosser Thue systems, e.g., (1) the word problem, (2) whether the monoid is trivial or finite or infinite? How far does the (obviously limited) parallel between the theory of finitely generated free monoids and the theory of monoids presented by finite (monadic, special) Church-Rosser Thue systems extend? One problem whose decidability remains open illustrates the problem.

Let Σ be a finite alphabet. Consider the following problem.

INSTANCE: a finite set $A \subset \Sigma^*$;

QUESTION: is A^* a free submonoid of Σ^* with A as its minimal generating set?

There are many different algorithms for solving this problem and some can be extended to the case where A is infinite but regular. One loses no generality by assuming that A is the minimal generating set of A^* since in the case of a free monoid one can always effectively construct that unique set from A. If T is a finite monadic Church-Rosser system on Σ, then one can determine whether a given finite set $A \subset \Sigma^*$ is an independent set by using the method of linear sentences mentioned above. It is shown in [12] that if M_T is cancellative, then one can decide whether the submonoid generated by the finite independent set A is free. But it is not known how to determine whether M_T is cancellative and it is not known how to decide the question of freeness when M_T is not cancellative.

It is important to note that many of the results reported in this section are quite recent and have not as yet been published. It appears that the general area has great potential for future exploration.

SECTION 6. One-Rule Systems

Thue systems with exactly one rewriting rule are a source of interesting problems and examples. Many of the examples are technical but serve to illustrate the difficulties of problems about finite systems and also suggest results that may be true in general. In order to discuss one-rule Thue systems and the monoids they present, it is useful to consider groups presented by a single defining relation, a topic that has been well studied in combinatorial group theory (see Magnus, Karrass, and Solitar [34]).

Every group presented by a single defining relation has a solvable word problem. This is a classic result of combinatorial group theory (see [34]). Adjan [1] showed that a monoid with a single defining relator can be embedded in the group presented by the same relator and so has a decidable word problem. Thus, we know that for every finite alphabet Σ and every $w \in \Sigma^*$, the Thue system $T = \{(w,e)\}$ has a decidable word problem. Unfortunately, knowing that these problems are decidable tells us nothing about the inherent complexity of the problems. Avenhaus and Madlener [3] have shown that the word problem for one relator groups has complexity that is at worst primitive recursive; this also true for a few other problems of one relator groups such as the power problem. However the work of Avenhaus and Madlener suggests that the word problem for one relator groups has complexity that is not bounded above by the functions in any one fixed level of the Grzegorczyk hierarchy. In particular, this problem appears not to be subelementary (i.e., not in the Grzegorczyk classes E_n for $n < 3$.

Consider a Thue system with a single rule (u,v) where $|u| \geq |v| \geq 1$. If $T = \{(u,v)\}$, then there exists a string w such that if $T' = \{(w,e)\}$, then $G_T = G_{T'}$; w is just uv^{-1}. That is, if there is a one relation presentation of a group, then there is also a one relator presentation. The parallel result for monoids does not hold and so one cannot use this strategy to show that the word problem for monoids presented by a single defining relation is decidable; in fact, the decidability of the word problem for monoids presented by a single defining relation, i.e., Thue systems of the form of $\{(u,v)\}$ with $u \neq e$ and $v \neq e$, is an open question.

Another topic of interest for monoids with a single defining relation is the structure of the congruence classes. Results in both of these areas will be discussed in this section.

Jantzen [28] studied monoids presented by a single defining relation in order to determine whether every such monoid had a Church-Rosser presentation on the same alphabet and to investigate the structure of the congruence classes for such monoids. His main results are summarized in the following theorem.

Theorem 6.1. Let $\Sigma = \{a,b\}$, let $w = abbaab$, and let $T = \{(w,e)\}$.
(a) The Thue system T is not Church-Rosser and there is no Church-Rosser Thue system that is equivalent to T.
(b) For each $x \in \Sigma^*$, the congruence class of x relative to T is not a context-free language, that is, no congruence class of the congruence generated by T is a context-free language.
(c) There is no infinite preperfect Thue system that is equivalent to T.

We denote the monoid presented by $[\{a,b\}, (abbaab,e)]$ by M_J and refer to it as the "Jantzen monoid." Jantzen's proof of Theorem 6.1(a) has been generalized to yield the following fact.

Theorem 6.2 [11]. If T is a special Thue system with exactly one rule, $T = \{(w,e)\}$, then either T is Church-Rosser or there is no finite Church-Rosser Thue system that is equivalent to T.

The situation of one-rule special Thue systems that are not Church-Rosser is interesting. Certain properties can be developed by considering the structure of the strings that serve as relators.

If $w = x^k$ for some $x \in \Sigma^*$ and $k > 1$, then w is imprimitive; otherwise, w is primitive. In either case, the shortest x such that $w = x^k$ for some $k \geq 0$ is the root of w, denoted $\rho(w)$. If w is primitive and for some u,v with $0 < |u| < |w|$, $uw = wv$, then w has overlap. If w is imprimitive or w has overlap, then there is a proper prefix of w that is also a proper suffix; the longest such common prefix and suffix is the overlap of w, denoted $ov(w)$.

Recall that a unit of a monoid is an element that has a two-sided inverse. The situation underlying Theorem 6.2 can be stated in the following way.

Theorem 6.3. [13] Let $T = \{(w,e)\}$.

(a) If w is primitive and w has no overlap, then M_T has no nontrivial units. In this case, T is Church-Rosser.

(b) If w is imprimitive and the root of w has no overlap, then the group of units of M_T is a finite cyclic group that is nontrivial. In this case, T is Church-Rosser.

(c) If w is primitive and w has overlap, then the group of units of M_T is infinite. In this case, T is not Church-Rosser.

(d) If w is imprimitive and $\rho(w)$ has overlap, then the group of units of M_T is infinite but has a finite (but nontrivial) cyclic subgroup. In this case, T is not Church-Rosser.

Thus, we have a situation where one feature of the algebraic structure of the monoid M_T presented by a Thue system T is closely related to the question of whether T is Church-Rosser.

If a finite Thue system is Church-Rosser, then there is a linear-time algorithm to solve the word problem (Theorem 3.5). Consider the Thue system $T = \{(aba,e)\}$. This system is not Church-Rosser but there is a linear-time algorithm to solve the word problem: ab is congruent to ba so that one can choose $\{a^n, b^n, ab^n \; n \geq 0\}$ to be the set of normal forms and then transform each $x \in \{a,b\}^*$ to its unique normal form; two strings are congruent if and only if they have the same normal form. This system is of interest because of an additional fact: for each $x \in \{a,b\}^*$, the congruence class $[x]$ is a deterministic context-free language. Thus, $T = \{(aba,e)\}$ is a Thue system that is not Church-Rosser, that is not equivalent to any Church-Rosser Thue system, and that has the property that every congruence class and every union of congruence classes where the union is taken over any regular subset of $\{a^n, b^n, ab^n \mid n \geq 0\}$ is a deterministic context-free language.

In order to establish his results on M_J, Jantzen used certain notions about matrix representations of monoids. This was developed further by Squier and Wrathall [54] who showed that M_J is faithfully represented by a specific group of 2×2 matrices of rational numbers. Using the results of Squier and Wrathall, Potts [52] constructed an infinite, but structurally simple presentation of M_J on four generators. Potts' presentation involves a finite number of rule schemata and is locally confluent but not Noetherian; however every element of M_J has a unique normal form. Otto [43] then showed that the presentation of M_J given by Jantzen (as in Theorem 6.1) does not admit a finite complete rewriting system that is based on a Knuth-Bendix ordering. (Otto did construct a finite complete rewriting system on four generators for M_J but the underlying ordering for this system is still not a Knuth-Bendix ordering.) Jantzen, Otto, and Potts have extended these results in different ways, sometimes by attacking other examples. However at this time the appropriate general theory has yet to be developed.

Now let us turn to one-rule systems that are not special. Such a system has the form $T = \{(u,v)\}$ where $|u| \geq |v| \geq 1$. As noted above the decidability of the word problem for this class of Thue systems is an open question.

It is clear that if $|u| = |v|$, then the word problem for T is decidable nondeterministically using at most linear space and hence is decidable deterministically in exponential time (in this case, $O(2^{c|uv|})$ for some $c > 0$). Metivier [35] has shown that if the rewriting is directed so that the rule (u,v) in $T = \{(u,v)\}$ must be applied as replacing u by v but not conversely, then the word problem is decidable nondeterministically in polynomial time. If $|u| > |v|$ and u is primitive and has no overlap, then just as in Theorem 6.3 the Thue system T is Church-Rosser so that there is a linear-time algorithm to solve the word problem. If u is not primitive or u has overlap, then ov(w) is defined. For this case Otto and Wrathall [48] established the following parallel to Theorem 6.3.

Let $OVL(w) = \{u \mid$ there exist nonempty v_1, v_2 such that $w = uv_1 = v_2u\}$. Let $\pi(w) = |w| - |ov(w)|$; $\pi(w)$ is the period of w. Let res(w) be the prefix of w of length equal to the remainder when $|w|$ is divided by $\pi(w)$.

Theorem 6.4. Let $T = \{(u,v)\}$ be a Thue system such that $0 < |v| < |ov(u)|$. Then T is Church-Rosser if and only if either (a) $|v| \geq \pi(u)$ and $v \in OVL(u)$, or (b) $v = res(u)$ and $OVL(u) \cap \{w \mid |res(u)| < |w| < \pi(u)\} = \emptyset$.

From Theorem 6.4 Otto and Wrathall were able to obtain the following parallel of Theorem 6.2.

Theorem 6.5. Let $T = \{(u,v)\}$ be a Thue system such that $0 \leq |v| \leq |ov(u)|$. Then T is Church-Rosser or there is no Church-Rosser Thue system that is equivalent to T.

If a finite Thue system is Church-Rosser, then the word problem is decidable in linear time. How many one-rule systems are Church-Rosser? This question can be approached by considering asymptotic density.

A string w is bordered if there exist x, y, z such that $w = xz = zy$ and $0 < |x| < |w|$; in this case, z is the border. If a string has no border, then it is unbordered.

For each positive integer k, fix an alphabet Σ of size k. For each integer $n > 1$, let $u_k(n)$ be the number of strings w in Σ^* of length n such that w is unbordered. Book and Squier [20] showed that for each n, the ratio of $u_k(n)$ to k^n goes to 1 as k goes to infinity. This fact can be interpreted in the following way.

Theorem 6.6. Almost all one-rule Thue systems are Church-Rosser and, hence, have word problems that are decidable in linear time.

Thus, while the decidability of the word problem for one-rule Thue systems remains an open question, the asymptotic density of systems with decidable word problems suggest that one should attempt to show that all such systems have decidable word problems.

Before leaving the subject of one-rule systems, one point should be made. The Jantzen monoid M_J has been the subject of a number of papers by different authors. To a very large extent this happened because the system $T = \{(abbaab,e)\}$ that presents M_J was the first known example of a Thue system with the following properties: (i) T is not Church-Rosser; (ii) there is no Church-Rosser Thue system on $\{a,b\}$ that is equivalent to T; and (iii) no congruence class of T is a context-free language. Clearly, one can not expect to build a theory based on one example. But all of this work is quite recent, Jantzen's paper having been published only in 1981, and so much more can be expected as more examples are extensively investigated. There is reason to hope that eventually a satisfactory general theory can be developed.

Acknowledgements

I wish to thank Maurice Nivat who introduced me to the study of Thue systems and Thue congruences in May 1975. The problems posed by his school have influenced much of my work in this area.

Friedrich Otto and Celia Wrathall provided valuable criticism of a preliminary version of this paper.

References

1. S. Adjan, Defining relations and algorithmic problems for groups and semigroups, Proc. Steklov Inst. Math. 85, 1966. (English version published by the American Mathematical Society, 1967.)

2. J. Avenhaus, R. Book, and C. Squier, On expressing commutativity by Church-Rosser presentations: a note on commutative monoids, R.A.I.R.O. Informatique Théorique 18 (1984), 47-52.

3. J. Avenhaus and K. Madlener, Algorithmische probleme bei einrelatorgruppen und ihre komplexität, Arch. Math. Logic 19 (1978), 3-12.

4. J. Avenhaus, K. Madlener, and F. Otto, Groups presented by finite two-monadic Church-Rosser Thue systems, Interner Bericht, Fachbereich Informatik, Univ. Kaiserslautern, 1984.

5. G. Bauer, Zur Darstellung von Monoiden durch Regelsysteme, Dissertation, Univ. Kaiserslautern, 1984.

6. G. Bauer, N-level rewriting systems, submitted for publication.

7. G. Bauer and F. Otto, Finite complete rewriting systems and the complexity of the word problem, Acta Informatica 21 (1984) 521-540.

8. J. Berstel, Congruences plus que parfaites et langages algébriques, Séminaire d'Informatique Théorique, Institut de Programmation, 1976-77, 123-147.

9. R. Book, Confluent and other types of Thue systems, J. Assoc. Computing Mach. 29 (1982), 171-183.

10. R. Book, When is a monoid a group? The Church-Rosser case is tractable, Theoret. Comput. Sci. 18 (1982), 325-331.

11. R. Book, A note on special Thue systems with a single defining relation, Math. Systems Theory 16 (1983), 301-312.

12. R. Book, Decidable questions of Church-Rosser congruences, Theoret. Comput. Sci. 24 (1983), 301-312.

13. R. Book, Homogeneous Thue systems and the Church-Rosser property, Discrete Math. 48 (1984), 137-145.

14. R. Book, M. Jantzen, and C. Wrathall, Monadic Thue systems, Theoret. Comput. Sci. 19 (1982), 231-251.

15. R. Book and C. Ó'Dúnlaing, Thue congruences and the Church-Rosser property, Semigroup Forum 22 (1981), 325-331.

16. R. Book and C. Ó'Dúnlaing, Testing for the Church-Rosser property, Theoret. Comput. Sci. 16(1981), 223-229.

17. R. Book and F. Otto, Cancellation rules and extended word problems, Information Proc. Letters 20 (1985), 5-11.

18. R. Book and F. Otto, On the security of two-party name-stamp protocols, Theoret. Comput. Sci., to appear.

19. R. Book and F. Otto, On the verifiability of two-party algebraic protocols, Theoret. Comput. Sci., to appear.

20. R. Book and C. Squier, Almost all one-rule Thue systems have decidable word problems, Discrete Math. 49 (1984), 237-240.

21. Y. Cochet, Sur l'algébricité des classes de certaines congruences définés sur le monoide libre. Thèse 3eme cycles, Rennes, 1971.

22. Y. Cochet, Church-Rosser congruences on free semigroups, Colloq. Math. Soc. Janos Bolyai: Algebraic Theory of Semigroups 20 (1976), 51-60.

23. Y. Cochet and M. Nevat, Une généralization des ensembles de Dyck, Israel J. Math. 9 (1971), 389-395.

24. D. Dolev and A. Yao, On the security of public-key protocols, IEEE Trans. Information Theory IT-22 (1976), 644-654.

25. R. Gilman, Computations with rational subsets of confluent groups, in J. Fitch (ed.), EUROSAM 1984, Lecture Notes in Computer Science 174 (1984), 207-212.

26. G. Huet, Confluent reductions: abstract properties and applications to term-rewriting systems, J. Assoc. Comput. Mach. 27 (1980), 797-821.

27. G. Huet and D. Oppen, Equations and rewrite rules, in R. Book (ed.), Formal Language Theory: Perspectives and Open Problems, Academic Press, 1980, 349-405.

28. M. Jantzen, On a special monoid with a single defining relation, Theoret. Comput. Sci. 16 (1981), 61-73.

29. D. Kapur, M. Krishnamoorthy, R. McNaughton, and P. Narendran, An $O(|T|^3)$ algorithm for testing the Church-Rosser property of Thue systems, Theoret. Comput. Sci., 35 (1985), 109-114.

30. D. Kapur and P. Narendran, A finite Thue system with decidable word problem and without equivalent finite canonical system, Theoret. Comput. Sci., 35 (1985), 337-344.

31. D. Kapur and P. Narendran, The Knuth-Bendix completion procedure and Thue systems, SIAM J. Computing, to appear.

32. D. Knuth and P. Bendix, Simple word problems in universal algebras, in J. Leech (ed.), Computational Problems in Abstract Algebra, Pergamon Press, 1970, 263-297.

33. K. Madlener and F. Otto, Pseudo-natural algorithms for decision problems in certain types of string-rewriting systems, submitted for publication.

34. W. Magnus, A. Karrass, and D. Solitar, Combinatorial Group Theory, Wiley-Interscience, 1966.

35. Y. Metivier, Calcul de longuerurs de chaines de reecriture dans le monoide libre, Theoret. Comput. Sci. 35 (1985), 71-88.

36. D. Muller and P. Schupp, Groups, the theory of ends, and context-free languages, J. Comput. System Sci. 26 (1983), 295-310.

37. P. Narendran, Church-Rosser and Related Thue systems, Ph.D. Dissertation, Rennesselaer Poly. Institute, 1983. Also appears as Report No. 84CRD176, General Electric Corporate Research and Development Center, Schenectady, NY, 1984.

38. M. Nivat (avec M. Benois), Congruences parfaites, Seminaire Dubriels, 25e Année, 1971-72, 7-01-09.

39. C. Ó'Dúnlaing, Finite and Infinite Regular Thue Systems, Ph.D. Dissertation, Univ. of California at Santa Barbara, 1981.

40. C. Ó'Dúnlaing, Infinite regular Thue systems, Theoret. Comput. Sci., 25 (1983), 339-345.

41. C. Ó'Dúnlaing, Undecidable questions of Thue systems, Theoret. Comput. Sci., 23 (1983), 339-345.

42. F. Otto, Some undecidability results for non-monadic Church-Rosser Thue systems, Theoret. Comput. Sci., 33 (1984), 261-278.

43. F. Otto, Finite complete rewriting systems for the Jantzen monoid and the Greendlinger group, Theoret. Comput. Sci., 32 (1984), 249-260.

44. F. Otto, Church-Rosser Thue systems that present free monoids, SIAM J. Computing, to appear.

45. F. Otto, Elements of finite order for finite monadic Church-Rosser Thue systems, Trans. American Math. Soc., to appear.

46. F. Otto, Deciding algebraic properties of monoids presented by finite Church-Rosser Thue systems, Proc. First International Conference on Rewriting Techniques and Applications, Dijon, France, May 1985, Lecture Notes in Computer Science, to appear.

47. F. Otto, Decision Problems and their Complexity for Monadic Church-Rosser Thue Systems, in preparaton.

48. F. Otto, and C. Wrathall, A note on Thue systems with a single defining relation, Math. Systems Theory, to appear.

49. L. Pan, On reduced Thue systems, Math. Systems Theory, to appear.

50. L. Pan, On the security of p-party protocols, submitted for publication.

51. D. Perrin and P. Schupp, Sure les monoids à un relateur qui sont des groupes, Theoret. Comput. Sci., 33 (1984), 331-334.

52. D. Potts, Remarks on an example of Jantzen, Theoret. Comput. Sci., 29 (1984), 277-284.

53. C. Squier, personal communication.

54. C. Squier and C. Wrathall, A note on representations of a certain monoid, Theoret. Comput. Sci., 17 (1982), 229-231.

56. A. Thue, Probleme über Veranderungen von Zeichenreihen nach gegeben Regeln, Skr. Vid. Kristianaia, I. Mat. Naturv. Klasse, No. 10 (1914), 34 pp.

57. C. Wrathall, On monoids and groups, in preparation.

DECIDING ALGEBRAIC PROPERTIES OF MONOIDS PRESENTED BY FINITE CHURCH-ROSSER THUE SYSTEMS

Friedrich Otto
Fachbereich Informatik
Universität Kaiserslautern
Postfach 3049

6750 Kaiserslautern
West Germany

1. Introduction

A Thue system T over alphabet Σ is a set of pairs of words over Σ. It induces a congruence $\overset{*}{\underset{T}{\longleftrightarrow}}$ on Σ^*, thus defining the factor monoid $\Sigma^*/\overset{*}{\underset{T}{\longleftrightarrow}}$. Hence, Thue systems can be used to describe monoids. An ordered pair $(\Sigma;T)$, where T is a Thue system over Σ, is called a presentation of the monoid $\Sigma^*/\overset{*}{\underset{T}{\longleftrightarrow}}$.

In 1911 Max Dehn formulated three fundamental decision problems for groups given by presentations of this type: the word problem, the conjugacy problem, and the isomorphism problem. Since then many more decision problems have been posed for groups as well as for monoids in general. However, as it turned out, all these problems are undecidable in general, even if only finite presentations are considered [cf., e.g., 14,15].

This fact led to the investigation of presentations involving only Thue systems that satisfy certain restrictions. One such restriction is to require that the Thue systems be finite and Church-Rosser. In fact, this restriction is a very severe one. Let T be a Thue system over Σ. In addition to the congruence $\overset{*}{\underset{T}{\longleftrightarrow}}$ T defines a reduction $\overset{*}{\underset{T}{\rightarrow}}$, which is the reflexive, transitive closure of the relation $\underset{T}{\rightarrow}$. For $u,v \in \Sigma^*$, $u \underset{T}{\rightarrow} v$ holds if and only if the word u is strictly longer than the word v, and v can be reached from u by a single application of a rule of T. A word $u \in \Sigma^*$ is called irreducible, if for no $v \in \Sigma^*$, we have $u \underset{T}{\rightarrow} v$. The Thue system T is Church-Rosser, if and only if in each congruence class of $\overset{*}{\underset{T}{\longleftrightarrow}}$, there is exactly one irreducible word. Hence, the set IRR(T) of irreducible words can be viewed as a set of representatives for the monoid $\Sigma^*/\overset{*}{\underset{T}{\longleftrightarrow}}$, if T is Church-Rosser.

For a finite Church-Rosser Thue system T over Σ, there is a linear-time algorithm that on input a word $u \in \Sigma^*$ computes the irreducible word that is congruent to u [3]. Thus, the word problem for a monoid M is decidable in linear time, if M can be presented by a finite

Church-Rosser Thue system. But also many other decision problems become decidable in this situation [5,20].

Here we are interested in finding out about the algebraic properties of a monoid M given by a presentation of the form $(\Sigma;T)$. Specifically, we investigate the following decision problems:

(1) Is M trivial ?

(2) Is M finite ?

(3) Is M a free monoid ?

(4) Is M a group ?

(5) Does M contain non-trivial idempotents ?

(6) Does M contain non-trivial elements of finite order ?

(7) Is M a free group ?

A property P of monoids is called invariant, if every monoid that is isomorphic to a monoid possessing property P itself possesses this property. An invariant property P of finitely presented monoids is a Markov property [16,see,e.g.,17], if it satisfies the following conditions:

(i) There is a finitely presented monoid M_1 which does not have property P, and which is not isomorphic to a submonoid of any finitely presented monoid having property P, and

(ii) there exists a finitely presented monoid M_2 having property P.

As can be checked easily, the properties asked for in problems (1) to (4) and (7) are Markov properties, while the properties of problems (5) and (6) are complements of Markov properties. Thus, by the main result of [16], all these decision problems are undecidable in general. However, we restrict our attention to monoids presented by finite Church-Rosser Thue systems or certain specializations thereof. Are these restrictions sufficiently powerful to guarantee the decidability of the problems listed above ?

After giving some basic definitions and notations, it is shown that problems (1) to (4) are decidable when being restricted to finite Church-Rosser Thue systems, while problems (5) to (7) are decidable when being restricted to finite Church-Rosser Thue systems that are monadic. However, it is not known so far whether this last result can be extended to all finite Church-Rosser Thue systems.

The decidability results stated above raise the following question: which monoids and groups can at all be presented by Thue systems of this restricted form ? For this question only a few partial answers are known so far. They are presented in the last section. So it remains a very challenging task to investigate the connection between syntactic properties of presentations and algebraic properties of the monoids and groups presented.

2. Preliminaries

An alphabet Σ is a finite set whose members are called letters. The set of words over Σ is denoted as Σ^*, and e denotes the empty word, i.e., Σ^* is the free monoid generated by Σ under the operation of concatenation with the empty word e as identity. In general, $|x|$ denotes the length of a word x. It is defined by $|e| = 0$, $|xa| = |x|+1$ for all $x \in \Sigma^*$, $a \in \Sigma$. The concatenation of words u and v is simply written as uv. For a set S, $|S|$ denotes the cardinality of S.

A Thue system T over Σ is a subset of $\Sigma^* \times \Sigma^*$. The members of T are called (rewriting) rules. Given a Thue system T over Σ, domain(T) = $\{\ell \mid \exists r \in \Sigma^*: (\ell,r) \in T\}$, and range(T) = $\{r \mid \exists \ell \in \Sigma^*: (\ell,r) \in T\}$. A Thue system T is called special, if $T \subseteq (\Sigma^*-\{e\}) \times \{e\}$, and it is called monadic, if all its rules are length-reducing, and range(T) $\subseteq \Sigma \cup \{e\}$. Finally, it is called two-monadic, if it is monadic with domain(T) $\subseteq \Sigma^2$.

For a Thue system T over Σ, $\underset{T}{\longleftrightarrow}$ denotes the following relation: $\forall u,v \in \Sigma^*$: $u \underset{T}{\longleftrightarrow} v$ if and only if $\exists x,y \in \Sigma^*, (\ell,r) \in T$: ($u = x\ell y$ and $v = xry$) or ($u = xry$ and $v = x\ell y$). The reflexive, transitive closure $\overset{*}{\underset{T}{\longleftrightarrow}}$ of $\underset{T}{\longleftrightarrow}$ is a congruence on Σ^*, the Thue congruence generated by T. If $u \overset{*}{\underset{T}{\longleftrightarrow}} v$, one says that u and v are congruent (modulo T). The congruence class $[u]_T$ of u is the set $\{v \in \Sigma^* \mid u \overset{*}{\underset{T}{\longleftrightarrow}} v\}$. It is well-known that the set of congruence classes $\{[u]_T \mid u \in \Sigma^*\}$ forms a monoid under the operation $[u]_T \circ [v]_T = [uv]_T$ with identity $[e]_T$. This monoid is denoted as $\Sigma^*/\overset{*}{\underset{T}{\longleftrightarrow}}$, and the ordered pair $(\Sigma;T)$ is called a presentation of this monoid.

Let T be a Thue system over Σ. Since the relation $\underset{T}{\longleftrightarrow}$ is symmetric, we may assume without loss of generality that for each rule $(\ell,r) \in T$, $|\ell| \geq |r|$. Now, for $u,v \in \Sigma^*$ with $u \underset{T}{\longleftrightarrow} v$ and $|u| > |v|$, we write $u \underset{T}{\rightarrow} v$. Then the Thue reduction $\overset{*}{\underset{T}{\rightarrow}}$ defined by T is the reflexive, transitive closure of $\underset{T}{\rightarrow}$. Obviously, this reduction is noetherian. If $u \overset{*}{\underset{T}{\rightarrow}} v$, one says that u reduces to v, u is an ancestor of v, and v is a descendant of u (modulo T). If u has no descendant except itself, then it is irreducible, otherwise it is reducible (modulo T). IRR(T) denotes the set of all irreducible words (modulo T), and for $L \subseteq \Sigma^*$, $\Delta_T^*(L) = \{v \mid \exists u \in L: u \overset{*}{\underset{T}{\rightarrow}} v\}$ is the set of all descendants of words of L.

Obviously, for each word $u \in \Sigma^*$, there is at least one irreducible descendant $v \in \Sigma^*$, but in general there are several irreducible words that are congruent. Following the notation of Book [3] we call a Thue system T over Σ Church-Rosser if and only if in each congruence class modulo T, there is exactly one irreducible word. This is equivalent to saying that every two congruent words have a common descendant, i.e., $u \overset{*}{\underset{T}{\leftrightarrow}} v$ implies that there exists some $z \in \Sigma^*$ such that $u \overset{*}{\underset{T}{\rightarrow}} z$ and $v \overset{*}{\underset{T}{\rightarrow}} z$. So in a Church-Rosser Thue system the irreducible words are unique representatives of their respective congruence classes, and since the reduction $\underset{T}{\rightarrow}$ is length-decreasing, each irreducible word u is the shortest word in its congruence class $[u]_T$.

3. Finite Church-Rosser Thue Systems

It is decidable in polynomial time whether or not a given finite Thue system T over alphabet Σ is Church-Rosser [7,13]. If T is Church-Rosser, then the word problem for the monoid $\Sigma^*/\overset{*}{\underset{T}{\leftrightarrow}}$ is decidable in linear time, since for each word $w \in \Sigma^*$, the unique irreducible descendant w_1 of w can be computed from w in linear time [3]. Actually, this procedure for computing irreducible descendants is uniform in T. Thus, we have the following.

<u>Theorem 3.1</u> (Book [3]). There exists a polynomial time algorithm that on input a finite Church-Rosser Thue system T over Σ and a word $w \in \Sigma^*$ computes the irreducible descendant w_1 of w modulo T.

Since $IRR(T) = \Sigma^* \setminus \Sigma^* \cdot L \cdot \Sigma^*$, where $L = \{\ell \in \Sigma^* \mid \exists r \in \Sigma^*: |\ell| > |r|$ and $(\ell, r) \in T\}$, IRR(T) is a regular subset of Σ^*, and from T we can effectively construct a finite state acceptor recognizing IRR(T). But from a finite state acceptor for IRR(T), one can determine the cardinality of IRR(T). Since for each element of the monoid $\Sigma^*/\overset{*}{\underset{T}{\leftrightarrow}}$, there exists exactly one irreducible representative in Σ^*, this implies the following.

<u>Theorem 3.2</u> (Book and O'Dunlaing [6]). Let T be a finite Thue system over Σ. If T is Church-Rosser, then one can effectively compute the cardinality of the monoid $\Sigma^*/\overset{*}{\underset{T}{\leftrightarrow}}$.

In particular, we have the following.

<u>Corollary 3.3</u>. The following problem is decidable:
INSTANCE: A finite Church-Rosser Thue system T over alphabet Σ.
QUESTION: Is the monoid $\Sigma^*/\overset{*}{\underset{T}{\leftrightarrow}}$ trivial ?

Corollary 3.3 can be interpreted as saying that it is decidable whether or not the monoid $\Sigma^*/\overset{*}{\underset{T}{\leftrightarrow}}$ presented by a finite Church-Rosser

Thue system T over Σ is free of rank 0. Recall that a monoid M is called free of rank n, if there exists an alphabet Γ of cardinality n such that the monoids M and Γ^* are isomorphic, and that a monoid M is free, if it is free of rank n for some n. This leads to the problem of deciding on input a finite Thue system T over Σ, whether or not the monoid $\Sigma^*/\overset{*}{\underset{T}{\leftrightarrow}}$ is free. Although this problem is undecidable in general, we do at least have the following information on presentations of free monoids.

Theorem 3.4. Let T be a finite Thue system over Σ. If the monoid $\Sigma^*/\overset{*}{\underset{T}{\leftrightarrow}}$ is free, then there exists a subset Σ_o of Σ that freely generates this monoid.

In particular, if the monoid $\Sigma^*/\overset{*}{\underset{T}{\leftrightarrow}}$ is freely generated by $\Sigma_o \subseteq \Sigma$, then for each $a \in \Sigma$, there exists a unique word $u_a \in \Sigma_o^*$ with $a \overset{*}{\underset{T}{\leftrightarrow}} u_a$. Define homomorphism $\varphi: \Sigma^* \to \Sigma_o^*$ by taking $\varphi(a) := u_a$ for all $a \in \Sigma$. Then for all words $u,v \in \Sigma^*$, $u \overset{*}{\underset{T}{\leftrightarrow}} v$ if and only if $\varphi(u) = \varphi(v)$ holds.

Now we restrict our attention to finite Church-Rosser Thue systems presenting free monoids. In this connection the notion of reduced Thue system is useful [19].

A Thue system $T = \{(\ell_i,r_i) \mid i \in I\}$ is called reduced if for each $i \in I$, the word r_i is irreducible modulo T, and the word ℓ_i is irreducible modulo $T-\{(\ell_i,r_i)\}$. For each finite Church-Rosser Thue system T, there exists a unique reduced Church-Rosser Thue system T' that is equivalent to T. In particular, T' is computable from T in polynomial time [19]. Therefore, we only need to consider finite reduced Church-Rosser Thue systems.

Lemma 3.5. Let T be a finite reduced Church-Rosser Thue system over Σ such that the monoid $\Sigma^*/\overset{*}{\underset{T}{\leftrightarrow}}$ is free, let $\Sigma_o \subseteq \Sigma$ be a set of free generators for this monoid, and let $\varphi: \Sigma^* \to \Sigma_o^*$ be the corresponding homomorphism. Further, let $\Sigma_1 = \{a \in \Sigma \mid \varphi(a) = e\}$, and let $\Sigma_2 = \Sigma-(\Sigma_o \cup \Sigma_1)$. Then the following statements hold:

(a) $T \cap (\Sigma^* \times \{e\}) = \Sigma_1 \times \{e\}$.

(b) $\text{range}(T) \cap \Sigma = \Sigma_2$.

So under the assumptions of Lemma 3.5 the only rules with right-hand side e that T contains are the rules $\{(a,e) \mid \varphi(a) = e\}$. Further, for each $a \in \Sigma_2$, there exists at least one word $u \in \Sigma^*$ such that $(u,a) \in T$, and these are the only rules of T with right-hand sides of length 1. Since T is reduced, the letters from Σ_1 do not occur in any rules of T other than $\{(a,e) | a \in \Sigma_1\}$. Obviously, $|\varphi(a)| > 0$ for each $a \in \Sigma_0 \cup \Sigma_2$. Hence, for each $a \in \Sigma_2$, if $u \overset{*}{\underset{T}{\leftrightarrow}} a$ for some $u \in (\Sigma_0 \cup \Sigma_2)^*$, then either $u = a$ or $|u|_a = 0$. Here $|u|_a$ denotes the <u>a-length</u> of u, i.e., the number of occurrences of the letter a in u. This shows that the letters from $\Sigma_1 \cup \Sigma_2$ can be deleted by applying Tietze-transformations to the presentation $(\Sigma;T)$ thus giving the presentation $(\Sigma_0;\emptyset)$ [15]. Using these observations it is rather straightforward to devise an algorithm that on input a finite reduced Church-Rosser Thue system T over Σ decides whether or not the monoid $\Sigma^*/\overset{*}{\underset{T}{\leftrightarrow}}$ is free. Together with Narendran's result mentioned above this gives the following.

<u>Theorem 3.6</u> [22]. The following problem is decidable:
INSTANCE: A finite Church-Rosser Thue system T over Σ.
QUESTION: Is the monoid $\Sigma^*/\overset{*}{\underset{T}{\leftrightarrow}}$ free ?
If the monoid $\Sigma^*/\overset{*}{\underset{T}{\leftrightarrow}}$ is free, then its rank can be computed effectively.

In fact, by using a somewhat different approach, Theorem 3.6 can be generalized to hold for each class $\mathfrak{C}$ of finite presentations for which there exists an algorithm $A(\mathfrak{C})$ that given a presentation $(\Sigma;T)$ from $\mathfrak{C}$ and a word $u \in \Sigma^*$ decides whether or not $u \overset{*}{\underset{T}{\leftrightarrow}} e$ holds. This means in particular that it is decidable whether or not a monoid $\Sigma^*/\overset{*}{\underset{R}{\leftrightarrow}}$, where R denotes a finite canonical string-rewriting system, is free.

The next problem we want to investigate is the following:
INSTANCE: A finite Thue system T over Σ.
QUESTION: Is the monoid $\Sigma^*/\overset{*}{\underset{T}{\leftrightarrow}}$ a group ?
Again, this problem is undecidable in general. However, for a finite Thue system T over Σ, we can inductively define a sequence of subsets of Σ as follows:

$\Sigma_1 = \{a \in \Sigma | \exists u,v \in \Sigma^*: (uav,e) \in T\}$,

$\Sigma_{i+1} = \{a \in \Sigma | \exists u,v \in \Sigma^*, w \in \Sigma_i^*: (uav,w) \in T\} \cup \Sigma_i$.

Obviously, we have $\Sigma_1 \subseteq \Sigma_2 \subseteq \ldots \subseteq \Sigma$, and if $\Sigma_i = \Sigma_{i+1}$ for some $i \geq 1$, then $\Sigma_{i+k} = \Sigma_i$ for all $k \geq 1$. Since Σ is finite, this implies that the above chain of inclusions contains at most n different sets, where n denotes the cardinality of Σ.

For each letter $a \in \Sigma_n$, we can determine a candidate for a^{-1} as follows: If $a \in \Sigma_1$, then $(uav,e) \in T$ for some $u,v \in \Sigma^*$. Choose a^{-1} to be vu. If $a \in \Sigma_{i+1}-\Sigma_i$ for some $i \geq 1$, then $(uav,w) \in T$ for some

$u, v \in \Sigma^*$ and $w \in \Sigma_i^*$. Let $w = a_1 \ldots a_m$ with $a_1, \ldots, a_m \in \Sigma_i$. Then words $a_1^{-1}, \ldots, a_m^{-1}$ have already been chosen. Hence, take a^{-1} to be $va_m^{-1} \ldots a_2^{-1} a_1^{-1} u$.

Now it is not hard to show that the monoid $\Sigma^*/\overset{*}{\underset{T}{\longleftrightarrow}}$ is a group if and only if $\Sigma_n = \Sigma$ and for all $a \in \Sigma_n$, $a \cdot a^{-1} \overset{*}{\underset{T}{\longleftrightarrow}} e$. Since the set Σ_n and the words a^{-1} for $a \in \Sigma_n$ can be computed effectively from T, we have the following.

<u>Theorem 3.7</u>. The following problem is decidable:

INSTANCE: A finite Church-Rosser Thue system T over Σ.

QUESTION: Is the monoid $\Sigma^*/\overset{*}{\underset{T}{\longleftrightarrow}}$ a group ?

Actually, Theorem 3.7 holds for each class $\mathbb{C}$ of finite presentations for which there exists an algorithm $A(\mathbb{C})$ that given a presentation $(\Sigma;T)$ from $\mathbb{C}$ and a word $u \in \Sigma^*$ decides whether or not $u \overset{*}{\underset{T}{\longleftrightarrow}} e$ holds. Of course, the complexity of our algorithm for deciding whether or not a monoid $\Sigma^*/\overset{*}{\underset{T}{\longleftrightarrow}}$ is a group depends on the lengths of the words a^{-1}, which may be exponential, and on the complexity of the algorithm $A(\mathbb{C})$. However, if only finite monadic Church-Rosser Thue systems are taken into account, then the above problem is decidable in polynomial time [4].

4. Finite Monadic Church-Rosser Thue Systems

Let T be a Thue system over Σ. A word $w \in \Sigma^*$ presents an <u>element of finite order</u> for $\Sigma^*/\overset{*}{\underset{T}{\longleftrightarrow}}$, if there exist integers $n \geq 0$ and $k \geq 1$ such that $w^{n+k} \overset{*}{\underset{T}{\longleftrightarrow}} w^n$. If, in addition, $w \overset{*}{\underset{T}{\not\longleftrightarrow}} e$ holds, then w presents a <u>non-trivial element of finite order</u> for $\Sigma^*/\overset{*}{\underset{T}{\longleftrightarrow}}$. Finally, w presents a <u>non-trivial idempotent</u>, if $w \overset{*}{\underset{T}{\not\longleftrightarrow}} e$ and $w^2 \overset{*}{\underset{T}{\longleftrightarrow}} w$ hold. Thus, idempotents are nothing but special elements of finite order. We are interested in the following two decision problems:

INSTANCE: A finite Thue system T over Σ.

(1) QUESTION: Does there exist a non-trivial idempotent in the monoid $\Sigma^*/\overset{*}{\underset{T}{\longleftrightarrow}}$?

(2) QUESTION: Does there exist a non-trivial element of finite order in the monoid $\Sigma^*/\overset{*}{\underset{T}{\longleftrightarrow}}$?

As already mentioned in the Introduction, these problems are undecidable in general. Therefore, we restrict our attention to finite Thue systems that are monadic and Church-Rosser. For a Thue system T over Σ and a letter $a \in \Sigma$, let $INT_T(a)$ denote the set $\{w \in IRR(T) \mid$

$awa \xrightarrow[T]{*} a\}$. Then we have the following.

Theorem 4.1. Let T be a monadic Church-Rosser Thue system over Σ. There exists a non-trivial idempotent in the monoid $\Sigma^*/\overset{*}{\underset{T}{\leftrightarrow}}$ if and only if one of the following three conditions is satisfied:

(i) $\exists u \in IRR(T)-\{e\}\ \exists x,y \in \Sigma^*$: $u = xy$ and $yx \xrightarrow[T]{*} e$, or

(ii) $\exists a \in \Sigma$: $|INT_T(a)| \geq 2$, or

(iii) $\exists a \in \Sigma\ \exists w \in IRR(T)$: $INT_T(a) = \{w\}$ and $aw \not\xrightarrow[T]{*} e$.

Condition (i) is equivalent to $e \in \Delta_T^*(CYCLE(IRR(T)-\{e\}))$, where for each $L \subseteq \Sigma^*$, $CYCLE(L) = \{vu \mid uv \in L\}$, i.e., CYCLE(L) is the language containing all the cyclic permutations of words of L. Given a finite monadic Thue system T over Σ, we can effectively construct a finite state acceptor A_1 for the regular set IRR(T)-{e}[3]. From A_1 we get a finite state acceptor A_2 for CYCLE(IRR(T)-{e}) [cf.12], from which we can construct a finite state acceptor A_3 for Δ_T^*(CYCLE (IRR(T)-{e})) [8]. Thus, condition (i) of Theorem 4.1 is decidable.

On the other hand, given a finite, monadic, Church-Rosser Thue system T over Σ and a letter $a \in \Sigma$, we can effectively construct a deterministic pushdown automaton M_a that recognizes $INT_T(a)$. Thus, also conditions (ii) and (iii) of Theorem 4.1 are decidable. This implies the following.

Theorem 4.2 [21]. Problem (1) is decidable when being restricted to finite, monadic, Church-Rosser Thue systems.

Let T be a finite, monadic, Church-Rosser Thue system over Σ. If there exists a non-trivial idempotent in $\Sigma^*/\overset{*}{\underset{T}{\leftrightarrow}}$, then this idempotent is a non-trivial element of finite order. However, there may exist non-trivial elements of finite order in $\Sigma^*/\overset{*}{\underset{T}{\leftrightarrow}}$, even if there are no non-trivial idempotents in this monoid. For example, this situation occurs when the monoid $\Sigma^*/\overset{*}{\underset{T}{\leftrightarrow}}$ is a finite group. Hence, the solution to problem (1) does not immediately give a solution to problem (2). Fortunately, we have the following.

Lemma 4.3. Let T be a finite, monadic, Church-Rosser Thue system over Σ, and let $\mu = \max\{|\ell| \mid \ell \in domain(T)\}$. If there is no non-trivial idempotent in the monoid $\Sigma^*/\overset{*}{\underset{T}{\leftrightarrow}}$, then the following are equivalent:

(i) There is a non-trivial element of finite order in $\Sigma^*/\overset{*}{\underset{T}{\leftrightarrow}}$.

(ii) There is a word $w \in \Sigma^*$ of length $|w| < \mu$ such that w presents a non-trivial element of finite order for $\Sigma^*/\overset{*}{\underset{T}{\leftrightarrow}}$.

Given a finite, monadic, Church-Rosser Thue system T over Σ and a word $w \in \Sigma^*$, we can decide effectively whether or not w presents a non-trivial element of finite order for the monoid $\Sigma^*/\overset{*}{\underset{T}{\leftrightarrow}}$. Thus, by combining Theorem 4.2 and Lemma 4.3 we get the following.

<u>Theorem 4.4</u> [21]. Problem (2) is decidable when being restricted to finite, monadic, Church-Rosser Thue systems.

Let $\Sigma = \{a_1,\ldots,a_n\}$ be an alphabet, let $\bar{\Sigma} = \{\bar{a}_1,\ldots,\bar{a}_n\}$ be an alphabet in 1-to-1 correspondence with Σ, and let T be the following Thue system on $\underline{\Sigma} := \Sigma \cup \bar{\Sigma}$: $T := \{(a_i\bar{a}_i,e),(\bar{a}_ia_i,e) \mid i = 1,2,\ldots,n\}$. Then the monoid $\underline{\Sigma}^*/\overset{*}{\underset{T}{\leftrightarrow}}$ presented by $(\underline{\Sigma};T)$ is a group, which is called the <u>free group of rank</u> n, since each group that is generated by Σ is a factor group of $\underline{\Sigma}^*/\overset{*}{\underset{T}{\leftrightarrow}}$. A finitely generated monoid is a <u>free group</u>, if it is isomorphic to the free group of rank n for some $n \in \mathbb{N}$.

Muller and Schupp [18] have shown that a finitely generated torsion-free group G is free if and only if it is context-free. Here a group G is called <u>torsion-free</u>, if it does not contain any non-trivial elements of finite order, and it is called <u>context-free</u>, if in any finite presentation of G, the set of words presenting the identity of G is a context-free language. Since each free group is torsion-free, this result of Muller and Schupp can be reformulated as follows.

<u>Theorem 4.5</u> (Muller and Schupp [18]).
A finitely generated context-free group G is free if and only if it is torsion-free.

If T is a finite, monadic, Church-Rosser Thue system over Σ such that the monoid $\Sigma^*/\overset{*}{\underset{T}{\leftrightarrow}}$ is a group, then this group is finitely generated and context-free, since $[e]_T$ is a deterministic context-free language [3]. Hence, this group is free if and only if it is torsion-free, i.e., if and only if it does not contain any non-trivial elements of finite order. Thus, from Theorem 4.4 we get the following.

<u>Theorem 4.6</u>. The following problem is decidable:
INSTANCE: A finite, monadic, Church-Rosser Thue system T over Σ.
QUESTION: Is the monoid $\Sigma^*/\overset{*}{\underset{T}{\leftrightarrow}}$ a free group ?

The results presented in this section lead to asking the following questions:

- Do problems (1) and (2) remain decidable when the class of all finite Church-Rosser Thue systems is considered ?

Actually, we do not even know whether the following problem is decidable:

- INSTANCE: A finite Church-Rosser Thue system T over Σ and a word $w \in \Sigma^*$.

  QUESTION: Does w present a non-trivial element of finite order for the monoid $\Sigma^*/\overset{*}{\underset{T}{\longleftrightarrow}}$?
- Is it decidable whether or not a given finite Church-Rosser Thue system presents a free group ?
- Which groups can at all be presented by finite, Church-Rosser Thue systems ?

For this last question some partial answers are known. They are presented in the next section.

5. Groups Presented By Certain Church-Rosser Thue Systems

Let $\mathfrak{C}$ be a class of finite Thue systems satisfying certain syntactical constraints, e.g., $\mathfrak{C}$ is the class of all one-rule Thue systems, or of all special, Church-Rosser Thue systems. Then for some decision problems there are uniform algorithms to solve these problems for all monoids or groups that can be presented by Thue systems from $\mathfrak{C}$. Therefore, it is of interest to find an algebraic characterization for those monoids or groups that can be presented in this way. However, up to now characterizations of this form are known only for a few classes of Thue systems of very restricted forms.

Theorem 5.1 (Cochet [9]).
A group G can be presented by a presentation of the form $(\Sigma;T)$, where T is a finite, special, Church-Rosser Thue system over Σ, if and only if G is the free product of finitely many cyclic groups.

In Theorem 5.1 the cyclic groups mentioned can be finite as well as infinite. If a finite, monadic, Church-Rosser Thue system T over Σ is reduced, and if each generator $a \in \Sigma$ has an inverse of length one, i.e., $\forall a \in \Sigma\ \exists b \in \Sigma$: $ab \overset{*}{\underset{T}{\longleftrightarrow}} e$, then T is two-monadic. On the other hand, there are finite, two-monadic, Church-Rosser Thue systems that present groups such that there does not exist an inverse of length one for each of the generators, although these Thue systems are reduced. Thus, the following is an extension of a result of Avenhaus and Madlener [1].

Theorem 5.2 (Avenhaus, Madlener, and Otto [2]).
A group G can be presented by a presentation of the form $(\Sigma;T)$, where T is a finite, two-monadic, Church-Rosser Thue system over Σ, if and only if G is a free product of a finitely generated free group and a finite number of finite groups.

As has been shown by Haring-Smith [11] the groups described by Theorem 5.2 are exactly those that can be presented by finitely generated presentations with simple reduced word problems. However, it is still an open problem to find an algebraic characterization for those groups that can be presented by finite, monadic, Church-Rosser Thue systems. The following has been conjectured.

Conjecture (Gilman [10]).
A group G can be presented by a presentation of the form $(\Sigma;T)$, where T is a finite, monadic, Church-Rosser Thue system over Σ, if and only if G is a free product of a finitely generated free group and a finite number of finite groups.

Remember that a group G that can be presented by a finite, monadic, Church-Rosser Thue system T over Σ is a context-free group, since the set $[e]_T$ is a (deterministic) context-free language. Hence, all the groups considered so far are specializations of the context-free groups investigated by Muller and Schupp [18]. However, nothing is known until now about an algebraic characterization for those groups that can be presented by finite, Church-Rosser Thue systems that are non-monadic. Further, no algebraic characterizations have been established for monoids that can be presented by these restricted kinds of Thue systems. So in this area there is still a lot of work to be done.

References

1. J. Avenhaus and K. Madlener, On groups defined by monadic Thue systems, Colloquium on Algebra, Combinatorics, and Logic in Computer Science, Györ, Hungary, Sept. 1983.

2. J. Avenhaus, K. Madlener and F. Otto, Groups presented by finite two-monadic Church-Rosser Thue systems, Technical Report 110/84, Fachbereich Informatik, Universität Kaiserslautern, 1984.

3. R.V. Book, Confluent and other types of Thue systems, Journal ACM 29 (1982), 171-182.

4. R.V. Book, When is a monoid a group ? The Church-Rosser case is tractable, Theoret. Comput. Sci. 18 (1982), 325-331.

5. R.V. Book, Decidable sentences of Church-Rosser congruences, Theoret. Comput. Sci. 24 (1983), 301-312.

6. R.V. Book and C. O'Dunlaing, Thue congruences and the Church-Rosser property, Semigroup Forum 22 (1981), 325-331.

7. R.V. Book and C. O'Dunlaing, Testing for the Church-Rosser property, Theoret. Comput. Sci. 16 (1981), 223-229.

8. R.V. Book and F. Otto, Cancellation rules and extended word problems, Inf. Proc. Letters 20 (1985), 5-11.

9. Y. Cochet, Church-Rosser congruences on free semigroups, Coll. Math. Soc. Janos Bolyai: Algebraic Theory of Semigroups 20 (1976), 51-60.

10. R.H. Gilman, Computations with rational subsets of confluent groups, Proceedings of EUROSAM 1984, LNCS 174 (1984), 207-212.

11. R.H. Haring-Smith, Groups and simple languages, Transactions of the Amer. Math. Soc. 279 (1983), 337-356.

12. J.E. Hopcroft and J.D. Ullman, Introduction to Automata Theory, Languages, and Computation, Addison-Wesley, 1979.

13. D. Kapur, M. Krishnamoorthy, R. Mc Naughton and P. Narendran, An $O(|T|^3)$ algorithm for testing the Church-Rosser property of Thue systems, Theoret. Comput. Sci. 35 (1985), 109-114.

14. G. Lallement, Semigroups and combinatorial applications, Wiley-Interscience, 1979.

15. W. Magnus, A. Karrass and D. Solitar, Combinatorial group theory, 2nd revised edition, Dover, N.Y., 1976.

16. A. Markov, Impossibility of algorithms for recognizing some properties of associative systems, Dokl. Akad. Nauk SSSR 77 (1951), 953-956.

17. A. Mostowski, Review of [16], J. Symbolic Logic 17 (1952), 151-152.

18. D.E. Muller and P.E. Schupp, Groups, the theory of ends, and context-free languages, J. Comput. Sys. Sci. 26 (1983), 295-310.

19. P. Narendran, Church-Rosser and related Thue systems, Ph.D. Dissertation, Rensselaer Polytechnic Institute, 1983. Also appears as Report No. 84 CRD 176, General Electric Corporate Research and Development, Schenectady, N.Y., 1984.

20. P. Narendran and F. Otto, Complexity results on the conjugacy problem for monoids, Theoret. Comput. Sci., 35 (1985), 227-243.

21. F. Otto, Elements of finite order for finite monadic Church-Rosser Thue systems, Transact. of the AMS, to appear.

22. F. Otto, Church-Rosser Thue systems that present free monoids, SIAM J. on Comput., to appear.

Two Applications of Equational Theories to Database Theory

Stavros S. Cosmadakis
MIT
Paris C. Kanellakis[1]
MIT

Abstract

Databases and equational theorem proving are well developed and seemingly unrelated areas of Computer Science Research. We provide two natural links between these fields and demonstrate how equational theorem proving can provide useful and tools for a variety of database tasks.

Our first application is a novel way of formulating functional and inclusion dependencies (the most common database constraints) using equations. The central computational problem of dependency implication is directly reduced to equational reasoning. Mathematical techniques from universal algebra provide new proof procedures and better lower bounds for dependency implication. The use of REVE, a general purpose transformer of equations into term rewriting systems, is illustrated on nontrivial sets of functional and inclusion dependencies.

Our second application demonstrates that the uniform word problem for lattices is equivalent to implication of dependencies expressing transitive closure, together with functional dependencies. This natural generalization of functional dependencies, which is not expressible using conventional database theory formulations, has a natural inference system and an efficient decision procedure.

1. Introduction

In order to deal formally with the problems of logical database design and data processing, database theory models data as sets of tables (*relations*). These relations are required to satisfy integrity constraints (*dependencies*), which intend to capture the semantics of a particular application. Various kinds of dependencies have been proposed in the literature (see [20, 13] for reviews of the area). For example, a *functional dependency* (FD) is a formal statement of the form EMPLOYEE→SALARY, which intuitively states that every employee has a unique salary. An *inclusion dependency* (IND) is a statement of the form MANAGER⊆EMPLOYEE, which intuitively states that every manager is an employee (the more general IND MANAGER.MANAGER-SALARY⊆EMPLOYEE.EMPLOYEE-SALARY expresses also the fact that managers make the same salary as managers as they make as employees). FD's and IND's are the most common database constraints.

A most general formulation of dependencies as sentences in first order logic (namely Horn clauses) was given in [13]. To handle the central computational problem of dependency *implication* a particular proof procedure was developed, the *chase* (see [20] for its wide applicability). Proof procedures for general data dependencies also appear in [23, 2, 3].The chase was seen to be a special case of a classical theorem proving technique, namely *resolution* [2, 3].

[1]On leave from Brown University; supported partly by NSF grant MCS-8210830 and partly by ONR-DARPA grant N00014-83-K-0146, ARPA Order No. 4786.

Alternative methods for theorem proving have been developed in the context of *equational theories*. This is a fragment of first order logic which has attracted a lot of attention because of its wide applicability in areas such as applicative languages, interpreters, and data types. See [15] for a survey of the area.

Given the formulation of database constraints as first order sentences, one would expect database theory to have been influenced by the developments in equational theories. However, not only did this never happen, but a constant effort has been made to minimize the role of equality in data dependencies (*multivalued dependencies*, the most widely studied after FD's, do not involve equality explicitly). This is even more impressive in view of the fact that the best algorithm for *losslessness of joins*, a basic computational problem, was derived from an efficient algorithm for *congruence closure* [12]. Also the best algorithm for implication of FD's [1] can be seen directly as a special case of an algorithm of [17] for the *generator problem in finitely presented algebras*; this last observation was made recently by the authors of this paper, and seems to have escaped the notice of the database theory community.

The *implication problem* for FD's and IND's (i.e., given a set Σ of FD's and IND's and an FD or IND σ, do all databases satisfying Σ also satisfy σ) has been studied in some detail; [6, 10, 19, 7, 16, 9]. In this paper we will use the FD,IND implication problem to illustrate a surprisingly close connection between dependency inference and equational theorem proving.

We first present a transformation of FD and IND implication into equational implication (Theorem 1). This not only reveals the underlying computational structure (Corollaries 1.1, 1.2), but also leads to a proof procedure very different from the standard technique (Theorem 2). We also demonstrate how database constraints can be compiled into rewrite rules, which can then be used to make inferences (Section 3.2). The full theoretical treatment of this transformation and its use in deriving upper and lower bounds for the implication problem appears in [10].

Our second transformation (Theorem 3) reveals the *semilattice* structure of FD's. The full treatment of this transformation requires the development of special semantics for relational databases [11]. We include it in our exposition because, despite its very different nature, it also illustrates a direct connection between database theory and equational theories. In fact, completing the semilattice into a lattice naturally provides transitive closure and *partition dependencies* to our arsenal of possible database constraints. The elegant Armstrong rules for FD implication [20] can now be seen as a special case of a proof system for equational implication in lattices (Theorem 4). This theorem also provides an efficient algorithm for the uniform word problem for lattices.

In summary, the purpose of this paper is to collect from [10, 11] the basic ideas which indicate that *equational theorem proving is the proper setting for database dependency implication*. Some experimentation in this direction has also been made, using the REVE system [14, 18]; the examples in Section 3.2 clearly demonstrate how a general-purpose equational theorem prover succesfully handles cases of nontrivial FD and IND implication.

2. Definitions

2.1. Equational Theories

Let M be a set of symbols and ARITY a function from M to the nonnegative integers $\mathcal{N}$. The set of finite strings over M is M*. Partition M into two sets:

$G=\{g\in M|\ \text{ARITY}(g)=0\}$ the *generators*,
$O=\{\theta\in M|\ \text{ARITY}(\theta)>0\}$ the *operators*.

The set of *terms* over M, $\mathcal{T}(M)$, is the smallest subset of M* such that,

1) every g in G is a term,
2) if $\tau_1,\ldots,\tau_m$ are terms and θ is in O with $\text{ARITY}(\theta)=m$, then $\theta\tau_1\ldots\tau_m$ is a term.

A *subterm* of τ is a substring of τ, which is also a term. Let $V=\{x,x_1,x_2,\ldots\}$ be a set of *variables*. Then the set of terms over operators O and generators G∪V will be denoted by $\mathcal{T}^+(M)$. For terms $\tau_1,\ldots,\tau_k$ in $\mathcal{T}^+(M)$ we can define the substitution $\varphi=\{\ (x_i\leftarrow\tau_i)\ |\ 1\leq i\leq k\ \}$ to be a function from $\mathcal{T}^+(M)$ to $\mathcal{T}^+(M)$. We use $\varphi(\tau)$ or $\tau[x_1/\tau_1,\ldots,x_k/\tau_k]$ for the result of replacing all occurences of variables x_i in term τ by term τ_i $(1\leq i\leq k)$, where these changes are made simultaneously.

An *equation* e is a string of the form $\tau=\tau'$, where τ,τ' are in $\mathcal{T}^+(M)$. We use the symbol E for a set of equations. We will be dealing with models for sets of equations, i.e., algebras. We consider each equation e as a sentence of first-order predicate calculus (with equality), with all variables *universally quantified.*
An *algebra* $\mathcal{A}=(A,F)$ is a pair, where A is a nonempty set and F a set of functions. Each f in F is a function from A^n to A, for some n in $\mathcal{N}$ which we call the *type(f)*.

Examples: (a) A *semigroup* $(A,\{+\})$ is an algebra with one associative binary operator, i.e., for all x,y,z in A $(x+y)+z=x+(y+z)$. An example of a semigroup is the algebra of the set of functions from $\mathcal{N}$ to $\mathcal{N}$, together with the composition operation. In semigroups we use ab instead of a+b and w.l.o.g. omit parentheses.
(b) $\mathcal{A}_M$ is an algebra with $A=\mathcal{T}(M)$. For each θ in O we define a function θ in F with $type(\theta)=\text{ARITY}(\theta)$; here we use the same symbol for the syntactic object θ and its interpretation. The function θ maps terms $\tau_1,\ldots,\tau_m$ from $\mathcal{T}(M)$ to the term $\theta\tau_1\ldots\tau_m$, (i.e., $\theta(\tau_1,\ldots,\tau_m)=\theta\tau_1\ldots\tau_m$). We will refer to $\mathcal{A}_M$ as the *free algebra* on M. From this example it is clear that we can without ambiguity use both $\theta\tau_1\ldots\tau_m$ and $\theta(\tau_1,\ldots,\tau_m)$ to denote the same term. One can similarly define an algebra with domain $\mathcal{T}^+(M)$.

Implication: Let e be an equation and $\mathcal{A}$ an algebra. $\mathcal{A}$ satisfies e, or is a model for e, if e becomes true when its operators and nonvariable generators are interpreted as the functions of $\mathcal{A}$ and its variables take *any* values in $\mathcal{A}$'s domain. The class of all algebras which are models for a set of equations E is called a *variety* or an *equational class.* We say that E implies e ($E\models e$) if equation e is true in every model of E. An *equational theory* is a set of equalities E (of terms over $\mathcal{T}^+(M)$), closed under *implication.*

We write $E \vdash e$, if there exists a finite proof of e starting from E and using only the following five rules:

$\tau = \tau$,

from $\tau_1 = \tau_2$ *deduce* $\tau_2 = \tau_1$,

from $\tau_1 = \tau_2$ *and* $\tau_2 = \tau_3$ *deduce* $\tau_1 = \tau_3$,

from $\tau_i = \tau_i'$ $(1 \leq i \leq m)$ *deduce* $\theta\tau_1 ... \tau_m = \theta\tau_1' ... \tau_m'$ $(\text{ARITY}(\theta) = m)$,

from $\tau_1 = \tau_2$ *deduce* $\varphi(\tau_1) = \varphi(\tau_2)$ (φ is any substitution).

Proposition 1: [4] $E \models \tau = \tau'$ iff $E \vdash \tau = \tau'$. ▮

A binary relation $\approx$ on $\mathcal{T}(M)$ or $\mathcal{T}^+(M)$ is a *congruence* provided that,

1) $\approx$ is an equivalence relation,
2) if $\text{ARITY}(\theta) = m$ and $\tau_i \approx \tau_i'$ $(1 \leq i \leq m)$ then $\theta\tau_1 ... \tau_m \approx \theta\tau_1' ... \tau_m'$.

Let $\approx$ be a congruence on $\mathcal{T}(M)$. Congruence guarantees that the operations in O are well-defined on $\approx$-equivalence (or congruence) classes. Thus we can form a *quotient* algebra $\mathcal{T}(M)/\approx$ with domain $\{[\tau] \mid \tau \text{ in } \mathcal{T}(M), [\tau] \text{ is the } \approx\text{-congruence class of } \tau\}$ and with functions corresponding to O's operators.

Let Γ be a set of equations over terms in $\mathcal{T}(M)$ (i.e., containing no variables). Consider the equational theory consisting of all $\tau = \tau'$ such that $\Gamma \models \tau = \tau'$. By Proposition 1 this theory induces a congruence $=_\Gamma$ on $\mathcal{T}(M)$, where $\tau =_\Gamma \tau'$ iff $\Gamma \models \tau = \tau'$. From the remark above we see that this congruence naturally defines an algebra $\mathcal{T}(M)/=_\Gamma$. If Γ is a finite set $\mathcal{T}(M)/=_\Gamma$ is known as a *finitely presented algebra* [17].

These are the only definitions needed to make our exposition self-contained. For an extended survey of the area, definitions of term rewriting systems and more general definitions, see [15].

2.2. Relational Database Theory

Let $\mathcal{U}$ be a finite set of *attributes* and $\mathcal{D}$ a countably infinite set of *values*, such that $\mathcal{U} \cap \mathcal{D} = \emptyset$. A *relation scheme* is an object R[U], where R is the *name* of the relation scheme and $U \subseteq \mathcal{U}$. A *tuple* t over U is a function from U to $\mathcal{D}$. Let A_i be an attribute in U and a_i a value, where $1 \leq i \leq |U|$; if $t[A_i] = a_i$ then we represent tuple t over U as $a_1 a_2 ... a_{|U|}$. We represent the restriction of tuple t on attributes $A_1 ... A_n$ of U as $t[A_1 ... A_n]$. A *relation* r over U (named R) is a (possibly infinite) nonempty set of tuples over U. A *database scheme* D is a finite set of relation schemes $\{R_1[U_1], ..., R_q[U_q]\}$ and a *database* $d = \{r_1, ..., r_q\}$ associates each relation scheme $R_i[U_i]$ in d with a relation r_i over U_i. A database is finite if all of its relations are finite. A database can be visualized as a set of tables, one for each relation, whose headers are the relation schemes (each column headed by an attribute), and whose rows are the tuples.

The logical constraints, which determine the set of legal databases, are called *database dependencies*. We will be examining two very common types of dependencies. These are sentences over relation names and attributes, which are either satisfied or falsified by relations.

FD $R: A_1 ... A_n \rightarrow A$ is a *functional dependency*.

Relation r (named R) satisfies this FD if, for tuples t_1, t_2 in r, $t_1[A_1 ... A_n] = t_2[A_1 ... A_n]$ implies $t_1[A] = t_2[A]$. If $n = 1$ we call the dependency a *unary functional dependency* (uFD).

It is quite common in the database literature to use the notation $R{:}A_1...A_n \rightarrow AB$ for $R{:}A_1...A_n \rightarrow A$ and $R{:}A_1...A_n \rightarrow B$ (i.e., for more than one FD with the same left-hand side).

IND $S{:}C_1...C_m \subseteq R{:}B_1...B_m$ is an *inclusion dependency.*
Relations s,r (named S,R respectively) satisfy this IND if, for each tuple t in s, there is a tuple t_1 in r with $t_1[B_i]=t[C_i]$ for $1 \leq i \leq m$. If $m=1$ we call the dependency a *unary inclusion dependency* (uIND).

Equality of two columns headed by attributes A, B in a relation named R can be expressed as a special case of IND's: use $R{:}AB \subseteq R{:}AA$. These dependencies are particularly illustrative of our analysis; we will use $A \equiv B$ to denote them.

Implication: We say that the set of dependencies Σ implies dependency σ ($\Sigma \models \sigma$) if, whenever a database d over scheme D satisfies Σ, it also satisfies σ. If we restrict ourselves to finite databases we have $\Sigma \models_{fin} \sigma$. Clearly if $\Sigma \models \sigma$ (*implication*) then $\Sigma \models_{fin} \sigma$ (*finite implication*), but the converse is not always true. Deciding implication of dependencies is a central problem in database theory. Since dependencies are sentences in first-order predicate calculus with equality, we have *proof procedures* for the implication problem (we denote proofs as $\Sigma \vdash \sigma$). A proof procedure is *sound* if when $\Sigma \vdash \sigma$ then $\Sigma \models \sigma$; and *complete* if it is sound and when $\Sigma \models \sigma$ then $\Sigma \vdash \sigma$ (similarly for finite implication). The standard complete proof procedure for database dependencies is the *chase.* We now present the chase for FD's and IND's.

Chase: Given a set of dependencies Σ over scheme D and a dependency σ, construct a set of tables T with D's relation schemes as headers. These tables are originally empty and will be filled with symbols from the countably infinite set $\mathfrak{I}$. Whenever we insert a new row of symbols from $\mathfrak{I}$ in a table of T and we do not specify some of the entries of this row, then we assume that distinct symbols from $\mathfrak{I}$, which have not yet appeared elsewhere in T, are used to fill these entries. We use t_i^r for the ith row of table R and $t_i^r[X]$ for this row's entries in the columns of attributes X.
The *initial configuration* of T depends on σ as follows:
(i) If $\sigma = R{:}A_1...A_n \rightarrow A$, insert rows t_1^r, t_2^r with the only restriction that $t_1^r[A_i]=t_2^r[A_i]$, where $1 \leq i \leq n$.
(ii) If $\sigma = S{:}C_1...C_m \subseteq R{:}B_1...B_m$, insert t_1^s.
Every dependency in Σ produces a *rule.* If f is an FD in Σ the corresponding FD-rule is:
<Consider T a database over symbols in $\mathfrak{I}$. If T does not satisfy f, because two symbols x and y are different then replace y by x in T>.
If $i = S{:}X \subseteq R{:}Y$ is an IND in Σ the corresponding IND-rule is:
<Consider T a database over symbols in $\mathfrak{I}$. If T does not satisfy i, because some $t^s[X]$ does not appear in the table R as some $t^r[Y]$, then insert t^r in R with $t^r[Y]=t^s[X]$.>

We will say that $\Sigma \vdash_{chase} \sigma$, if there is a finite sequence of applications of the FD-rules and IND-rules produced by Σ that transforms T's initial configuration to a final configuration satisfying:
(i) If $\sigma = R{:}A_1...A_n \rightarrow A$, then $t_1^r[A]=t_2^r[A]$
(ii) If $\sigma = S{:}C_1...C_m \subseteq R{:}B_1...B_m$, then $t_1^s[C_i]=t_j^r[B_i]$, where $1 \leq i \leq m$, for some j.

Proposition 2: $\Sigma \vdash_{chase} \sigma$ iff $\Sigma \models \sigma$. ∎

3. Functional and Inclusion Dependencies as Equations

3.1. Basic Transformation

Let Σ be a set of FD's and IND's over a database scheme D and σ an FD or IND. We will transform Σ into two sets of equations E_Σ and $\mathcal{E}_\Sigma$ such that the following holds: $\Sigma \models \sigma$ iff $E_\Sigma \models E_\tau$ iff $\mathcal{E}_\Sigma \models \mathcal{E}_\tau$, for sets of equations $E_\tau, \mathcal{E}_\tau$ whose form depends on Σ and σ. We assume that D only contains one relation scheme; this simplifies notation, and there is no loss of generality.

Transformation: From the dependencies in Σ construct the following sets of symbols,

$M_f = \{f_k \mid$ for each FD with an n attribute left-hand side include one operator f_k of ARITY n$\}$,
$M_i = \{i_k \mid$ for each IND include one operator i_k of ARITY 1$\}$,
$M_a = \{a_k \mid$ for each attribute A_k include one operator a_k of ARITY 1$\}$,
$M_\alpha = \{\alpha_k \mid$ for each attribute A_k include one generator $\alpha_k\}$.

Now let $M = M_f \cup M_i \cup M_a \cup M_\alpha$ and $V = \{x, x_1, x_2, ...\}$ be a set of variables. $\mathcal{T}^+(M_f)$ ($\mathcal{T}^+(M_i)$) are the sets of terms constructed using operators in M_f (M_i) and generators in V.

The set E_Σ consists of the following equations
1) one equation for each $\sigma_k = A_1...A_n \rightarrow A$: $f_k a_1 x ... a_n x = ax$,
2) m equations for each $\sigma_k = B_1...B_m \subseteq A_1...A_m$: $a_1 i_k x = b_1 x$ and ... and $a_m i_k x = b_m x$.

The set $\mathcal{E}_\Sigma$ consists of the following equations:
3) one equation for each $\sigma_k = A_1...A_n \rightarrow A$: $f_k \alpha_1 ... \alpha_n = \alpha$,
4) m equations for each $\sigma_k = B_1...B_m \subseteq A_1...A_m$: $i_k \alpha_1 = \beta_1$ and ... and $i_k \alpha_m = \beta_m$,
5) for each pair of symbols f_p in M_f and i_q in M_i the equation $f_p i_q x_1 ... i_q x_n = i_q f_p x_1 ... x_n$ (ARITY$(f_p) = n$).

The transformation is illustrated in Figure 1. Note that in $\mathcal{E}_\Sigma$ only equations 5) contain variables. Equations 5) are *commutativity* conditions between f and i operators. The transformation can also be thought of as the Skolemization of the definitions from Section 2.2. We now present Theorem 1, which is central to our approach. A slightly more general version of the Theorem is presented in [10].

Theorem 1: In each of the following three cases, (i),(ii),(iii) are equivalent.

$\equiv$ Case:
i) $\Sigma \models A \equiv B$
ii) $E_\Sigma \models ax = bx$
iii) $\mathcal{E}_\Sigma \models \alpha = \beta$.

FD Case:
i) $\Sigma \models A_1...A_n \rightarrow A$
ii) $E_\Sigma \models \tau[x_1/a_1x, ..., x_n/a_nx] = ax$, for some τ in $\mathcal{T}^+(M_f)$
iii) $\mathcal{E}_\Sigma \models \tau[x_1/\alpha_1, ..., x_n/\alpha_n] = \alpha$, for some τ in $\mathcal{T}^+(M_f)$.

IND Case:

i) $\Sigma \models B_1 \ldots B_m \subseteq A_1 \ldots A_m$

ii) $E_\Sigma \models a_1\tau = b_1 x$ and ... and $a_m\tau = b_m x$, for some τ in $\mathcal{T}^+(M_i)$

iii) $\mathcal{E}_\Sigma \models \tau[x/\alpha_1] = \beta_1$ and ... and $\tau[x/\alpha_m] = \beta_m$, for some τ in $\mathcal{T}^+(M_i)$.

Proof Sketch: We use E_τ ($\mathcal{E}_\tau$) to denote the set of equations corresponding to term τ in (ii),(iii).
(ii)$\Rightarrow$(i) Suppose $E_\Sigma \models E_\tau$, and let relation r satisfy Σ; we will show that r satisfies σ. Relation r is, by definition, nonempty and its entries can be w.l.o.g. positive integers. Number its tuples 1,2,... etc., (it could contain a countably infinite number of tuples). Define $A(.)$: $\mathcal{N} \rightarrow \mathcal{N}$, such that, if x is the number of a tuple in r, then A(x) is the entry in tuple x at attribute A, else A(x) is 0 ($\mathcal{N}$ are the nonnegative integers). If f is the FD $C_1 \ldots C_k \rightarrow C$ in Σ define $F(\ldots)$: $\mathcal{N}^k \rightarrow \mathcal{N}$, such that, if x is the number of a tuple in r, then $F(C_1(x), \ldots, C_k(x)) = C(x)$, else F is 0. This is a well defined function since r satisfies f. If i is the IND $D_1 \ldots D_k \subseteq C_1 \ldots C_k$ in Σ define $I(.)$: $\mathcal{N} \rightarrow \mathcal{N}$, such that, if x is the number of a tuple in r and x' is the number of the first tuple in r where $t_x[D_1 \ldots D_k] = t_{x'}[C_1 \ldots C_k]$, then $I(x) = x'$, else I(x) is 0. This is also a well defined function since r satisfies i. We have constructed an algebra with domain $\mathcal{N}$ and functions A(.),...,F(...),...,I(.),..., which, as is easy to verify, is a model for E_Σ. Let σ be an IND. By interpreting each symbol in τ as an I(.), we see that when x is a tuple number $\tau(x)$ is another tuple number. Since $E_\Sigma \models E_\tau$, we must have $A_i(\tau) = B_i(x)$ $1 \leq i \leq m$, which means that r satisfies σ. The case of an FD is similar.

(iii)$\Rightarrow$(ii) Suppose $\mathcal{E}_\Sigma \models \mathcal{E}_\tau$, and let $\mathcal{M}$ be a model of E_Σ; we will show that $\mathcal{M}$ satisfies E_τ. From $\mathcal{M}$ we will construct a model $\mathcal{A}(\mathcal{M})$ for $\mathcal{E}_\Sigma$. The algebra $\mathcal{A}(\mathcal{M})$ will have domain all functions from $\mathcal{M}$ to $\mathcal{M}$, i.e., $\mathcal{M} \rightarrow \mathcal{M}$. In $\mathcal{A}(\mathcal{M})$ the interpretation of α will be the function $a(x)$, which is the interpretation of a(.) in $\mathcal{M}$. The interpretation of i(.) will be the function $\lambda h.h(i(x))$, where $i(x)$ is the interpretation of i(.) in $\mathcal{M}$ (this is a function from $\mathcal{M} \rightarrow \mathcal{M}$ to $\mathcal{M} \rightarrow \mathcal{M}$). The interpretation of f(...) will be the function $\lambda h_1 \ldots h_n . f(h_1(x), \ldots, h_n(x))$, where $f(x_1, \ldots, x_n)$ is the interpretation of f(...) in $\mathcal{M}$ (this is a function from $(\mathcal{M} \rightarrow \mathcal{M})^n$ to $\mathcal{M} \rightarrow \mathcal{M}$). It is straightforward to check that equations 3),4) hold in $\mathcal{A}(\mathcal{M})$, because $\mathcal{M}$ is a model for E_Σ. Also equations 5) hold in $\mathcal{A}(\mathcal{M})$: For example, if n=1 the interpretation of f(i(h)) in $\mathcal{A}(\mathcal{M})$ is $f(h(i(x)))$, which is also the interpretation of i(f(h)) (h is any element of $\mathcal{M} \rightarrow \mathcal{M}$). Thus $\mathcal{A}(\mathcal{M})$ is a model for $\mathcal{E}_\Sigma$. Since $\mathcal{E}_\Sigma \models \mathcal{E}_\tau$, $\mathcal{A}(\mathcal{M})$ satisfies $\mathcal{E}_\tau$, and it easily follows that $\mathcal{M}$ satisfies E_τ.

(i)$\Rightarrow$(iii) By induction on the number of steps of a chase proof of σ from Σ (see [8]). ∎

A proof procedure for IND's and FD's which is different from the chase is given in [19]. We can show that each of the rules in [19] can be simulated using the equational reasoning of Proposition 1, and thus give an alternate proof of the (i)$\Rightarrow$(iii) step. Let us illustrate this with an example: From $A \rightarrow B$ and $CD \subseteq AB$ the *pullback rule* of [19] derives $C \rightarrow D$. In equational language $f\alpha = \beta$, $i\alpha = \gamma$, $i\beta = \delta$ and $fix = ifx$ imply $f\gamma = fi\alpha = if\alpha = i\beta = \delta$.

Corollary 1.1: Let Σ be a set of FD's and σ an FD. The implication problem $\Sigma \models \sigma$ is equivalent to a *generator problem for a finitely presented algebra* [17].
Proof: $\mathcal{E}_\Sigma$ is now a finite set of equations with no variables. If $\approx$ is the congruence induced by $\mathcal{E}_\Sigma$ on $\mathcal{T}(M)$ then $\mathcal{T}(M)/\approx$ is a finitely presented algebra. The equational implication in Theorem 1 is known, in this case, as a generator problem for the finitely presented algebra $\mathcal{T}(M)/\approx$. ∎

Using Corollary 1.1, one can observe that the linear time algorithm of [1] for FD inference can be derived in a straightforward way from the general algorithm of [17] for the generator problem.

For the special case of uFD's and IND's, the equations resulting from our transformation can be viewed as *string equations*:

Semigroup Transformation: Let Σ be a set of IND's and uFD's. Produce the set of symbols M_s from M as follows: for each $f_k(.)$ in M_f add one generator f_k in M_s; for each $i_k(.)$ in M_i add one generator i_k in M_s; for each $a_k(.)$ in M_a add one generator a_k in M_s; add one binary operator + in M_s.
E_S consists of the associative axiom for + and the following word (string) equations (we omit + and parentheses):
1) one equation for each uFD $\sigma_k = A_1 \rightarrow A$: $f_k a_1 = a$
2) m equations for each IND $\sigma_k = B_1...B_m \subseteq A_1...A_m$: $a_1 i_k = b_1$ and ... and $a_m i_k = b_m$.

Corollary 1.2: Let Σ be a set of uFD's and IND's
$\Sigma \models A \equiv B$ iff $E_S \models a = b$
$\Sigma \models A_1 \rightarrow A$ iff $E_S \models wa_1 = a$, for some string w in M_s^*
$\Sigma \models B_1...B_m \subseteq A_1...A_m$ iff $E_S \models a_1 w = b_1$ and ... and $a_m w = b_m$, for some string w in M_s^*. ∎

Note that the first case is an instance of the *uniform word problem for semigroups*. The other two cases are known as E_S-*unification* problems [15]. Corollary 1.2 is used in [10] to study the computational complexity of the inference problem for FD's and IND's.

The approach of Theorem 1 can in fact be extended to more general database dependency statements [10, 8]. What we present here is the application of this transformation to the most practical database constraints, in order to illustrate the basic ideas involved.

3.2. Dependency Inference

In this section we will be dealing with the inference problem for IND's and uFD's. As demonstrated in [19, 7, 10] this is an undecidable problem, with a number of interesting decidable subcases [10]. We will first present a proof procedure for IND's and uFD's, which differs from the chase because it is based on equational reasoning. This procedure also differs from that of [19], because of the simplicity and symmetry of its rules. We use the graph notation developed in [9, 10].

Graph Notation: Let Σ be a set of IND's and uFD's over relation scheme R (it is very simple to generalize both the notation and the proof procedure to handle several relation schemes). We construct a labeled directed graph G_Σ, which has exactly one node a_i for each attribute A_i in R. Let $i = B_1...B_m \subseteq A_1...A_m$ be an IND in Σ. Then G_Σ contains m *black* arcs $(a_1,b_1),...,(a_m,b_m)$, each arc labeled by the name i of the IND. Let $f = A \rightarrow B$ be a uFD in Σ. Then G_Σ contains one *red* arc (a,b) labeled by the name f of the uFD.

The graph notation is illustrated in the two examples of Figure 2.

The Proof Procedure G: Given a set Σ of uFD's and IND's construct their graphical representation G_{Σ}. Each attribute in Σ is associated with one of the nodes of G_{Σ}.

Rules: Apply some finite sequence of the graph manipulation rules 1,2,3 and 4 of Figure 3 on G_{Σ}. Rules 1 and 2 introduce new unnamed nodes. Rules 3 and 4 identify two existing nodes; the node resulting from this identification is associated with the union of the two sets of attribute names, that were associated with each of the identified nodes. Note that rules 1,2 w.l.o.g. need be applied at most once to every left-hand side configuration.

Let G be the resulting graph.

We say that $\Sigma \vdash_G \sigma$ when:

σ is $A \equiv B$ and A,B are associated with the same node;

σ is a uFD $A \rightarrow B$ and there is a path of red arcs in G starting at A and ending at B;

σ is an IND $B_1 ... B_m \subseteq A_1 ... A_m$ and there are m black directed paths in G, all with the same sequence of labels, path i starting at A_i and ending at B_i.

Theorem 2: $\Sigma \models \sigma$ iff $\Sigma \vdash_G \sigma$.

Proof Sketch: We outline the proof for σ being $A \equiv B$.

($\Leftarrow$): Rules 3,4 are obviously sound. Rules 1 and 2 are sound in the sense of the *attribute introduction rule* of [19], which we illustrate as rule 5 of Figure 3.

($\Rightarrow$): We assume that we cannot prove σ, and construct a model for $\mathcal{E}_{\Sigma}$ in which $\alpha \neq \beta$; then by Theorem 1 Σ does not imply σ. If σ is not provable, then there is a (possibly infinite) graph G which represents Σ, is closed under the rules, and in which the names A and B correspond to different nodes. We add one special node $\perp$ to G. The labels of G are symbols corresponding to INDs (i symbols) or uFDs (f symbols) of Σ. If a node in $G \cup \{\perp\}$ has no outgoing arc labeled with some i, add one going to $\perp$. Repeat for the f symbols. The resulting graph represents functions interpreting the operators and generators in $\mathcal{E}_{\Sigma}$: This is because closure with respect to rules 3 and 4 and the padding of G we performed, guarantees functionality. The node A (B) is the interpretation of α (β). Now closure with respect to rules 1 and 2 guarantees the commutativity conditions of $\mathcal{E}_{\Sigma}$, and the fact that G represents Σ guarantees equations 3),4) of $\mathcal{E}_{\Sigma}$. Thus there is a model of $\mathcal{E}_{\Sigma}$ in which $\alpha \neq \beta$. ∎

A different (*heuristic*) approach to dependency inference could proceed as follows: We first translate the dependencies into equations using the Semigroup Transformation of Section 3.1. We then try to compile them into a (confluent and noetherian) rewrite rule system using some generalized Knuth-Bendix type procedure. If we succeed, the resulting rewrite rule system would be very useful in making many of the desired inferences.

We demonstrate this general approach on three examples. Each example illustrates some of the inherent difficulties of the FD and IND implication problem. The REVE system [14, 18] has been used in all cases. See [15] for rewrite rule notations and definitions.

Example 1: Consider the uFD's and uIND's in Figure 2a. As shown in [16], uFD and uIND statements can be handled independently (i.e.. they do not interact). However, implication is still non-trivial because it differs from *finite* implication (which, nonetheless, can also be decided in polynomial time [16]). The instances which differentiate between finite and unrestricted implication are exactly those containing mixed cycles of uIND's and uFD's, such as the one in Figure 2a. We translated these statements into equations and compiled them into the following rewrite rule system, using REVE:

Rules:

(fa) → b ((xf)a) → (xb)

(bi) → c ((xb)i) → (xc)

(gc) → d ((xg)c) → (xd)

(bj) → a ((xb)j) → (xa)

(x(yz)) → ((xy)z)

As expected, the rules clearly show that the uIND and FD statements decouple.

Example 2: Consider the dependencies f=C→D, i=AB⊆CD, j=BA⊆CD, k=B⊆A. This is the example used in [19] to illustrate the necessity of the *attribute introduction* rule. REVE succeeded in compiling the dependencies into the following rewrite rule system:

Rules:

(fc) → d ((xf)c) → (xd)

(ci) → a ((xc)i) → (xa)

(di) → b ((xd)i) → (xb)

(dj) → a ((xd)j) → (xa)

(cj) → b ((xc)j) → (xb)

(ak) → b ((xa)k) → (xb)

(x(yz)) → ((xy)z)

(fa) → b ((xf)a) → (xb)

(fb) → a ((xf)b) → (xa)

(bk) → a ((xb)k) → (xa)

The non-trivial inference made in this case is that AB⊆BA follows from the dependencies in Figure 2b: observe the "inferred" rule (bk) → a.

Example 3: The dependencies in Figure 2b correspond to the base case of the proof in [9] that certain restricted proof procedures cannot exist for FD's and IND's (the argument uses the chase procedure in a structured fashion). REVE compiled these dependencies into the following rewrite rule system:

Rules:

$(fa_1) \rightarrow c_1 \quad ((xf)a_1) \rightarrow (xc_1)$
$(gc_2) \rightarrow b_2 \quad ((xg)c_2) \rightarrow (xb_2)$
$(hd_2) \rightarrow b_2 \quad ((xh)d_2) \rightarrow (xb_2)$
$(c_2i) \rightarrow c_1 \quad ((xc_2)i) \rightarrow (xc_1)$
$(d_2i) \rightarrow d_1 \quad ((xd_2)i) \rightarrow (xd_1)$
$(a_1j) \rightarrow a_3 \quad ((xa_1)j) \rightarrow (xa_3)$
$(d_1j) \rightarrow d_3 \quad ((xd_1)j) \rightarrow (xd_3)$
$(d_2k) \rightarrow d_3 \quad ((xd_2)k) \rightarrow (xd_3)$
$(b_2k) \rightarrow b_3 \quad ((xb_2)k) \rightarrow (xb_3)$
$(x(yz)) \rightarrow ((xy)z)$

$(hd_3) \rightarrow b_3 \quad ((xh)d_3) \rightarrow (xb_3)$
$(b_2i) \rightarrow (hd_1) \quad ((xb_2)i) \rightarrow ((xh)d_1)$
$(c_1j) \rightarrow (fa_3) \quad ((xc_1)j) \rightarrow ((xf)a_3)$
$(gc_1) \rightarrow (hd_1) \quad ((xg)c_1) \rightarrow ((xh)d_1)$
$((gf)a_3) \rightarrow b_3 \quad (((xg)f)a_3) \rightarrow (xb_3)$

The non-trivial inference here is that $A_3 \rightarrow B_3$ follows from the dependenies of Figure 2c: observe the "inferred" rule $((gf)a_3) \rightarrow b_3$.

4. Functional Dependencies, Transitive Closure and Lattices

4.1. Functional Dependency Inference Revisited

The implication problem for functional dependencies was one of the first computational problems identified as central to database theory [1]. As we saw in Corollary 1.1, it is directly related to the generator problem for finitely presented algebras. In this section we will reformulate it as a word problem in a lattice, which will reveal much more of its algebraic structure.

Let $+, \cdot$ be two operators satisfying the *lattice axioms* (LA):

1. $x+x=x$, $x \cdot x=x$ (idempotency)

2. $x+y=y+x$, $x \cdot y=y \cdot x$ (commutativity)

3. $x+(y+z)=(x+y)+z$, $x \cdot (y \cdot z)=(x \cdot y) \cdot z$ (associativity)

4. $x+(x \cdot y)=x$, $x \cdot (x+y)=x$ (absorption)

Let us assume, again for simplicity, that we have one relation scheme R[U] with attributes U. For every attribute A in U, introduce a constant symbol A. Using these constants and the operators $+,\bullet$ we can form expressions, which we call *partition expressions.* An equation $p=q$ involving two partition expressions is a *partition dependency* (PD). For example, $A=A\bullet B$, $A+B=C$ are PD's.

In [11] we develop the semantics of PD's and show that they are a proper generalization of FD's. Let E be a set of PD's and e a PD: $E\models_{lat}e$ iff e is implied from EULA.

ACI-Transformation: Given a set of FD's F we transform them into a set of equations E_F as follows: $f=A_1A_2...A_n\rightarrow A$ is transformed into e_f: $A_1\bullet A_2\bullet...\bullet A_n=A\bullet A_1\bullet A_2\bullet...\bullet A_n$, where $\bullet$ is associative, commutative and idempotent.

Theorem 3 [11]: $F\models f$ iff $E_F\models_{lat}e_f$ ∎

In fact, this is a more useful approach than the generator formulation of Corollary 1.1. The implication problem for FD's can thus be reduced, in this straightforward way, to the (uniform) *word problem for semilattices* (structures with a single associative, commutative and idempotent operator). On the other hand, since $X=Y$ is equivalent to $X=X\bullet Y$ *and* $Y=Y\bullet X$, we can also reduce the above word problem to the implication problem for FD's.

In order to complete our exposition we would like to comment on the semantics of a PD which contains the + operator (for FD's we have been using • only).
From [11], it follows that a relation r satisfies the PD $C=A+B$ when, for any tuples $t,s\in r$,
$t[C]=s[C]$ iff there are tuples $s_0,...,s_n$ of r with $t=s_0$, $s_n=s$, and for $i=0,...,n\text{-}1$ $s_i[A]=s_{i+1}[A]$ *or* $s_i[B]=s_{i+1}[B]$.

Example: Consider a database d with only one relation r representing an undirected graph. This relation has three attributes: HEAD, TAIL and COMPONENT. For every edge {a,b} in the graph we have in the relation tuples abc, bac, aac, bbc, where c is a number which could vary with a and b. These are the only tuples in r. We would like to express that: *component is the connected component in which the arc (head, tail) belongs.* We can do this by enforcing the PD COMPONENT = HEAD + TAIL.

4.2. On the Uniform Word Problem for Lattices

We have seen how FD implication is equivalent to the uniform word problem for semilattices (idempotent commutative semigroups). We have also motivated a larger class of dependencies, partition dependencies, which can naturally express transitive closure. The problem of partition dependency implication is equivalent to the *uniform word problem for lattices*. This problem is studied in [11]. From the analysis in [11] it follows that there is a polynomial-time algorithm for this word problem, and therefore for PD implication. Specifically, one has the following proof procedure for implication:

Theorem 4 [11]: $E \models_{lat} p=q$ iff $p \leq_E q$ and $q \leq_E p$ can be proved using the following rules:

1. $A \leq_E A$, A in $\mathcal{U}$.

2. $z \leq_E w$, $w \leq_E z$ for $z=w$ in E.

3. *from* $p \leq_E q$, $q \leq_E r$ *derive* $p \leq_E r$.

4. *from* $p \leq_E r$, $q \leq_E r$ *derive* $p+q \leq_E r$.

5. *from* $p \leq_E r$ *derive* $p \cdot q \leq_E r$.

6. *from* $r \leq_E p$, $r \leq_E q$ *derive* $r \leq_E p \cdot q$.

7. *from* $r \leq_E p$ *derive* $r \leq_E p+q$. ∎

The above proof procedure directly leads to a polynomial-time algorithm for PD implication: Observe that, if there is a proof that $p \leq_E q$, then this proof need only mention subexpressions of p, q, and of the expressions appearing in E. Thus, we can just write down these expressions (say, as in [17]) and repeatedly apply the rules, until no new inference can be made.

If E is empty we obtain a special case of the uniform word problem, namely that of recognizing *identities.* It had been shown [22] that rules 1, 4-7 above form a complete inference system for identities. We also remark that the proof procedure of Theorem 4 is a generalization of the Armstrong rules for FD's [20].

Since inference of FD's can be seen as a special case of inference of PD's, the problem is actually *logspace complete* for PTIME [21]. However, in the special case where E is empty (i.e. the identities) it can be solved in *logarithmic space* as follows: we first rewrite $p=q$ as a Boolean tree with leaves of the form $A \leq B$, A,B in $\mathcal{U}$. We then replace $A \leq A$ by *true* and $A \leq B$ by *false* if $A \neq B$, and evaluate the resulting tree.

Example: $A+B=C \cdot D$ is (recursively) rewritten as

$A+B \leq C \cdot D \wedge C \cdot D \leq A+B$

$(A+B \leq C \wedge A+B \leq D) \wedge (C \cdot D \leq A \vee C \cdot D \leq B)$

$((A \leq C \wedge B \leq C) \wedge (A \leq D \wedge B \leq D)) \wedge ((C \leq A \vee D \leq A) \vee (C \leq B \vee D \leq B))$

5. Conclusions

We have shown how the problem of FD,IND implication can be transformed to an equational implication problem (Theorem 1). Our approach can in fact be generalized to handle the implication problem for the most general dependencies of [13] (see [8]). We have solved the uniform word problem for lattices in polynomial time; for distributive lattices, this problem becomes NP-hard [5].

We have experimented with REVE on FD and IND implication. We believe that an equational theorem prover based on ACI-unification could be useful for the problems outlined in Section 4.
A shortcoming of our approach is that it cannot directly handle *finite* implication. A number of positive results in that area are contained in [10, 16].

Acknowledgement

We would like to thank the REVE group at M.I.T., and in particular John Guttag, Kathy Yelick and Dave Detlefs.

References

1. Beeri, C. and Bernstein, P.A. "Computational Problems Related to the Design of Normal Form Relational Schemas". *ACM Transactions on Database Systems 4*, 1 (March 1979), 30-59..

2. Beeri, C. and Vardi, M.Y. "Formal Systems for Tuple and Equality Generating Dependencies". *SIAM Journal of Computing 13*, 1 (February 1984), 76-98..

3. Beeri, C. and Vardi, M.Y. "A Proof Procedure for Data Dependencies". *Journal of the Association for Computing Machinery 31*, 4 (October 1984), 718-741..

4. Birkhoff, G. "On the Structure of Abstract Algebras". *Proceedings of the Cambridge Philosophical Society 31*, (1935).

5. Bloniarz, P.A., Hunt, H.B. III and Rosenkrantz, D.J. "Algebraic Structures with Hard Equivalence and Minimization Problems". *Journal Of The ACM 31*, 4 (October 1984), 879-904..

6. Casanova, M.A., Fagin, R. and Papadimitriou, C.H. "Inclusion Dependencies and Their Interaction with Functional Dependencies". *Journal of Computer and System Sciences 28*, 1 (February 1984), 29-59..

7. Chandra, A.K. and Vardi, M.Y. The Implication Problem for Functional and Inclusion Dependencies is Undecidable. IBM Tech. Rep. RC 9980, , , 1983.

8. Cosmadakis, S.S. *Equational Theories and Database Constraints.* Ph.D. Th., Massachusetts Institute of Technology, 1985.

9. Cosmadakis, S.S. and Kanellakis, P.C. "Functional and Inclusion Dependencies: A Graph Theoretic Approach". *Proceedings of the 3rd ACM Symposium on Principles of Database Systems* (April 1984), 24-37.

10. Cosmadakis, S.S. and Kanellakis, P.C. "Equational Theories and Database Constraints". *Proceedings of the 17th Annual ACM Symposium on Theory of Computing* (May 1984), .

11. Cosmadakis, S.S., Kanellakis, P.C. and Spyratos, N. "Partition Semantics for Relations". *Proceedings of the 4th ACM Symposium on Principles of Database Systems* (March 1985), .

12. Downey, P.J., Sethi, R. and Tarjan, R.E. "Variations on the Common Subexpression Problem". *Journal of the Association for Computing Machinery 27*, 4 (October 1980), 758-771..

13. Fagin, R. "Horn Clauses and Database Dependencies". *Journal of the ACM 29*, 4 (October 1982), 952-985..

14. Forgaard, R. and Guttag, J.V. "REVE: A Term Rewriting System Generator with Failure Resistant Knuth-Bendix". *Proceedings of an NSF Workshop on the Rewrite Rule Laboratory* (April 1984), 5-31.

15. Huet, G. and Oppen, D. Equations and Rewrite Rules: a Survey. In *Formal Languages: Perspectives and Open Problems.* , Eds., Academic Press, , 1980.

16. Kanellakis, P.C., Cosmadakis, S.S. and Vardi, M.Y. "Unary Inclusion Dependencies Have Polynomial Time Inference Problems". *Proceedings of the 15th Annual ACM Symposium on Theory of Computing* (1983).

17. Kozen, D. "Complexity of Finitely Presented Algebras". *Proceedings of the Ninth Annual ACM Symposium on Theory of Computing, ACM SIGACT* (May 1977), .

18. Lescanne, P. "Computer Experiments with the REVE Term Rewriting System Generator". *Proceedings of the 10th ACM Symposium on Principles of Programming Languages* (January 1983), 99-108.

19. Mitchell, J.C. "The Implication Problem for Functional and Inclusion Dependencies". *Information and Control 56*, 3 (March 1983), 154-173. .

20. Ullman, J.D.. *Principles of Database Systems.* Computer Science Press, Inc., , 1983.

21. Vardi, M.Y. "Personal Communication". ( ).

22. Whitman, P.M. "Free Lattices". *Annals of Mathematics 42*, (1941).

23. Yannakakis, M. and Papadimitriou C.H. "Algebraic Dependencies". *J. Comput. Systems Sci. 21*, 1 (August 1982), 2-41. .

$\underline{\Sigma}$: $A \to B$, $C \to D$

$CD \subseteq AB$

$A'B' \to C'$

$\underline{E_\Sigma}$:

$$fax = bx$$
$$gcx = dx$$
$$aix = cx$$
$$bix = dx$$
$$f'a'xb'x = c'x$$

$\underline{\mathcal{E}_\Sigma}$:

$$f\alpha = \beta$$
$$g\gamma = \delta$$
$$i\alpha = \gamma$$
$$i\beta = \delta$$
$$f\alpha'\beta' = \gamma'$$

$$fix = ifx \qquad gix = igx$$
$$f'ix_1ix_2 = if'x_1x_2$$

$\underline{M}$:

M_f : $f(\cdot)$ $g(\cdot)$ $f'(\cdot,\cdot)$

M_i : $i(\cdot)$

M_a : $a(\cdot)$ $b(\cdot)$ $c(\cdot)$ $d(\cdot)$ $a'(\cdot)$ $b'(\cdot)$ $c'(\cdot)$

M_α : α β γ δ α' β' γ'

Figure 1

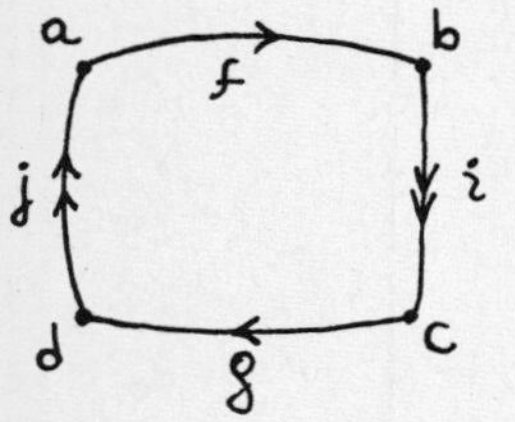

$A \to B$, $C \to D$

$C \subseteq B$, $A \subseteq D$

(a)

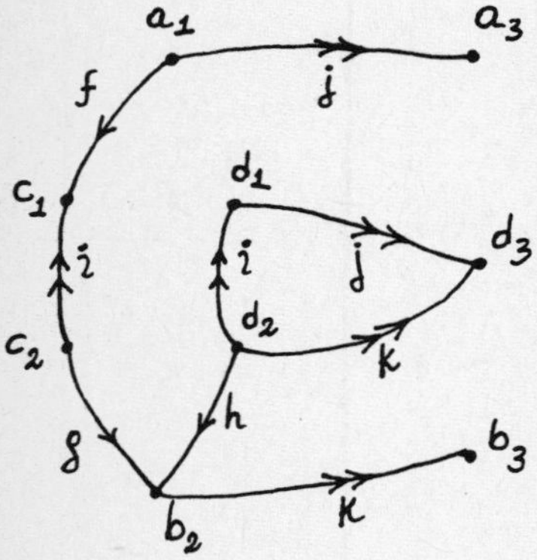

$A_1 \to C_1$, $C_2 \to B_2$, $D_2 \to B_2$

$C_1D_1 \subseteq C_2D_2$

$A_3D_3 \subseteq A_1D_1$

$D_3B_3 \subseteq D_2B_2$

(b)

→ red

↠ black

Figure 2

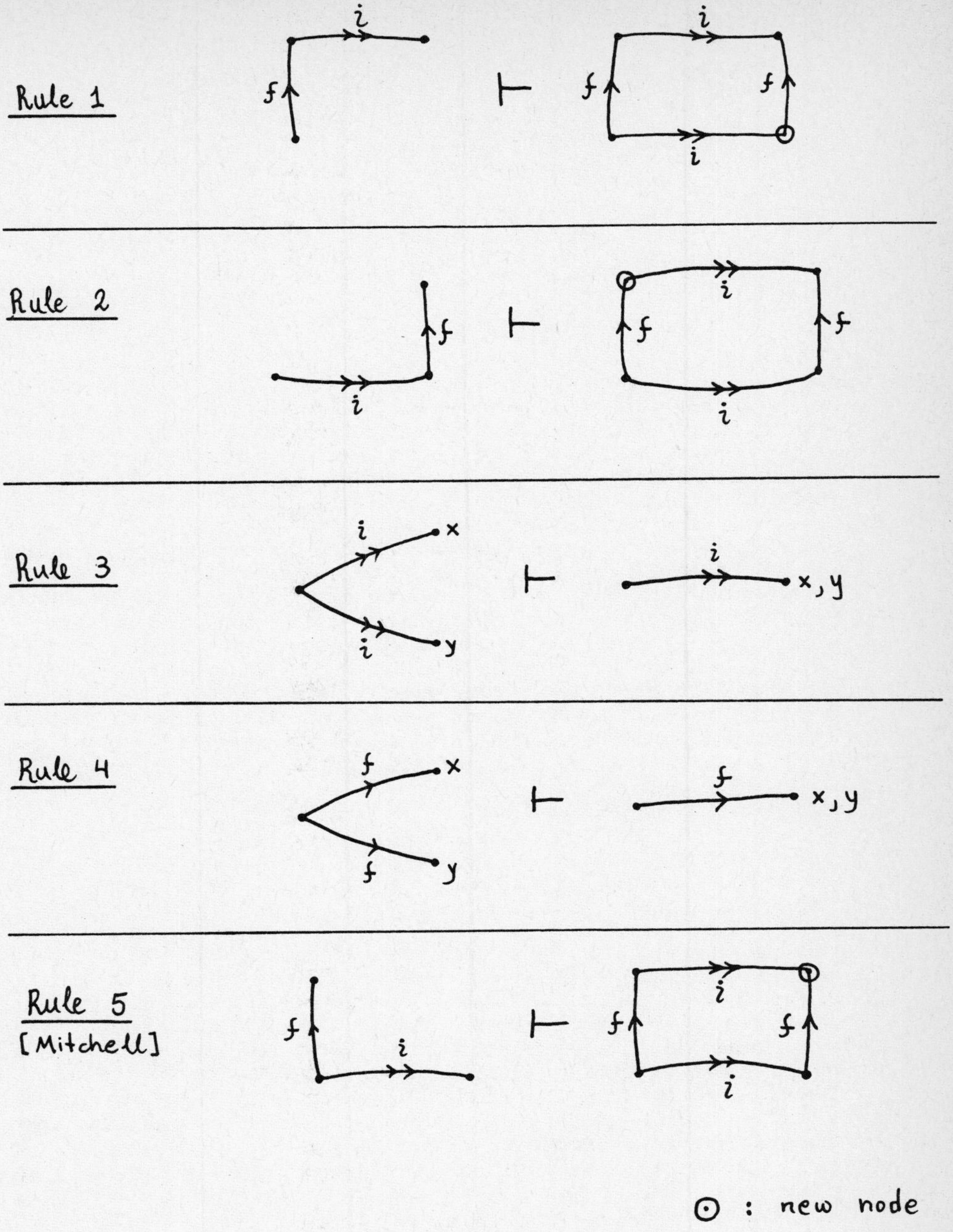
Rule 1
f
i
f
f
i
i
Rule 2
f
i
i
f
f
i
Rule 3
i
x
i
y
i
x, y
Rule 4
f
x
f
y
f
x, y
Rule 5
[Mitchell]
f
i
i
f
f
i
⊙ : new node

Figure 3

AN EXPERIMENT IN PARTIAL EVALUATION: THE GENERATION OF A COMPILER GENERATOR [1]

Neil D. Jones
Peter Sestoft
Harald Søndergaard

DIKU
University of Copenhagen
Sigurdsgade 41, DK-2200 Copenhagen N., Denmark

1. Introduction

It has been known for several years that in theory the program transformation principle called *partial evaluation* or *mixed computation* can be used for compiling and compiler generation (given an interpreter for the language to be implemented), and even for the generation of a compiler generator.

The present paper describes an experimental partial evaluator able to generate stand-alone compilers and compiler generators. As far as we know, such generations had not been done in practice prior to summer 1984.

Partial evaluation of a *subject program* with respect to some of its input parameters results in a *residual program*. By definition, running the residual program on any remaining input yields the same result as running the original subject program on all of its input. Thus a residual program can be considered a *specialization* of the subject program to known, fixed values of some of its parameters. A *partial evaluator* is a program that performs partial evaluation given a subject program and fixed values for some of the program's parameters.

1.1. Application to Compiler Generation

The significance of partial evaluators for compiling, compiler generation, and compiler generator generation stems from the following fact: Consider an interpreter for a given language S. The specialization of this interpreter to a known source program s (written in S) *already is* a target program for s, written in the same language as the interpreter. Thus, partial evaluation of an interpreter with respect to a fixed source program amounts to compiling. From this viewpoint then, partial evaluation and compilation are nothing but special cases of program transformation for the purpose of optimization.

Furthermore, partially evaluating a partial evaluator with respect to a fixed interpreter yields a compiler for the language implemented by the interpreter. And even more mind-boggling: Partially evaluating the partial evaluator with respect to itself yields a compiler generator, namely, a program that transforms interpreters into compilers.

It is nearly always easier to implement a new language by writing an interpreter than by writing a compiler for the language since in the latter case, one has to think of two binding times, compile time and run time. Interpretive implementations have only one binding time, but are usually too

---

[1] Presented May 1985 at the First International Conference on Rewriting Techniques and Applications, Dijon, France

inefficient for practical use. The potential significance of a good partial evaluator is thus that it allows for the automatic construction of efficient compilers from more intelligible interpretive specifications of programming languages (by automatically splitting the binding time into two).

In our experience, the compilers produced turn out to be natural in structure, reasonably efficient, and to produce reasonably efficient target programs, which typically run one order of magnitude faster than the interpreted source programs.

It could be argued that the restriction to language definitions in interpretive form is too limiting, since in practice one often chooses to define languages by denotational or axiomatic semantics, rather than operationally. However, denotational semantics provides "runnable specifications" of programming languages (as shown by the existence of several semantics-based compiler generators: [Mos79], [Set81], [Pau82], [ChJ83]), and these may in principle be regarded as interpreters.

1.2. Relation to Other Work

A very extensive list of references to partial evaluation literature is given in [Fut83]. The applicability of partial evaluation to compiler generation is mentioned in [Fut71], and to compiler generator generation in [Tur80], and [Ers82]. Some steps have been taken towards realizing these goals in practice ([Bec76], [EmH80], and [Tur82]), but as far as we know, we are the first to give a complete solution to this open problem.

Our partial evaluator differs from those presented in the literature mainly by being itself written in the same language it partially evaluates, and thus being self-applicable (whence it is called an *autoprojector*). This is essential for the generation of compilers and compiler generators.

Also, it uses a separate stage of preprocessing to determine statically (by flow analysis) which parts of a program may be reduced away during partial evaluation, and which parts will possibly appear in the residual program produced. The partial evaluators reported in the literature determine this dynamically during partial evaluation, but preprocessing appears to be advantageous for the realization of compiler generation and compiler generator generation. Finally, while this preprocessing is done automatically, the user is required to annotate (by hand, presently) the function calls appearing in the subject program.

1.3. The Paper

First, this paper gives an introduction to partial evaluation and presents the results from its application to compiler generation. Second, the subject language and the autoprojector are described, and special attention is paid to some rather subtle problems which had to be solved during the construction. Finally, the project is reviewed, and suggestions for further work are given.

2. Partial Evaluation

In this section we set up the framework for discussing partial evaluation and its applications.

2.1. Preliminaries

We assume there is given a single, fixed set D whose elements may represent programs in various languages, as well as their input and their output. Sequences of elements of D are denoted by $\langle d_1, \ldots, d_n \rangle$. The set of all finite sequences of elements of D is denoted by D*.

Parentheses will usually be put to use only when necessary to disambiguate expressions. We write $X \rightarrow Y$ to denote the set of all total functions from X to Y, and $X \dashrightarrow Y$ for the partial functions. An expression $X \rightarrow Y \rightarrow Z$ is parenthesized as $X \rightarrow (Y \rightarrow Z)$, and a double function application f x y is parenthesized (f x) y (so f, x, and y have types $f: X \rightarrow Y \rightarrow Z$, x: X, y: Y for some X, Y, and Z).

We identify a *programming language* L with its semantic function on whole programs (assumed to be computable):

$$L: D \dashrightarrow D^* \dashrightarrow D$$

and the well-formed L-programs are those to which L assigns a meaning:

$$\text{L-programs} = \text{domain}(L).$$

The *input-output function* computed by $\ell \in$ L-programs is $(L\ \ell): D^* \dashrightarrow D$ (which is partial since ℓ may loop). Input is always a sequence. If it is the singleton $\langle d \rangle$, we shall simply write $L\ \ell\ d$ instead of $L\ \ell\ \langle d \rangle$.

Thus, $L\ \ell\ \langle d_1, \ldots, d_n \rangle$ denotes the output (if any) obtained by running the L-program ℓ on input data $d_1, \ldots, d_n$. For an example, consider the following exponentiation algorithm:

```
          f(n,x)  =  if n=0 then 1
power =              else if even(n) then f(n/2,x)^2
                     else x*f(n-1,x)
```

We see that L power <3, 2> = 8. The equality sign shall always mean that either both sides are undefined, or else they are defined and equal.

2.2. Definition of Partial Evaluation

Definition 2.1. Let ℓ be an L-program and let $d_1, \ldots, d_m$ be values in D. The L-program r is a *residual program for ℓ with respect to* $\langle d_1, \ldots, d_m \rangle$ iff

$$L\ \ell\ \langle d_1, \ldots, d_m, \ldots, d_{m+n} \rangle = L\ r\ \langle d_{m+1}, \ldots, d_{m+n} \rangle$$

for all $d_{m+1}, \ldots, d_{m+n}$ in D. ∎

Definition 2.2. A P-program p is an *L-partial evaluator* iff

$P\ p\ \langle \ell, d_1, \ldots, d_m \rangle$ is a residual L-program for ℓ with respect to $\langle d_1, \ldots, d_m \rangle$

for all L-programs ℓ and values $d_1, \ldots, d_m$ in D. ∎

Hence, a partial evaluator takes a subject program and part of its input and produces a (residual) program; the residual program applied to any remaining input produces the same result as the subject program applied to all of its input. The characteristic equation therefore is

$$L\ \ell\ \langle d_1,\ldots,d_m,\ldots,d_{m+n}\rangle \;=\; L\ (P\ p\ \langle \ell, d_1,\ldots,d_m\rangle)\ \langle d_{m+1},\ldots,d_{m+n}\rangle.$$

For a simple example, let the L-program ℓ be "power" from Section 2.1, and suppose we are given that n equals 5. A trivial residual program $resid_1$ may easily be constructed by adding a single equation:

$resid_1$ =

```
g(x)    =   f(5,x)
f(n,x)  =   if n=0 then 1
            else if even(n) then f(n/2,x)^2
            else x*f(n-1,x)
```

The general possibility of partial evaluation in recursive function theory is known as the S-m-n Theorem, and is shown in just this way (e.g. see [Rog67]). A less trivial residual program may be obtained by symbolically executing the program $resid_1$ (which is possible since its control flow is completely determined by n), yielding a program with only one equation:

$resid_2$ =

$$g(x) \;=\; x*(x^2)^2$$

Partial evaluation thus can be viewed as substitution of known values for some parameters, possibly followed by equivalence preserving program transformations, and can result in residual programs which are much faster (though usually larger) than the original. See [Bec76] and [EmH80] for examples. Partial evaluation followed by evaluation of the resulting program may be even faster than normal evaluation, because of the optimizing transformations.

In practice it seems difficult to obtain efficient residual programs without compromising halting properties. For example, a residual program in a call-by-value language may terminate more often than the original subject program because of the call-by-name nature of symbolic execution. Further, partial evaluators are notorious for entering infinite PE-time loops, even on some subject programs which terminate at run time.

Note that here and in the sequel, PE abbreviates "partial evaluation".

3. Compiling and Compiler Generation

We now turn to the applications of partial evaluation to compiler generation - in theory and in practice.

3.1. Compiling by Partially Evaluating an Interpreter

Definition 3.1. An L-program int is an *interpreter* for the language S iff

$$S\ s\ \langle d_1,\ldots,d_n\rangle \;=\; L\ int\ \langle s, d_1,\ldots,d_n\rangle$$

for all S-programs s and data $d_1,\ldots,d_n$. ∎

By this definition an interpreter takes as input both the program to be interpreted and its input data.

Let the P-program p be an L-partial evaluator. If an S-interpreter int is partially evaluated with respect to a given S-program s, the result will be an L-program with the same input-output behaviour as s, since

$$\begin{aligned} S\ s\ \langle d_1, \ldots, d_n\rangle &= L\ int\ \langle s, d_1, \ldots, d_n\rangle \\ &= L\ (P\ p\ \langle int, s\rangle)\ \langle d_1, \ldots, d_n\rangle. \end{aligned}$$

Note that the last line describes the application of a certain L-program (namely P p <int, s>) to input $\langle d_1, \ldots, d_n\rangle$. The result of this is the same as the result of applying the S-program s to $\langle d_1, \ldots, d_n\rangle$, so we may reasonably call this

$$target = P\ p\ \langle int, s\rangle$$

since it is an L-program with the same input-output behaviour as s. In other words we have compiled the source S-program s into an L-program target by partially evaluating the S-interpreter with respect to the source program s. For an example, see Figures 4.1 (interpreter), 4.2 (source program), and 4.3 (target program) below.

3.2. Compiler Generation

Definition 3.2. An L-program mix is an *L-autoprojector* iff it is an L-partial evaluator. ∎

An autoprojector is thus a partial evaluator for the language in which it is itself written. In the following we will assume that an autoprojector mix is given. Letting mix play the role of the partial evaluator p from above, we have that

$$target = L\ mix\ \langle int, s\rangle.$$

Note that in the following generations it is essential that mix is self-applicable, i.e. an autoprojector. A compiler from S to L may be generated by computing:

$$comp = L\ mix\ \langle mix, int\rangle$$

that is, by partially evaluating the autoprojector itself with respect to the S-interpreter. To see this, observe that

$$\begin{aligned} L\ comp\ s &= L\ (L\ mix\ \langle mix, int\rangle)\ s && \text{- by the definition of comp} \\ &= L\ mix\ \langle int, s\rangle && \text{- since mix is a partial evaluator} \\ &= target. \end{aligned}$$

Thus comp is a compiler since given s it produces a target program for s.

3.3. Compiler Generator Generation

By the same reasoning a compiler generator may be obtained:

$$cocom = L\ mix\ \langle mix, mix\rangle.$$

This L-program transforms interpreters into compilers; it is easy to verify that

$$comp = L\ cocom\ int.$$

In fact, cocom is more than a compiler generator. It is the realization of a general currying function, able to transform a program for a two-argument function f(x,y) into a program which, when given data $x=x_0$, will yield as output a program for the function $\lambda y. f(x_0, y)$. In other words cocom maps $rep(X \times Y \rightarrow Z)$ to $rep(X \rightarrow rep(Y \rightarrow Z))$, where $rep(A \rightarrow B)$ denotes the set of program representations of functions from A to B. In particular, cocom transforms an interpreter into its curried form, a compiler.

3.4. Theory versus Practice

Futamura was apparently the first to propose compiler construction by partially evaluating the partial evaluator [Fut71]. The idea that L mix <mix, mix> is a compiler generator seems to have been realized independently in the USSR, Sweden, and presumably Japan at about the same time. See [Bec76], [Tur80] (reporting work done earlier in the USSR), and [Ers82].

Practice has, however, lagged behind theory. A large partial evaluator for Lisp as used in practice, with imperative features and property lists, is described in [Bec76]. Use of partial evaluators to compile programs in various languages may be found in [Bec76], [EmH80], and [Tur82], and a handwritten version of cocom is described in [Bec76], where it is called REDCOMPILE. Partial evaluation of Prolog is described in [Kom82], and *of* Lisp *by* Prolog in [Kah83].

In [KaC84] Kahn and Carlsson give an indirect method for compiling Prolog. A Prolog interpreter is first partially evaluated on a Prolog program, yielding an equivalent Lisp program, which is then compiled further into machine language using an already-written Lisp compiler. The resulting target programs are faster than those produced by Warren's cleverly handwritten Prolog compiler [War77], but compilation is slower by two orders of magnitude.

As far as we have been able to determine, our experiments are the first which have succeeded in automatically producing either stand-alone compilers or compiler generators.

3.5. Results

One could expect compilation by computing

target = L comp s

(where comp = L mix <mix, int>) to be considerably faster than by computing

target = L mix <int, s>.

The reason is that the latter involves applying a general-purpose partial evaluation algorithm, while comp is on the other hand specialized to the language implemented by int. This expectation is verified in practice. The compilers produced by the present mix have a surprisingly natural structure and are reasonably small and efficient, as the figures below indicate. Even cocom is of reasonable size, although its logic is harder to follow.

A mix-produced compiler works like a traditional compiler in that it translates a composite program structure by first compiling its substructures and then combining the resulting target program fragments. Unlike traditional compilers, the mix-produced ones first examine the fragments to see whether they contain operations that can be done at compile time, thus automatically doing what is often a separate pass: peephole optimization and constant folding. For example, the compiler generated from a simple two-register machine interpreter (actually the one given shortly in Figure 4.1) compiles the program X:=X+1; Y:=Y+1; X:=X-1 into the same code as Y:=Y+1.

Following are some results regarding size and run time of some of the target programs, compilers, and the compiler generator generated by mix. In the figures, "int" denotes an interpreter for a simple language S with list-valued expressions, <u>while</u>, <u>if</u>, and assignment, and "source" is an example S-program. The programs target, comp, and cocom were produced as described above.

Program	# functions	# lines	Ratio
source	-	30	
target	13	47	1.6
int	9	105	
comp	29	382	3.6
mix	23	461	
cocom	58	1294	2.8

<u>Figure 3.1: Size measurements</u>

Run		Time in seconds	Ratio
output	= L int <source, data>	5.54 + 0.58	
	= L target data	0.30 + 0.64	6.5
target	= L mix <int, source>	3.10 + 0.00	
	= L comp source	0.18 + 0.00	17.2
comp	= L mix <mix, int>	54.74 + 4.26	
	= L cocom int	1.92 + 5.16	8.3
cocom	= L mix <mix, mix>	255.52 + 16.30	
	= L cocom mix	8.72 + 17.62	10.3

<u>Figure 3.2: Time measurements</u>

The running times in Figure 3.2 are given in the form: Computation time + Garbage collection time. *Note that comp and cocom are an order of magnitude faster than their non-partially evaluated counterparts int and mix.* For a more realistic interpreter, at least the first ratio would be higher.

The running times do not include the preprocessing mentioned in Section 1.2. Preprocessing is hard to account for fairly in the tables because it has an earlier binding time than partial evaluation (e.g. should one count preprocessing of both mix *and* int in compiler generation, or just int?) In any case preprocessing is an order of magnitude faster than mix application, so it doesn't make much difference.

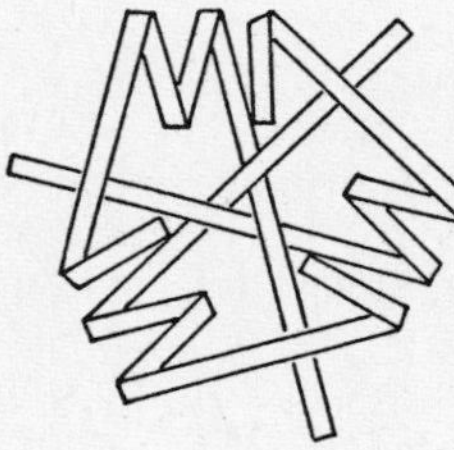

4. The Language L

The choice of subject language for an autoprojector seems crucial. On the one hand, the language should be simple to process. On the other hand it should be strong enough to express a non-trivial autoprojector. The autoprojector may be viewed as a generalized interpreter (if applied to a one-argument program for example). Thus we obviously cannot hope to build it unless the language is *self-interpretable*. But then the language cannot possibly express its own halting function [HoA72] (and this is surely the root of some of the termination problems we have encountered). Applicative languages seem preferable to imperative ones due to the ease with which source-to-source transformations may be performed.

4.1. Description

The subject language of the present autoprojector may be thought of as a dialect of pure Lisp with static scoping. An L-program takes the form of a system of recursive equations as shown here in abstract form (Figure 4.1 gives an example in the concrete syntax):

$f_1(x_1,\ldots,x_m)$	=	expression_1
...		...
$f_n(x_1,\ldots,x_p)$	=	expression_n

Variables range over D = { d | d is a Lisp list } and the expressions are constructed from variables (Lisp atoms) and constants of form (**quote** list) by operators: **car**, **cdr**, **cons**, **equal**, and **atom**. In addition there is a conditional: (**if** cond **then** exp_1 **else** exp_2) and a function call: (**call** f_j exp_1 exp_2 ... exp_n).

Programs are evaluated using static scoping, call-by-value, and greedy evaluation. The program's input is through the first function's arguments. L is first order - functions may *not* be manipulated as data objects.

4.2. An Example Use

Figure 4.1 shows an example interpreter written in L. **callr** is a special form of **call** which will be explained shortly. The interpreter implements an imperative two-register machine, and the registers, X and Y, are each capable of holding any natural number. In the interpreter, value m is represented by a list of m ones. A program is a list (ins_1 ins_2 ... ins_n) where the instructions ins_j may take the following forms:

X:=X+1, X:=X-1, Y:=Y+1, Y:=Y-1, (GOTO 1^m), (IFX=0 1^m), or (IFY=0 1^m)

The destinations of GOTO and IF are indicated in unary, so 1^m means the program's m-th instruction (the first has number 0). Input is through X, output is through Y, and Y is initialized to 0 = () = nil.

Although very simple, the language is capable of computing any recursive function (modulo a little encoding of data). The compiler generated automatically translates imperative programs into equivalent applicative ones using the technique of continuations (although this is in no way explicitly built into the autoprojector).

```
(
   (Execute (pgm x) = (callr Run pgm pgm x 'nil))

   (Run (pgm suf x y) =
      (if (equal suf 'nil) then y else
      (if (equal (car suf) 'X:=X+1) then
         (call Run pgm (cdr suf) (cons '1 x) y) else
      (if (equal (car suf) 'Y:=Y+1) then
         (call Run pgm (cdr suf) x (cons '1 y)) else
      (if (equal (car suf) 'X:=X-1) then
         (call Run pgm (cdr suf) (cdr x) y) else
      (if (equal (car suf) 'Y:=Y-1) then
         (call Run pgm (cdr suf) x (cdr y)) else
      (if (equal (car (car suf)) 'GOTO) then
         (callr Run pgm (call Hop pgm (cdr (car suf))) x y) else
      (if (equal (car (car suf)) 'IFX=0) then
         (if (equal x 'nil) then
            (callr Run pgm (call Hop pgm (cdr (car suf))) x y)
         else (call Run pgm (cdr suf) x y)
         ) else
      (if (equal (car (car suf)) 'IFY=0) then
         (if (equal y 'nil) then
            (callr Run pgm (call Hop pgm (cdr (car suf))) x y)
         else (call Run pgm (cdr suf) x y)
         ) else
         'error
      ))))))))
   )

   (Hop (pgm dest) =
      (if (equal dest 'nil) then pgm
      else (call Hop (cdr pgm) (cdr dest)))
   )
)
```

Figure 4.1: Interpreter written in L

Figure 4.2 shows an example program (including comments) in the language implemented by the above interpreter. The program Twice computes 2*x where x is the input. Figure 4.3 shows the corresponding target program, which has a nice structure. Note that Run-2 could be eliminated and the call to it replaced by y, using simple peephole postprocessing.

```
(
   (IFX=0 . (1 1 1 1 1))    ; 0: if X=0 then halt
   Y:=Y+1                   ; 1: Y:=Y+2
   Y:=Y+1                   ; 2:
   X:=X-1                   ; 3: X:=X-1
   (GOTO . ())              ; 4: goto 0
)
```

Figure 4.2: The program Twice

```
(
    (Execute-1 (x) = (call Run-1 x 'nil) )

    (Run-1 (x y) =
       (if x then (call Run-1 (cdr x) (cons '1 (cons '1 y) ) )
       else (call Run-2 x y)
       )
    )

    (Run-2 (x y) = y)
)
```

Figure 4.3: Target program for Twice

5. General Methods and Problems

5.1. Strategy for Rewriting Programs

The residual program for an equation system

$$\{ f_i (x_1, \ldots, x_{n_i}) = e_i \}_{i=1..m}$$

is naturally another system of equations each of form

$$f_i\text{-}j\ (y_1, \ldots) = e_i\text{-}j$$

where f_i-j represents a *specialized* version of f_i, and the variables of f_i-j are a subset of the variables of f_i. Specialization is done on the basis of PE-time knowledge about the arguments to f_i. For example, if it is discovered that in one call to f_i, the first argument always has value 5, the partial evaluator could exploit this fact by constructing an f_i-variant with the first variable removed, and in which e_i-j is a simplified version of e_i.

Expression e_i may be simplified to obtain e_i-j by a symbolic evaluation, which is done in a *PE-time environment* containing information known at PE-time about the arguments of f_i. In our autoprojector this environment is a set of bindings of variable names to expressions

$$\text{env} = [\, x_1 \mapsto e_1' , \ldots, x_{n_i} \mapsto e_{n_i}' \,].$$

In a more sophisticated partial evaluator, environments containing various other kinds of descriptive information may be used, for example see [Bec76].

For a simple example, let $\overline{e}$ represent the result of partially evaluating e in the current PE-time environment. Then **(car** e) may be partially evaluated as follows:

$$\overline{(\textbf{car}\ e)} = \left\{ \begin{array}{lll} \underline{\text{case}}\ \text{form of}\ \overline{e}\ \underline{\text{of}} & & \\ (\textbf{quote}\ (hd\ .\ tl)) & : & (\textbf{quote}\ hd) \\ (\textbf{cons}\ e_1\ e_2) & : & e_1 \\ \underline{\text{otherwise}} & : & (\textbf{car}\ \overline{e}) \\ \underline{\text{end}} & & \end{array} \right.$$

A critical problem is the treatment of a function call (**call** f_j e_1 ... e_n). There are two possibilities - either to produce a residual call (possibly to a specialized version of f_j, in case some of $\overline{e}_1,\ldots,\overline{e}_n$ are constant) or to *unfold* the call. To do this, the equation $f_j(x_1,\ldots,x_n) = e$ defining f_j is found, and (**call** f_j e_1 ... e_n) is reduced to the result of partially evaluating e in the PE-time environment $[x_1 \mapsto \overline{e}_1, \ldots, x_n \mapsto \overline{e}_n]$.

5.2. Three Pitfalls

Several problems can occur, mainly in connection with choice of a good call unfolding strategy. First, a too conservative strategy can result in trivial residual programs like $resid_1$ from Section 2.2, and so in interpretive execution of target programs. Second, a too liberal strategy can lead to PE-time loops in which the same function is unfolded infinitely. Third, the residual programs may turn out to be *less* efficient than the original subject programs, due to the call-by-name nature of symbolic evaluation. For example,

```
f(n)  =  if n=0 then 1 else g(f(n-1))
g(n)  =  n + n + 1
```

should *not* be unfolded to

```
f(n)  =  if n=0 then 1 else f(n-1) + f(n-1) + 1
```

since the first runs in linear time while the second requires exponential time. We have experienced all of these problems during the development of the autoprojector.

5.3. When to Unfold? Structural Induction Is Not Enough

Consider a call appearing in a recursively defined function

$$f(x_1,\ldots,x_n) \;=\; \ldots\; f(e_1,\ldots,e_n)\; \ldots$$

If there exists an argument x_i which always decreases (according to some well-founded partial order), then the call may safely be unfolded, provided x_i is evaluable to a constant at PE-time. For example, the exponentiation program given in Section 2.1 may be unfolded with respect to a known value of n, but not with respect to x.

While general, this rule does not cover all cases of interest, in particular compilation by partial evaluation of an interpreter:

$$\text{target} \;=\; L\ \text{mix} \langle \text{int}, s \rangle.$$

The critical point is that in the great majority of programming languages, most commands/expressions may be performed/evaluated on the basis of their subcomponents, without reference to other parts of the enclosing program s. Such "descents" by the interpreter to smaller parts of s may always safely be unfolded, but whenever the interpreter shifts its attention to a different or a larger part of s, its corresponding call (or "go") must not be unfolded due to the risk of infinite expansion.

For example in Figure 4.1 the calls implementing GOTO, IFX=0, and IFY=0 may *not* be unfolded, but all others may. The problem arises because of the mixture of static actions (dependent only on the source program) and program-execution actions found in interpreters.

Our autoprojector does not solve the problem of deciding which calls to unfold. Instead, the user is required to classify all calls appearing in the input program as residual (never unfolded) or eliminable (always unfolded), as may be seen in Figure 4.1 (**callr** and **call**, respectively). We return to the problem of call annotation in Section 7.3.

5.4. Cause and Effect in L mix ⟨mix, int⟩

Our early partial evaluation algorithms produced reasonable code on small examples:

$$\text{resid} \;=\; \text{L mix} \langle \ell, \text{d} \rangle$$

and

$$\text{target} \;=\; \text{L mix} \langle \text{int}, \text{s} \rangle$$

but turned out to produce enormous and slow compilers when self-applied:

$$\text{comp} \;=\; \text{L mix} \langle \text{mix}, \text{int} \rangle .$$

We finally overcame this problem (as shown by the figures in Section 3.5) by the following analysis. Considering L mix ⟨ℓ, d⟩, it is clear that production of a smaller, more efficient residual program will require a larger, more sophisticated mix algorithm. On the other hand, a larger input program ℓ will in general yield a larger residual program. The generation of a small compiler L mix ⟨mix, int⟩ thus requires that mix be simultaneously large and small! To be more precise, the size of

$$\text{comp} \;=\; \text{L mix}_1 \langle \text{mix}_2, \text{int} \rangle$$

will depend on the number of operations in mix_2 which are 1) encountered while running mix_1, and 2) not evaluable at mix_1-time.

For example, consider the reduction of an occurrence of (**car** e) in int, done by mix_2 in the way mentioned earlier. After a recursive call in mix_2 to compute $\overline{e}$, a series of tests are done on $\overline{e}$, each ending in construction of a residual expression. The tests and constructions are based on $\overline{e}$, which is dependent on *both* of mix_2's arguments (int and s). Mix_1 has available only the first of mix_2's arguments, so the tests and constructions for (**car** e) cannot be performed by mix_1. They will thus appear in mix_2's residual program, the compiler being produced.

On the other hand, the recursive call in mix_2 to compute $\overline{e}$ descends to a smaller part of mix_2's argument int, and so will be unfolded. Consequently *every* occurrence of **car** in int will result in a distinct occurrence in comp of the code for reduction of (**car** e). The code for **cdr** is similar, and that for **cons** and **if** is larger - which explains the large size of our first automatically produced compilers.

This problem was solved by two methods. The first is a straightforward encapsulation. For example, the code for (**car** e) was moved to a separate function which is only called residually, and which has no eliminable arguments. Consequently the equation for this function appears only once in the generated compiler. The second method reduces the number of mix_2's residual operations, and will be discussed in the next section.

6. How the Autoprojector Works

Partial evaluation is done in two steps, preprocessing and mix application. The preprocessor transforms an L-program ℓ into a new version ℓ^{ann} containing various annotations. Compiler generation etc. is now a bit more involved, due to the need for annotation:

$$\text{target} = \text{L mix} \langle \text{int}^{ann}, \text{s} \rangle$$

$$\text{comp} = \text{L mix} \langle \text{mix}^{ann}, \text{int}^{ann} \rangle$$

$$\text{cocom} = \text{L mix} \langle \text{mix}^{ann}, \text{mix}^{ann} \rangle$$

6.1. Preprocessing

Input to the preprocessor consists of:

1. An L-program ℓ, in which each function call is classified as residual or eliminable.
2. An indication of which of ℓ's parameters will be known during partial evaluation.

Output is ℓ^{ann}, a heavily annotated version of ℓ, obtained by the following three preprocessing steps:

1. For every function f_i, the variables are classified as either *known* (ultimately dependent only on the known variables of the first function f_1) or *unknown* (possibly depending on unknown variables of f_1).
2. The variables of f_i are permuted so the known variables come first, and call arguments are permuted accordingly. Input to mix is thus a system of equations (ev_i = "eliminable variable i", rv_i = "residual variable i"):

$$\boxed{f_i(ev_1,\ldots,ev_m,rv_1,\ldots,rv_n) = e_i}$$

3. All expressions (op e_1 ... e_n) appearing in ℓ (other than calls) are rewritten, so "op" becomes "ope" if (op e_1 ... e_n) may be evaluated at PE-time, and "opr" if not. For example, **car** in (**car** e) becomes **care** (meaning "eliminable **car**") if e contains no residual variables or calls.

6.2. Comments on Preprocessing

The classification of all function variables as known or unknown makes it easier for mix to build residual programs. Also, it is needed for the third step of preprocessing. The partitioning is obtained by a simple flow analysis in which the subject program is executed abstractly using {Unknown, Known} as variables' value domain.

Permutation of variables and annotation of operators is straightforward using the results of the first step. One purpose of the third step is to reduce the workload of mix. For example, the argument of **care** will always be a known constant, so one may simplify the <u>case</u> expression of Section 5.1 to:

$$\overline{(\textbf{care}\ e)} = (\textbf{quote}\ \text{car}(\ \text{car}(\ \text{cdr}(\overline{e}))))$$

The main advantage, however, of annotating all operators, only becomes obvious during compiler generation:

$$\text{comp} = L\ \text{mix}_1 \langle \text{mix}_2^{\text{ann}}, \text{int}^{\text{ann}} \rangle.$$

Each **care**, etc. appearing in int^{ann} results in the performance of fewer residual operations in mix_2 than would have been caused by an unannotated **car**. These shorter sequences result in the production of a smaller compiler by mix_1 than would have otherwise been the case. Experiments show that using an unannotated interpreter increases the generated compiler's size by a factor 50.

6.3. Application of Mix

Input consists of an annotated program ℓ^{ann} together with the values of some of its parameters. Mix's output is a system of specialized versions of ℓ's equations:

$$(f_i . \text{evv})(rv_1, \ldots, rv_n) = \bar{e}$$

Here $(f_i . \text{evv})$ is a new function name consisting of an original name f_i and a tuple evv of values of f_i's eliminable variables. The rv_j are f_i's residual variables, and $\bar{e}$ is the result of reducing the right side of the original equation $f_i(\ldots) = e$ according to the known values evv. The techniques used are just those which were discussed in Section 5.1.

A simple postprocessing replaces the $(f_1 . \text{evv})$ pairs by new function names f_i-1, f_i-2, etc.

7. Conclusions

7.1. Review

The mix project was undertaken after a conversation with A. P. Ershov in fall 1983, in which it was learned that no one had yet succeeded in constructing a non-trivial L mix <mix, mix> by computer. The problem turned out to be more subtle than expected, and we have had to throw away numerous earlier versions of mix for various languages. In particular, it was very difficult to anticipate the structure, size, or efficiency of a mix-produced compiler, although these have (at last, and somewhat to our surprise) turned out to be quite reasonable.

There were essentially three conceptual breakthroughs that were necessary to carry out the project. The first was the realization that interpreters *almost* always handle their structural argument by recursive descent, with the consequence that *calls* should be annotated as residual or eliminable (and not *functions*, as has been done with other partial evaluators). The second insight was to see the value of preprocessing the program, to classify each function's arguments as residual or eliminable *in advance*, rather than doing this adaptively *during partial evaluation*. The third came from an analysis of the effects of mix's structure and call annotations on the size of

$$\text{comp} = L\ \text{mix} \langle \text{mix}, \text{int} \rangle$$

and resulted in extending the preprocessor to classify each of an L-program's operations as residual or eliminable.

7.2. Programming Style and Language L

A somewhat different programming style is needed in order to realize the full benefits possible with partial evaluation. For one example, for compiler generation purposes the traditional interpreter's "A-list"

$$((\text{name}_1 \ . \ \text{value}_1) \ \ldots \ (\text{name}_n \ . \ \text{value}_n))$$

is best split into a separate name list and value list. The reason is that the name list and its associated lookup and updating functions need not appear in the residual target program, since they depend only on the source program's syntax, whereas the value list *must* be present.

As regards the choice of language which mix accepts and in which it is written, we think that the following characteristics of our Lisp variant have contributed much to the success of the project:

1. Programs can both accept programs as input data and produce them as output.
2. The language's semantics makes it easy to do symbolic evaluation and to do the flow analysis used by the preprocessor.
3. The natural recursivity of partial evaluation is easy to program.
4. The referential transparency of L-programs facilitates specialization of an arbitrary program part without disturbing other parts.

It seems more difficult to write an autoprojector for an imperative language, owing to the need for more sophisticated partial evaluation techniques, and because of the difficulty of recognizing "descents" by a program into a smaller part of a structured known argument.

One problem has to do with program "topology". An imperative interpreter typically contains a single outermost loop to determine the type of program construct to be processed. Residual programs L mix <int, s> thus naturally consist of a collection of nested loops, *regardless* of the structure of the interpreted program. Ershov makes the observation that sophisticated methods seem to be required to synthesize target programs with a structure which is natural for the input program s. We have not encountered this problem in our work, presumably because of the use of systems of recursion equations as a programming formalism. Here the topological transformations are implicit in the generation of residual programs as equation systems.

7.3. Discussion

Program transformation is concerned with deriving "better" equivalent programs. The *quality criteria* are implicit in the rewrite rules used; so the set of rewrite rules determine the strength of a partial evaluator. The present set contains only 20 simple rules, excluding even standard rules like those known as "condition propagation". These are easily included but were deemed unnecessary for our purpose. The aim has been to construct an *autoprojector*, well suited for the special purpose of compiler generation, rather than a general-purpose partial evaluator.

One may think of the transformations performed by mix as split into two categories. One consists of simple local *reductions*, while the other is concerned with function transformation and includes *unfolding* and *specialization* of functions. Although specializations constitute a limited class of transformations (as compared to that of [BuD77] for example), they may imply considerable changes in program topology.

The use of preprocessing appears to be novel in comparison to other approaches to program transformation. Preprocessing serves two purposes: To classify function variables, thereby determining the number of variables for each residual function; and to annotate all operators as "definitely eliminable" or "possibly residual". It appears difficult to make the first decision dynamically during partial evaluation (and most program transformation systems require human intervention here). Operator annotation also appears to be essential - without it, the generated compilers in our experiments have turned out to be *much* larger and less efficient.

The main drawback of the present solution is the need for annotation by hand of function calls. A certain amount of automatic call annotation can certainly be done (since it is easy in Lisp to see when a known argument is replaced by a substructure). However, there appears to be much more to a good call rewriting strategy than that, like ensuring termination and avoiding manifolded function calls in residual programs. In particular, function tabulation techniques like that of [Fut83] prove too liberal for our purpose. Since mix cannot rely on structural induction as do these techniques, applying them leads to infinite partial evaluation.

7.4. Future Work

The development of a good autoprojector is harder than that of a partial evaluator in general. The reason is that attempts to increase *strength* almost certainly imply great penalties as regards *efficiency*. In connection with the present work, at least three tasks deserve attention:

1. It should be investigated whether a generally useful call annotation algorithm is possible. In case it is not, a dynamic call processing algorithm based on a more complex PE-time environment may be developed.
2. Logic programming languages such as Prolog seem to have all the desirable characteristics mentioned in Section 7.2, in addition to other virtues. It therefore seems likely that a Prolog-based autoprojector could profitably be constructed.
3. A natural next step would be to apply the present autoprojector to the Prolog interpreter of [KaC84]. This should speed up Prolog compilation by an order of magnitude.

8. References

[Bec76]
Beckman, L. *et al*, A partial evaluator, and its use as a programming tool, *Art. Int.* **7**,4 (1976) 319-357

[BuD77]
Burstall, R. & J. Darlington, A transformation system for developing recursive programs, *JACM* **24**,1 (1977) 44-67

[ChJ83]
Christiansen, H. & N. D. Jones, Control flow treatment in a simple semantics-directed compiler generator, in *Proc. IFIP WG 2.2: Formal Description of Programming Concepts II* (D. Bjørner, ed.) 73-99, North-Holland 1983

[EmH80]
Emanuelson, P. & A. Haraldsson, On compiling embedded languages in Lisp, *Proc. 1980 ACM Lisp Conference*, Stanford, California (1980) 208-215

[Ers77]
Ershov, A., On the partial evaluation principle, *Inf. Proc. Letters* **6**,2 (April 1977) 38-41

[Ers82]
Ershov, A., Mixed computation: potential applications and problems for study, *Theor. Comp. Sci.* **18** (1982) 41-67

[Fut71]
Futamura, Y., Partial evaluation of computation process - an approach to a compiler-compiler, *Systems, Computers, Controls* **2**,5 (1971) 45-50

[Fut83]
Futamura, Y., Partial computation of programs, in *LNCS 147: Proc. RIMS Symp. Software Science and Engineering*, Kyoto, Japan (1982) 1-35, Springer 1983

[HoA72]
Hoare, C. & D. Allison, Incomputability, *Comp. Surveys* **4**,3 (September 1972) 169-178

[Kah83]
Kahn, K., *A Partial Evaluator of Lisp Written in Prolog*, UPMAIL Technical Report no. 17, University of Uppsala, Sweden (1983)

[KaC84]
Kahn, K. & M. Carlsson, The compilation of Prolog programs without the use of a Prolog compiler, *Proc. Int. Conf. Fifth Generation Computer Systems*, Tokyo, Japan (1984) 348-355

[Kom82]
Komorowski, H. J., Partial evaluation as a means for inferencing data structures in an applicative language: a theory and implementation in the case of Prolog, *Proc. 9th ACM POPL Symp.*, Albuquerque, New Mexico (1982) 255-267

[Mos79]
Mosses, P., *SIS - Semantics Implementation System, Reference Manual and User Guide*, DAIMI MD-30, University of Aarhus, Denmark (1979)

[Pau82]
Paulson, L., A semantics-directed compiler generator, *Proc. 9th ACM POPL Symp.*, Albuquerque, New Mexico (1982) 224-233

[Rog67]
Rogers, H., *Theory of Recursive Functions and Effective Computability*, McGraw-Hill 1967

[Set81]
Sethi, R., *Control Flow Aspects of Semantics Directed Compiling*, Technical report, Bell Labs, Murray Hill, New Jersey (1981)

[Tur80]
Turchin, V., Semantic definitions in REFAL and the automatic production of compilers, in *LNCS 94: Semantics-Directed Compiler Generation* (N. D. Jones, ed.) 441-474, Springer 1980

[Tur82]
Turchin, V. *et al*, Experiments with a supercompiler, *Proc. 1982 ACM Symp. on Lisp and Functional Programming*, Pittsburgh, Pennsylvania (1982) 47-55

[War77]
Warren, D., *Implementing Prolog - Compiling Predicate Logic Programs*, DAI Research Report nos. 39-40, University of Edinburgh, Scotland (1977)

NARROWER: a new algorithm for unification and its application to Logic Programming.(*)

Pierre RETY
Claude KIRCHNER
Hélène KIRCHNER
Pierre LESCANNE

Centre de Recherche en Informatique de Nancy
BP 239
54506 Vandoeuvre Les Nancy Cedex
France

1. INTRODUCTION

In this paper, an algorithm for solving equations in equational theories is proposed. Its correctness and its completeness are proved and an implementation called NARROWER is described. It is made by extending the software REVE. Some experiments are also presented. The algorithm and its implementation have the nice property that when the set of solutions is infinite, it can detect regularity and describes the solutions. We also try to show the connection of such an algorithm with the design of a logic programming language, the purpose of which is to solve equations.

We would like to explain our ideas on an example. As usual, we suppose that we provide a convergent set of rules that some people would call an "abstract data type" and others an "universe". We give an example in the classical frame of the integers. A convergent set of rules, later referred to as R, for describing properties of INTEGER is proposed in Figure 1.

In this framework, we may want to solve classical equations as we learn in high school, such as linear equations or quadratic equations. This works well with NARROWER. Suppose we would like to know the solution of the equation

$$2x - 1 = 1$$

that we code here into

$$x + x + p(0) = s(0).$$

We just type the command **narrow** followed by the equation and the system starts by adding a rule of the form

(*) This research was partly supported by the GRECO of programmation and by ADI under Grant 82/767.

```
% relations between constructors 1..2
s(p(x)) → x
p(s(x)) → x

% definitions of "+"
(0 + x) → x
(s(x) + y) → s((x + y))
(p(x) + y) → p((x + y))

% proprieties of "+"
(x + 0) → x
(x + s(y)) → s((x + y))
(x + p(y)) → p((x + y))
((x + y) + z) → (x + (y + z))

% definitions of "-"
-(0) → 0
-(s(x)) → p(-(x))
-(p(x)) → s(-(x))

% proprieties of "-"
-(-(x)) → x
(-(x) + x) → 0
x + -(x) → 0
(x + (-(x) + z)) → z
(-(x) + (x + z)) → z
-((x + y)) → (-(y) + -(x))

% definitions of "*"
(0 * x) → 0
(s(x) * y) → (y + (x * y))
(p(x) * y) → (-(y) + (x * y))

% proprieties of "*"
(x * 0) → 0
(x * s(y)) → ((x * y) + x)
(x * p(y)) → ((x * y) + -(x))
```

Figure 1. A possible specification of INTEGER.

$$x === x \rightarrow \textbf{true}$$

whose superposition with a term means that a solution is discovered. The new set of rules will be called R1. NARROWER also creates a pair of terms of the form

$$\langle t === t', \textbf{solution}(x_1,\ldots,x_n)\rangle$$

where the right-hand side is for storing parts of the substitutions. Then it is ready to compute the solution of the equations. In some cases t === t' unifies with x === x, which means that t can be made equal to t' by a substitution τ. $\tau(x_1,\ldots,x_n)$ is a solution of the equation. Otherwise the left-hand side t === t' is compared with the left-hand side g of a rule g → d in R. More precisely a unifier of g with a subterm of t is looked for. If such a unifier σ exists, say at occurrence u, then NARROWER creates a new pair of the form

<σ(t === t')[u <- σ(d)], **solution**($\sigma(x_1),\ldots,\sigma(x_n)$)>.

Usually, this last pair can be reduced by R, thus it could be more useful or more efficient to work only with the normal forms. Thus NARROWER appends a pair <s === s', **solution**($t_1,\ldots,t_n$)> where s === s', $t_1,\ldots,t_n$ are the normal forms of the previous terms. The process that goes from t === t' to s === s' is called **narrowing.** In the previous example, the system first reduces

<x + x + p(0) === s(0), **solution**(x)>

to

<p(x + x) === s(0), **solution**(x)>.

It then superposes the pair with 0 + x → x which gives

<p(0) === s(0), **solution**(0)>

that leads to no solution. It also superposes, among others, with s(x) + y → s(x + y) which gives

<p(s(x + s(x)) === s(0), **solution**(s(x))>

before reduction and

<s(x + x) === s(0), **solution**(s(x))>

after normalization. This pair superposes with 0 + x → x and produces

<s(0) === s(0), **solution**(s(0))>

which superposes with x === x → **true** yielding

<**true**, **solution**(s(0))>

showing that x / s(0) is the solution. If the equation x + x = s(0) is submitted to NARROWER, then it will answer that there is no solution. In Section 7, we will look at other examples.

In Section 2, we introduce the basic concepts and notations, including the narrowing process and the NARROWER procedure. In Section 3, we describe how this procedure can be optimized and we give more details on our implementation in Section 4. In some cases the solutions i.e., the substitutions generated by the system are infinitely many, but they usually share the same structure and can be described recursively. One of the originalities of the procedure proposed here is that it discovers regularities and suggests a recursive equation to describe infinite sets of solutions. This feature is explained in Section 5. In Section 6, we use examples to show what can be expected from such a procedure from the logic programming point of view.

2. NARROWING

In this section we introduce the concept of narrowing and show that it provides a complete method for solving equation in a theory described by a confluent and noetherian term rewriting system. The following notations and properties are valid for the whole paper. They are consistent with [8,11].

Let A be an equational theory, and R a convergent (that is confluent and noetherian) term rewriting system equivalent to A. F is the set of symbols of A, X a set of variables, and T(F, X) the set of terms on F and X. $\rightarrow$ is the rewriting relation derived from R and $t{\downarrow}R$ denotes the normal form of the term t using R.

Substitutions σ are defined as endomorphisms on T(F,X) that extend mappings from X to T(F,X) with a finite domain $D(\sigma)$. A substitution σ is denoted by $\{(x_1/t_1),\ldots,(x_n/t_n)\}$. $\sigma|W$ is the restriction of the substitution σ to the subset W of X and $I(\sigma)$ is the union of all $V(\sigma(x))$ for any x in $D(\sigma)$.

We write $<$ the subsumption quasi-ordering on M(F,X) defined by: $t<t'$ iff $t'=\sigma(t)$ for a substitution σ (called a match from t to t'). Composition of substitutions σ and ρ is denoted by $\sigma.\rho$.

Given an equational theory A, two terms t and t' are said to be A-unifiable [14,7] iff there exists a substitution σ such that $\sigma(t) =_A \sigma(t')$. σ is also called an A-solution of the equation t=t'. Given a subset V of X, we define $\sigma \leq_A \sigma'[V]$ iff $\sigma' =_A \sigma''.\sigma\ [V]$ for a substitution σ''. If V=X, V is omitted. Σ is a complete set of A-unifiers of t and t' away from W containing the set V of the variables of t and t' iff:

- for all $\sigma \in \Sigma$, $D(\sigma) \subseteq V$ and $I(\sigma) \cap W = \{\}$ (The goal of this technical restriction is only to avoid conflict between variables)
- for all $\sigma \in \Sigma$, $\sigma(t) =_A \sigma(t')$
- for all unifiers σ', there exists an $\sigma \in \Sigma$ such that $\sigma \leq_A \sigma'[V]$.
  In addition Σ is said to be minimal if it satisfies the further condition:
  for all σ and $\sigma' \in \Sigma$, $\sigma \leq_A \sigma'$ implies $\sigma=\sigma'$.

An A-unification algorithm is complete if it generates a complete set of A-unifiers. Note that this set may not be finite.

2.1. The narrowing: a method for solving equations in equational theories

The interest of the narrowing is to reduce the problem of unification in an equational theory A to the well-known problem of term unification, provided a convergent term rewriting system equivalent to A exists.

2.1.1. Definitions

Informally, the narrowing of a term consists of three steps. First, a substitution is used to create a subterm $\sigma(t)$ that matches a left hand side of a rule in R. Second, this rule is applied to $\sigma(t)$ in order to reduce it to s. The third step computes the R-normal form of s. Let us remark that if t is a term, W a finite set of variables containing V(t) and $g \rightarrow d$ a rule of R, it is always possible to rename the variables of g such that the intersection of V(g) and W is empty. W' is the union of V(g) and W.

Definition 1:[4] Let t and t' be two terms, u a non variable occurrence of t, $g \to d$ a rule of R and σ a substitution, we write

$$t \text{ -\^{}-> } t' \quad [u, g\to d, \sigma]$$

iff

- The subterm of t at the occurrence u (written $t|u$) and g are unifiable, and σ is the most general unifier of these two terms away from W'.
- $t' = \sigma(t)[u \leftarrow d]{\downarrow}R$

The substitution σ is called a **narrowing substitution**, the process that transforms t into t' is called **narrowing**, and a **narrowing derivation** (written -^*^->) is any sequence of narrowings issued from a term. The transformation of t into $\sigma(t[u\leftarrow d])$ is sometimes called **paramodulation.** We propose the name **U-reduction** (U for unification).

2.1.2. A method for equation solving

We now make clear the connection between the narrowing process and equation solving in an equational theory described by a convergent term rewriting system R. Let $t_0 = t_0'$ be the equation to be solved. The method consists of building from $(t_0 = t_0')$ all the possible narrowing derivations and to collect the corresponding narrowing substitutions, until we obtain equations $(t_n=t_n')$ such that t_n and t_n' are unifiable. The unification problem in the equational theory is then reduced to narrowing plus standard unification of terms.

To establish the correctness and the completeness of this method is the purpose of the following theorem. Correctness means that the method provides effectively solutions of the given equation $(t_0=t_0')$. Completeness means that for any solution θ, the method provides a solution σ such that σ is less than or equal to θ for the subsumption quasi-ordering $\leq_A$ on substitutions. Similar results on narrowing were established by J.M.Hullot [9,10], but only for U-reduction, while ours are for narrowing in general.

In order to iterate the narrowing process on the two terms in parallel, we introduce a special operator === which does not belong to the operator set F, and the process starts with the term t_0===t_0'. It is obvious that if t_0===t_0' -^^-> t then t can be written as t_i===t_i'.

COMPLETENESS THEOREM: Let t_0, t_0' be two terms, W a finite set of variables that contains $V(t_0) \cup V(t_0')$ and B the set of substitutions σ that satisfies the following conditions.

- There exists a narrowing derivation issued from t_0===t_0'

$$t_0\text{===}t_0' \text{ -\^{}->}[\sigma_1]\ t_1\text{===}t_1' \text{ -\^{}->}[\sigma_2] \ \ldots \text{ -\^{}->}[\sigma_n]\ t_n\text{===}t_n'$$

such that the substitutions $\sigma_1,\ldots,\sigma_n$ are away from W, t_n and t_n' are unifiable by the most general unifier β away from W
- $\sigma = \beta.\sigma_n\ldots\sigma_1$ [W]

Then B is a complete set of R-unifiers of t_0 and t_0' away from W.

The theorem is still valid if the narrowing is restricted to normalized substitutions $(\sigma_i \ldots \sigma_1)|W$.

Theoretically the process can be seen as building a tree whose nodes are labeled by equations and whose edges are labeled by substitutions. The equations are those successively generated by the narrowing process and the substitutions are the narrowing substitutions used at each step to get the corresponding equation. A solution can be seen as a path of the tree leading to a node labeled by an equation whose members are unifiable. Such a node is called successful. This tree, hereafter called **narrowing tree**, can be infinite.

2.2. A narrowing procedure

We propose here a narrowing procedure. Clearly two operations enable us to perform the method: normalization and overlapping (also called superposition). Let us first remind the notion of overlapping and the related concept of critical pairs.

Definition 2: Let (l,r) and (g,d) be two directed pairs of terms such that

- V(l) and V(g) are disjoint
- g overlaps l at the occurrence u with the substitution σ iff σ is the most general unifier away from V(l) U V(g) of the term g and the subterm of l at the occurrence u.

The pair of terms (σ(l[u←d]), σ(r)) is called a critical pair of the pair (g,d) on the pair (l, r) at the occurrence u. In what follows the pair (g,d) will often be built from a rule g→d.

In the narrowing process, the rules of R are overlapped on the terms t===t' and normalizations are performed using R. On the other hand we are interested in recording the values substituted to the variables of t and t'. For this purpose, we consider directed pairs (u===u', **solution**$(\sigma(x_1),\ldots,\sigma(x_n))$) where === and **solution** are new function symbols, $x_1,\ldots,x_n$ are the variables of t and t', and σ is the composition of the narrowing substitutions. Such a pair can be interpreted as follows: in the context where the values of $x_1,\ldots x_n$ are respectively $\sigma(x_1),\ldots,\sigma(x_n)$, the initial equation is equivalent to u===u', which means that both have the same set of solutions. The normalized left-hand side of a critical pair obtained by overlapping a rule of R on such a pair can be interpreted as the result of one step of narrowing, while its right-hand side is the new values of the variables $x_1,\ldots,x_n$. The narrowing process provides a solution as soon as t and t' are unifiable. For this purpose, we add to R the rule x===x → **true**. Notice that the new term rewriting system R U {x===x → **true**} denoted Rl is always convergent. Overlapping this rule on a pair produces the critical pair (**true**, **solution**$(\theta(x_1),\ldots,\theta(x_n))$) and θ can be interpreted as a solution of the initial equation.

2.2.1. The procedure

Let t_0 and t_0' be the terms to unify, $W = V(t_0) \cup V(t_0') = \{x_1,\ldots,x_n\}$. The parameters of the procedure are a convergent term rewriting system $Rl = R \cup$ {x===x → **true**}, a set C of directed pairs (t===t', **solution**$(\sigma(x_1),\ldots,\sigma(x_n))$) and a set P of critical pairs obtained by overlapping rules of Rl into directed pairs of C.

Each element of C is obtained by normalizing a critical pair in P. Its left part can be understood as the label of a node in the narrowing tree, while its right part can be seen as the path which leads to this node. Figure 2 gives a description of the NARROWER procedure.

```
Initialization
R1 = R U { x===x → true }
C = {(t0===t0', solution(x1,...,xn)}
P = {}

NARROWER(P, R1, C)
  if P is not empty
    then choose a critical pair (p, q) in P
         g = p↓R, d = q↓R
         NARROWER(P - {(p, q)}, R1, C U {(g, d)})
    else if all the critical pairs between the left-hand sides in C and R1
            have been computed
            then STOP
            else choose a directed pair (l, r) of C
                 with which critical pairs have not been computed
                 P = CRITICAL_PAIRS((l, r), R1)
                 NARROWER(P, R1, C)
            endif
    endif
end
```

Figure 2. NARROWER

CRITICAL_PAIRS((l, r), R1) computes the critical pairs of all the rules of R1 on l. We always suppose that the strategy for choosing the pairs of C in order to compute critical pairs satisfies the following fairness hypothesis.

Fairness hypothesis:

Let H be the union (possibly infinite) of the values of the parameter C at each recursive call of NARROWER. For any directed pair (l, r) in H, there exists eventually a recursive call such that (l, r) is chosen so that CRITICAL_PAIRS((l, r), R1) is called.

This hypothesis is necessary to insure the completeness of the procedure. Now notice two facts. NARROWER never adds rules in R1 and the directed pairs (l, r) of C could not be considered as rewrite rules because V(l) does not always contain V(r).

The proof of the NARROWER procedure consists of two steps: correctness and completeness. NARROWER is correct in the sense that with any pair in H, we can associate a narrowing derivation issued from t_0===t_0'. NARROWER is complete: that is, any term issued from t_0===t_0' by a narrowing derivation is produced by the procedure in H. From these two results we deduce that NARROWER correctly simulates the narrowing process. Hence the following theorem can be stated:

VALIDITY THEOREM:

The set of solutions of the procedure NARROWER applied on t_0 and t_0' is a complete set of R-unifiers of t_0 and t_0'.

3. OPTIMIZATIONS

The aim of this section is to find optimizations of the NARROWER procedure. This means to decide that in some cases, the subtree issued from a given node in the narrowing tree is redundant and can be dropped without loosing the completeness of the returned set of unifiers.

Such optimizations have been studied in automatic theorem proving and logic programming. One of them is subsumption. This plays the same role as the simplification of a left-hand side of a rule in term rewriting system. A rule $g \to d$ is said simplifiable by $g' \to d'$ if a subterm of g is an instance of g'. The question then arises to know whether such simplifications can be performed in the narrowing process in order to restrict the narrowing tree. But care must be taken to avoid loosing the completeness. Let us give an example of such a situation.

Example: Integers modulo 2. To transform the integers of the introduction into the integers modulo 2, let us add the axiom of + : $x + x = 0$ directed into the rule $x + x \to 0$. The resulting term rewriting system is still convergent and the narrowing process may be used to solve the equation $0 = (x + y)$. Among other possible solutions, the process will generate the following narrowing derivations:

```
0 = (x + y) -^^->[y\0] 0 = x  -^^->[x\0] 0 = 0      (1)
            -^^->[y\x] 0 = 0                         (2)
```

with the corresponding solutions:

(1) (x=0, y=0)
(2) (y=x)

NARROWER creates two pairs:

(0 === 0, **solution**(0,0)
(0 === 0, **solution**(x,x)

and since they have the same left-hand side, the first, is "useless". But care must be taken that also the set of solutions is subsumed, otherwise solutions can be lost this way. We know example where this can happen.

Restricting the kind of allowed simplifications, we propose here the following optimization: if NARROWER generates two directed pairs such that one is an instance of the other, the first one is useless. This is equivalent to say that the subtree issued from the first node does not lead to new solutions in the narrowing tree. More formally:

SUBSUMPTION THEOREM:

Let c_i and c_j be two pairs such that $c_i = (b_i, \delta_i)$, $c_j = (b_j, \delta_j)$, $b_i = \theta(b_j)$ and $\delta_i = \theta.\delta_j$. Then c_i can be dropped without loosing the completeness of the set of unifiers.

Let us now give an example where the hypotheses of the theorem are satisfied:

Example: Let R be the convergent rewriting system $\{g(f(x,x),0) \to g(x,0)$, $g(g(f(x,x),y),z) \to g(g(x,y),z)$ and $(g(f(x_1,x_2),0)$ === $g(g(f(x_1,x_2),x_3),x_4))$ the equation to be solved,

By narrowing two equations are found:

$g(x_1,0) === g(g(x_1,0),x_4)$

when using the narrowing substitution $(x_2/x_1,x_3/0)$ and the first rule at occurrence 1 in the right-hand side of the equation and

$g(x_1,0) === g(g(x_1,x_3),x_4)$

when using the narrowing substitution (x_2/x_1) and the first rule at the top of the left-hand side of the equation. NARROWER generates the corresponding pairs:

$(g(x_1,0) === g(g(x_1,0),x_4))$, **solution**$(x_1,x_1,0,x_4)$

$(g(x_1,0) === g(g(x_1,x_3),x_4))$, **solution**(x_1,x_1,x_3,x_4).

With $\theta = (x_3/0)$, the hypotheses of the previous theorem are satisfied and the first pair is useless.

4. IMPLEMENTATION

The aim of this section is to show how the completion procedure has been adapted to perform narrowing and implemented as an extension of REVE [13].

Remind first that the Knuth-Bendix completion procedure attempts to transform a set of equations that defines an equational theory into an equivalent term rewriting system which is confluent, noetherian and interreduced. For this purpose, the completion procedure computes critical pairs between rules, normalizes them and directs them using a noetherian ordering on terms, in order to produce new rules. Whenever a new rule is introduced, it simplifies all the other existing rules. Thus completion and narrowing are both based on overlapping and normalization. Nevertheless let us point out some differences.

- From the proof of correctness of NARROWER, we can see that the overlapping is always computed in the left-hand side of the pair (t, **solution**$(t_1,..,t_n)$). However these directed pairs could not be made into a rule because they violate the condition on variables.

- Assume that the pair of terms (t===t', **solution**$(\sigma(x_1),...,\sigma(x_n))$) is implemented as a "rule" t===t' $\rightarrow$ **solution**$(\sigma(x_1),...,\sigma(x_n))$. Such a "rule" would never be used to reduce a term, and could not be merged into the rewriting system like in the completion procedure. Thus the directed pairs generated by overlapping are put in a set DP.

- The normalization of a critical pair is only performed using rules of R. Neither {x === x $\rightarrow$ **true**}, nor the directed pairs are used for simplification. However, as said in the previous section, subsumption tests are performed.

- Only rules of R U {x === x $\rightarrow$ **true**} are overlapped on directed pairs to produce critical pairs.

Among other functionalities, the system REVE provides an implementation of the Knuth-Bendix completion procedure. The modularity of the system enabled us to extend it by adding a new command **narrow** which solves equations by narrowing. The implementation has been derived from the Knuth-Bendix algorithm using the described modifications.

5. RECURSIVE DEFINITION OF THE SET OF SOLUTIONS

In this section we discuss the case of infinite narrowing derivations where the same equation occurs many times. We first give an example of this situation due to F.Fages [3]. Let us consider the following confluent and noetherian term rewriting system R:

$g(f(x, y)) \rightarrow g(y)$

and the following equation:

$g(x) === g(0)$

If we superpose the left-hand side of the equation with the second rule, we obtain the equation g(f(u, z)) === g(0) which normalizes to g(z) === g(0). Up to a renaming of the variables it is the same equation as the given equation. The narrowing derivation:

$$(g(x) === g(0)) \text{ -\^{}\^{}->}[x \rightarrow f(u,x)]\ (g(x) === g(0)) \text{ -\^{}\^{}->}[x \rightarrow f(u,x)] \ldots$$
$$\ldots (g(x) === g(0)) \text{ -\^{}\^{}->}[x \rightarrow f(u,x)]\ (g(x) === g(0)) \text{ -\^{}\^{}->}[x \rightarrow f(u,x)] \ldots$$

is an example of a serious difficulty with the narrowing process: it does not terminate. The purpose of this section is to give a finite description of the solutions, which allows the termination of NARROWER. To support the intuition, let us consider the narrowing tree corresponding to such a situation. There exists at least one node labeled by an equation e such that e -^+^-> e. Such a tree can be represented as a directed cyclic graph and the path corresponding to this narrowing derivation is called a loop starting at the node labeled by e. We call this kind of narrowing tree a rational narrowing tree. A finite description of a complete set of unifiers of the given equation will be obtained by looking for all the possible paths in the narrowing tree leading to a successful node.

5.1. Characterization of the loops

In what follows, we consider that we have to solve the equation e_0 = (t_0 === t_0') and that all the equations derived from e_0 by narrowing are labeled by integers 1,...,n. Different equations have different labels. This is possible since the narrowing tree is supposed to be rational and thus the set of different equations generated by NARROWER from e_0 is finite.

We denote by Loop_Eq the set of all "loop equations" e from which a narrowing derivation containing e is issued. Loop_Eq is the set of nodes where a loop starts, i.e.,

Loop_Eq = { e | e -^+^-> e and e_0 -^*^-> e}

Let End_i be the set of all the substitutions leading to the success of the narrowing process from e_i without encountering a loop equation:

End_i = { σ | e_i -^->[α_1] e_{i1} ... -^->[α_n] e_{in} such that

* e_{in} = (t === t') has θ as the most general unifier,
* for any j∈{i, il, ..., in}, e_j does not belong to Loop_Eq
* and $\sigma = \theta.\alpha_n...\alpha_1$}

An element of End_i can be seen as a path without loop, leading to a successful node and starting at the node labeled by e_i. End_0 is the set of paths without loops starting at the root and issuing at a successful node.

Let $Loop_p$ be the set of substitutions obtained from a loop in a narrowing derivation which starts from e_p.

$Loop_p$ = { σ | $\sigma = \sigma_k...\sigma_1$ such that there exist narrowing derivations

* e_0 -^*^-> e_p
* e_p -^->[σ_1] e_{p1} -^->[σ_2] ... -^->[σ_k] e_{pk} = e_p
* for k,j∈{1,...,k}, k≠j => $e_{pk} \neq e_{pj}$ (no loop)}

An element of $Loop_p$ corresponds to a path looping once which starts at the node labeled by e_p.

Let $First_p$ be the set of substitutions obtained as the first part of a narrowing derivation issued from e_0 without loop:

$First_p$ = { σ | there exists a narrowing derivation e_0 -^->[σ_1] e_{01} ... e_{0n-1} -^->[σ_n] e_{0n} such that

* $e_{0n} = e_p$
* e_p belongs to Loop_Eq
* $\sigma = \sigma_n...\sigma_1$
* for i,j∈{1,...,n} i≠j => $e_{0i} \neq e_{0j}$ (no loop)}

An element of $First_p$ corresponds to a path from the root labeled by e_0 and leading to a node where a loop starts.

For each loop equation e_p, the following set describes the interloop substitutions:

$Inter\_Loop_q$ = {σ | there exists a narrowing derivation

e_p -^->[σ_1] e_{p1} -^->[σ_2] ... -^->[σ_k] e_{pk} with

* $e_q = e_{pk}$
* e_p and e_q belong to Loop_Eq
* p ≠ q
* for i,j∈{1,...,k} i≠j => $e_{pi} \neq e_{pj}$ (no loop)}

An element of $Inter\_Loop_q$ corresponds to a path going from a node labeled by e_p where a loop starts, to another node labeled by e_q where another loop starts.

We are now ready to describe a complete set of solutions of the equation e_0. Let us define the set S_i associated to each loop equation e_i by the following recursive definition:

* S_i contains $First_i$,
* For any substitution β in $Loop_i$ and any substitution α in S_i, β.α belongs to S_i,
* For any substitution γ in $Inter\_Loop_{ji}$ and any substitution β in Sj, γ.β

belongs to S_i.

An element of S_i corresponds to a possible paths from the root to the node labeled by e_i, after possible loops at other nodes labeled by an ej.

Let Z be the set of substitutions defined by:

* Z contains End_0,
* For any substitutions α in S_i and λ in End_i, $\lambda.\alpha$ belongs to Z.

Intuitively an element of Z is either a path without loop from the root to a successful node or is decomposed into the path from the root to a node labeled by e_i where a loop starts, followed by a path leading to a successful node.

Theorem: Z is a complete set of unifiers of the equation e_0.

Proof: It is an easy consequence of the above definitions. Each element of Z is an unifier of e_0 since such an element is obtained by a narrowing derivation leading to a successful node and associated with an equation whose members are unifiable.
Conversely, let σ be a substitution issued from a narrowing derivation: $\sigma = \theta.\alpha_n...\alpha_1$ with e_0 -^->[α_1] e_1 -^->[α_2] e_2 ... -^->[α_n] en = (t_n === t_n') θ the most general unifier of t_n and t_n', where e_1, ..., en, are all the loop equations occurring in this narrowing derivation. One can see that all the substitutions α_i belong to one of the sets $First_i$, End_i, $Loop_i$ or $Inter\_loop_{ij}$. Thus σ belongs to Z. □

From this finite description of the complete set of unifiers, one can modify the NARROWER procedure in such a way that it terminates if the narrowing tree is rational. We now describe these modifications.

5.2. A rational narrowing procedure

As a consequence of the previous theorem, we remove the loops e -^+^-> e of the narrowing tree. We denote by RATIONAL_NARROWER the procedure obtained from the NARROWER procedure as follows.

In order to cut the loops, new symbols are introduced whenever a loop equation appears. Their goal is to stop the superposition process. More formally, whenever a pair (e, **solution**(t_1,...,t_n)) is generated, if e appears as a left-hand side of a directed pair of DP, then the pair (e, **solution**(t_1,...,t_n)) is replaced by (loop_e, **solution**(t_1,...,t_n)) where loop_e is a new function symbol attached to each loop equation e.

If the rational narrowing procedure terminates, that is if the narrowing tree generated is rational, then the sets $First_i$, End_i, $Loop_i$, $Inter\_loop_{ij}$ have to be computed in order to provide a complete set of unifiers of the equation. It is out of the scope of this paper to describe in details such a computation. Let us only say that it takes into account a part of the history of the computation of the narrowing tree.

6. NARROWING AND LOGIC PROGRAMMING

The main mechanism of the Prolog language is the linear resolution principle which has some similarities with the U-reduction presented here. Dershowitz was the first to point out to us [1,2] this similarity. In [5] Goguen and Meseguer presented a close idea in their language EQLOG. They all claim that the future logic programming languages will be built upon a principle that joints U-reduction from Prolog and the normalization from Functional Programming. Unfortunately "the mechanism that joins the predicate logic and equational logic features, namely narrowing, has not been implemented in a programming language context" (loc. cit.) NARROWER is an attempt to propose such tools in order to make experiments.

The main difference between the Prolog strategy and the NARROWER strategy is that Prolog only does resolution, i.e., U-reduction only at the top, when NARROWER does U-reduction followed by a step of reductions. If we assimilate the U-reduction to the resolution, we see that NARROWER performs a crucial action that simplifies the form of the expression it manipulates. Usually the U-reduction is rather expansive since it is based on unification and the reductions are much cheaper since they are based on matching. Therefore the power of NARROWER lies in mixing programming logic features to infer new facts from old ones and functional programming features to simplify the form of the new facts in order to keep them always in a more manageable form. This combination of the two strategies makes logic programming languages based on narrowing good candidates to succeed Prolog.

As usual in logic programming the universe of the program is described by a set of facts that state its basic properties. This set is also called specification of the abstract data type of the program and this specification is given in an algebraic style. In the current implementation, these properties are only equalities. They have to be presented as a noetherian and confluent set of rules. Such properties are usually provided from any presentation using the tools available in REVE. In the future it would be possible to also assert statements in the first order predicate calculus, based on Hsiang's works [6]. These statements will be equalities in the boolean ring, in other words equivalences between predicates, unlike Prolog that deals only with implications. This will require mechanisms for handling associative and commutative equations that are now present in REVEUR 3 [12]. Such mechanisms exist and we plan to extend the current attempt to this framework. Another restriction lies in the absence of sorts or types in our system. They will also be introduced in the future.

Here we would like to present our ideas on two examples, the "integers" (Figure 1) and the " map coloration" (Figure 3 in Appendix). In the introduction we have seen how to solve linear equations, here we propose to solve the quadratic equation

$$x^2 + 3x + 2 = 0$$

This is transformed into

$$\langle s(s((x * x) + x + x + x)) === 0, \textbf{solution}(x)\rangle$$

NARROWER finds the solution p(0) into two steps. A superposition for example with $p(x) + y \rightarrow p(x + y)$ yields

<s(s((p(x) * p(x)) + p(x + p(x)) + p(x)))) === 0, **solution**(x)>

that reduces to

<-(x) + ((x * x) + (x + x)) === 0, **solution**(p(x))>

and a new superposition with x + 0 → x gives the solution p(0). NARROWER finds also the solution p(p(0)), but does not terminate because it does not know that the equation has only two solutions and so it runs forever, looking for other solutions. Obviously a strategy that works depth-first and stops after finding the first solution would terminate in this case.

References

1. N. Dershowitz, "Computing With Term Rewriting Systems," Procedings of An NSF Workshop On The Rewrite Rule Laboratory, April 1984.

2. N. Dershowitz, "Equations as programming language," Fourth Jerusalem Conference on Information Technology, pp. 114-123, Jerusalem (Israel), May 1984.

3. F. Fages and G. Huet, "Unification and Matching in Equational Theories," Proceedings of CAAP 83, vol. 159, pp. 205-220, Springer Verlag, l'Aquilla, Italy, 1983.

4. M. Fay, "First-Order Unification in an Equational Theory," Proceedings of the 4th Workshop on Automated Deduction, pp. 161-167, Austin, Texas, 1979.

5. J. Goguen and J. Meseguer, "Equality, Types, Modules and Generics for Logic Programming," SRI Internal Publication, Menlo Park, 1984.

6. J. Hsiang, "Refutational Theorem Proving Using Term Rewriting Systems," Ph.D Thesis, University of Illinois, Urbana, 1981.

7. G. Huet, "Resolution d'Equations dans des Langages d'Ordre 1,2, ... ω," Thèse d'Etat, Université de Paris VII, 1976.

8. G. Huet and D. Oppen, "Equations and Rewrite Rules: A Survey," in Formal Languages: Perspectives And Open Problems, ed. Book R., Academic Press, 1980.

9. J.M. Hullot, "Canonical Forms And Unification," in Proceedings of the Fifth Conference on Automated Deduction, Lecture Notes in Computer Science, vol. 87, pp. 318-334, Springer Verlag, Les Arcs, France, July 1980.

10. J.M. Hullot, "Compilation de Formes Canoniques dans les Théories Equationnelles," Thèse de 3ème Cycle, Université de Paris Sud, 1980.

11. J. P. Jouannaud, C. Kirchner, and H. Kirchner, "Incremental Construction of Unification Algorithms in Equational Theories," in Proceedings of the International Conference On Automata, Languages and Programming, Lecture Notes in Computer Science, vol. 154, pp. 361-373, Springer Verlag, Barcelona Spain, 1983.

12. C. Kirchner and H. Kirchner, "Implementation of a General Completion Procedure Parameterized by Built-in Theories And Strategies," Rapport Crin 84-R-85, 1984.

13. P. Lescanne, "Computer Experiments with the REVE Term Rewriting System Generator," in 10th ACM Conf. on Principles of Programming Languages, pp. 99-108, Austin Texas, January 1983.

14. G. Plotkin, "Building-In Equational Theories," Machine Intelligence, vol. 7, pp. 73-90, 1972.

APPENDIX The map coloration

The map coloration is a classical problem in logic programming. Figure 3 shows the universe as it was presented to NARROWER and Figure 4 is a picture of the map. The problem that was asked to NARROWER was to find the color of a map where 1 is "b" and 2 is "y". NARROWER found the 8 possible solutions as shown in Figure 5.

```
% Boolean operations

x & ff == ff
ff & x == ff
tt & x == x
x & tt == x
(x & ( y & z)) == ((x & y) & z)

% Colors

next(b, y) == tt
next(b, g) == tt
next(b, r) == tt

next(g, y) == tt
next(g, b) == tt
next(g, r) == tt

next(y, b) == tt
next(y, g) == tt
next(y, r) == tt

next(r, y) == tt
next(r, g) == tt
next(r, b) == tt

next(x, x) == ff

% The map
```

map(x_1, x_2, x_3, x_4, x_5) == next(x_1, x_2) & next(x_1, x_3) &
next(x_1, x_5) & next(x_2, x_3) & next(x_2, x_4) & next(x_2, x_5) & next(x_3, x_4)

Figure 3. Map Coloration

```
 ---------------------------------------------------------------
|                              |                                |
|              1               |               3                |
|                              |                                |
|                              |                                |
|---------------------------------------------------------------
|                    |                    |                    |
|                    |                    |                    |
|         5          |         2          |         4          |
|                    |                    |                    |
|                    |                    |                    |
 ---------------------------------------------------------------
```

Figure 4. A map

The equation map(b, y, x_3, x_4, x_5) === tt has the set of r-unifiers as follows:

1.
x_3 / g
x_4 / b
x_5 / g

2.
x_3 / g
x_4 / b
x_5 / r

3.
x_3 / g
x_4 / r
x_5 / g

4.
x_3 / g
x_4 / r
x_5 / r

5.
x_3 / r
x_4 / g
x_5 / g

6.
x_3 / r
x_4 / g
x_5 / r

7.
x_3 / r
x_4 / b
x_5 / g

8.
x_3 / r
x_4 / b
x_5 / r

Figure 5. The answer of NARROWER to the map problem.

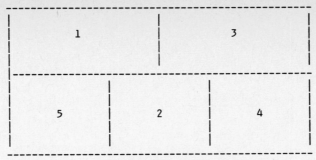

Solving Type Equations by Graph Rewriting

Hassan Ait-Kaci

Microelectronics and Computer Technology Corporation[1]
9430 Research Boulevard
Austin, Texas 78759-6509
(512) 834-3354

1. Introduction

The first part of this paper focuses on syntactic properties of record-like type structures. A syntax of structured types is introduced as labelled infinite trees, which may be seen as extrapolated from the syntax of first-order terms as used in algebraic semantics [8, 14, 15]. However, since the terms defined here are not to be interpreted as operations, the similarity is purely syntactic. A calculus of partially-ordered record structures is presented. It is then extended to variant record structures through a powerlattice construction. The second part deals with solving recursive type equations in a lattice of variant records. An operational semantics of type structure rewriting is first informally described. Then, a fixed-point semantics is discussed. Finally, a discussion of the correctness of the former with respect to the latter concludes the paper.

2. A Calculus of Type Subsumption

The notion of subtyping has recently been integrated as a feature in some programming languages, although in a limited fashion. For example, in PASCAL it is provided only for so-called *simple* types like enumeration or range types. For more complex types, in general, subtyping is not *implicitly* inferred. For example, in ADA, one must declare *explicitly* most subtyping relationships. This is true even in those formalisms like KL-ONE [5] or OBJ [11] where subtyping is a central feature. The only formalism which may be used for implicit subtyping is provided by first-order terms in PROLOG as first-order term instantiation. However, even this representation is limited as a model for partially ordered type structures. Nevertheless, it is of great inspiration for what is desired, which is a practical system of type structures which must have at least as much expressive power as offered by, say, classical record structures, as well as the capability of efficiently automating subtyping inference, and the construction of new structures from old ones.

A specific *desideratum* can be informally sketched as follows. a structured data type must have:

- a *head symbol* which determines a class of objects being restricted;
- *attributes (or fields, or slots, etc.,)* possessed by this type, which are typed by structured types themselves;
- *coreference constraints* between attributes, and attributes of attributes, *etc.*, denoting the fact that the *same* substructure is to be shared by different compositions of attributes.

Then, a type structure t_1 is a *subtype* of a type structure t_2 if and only if:

- the class denoted by the head of t_1 is contained in the class denoted by the head of t_2; *and,*
- *all* the attributes of t_2 are present in t_1 and have types which are subtypes of their counterparts in t_2; *and,*

[1]Research described in this paper was done while the author was at the University of Pennsylvania, Philadelphia.

- *all* the coreference constraints binding in t_2 are also binding in t_1.

For example, understanding the symbols student, person, philadelphia, cityname to denote sets of objects, and if student $<$ person and philadelphia $<$ cityname denote set inclusion, then the type:

```
student(id => name(last => X:string);
        lives_at => Y:address(city => philadelphia);
        father => person(id => name(last => X);
                         lives_at => Y));
```

should be a subtype of:

```
person(id => name;
       lives_at => address(city => cityname);
       father => person);
```

The letters X, Y in this example denote coreference constraints as will be explained. Formalizing the above informal wish is what this section attempts to achieve.

2.1. A Syntax of Structured Types

Let Σ be a partially ordered *signature* of *type symbols* with a *top* element $\top$, and a *bottom* element $\bot$. Let $\mathcal{L}$ be a set of *label symbols*, and let $\mathcal{T}$ be a set of *tag symbols*, both non-empty and countably infinite. I shall represent type symbols and labels by strings of characters starting with a *lower-case* letter, and tags by strings of characters starting with an *upper-case* letter.

A simple "type-as-set" semantics for these objects is elaborated in [1]. It will suffice to mention that type symbols in Σ denote sets of objects, and label symbols in $\mathcal{L}$ denote the *intension* of functions. This semantics takes the partial ordering on type symbols into set inclusion, and label concatenation as function composition. Thus, the syntax of terms introduced next can be interpreted as describing commutative composition diagrams of attributes.

In a manner akin to tree addressing as defined in [8, 12, 13], I define a *term domain on* $\mathcal{L}$ to be the *skeleton* built from label symbols of a such a commutative diagram. This is nothing but the graph of arrows that one draws to picture functional maps. Formally,

Definition 1: A *term (or tree) domain* Δ on $\mathcal{L}$ is a set of finite strings of labels of $\mathcal{L}$ such that:

- Δ is *prefix-closed; i.e.,* if $u, v \in \mathcal{L}^*$ and $u.v \in \Delta$ then $u \in \Delta$;
- Δ is *finitely branching; i.e.,* if $u \in \Delta$, then the set $\{u.a \in \Delta \mid a \in \mathcal{L}\}$ is finite.

It follows from this definition that the empty string e must belong to all term domains. Elements of a term domain are called *(term) addresses*. Addresses in a domain which are not the prefix of any other address in the domain are called *leaves*. The empty string is called the *root* address. For example, if $\mathcal{L}$ = {id, born, day, month, year, first, last, father}, a term-domain on $\mathcal{L}$ may be Δ_1 = {e, born, born.day, born.month, born.year, id, id.last, father, father.id, father.id.first}. A term domain need not be finite; for instance, the regular expression Δ_2 = a(ba)*+(ab)*, where a, b $\in \mathcal{L}$, denotes a regular set (on {a,b}, say) which is closed under prefixes, and finitely branching; thus, it is a term domain and it is infinite.

Given a term domain Δ, an address w in Δ, we define the *sub-domain of* Δ *at address* w to be the term domain $\Delta\backslash w = \{w' \mid w.w' \in \Delta\}$. In the last example, the sub-domain at address born of Δ_1 is the set {e, day, month, year}, and the sub-domain of Δ_2 at address a.b is Δ_2 itself.

Definition 2: A term domain Δ is a *regular* term domain if the set of all sub-domains of Δ defined as **Subdom**$(\Delta) = \{\Delta\backslash w \mid w \in \Delta\}$ is finite.

In the previous examples, the term domain Δ_1 is a finite (regular) term domain, and Δ_2 is a regular infinite term domain since **Subdom**$(\Delta_2) = \{\Delta_2, b.\Delta_2\}$. In what follows, I will consider only regular term-domains.

The "flesh" that goes on the skeleton defined by a term domain consists of signature symbols labelling the nodes which are arrow extremities. Keeping the "arrow graph" picture in mind, this stands for information about the origin and destination sets of the arrow representation of functions. As for notation, I proceed to introduce a specific syntax of terms as record-like structures. Thus, a term has a *head* which is a type symbol, and a *body* which is a (possibly empty) list of pairs associating labels with terms in a unique fashion -- an *association list*. An example of such an object is shown in figure 2-1.

```
person(id => name;
       born => date(day => integer;
                    month => monthname;
                    year => integer);
       father => person);
```

Figure 2-1: An example of a term structure

The domain of a term is the set of addresses which explicitly appear in the expression of the term. For example, the domain of the above term is the set of addresses {e, id, born, born.day, born.month, born.year, father}.

The example in figure 2-1 shows a possible description of what one may intend to use as a structure for a person. The terms associated with the labels are to *restrict* the types of possible values that may be used under each label. However, there is no explicit constraint, in this particular structure, *among* the sub-structures appearing under distinct labels. For instance, a person bearing a last-name which is not the same as his father's would be a legal instance of this structure. In order to capture this sort of constraints, one can *tag* the addresses in a term structure, and *enforce* identically tagged addresses to be identically instantiated. For example, if in the above example one is to express that a person's father's last-name must be the same as that person's last-name, a better representation may be the term in figure 2-2.

```
person(id => name(last => X:string);
       born => date(day => integer;
                    month => monthname;
                    year => integer);
       father => person(id => name(last => X:string)));
```

Figure 2-2: An example of tagging in a term structure

Definition 3: A *term* is a triple (Δ, ψ, τ) where Δ is a term domain on $\mathcal{L}$, ψ is a *symbol* function from $\mathcal{L}^*$ to Σ such that $\psi(\mathcal{L}^* - \Delta) = \{\top\}$, and τ is a *tag* function from Δ to $\mathcal{T}$. A term is finite (*resp.* regular) if its domain is finite (*resp.* regular).

Such a definition illustrated for the term in figure 2-2 is captured in the table in figure 2-3. Note the *"syntactic sugar"* implicitly used in figure 2-2. Namely, I shall omit writing explicitly tags for addresses which are not sharing theirs. In the sequel, by "term" it will be meant "regular term".

Given a term $t = (\Delta, \psi, \tau)$, an address w in Δ, the *subterm of t at address* w is the term $t \backslash w = (\Delta \backslash w, \psi \backslash w, \tau \backslash w)$ where $\psi \backslash w\colon \mathcal{L}^* \to \Sigma$ and $\tau \backslash w\colon \Delta \backslash w \to \mathcal{T}$ are defined by:

- $\psi \backslash w(w') = \psi(w.w') \ \forall w' \in \mathcal{L}^*$;
- $\tau \backslash w(w') = \tau(w.w') \ \forall w' \in \Delta \backslash w$.

From these definitions, it is clear that $t \backslash e$ is the same as t. In example of figure 2-2, the subterm at address father.id is name(last => X:string).

Given a term $t = (\Delta, \psi, \tau)$, a symbol f, (*resp.*, a tag X, a term t') is said to *occur* in t if there is an address w

Addresses (Δ)	*Symbols* (ψ)	*Tags* (τ)
e	person	X_0
id	name	X_1
id.last	string	X
born	date	X_2
born.day	integer	X_3
born.month	monthname	X_4
born.year	integer	X_5
father	person	X_6
father.id	name	X_7
father.id.last	string	X

Figure 2-3: (Δ, ψ, τ)-definition of the term in figure 2-2

in Δ such that $\psi(w) = f$ (*resp.*, $\tau(w) = X$, $t\backslash w = t'$). The following proposition is immediate and follows by definition.[2] .

Proposition 4: Given a term $t = (\Delta, \psi, \tau)$, the following statements are equivalent:

- t is a regular term;
- The number of subterms occurring in t is finite;
- The number of symbols occurring in t is finite;
- The number of tags occurring in t is finite.

It follows that a coreference relation on a regular term domain has finite index.

Definition 5: In a term, any two addresses bearing the same tag are said to corefer. Thus, the *coreference* relation κ of a term $t = (\Delta, \psi, \tau)$ is a relation defined on Δ as the *kernel* of the tag function τ; *i.e.*, $\kappa = \mathrm{Ker}(\tau) = \tau \bullet \tau^{-1}$.

We immediately note that κ is an equivalence relation since it is the kernel of a function. A κ-class is called a *coreference class*. For example, in the term in figure 2-2, the addresses father.id.last and id.last corefer.

A term t is *referentially consistent* if the same subterm occurs at all addresses in a coreference class. That is, if C is a coreference class in Δ/κ then $t\backslash w$ is *identical* for *all* addresses w in C. Thus, if a term is referentially consistent, then by definition for any w_1, w_2 in Δ, if $\tau(w_1) = \tau(w_2)$ then for all w such that $w_1.w \in \Delta$, necessarily $w_2.w \in \Delta$ also, and $\tau(w_1.w) = \tau(w_2.w)$. Therefore, if a term is referentially consistent, κ is in fact more than a simple equivalence relation: it is a *right-invariant* equivalence, or a *right-congruence*, on Δ. That is, for any two addresses w_1, w_2, if $w_1 \kappa w_2$ then $w_1.w \kappa w_2.w$ for any w such that $w_1.w \in \Delta$ and $w_2.w \in \Delta$.

Definition 6: A *well-formed term* (wft) is a term which is referentially consistent.

I shall use this property to justify another syntactic "sweetness": whenever a tag occurs in a term without a subterm, what is meant is that the subterm elsewhere referred to in the term by an address bearing this tag is implicitly present. If there is no such subterm, the implicit subterm is $\top$. For example, in the term $\mathrm{foo}(l_1 \Rightarrow X;\ l_2 \Rightarrow X{:}\mathrm{bar};\ l_3 \Rightarrow Y;\ l_4 \Rightarrow Y)$, the subterm at address l_1 is bar, and the subterm at address l_4 is $\top$. In what follows, $\top$ will never be written explicitly in a term.

Note that it is quite possible to consider *infinite* terms such as shown in figure 2-4. For example, at the addresses father and father.son.father, is a phenomenon which I call *cyclic tagging*.

Syntactically, cycles may also be present in more pathological ways such as pictured in figure 2-5, where one must follow a path of cross-references.

---

[2] Also established in [8]

```
person(id => name(last => X:string);
       born => date(day => integer;
                    month => monthname;
                    year => integer);
       father => Y:person(id => name(last => X:string);
                          son => person(father => Y)));
```

Figure 2-4: An example of simple cyclic tagging in a term structure

```
foo(l_1 => X_1:foo_1(k_1 => X_2);
    l_2 => X_2:foo_2(k_2 => X_3);
    ...
    l_i => X_i:foo_i(k_i => X_i+1);
    ...
    l_n => X_n:foo_n(k_n => X_1));
```

Figure 2-5: An example of complex cyclic tagging in a term structure

A term is *referentially acyclic* if there is no cyclic tagging occurring in the term. A *cyclic term* is one which is not referentially acyclic. Thus, the terms in figures 2-4 and 2-5 are *not* referentially acyclic. A wft is then best pictured as a *labelled directed graph* as illustrated in figure 2-6 which is the *graph representation* of the wft below. Thus, labels act as arcs between nodes bearing type symbols. Tags are *physical pointers* to nodes, indicating which nodes are shared.

```
X_0:f_1(l_1 => X_1:f_2(l_2 => X_2;
                       l_3 => f_3);
        l_4 => X_2;
        l_5 => f_4(l_6 => X_1;
                   l_7 => X_3:f_5;
                   l_8 => X_3);
                   l_9 => X_0))
```

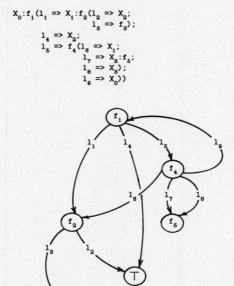

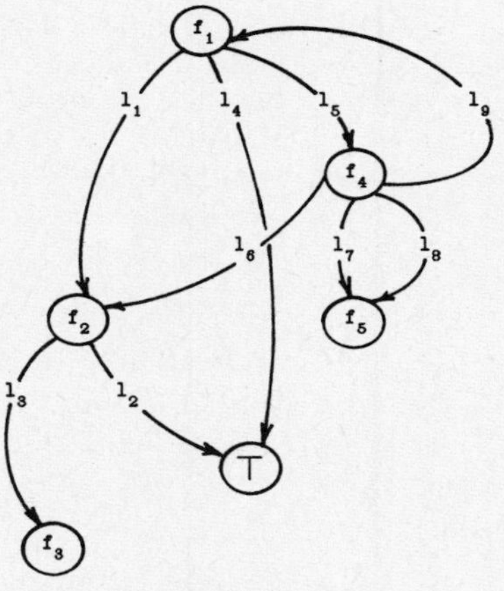

Figure 2-6: Graph representation of a wft

In figure 2-6, the similarity with finite states diagrams is not coincidental. And thus, it follows that a term is referentially acyclic if and only if its term domain is finite. Also, any term (cyclic or not) expressed in the above syntax is a regular term.

The set of well-formed terms is denoted $\mathcal{WFT}$. The set of well-formed acyclic terms is denoted $\mathcal{WFAT}$ and is a subset of $\mathcal{WFT}$.

I shall not give any semantic value to the tags aside from the coreference classes they define. The following relation α on $\mathcal{WFT}$ is to handle *tag renaming*. This means that α is relating wft's which are identical up to a renaming of the tags which preserves the coreference classes.

Definition 7: Two terms $t_1 = (\Delta_1, \psi_1, \tau_1)$ and $t_2 = (\Delta_2, \psi_2, \tau_2)$ are *alphabetical variants* of one another (noted $t_1 \ \alpha \ t_2$) if and only if:

1. $\Delta_1 = \Delta_2$;
2. $\mathrm{Ker}(\tau_1) = \mathrm{Ker}(\tau_2)$;
3. $\psi_1 = \psi_2$.

Interpreting these structures as commutative diagrams betweens sets, it comes that the symbols $\top$ and $\bot$ denote, respectively, the whole universe -- *"anything"* -- and the empty set -- *"inconsistent"*. Hence, a term in which the symbol $\bot$ occurs is to be interpreted as being inconsistent. To this end, we can define a relation $\Downarrow$ on $\mathcal{WFT}$ -- *smashing* --, where $t_1 \Downarrow t_2$ if and only if $\bot$ occurs in both t_1 *and* t_2, to be such that all equivalence classes except $[\bot]$ are *singletons*. Clearly, if $\bot$ occurs in a term, it also occurs in all terms in its α-class. In the way they have been defined, the relations α and $\Downarrow$ are such that their *union* $\approx \, = \alpha \cup \Downarrow$ is an equivalence relation. Thus,

Definition 8: A *ψ-type* is an element of the quotient set $\Psi = \mathcal{WFT}/\approx$. An *acyclic* ψ-type is an element of the quotient set $\Psi_0 = \mathcal{WFAT}/\approx$.

2.2. The Subsumption Ordering

The partial ordering on symbols can be extended to terms in a fashion which is reminiscent of the algebraic notion of *homomorphic extension*. I define the *subsumption* relation on the set Ψ as follows.

Definition 9: A term $t_1 = (\Delta_1, \psi_1, \tau_1)$ *is subsumed* by a term $t_2 = (\Delta_2, \psi_2, \tau_2)$ (noted $t_1 \preceq t_2$), if and only if *either*, $t_1 \approx \bot$; *or*,

1. $\Delta_2 \subseteq \Delta_1$;
2. $\mathrm{Ker}(\tau_2) \subseteq \mathrm{Ker}(\tau_1)$;
3. $\psi_1(w) \leq \psi_2(w), \ \forall w \in \mathcal{L}^*$.

It is easy to verify that a subsumption relation on Ψ defined by $[t_1] \preceq [t_2]$ if and only if $t_1 \preceq t_2$ is well-defined (*i.e.*, it does not depend on particular class representatives) and it is an *ordering* relation.[3]

This notion of subsumption is related to the (in)famous *IS-A* ordering in semantic networks [5, 6], and the *tuple ordering* in the so-called semantic relation data model [4]. It expresses the fact that, given a ψ-type t, any ψ-type t' defined on at least the same domain, with at least the same coreference classes, and with symbols at each address which are less than the symbols in t at the corresponding addresses, is a subtype of t. Indeed, such a t' is *more specified* than t.

The "homomorphic" extension of the ordering on Σ to the subsumption ordering on Ψ can be exploited further. Indeed, if *least upper bounds* (LUB) and *greatest lower bounds* (GLB) are defined for any subsets of Σ, then this property carries over to Ψ.

Theorem 10: If the signature Σ is a lattice, then so is Ψ.

Rather than giving formal definitions for the meet and join operations on Ψ, let us illustrate the extended lattice

[3]In the sequel, I shall use the (*abusive*) convention of denoting a ψ-type by one of its class representatives, understanding that what is meant is modulo *tag renaming* and *smashing*.

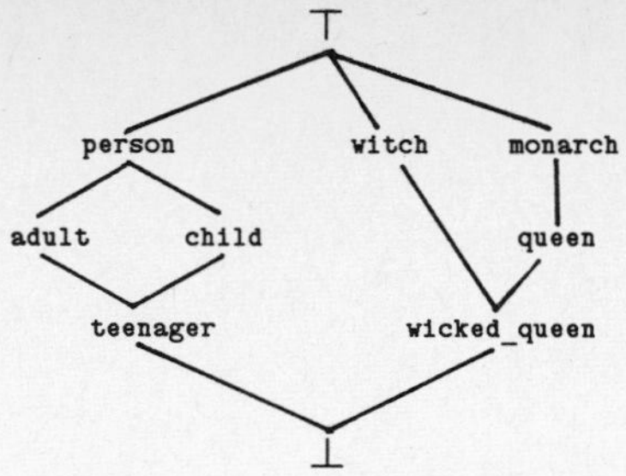

Figure 2-7: A signature which is a lattice

operations with an example. Figure 2-7 shows a signature which is a finite (non-modular) lattice. Given this signature, the two types in figure 2-8 admit as meet and join the types in figure 2-9.

```
child(knows => X:person(knows => queen;
                        hates => Y:monarch);
      hates => child(knows => Y;
                     likes => wicked_queen);
      likes => X);

adult(knows => adult(knows => witch);
      hates => person(knows => X:monarch;
                      likes => X));
```

Figure 2-8: Two wft's

```
person(knows => person;
       hates => person(knows => monarch;
                       likes => monarch));

teenager(knows => X:adult(knows => wicked_queen;
                          hates => Y:wicked_queen);
         hates => child(knows => Y;
                        likes => Y);
         likes => X);
```

Figure 2-9: LUB and GLB of the two types in figure 2-8

The reader is referred to [1] for the detailed definitions of the meet and join operation on Ψ. It suffices here to say that they are essentially extensions of the *unification* [15, 20] and *generalization* [19] operations on regular first-order terms. Indeed, these operations are special cases of my definitions when *(i)* Σ is a *flat* lattice, *(ii)* a coreference class may contain more than one element *iff* all of its elements are leaves and the symbols occurring at these leaves are restricted to be $\top$.

An important remark is that the set Ψ_0 of acyclic ψ-types also has a lattice structure.

Theorem 11: If Σ is a lattice, then so is Ψ_0. However Ψ_0 is *not* a sublattice of Ψ.

The join operation is the same, but the meet operation is modified so that if the GLB in Ψ of two acyclic terms contains a cycle, then their GLB in Ψ_0 is $\perp$. However, Ψ_0 is not a sublattice of Ψ, since the meet in Ψ of two acyclic wft's is not necessarily acyclic. Consider, for example[4]

$$t_1 = \mathtt{f}(l_1 \Rightarrow X : \mathtt{f};\ l_2 \Rightarrow \mathtt{f}(l_3 \Rightarrow X))$$

$$t_2 = \mathtt{f}(l_1 \Rightarrow X : \mathtt{f};\ l_2 \Rightarrow X)$$

$$t_1 \wedge t_2 = \mathtt{f}(l_1 \Rightarrow X : \mathtt{f}(l_3 \Rightarrow X)\ ;\ l_2 \Rightarrow X)$$

2.3. A Distributive Lattice of Types

Accepting the "type-as-set" interpretation of the calculus of ψ-types, it is yet necessary to wonder whether lattice-theoretic properties of meet and join reflect those of intersection and union. Unfortunately, this is not the case with Ψ. The lattice of ψ-types is not so convenient as to be ***distributive***, even if the signature Σ is itself distributive. As a counter-example, consider the flat (distributive) lattice $\Sigma = \{\top,\ \mathtt{a},\ \mathtt{f},\ \bot\}$. Indeed,

$$\mathtt{f} \wedge (\mathtt{f}(l \Rightarrow \mathtt{a}) \vee \mathtt{a}) = \mathtt{f}$$

$$(\mathtt{f} \wedge \mathtt{f}(l \Rightarrow \mathtt{a})) \vee (\mathtt{f} \wedge \mathtt{a}) = \mathtt{f}(l \Rightarrow \mathtt{a})$$

and this proves that $\mathcal{WFT}$ is not distributive.[5]

This is not the only ailment of $\mathcal{WFT}$ as a type system. Recall that in order to obtain the benefit of a lattice structure as stated in theorem 10, there is a rather strong demand that the type signature Σ be itself a lattice. For a signature that would be any poset, this nice result is unfortunately lost. In practice, programs deal with finite sets of primitive types. Even then, it would be quite unreasonable to require that all meets and joins of those primitive types be explicitly defined. What should be typically specified in a program is the minimal amount of type information which is to be relevant to the program. Clearly, such a signature of type symbols should be not necessarily more than a finite incompletely specified poset of symbols.

It is hence necessary to go further than the construction of $\mathcal{WFT}$ in order to obtain a satisfactory type system which would not make unreasonable demand for primitive type information. Fortunately, it is possible not to impose so drastic demands on Σ and yet construct a more powerful lattice than $\mathcal{WFT}$; *i.e.,* a distributive lattice. The idea is very simple, and is based on observing that the join operation in Ψ is too "greedy". Indeed, if one wants to specify that an object is of type `foo` or `bar` when no explicit type symbol in Σ is known as their GLB, then $\top$ is returned. Clearly, it is not correct to infer that the given object is of type *"anything"* just because Σ does not happen to contain explicitly a symbol for the GLB `foo` and `bar`. All that can be correctly said is that the given object is of *disjunctive* type $\mathtt{foo}\vee\mathtt{bar}$.

I next give a brief summary of a construction of such a more adequate type lattice. It may be construed as a powerdomain construction to handle indeterminacy [17]; in our case, ***variant records***. It is not possible to detail this construction here. The interested reader is referred to [1].

A poset is *Noetherian* if it does not contain infinitely ascending chains. Given a set S, the set $\mathfrak{L}^{(S)}$ of finite non-empty subsets of ***maximal elements*** of S is called the ***restricted power of*** S. If S is a Noetherian poset, the set $\mathfrak{L}^{[S]}$ of *all* such subsets of maximal elements is called the *complete* restricted power of S. Given a Noetherian poset S, and $S' \subseteq S$, $\Re(S')$ is the set of maximal elements of S'.

I shall call £ the set $\mathfrak{L}^{[\Psi]}$, and $£_0$ the set $\mathfrak{L}^{[\Psi_0]}$. Clearly, $£_0$ is a subset of £. I shall denote a singleton `{t}` in £ simply by `t`.

---

[4]A similar phenomenon happens in unification of first-order terms where it is reason for the so-called *"occur-check"* testing whether a variable occurs in a term when trying to unify that variable with the term.

[5]A similar result was pointed out by G.Plotkin in [18].

Definition 12: Subsumption in $\pounds$ is defined by, $T_1 \sqsubseteq T_2$ if and only if *every* ψ-type in T_1 is subsumed by *some* ψ-type in T_2.

Let's define a notational variant of elements of $\pounds$ which will have the advantage of being more *compact* syntactically. Consider the object shown in figure 2-10. The syntax used is similar to the one which has expressed ψ-types up to now. However, *sets* of terms rather that terms may occur at some addresses.

```
person(sex => {male, female};
       father => Y:person(sex => male);
       mother => Z:person(sex => female);
       parent => {Y, Z});
```

Figure 2-10: Example of a ϵ-term

This notation may be viewed as a compact way of representing a sets of ψ-types. For example, the object in figure 2-10 represents a set of *four* ψ-types which can be obtained by expansion, keeping *one* element at each address. Such terms are called ϵ-terms. An ϵ-term can be transformed into a set of ψ-types -- its *ψ-expansion*; *i.e.*, the ψ-expansion of an ϵ-term is the set of all possible ψ-types which can be inductively obtained by keeping only one ψ-type at each address. The reader familiar with first-order logic could construe this process as being similar to transforming a logical formula into its disjunctive normal form.

We are now ready to construct a distributive lattice of ϵ-types. First, we relax the demand that the signature Σ be lattice. Assuming it is a Noetherian poset we can embed it in a meet-semilattice $2^{[\Sigma]}$ preserving existing GLB's. Then, we can define the meet operation on Ψ so that whenever the meet of two symbols in not a singleton, the result is expanded using ψ-expansion.

Theorem 13: If the signature Σ is a Noetherian poset then so is the lattice Ψ_0; but the lattice Ψ is *not* Noetherian.

The following counter-example exhibits an infinitely ascending chain of wfts in Ψ. For any a in $\mathcal{L}$ and any f in Σ, define the sequence $t_n = (\Delta_n, \psi_n, \tau_n), n \geq 1$ as follows:

$$\Delta_n = a^*;$$

$$\psi_n(\Delta_n) = f;$$

$$\Delta_n/\kappa_n = \Delta_n/\mathrm{Ker}(\tau_n) = \{\{e\}, \{a\}, \ldots, \{a^{n-1}\}, a^n.a^*\}.$$

This clearly defines an infinite strictly ascending sequence of regular wft's since, for all $n \geq 0$:

$$\Delta_{n+1} \subseteq \Delta_n;$$

$$\psi_n(\Delta_n) \leq \psi_{n+1}(\Delta_{n+1});$$

$$\kappa_{n+1} \subset \kappa_n.$$

In our syntax, this corresponds to the sequence:

```
t0 = X : f(a => X),

t1 = f(a => X : f(a => X)),

t2 = f(a => f(a => X : f(a => X))), ... ,

tn = f(a => f(a => ... f(a => X : f(a => X))...)), ...
           <---- n+1 a's ---->
```

We define two binary operations $\sqcap$ and $\sqcup$ on the set $\pounds_0$. For any two sets T_1 and T_2 in $\pounds_0$:

$$T_1 \sqcap T_2 = \Re(\{t \mid t = t_1 \wedge t_2,\ t_1 \in T_1,\ t_2 \in T_2\});$$

$$T_1 \sqcup T_2 = \Re(T_1 \cup T_2).$$

where $\wedge$ is the meet operation defined on Ψ_0. Then, for *any* poset Σ containing $\top$ and $\bot$,

> **Theorem 14:** The poset $\mathcal{L}_0$ is a *distributive* lattice whose meet is $\sqcap$, whose join is $\sqcup$, and whose top and bottom are $\{\top\}$ and $\{\bot\}$.

It is not possible to define lattice operations for $\mathcal{L}$ because Ψ is not Noetherian. Hence, the set of maximal elements of a set cannot be defined for *all* sets. However, if only finite sets of regular wft's are considered, then:

> **Theorem 15:** The poset $\mathcal{Q}^{(\Psi)}$ of *finite* sets of incomparable regular wft's is a distributive lattice.

However, it is not complete. It is also true that $\mathcal{Q}^{(\Psi_0)} \subseteq \mathcal{Q}^{(\Psi)}$ and $\mathcal{Q}^{(\Psi_0)}$ is a distributive lattice, but it is not a sublattice of $\mathcal{L}$. In general, the GLB of elements of $\mathcal{Q}^{(\Psi_0)}$ is a lower bound of the GLB of these elements taken in $\mathcal{Q}^{(\Psi)}$.

A *Brouwerian lattice* L is a lattice such that for any given elements a and b, the set $\{x \in L \mid a \wedge x \leq b\}$ contains a greatest element, written as $a \rightarrow b$. An interesting point is that *(i)* any Brouwerian lattice is distributive but, *not conversely*; and *(ii)* any Boolean lattice is Brouwerian, but *not conversely* [3]. Thus, the class of Brouwerian lattices lies strictly *between* the class of distributive lattices and the class of Boolean lattices.

> **Theorem 16:** If the signature Σ is a Noetherian poset then the lattice $\mathcal{L}_0$ of *all* sets of finite wfts is a complete Brouwerian lattice.

To answer the question that might be hovering in the reader's mind,[6] the fact that the lattice $\mathcal{L}_0$ is a complete Brouwerian lattice reveals itself invaluable for showing the existence of solutions to systems of equations. Apart from its lattice theoretic properties, a Brouwerian lattice is interesting as it forms the basis of an *intuitionistic* propositional logic, due to L.E.J.Brouwer [7, 10].

Unfortunately, theorem 16 does not hold for $\mathcal{L}$ the lattice of all regular terms since the lattice $\mathcal{L}$ is not complete. On the other hand, I do not know whether $\mathcal{L}$ is Brouwerian.

3. Programs as Recursive Type Equations

Consider the equations in figure 3-1. Each equation is a pair made of a symbol and an ϵ-term, and may intuitively be understood as a *definition*. I shall call a set of such definitions a *knowledge base*.[7]

> **Definition 17:** A *knowledge base* is a function from $\Sigma - \{\bot\}$ to $\mathcal{L}_0$ which is the identity almost everywhere except for a finite number of symbols.

So far, the partial order on Σ has been assumed predefined. However, given a knowledge base, it is quite easy to quickly infer what I shall call its *implicit symbol ordering*. For example, examining the knowledge base in figure 3-1, it is evident that the signature Σ must contain the set of symbols {list, cons, nil, append, append_0, append_1}, and that the partial ordering on Σ is such that nil < list, cons < list, append_0 < append, append_1 < append. In general, this ordering can always be extracted from the specification of a knowledge base.

> **Definition 18:** A knowledge base is *well-defined* if and only if it admits an implicit symbol ordering.

---

[6]Namely, *"So what?..."*

[7]Or *program*, or *type environment*... Nevertheless, *knowledge base* is a deliberate choice since what is defined is in essence an *abstract semantic network*.

```
list = {nil, cons};

append = {append_0, append_1};

append_0 =
      (front => nil;
       back => X:list;
       whole => X);

append_1 =
      (front => cons(head => X; tail => Y);
       back => Z:list;
       whole => cons(head => X; tail => U);
       patch => append(front => Y; back => Z; whole => U));
```

Figure 3-1: A specification for appending two lists

I want to describe an *interpretation* of any given type in the context of this knowledge base so that *expanding* the input according to the specifications will produce a consistently typed object. A ψ-type is evaluated by "*expanding*" its root symbol if its knowledge base value is not itself; *i.e.*, substituting the root symbol by its knowledge base value by taking the meet of this value and the ψ-type whose root symbol has been erased (replaced by $\top$). If the root symbol is mapped to itself by the knowledge base, the process is applied recursively to the subterms. Recalling the "type-as-set" semantics of ϵ-types and ψ-types, this process essentially computes unions and intersections of sets. The symbol substitution process is to be interpreted as *importing* the information encapsulated in the symbol into the context of another type.

Let's *trace* what the interpreter does, one step at a time, on an example. Let's suppose that the knowledge base in figure 3-1 is defined. Consider the following input:

```
append(front => cons(head => 1;
                     tail => cons(head => 2;
                                  tail => nil));
       back => cons(head => 3;
                    tail => nil));
```

Next, the interpreter expands append into {append_0, append_1}:

```
{append_0(front => cons(head => 1;
                        tail => cons(head => 2;
                                     tail => nil));
          back => cons(head => 3;
                       tail => nil)),

 append_1(front => cons(head => 1;
                        tail => cons(head => 2;
                                     tail => nil));
          back => cons(head => 3;
                       tail => nil))};
```

Each of these two basic ϵ-terms is further expanded according to the definitions of their heads. However, the first one (append_0) yields $\perp$ since the meet of the subterms at front is $\perp$. Hence, by $\Re$-reduction, we are left with only:

```
(front => cons(head => 1;
               tail => cons(head => 2;
                            tail => nil));
 back => cons(head => 3;
              tail => nil);
 whole => cons(head => 1;
               tail => U);
 patch => append(front => cons(head => 2;
                               tail => nil);
                 back => cons(head => 3;
                              tail => nil);
                 whole => U));
```

The process continues, expanding the subterms:[8]

```
(front => cons(head => 1;
               tail => cons(head => 2;
                            tail => nil));
 back => cons(head => 3;
              tail => nil);
 whole => cons(head => 1;
               tail => cons(head => 2;
                            tail => U));
 patch => (front => cons(head => 2;
                         tail => nil);
           back => cons(head => 3;
                        tail => nil);
           patch => append(front => nil;
                           back => cons(head => 3;
                                        tail => nil);
                           whole => U);
           whole => cons(head => 2;
                         tail => U)));
```

Finally, the following term is obtained which cannot be further expanded. The interpretation of `append` has thus correctly produced a type whose `whole` is the concatenation of its `front` to its `end`. The result could be isolated by projection on the field `whole` if desired. The attribute `patch` is the history of the computation.

```
(front => cons(head => 1;
               tail => cons(head => 2;
                            tail => nil));
 back => cons(head => 3;
              tail => nil);
 whole => cons(head => 1;
               tail => cons(head => 2;
                            tail => cons(head => 3;
                                         tail => nil)));
 patch => (front => cons(head => 2;
                         tail => nil);
           back => cons(head => 3;
                        tail => nil);
           patch => (front => nil;
                     back => cons(head => 3;
                                  tail => nil);
                     whole => cons(head => 3;
                                   tail => nil));
           whole => cons(head => 2;
                         tail => cons(head => 3;
                                      tail => nil))));
```

Computation in KBL amounts essentially to term rewriting. In fact, it bears much resemblance with computation with non-deterministic program schemes [9, 16], and macro-languages and tree grammars [14]. This section attempts a formal characterization of computation in KBL along the lines of the algebraic semantics of

[8] For what remains, I shall leave out the details of cleaning-up $\perp$ by $\Re$-reduction.

tree grammars [2, 14]. Symbol rewriting presented in this section is very close to the notion of second-order substitution defined in [8] and macro-expansion defined in [14].

It is next shown that a KBL program can be seen as a system of equations. Thanks to the lattice properties of finite wft's, such a system of equations admits a least fixed-point solution. The particular order of computation of KBL, the *"fan-out computation order"*, which rewrites symbols closer to the root first is formally defined and shown to be maximal; *i.e.*, it yields "greater" ϵ-types than any other order of computation. Unfortunately, the complete "correctness" of KBL is not established. That is, it is not known (yet) whether the normal form of a term is equal to the fixed-point solution. However, as steps in this direction, two technical lemmas are conjectured to which a proof of the correctness is corollary.

All wft's considered hereafter are *finite*. Hence, I shall not bother mentioning the adjective "finite" when dealing with wft's for the rest of this paper.

3.1. Wft substitution

I next introduce and give some properties of the concept of wft substitution. Roughly, given a wft t such that a symbol f occurs at address u in t, one can substitute some other wft t' for f at address u in t by "pasting-in" t' in t at that address.

Given a wft $t = (\Delta, \psi, \tau)$ and some string u in $\mathcal{L}^*$, I define the wft u.t to be the smallest wft containing t at address u; that is, $u.t = (u.\Delta, u.\psi, u.\tau)$ where

- $u.\Delta = \{w \in \mathcal{L}^* \mid w = u.v,\ v \in \Delta\}$;
- $u.\psi(w) =$ *if* $w = u.v$ *then* $\psi(v)$ *else* $\top$;
- $u.\tau : u.\Delta \rightarrow \mathcal{T}$ *such that* $u.\tau(v) = u.\tau(w)$ *iff* $v = u.v'$, $w = u.w'$ *and* $\tau(v') = \tau(w')$.

This can be better visualized as the wft obtained by attaching the wft t at the end of the string u.

Let u_i, $i=1,\ldots,n$ be mutually non-coreferring addresses in Δ and let f_i, $i=1,\ldots,n$ be symbols in Σ. Then, the wft $t[u_1:f_1,\ldots,u_n:f_n]$ is the wft (Δ, ϕ, τ), where ϕ coincides with ψ everywhere except for the coreference classes of the u_i's where $\phi([u_i]) = f_i$ for $i=1,\ldots,n$. It is clear that the term obtained is still well-formed.

> **Definition 19:** Let $t = (\Delta, \psi, \tau)$ be a wft and u some address in Δ, and let t' be a wft. The term $t[t'/u]$ is defined as $t[t'/u] = t[u:\top] \wedge u.t'$.

This operation must not be confused with the classical tree *grafting* operation which *replaces* a subtree with another tree. The operation defined above *super-imposes* a term on a subterm with the exception of the root symbol of that subtree which becomes equal to the root of the replacing tree. Note that $\perp$ may result out of such a substitution. To illustrate this operation, if t is the wft

```
(front => cons(head => X1 : 1;
               tail => X2 : cons(head => 2;
                                 tail => nil));
 back => X3 : cons(head => 3; tail => nil);
 whole => cons(head => X1; tail => X4);
 patch => append(front => X2; back => X3; whole => X4));
```

and t' is the wft

```
(front => cons(head => X; tail => Y);
 back => Z;
 whole => cons(head => X; tail => U);
 patch => append(front => Y; back => Z; whole => U));
```

then t[t'/patch] is

```
(front => cons(head => X1 : 1;
               tail => X2 : cons(head => X5 : 2;
                                 tail => X6 : nil));
 back => X3 : cons(head => 3;
                   tail => nil);
 whole => cons(head => X1;
               tail => X7 : cons(head => X5;
                                 tail => X4));
 patch => (front => X2;
           back => X3;
           patch => append(front => X6;
                           back => X3;
                           whole => X4);
           whole => X7)).
```

Next, I give a series of "surgical" lemmas about this substitution operation which will be needed in proving key properties of KBL's computation rule. The first lemma states the intuitively clear fact that which address is picked out of a coreference class in a substitution does not affect the result. This is made apparent as depicted in figure 3-2.

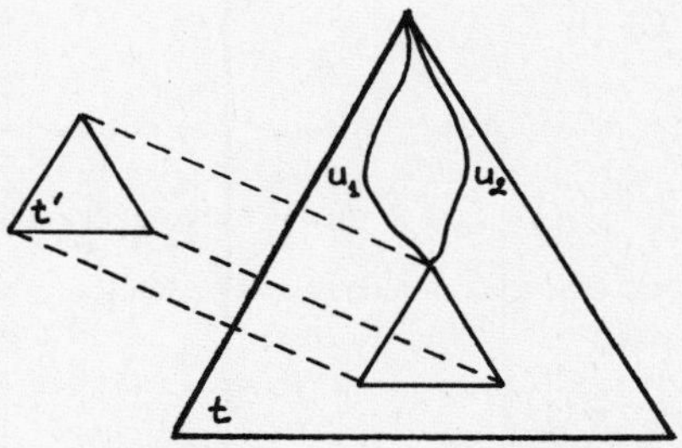

Figure 3-2: Substitution at coreferring addresses

Lemma 20: Let $t = (\Delta, \psi, \tau)$ and t' be wft's, and let u_1, u_2 be two coreferring addresses in Δ. Then, $(t[t'/u_1])[t'/u_2] = t[t'/u_1] = t[t'/u_2] = (t[t'/u_2])[t'/u_1]$

An address u *covers* an address v in a wft if there exists an address u' in $[u]$ such that $v = u'.w$ for some w in $\mathcal{L}^*$. That is, u covers v in t if v occurs in $t\backslash u$.

Next, it is important to analyze the extent to which a sequence of substitutions is affected by the particular order in which they are performed. Specifically, order of two substitutions will not matter if the addresses do not cover each other; however, order of substitutions will matter if one of the two addresses covers the other. We first need a small technical lemma.

Lemma 21: If u and v are addresses in a wft t which do not cover each other, then for any wft t',

$$(t[u{:}\top] \wedge u.t')[v{:}\top] = t[u{:}\top, v{:}\top] \wedge u.t'$$

The next lemma gives a sufficient condition for commutativity.

Lemma 22: Let $t = (\Delta, \psi, \tau)$, t_1, t_2 be wft's, and let u_1, u_2 be two addresses in Δ which do not cover each other. Then,

$$(t[t_1/u_1])[t_2/u_2] = (t[t_2/u_2])[t_1/u_1]$$

The second lemma complements the previous one and shows that the order of substitution matters for covering addresses. However, the wft resulting from performing the "outermost" substitution first subsumes the wft resulting from performing the "innermost" substitution first. The picture in figure 3-3 may help illustrate the argument.

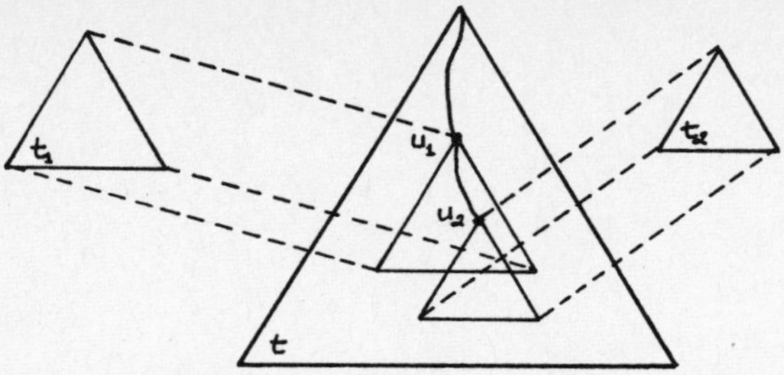

Figure 3-3: Substitutions at covering addresses

> **Lemma 23:** If two addresses u_1 and u_2 in a wft t are such that u_1 covers u_2, then
>
> $$(t[t_2/u_2])[t_1/u_1] \preceq (t[t_1/u_1])[t_2/u_2]$$
>
> for any wft's t_1 and t_2.

The objective of these lemmas is to help show that the particular order of performing substitution performed by the KBL interpreter yields an ϵ-type that subsumes all ϵ-types obtained by any other order of computation. Next, the *fan-out computation* theorem 26 is proposed to that effect, using the above technical lemmas.

The following notion will be useful in expressing an ordering on the addresses of a wft. The notion of *radius* of an address is a measure how "close to the root" an address is; that is, the shortest (in length) in the coreference its class. Given a string u in $\mathcal{L}^*$, $|u|$ denotes its length; *i.e.*, the number of labels which constitute u.

> **Definition 24:** Let $t = (\Delta, \psi, \tau)$ be a wft; then, the *radius* of an address u in Δ is defined as $\rho(u) = \mathrm{Min}(\{|v| \mid v \in [u]\})$.

That such a minimum number exists for all classes is clear. Recall that lemma 20 states that a substitution can be performed at any address in a coreference class with the same result. For this reason, it will be implicit in all substitutions considered hereafter that the address at which the substitution is performed is a minimal length in its class.

> **Definition 25:** A sequence of addresses u_i, $i=1,\ldots,n$ of a wft t is in *"fan-out"* order if and only if $i<j$ implies $\rho(u_i) \leq \rho(u_j)$.

For example, in the wft:

$$
\begin{array}{lll}
t = & f_1(l_1 \Rightarrow X_1{:}f_2(l_2 \Rightarrow X_2; & \\
 & \qquad\qquad\qquad l_3 \Rightarrow f_3); & \\
 & \quad l_4 \Rightarrow X_2; & \\
 & \quad l_5 \Rightarrow f_4(l_6 \Rightarrow X_1; & \\
 & \qquad\qquad\qquad l_7 \Rightarrow X_3{:}f_5; & \\
 & \qquad\qquad\qquad l_8 \Rightarrow X_3)) &
\end{array}
$$

the sequence e, $l_5.l_6$, l_4, $l_5.l_7$, $l_1.l_3$ is in fan-out order. However, the sequence e, $l_5.l_6$, l_4, $l_1.l_3$, l_5 is not. In the sequel, I shall lighten the notation $(t[t_1/u_1])[t_2/u_2]$ to $t[t_1/u_1][t_2/u_2]$.

The following theorem is a consequence of the lemmas just presented.

> **Theorem 26:** Let t be a wft, and $U = \{u_1, \ldots, u_n\}$ a set of mutually non-coreferring addresses of t such that the sequence u_i, $i=1,\ldots,n$ is in fan-out order. Let π be a permutation of the set

$\{1,\ldots,n\}$ such that $\pi(u_i)$, $i=1,\ldots,n$ is also in fan-out order. Then, for any set of wft's $\{t_1,\ldots,t_n\}$,

$$t[t_1/u_1]\ldots[t_n/u_n] = t[t_{\pi(1)}/u_{\pi(1)}]\ldots[t_{\pi(n)}/u_{\pi(n)}]. \tag{1}$$

Moreover, if the permutation π destroys fan-out order, then

$$t[t_1/u_1]\ldots[t_n/u_n] \preceq t[t_{\pi(1)}/u_{\pi(1)}]\ldots[t_{\pi(n)}/u_{\pi(n)}]. \tag{2}$$

Substitution is extended to ϵ-types as follows: for any t in Ψ_0, T in $\pounds_0$, and any u in Δ_t,

$$t[T/u] = \sqcup_{t'\in T} t[t'/u].$$

3.2. Symbol Rewriting Systems

Definition 27: A *Symbol Rewriting System* (SRS) on Σ is a system S of n equations $S: s_i = E_i$, where $s_i \in \Sigma$ and $E_i \in \pounds_0$, for $i = 1,\ldots,n$.

Given such a system S, I shall denote by E the subset $\{s_1,\ldots,s_n\}$ of Σ of S-*expandable* symbols, and N the set $\Sigma - E$ of *non*-S-*expandable* symbols of Σ. An example of a SRS is given by figure 3-1. There, we have E = {list, append, append_0, append_1} and N = {nil, cons}.

Definition 28: Let $S: s_i = T_i$ be a SRS. It defines a *one-step rewriting* relation $\xrightarrow[S]{}$ on $\pounds_0$ as follows: $T_1 \xrightarrow[S]{} T_2$ if and only if there is a wft $t \in T_1$, some address u in Δ_t and some index $i\in\{1,\ldots,n\}$ for which $\psi_t(u)=s_i$, such that $T_2 = (T_1-\{t\}) \sqcup t[E_i/u]$.

In words, this expresses the fact that the ϵ-type T_2 is obtained from the ϵ-type T_1 by picking out some element of T_1, substituting for *one* of its occurrences of some expandable symbol the right-hand side of this symbol in S, and adjoin the result to the set keeping only maximal elements. This process is illustrated by the first step of the trace of KBL shown on page 11.

I shall denote by $\xrightarrow[S]{k}$ for $k\geq 0$ the relation $\xrightarrow[S]{}$ composed with itself k times, and by $\xrightarrow[S]{*}$ the reflexive and transitive closure of $\xrightarrow[S]{}$; that is, the relation $\cup_{k=0}^{\infty} \xrightarrow[S]{k}$.

In the foregoing, the notation for the sets Ψ of ψ-types and $\pounds$ of ϵ-types was implicitly understood to depend on the signature of symbols Σ. Whenever it will be necessary to make this more explicit I shall use the notation $\Psi[\Sigma]$ and $\pounds[\Sigma]$.

Definition 29: Let S be a SRS, and t be a wft. The S-*normal form* of an ϵ-type T is defined as

$$\mathcal{N}(T) = \sqcup\{T' \in \pounds_0[N] \mid T \xrightarrow[S]{*} T'\}$$

That is the LUB of all terms containing no more expandable symbols that can be rewritten from T. Since $\pounds_0$ is a complete lattice, this is well-defined. Notice that a normal form is defined as a join of *all* possible rewriting of an ϵ-type. Thus, by theorem 26, we can restrict this definition only to sequences of rewritings in fan-out order without losing anything in the definition of a normal form.

To lighten notation, I shall make use of vector notation to denote elements of $\pounds_0^n$ the set of n-tuples of ϵ-types ; *e.g.*, $\vec{T} = \langle T_1,\ldots,T_n\rangle$, $T_i \in \pounds_0$, $i=1,\ldots,n$. Hence, a symbol rewriting system S of n equations, is denoted by a single vector equation $\vec{s} = \vec{E}$. Given such a SRS, I shall use either indices in $\{1,\ldots,n\}$ or the symbols s_i to index the components of a vector $\vec{T}$ in $\pounds_0^n$; *i.e.*, $T_{s_i} = T_i$. There should be no confusion since the s_i's will be assumed distinct. Vector rewriting is the appropriate obvious extension to vectors of ϵ-types of the $\xrightarrow[S]{}$ relation, and so is the definition of vector normal form $\vec{\mathcal{N}}(\vec{T})$.

Given a SRS $\mathbf{S}$: $\vec{s} = \vec{E}$ and a wft $\mathtt{t}$, $\mathbf{X}(\mathtt{t},\vec{s})$ denotes the set of (minimum radius) addresses in $\mathtt{t}$ whose symbols are S-expandable. That is,

$$\mathbf{X}(\mathtt{t},\vec{s}) = \{\mathtt{u} \in \Delta_{\mathtt{t}} \mid \psi_{\mathtt{t}}(\mathtt{u}) = \mathtt{s}_i, \textit{ for some } \mathtt{i}=1,\ldots,\mathtt{n}\}.$$

Any indexing of $\mathbf{X}(\mathtt{t},\vec{s}) = \{\mathtt{u}_1,\ldots,\mathtt{u}_m\}$ will be assumed to be a *fan-out indexing.* That is, one such that the sequence $(\mathtt{u}_1,\ldots,\mathtt{u}_m)$ is in fan-out order. For example, taking the wft $\mathtt{t}$ on page 15 and $\vec{s} = \langle \mathtt{f}_2,\mathtt{f}_4,\mathtt{f}_5\rangle$ we have $\mathbf{X}(\mathtt{t},\vec{s}) = \{1_1,\ 1_5,\ 1_5.1_7\}$.

The objective here is to define the operation of applying a fan-out sequence of substitutions of ϵ-types to a wft $\mathtt{t}$ at all expandable addresses of $\mathtt{t}$. This operation is denoted $\mathtt{t}[\vec{T}/\vec{s}]$ and defined as:

$$\mathtt{t}[\vec{T}/\vec{s}] = \mathtt{t}[T_{\psi_t(u_1)}/u_1]\ldots[T_{\psi_t(u_m)}/u_m] \tag{3}$$

where $\{\mathtt{u}_1,\ldots,\mathtt{u}_m\} = \mathbf{X}(\mathtt{t},\vec{s})$. By theorem 26, it is evident that this is a well-defined operation. I shall condense notation in 3 to:

$$\mathtt{t}[\vec{T}/\vec{s}] = \mathtt{t}[T_{\psi_t(u)}/u]_{u\in \mathbf{X}(t,\vec{s})}$$

Let's illustrate this operation on a small example. Let's take $\vec{s} = \langle s_1,s_2\rangle$ and $\vec{T} = \langle T_1,T_2\rangle$ with

$$T_1 = \{f(1_1 \Rightarrow X;\ 1_2 \Rightarrow X),\ g\}$$

$$T_2 = h(1_2 \Rightarrow X;\ 1_3 \Rightarrow X)$$

and the term

$$t = s_1(1_1 \Rightarrow s_2;\ 1_3 \Rightarrow s_1).$$

The set of expandable addresses for $\vec{s}$ in $\mathtt{t}$ thus is:

$$\mathbf{X}(t,\vec{s}) = \{e,\ 1_1,\ 1_2\}$$

corresponding to the symbols (in fan-out order) s_1, s_2, s_1. Hence, the sequence of substitutions starts with s_1 at e:

$$\begin{array}{l} \{\ f(1_1 \Rightarrow X : s_2; \\ \quad 1_2 \Rightarrow X; \\ \quad 1_3 \Rightarrow s_1), \\ \ \ g(1_1 \Rightarrow s_2; \\ \quad 1_3 \Rightarrow s_1)\ \} \end{array}$$

then continues with s_2 at 1_1:

$$\begin{array}{l} \{\ f(1_1 \Rightarrow X : h(1_2 \Rightarrow Y;\ 1_3 \Rightarrow Y); \\ \quad 1_2 \Rightarrow X; \\ \quad 1_3 \Rightarrow s_1), \\ \ \ g(1_1 \Rightarrow h(1_2 \Rightarrow X;\ 1_3 \Rightarrow X); \\ \quad 1_3 \Rightarrow s_1)\ \} \end{array}$$

and finally ends with s_1 at 1_2:

```
{ f(l₁ => X : h(l₂ => Y; l₃ => Y);
    l₂ => X;
    l₃ => f(l₁ => Y : l₁; l₂ => Y),
  g(l₁ => h(l₂ => X; l₃ => X);
    l₃ => h(l₂ => Y; l₃ => Y)),
  f(l₁ => X : h(l₂ => Y; l₃ => Y);
    l₂ => X;
    l₃ => g),
  g(l₁ => h(l₂ => X; l₃ => X);
    l₃ => g) }
```

which is the value of $\mathtt{t}[\vec{\mathtt{T}}/\vec{\mathtt{s}}]$

This operation is extended to $\mathcal{L}_0^{\mathtt{n}}$ to vectors of ϵ-types as follows: $\vec{\mathtt{T}}[\vec{\mathtt{T}}'/\vec{\mathtt{s}}]$ is the vector of $\mathcal{L}_0^{\mathtt{n}}$ whose $\mathtt{i}^{th}$ component is defined as

$$(\vec{\mathtt{T}}[\vec{\mathtt{T}}'/\vec{\mathtt{s}}])_{\mathtt{i}} = \sqcup_{\mathtt{t}\in\mathtt{T}_{\mathtt{i}}} \mathtt{t}[\vec{\mathtt{T}}'/\vec{\mathtt{s}}]. \tag{4}$$

Definition 30: An element $\vec{\mathtt{T}}$ of $\mathcal{L}_0^{\mathtt{n}}$ is a *solution* of the equation $\vec{\mathtt{s}} = \vec{\mathtt{E}}$ if and only if

$$\vec{\mathtt{E}}[\vec{\mathtt{T}}/\vec{\mathtt{s}}] = \vec{\mathtt{T}}.$$

We now proceed to show that a SRS viewed as a system of equations in $\mathcal{L}_0^{\mathtt{n}}$ always has a solution which corresponds to the least fixed-point of a vector function from $\mathcal{L}_0^{\mathtt{n}}$ to itself. Such a function $\mathcal{F}$ is defined for a SRS $\vec{\mathtt{s}} = \vec{\mathtt{E}}$ as follows:

$$\mathcal{F}(\vec{\mathtt{T}}) = \vec{\mathtt{E}}[\vec{\mathtt{T}}/\vec{\mathtt{s}}]. \tag{5}$$

Proposition 31: The function $\mathcal{F}$ from $\mathcal{L}_0^{\mathtt{n}}$ to itself defined by 5 is continuous.[9]

As a result, $\mathcal{F}$ has a least fixed-point given by

$$\mathbf{Y}\mathcal{F} = \mathcal{F}^*(\vec{\bot}) = \sqcup_{k=0}^{\infty} \mathcal{F}^k(\vec{\bot}).$$

Now, since

$$\vec{\mathtt{E}}[\mathbf{Y}\mathcal{F}/\vec{\mathtt{s}}] = \mathbf{Y}\mathcal{F}$$

$\mathbf{Y}\mathcal{F}$ is the solution of the equation $\vec{\mathtt{s}} = \vec{\mathtt{E}}$.

Let's take again a small example to illustrate. Consider the single equation:

```
tree = {leaf, node(left => tree; right => tree)}
```

with **leaf** $<$ **tree**, **node** $<$ **tree**. Hence, $\mathcal{F}_{\mathtt{tree}}(\vec{\bot}) = \{\mathtt{leaf}\}$; then, $\mathcal{F}^2_{\mathtt{tree}}(\vec{\bot})$ is given by:

```
{leaf, node(left => leaf; right => leaf}
```

and so $\mathcal{F}^3_{\mathtt{tree}}(\vec{\bot})$ is:

[9] This is where the fact that $\mathcal{L}_0$ is a complete Brouwerian lattice is important. Indeed, the proof of this proposition uses a characteristic property of these structures.

```
{leaf, node(left => leaf; right => leaf),
       node(left => leaf;
            right => node(left => leaf;
                          right => leaf)),
       node(left => node(left => leaf;
                         right => leaf));
            right => leaf),
       node(left => node(left => leaf;
                         right => leaf));
            right => node(left => leaf;
                          right => leaf))}
```

and so on... The reader should see now that the successive powers of the **tree** component function $\mathcal{F}$ generate all possible binary trees. Indeed, the *meaning* of the type **tree** *is* precisely $\mathcal{F}^{*}_{\mathtt{tree}}(\vec{\bot})$ the infinite set (ϵ-type) of all such terms. Hence, solving type equation does give the meaning of recursively defined types.

The reader may wonder at this point how the example given in the beginning of this section on appending two lists is related to computing a *vector* fixed-point. To see this, given a knowledge base KB, we can add a new equation called *query* of the form ? = E, where ? is a special symbol not already in Σ. Then, the *answer* to the query is the component $(\mathbf{Yf})_?$ of the solution of the augmented system.

3.3. Correctness

In order to establish that the fixed-point solution of a SRS does correspond to the value computed by KBL, it is necessary to establish the *correctness* of the KBL interpreter. Namely, one must show that the normal form obtained by infinite rewritings is equal to the least solution of the system of equations.

Unfortunately, I have not *(yet)* worked out a complete proof for the correctness theorem. A *"conditional"* proof is obtained if two technical lemmas can be proved. These lemmas make intuitive sense and are extrapolations of similar facts for tree-grammars.[10] I conjecture them for now.

For any $\vec{T}$ in $\mathcal{L}^n_0$ define

$$\mathcal{G}(\vec{T}) = \vec{T} \sqcup \mathcal{F}(\vec{T})$$

and

$$\mathcal{G}^{*}(\vec{T}) = \sqcup_{k=0}^{\infty}\mathcal{G}^{k}(\vec{T})$$

Then, provided that, for any $\vec{T}_1, \vec{T}_2, \vec{T}_3$, in $\mathcal{L}^n_0$,

Lemma 32: $\vec{T}_1 \overset{*}{\underset{S}{\rightarrow}} \vec{T}_2$ *implies* $\vec{T}_2[\vec{T}_3/\vec{s}] \sqsubseteq \vec{T}_1[\mathcal{G}^{*}(\vec{T}_3)/\vec{s}]$;

and,

Lemma 33: $\vec{T}_2 \subseteq \vec{T}_1[\vec{\mathcal{N}}(\vec{s})/\vec{s}]$ *implies* $\vec{T}_1 \overset{*}{\underset{S}{\rightarrow}} \vec{T}_2$;

then,

Theorem 34: $\mathbf{Y}\mathcal{F} = \vec{\mathcal{N}}(\vec{s})$.

---

[10] See [14], pages 28-29, lemmas 2.38 and 2.39.

4. Conclusion

I have described a syntactic calculus of partially ordered structures and its application to computation. A syntax of record-like terms and a "type subsumption" ordering were defined and shown to form a lattice structure. A simple "type-as-set" interpretation of these term structures extends this lattice to a distributive one, and in the case of finitary terms, to a complete Brouwerian lattice. As a result, a method for solving systems of type equations by iterated rewriting of type symbols was proposed which defines an operational semantics for KBL -- a Knowledge Base Language. It was shown that a KBL program can be seen as a system of equations. Thanks to the lattice properties of finite structures, a system of equations admits a least fixed-point solution. The particular order of computation of KBL, the *"fan-out computation order"*, which rewrites symbols closer to the root first was formally defined and shown to be maximal. Unfortunately, the complete "correctness" of KBL is not yet established. That is, it is not known at this point whether the normal form of a term is equal to the fixed-point solution. However, as steps in this direction, two technical lemmas were conjectured to which a proof of the correctness is corollary.

References

[1] Ait-Kaci, H.
A Lattice Theoretic Approach to Computation Based on a Calculus of Partially Ordered Type Structures.
PhD thesis, Computer and Information Science, University of Pennsylvania, 1984.

[2] Berry, G., and Levy, J.J.
Minimal and Optimal Computations of Recursive Programs.
Journal of the ACM 26:148-75, 1979.

[3] Birkhoff, G.
Colloquium Publications. Volume 25: *Lattice Theory.*
American Mathematical Society, Providence, RI, 1940.
Third (revised) edition, 1979.

[4] Borkin, S.A.
Series in Computer Science. Volume 4: *Data Models: A Semantic Approach for Database Systems.*
The M.I.T. Press, Cambridge, MA, 1980.

[5] Brachman, R.J.
A New Paradigm for Representing Knowledge.
BBN Report 3605, Bolt Beranek and Newman, Cambridge, MA, 1978.

[6] Brachman, R.J.
What IS-A Is and Isn't: An Analysis of Taxonomic Links in Semantic Networks.
Computer 16(10):30-35, October 1983.

[7] Brouwer, L.E.J.
On Order in the Continuum, and the Relation of Truth to Non-Contradictority.
In *Proceedings of the Section of Sciences 54*, pages 357-358. Koninklijke Nederlandse Akademie Van Wetenschappen, 1951.
Series A, Mathematical Sciences.

[8] Courcelle, B.
Fundamental Properties of Infinite Trees.
Theoretical Computer Science 25:95-169, 1983.

[9] Courcelle, B., and Nivat, M.
The Algebraic Semantics of Recursive Program Schemes.
In J.Winkowski (editor), *Mathematical Foundations of Computer Science Proceedings*, pages 16-30. Springer-Verlag, Berlin, W.Germany, 1978.
Lecture Notes in Computer Science *64*.

[10] Dummett, M.
Elements of Intuitionism.
Oxford University Press, Oxford, UK, 1977.

[11] Goguen, J.A., and Tardo, J.J.
An Introduction to OBJ: a Language for Writing and Testing Formal Algebraic Program Specifications.
In *Proceedings of the IEEE Conference on Specifications of Reliable Software*, pages 170-189. Cambridge, MA, 1979.

[12] Gorn, S.
Explicit Definitions and Linguistic Dominoes.
In J.F. Hart and S. Takasu (editors), *Systems and Computer Science*, pages 77-105. University of Toronto Press, Toronto, Ontario, 1965.

[13] Gorn, S.
Data Representation and Lexical Calculi.
Information Processing & Management 20(1-2):151-174, 1984.
Also available as technical report MS-CIS-82-39, Department of Computer and Information Science, University of Pennsylvania, Philadelphia, PA.

[14] Guessarian, I.
Lecture Notes in Computer Science. Volume 99: *Algebraic Semantics*.
Springer-Verlag, Berlin, W.Germany, 1981.

[15] Huet, G.
Resolution d'Equations dans des Langages d'Ordre 1, 2, ..., ω.
PhD thesis, Universite de Paris VII, France, September, 1976.

[16] Nivat, M.
On the Interpretation of Recursive Polyadic Program Schemes.
In *Symposia Mathematica*, pages 225-81. Istituto Nazionale di Alta Mathematica, Rome, Italy, 1975.

[17] Plotkin, G.D.
A Powerdomain Construction.
SIAM Journal on Computing 5, 1976.

[18] Plotkin, G.D.
Lattice Theoretic Properties of Subsumption.
Memorandum MIP-R-77, Department of Machine Intelligence and Perception, University of Edinburgh, June, 1977.

[19] Reynolds, J.C.
Transformational Systems and the Algebraic Structure of Atomic Formulas.
In D. Michie (editor), *Machine Intelligence 5,* chapter 7. Edinburgh University Press, 1970.

[20] Robinson, J.A.
A Machine-Oriented Logic Based on the Resolution Principle.
Journal of the ACM 12(1):23-41, 1965.

TERMINATION*

Nachum Dershowitz

Department of Computer Science
University of Illinois at Urbana-Champaign
Urbana, Illinois 61801
U.S.A.

ABSTRACT

This survey describes methods for proving that systems of rewrite rules terminate. Illustrations of the use of path orderings and other simplification orderings in termination proofs are given. The effect of restrictions, such as linearity, on the form of rules is considered. In general, though, termination is an undecidable property of rewrite systems.

1. INTRODUCTION

A *term-rewriting (rewrite) system* R over a set of terms $\mathcal{T}$ is a set of *rewrite rules,* each of the form $l \rightarrow r$, where l and r are terms in $\mathcal{T}$ or are terms containing *variables* ranging over $\mathcal{T}$. Such a rule applies to a term t in $\mathcal{T}$ if a subterm s of t matches the left-hand side l with some substitution σ of terms in $\mathcal{T}$ for variables appearing in l (i.e. $s = l\sigma$). The rule is applied by replacing the subterm s in t with the corresponding right-hand side $r\sigma$ of the rule, within which the same substitution σ of terms for variables has been made. We write $t \Rightarrow_R u$, or just $t \Rightarrow u$, to indicate that a term u in $\mathcal{T}$ is *derivable* in this way from the term t in $\mathcal{T}$ by a single application of some rule in R. If $t \Rightarrow \cdots \Rightarrow u$ in zero or more steps, abbreviated $t \Rightarrow^* u$, then we say that t *reduces* to u; if no rule can be applied to t, we say that t is *irreducible;* when t reduces to an irreducible term u, we say that u is a *normal form* of t.

There are five properties involved in the verification of rewrite systems:

1) *termination*—no infinite derivations are possible,

2) *confluence*—each term has at most one normal form,

3) *soundness*—terms are only rewritten to equal terms,

4) *completeness*—equal terms have the same normal form,

5) *correctness*—all normal forms satisfy given requirements.

---

*The preparation of this survey was supported in part by the National Science Foundation under Grant MCS 83-07755.

This survey is devoted to a discussion of the first aspect, namely termination, generally a prerequisite for demonstrating other properties. Two related concepts, only briefly discussed, are "quasi-termination" and "weak termination." A quasi-terminating rewrite system is one for which only a *finite* number of different terms are derivable from any given term. A weakly-terminating system is one for which every term has at least one normal form.

Consider, for example, the following simple system consisting of three rules:

$$\begin{aligned} white, red &\rightarrow red, white \\ blue, red &\rightarrow red, blue \\ blue, white &\rightarrow white, blue \end{aligned} \tag{0}$$

This program plays the "Dutch National Flag" game. Given a sequence of marbles, colored *red*, *white*, or *blue* and placed side by side in no particular order, the program rearranges the marbles so that all *red* ones are on the left, all *blue* ones are on the right, and all *white* ones are in the middle. The first rule, for example, states that if anywhere in the series there is an adjacent pair of marbles, the left one *white* and the right one *red*, then they should be exchanged so that the *red* marble is on the left and the *white* one is on the right. It is not hard to prove that, regardless of the initial arrangement of marbles, applying the above rules in any order always results in a sequence of correctly arranged marbles. As we will see, a termination proof can be based on the ordering

blue is greater than *white* and *white* is greater than *red*.

Each rule replaces two marbles, the one on the left with "greater" color is exchanged with the "smaller" one to its right.

To illustrate the difficulty often encountered when attempting to determine if, and why, a rewrite system terminates, consider the following system (for disjunctive normal form):

$$\begin{aligned} --\alpha &\rightarrow \alpha \\ -(\alpha+\beta) &\rightarrow -\alpha\times-\beta \\ -(\alpha\times\beta) &\rightarrow -\alpha+-\beta \\ \alpha\times(\beta+\gamma) &\rightarrow (\alpha\times\beta)+(\alpha\times\gamma) \\ (\beta+\gamma)\times\alpha &\rightarrow (\beta\times\alpha)+(\gamma\times\alpha) \end{aligned} \tag{1}$$

The first rule eliminates double negations; the second and third rules apply DeMorgan's laws to push negations inward; the last two apply the distributivity of $\times$ over $+$. The difficulty in proving termination for systems such as this stems from the fact that while some rewrites may decrease the size of a term, other rewrites may increase its size *and* duplicate occurrences of subterms. Furthermore, applying a rule to a subterm not only affects the structure of that subterm, but also changes the structure of its superterms. And a proof of termination must take into consideration the many different possible rewrite sequences generated by the non-deterministic choice of rules and subterms.

Various methods for proving termination of rewrite systems have been suggested, including [Gorn-67, Iturriaga-67, Knuth-Bendix-70, Manna-Ness-70, Gorn-73, Lankford-75, Lipton-Snyder-77, Plaisted-78, Plaisted-78b, Dershowitz-Manna-79, Lankford-79, Kamin-Levy-80, Pettorossi-81, Dershowitz-82, Jouannaud,*etal.*-82, Dershowitz,*etal.*-83, Lescanne-84, Jouannaud-Munoz-84, Kapur,*etal.*-85, Bachmair-Plaisted-85, Bachmair-Dershowitz-85, Rusinowitch-85]. Termination is in general an undecidable property of rewrite systems (as it is for Markov systems on strings; see [Huet-Lankford-78]). For a lively discussion of tasks that are difficult to show terminating, see [Gardner-83].

In the next section we prove that termination is undecidable. In Section 3 we show how *well-founded orderings* are used in termination proofs, and in Section 4 we show how *simplification orderings* are used. Similar methods are described in Section 5 for using *quasi-orderings* to prove termination (or quasi-termination). Section 6 presents *multiset orderings*. Then, in Section 7, we define *path orderings* based on an underlying operator "precedence". This is followed in the last two sections with methods for determining if rewrite systems of restricted form terminate (or weakly-terminate). Examples are provided throughout; proofs are generally omitted.

2. NONTERMINATION

Given a set of operators F, we consider the set $\mathcal{T}(F)$ of all terms constructed from operators in F. Operators in F may be *varyadic,* i.e. have variable arity, in which case if f is an operator and $t_1, ..., t_n$ $(n \geq 0)$ are terms in $\mathcal{T}(F)$, then $f(t_1, \ldots, t_n)$ is also a term in $\mathcal{T}(F)$. Or an operator f may be restricted to a fixed arity, in which case $f(t_1, \ldots, t_n) \in \mathcal{T}$ only if f is of arity n.

Definition 1. A rewrite system R is *terminating* for a set of terms $\mathcal{T}$, if there exist no infinite sequence of terms $t_i \in \mathcal{T}$ such that $t_1 \Rightarrow t_2 \Rightarrow t_3 \Rightarrow \cdots$. A system is *nonterminating* if there exists any such infinite derivation. A system is *weakly-terminating* if for each term $t \in \mathcal{T}$ there is an irreducible term derivable from t.

Terminating systems are variously called *finitely terminating, uniformly terminating, strongly terminating,* and *noetherian.* Unless indicated otherwise, when we speak of termination, we mean with respect to *all* terms constructed from a given set of (fixed or variable) operators F. Rules of a terminating system are called *reductions.*

Example. A trivial example of a terminating system is

$$--\alpha \rightarrow \alpha. \tag{2}$$

An equally trivial example of a nonterminating system is

$$-\alpha \rightarrow ---\alpha. \tag{3}$$

A less trivial example (of what?) is

$$-(\alpha+\beta) \rightarrow (--\alpha+\beta)+\beta. \tag{4}$$

An example of a non-weakly-terminating system is

$$f(g(\alpha)) \quad \rightarrow \quad g(g(f(f(\alpha)))). \tag{5}$$

Theorem 1. *Termination of rewrite systems is undecidable, even if the system has only two rules.*

Proof. Turing machines can be simulated by rewrite systems. Given any Turing machine M, there exists a two-rule system R_M such that R_M terminates for all initial terms if, and only if, M halts for all input tapes. Since it is undecidable (not even semi-decidable) if a Turing machine halts uniformly, it is also undecidable if rewrite systems terminate.

Each state symbol and tape symbol of the machine will be a constant in the system. Additionally, we need three operators: a binary operator (which we will denote by adjacency and assume associates to the right), a unary operator ∂ (the *erase* function), and a ternary operator C.[1] We use an additional constant $\square$ to denote the end of the tape. Corresponding to a machine in state q with nonblank left portion of the tape $a_1a_2 \cdots a_m$ (from the left end until the symbol preceding the read head) and right portion $b_1b_2 \cdots b_n$ (from the symbol being scanned to the end), is the term

$$C(a_m \cdots a_2a_1\square, qb_1b_2 \cdots b_n\square, machine),$$

where *machine* is a term encoding transitions as subterms of the form

$$\partial(\alpha\sigma\beta \; \gamma\gamma'\sigma'\delta'\delta)$$

signifying "if the machine is in state σ reading the symbol β and the symbol immediately to left of β is α, then replace the tape segment $\alpha\beta$ with $\gamma\gamma'\delta'\delta$, position the head on δ', and go into state σ'." Any extra tape symbols introduced in this way, are placed within an "erase" term ∂. Thus, for each left-moving instruction of the form "if in state q reading a, write a', move left, and go into state q'," there are subterms of the form

$$\partial(sqa \;\; \partial(\#)\partial(\#)q'sa')$$

for *every* tape symbol s, as well as an extra subterm of the form

$$\partial(\square qa \;\; \square\,\partial(\#)q'\#a')$$

(where $\#$ is the blank symbol) to handle the left end of the tape. For each right-moving instruction of the form "if in state q reading a, write a', move right, and go into state q'," there are subterms of the form

$$\partial(sqa \;\; sa'q'\partial(\#)\partial(\#))$$

for *every* tape symbol s, as well as extra subterm of the form

$$\partial(sq\square \;\; sa'q'\partial(\#)\square)$$

when a is the blank symbol $\#$ (to handle the right end of the tape). The term *machine* is

---

[1]Cf. [Bergstra-Tucker-80], where it is shown that *six* "hidden" functions suffice for the specification of com-

the concatenation of all transitions.

The rewrite system $R_{\mathcal{M}}$ consists of exactly two rules:

$$\begin{array}{rcl} \partial(\xi)\tau & \rightarrow & \tau \\ C(\alpha\lambda,\sigma\beta\rho,\partial(\alpha\sigma\beta\ \gamma\gamma'\sigma'\delta'\delta)\tau) & \rightarrow & C(\gamma'\gamma\lambda,\sigma'\delta'\delta\rho,machine). \end{array}$$

The first rule erases transitions from the machine description until an applicable one reaches the beginning of the description, at which time the second rule can be applied to simulate a move. Though there are rewrite sequences that erase all applicable transitions and therefore do not correspond to a machine computation, those sequences all terminate. Clearly, if the machine $\mathcal{M}$ does not terminate for some input tape, then the system $R_{\mathcal{M}}$ does not terminate for the corresponding input term. Note that no rewrite step can increase the number of occurrences of the operator C in a term. Thus, the only way for $R_{\mathcal{M}}$ not to terminate is for one of the occurrences of C to be infinitely rewritten, in a manner corresponding to an infinite computation of $\mathcal{M}$. □

An alternative proof of undecidability of termination is given in [Huet-Lankford-78]; see Section 9. The number of rules in that proof depends on the number of machine transitions.[2]

Though termination of a rewrite system means that all (infinitely many) possible derivations are finite, one need only consider derivations that begin with certain terms:

Lemma 1. *A rewrite system is terminating (for all terms) if, and only if, it terminates for all instances of its left-hand sides.*

By an *instance* of a left-hand side l we mean a term $l\sigma$ with terms substituted for the variables of the left-hand side. Certainly, if a derivation repeats a term, the system is nonterminating. We say that

Definition 2. A derivation $t_1 \Rightarrow t_2 \Rightarrow \cdots \Rightarrow t_j \Rightarrow \cdots \Rightarrow t_k \Rightarrow \cdots$ *cycles* if $t_j = t_k$ for some $j<k$. A rewrite system *cycles* if it has a cycling derivation.

Cycling is a special case of "looping":

Definition 3. A derivation $t_1 \Rightarrow t_2 \Rightarrow \cdots \Rightarrow t_j \Rightarrow \cdots \Rightarrow t_k \Rightarrow \cdots$ *loops* if t_j is a (not necessarily proper) subterm of t_k for some $j<k$. A rewrite system *loops* if it has a looping derivation.

It is also obvious that looping systems do not terminate. But a system need not be looping to be nonterminating.

Example. System (4) does not terminate. The following infinite derivation begins with an instance of its left-hand side, but the system is nonlooping:

---

putable data types. In fact, *three* do.

[2]Perhaps a proof along the lines of the one given above was intended by [Lipton-Snyder-77] when they asserted, *sans* proof, that *three* rules suffice for undecidability.

$$\begin{aligned} --(0+1) &\Rightarrow -((--0+1)+1) \\ &\Rightarrow (--(--0+1)+1)+1 \\ &\Rightarrow (-((----0+1)+1)+1)+1 \\ &\Rightarrow (((--(----0+1)+1)+1)+1)+1 \\ &\Rightarrow \cdots \end{aligned}$$

To characterize nontermination, therefore, a notion weaker than looping is needed. Viewing terms as ordered trees suggests the following definition:

Definition 4. A term s is *homeomorphically embedded* in a term t written $s \trianglelefteq t$, if, and only if, s is of the form $f(s_1,s_2, \ldots, s_m)$, t is of the form $g(t_1,t_2, \ldots, t_n)$, and either
(a) $f=g$ and $s_i \trianglelefteq t_{j_i}$ for all i, $1 \le i \le m$, where $1 \le j_1 < j_2 < \cdots < j_m \le n$, or
(b) $s \trianglelefteq t_j$ for some j, $1 \le j \le n$.

Thus, this relation embodies a notion of "syntactic simplicity": $s \trianglelefteq t$ if s may be obtained from t by deletion of selected operators and operands. If s is embedded in t, but $s \neq t$, then we write $s \triangleleft t$. For example,

$$--(0+1) \triangleleft (((--(----0+1)+1)+1)+1)+1.$$

Definition 5. A derivation $t_1 \Rightarrow t_2 \Rightarrow \cdots \Rightarrow t_j \Rightarrow \cdots \Rightarrow t_k \Rightarrow \cdots$ is *self-embedding* if $t_j \trianglelefteq t_k$ for some $j<k$. A rewrite system is *self-embedding* if it allows a self-embedding derivation.

Theorem 2 [Dershowitz-82]. *If a rewrite system is nonterminating, then it is self-embedding.*

The proof of this is based on the Tree Theorem [Higman-52, Kruskal-60, Nash-Williams-63].[3]

This theorem means that, to show termination of a system, one can prove it to be non-self-embedding. The converse, however, does not hold: self-embedding does not imply nontermination.

Example. The rewrite system

$$f(f(\alpha)) \quad \rightarrow \quad f(g(f(\alpha))) \tag{6}$$

is both self-embedding and terminating.

Unfortunately, even this sufficient condition for termination is undecidable:

Theorem 3 [Plaisted-85]. *It is undecidable whether a rewrite system is self-embedding.*

Of course, self-embedding is partially decidable: just search through all derivations until an embedding is discovered. It is similarly undecidable if a system cycles or loops. (For details,

[3] A weaker form of "embedding" and correspondingly weaker results appear as an exercise in [Knuth-73], where it was suggested that embedding has applications to proofs of termination.

see [Plaisted-85].)

3. TERMINATION

To express proofs of termination, we need the following concepts: A *partially-ordered* set $(S,\succ)$ consists of a set S and a transitive and irreflexive binary relation $\succ$ defined on elements of S.[4] As usual, $s \succeq t$ means that either $s \succ t$ or $s = t$, $s \prec t$ means the same as $t \succ s$, and $s \preceq t$ means $t \succeq s$. A partially ordered set is said to be *totally ordered* if for any two distinct elements s and s' of S, either $s \succ s'$ or $s' \succ s$. For example, both the set of integers and the set of natural numbers are totally ordered by the "greater-than" relation $>$. The set of all subsets of the integers is partially ordered by the "proper subset" relation $\subseteq$. An *extension* of a partial ordering $\succ$ on S is a partial ordering $\succ'$ also on S such that $s \succ s'$ implies $s \succ' s'$ for all $s, s' \in S$. Partial orderings of component elements can also be extended to a partial ordering of tuples of elements: a tuple $(s_1, s_2, \ldots, s_n)$ in $(S_1,\succ_1)\times(S_2,\succ_2)\times \cdots (S_n,\succ_n)$ is *lexicographically* greater than another tuple $(t_1, t_2, \ldots, t_n)$ if for some i $(1 \leq i \leq n)$ $s_i \succ_i t_i$ while $s_j = t_j$ for all $j < i$.

A partially ordered set $(S,\succ)$ is said to be *well-founded* if there are no infinite descending sequences $s_1 \succ s_2 \succ s_3 \succ \cdots$ of elements of S. Thus, the natural numbers $\mathbf{N}$ under their "natural" ordering $>$ is well-founded, since no sequence of natural numbers can descend beyond 0. But $>$ is not a well-founded ordering of all the integers, since, for example, $-1 > -2 > -3 > \cdots$ is an infinite descending sequence. Nor is $>$ a well-founded ordering of the reals. If $(S_1,\succ_1)$ and $(S_2,\succ_2)$ are two well-founded sets, then their lexicographically ordered cross-product $(S_1 \times S_2, \succ^*)$ is also well-founded, where a pair (s_1, s_2) in $S_1 \times S_2$ is greater than another pair (t_1, t_2) in $S_1 \times S_2$ if either $s_1 \succ_1 t_1$ or else $s_1 = t_1$ and $s_2 \succ_2 t_2$. Similarly, a lexicographic ordering of tuples of any fixed length is well-founded, if the orderings of the components are. For example, the tuple (2,5,1,6) is greater than (2,4,9,8) in the well-founded lexicographic ordering of tuples of naturally ordered natural numbers. (See, e.g., [Manna-74].)

The notion of well-foundedness suggests the following straightforward method of proving termination:

Theorem 4. *A rewrite system R over a set of terms $\mathcal{T}$ is terminating if, and only if, there exists a well-founded ordering $\succ$ over $\mathcal{T}$ such that*

$$t \Rightarrow u \text{ implies } t \succ u$$

for all terms t and u in $\mathcal{T}$.

Example. System (0) terminates, since the lexicographic ordering of tuples of colors (with $blue > white > red$) is well-founded and the tuple of colors corresponding to a sequence of marbles is reduced with each rule application. By the nature of the lexicographic ordering, one

[4]Asymmetry of a partial ordering follows from transitivity and irreflexivity.

need only consider the change in the leftmost of the two affected components: if it was *white* before, then it is *red* after; if it was *blue* before, then it is either *red* or *white* after.

The following equivalent formulation (see[Kamin-Levy-80]) takes advantage of the structure of terms:

Corollary . *A rewrite system R over a set of terms $\mathcal{T}$ is terminating if, and only if, there exists a well-founded ordering $\succ$ over $\mathcal{T}$ such that*

$$l \succ r$$

for each rule $l \rightarrow r$ in R and for any substitution of terms in $\mathcal{T}$ for the variables of the rule, and such that

$$t \Rightarrow u \text{ and } t \succ u \text{ imply } f(\cdots t \cdots) \succ f(\cdots u \cdots)$$

for all terms in $\mathcal{T}$.

Example. The system

$$f(f(\alpha)) \quad \rightarrow \quad f(g(f(\alpha))) \tag{6}$$

is terminating, since the number of adjacent f's is reduced with each application. Note that counting the number of adjacencies makes $g(f(f(a))) > f(a)$, though $f(g(f(f(a)))) \not\succ f(f(a))$.

The following definition and theorem eliminate the need to consider all derivations $t \Rightarrow u$ and are often used to prove termination:

Definition 6. A partial ordering $\succ$ over a set of terms $\mathcal{T}$ is *monotonic* (with respect to term structure) if it has the *replacement property,*

$$t \succ u \text{ implies } f(\cdots t \cdots) \succ f(\cdots u \cdots),$$

for all terms in $\mathcal{T}$.

In other words, reducing a subterm, reduces any superterm containing it.

Theorem 5 [Manna-Ness-70]. *A rewrite system R over a set of terms $\mathcal{T}$ is terminating if, and only if, there exists a monotonic well-founded ordering $\succ$ over $\mathcal{T}$ such that*

$$l \succ r$$

for each rule $l \rightarrow r$ in R and for any substitution of terms in $\mathcal{T}$ for the variables of the rule.

Note that the ordering $\succ$ is defined on $\mathcal{T}$, not on terms like l and r containing variables. That is why we require that $l \succ r$ for all *substitutions* that yields terms in $\mathcal{T}$. With monotonicity, this ensures that $t \succ u$ whenever t reduces to u. As we will see, it is sometimes possible to "lift" an ordering on $\mathcal{T}$ to an orderings on terms with variables so that $l \succ r$ in the lifted ordering guarantees that in fact $l \succ r$ for all substitutions.

Example. The system

$$f(g(\alpha)) \rightarrow g(f(\alpha)) \tag{7}$$

terminates. To see this, consider the following well-founded monotonic ordering on monadic terms: given an ordering on operators, a term s is greater than a term t if s has more operators than does t, or if they have the same number of operators, but the outermost operator of s is greater than that of t, or if they are of the same length and their outermost operators are identical, but the operand of s is (recursively) greater than that of t. Choosing an operator ordering $f > g$, the above rule is a reduction.

It is frequently convenient to separate a well-founded ordering on terms into two parts: a *termination function* τ that maps terms in $\mathcal{T}$ to a set $\mathcal{W}$ and a "standard" well-founded ordering $\succ$ on $\mathcal{W}$.

Definition 7. A *termination function* $\tau:\mathcal{T} \rightarrow \mathcal{W}$ is composed of a set of functions $f_\tau:\mathcal{W} \rightarrow \mathcal{W}$, one for each operator f, and is defined by

$$\tau(f(t_1, \ldots, t_n)) = f_\tau(\tau(t_1), \ldots, \tau(t_n))$$

for every term $f(t_1, \ldots, t_n)$ in $\mathcal{T}$, and for which

$$x \succ x' \text{ implies } f_\tau(\cdots x \cdots) \succ f_\tau(\cdots x' \cdots)$$

for all $x, x', \cdots$ in $\mathcal{W}$.

In other words a termination function is a monotonic morphism on terms.

Theorem 6 [Manna-Ness-70]. *A rewrite system R over a set of terms $\mathcal{T}$ is terminating if, and only if, there exists a well-founded set $(\mathcal{W}, \succ)$ and termination function $\tau:\mathcal{T} \rightarrow \mathcal{W}$, such that*

$$\tau(l) \succ \tau(r)$$

for each rule $l \rightarrow r$ in R and for any substitution of terms in $\mathcal{T}$ for the variables of the rule.

The use of monotonic *polynomial interpretations* was suggested in [Manna-Ness-70, Lankford-75, Lankford-79]. Using this method, an integer polynomial $F(x_1, \ldots, x_n)$ of degree n is associated with each n-ary operator f. The choice of coefficients must ensure monotonicity and that terms are mapped into nonnegative integers only; this is the case if all coefficients are positive. (A number of examples may be found in [Dershowitz-Manna-79]; some work on automated polynomial proofs is in progress [BenCherifa-84].) The use of rewrite systems as termination functions and the formulation of abstract monotonicity conditions are explored in [Bachmair-Dershowitz-85, Gnaedig-85].

Example. Consider the following system (for symbolic differentiation with respect to x):

$$\begin{array}{rcl}
D_x\, x & \rightarrow & 1 \\
D_x\, a & \rightarrow & 0 \\
D_x\,(\alpha+\beta) & \rightarrow & D_x\,\alpha + D_x\,\beta \\
D_x\,(\alpha-\beta) & \rightarrow & D_x\,\alpha - D_x\,\beta \\
D_x\,(-\alpha) & \rightarrow & -D_x\,\alpha \\
D_x\,(\alpha\times\beta) & \rightarrow & \beta\times D_x\,\alpha + \alpha\times D_x\,\beta \\
D_x\,(\frac{\alpha}{\beta}) & \rightarrow & \frac{D_x\,\alpha}{\beta} - \alpha\frac{D_x\,\beta}{\beta^2} \\
D_x\,(\ln\ \alpha) & \rightarrow & \frac{D_x\,\alpha}{\alpha} \\
D_x\,(\alpha^\beta) & \rightarrow & \beta\times\alpha^{\beta-1}D_x\,\alpha + \alpha^\beta\times(\ln\ \alpha)\times D_x\,\beta
\end{array} \qquad (8)$$

where a is any constant symbol other than x. Let the termination function $\tau: \mathcal{T} \rightarrow \mathbf{N}$ be defined as follows:

$$\begin{array}{rcl}
\tau(\alpha+\beta) & = & \tau(\alpha) + \tau(\beta) \\
\tau(\alpha\times\beta) & = & \tau(\alpha) + \tau(\beta) \\
\tau(\alpha-\beta) & = & \tau(\alpha) + \tau(\beta) \\
\tau(\frac{\alpha}{\beta}) & = & \tau(\alpha) + \tau(\beta) \\
\tau(\alpha^\beta) & = & \tau(\alpha) + \tau(\beta) \\
\tau(D_x\,\alpha) & = & \tau(\alpha)^2 \\
\tau(-\alpha) & = & \tau(\alpha) + 1 \\
\tau(\ln\ \alpha) & = & \tau(\alpha) + 1 \\
\tau(u) & = & 4
\end{array}$$

where u is any constant (including x). For each of the nine rules $l \rightarrow r$, the value of τ decreases, i.e. $\tau(l) > \tau(r)$. For example,

$$\tau(D_x\,(\frac{\alpha}{\beta})) = \tau(\frac{\alpha}{\beta})^2 = (\tau(\alpha)+\tau(\beta))^2 = \tau(\alpha)^2+\tau(\beta)^2+2\tau(\alpha)\tau(\beta),$$

while

$$\tau(\frac{D_x\,\alpha}{\beta} - \alpha\frac{D_x\,\beta}{\beta^2}) = \tau(\alpha)^2+\tau(\beta)^2+\tau(\alpha)+2\tau(\beta)+4.$$

This is a decrease, since $\tau(\alpha)$ and $\tau(\beta)$ are at least 4 and therefore

$$2\tau(\alpha)\tau(\beta) \geq 4\tau(\alpha)+4\tau(\beta) > \tau(\alpha)+2\tau(\beta)+4.$$

Integer polynomials cannot, however, suffice for termination proofs in general, since that would place a polynomial bound on computations (see, e.g., [Huet-Oppen-80]).

Example. It seems that System (1) cannot be proved to terminate with any monotonic polynomial interpretation [Dershowitz-83]. But termination can be proved using exponentials [Filman-78], defining $\tau: \mathcal{T} \rightarrow \mathbf{N}$ as follows:

$$\begin{aligned}\tau(\alpha+\beta) &= \tau(\alpha) + \tau(\beta)+1\\ \tau(\alpha\times\beta) &= \tau(\alpha)\tau(\beta)\\ \tau(-\alpha) &= 3^{\tau(\alpha)}\\ \tau(u) &= 3,\end{aligned}$$

where u is any constant. Since the value of any term is at least 3, each rule is a reduction.

Proving termination of *rewriting modulo equations* is, in practice, considerably more difficult than for plain rewrite systems. Here, given an equational theory (congruence relation) E, a rule $l \rightarrow r$ in R applies to a term $t \in \mathcal{T}$ if there is a substitution σ such that $l\sigma = s$ for some subterm s of a term v such that $v =_E t$ in the theory E. If $l \rightarrow r$ applies in this sense, then we write $t \Rightarrow_{R/E} u$, where u is any term equal (in E) to that v with s replaced by $r\sigma$. The question then is: for given R and E, does there exist an infinite sequence of terms $t_i \in \mathcal{T}$ such that $t_1 \Rightarrow_{R/E} t_2 \Rightarrow_{R/E} \cdots$?

Example. Let I denote the equational theory (idempotence):

$$\alpha+\alpha = \alpha.$$

For any nonempty R, R/I cannot be terminating, since there must be an infinite derivation $l =_I l+l \Rightarrow_R l+r =_I (l+l)+r \Rightarrow_R \cdots$ for any $l \rightarrow r \in R$.

The equational theory AC, consisting of the associative and commutative axioms,

$$\begin{aligned}f(\alpha,f(\beta,\gamma)) &= f(f(\alpha,\beta),\gamma)\\ f(\alpha,\beta) &= f(\beta,\alpha),\end{aligned}$$

is particularly important in practice. Let $\bar{t}$ denote the flattened version of a term t, with all nested occurrences of associative-commutative operators stripped, and where the order of arguments of such operators is not significant, and let $\bar{\mathcal{T}} = \{\bar{t} : t \in \mathcal{T}\}$. Two terms u and v are equal in AC if, and only if, $\bar{u}$ and $\bar{v}$ are the same. It is natural, therefore, to consider orderings on flattened terms.

Theorem 7 [Dershowitz,*etal.*-83]. *Let R be a rewrite system over some set of terms $\mathcal{T}$ and F a set of associative-commutative operators. The rewrite relation R/AC is terminating if, and only if, there exists a well-founded ordering $\succ$ on $\overline{\mathcal{T}}$ such that*

$$\overline{l} \succ \overline{r}$$

for each rule $l \to r$ in R and for any substitution of terms for the variables of the rule, and

$$\overline{f(l,\xi)} \succ \overline{f(r,\xi)}$$

for each rule $l \to r$ in R whose left-hand side l or right-hand side r has outermost associative-commutative symbol $f \in F$ or whose right-hand side is just a variable (where ξ is a variable otherwise not occurring in the rule), and such that

$$u \Rightarrow_{R/AC} v \text{ and } \overline{u} \succ \overline{v} \text{ imply } f(\cdots \overline{u} \cdots) \succ f(\cdots \overline{v} \cdots)$$

for all terms u and v in $\mathcal{T}$ and $f(\cdots \overline{u} \cdots)$ and $f(\cdots \overline{v} \cdots)$ in $\overline{\mathcal{T}}$.

Since addition and multiplication are themselves associative and commutative, monotonic polynomial interpretations are frequently helpful. To provide an ordering for flattened terms, a polynomial interpretation of a term should preserve its value under associativity and commutativity. The interpretations, $F(x,y)=xy$ and $F(x,y)=x+y+1$, for example, preserve value, whereas $F(x,y)=xy+1$, though symmetric, does not.

Example. Consider the following system (for Boolean rings):

$$\begin{array}{rcl} \alpha\cdot 1 & \to & \alpha \\ \alpha\cdot 0 & \to & 0 \\ \alpha\cdot\alpha & \to & \alpha \\ \alpha+0 & \to & \alpha \\ \alpha+\alpha & \to & 0 \\ (\alpha+\beta)\cdot\gamma & \to & (\alpha\cdot\gamma)+(\beta\cdot\gamma) \end{array} \tag{9}$$

One can use the following polynomial interpretation to prove its termination:

$$\begin{array}{rcl} \tau(\alpha+\beta) & = & \tau(\alpha)+\tau(\beta)+1 \\ \tau(\alpha\cdot\beta) & = & \tau(\alpha)\cdot\tau(\beta) \\ \tau(u) & = & 2, \end{array}$$

where u is any constant.

4. SIMPLIFICATION ORDERINGS

In proving termination, one can use any ordering $\succ$ that is well-founded over all terms that could appear in any one derivation; the ordering need not be well-founded over all terms that appear in all derivations. We call an ordering for which $\succ \cap \Rightarrow^*$ is always well-founded, regardless of what rules are in R, *well-founded for derivations*. Thus, to apply Theorem 4, we need only that $\succ$ be a well-founded ordering for derivations. In particular, Theorem 2 implies the following:

Theorem 8. *A partial ordering $\succ$ is well-founded for derivations if it has an extension that contains the embedding relation $\triangleright$.*

To apply Theorem 5, we need $\succ$ to be monotonic, as well as well-founded for derivations. The following definition describes monotonic extensions of $\triangleright$:

Definition 8 [Dershowitz-82]. A monotonic partial ordering $\succ$ is a *simplification ordering* for a set of terms $\mathcal{T}$ if it possesses the *subterm property,*

$$f(\cdots t \cdots) \succ t,$$

and the *deletion property,*

$$f(\cdots t \cdots) \succ f(\cdots \quad \cdots),$$

for all terms in $\mathcal{T}$.

By iterating the subterm property, any term is also greater than any of the (not necessarily immediate) subterms contained within it. The deletion condition asserts that deleting subterms of a (variable arity) operator reduces the term in the ordering; if the operators f have fixed arity, the deletion condition is superfluous. Together these conditions imply that "syntactically simpler" terms are smaller in the ordering.

Theorem 9 [Dershowitz-79]. *Any simplification ordering is a monotonic well-founded ordering for derivations.*

In the previous section, we saw the use of polynomial interpretations for termination proofs. That method requires that terms be mapped onto the well-founded nonnegative integers; using simplification orderings, on the other hand, allows the methods to be extended to domains that are not themselves well-founded. For example, one can associate a monotonic polynomial $F(x_1, \ldots, x_n)$ over the *reals* with each n-ary operator f [Dershowitz-79]. For any given choice of polynomials F to provide a simplification ordering, we must have that

$$x_i > x_i' \textit{ implies } F(\cdots x_i \cdots) > F(\cdots x_i' \cdots)$$

and

$$F(\cdots x_i \cdots) > x_i$$

for all positions i and for all real-valued xs.[5] For termination, we need

$$\tau(l) > tau(r),$$

for all rules $l \rightarrow r$ and for all real value assignments to the variables $\tau(\alpha)$ in $\tau(l)$. Allowing the x's to take on any real value is usually too strong a requirement; instead one may show that terms always map into some subset R' of the reals, i.e. x_1, ..., x_n in R' implies $F(x_1, \ldots, x_n)$ in R'. Then one need only show that the conditions hold for all x in R'. The above conditions are all decidable (albeit in superexponential time), since they are logical combinations of multivariate polynomial inequalities over the reals [Tarski-51] (see [Cohen-69] for a much

[5]The methods of the next section allow the strict inequalities $>$ in these two conditions to be replaced by $\geq$.

briefer decision procedure and [Collins-75] for a more efficient one). Thus, the polynomial ordering can be effectively "lifted" to open (i.e. nonground) terms. It is similarly decidable if there exists polynomials (and a suitable definition of R') of a given maximum degree that satisfy the conditions and thereby prove termination. (The decision procedure, however, cannot point to the appropriate polynomials). For polynomials over the natural numbers, these conditions are not decidable (see [Lankford-79]).

Example. Consider the set of expressions $\mathcal{T}$ constructed from some set of constants and the single operator $\times$ and the system (for semigroups)

$$(\alpha\times\beta)\times\gamma \quad \rightarrow \quad \alpha\times(\beta\times\gamma) \tag{10}$$

Terms t and u are compared by comparing their real value interpretations, $\tau(t)$ and $\tau(u)$. The real polynomials used are

$$\tau(\alpha\times\beta) = d\cdot\tau(\alpha) + \tau(\beta)$$

for some real $d>1$, for products, and

$$\tau(u) = e$$

for some $e>0$, for constants u. The value of the function τ decreases for the subexpression that the rule is applied to: for any terms α, β, and γ,

$$\tau((\alpha\times\beta)\times\gamma) = d\cdot\tau(\alpha\times\beta)\times\tau(\gamma) = d^2\cdot\tau(\alpha) + d\cdot\tau(\beta) + \tau(\gamma),$$

while

$$\tau(\alpha\times(\beta\times\gamma)) = d\cdot\tau(\alpha)+\tau(\beta\times\gamma) = d\cdot\tau(\alpha)+d\cdot\tau(\beta)+\tau(\gamma).$$

This is a reduction, i.e.

$$\tau((\alpha\times\beta)\times\gamma) > \tau(\alpha\times(\beta\times\gamma)),$$

since $d^2>d$ and $\tau(\alpha)>0$.

Most orderings used in conjunction with Theorem 5 to prove termination of rewrite systems are simplification orderings. In fact:

Theorem 10. *Any total monotonic ordering $\succ$ is well-founded for derivations if, and only if, it is a simplification ordering.*

In general, however, total monotonic orderings, and hence simplification orderings, do not suffice for termination proofs.

Example. Consider the system

$$\begin{array}{lcl} f(a) & \rightarrow & f(b) \\ g(b) & \rightarrow & g(a). \end{array} \tag{11}$$

If an ordering $>$ is total, then either $a>b$ or $b>a$. If $a>b$, then we would also have $g(a)>g(b)$, and the second rule would not be a reduction; analogously, if $b>a$, the first rule would not be.

We have seen above (Theorem 1) that termination is undecidable for two-rule systems; for one-rule systems, the question of decidability is open. On the other hand,

Theorem 11 [Jouannaud-Kirchner-82]. *It is decidable if a system of only one rule reduces under any simplification ordering.*

5. QUASI-ORDERINGS

This section describes methods for proving termination using quasi-orderings. A *quasi-ordered* set $(S,\succsim)$ consists of a set S and a transitive and reflexive binary relation $\succsim$ defined on elements of S. For example, the set of integers is quasi-ordered under the relation "greater or congruent modulo 10." Given a quasi-ordering $\succsim$ on a set S, define the equivalence relation $\approx$ as both $\succsim$ and $\precsim$ and the partial ordering $\succ$ as $\succsim$ but not $\precsim$. A quasi-order $\succsim$ on S is *total* if, for any two elements s and s' in S, either $s\succsim s'$ or else $s\precsim s'$. Note that the strict part $\succ$ is well-founded if, and only if, all infinite *quasi-descending* sequences $s_1\succsim s_2\succsim s_3\succsim \cdots$ of elements of S contain a pair $s_j\precsim s_k$ for some $j<k$. In other words, if $\succ$ is well-founded, then from some point on, in any infinite quasi-descending sequence, all elements are equivalent.

A stronger notion than well-foundedness is accordingly the following:

Definition 9 [Kruskal-60]. A set S is *well-quasi-ordered* under a quasi-ordering $\precsim$ if every infinite sequence $s_1,s_2,\cdots$ of elements of S contains a pair of elements s_j and s_k, $j<k$, such that $s_j\precsim s_k$.

Thus, the strict part of any well-quasi-ordering is well-founded. Well-quasi-ordered sets are said to have the *finite basis property* in [Higman-52]; for a survey of the history and applications of well-quasi-orderings, see [Kruskal-72]. A generalization, limiting the contexts in which an embedding may occur, and possibly having applications to proofs of termination, can be found in [Ehrenfeucht,*etal.*-83, Bucher,*etal.*-84, Puel-85]. A even stronger notion than well-quasi-ordering, namely *better-quasi-ordering,* is exploited in [Laver-78].

Note that any finite set is well-quasi-ordered under any quasi-ordering (including equality). It follows from the definitions that if a set is well-quasi-ordered under $\precsim$, then it is well-founded under (any extension of) the partial ordering $\succ$; the converse is true for total orderings, i.e. if a set is well-founded under a total ordering $\succ$, then it is well-quasi-ordered under $\precsim$.

Theorem 12. *A rewrite system R over a set of terms $\mathcal{T}$ is terminating if there exists a quasi-ordering $\succsim$, which extends a well-founded ordering $\succ$ and has the strict subterm property*

$$f(\cdots t \cdots) \succ t,$$

such that

$$l \succ r$$

for each rule $l \rightarrow r$ in R and for any substitution of terms in $\mathcal{T}$ for the variables of the rule, such that

$$s \Rightarrow t \text{ and } s \succsim t \text{ imply } f(\cdots s \cdots) \succsim f(\cdots t \cdots).$$

(Cf. [Kamin-Levy-80].)

The quasi-ordering used in the above theorem can be a combination of two quasi-orderings, one used to show that eventually all terms in a derivation are equivalent and the second to show that there can only be a finite number of equivalent terms in any such derivation.

Definition 10. A rewrite system R is *quasi-terminating* for a set of terms $\mathcal{T}$, if all (infinite) derivations contain only a finite number of different terms. Equivalently (for finite systems), any infinite derivation must cycle.

Quasi-terminating systems are also referred to as *globally finite*. To prove that a system is quasi-terminating, one can use quasi-orderings in the obvious way:

Theorem 13. *A rewrite system R over a set of terms $\mathcal{T}$ is quasi-terminating if there exists a quasi-ordering $\succsim$, which extends a well-founded ordering $\succ$ and whose equivalence relation $\approx$ admits only finite equivalence classes, such that*

$$t \Rightarrow u \text{ implies } t \succsim u$$

for all terms t and u in $\mathcal{T}$.

The following theorem gives one method for establishing finiteness of equivalence classes:

Theorem 14. *If the strict part $\succ$ of a quasi-ordering $\succsim$ on a set of terms $\mathcal{T}$ is an extension of the embedding relation $\rhd$, then $\approx$ admits only finite equivalence classes.*

Example. Consider the polynomial interpretation

$$\tau(if(\alpha,\beta,\delta)) = \tau(\alpha)\times(\tau(\beta)+\tau(\gamma))$$

with constants assigned the value 2. The partial ordering $t \succ u$ if, and only if, $\tau(t) > \tau(u)$ does contain the embedding relation. Since, for the system (for normalizing conditionals)

$$if(if(\alpha,\beta,\gamma),\delta,\epsilon) \rightarrow if(\alpha,if(\beta,\delta,\epsilon),if(\gamma,\delta,\epsilon)) \qquad (12)$$

$\tau(l)=\tau(r)$, the system is quasi-terminating.

Another method is the following:

Theorem 15. *If the strict part $\succ$ of a quasi-ordering $\succsim$ on a set of terms $\mathcal{T}$ is well-founded and has the subterm property*

$$f(\cdots t \cdots) \succ t,$$

the deletion property

$$f(\cdots t \cdots) \succ f(\cdots \quad \cdots),$$

and admits only a finite number of terms smaller than any given one, then $\approx$ admits only finite equivalence classes.

Note that the ordering need not be monotonic. (Cf. [Lipton-Snyder-77].)

Example. Consider the following system (for distributivity):

$$\begin{array}{rcl} \alpha\times(\beta+\gamma) & \rightarrow & (\alpha\times\beta)+(\alpha\times\gamma) \\ (\beta+\gamma)\times\alpha & \rightarrow & (\beta\times\alpha)+(\gamma\times\alpha) \\ \alpha\times 1 & \rightarrow & \alpha \\ 1\times\alpha & \rightarrow & \alpha \end{array} \qquad (13)$$

Under the natural interpretation (+ as addition and × as multiplication, but constants as 2) terms can be mapped into natural numbers (and hence the term ordering has order-type ω) while satisfying the subterm property. Since $l \approx r$ under this interpretation the system quasi-terminates.

Of course:

Theorem 16 [Guttag,*etal.*-83]. *Quasi-termination of rewrite systems is undecidable.*

On the other hand, nontermination of any quasi-terminating system is clearly semi-decidable. Also, termination of a quasi-terminating system for a *given* input term is decidable (construct all derivations initiated by that term until they terminate or cycle).

Example. System (10) quasi-terminates, as does any (finite) system that never increases the size of terms.

Another notion that has been investigated is *fair termination* (of quasi-terminating systems), in which all infinite derivations must include an application of each rule that is infinitely often applicable. See [Porat-Francez-85].

Using a definition of monotonicity, we can give a local condition for quasi-termination:

Definition 11. A quasi-ordering $\succsim$ over a set of terms $\mathcal{T}$ is *monotonic* if

$$t \succsim u \textit{ implies } f(\cdots t \cdots) \succsim f(\cdots u \cdots)$$

for all terms in $\mathcal{T}$.

Theorem 17 [Dershowitz-82]. *A rewrite system R over a set of terms $\mathcal{T}$ is quasi-terminating if there exists a monotonic quasi-ordering $\succsim$, which extends a simplification ordering $\succ$, such that*

$$l \succsim r$$

for each rule $l \rightarrow r$ in R and for any substitution of terms in $\mathcal{T}$ for the variables of the rule.

Example. System (13) can be shown to be quasi-terminating using the "natural" interpretation which preserves the value of a term under rewriting, i.e. $\tau(l)=\tau(r)$ for both rules. By letting constants have a positive value, the quasi-ordering $\geq$ is an extension of the simplification ordering $>$.

Given quasi-termination, the following method may be used to prove full termination:

Theorem 18. *A quasi-terminating rewrite system R over a set of terms $\mathcal{T}$ is terminating if there exists a monotonic quasi-ordering $\succsim$ such that*

$$l \succ r$$

for each rule $l \rightarrow r$ in R and for any substitution of terms in $\mathcal{T}$ for the variables of the rule.

Thus, to prove termination one can first find a monotonic quasi-ordering $\succsim$ guaranteeing quasi-termination, and then find any monotonic quasi-ordering $\succsim'$ under which each rule is a reduction.[6]

Example. The proof of termination of System (12) may be completed using the monotonic quasi-ordering $t \succsim' u$ if, and only if, $|t| \leq |u|$, which "decreases" with application of the length-increasing rules.

Example. To complete a proof of termination for the quasi-terminating System (10), a monotonic quasi-ordering $\succsim$ can be used, under which $t_1 \times t_2 \succsim t_1' \times t_2'$ if, and only if, $|t_1 \times t_2| = |t_1' \times t_2'|$ and $|t_1| \geq |t_1'|$.

Extending the results of the previous section, we have

Definition 12 [Dershowitz-82]. A monotonic quasi-ordering $\succsim$ is a *quasi-simplification ordering* for a set of terms $\mathcal{T}$ if it possesses the subterm property

$$f(\cdots t \cdots) \succsim t,$$

and deletion property,

$$f(\cdots t \cdots) \succsim f(\cdots \quad \cdots),$$

for all terms in $\mathcal{T}$.

That is, a quasi-simplification ordering is a monotonic extension of the embedding relation $\trianglerighteq$. A quasi-simplification ordering for fixed-arity operators is called a *divisibility order* in [Higman-52]. The strict part $\succ$ of any quasi-simplification ordering $\succsim$ is well-founded for

[6] [Lipton-Snyder-77, Guttag, *etal.*-83] use "increasing length" where any monotonic quasi-ordering would do.

derivations. For proving termination, it is enough that $\succsim$ be monotonic:

Theorem 19 [Dershowitz-82]. *A rewrite system R over a set of terms $\mathcal{T}$ is terminating if there exists a quasi-simplification ordering $\succsim$ such that*

$$l \succ r$$

for each rule $l \rightarrow r$ in R and for any substitution of terms in $\mathcal{T}$ for the variables of the rule.

6. MULTISET ORDERINGS

Multisets, or *bags,* are like sets, but allow multiple occurrences of identical elements. A partial ordering $\succ$ on any given set S can be extended to form an ordering $\succ\!\!\succ$ on finite multisets over S. In this extended ordering, $M \succ\!\!\succ M'$, for two finite multisets M and M' over S, if M' can be obtained from M by replacing one or more elements in M by any (finite) number of elements taken from S, each of which is smaller than one of the replaced elements. More formally, let $\mathcal{M}(S)$ denote the set of finite multisets of elements of S. Then:

Definition 13 [Dershowitz-Manna-79]. For a partially-ordered set $(S, \succ)$, the *multiset ordering* $\succ\!\!\succ$ on $\mathcal{M}(S)$ is defined as follows:

$$M \succ\!\!\succ M'$$

if, and only if, for some multisets $X, Y \in \mathcal{M}(S)$, where X is a nonempty subset of M,

$$M' = (M - X) \cup Y$$

and for all $y \in Y$ there is an $x \in X$ such that

$$x \succ y.$$

Definition 14. For a quasi-ordered set $(S, \succsim)$, the *multiset quasi-ordering* $\succsim\!\!\succsim$ on $\mathcal{M}(S)$ is defined as follows:

$$M \succsim\!\!\succsim M'$$

if, and only if, for some multisets $X, Y \in \mathcal{M}(S)$,

$$M' \approx (M - X) \cup Y$$

and for all $y \in Y$ there is an $x \in X$ such that

$$x \succ y,$$

where two multisets are considered equivalent if the equivalence classes of their elements (under $\approx$) are the same.

For example, the multiset {3,3,3,4,0,0} of natural numbers is identical to the multiset {0,3,3,0,4,3}, but distinct from {3,4,0}. If **N** is the set of natural numbers 0, 1, 2, ... with the $>$ ordering, then under the corresponding *multiset ordering* $\gg$ over **N**, the multiset {3,3,4,0} is greater than each of the three multisets {3,4}, {3,2,2,1,1,1,4,0}, and {3,3,3,3,2,2}. In the first case, two elements have been removed (i.e. replaced by zero elements); in the second case, an occurrence of 3 has been replaced by two occurrences of 2 and three occurrences of 1; and in the third case, the element 4 has been replaced by two occurrences each of 3 and 2, and in addition the element 0 has been removed. (See also [Smullyan-79, Gardner-83].)

This ordering on multisets enjoys the following minimality property:

Theorem 20 [Lescanne-Jouannaud-82]. *For a given partial ordering $\succ$ on a set S, any partial ordering $\gg'$ on $\mathcal{M}(S)$ that satisfies the property*

$$s \succ s' \text{ implies } \{\cdots s \cdots\} \gg' \{\cdots s' \cdots\}$$

is contained in the multiset ordering $\gg$.

Multiset orderings are used in termination proofs on account of the following:

Theorem 21 [Dershowitz-Manna-79]. *The multiset ordering $\gg$ is well-founded if, and only if, $\succ$ is.*

Example. To prove termination of System (8), we use a ***simple path ordering*** of [Plaisted-78]. Terms are mapped into multisets of sequences of operators; sequences are compared in the *monadic path ordering* $>_{mpo}$, as we did for System (7). The monotonic termination function used for the simple path ordering is

$$\tau(t) = \{(f_1, f_2, \ldots, f_k) \mid (f_1, f_2, \ldots, f_k) \text{ is a path in } t\},$$

where a *path* is a sequence of operators, starting at the outermost one of the whole term (the root, viewing terms as trees) and taking subterms until a constant (leaf) is reached. For the operator ordering, we take D to be greater than all else. For example, consider the expression

$$t = D_x D_x (D_x y \times (y + D_x D_x x)),$$

or with the D's numbered for expository purposes,

$$t = D_1 D_2 (D_3 y \times (y + D_4 D_5 x)).$$

There are three paths, and

$$\tau(t) = \{(D_1, D_2, \times, D_3, y), (D_1, D_2, \times, +, y), (D_1, D_2, \times, +, D_4, D_5, x)\}.$$

Applying the rule

$$D_x(\alpha \times \beta) \quad \rightarrow \quad \beta \times D_x \alpha \; + \; \alpha \times D_x \beta$$

to t yields

$$u = D_1(((y + D_4 D_5 x) \times D_2 D_3 y) + (D_3 y \times D_2 (y + D_4 D_5 x)))$$

(with the labeling of the D_x's retained), and accordingly

$$\tau(u) = \{(D_1, +, \times, +, y), (D_1, +, \times, +, D_4, D_5, x), (D_1, +, \times, D_2, D_3, y),$$
$$(D_1, +, \times, D_3, y), (D_1, +, \times, D_2, +, y), (D_1, +, \times, D_2, +, D_4, D_5, x)\}.$$

We have $\tau(t) \gg_{mpo} \tau(u)$, since

$$\begin{array}{rcl}
(D_1,D_2,\times,D_3,y) & >_{mpo} & (D_1,+,\times,+,y) \\
(D_1,+,\times,D_2,+,D_4,D_5,x) & >_{mpo} & (D_1,+,\times,+,D_4,D_5,x) \\
(D_1,D_2,\times,D_3,y) & >_{mpo} & (D_1,+,\times,D_2,D_3,y) \\
(D_1,D_2,\times,D_3,y) & >_{mpo} & (D_1,+,\times,D_3,y) \\
(D_1,D_2,\times,D_3,y) & >_{mpo} & (D_1,+,\times,D_2,+,y) \\
(D_1,+,\times,D_2,+,D_4,D_5,x) & >_{mpo} & (D_1,+,\times,D_2,+,D_4,D_5,x).
\end{array}$$

In the monadic path ordering, sequences are compared left-to-right: At each step, any operator or constant less than or equal to the corresponding one in the other sequence is skipped over. Whichever sequence is finished first is smaller; if both finish together, whichever last had a smaller operator is larger.[7]

If $(S,\succ)$ is totally ordered, then for any two multisets $M,M' \in \mathcal{M}(S)$, one may determine whether $M \gg M'$ by first sorting the elements of both M and M' in descending order (with respect to the relation $\succ$) and then comparing the two sorted sequences lexicographically.[8] For example, to compare the multisets {3,3,4,0} and {3,2,1,2,0,4}, one may compare the sorted sequences (4,3,3,0) and (4,3,2,2,1,0). Since (4,3,3,0) is lexicographically greater than (4,3,2,2,1,0), it follows that {3,3,4,0}$\gg${3,2,1,2,0,4}. [Lescanne-Jouannaud-82] describes an implementation of multiset orderings for the nontotal case.

Consider the case where there is a bound k on the number of replacement elements. Any termination proof using this bounded multiset ordering over $\mathbf{N}$ may be translated into a proof using natural numbers. This may be done using the termination function

$$\psi(M) = \sum_{n \in M} \frac{k^n - 1}{k-1}$$

which maps multisets over the natural numbers into the natural numbers. When exactly k elements $n-1$ replace one element n, the above function gives the exact number of replacements until termination.

In general, if $(S,\succ)$ is of order type α, then the multiset ordering $(\mathcal{M}(S),\gg)$ over $(S,\succ)$ is of order type ω^α. This follows from the fact that there exists a mapping ψ from $\mathcal{M}(S)$ onto ω^α that is one-to-one and *order-preserving,* i.e. if $M \gg M'$ for $M,M' \in \mathcal{M}(S)$, then the ordinal $\psi(M)$ is greater than $\psi(M')$. That mapping is

$$\psi(M) = \sum_{m \in M} \omega^{\phi(m)}$$

where $\sum$ denotes the natural (i.e. commutative) sum of ordinals and ϕ is the one-to-one order-preserving mapping from S onto α.

---

[7][Gorn-73] uses a "stepped" lexicographic ordering (under which longer sequences are larger) to prove termination of differentiation, but without using multisets, his proof applies only when D's are not nested.

[8]This is the ordering I_ω^+ in [Manna-69].

Example. The simple path ordering does not work for the system:

$$\begin{array}{lcl} --\alpha & \rightarrow & \alpha \\ -(\alpha+\beta) & \rightarrow & ---\alpha\times---\beta \\ -(\alpha\times\beta) & \rightarrow & ---\alpha+---\beta \end{array} \tag{14}$$

Instead, we use Theorem 19 and define the following quasi-simplification ordering: $t \gg u$ for two terms t and u if, and only if,

$$|t|_{+\times} \geq |u|_{+\times} \text{ and } \{|\alpha|_{+\times}: -\alpha \text{ in } t\} \geq \{|\alpha|_{+\times}: -\alpha \text{ in } u\},$$

where the multisets contain the value $|\alpha|_{+\times}$ (the number of occurrences of operators other than $-$ in α) for each subterm of the form $-\alpha$, and multisets are compared using $\geq$. It is easy to see that this quasi-ordering satisfies the replacement and subterm properties of quasi-simplification orderings on fixed-arity terms. It remains to show that each rule reduces the subterm it is applied to. For all three rules, the number of operators other than $-$ is the same on both sides. To see that

$$--\alpha \succ \alpha,$$

note that there are two less elements in the multiset of numbers of operators for the right-hand side than for the left-hand side. To see that

$$-(\alpha+\beta) \succ ---\alpha\times---\beta$$

$$-(\alpha\times\beta) \succ ---\alpha+---\beta$$

note that the number of operators other than $-$ in $\alpha+\beta$ and $\alpha\times\beta$ is greater than that of $--\alpha$, $-\alpha$, α, $--\beta$, $-\beta$, and β.

7. PRECEDENCE ORDERINGS

We use the multiset ordering in the following:

Definition 15 [Dershowitz-82]. Let $\succ$ be a partial ordering on a set of operators F. The *recursive path ordering* $\succ_{rpo}$ on the set $\mathcal{T}(F)$ of terms over F is defined recursively as follows:

$$s = f(s_1, \ldots, s_m) \succ_{rpo} g(t_1, \ldots, t_n) = t$$

if

$$s_i \succsim_{rpo} t \quad \text{for } some\ i=1,\ldots,m$$

or

$$f \succ g \text{ and } s \succ_{rpo} t_j \quad \text{for } all\ j=1,\ldots,n$$

or

$$f = g \text{ and } \{s_1, \ldots, s_m\} \gg_{rpo} \{t_1, \ldots, t_n\},$$

where $\gg_{rpo}$ is the extension of $\succ_{rpo}$ to multisets and $\succsim_{rpo}$ means $\succ_{rpo}$ or permutatively congruent (equivalent up to permutations of subterms).

This definition is similar to a characterization of the *path of subterms ordering* given in

[Plaisted-78b].[9] The idea is that a term is decreased by replacing a subterm with any number of smaller (recursively) subterms connected by any structure of operators smaller (in the operator ordering) than the outermost operator of the replaced subterm.

To determine, then, if a term s is greater in this ordering than a term t, the outermost operators of the two terms are compared first. If the operators are equal, then those (immediate) subterms of t that are not also subterms of s must each be smaller (recursively in the term ordering) than some subterm of s. If the outermost operator of s is greater than that of t, then s must be greater than each subterm of t; while if the outermost operator of s is neither equal nor greater that that of t, then some subterm of s must be greater or equal to t. For example, suppose $- > +$, and let $s = -(1\times(1+0))$ and $t = -1 + -(0\times 1)$. The term s is greater than t under the corresponding recursive path ordering $>_{rpo}$ by the following line of reasoning:

$$s >_{rpo} t \text{ since } - > + \text{ and } s >_{rpo} -1, -(0\times 1)$$

$$s >_{rpo} -1 \text{ since } 1\times(1+0) >_{rpo} 1$$

$$1\times(1+0) >_{rpo} 1 \text{ since } 1 \geq_{rpo} 1$$

$$s >_{rpo} -(0\times 1) \text{ since } 1\times(1+0) >_{rpo} 0\times 1$$

$$1\times(1+0) >_{rpo} 0\times 1 \text{ since } 1=1 \text{ and } 1+0 >_{rpo} 0$$

$$1+0 >_{rpo} 0 \text{ since } 0 \geq 0.$$

Theorem 22 [Dershowitz-82]. *The recursive path ordering is a simplification ordering.*

Using the recursive path ordering to prove the termination of rewrite systems generalizes the (exponential interpretation) method in [Iturriaga-67].[10]

Example. We can use a recursive path ordering to prove termination of System (1). Let the operators be ordered by $- > \times > +$. Since this is a simplification ordering on terms, by Theorem 9, we need only show that

$$\begin{array}{rcl} --\alpha & >_{rpo} & \alpha \\ -(\alpha+\beta) & >_{rpo} & -\alpha\times-\beta \\ -(\alpha\times\beta) & >_{rpo} & -\alpha+-\beta \\ \alpha\times(\beta+\gamma) & >_{rpo} & (\alpha\times\beta)+(\alpha\times\gamma) \\ (\beta+\gamma)\times\alpha & >_{rpo} & (\beta\times\alpha)+(\gamma\times\alpha) \end{array}$$

for any terms α, β, and γ. The first inequality follows from the subterm condition of simplification orderings. By the definition of the recursive path ordering, to show that

---

[9]This ordering addresses the problem posed in [Levy-80].

[10]The cases where Iturriaga's method works are those for which the operators are partially ordered so that the outermost ("virtual") operators of the left-hand side of the rules are greater than any other operators.

$-(\alpha+\beta)>_{rpo}(-\alpha\times-\beta)$ when $->\times$, we must show that $-(\alpha+\beta)>_{rpo}-\alpha$, and $-(\alpha+\beta)>_{rpo}-\beta$. Now, since the outermost operators of $-(\alpha+\beta)$, $-\alpha$, and $-\beta$ are the same, one must show that $\alpha+\beta>_{rpo}\alpha$ and $\alpha+\beta>_{rpo}\beta$. But this is true by the subterm condition. Thus the second inequality holds. By an analogous argument, the third inequality also holds. For the fourth inequality, since $\times>+$, we must show $\alpha\times(\beta+\gamma)>_{rpo}\alpha\times\beta$ and $\alpha\times(\beta+\gamma)>_{rpo}\alpha\times\gamma$. By the definition of the recursive path ordering for the case when two terms have the same outermost operator, we must show that $\{\alpha,\beta+\gamma\}\gg_{rpo}\{\alpha,\beta\}$ and $\{\alpha,\beta+\gamma\}\gg_{rpo}\{\alpha,\gamma\}$. These two inequalities between multisets hold, since the elements $\beta+\gamma$ is greater than both β and γ with which it is replaced. Similarly the fifth inequality may be shown to hold. Therefore, by Theorem 9, this system terminates for all inputs.

The *multiset ordering* described above, *nested multiset ordering* [Dershowitz-Manna-79], and *simple path ordering* may all be thought of as special cases of the *recursive path ordering*, in which the multiset constructor $\{\cdots\}$ is greater than other operators. The nested multiset ordering is just a recursive path ordering on all terms constructed from one varyadic operator, and (with just that one operator) is of order type ϵ_0.[11] Gentzen used such an ordering to show termination of his "normalization procedure" [Gentzen-38]. Two other interesting examples of ϵ_0 termination arguments may be found in [Kirby-Paris-82].

The above definition of the *recursive path ordering* is not particularly well-suited for computation. The *recursive decomposition ordering* $\succ_{rdo}$ (defined in [Lescanne-84, Plaisted-79] for the case when the ordering $\succ$ on operators is total) "preprocesses" terms in an attempt to improve efficiency. Suppose $\succ$ is total, and let $\bar{t}$ denote the term $t=g(t_1,\ldots,t_n)$ with all subterms sorted according to $\succ_{rdo}$, i.e. $\bar{t}=g(\bar{t}_{j_1},\ldots,\bar{t}_{j_n})$, where $\bar{t}_{j_1}\succeq_{rdo}\cdots\succeq_{rdo}\bar{t}_{j_n}$ and $\{t_{j_1},\ldots,t_{j_n}\}$ is permutatively congruent to $\{t_1,\ldots,t_n\}$. Consider two sorted terms $\bar{s}=u[f(s_1,\ldots,s_m)]$ and $\bar{t}=v[g(t_1,\ldots,t_n)]$, where f and g are the greatest operators in s and t, and u and v are the "contexts" surrounding the leftmost (maximal) occurrences of f and g in s and t, respectively. Then,

$$s \succ_{rdo} t$$

if, and only if, the decomposition of $\bar{s}$,

$$\langle f,(s_1,\ldots,s_m),u[\circ]\rangle,$$

is greater than the decomposition of $\bar{t}$,

$$\langle g,(t_1,\ldots,t_n),v[\circ]\rangle,$$

where the three components are compared lexicographically, the operators f and g according to $\succ$, the subterms s_i and t_j lexicographically (using $\succ_{rdo}$ recursively), and the contexts u and v recursively. In comparing contexts, the operator $\circ$ is considered to be greater than any term not containing $\circ$; in choosing greatest f and g, circles are ignored. For example, suppose $0>->\times>+>1$, $s=-(1\times(1+0))$, and $t=-1+-(0\times1)$. Their sorted terms are

[11]That the nested multiset ordering has the properties of simplification orderings was pointed out in

$\bar{s}=-((0+1)\times 1)$ and $\bar{t}=-(0\times 1)+-1$. The full decomposition of $\bar{s}$ is

$$\langle 0,(\ ),\langle -,(\langle \times,(\langle +,(\circ,1),\circ\rangle,1),\circ\rangle),\circ\rangle\rangle;$$

that of $\bar{t}$ is

$$\langle 0,(\ ),\langle -,(\langle \times,(\circ,1),\circ\rangle),\langle +,(\circ,\langle -,(\ ),\circ\rangle),\circ\rangle\rangle\rangle.$$

The first decomposition is greater, since $\langle +,(\circ,1),\circ\rangle$ is greater than just $\circ$.

With the above definition, the comparison of two sorted terms is essentially lexicographic. Sorting a list of sorted terms and building the decomposition are believed to be relatively inexpensive [Dershowitz-Zaks-81, Lescanne-Steyaert-83]. The definition of "decomposition" can be extended to the nontotal case [Jouannaud,*etal.*-82, Rusinowitch-85]. The *recursive decomposition ordering* as well as the *path of subterms ordering* [Plaisted-78b] and *path ordering* [Kapur-Sivakumar-83], extend the recursive path ordering somewhat when the ordering $\succ$ on operators is partial. The four are are equivalent in the total case. For example, the path of subterms ordering makes $h(f(\alpha),f(\beta)) >_{pso} h(g(\alpha,\beta),g(\alpha,\beta))$ if $f > g$, but the two are incomparable under $>_{rpo}$. With a total ordering on operators, terms are also totally ordered. Thus, one can determine that $h(f(\alpha),f(\beta)) >_{rpo} h(g(\alpha,\beta),g(\alpha,\beta))$ in all three possible cases: $\alpha > \beta$, $\beta > \alpha$, and $\alpha = \beta$. The exact relation between them is investigated in [Rusinowitch-85]. These orderings are also equivalent for monadic terms, even when the operator ordering is partial; an efficient implementation of the monadic case is given in [Lescanne-81].

These precedence orderings may be conveniently lifted to apply to nonground terms (containing variables) by considering variables as (zeroary) constant symbols, unrelated to any other symbol. For the *recursive path ordering* this idea is illustrated in [Dershowitz-82] and formalized in [Huet-Oppen-80]; for the *recursive decomposition ordering* this is done in [Jouannaud,*etal.*-82]; for the *path of subterms ordering,* see [Plaisted-78b]. For example, we have $-(\alpha+\beta) >_{rpo} -\alpha \times -\beta$, where α and β are variables, since $-$ is greater than $\times$ (under $>$) and $-(\alpha+\beta)$ is greater than both $-\alpha$ and $-\beta$ (under $>_{rpo}$). For $-(\alpha+\beta) >_{rpo} -\alpha$, it must be that $\alpha+\beta >_{rpo} \alpha$, which is true since $+ \not\gtrless \alpha$ and $\alpha \geq_{rpo} \alpha$. Given a partial ordering $\succ$ of operators F, the following lifted ordering can also be used:

$$\bigcap_{\succ^{+} \supseteq \succ} \succ^{+}_{rpo},$$

where orderings are viewed as relations and all possible total extensions of the given precedence are considered. (See, for example, [Forgaard-84].)

These orderings are also *incremental*. That is, one can start with an empty ordering on operators, and add to it only as necessary to satisfy given inequalities between terms. How this may be done with the *recursive decomposition ordering* is described in [Jouannaud,*etal.*-82] (see also [AitKaci-83]). When comparing two terms, the comparison may stop when two decompositions have incomparable symbols, say f and g, as their first components. The idea is to add $f > g$ to the ordering at that point. (This method has been implemented in the

---

[Scherlis-80]. For a "constructive" discussion of this ordering, see [Paulson-84].

REVE system [Lescanne-83]. Details may be found in [Choque-83, Detlefs-Forgaard-85].) For instance, in order for $\alpha\times(\beta+\gamma)>_{rdo}(\alpha\times\beta)+(\alpha\times\gamma)$ to hold, one needs $\times>+$; if $\times>+$, then for $-(\alpha+\beta)>_{rdo}-\alpha\times-\beta$ to hold, it must be that $->\times$. But choosing an ordering on operators so that two terms are comparable under the *recursive path ordering* is NP-complete [Krishnamoorthy-Narendran-84] in the number of different operators.

It is sometimes necessary to transform terms before comparing them in the recursive path ordering. As long as the ordering on the operators of the transformed terms is well-founded, the recursive path ordering on transformed terms will also be:

Theorem 23 [Dershowitz-82]. *The recursive path ordering $\succ_{rpo}$ on the set of terms $\mathcal{T}(F)$ is well-founded if, and only if, the partial ordering $\succ$ on the set of operators F is well-founded.*

But the transform τ, which acts as termination function, needs to satisfy the monotonicity condition

$$\tau(t)\succ_{rpo}\tau(u) \textit{ implies } \tau(f(\cdots t \cdots))\succ_{rpo}\tau(f(\cdots u \cdots)).$$

Depending on the particular τ, this condition may or may not hold. One way in which terms may be transformed is to let the kth operand of a term act as its operator. Then to compare two terms one must first *recursively* compare their kth operands and then use the recursive path ordering. With this transform, the result is a monotonic simplification ordering. (See [Dershowitz-82].)

Example. To prove that System (12) terminates we consider the condition to be the operator. The condition $if(\alpha,\beta,\gamma)$ of the left-hand side is greater (by the subterm property) than the condition α of the right-hand side. Thus, we need to show that the left-hand side is greater than both right-hand-side operands $if(\beta,\delta,\epsilon)$ and $if(\gamma,\delta,\epsilon)$. Again, $if(\alpha,\beta,\gamma)$ is greater than both operators β and γ, and now the left-hand side is clearly greater than the remaining operands δ and ϵ.

Example. The following system (for a combinator C) terminates:

$$(C\cdot((\alpha\cdot\beta)\cdot\gamma)\cdot\delta \qquad \rightarrow \qquad (\alpha\cdot\gamma)\cdot((\beta\cdot\gamma)\cdot\delta). \tag{15}$$

One way to see that is to consider the left operand of $\cdot$ to be the operator.[12]

This particular ordering, considering the first operand to be the operator and applied to terms constructed only from one varyadic operator f, is of order type Γ_0 (see [Veblen-08, Feferman-68].) This can be shown with the following order-preserving mapping [Dershowitz-80] ψ from $\mathcal{T}(\{f\})$ onto Γ_0:

---

[12] This kind of proof is possible when the combinator has a *non-ascending property* described in [Pettorossi-78, Pettorossi-81].

$$\psi(f) = 0$$

$$\psi(f(f, \ldots, f)) = n \text{ where } n \text{ is the number of operands } f$$

$$\psi(f(\alpha, \beta_1, \beta_2, \ldots, \beta_n)) = \phi^{\psi(\alpha)}(\sum_{i=1}^{n} \omega^{\psi(\beta_i)}) + \delta(t)$$

where $\phi^0(\beta)=\beta$, $\phi^1(\beta)=\epsilon_\beta$ (the β-th epsilon number), $\phi^\alpha(\beta)$ is the βth fixpoint ξ of $\phi^\mu(\xi)=\xi$ common to ϕ^μ for all ordinals $\mu<\alpha$, $\sum$ is the natural (commutative) sum of ordinals, and δ is 1 if $\psi(\alpha)=1$, $n=1$, and $\psi(\beta_1)$ is an epsilon number and is 0 otherwise. (The purpose of δ is to ensure that $\psi(f(f,\beta))>\psi(\beta)$ even if $\psi(\beta)$ is an epsilon number.) That this mapping is order-preserving follows from the fact ([Feferman-68, Weyhrauch-78]) that $\phi^\alpha(\beta)>\phi^{\alpha'}(\beta')$ if and only if $\alpha=\alpha'$ and $\beta>\beta'$, or else $\alpha>\alpha'$ and $\phi^\alpha(\beta)>\beta'$, or else $\alpha<\alpha'$ and $\beta>\phi^{\alpha'}(\beta')$.

More generally, terms may be mapped by replacing their operators with the whole term itself, where the new operator is the whole term itself ordered by some *other* well-founded ordering:

Definition 16 [Kamin-Levy-80, Plaisted-79]. Let $\succsim$ be a quasi-ordering on a set of terms $\mathcal{T}$. The *semantic path ordering* $\succ_{spo}$ on $\mathcal{T}$ is defined recursively as follows:

$$s = f(s_1, \ldots, s_m) \succ_{spo} g(t_1, \ldots, t_n) = t$$

if

$$s_i \succsim_{spo} t \quad \text{for some } i=1,\ldots,m$$

or

$$s \succ t \text{ and } s \succ_{spo} t_j \quad \text{for all } j=1,\ldots,n$$

or

$$s \approx t \text{ and } \{s_1, \ldots, s_m\} \succ\!\!\succ_{spo} \{t_1, \ldots, t_n\},$$

where $\succ\!\!\succ_{spo}$ is the extension of $\succ_{spo}$ to multisets and $\succsim_{spo}$ means $\succ_{spo}$ or permutatively congruent (equivalent up to permutations of subterms).

To use this semantic path ordering in a termination proof, the monotonicity condition

$$t \Rightarrow u \text{ implies } f(\cdots t \cdots) \succ f(\cdots u \cdots)$$

must hold.

Example. Consider the system

$$\begin{array}{rcl} g(\alpha,\beta) & \rightarrow & h(\alpha,\beta) \\ h(f(\alpha),\beta) & \rightarrow & f(g(\alpha,\beta)). \end{array} \qquad (16)$$

The first rule suggests $g>h$; the second requires $h>f$ and $h\gtrsim g$. This conflict can be overcome by letting $>$ be a lexicographic combination of a recursive path ordering with $g \equiv h > f$ and one with $g>h$. Comparing terms under the corresponding $>_{spo}$ shows a reduction for both rules.

The recursive path ordering has also been adapted to handle associative-commutative operators by flattening and transforming terms (distributing large operators over small ones) before comparing them [Plaisted-83, Bachmair-Plaisted-85]. Here, too, the difficulty is in ensuring monotonicity. Flattening alone would not be monotonic. For instance, if $f > g$ then $f(a,a) >_{rpo} g(a,a)$, but $\overline{f(f(a,a),a)} = f(a,a,a) <_{rpo} f(g(a,b),c) = \overline{f(g(a,b),c)}$.

Another well-founded ordering is the following lexicographic version of the recursive path ordering:

Definition 17 [Kamin-Levy-80]. Let $\succ$ be a partial ordering on a set of operators F. The *lexicographic path ordering* $\succ_{lpo}$ on the set $\mathcal{T}(F)$ of terms over F is defined recursively as follows:

$$s = f(s_1, \ldots, s_m) \succ_{lpo} g(t_1, \ldots, t_n) = t$$

if

$$s \succ_{lpo} t_j \quad \text{for } all \ j=1,\ldots,n$$

and either

$$s_i \succeq_{lpo} t \quad \text{for } some \ i=1,\ldots,m$$

or

$$f = g \ and \ (s_1, \ldots, s_m) \succ_{lpo}^{*} (t_1, \ldots, t_n),$$

where $\succ_{lpo}^{*}$ is the lexicographic extension of $\succ_{lpo}$.

By the same token, some operators may have their operands compared lexicographically, while others are compared using multisets. [13] Multiset and lexicographic versions of these path orderings have been implemented in REVE [Lescanne-84, Detlefs-Forgaard-85] and RRL [Kapur-Sivakumar-83]. In [Kamin-Levy-80] it is pointed out that any well-founded manner of comparing operands that depends only on recursive comparisons of subterms would work as well.

Example. The following system (for Ackermann's function) can easily be seen to terminate with a lexicographic path ordering with empty precedence:

$$a(s(\alpha),s(\beta)) \rightarrow a(\alpha,a(s(\alpha),\beta)) \tag{17}$$

Sometimes, it is possible to adapt one of the above path orderings to work where otherwise it would not.

Example. The lexicographic path ordering cannot directly handle

[13]The same lexicographic path ordering has been described in [Sakai-84], where it is erroneously claimed to be an extension of the recursive path ordering; in fact, the two orderings are incomparable. How one might transform terms so that $t \succ_{lpo} u$ if, and only if, $\tau(t) \succ rpo \tau(u)$ is examined in [Pettorossi-81].

$$
\begin{array}{lcl}
(\alpha\cdot\beta)\cdot\gamma & \rightarrow & \alpha\cdot(\beta\cdot\gamma) \\
(\alpha+\beta)\cdot\gamma & \rightarrow & (\alpha\cdot\gamma)+(\beta\cdot\gamma) \\
\gamma\cdot(\alpha+f(\beta)) & \rightarrow & g(\gamma,\beta)\cdot(\alpha+a).
\end{array}
\tag{18}
$$

One needs to differentiate between $\cdot$ in general and $g(\cdots)\cdot\cdots$, making the operator larger in the former case.

Suppose we are given a quasi-ordering $\succsim_F$ on (fixed arity) operators and a quasi-simplification ordering $\succsim_T$ on terms, such that $f(\cdots t\cdots)\succ_T t$ only when f is unary and $f\succsim_F g$ all operators g. Then we can define a quasi-simplification ordering $\succsim$ in the following manner:

$$s = f(s_1, \ldots, s_m) \succsim g(t_1, \ldots, t_n) = t,$$

if, and only if,

$$(s, f, s_1, \ldots, s_m) \succsim (t, g, t_1, \ldots, t_n)$$

where the two tuples are compared lexicographically, first according to the terms $s\succsim_T t$, then according to the operators $f\succsim_F g$, and finally according to the subterms $s_i\succsim_T t_i$, (or, alternatively, $s_i\succsim t_i$ recursively). The condition on the operator ordering $\succsim_F$ ensures that $\succsim$ possesses the subterm property. To prove termination, one must find appropriate quasi-orderings $\succsim_F$ and $\succsim_T$ for which $l\succ r$ for all rules $l\rightarrow r$ in the given system.

Other examples of simplification orderings are the *recursive lexicographic ordering* in [Knuth-Bendix-70] and the *polynomial ordering* in [Lankford-79]. The method of [Knuth-Bendix-70] assigns a positive integer weight to each zeroary operator and a nonnegative integer weight to each other operator, with $\succsim_T$ comparing terms according to the sum of the weights of their respective operators, $\succsim_F$ a total ordering of operators, and subterms compared recursively. Thus, the condition on $\succsim_F$ requires that a unary operator have zero weight only if it is the largest operator under $\succsim_F$. [Lankford-79] replaces the linear sum of weight function with monotonic polynomials having nonnegative integer coefficients. Since both these methods use total monotonic orderings, the subterm condition is both necessary and sufficient for the orderings to be well-founded; the integer requirements are not themselves necessary.

Example. For System (10) we can use the Knuth-Bendix ordering, taking $t\succsim_T u$ to be $|t|\geq|u|$ and $\succsim_F$ to be equality, and comparing subterms recursively.

Example. This method applies also to System (14) with $t\succsim_T u$ if, and only if, $|t|_{+\times}\geq|u|_{+\times}$, the largest operator under $>_F$ is $-$, and subterms compared recursively.

8. COMBINED SYSTEMS

In this section we consider the termination of combinations of rewrite systems. If R and S are two (strongly or weakly) terminating systems, we wish to know under what conditions the system $R\cup S$, containing all the rules of both R and S, also (strongly or weakly) terminates.

Definition 18. A rewrite relation R *commutes over* another relation S, if whenever $t \Rightarrow_S u \Rightarrow_R v$, there is an alternative derivation of the form $t \Rightarrow_R w \Rightarrow^*_{R \cup S} v$.

With it we can reduce termination of the union of R and S to termination of each:

Theorem 24 [Bachmair-Dershowitz-85]. *Let R and S be two rewrite systems over some set of terms $\mathcal{T}$. Suppose that R commutes over S. Then, the combined system $R \cup S$ is terminating if, and only if, R and S both are.*

For rewriting modulo equations, we have the following analogous results:

Theorem 25 [Jouannaud-Munoz-84]. *If the rewrite relation R commutes over the congruence relation E, then R/E is terminating if, and only if, R is terminating.*

Furthermore,

Theorem 26. *Let E be a congruence relation and R and S two E-terminating rewrite systems (over some set of terms $\mathcal{T}$). If whenever $t \Rightarrow_S u \Rightarrow_{R/E} v$, there is an alternative derivation of the form $t \Rightarrow_{R/E} w \Rightarrow^*_{(R \cup S)/E} v$, then the combined system $(R \cup S)/E$ is also terminating.*

Some suggestions of how noncommuting R and E might be handled are given in [Jouannaud-Munoz-84].

To show that two relations commute, we can make use of the following properties:

Definition 19. A system is *left-linear* if no variable occurs more than once on the left-hand side of a rule; it is *right-linear* if no variable has more than one occurrence on the right-hand side. We say that a system is *linear* if it is both left- and right-linear.

Definition 20. A term u is said to *overlap* (or *superposes*) a term t if u can be unified with some (not necessarily proper) subterm s of t, i.e. if the two can be made the same by substituting terms for the variables in t and u (Whenever we speak in this section of unifying two terms, we consider their variables to be disjoint and insist that neither of the terms be just a variable.) We say that there is no overlap between two terms t and u if neither t overlaps u nor u overlaps t. A rewrite system R is said to be *non-overlapping* if there is no overlap among the left-hand sides of R, i.e. no left-hand side l_i overlaps a different left-hand side l_j and no left-hand side l_i overlaps a proper subterm of itself.

Example. The linear system

$$(\alpha \times \beta) \times \gamma \quad \rightarrow \quad \alpha \times (\beta \times \gamma) \tag{10}$$

is overlapping since $(\alpha \times \beta) \times \gamma$ is unifiable with $\alpha \times \beta$. The system

$$\alpha \times (\beta + \gamma) \quad \rightarrow \quad (\alpha \times \beta) + (\alpha \times \gamma) \tag{19}$$

is left-linear but not right-linear; the system

$$(\alpha \times \beta) + (\alpha \times \gamma) \quad \rightarrow \quad \alpha \times (\beta + \gamma) \tag{20}$$

is right-linear but not left-linear. Both are non-overlapping.

Other investigations of some of commuting systems include [Rosen-73, O'Donnell-77, Huet-Levy-79, Huet-80, Raoult-Vuillemin-80]

Using these properties to establish commutation, we have the following results:

Corollary [Dershowitz-81]. *Let R and S be two rewrite systems (over some set of terms $\mathcal{T}$). Suppose that R is left-linear, S is right-linear, and there is no overlap between left-hand sides of R and right-hand sides of S. Then, the combined system $R \cup S$ is terminating if, and only if, R and S both are.*

This generalizes the case exploited in [Bidoit-].

Example. The systems

$$\begin{array}{rcl} \alpha\times(\beta+\gamma) & \rightarrow & (\alpha\times\beta)+(\alpha\times\gamma) \\ (\beta+\gamma)\times\alpha & \rightarrow & (\beta\times\alpha)+(\gamma\times\alpha) \\ \alpha\times 1 & \rightarrow & \alpha \\ 1\times\alpha & \rightarrow & \alpha \end{array} \tag{13}$$

and

$$\begin{array}{rcl} \alpha\times\alpha & \rightarrow & \alpha \\ \alpha+\alpha & \rightarrow & \alpha \end{array} \tag{21}$$

each terminate; therefore their union also does.

Each of the three requirements of the above theorem is necessary, as evidenced by the following examples of nonterminating systems.

Example. The system

$$\begin{array}{rcl} f(\alpha,\alpha) & \rightarrow & f(a,b) \\ b & \rightarrow & a \end{array} \tag{22}$$

has the infinite derivation $f(a,a) \Rightarrow f(a,b) \Rightarrow f(a,a) \Rightarrow \cdots$, though each rule terminates, the first is right-linear, the second is linear, and there is no overlap (but the first is not left-linear).

Example. The system

$$\begin{array}{rcl} b & \rightarrow & a \\ f(a,b,\alpha) & \rightarrow & f(\alpha,\alpha,\alpha) \end{array} \tag{23}$$

has the infinite derivation $f(a,b,b) \Rightarrow f(b,b,b) \Rightarrow f(a,b,b) \Rightarrow \cdots$, though each rule terminates, the first is linear, the second is left-linear, and there is no overlap (but the second is not right-linear).

Example. The system

$$\begin{array}{ccc} b & \rightarrow & g(a) \\ a & \rightarrow & g(b) \end{array} \tag{24}$$

has the infinite derivation $b \Rightarrow g(a) \Rightarrow g(g(b)) \Rightarrow \cdots$, though each rule terminates and both are linear (but there is overlap).

Similarly for rewriting modulo equations, we have:

Theorem 27. *If R/E is left-linear, S is right-linear, and there is no overlap between left-hand sides of R/E and right-hand sides of S, then the combined system $(R \cup S)/E$ is also terminating.*

Example. Let E be AC, S be

$$\begin{array}{ccc} \alpha \cdot 1 & \rightarrow & \alpha \\ \alpha \cdot 0 & \rightarrow & 0 \\ \alpha \cdot \alpha & \rightarrow & \alpha \\ \alpha + 0 & \rightarrow & \alpha \\ \alpha + \alpha & \rightarrow & 0 \end{array} \tag{9a}$$

and R be

$$(\alpha + \beta) \cdot \gamma \quad \rightarrow \quad (\alpha \cdot \gamma) + (\beta \cdot \gamma) \tag{9b}$$

The system S is right-linear; the relation R/AC is left-linear, since R is left-linear and AC is linear. There are no occurrences of $\mathbf{0}$ on the left-hand sides of R, so there is no overlap. Therefore, R/AC commutes over S. If, say,

$$(d \cdot (a \cdot a)) \cdot (b + c) \Rightarrow_S (d \cdot a) \cdot (b + c) \Rightarrow_{R/AC} d \cdot (a \cdot b + a \cdot c)$$

then by the same token

$$(d \cdot (a \cdot a)) \cdot (b + c) \Rightarrow_{R/AC} d \cdot ((a \cdot a) \cdot b + (a \cdot a) \cdot c) \Rightarrow_S \Rightarrow_S d \cdot (a \cdot b + a \cdot c).$$

Recall that a system is *weakly* terminating if every term rewrites to an irreducible term.

Example. The following system [cf. System (1)] does not always terminate but is weakly-terminating and its irreducible terms are in disjunctive normal form:

$$\begin{array}{rcl} --\alpha & \rightarrow & \alpha \\ -(\alpha+\beta) & \rightarrow & ---\alpha\times---\beta \\ -(\alpha\times\beta) & \rightarrow & ---\alpha+---\beta \\ \alpha\times(\beta+\gamma) & \rightarrow & (\alpha\times\beta)+(\alpha\times\gamma) \\ (\beta+\gamma)\times\alpha & \rightarrow & (\beta\times\alpha)+(\gamma\times\alpha) \end{array} \qquad (25)$$

To see that it does not terminate, consider the derivation

$$\begin{array}{l} --(0\times(0+1)) \Rightarrow --((0\times0)+(0\times1)) \Rightarrow -(---(0\times0)\times---(0\times1)) \\ \quad\Rightarrow \cdots \Rightarrow -(-(0\times0)\times-(0\times1)) \\ \quad\Rightarrow \cdots \Rightarrow -((---0+---0)\times(---0+---1)) \\ \quad\Rightarrow \cdots \Rightarrow -((-0+-0)\times(-0+-1)) \Rightarrow -((-0\times(-0+-1))+(-0\times(-0+-1))) \\ \quad\Rightarrow ---(-0\times(-0+-1))\times---(-0\times(-0+-1)) \Rightarrow \cdots . \end{array}$$

Thus, beginning with a term of the form $--(\alpha\times(\alpha+\beta))$, a term containing a subterm of the same form is derived, and the process may continue *ad infinitum*. On the other hand, any application of the second or third rule can be followed immediately by two applications of the first rule, thus simulating a derivation of System (1) and guaranteeing termination.

To prove that a system is weakly terminating, one can choose a particular evaluation strategy and show that the value of a term is reduced in some well-founded ordering for those rewrites allowed by the chosen strategy. Thus, for the union of two weakly terminating systems R and S, one can choose to first reduce to an R-normal form and only then apply S. Then, if one can show that applying S to an R-normal form results in an R-normal form, weak termination of $R \cup S$ follows.

Example. The nonterminating System (25) is weakly terminating by the following line of reasoning: The first three rules alone are weakly terminating, since applying one of those rules to an *outermost* occurrence of $-$ reduces the multiset of sizes of arguments of $-$. (Note that this is not, and need not be, a monotonic ordering.) Similarly, the last two rules can be shown weakly terminating. Since the first three rules eliminate all negations of nonconstants and the two distributivity rules cannot introduce other negations, weak termination is proved.

9. RESTRICTED SYSTEMS

In this section, we consider how linearity and nonoverlapping of rules make it possible to restrict the derivations that must be considered when proving termination or nontermination of a rewrite system. Unfortunately:

> **Theorem 28** [Huet-Lankford-78]. *Termination of a rewrite system is undecidable, even if the system is linear and nonoverlapping and has only monadic operators and constants.*

In the extreme case of a single monadic rule with right-hand side no longer than left-hand side, deciding termination is trivial. [Metivier-83, Calladine-85] provide upper bounds on the length of a derivation in that case. Similarly:

Theorem 29 [Guttag, *etal.*-83]. *Quasi-termination of a rewrite system is undecidable, even if the system is linear and nonoverlapping and has only monadic operators and constants.*

We need the following definitions:

Definition 21 [Lankford-Musser-78]. The set of *forward closures* for a given rewrite system R may be inductively defined as follows: Every rule in R is a forward closure. Let

$$c_1 \Rightarrow c_2 \Rightarrow \cdots \Rightarrow c_m$$

and

$$d_1 \Rightarrow d_2 \Rightarrow \cdots \Rightarrow d_n$$

be two forward closures already included. If c_m has a (nonvariable) subterm s within some context u such that s unifies with d_1 via most general unifier σ, then

$$c_1\sigma \Rightarrow c_2\sigma \Rightarrow \cdots \Rightarrow c_m\sigma = u\sigma[d_1\sigma] \Rightarrow u\sigma[d_2\sigma] \Rightarrow \cdots \Rightarrow u\sigma[d_n\sigma]$$

is also a forward closure. (Two forward closures are considered equal if they can be obtained one from the other by variable renaming.)

This definition is related to the *narrowing process,* as defined in [Slagle-74, Hullot-80].

Definition 22 [Guttag, *etal.*-83]. The set of *overlap closures* for a given rewrite system R may be inductively defined as follows: Every rule in R is a forward closure. Let

$$c_1 \Rightarrow c_2 \Rightarrow \cdots \Rightarrow c_m$$

and

$$d_1 \Rightarrow d_2 \Rightarrow \cdots \Rightarrow d_n$$

be two overlap closures already included. If c_m has a (nonvariable) subterm s within some context u such that s unifies with d_1 via most general unifier σ, then

$$c_1\sigma \Rightarrow c_2\sigma \Rightarrow \cdots \Rightarrow c_m\sigma = u\sigma[d_1\sigma] \Rightarrow u\sigma[d_2\sigma] \Rightarrow \cdots \Rightarrow u\sigma[d_n\sigma]$$

is also an overlap closure. If d_1 has a (nonvariable) subterm t within some context v such that t unifies with c_m via most general unifier τ, then

$$v\tau[c_1\tau] \Rightarrow v\tau[c_2\tau] \Rightarrow \cdots \Rightarrow v\tau[c_m\tau] = d_1\tau \Rightarrow d_2\tau \Rightarrow \cdots \Rightarrow d_n\tau$$

is also an overlap closure. (Two overlap closures are considered equal if they can be obtained one from the other by variable renaming.)

Example. Consider the system

$$\begin{array}{lcl} --\alpha & \rightarrow & \alpha \\ -(\alpha+\beta) & \rightarrow & -\alpha+-\beta \end{array} \qquad (26)$$

The derivation

$$-((\alpha+-\beta)+-\gamma) \Rightarrow -(\alpha+-\beta)+--\gamma \Rightarrow$$
$$(-\alpha+--\beta)+--\gamma \Rightarrow (-\alpha+\beta)+--\gamma \Rightarrow (-\alpha+\beta)+\gamma$$

is a forward closure for that system; the derivation

$$-(\alpha+--\beta) \Rightarrow -\alpha+---\beta \Rightarrow -\alpha+-\beta$$

is an overlap closure, but not a forward one; the derivation

$$-(\alpha+--\beta) \Rightarrow -(\alpha+\beta) \Rightarrow -\alpha+-\beta$$

is neither.

Theorem 30 [Dershowitz-81]. *A right-linear rewrite system is terminating if, and only if, it has no infinite forward closures.*

Example. The self-embedding rewrite system

$$f(h(\alpha)) \rightarrow f(g(h(\alpha))) \tag{27}$$

is right-linear and has only one forward closure:

$$f(h(\alpha)) \Rightarrow f(g(h(\alpha)))$$

Since this forward closure is finite, the system must terminate. Note that, by Theorem **10**, no total monotonic ordering could prove termination of this system.

Example. The forward closures of

$$f(g(\alpha)) \rightarrow g(g(f(\alpha))) \tag{28}$$

are all of the form

$$f(g(g^i(\alpha))) \Rightarrow g(g(f(g^i(\alpha)))) \Rightarrow \cdots \Rightarrow g^{2i}(f(\alpha))$$

where $i \geq 0$. Since the system is right-linear and all its forward closures are finite, by the theorem, it must terminate for all inputs.

Example. The forward closures of

$$f(g(\alpha)) \rightarrow g(g(f(f(\alpha)))) \tag{29}$$

include

$$f(g(\alpha)) \Rightarrow g(g(f(f(\alpha))))$$

and the infinite forward closures

$$f(g(g(g^i(\alpha)))) \Rightarrow g(g(f(f(g(g^i(\alpha)))))) \Rightarrow g(g(f(g(g(f(f(g^i(\alpha)))))))) \Rightarrow \cdots$$

for all $i \geq 0$. Thus, the system does not terminate.

Theorem 31 [Dershowitz-81]. *A non-overlapping left-linear rewrite system is terminating if, and only if, it has no infinite forward closures.*

It has been conjectured [Dershowitz-81] that left-linearity is unnecessary.

Example. None of the forward closures of the non-overlapping left-linear System (8) have nested D operators. (This can be shown by induction.) Thus, the finiteness of those forward closures—and consequently the termination of the system—can be easily proved by considering the multiset of the sizes of the arguments of the D's. Any rule application reduces that value under the multiset ordering.

In general, though, a term-rewriting system need not terminate even if all its chains do:

Example. The non-right-linear and overlapping system

$$\begin{array}{rcl} f(a,b,\alpha) & \rightarrow & f(\alpha,\alpha,b) \\ b & \rightarrow & a \end{array} \tag{30}$$

has two finite forward closures. Nevertheless, the system does not terminate. To wit,

$$f(a,b,b) \Rightarrow f(b,b,b) \Rightarrow f(a,b,b).$$

Theorem 32 [Guttag, *etal.*-83]. *A quasi-terminating left-linear rewrite system is terminating if, and only if, it has no infinite overlap closures.*

Example. System (30) has the following infinite overlap closure:

$$f(b,b,b) \Rightarrow f(a,b,b) \Rightarrow f(b,b,b) \Rightarrow \cdots$$

It is unknown whether quasi-termination and/or left-linearity are necessary in the above theorem.

The above theorems give necessary and sufficient conditions for a left-linear or right-linear system to terminate. One of the advantages in using closures is that nontermination is more easily detectable, as the next theorem will demonstrate. First, we must extend the definition of "looping."

Definition 23. A derivation $t_1 \Rightarrow t_2 \Rightarrow \cdots \Rightarrow t_i \Rightarrow \cdots$ *loops* if for some $j > i$ t_j has a subterm that is an *instance* of t_i.

Theorem 33 [Dershowitz-81]. *A right-linear or non-overlapping left-linear rewrite system is nonterminating if, and only if, it has infinitely many nonlooping infinite forward closures or it has a looping forward closure.*

Example. The system

$$\begin{array}{rcl} g(\alpha) & \rightarrow & h(\alpha) \\ f(\alpha,\alpha) & \rightarrow & f(a,\alpha) \\ b & \rightarrow & a \\ a & \rightarrow & b \end{array} \tag{31}$$

has two finite forward closures $b \Rightarrow a$ and $b \Rightarrow c$, one infinite looping forward closure $f(\alpha,\alpha) \Rightarrow f(a,b) \Rightarrow f(a,a) \Rightarrow \cdots$, and an infinite number of finite forward closures

$f(\alpha,\alpha) \Rightarrow f(a,b) \Rightarrow f(a,a) \Rightarrow \cdots \Rightarrow f(a,b) \Rightarrow f(a,c)$ with the same initial term.

Example. Consider again the right-linear System (26). Since forward closures cannot begin with a term having $-$ other than as outermost or innermost operator, the termination of all closures can be easily proved using a multiset ordering on the sizes of the arguments to $-$.

Corollary . *The termination of a right-linear or non-overlapping left-linear rewrite system is decidable if the number of forward closures issuing from different initial terms is finite.*

Example. The non-overlapping left-linear system

$$\begin{array}{lcl} f(a,\alpha) & \rightarrow & f(\alpha,g(\alpha)) \\ g(a) & \rightarrow & a \end{array} \tag{32}$$

has three forward closures:

$$\begin{array}{l} g(a) \Rightarrow a \\ f(a,\alpha) \Rightarrow f(\alpha,g(\alpha)) \\ f(a,a) \Rightarrow f(a,g(a)) \Rightarrow f(a,a) \Rightarrow \cdots \end{array}$$

Since its third forward closure cycles, it does not terminate. On the other hand, the system

$$\begin{array}{lcl} f(a,\alpha) & \rightarrow & f(\alpha,g(\alpha)) \\ g(a) & \rightarrow & b \end{array} \tag{33}$$

has the forward closures:

$$\begin{array}{l} g(a) \Rightarrow b \\ f(a,\alpha) \Rightarrow f(\alpha,g(\alpha)) \\ f(a,a) \Rightarrow f(a,g(a)) \Rightarrow f(a,b) \Rightarrow f(b,g(b)) \end{array}$$

Since none of its three forward closures loops, it does terminate.

Example. The forward closures of

$$\begin{array}{lcl} f(\alpha,\alpha) & \rightarrow & f(a,b) \\ b & \rightarrow & c \end{array} \tag{34}$$

are

$$b \Rightarrow c$$

and

$$f(\alpha,\alpha) \Rightarrow f(a,b) \Rightarrow f(a,c)$$

Since the forward closures do not loop, the system terminates.

In particular,

Corollary [Huet-Lankford-78]. *The termination of a rewrite system containing no variables (a ground system) is decidable.*

Quasi-termination of ground systems is similarly decidable [Dauchet-Tison-84].

REFERENCES

[AitKaci-83] Ait-Kaci, H. "An algorithm for finding a minimal recursive path ordering", Report MS-CIS-83-7, Department of Computer and Information Science, University of Pennsylvania, Philadelphia, PA, 1983.

[Bachmair-Dershowitz-85] Bachmair, L., and Dershowitz, N. "Commutation, transformation, and termination". (1985) (submitted).

[Bachmair-Plaisted-85] Bachmair, L., and Plaisted, D. A. "Associative path ordering". *Proceedings of the First International Conference on Rewriting Techniques and Applications*, Dijon, France (May 1985).

[BenCherifa-84] Ben Cherifa, A. "Preuve de la terminaison finie d'un système de reécriture par l'ordre polynômial", Unpublished manuscript, Centre de Recherche en Informatique de Nancy, Nancy, France, 1984.

[Bergstra-Tucker-80] Bergstra, J. A., and Tucker, J. V. "Equational specifications for computable data types: Six hidden functions suffice and other sufficiency bounds", Preprint IW 128/80, Mathematisch Centrum, Amsterdam, The Netherlands, January 1980.

[Bidoit-] Bidoit, M. "Thesis", Thèse.

[Bucher,*etal.*-84] Bucher, W., Ehrenfeucht, A., and Haussler, D. "On total regulators generated by derivation relations", University of Denver, 1984.

[Calladine-85] Calladine, P. "Personal communication", Laboratoire d'Informatique, Université de Poitiers, May 1985.

[Choque-83] Choque, G. "Calcul d'un ensemble complet d'incrementations minimales pour l'ordre recursif de decomposition", Technical report, Centre de Recherche en Informatique de Nancy, Nancy, France, 1983.

[Cohen-69] Cohen, P. J. "Decision procedures for real and p-adic fields". *Communications of Pure and Applied Mathematics*, Vol. 22, No. 2 (1969), pp. 131-151.

[Collins-75] Collins, G. "Quantifier elimination for real closed fields by cylindrical algebraic decomposition". *Proceedings Second GI Conference on Automata Theory and Formal Languages* (1975), pp. 134-183.

[Dauchet-Tison-84] Dauchet, M., and Tison, S. "Decidability of confluence for ground term rewriting systems", Unpublished report, Université de Lille I, Lille, France, 1984.

[Dershowitz,*etal.*-83] Dershowitz, N., Hsiang, J., Josephson, N. A., and Plaisted, D. A. "Associative-commutative rewriting". *Proceedings of the Eighth International*

Joint Conference on Artificial Intelligence, Karlsruhe, West Germany (August 1983), pp. 940-944.

[Dershowitz-79] Dershowitz, N. "A note on simplification orderings". *Information Processing Letters*, Vol. 9, No. 5 (November 1979), pp. 212-215.

[Dershowitz-80] Dershowitz, N. "On representing ordinals up to Γ_0", Unpublished note, Department Computer Science, University of Illinois, Urbana, IL, June 1980.

[Dershowitz-81] Dershowitz, N. "Termination of linear rewriting systems". *Proceedings of the Eighth EATCS International Colloquium on Automata, Languages and Programming*, Vol. 115, Acre, Israel (July 1981), pp. 448-458.

[Dershowitz-82] Dershowitz, N. "Orderings for term-rewriting systems". *J. Theoretical Computer Science*, Vol. 17, No. 3 (March 1982), pp. 279-301 (previous version appeared in Proceedings of the Symposium on Foundations of Computer Science, San Juan, PR, pp. 123-131 [October 1979]).

[Dershowitz-83] Dershowitz, N. "Well-founded orderings", Technical Report ATR-83(8478)-3, Information Sciences Research Office, The Aerospace Corporation, El Segundo, CA, May 1983.

[Dershowitz-Manna-79] Dershowitz, N., and Manna, Z. "Proving termination with multiset orderings". *Communications of the ACM*, Vol. 22, No. 8 (August 1979), pp. 465-476 (also in Proceedings of the International Colloquium on Automata, Languages and Programming, Graz, 188-202 [July 1979]).

[Dershowitz-Zaks-81] Dershowitz, N., and Zaks, S. "Applied tree enumerations". *Proceedings of the Sixth Colloquium on Trees in Algebra and Programming*, Vol. 112, Genoa, Italy (March 1981), pp. 180-193.

[Detlefs-Forgaard-85] Detlefs, D., and Forgaard, R. "A procedure for automatically proving the termination of a set of rewrite rules". *Proceedings of the First International Conference on Rewriting Techniques and Applications*, Dijon, France (May 1985).

[Ehrenfeucht,*etal.*-83] Ehrenfeucht, A., Haussler, D., and Rozenberg, G. "On regularity of context-free languages". *Theoretical Computer Science*, Vol. 27 (1983), pp. 311-32.

[Feferman-68] Feferman, S. "Systems of predicative analysis II: Representation of ordinals". *J. Symbolic Logic*, Vol. 33 (1968), pp. 193-220.

[Filman-78] Filman, R. E. "personal communication", 1978.

[Forgaard-84] Forgaard, R. "A program for generating and analyzing term rewriting systems", Master's thesis, Laboratory for Computer Science, Massachusetts Institute of

Technology, Cambridge, MA, September 1984.

[Gardner-83] Gardner, M. "Mathematical games: Tasks you cannot help finishing no matter how hard you try to block finishing them". *Scientific American*, Vol. 24, No. 2 (August 1983), pp. 12-21.

[Gentzen-38] Gentzen, G. "New version of the consistency proof for elementary number theory". In: *Collected Papers of Gerhard Gentzen*, M. E. Szabo, ed (1938). North-Holland, 1969, pp. 252-286 (1938).

[Gnaedig-85] Gnaedig, I. "personal communication", 1985.

[Gorn-67] Gorn, S. "Handling the growth by definition of mechanical languages". *Proceedings of the Spring Joint Computer Conference* (Spring 1967), pp. 213-224.

[Gorn-73] Gorn, S. "On the conclusive validation of symbol manipulation processes (How do you know it has to work?)". *J. of the Franklin Institute*, Vol. 296, No. 6 (December 1973), pp. 499-518.

[Guttag,*etal.*-83] Guttag, J. V., Kapur, D., and Musser, D. R. "On proving uniform termination and restricted termination of rewriting systems". *SIAM Computing*, Vol. 12, No. 1 (February 1983), pp. 189-214.

[Higman-52] Higman, G. "Ordering by divisibility in abstract algebras". *Proceedings of the London Mathematical Society (3)*, Vol. 2, No. 7 (September 1952), pp. 326-336.

[Huet-80] Huet, G. "Confluent reductions: Abstract properties and applications to term rewriting systems". *J. of the Association for Computing Machinery*, Vol. 27, No. 4 (1980), pp. 797-821 (previous version in Proceedings of the Symposium on Foundations of Computer Science, Providence, RI, pp. 30-45 [1977]).

[Huet-Lankford-78] Huet, G., and Lankford, D. S. "On the uniform halting problem for term rewriting systems", Rapport Laboria 283, IRIA, March 1978.

[Huet-Levy-79] Huet, G., and Levy, J. J. "Call by need computations in non-ambiguous linear term rewriting systems", Rapport laboria 359, INRIA, Le Chesnay, France, August 1979.

[Huet-Oppen-80] Huet, G., and Oppen, D. C. "Equations and rewrite rules: A survey". In: *Formal Language Theory: Perspectives and Open Problems*, R. Book, ed. Academic Press, New York, 1980, pp. 349-405.

[Hullot-80] Hullot, J. M. "Canonical forms and unification". *Proceedings of the Fifth Conference on Automated Deduction*, Les Arcs, France (July 1980), pp. 318-334.

[Iturriaga-67] Iturriaga, R. "Contributions to mechanical mathematics", Ph.D. Thesis, Carnegie-Mellon University, Pittsburgh, Pennsylvania, 1967.

[Jouannaud,*etal.*-82] Jouannaud, J. P., Lescanne, P., and Reinig, F. "Recursive decomposition ordering". *Proceedings of the Second IFIP Workshop on Formal Description of Programming Concepts*, Garmisch-Partenkirchen, West Germany (June 1982), pp. 331-348.

[Jouannaud-Kirchner-82] Jouannaud, J. P., and Kirchner, H. "Construction d'un plus petit order de simplification", Unpublished note, Centre de Recherche en Informatique de Nancy, Nancy, France, 1982.

[Jouannaud-Munoz-84] Jouannaud, J. P., and Muñoz, M. "Termination of a set of rules modulo a set of equations". *Proceedings of the Seventh International Conference on Automated Deduction*, Napa, CA (May 1984), pp. 175-193.

[Kamin-Levy-80] Kamin, S., and Levy, J. J. "Two generalizations of the recursive path ordering", Unpublished note, Department of Computer Science, University of Illinois, Urbana, IL, February 1980.

[Kapur,*etal.*-85] Kapur, D., Narendran, P., and Sivakumar, G. "A path ordering for proving termination of term rewriting systems". *Proceedings of the Tenth Colloquium on Trees in Algebra and Programming* (1985).

[Kapur-Sivakumar-83] Kapur, D., and Sivakumar, G. "Experiments with and architecture of RRL, a rewrite rule laboratory". *Proceedings of an NSF Workshop on the Rewrite Rule Laboratory*, Schenectady, NY (September 1983), pp. 33-56 (available as Report 84GEN008, General Electric Research and Development [April 1984]).

[Kirby-Paris-82] Kirby, L., and Paris, J. "Accessible independence results for Peano arithmetic". *Bulletin London Mathematical Society*, Vol. 14 (1982), pp. 285-293.

[Knuth-73] Knuth, D. E. *Fundamental algorithms.* Addison-Wesley, Reading, MA, 1973 (second edition).

[Knuth-Bendix-70] Knuth, D. E., and Bendix, P. B. "Simple word problems in universal algebras". In: *Computational Problems in Abstract Algebra*, J. Leech, ed. Pergamon Press, 1970, pp. 263-297.

[Krishnamoorthy-Narendran-84] Krishnamoorthy, M. S., and Narendran, P. "A note on recursive path ordering", Unpublished note, General Electric Corporate Research and Development, Schenectady, NY, 1984.

[Kruskal-60] Kruskal, J. B. "Well-quasi-ordering, the Tree Theorem, and Vazsonyi's conjecture". *Transactions of the American Mathematical Society*, Vol. 95 (May 1960), pp. 210-225.

[Kruskal-72] Kruskal, J. B. "The theory of well-quasi-ordering: A frequently discovered concept". *J. Combinatorial Theory Ser. A*, Vol. 13 (1972), pp. 297-305.

[Lankford-75] Lankford, D. S. "Canonical algebraic simplification in computational logic", Memo ATP-25, Automatic Theorem Proving Project, University of Texas, Austin, TX, May 1975.

[Lankford-79] Lankford, D. S. "On proving term rewriting systems are Noetherian", Memo MTP-3, Mathematics Department, Louisiana Tech. University, Ruston, LA, May 1979.

[Lankford-Musser-78] Lankford, D. S., and Musser, D. R. "A finite termination criterion", Unpublished draft, 1981.

[Laver-78] Laver, R. "Better-quasi-orderings and a class of trees". *Studies in Foundations and Combinatorics* (1978), pp. 31-48.

[Lescanne-81] Lescanne, P. "Two implementations of the recursive path ordering on monadic terms". *Proceedings of the Nineteenth Allerton Conference on Communication, Control, and Computing*, Monticello, IL (September 1981), pp. 634-643.

[Lescanne-83] Lescanne, P. "Computer experiments with the REVE term rewriting system generator". *Proceedings of the Tenth Symposium on Principles of Programming Languages*, Austin, TX (January 1983), pp. 99-108.

[Lescanne-84] Lescanne, P. "Some properties of decomposition ordering, A simplification ordering to prove termination of rewriting systems". *RAIRO Theoretical Informatics*, Vol. 16, No. 4, pp. 331-347.

[Lescanne-84] Lescanne, P. "Uniform termination of term-rewriting systems with status". *Proceedings of the Ninth Colloquium on Trees in Algebra and Programming*, Bordeaux, France (March 1984).

[Lescanne-Jouannaud-82] Lescanne, P., and Jouannaud, J. P. "On multiset orderings". *Information Processing Lett.*, Vol. 15, No. 2 (September 1982), pp. 57-62.

[Lescanne-Steyaert-83] Lescanne, P., and Steyaert, J. M. "On the study of data structures: Binary tournaments with repeated keys". *Proceedings of the Tenth EATCS International Colloquium on Automata, Languages and Programming*, Barcelona, Spain (July 1983), pp. 466-475.

[Levy-80] Levy, J. J. "Problem 80-5". *J. of Algorithms*, Vol. 1, No. 1 (March 1980), pp. 108-109.

[Lipton-Snyder-77] Lipton, R., and Snyder, L. "On the halting of tree replacement systems". *Proceedings of the Conference on Theoretical Computer Science*, Waterloo, Canada (August 1977), pp. 43-46.

[Manna-69] Manna, Z. "Termination of algorithms", Ph.D. thesis, Department of Computer Science, Carnegie-Mellon University, Pittsburgh, PA, April 1969.

[Manna-74] Manna, Z. *Mathematical Theory of Computation*. McGraw-Hill, New York, 1974.

[Manna-Ness-70] Manna, Z., and Ness, S. "On the termination of Markov algorithms". *Proceedings of the Third Hawaii International Conference on System Science*, Honolulu, HI (January 1970), pp. 789-792.

[Metivier-83] Metivier, Y. "About the rewriting systems produced by the Knuth-Bendix completion algorithm". *Information Processing Letters*, Vol. 16 (January 1983), pp. 31-34.

[Nash-Williams-63] Nash-Williams, C. S. J. A. "On well-quasi-ordering finite trees". *Proceedings of the Cambridge Philosophical Society*, 59 (1963), pp. 833-835.

[O'Donnell-77] O'Donnell, M. J. "Computing in systems described by equations". *Lecture Notes in Computer Science*, Vol. 58, Berlin (1977).

[Paulson-84] Paulson, L. C. "Constructing recursion operations in intuitionistic type theory", Technical Report 57, Computer Laboratory, University of Cambridge, Cambridge, UK, October 1984.

[Pettorossi-78] Pettorossi, A. "A property which guarantees termination in weak combinatory logic and subtree replacement systems", Report R.78-23, Instituto di Automatica, Università di Roma, Rome, Italy, November 1978.

[Pettorossi-81] Pettorossi, A. "Comparing and putting together recursive path orderings, simplification orderings and non-ascending property for termination proofs of term rewriting systems". *Proceedings of the Eighth International Colloquium on Automata, Languages and Programming*, Acre, Israel (July 1981), pp. 432-447.

[Plaisted-78] Plaisted, D. A. "Well-founded orderings for proving termination of systems of rewrite rules", Report R78-932, Department of Computer Science, University of Illinois, Urbana, IL, July 1978.

[Plaisted-78b] Plaisted, D. A. "A recursively defined ordering for proving termination of term rewriting systems", Report R-78-943, Department of Computer Science, University of Illinois, Urbana, IL, September 1978.

[Plaisted-79] Plaisted, D. A. "personal communication", 1979.

[Plaisted-83] Plaisted, D. A. "An associative path ordering". *Proceedings of an NSF Workshop on the Rewrite Rule Laboratory*, Schenectady, NY (September 1983), pp. 123-136 (available as Report 84GEN008, General Electric Research and Development [April 1984]).

[Plaisted-85] Plaisted, D. A. "The undecidability of self embedding for term rewriting systems". *Information Processing Lett.*, Vol. 20, No. 2 (February 1985), pp. 61-64.

[Porat-Francez-85] Porat, S., and Francez, N. "Fairness in term rewriting systems".

Proceedings of the First International Conference on Rewriting Techniques and Applications, Dijon, France (May 1985).

[Puel-85] Puel, L. "personal communication", May 1985.

[Raoult-Vuillemin-80] Raoult, J. C., and Vuillemin, J. "Operational and semantic equivalence between recursive programs". *J. of the Association of Computing Machinery*, Vol. 27, No. 4 (October 1980), pp. 772-796.

[Rosen-73] Rosen, B. "Tree-manipulating systems and Church-Rosser theorems". *J. of the Association for Computing Machinery*, Vol. 20 (1973), pp. 160-187.

[Rusinowitch-85] Rusinowitch, M. "Plaisted ordering and recursive decomposition ordering revisited". *Proceedings of the First International Conference on Rewriting Techniques and Applications*, Dijon, France (May 1985).

[Sakai-84] Sakai, K. "An ordering method for term rewriting systems". *Proceedings of the First International Conference on Fifth Generation Computer Systems*, Tokyo, Japan (November 1984).

[Scherlis-80] Scherlis, W. L. "Expression procedures and program derivation", Ph.D. Dissertation, Department Computer Science, Stanford University, Stanford, CA, August 1980.

[Slagle-74] Slagle, J. R. "Automated theorem-proving for theories with simplifiers, commutativity, and associativity". *J. of the Association for Computing Machinery*, Vol. 21, No. 4 (1974), pp. 622-642.

[Smullyan-79] Smullyan, R. M. "Trees and ball games". *Annals of the New York Academy of Science*, Vol. 321 (1979), pp. 86-90.

[Tarski-51] Tarski, A. *A Decision Method for Elementary Algebra and Geometry.* University of California Press, Berkeley, CA, 1951.

[Veblen-08] Veblen, O. "Continuous increasing functions of finite and transfinite ordinals". *Transactions of the American Mathematical Society*, Vol. 9 (1908), pp. 280-292.

[Weyhrauch-78] Weyhrauch, R. W. "Some notes on ordinals up to Γ_0", Informal note 13, Stanford University, Stanford, CA, March 1978.

PATH OF SUBTERMS ORDERING AND RECURSIVE DECOMPOSITION ORDERING REVISITED .

Michael Rusinowitch

Centre de Recherche en Informatique de Nancy
Campus Scientifique BP 239
54506 Vandoeuvre Cedex France

ABSTRACT

The relationship between several simplification orderings is investigated: PSO, RPO, RDO. RDO is improved in order to deal with more pairs of terms, and made more efficient and easy to handle, by removing useless computations.

INTRODUCTION

Rewriting Systems enable us to prove equalities in systems described by equations. Their principle is based on orienting axioms (and some of their consequencies called critical pairs) so that they are always applied in the same direction. Oriented equations are called rewrite rules and applying the equations is called rewriting. Each term is associated with a normal form, that is, a term that cannot undergo more reducing by the rewrite rules. Equality between two terms is then equivalent to identity of their normal forms.

To be able to compute normal forms, rewritings must terminate. This is usually obtained by exhibiting a well founded ordering that contains the rewriting relation. Dershowitz has shown that the simplification orderings fitted well such a purpose.

In the following, we study three of the most well-known ones:
-the Path of Subterms Ordering (PSO) of PLAISTED [1].
-the Recursive Path Ordering (RPO) of DERSHOWITZ [5].
-the Recursive Decomposition Ordering (RDO) of JOUANNAUD-LESCANNE-REINIG [2].

All these orderings are defined by extending a basic ordering on function symbols, called a "precedence".

In the first part of this work, we extend PSO to the case of a partial precedence and show that it contains RPO. As a consequence, we get that PSO is well founded if and only if the precedence is well founded. A counter example which shows that PSO is not included in RDO is given. With slight change in the definition of PSO, we get a new ordering which possesses the following property called incrementality (cf [2]): given two terms, the precedence can be automatically extended in order to orient them.

Our goal in the second part, is to improve RDO by eliminating many unnecessary comparaisons. For example, comparing the terms a(b(c)) and A(b(c)) with the precedence $a<A$, generate 4 checks of "$a<A$" . The idea is to first simplify the terms by their common suffix, then compare the left parts of these terms: the result is now obtained with a single use of "$a<A$". The same remark is true for the ordering of KAPUR-NARENDRAN-SIVAKUMAR [6]. Based on this idea, a simplified version of RDO is proposed, which does not use anymore the fourth part of the elementary decompositions called the "context" in [2]. We prove that the obtained ordering is equivalent to RDO. But this definition of RDO generates less computations than the previous ones. The section ends with an extension of RDO which is proven equivalent to the ordering given in [6].

I-PRELIMINARIES

1-MULTISET ORDERINGS (see[4])

A **multiset** is a set with possibly repeated elements. More formally, a multiset M is a mapping $E \longrightarrow N$, where E is a set and N is the set of natural numbers. M(E) denotes the set of all the multisets on E with finite carrier. For x in E, we say that M(x) is the number of occurrences of x in M, and we write $x \in M$ instead of $M(x) > 0$.

Each ordering on E can be extended to M(E) :

Definition 1-1:

Let $<_E$ be an ordering on E. We can define an ordering on M(E) by :

$M1 \ll_E M2$ iff $M1 \neq M2$ and

$$\forall x \in E \ (M2(x) < M1(x) \Rightarrow \exists y \in E \ x <_E y \text{ and } M1(y) < M2(y))$$

If we denote the inf of two mappings M1 and M2 by $M1 \sqcap M2$, we get a generalisation of the intersection of two sets. The next lemma states that, to compare multisets, we may first delete their common instances :

Lemma 1-2:

$$M1 \ll_E M2 \text{ iff } (M2 \neq \emptyset \text{ and } \forall x \in M1-(M1 \sqcap M2) \ \exists y \in M2-(M1 \sqcap M2) \ x <_E y).$$

Inclusion of orderings is preserved when extended to multisets :

Lemma 1-3:

The multiset extension of an ordering is monotonic, that is to say :

$$(\forall x,y \in E \ x <_E y \Rightarrow x <'_E y) \Rightarrow (\forall \ M1,M2 \in M(E) \ M1 \ll_E M2 \Rightarrow M1 \ll'_E M2)$$

We can use this property to prove that well foundedness is preserved, too, by the multiset extension. Our proof does not use Konig 's lemma as others usually do.

Lemma 1-4:

<<E is well founded iff <E is well founded.

Proof: <E can be extended to a total well founded ordering <'E ; now, <<'E is well founded because it can be seen as a lexicographical ordering on ordered words on E. Since <<E is included in <<'E by lemma 1-3, it is also well founded.

2-TERMS-OCCURRENCES.

F denotes a finite set of function symbols, and ar is the arity of symbols in F. X is a set of variables. N+ is the free monoid on N, and the empty word is denoted by ε. T(F,X) is the set of terms, that is the set of functions: t :N+---->FUX whose domain occ(t) is finite and satisfies :

$\varepsilon \in occ(t)$

$ui \in occ(t)$ iff $u \in occ(t)$ and $i \in [1..ar(t(u))]$

t/u is the subterm of t at the occurence u. t(u) is the symbol of t at u. |t| = card(occ(t)) is the size of t. T(F) is the set of closed terms.

3-SIMPLIFICATION ORDERINGS .

Simplification orderings have been introduced by Dershowitz.

Definition 1-5:

An ordering < on T(F,X) is a simplification ordering if it has the following properties for every function symbol f :

compatibility property : $t_1 < t_2 \Rightarrow f(..,t_1,..) < f(..,t_2,..)$

subterm property : $t < f(..,t,..)$

Orienting rules from left to right according to a simplification ordering ensure that the rewriting process terminates :

Theorem 1-6: (see[5]).

A rewriting system with a finitely many symbols is finitely terminating if there exists a simplification ordering < such that for all substitution s and for all rule g —> d , s(d) < s(g).

Now, we are going to study two particular simplification orderings : the Path of Subterms Ordering (PSO) and the recursive decomposition ordering (RDO).

II-PATH OF SUBTERMS ORDERING .

Rather than comparing two terms directly, PSO compares two data structures built up from these terms: their paths of subterms. A path of subterms is the sequence of subterms on a path from the root to the leaf.

1-PATHS OF SUBTERMS.

Definition 2-1: path of subterms.

The multiset of paths of subterms of t is

$$\mathrm{SPATH}(t)=\begin{cases}\{t\} \text{ if } t \text{ is a constant or a variable}\\ \sum_{i=1}^{m} \{t\}.\ \mathrm{SPATH}\ (t_i) \text{ if } t=f(t_1,t_2,\ldots.t_m)\ .\end{cases}$$

where $\{t\}.\mathrm{SPATH}\ (t_i) = \sum_{g \in \mathrm{SPATH}(t_i)} \{t.g\}$

We define also :

$$\mathrm{PSPATH}(t) = \begin{cases}\sum_{i=1}^{m} \mathrm{SPATH}\ (t_i) \text{ if } t=f(t_1,\ldots,t_m)\\ \emptyset \text{ otherwise}\end{cases}$$

Example :

t= f(a,a,g(c))
SPATH(t)={(t,a),(t,a),(t,g(c),c)}
PSPATH(t)={(a),(a),(g(c),c)}

Definition 2-2: congruence of permutation ~ .

$f(s_1,\ldots,s_n) \sim g(t_1,\ldots,t_n)$ iff f=g and $s_i \sim t_i$ up to a permutation

Definition 2-3:

Let a be a sequence of terms, then subsequ(a) is the multiset of subsequences of a : subsequ(ø)=ø
subsequ(t.b)={t,ε}.subsequ(b) = t.subsequ(b) + subsequ(b)

Remark 2-4: If a is a path of subterms of t then subsequ(a) is a set.

Definition 2-5:

If R is an ordering on terms, then Rlex is a lexicographic-like ordering on sequences of terms defined by : s Rlex t iff $s = \emptyset$ and $t \neq \emptyset$

or s_1 R t_1
or $s_1 \sim t_1$ and $(s_2,\ldots s_m)$ Rlex $(t_2,\ldots t_n)$

where $s = s_1.s_2.\ldots.s_m$ and $t = t_1.t_2.\ldots.t_n$

And now, we are going to use the lexicographic extension of an intermediate ordering <i on terms to get an ordering on paths of subterms, and then the PSO.

2-THE PATH OF SUBTERMS ORDERING ON T(F).

Definition 2-6:

Let < be a precedence on F, <pso is defined recursively by

s <pso t iff SPATH(s) <<l SPATH(t)
where <l is an ordering on paths of subterms
with a <l b iff subsequ(a) <<ilex subsequ(b)
and <i an ordering on terms
with $u = f(u_1,\ldots)$ <i $v = g(v_1,\ldots)$

iff f<g or (f=g and PSPATH(u) <<l PSPATH(v))

Example 2-7:

```
       g
       |
s=     +          t=   +        with the precedence 0<+ , g<f
     /   \            / \
   0       g         0   f
```

SPATH(s) = {(s,0+g,0) , (s,0+g,g)}   SPATH(t) = {(t,0),(t,f)}

(s,0+g,0) <l (t,f) because s <i f , 0+g <i t , 0 <i t

(s,0+g,g) <l (t,f) in a similar way and then s <pso t.

We can prove exactly like in [1] :

Proposition 2-8:

<pso is a simplification ordering .

Moreover, <pso satisfies a compatibility property stronger than the one which is required in the definition of a simplification ordering :

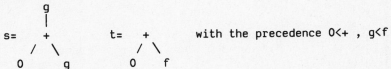

Proposition 2-9:

If $\{s_1....s_n\}$ <<pso $\{t_1,...t_n\}$ then $f(s_1,...s_n)$ <pso $f(t_1,....t_n)$

<pso is also monotonic with respect to the precedence :

Proposition 2-10:

If < is included as a relation in <' then <pso is included in <'pso .

3-COMPARISON OF PSO AND RPO .

Let us now recall the definition of RPO (see[5]):

$t = g(t_1,t_2,..,t_n)$ <rpo $s = f(s_1,s_2,..,s_m)$

iff (rpo1) f=g and $(t_1,t_2,..t_n)$ <<rpo $(s_1,s_2,..s_m)$

or (rpo2) g<f and for all ti: t_i <rpo s

or (rpo3) not(g≦f) and for some s_i: t ≦rpo s_i

The main result of this section is :

Theorem 2-11:

t <rpo s => t <pso s

Sketch of the proof : by induction on $|s|+|t|$. If t <rpo s with :

rpo1 : then $(t_1,t_2,..)$<<rpo $(s_1,s_2,..)$, and by induction hypothesis $(t_1,t_2,..)$<<pso $(s_1,s_2,..)$; we can conclude from f=g and the generalized compatibility property of <pso.

rpo2 : then g<f and for all t_i , t_i <rpo s. Since we have s ≠ t_i , SPATH(s) ⊓ SPATH(t_i)=ø . So, if a ∈ SPATH(t_i), there exists b ∈ SPATH(s) with a<l b.

Lemma : t.a <l b.

Indeed, t.subsequ(a)<<ilex (s) since t<i s due to g<f ; subsequ(a)<<ilex subsequ(b) because a <l b ; so, subsequ(t.a)= t.subsequ(a)+subsequ(a) <<ilex subsequ(b) because (s) belongs to the right member, but not to the left one.

From the last lemma, we get SPATH(t)<<l SPATH(s) and so, t<pso s.

rpo3 : then t ≦rpo s_i ; by induction t ≦pso si; we conclude from the sub-term property of <pso.

Corollary 2-12:

If the precedence < is total then RPO and PSO are the same ordering.

Proof : If < is total then rpo is total on T(F)/~ and so is pso from the last theorem. But, if s~t, s and t are neither comparable by rpo nor by pso.

Corollary 2-13:

If < is well founded then pso is well founded .

Proof : < is included in a total well founded ordering <'. It is known that RPO(<') is well founded (see[3]); but rpo(<')=pso(<') and pso(<) is included in pso(<') from the monotonic property of the PSO; the corollary follows as in lemma 1-4. Compare this proof with PLAISTED 's [1]!

Remark 2-14: PSO is not included in RDO. As shown in a previous example:

```
          g
          |
    s =   +        <pso    t =   +      with 0<+ and g<f
         / \                    / \
        0   g                  0   f
```

But we do not have s <rdo t because it is impossible to bound $d^{ll}(s)$ with a decomposition along a path of t . A consequence is that PSO is strictly better than RPO. An example given in [2] shows that RDO is not included in PSO. However, it is possible to prove that PSO and RDO are the same ordering when restricted to monadic terms.

4-A VARIANT OF PSO .

In most cases, the use of subsequences for comparing paths of subterms yields redundant computations. Considering paths of subterms as multisets provides a simple variant of PSO, with an additional property of incrementality.

Definition 2-15:

Let < be a precedence. We define <ps recursively : s <ps t iff SPATH(s) <<2 SPATH(t) where a<<2 b iff α <<j β (α(resp β) denotes the multiset of subterms occurring in the path a (resp b))

and u <j v iff (f < g) or (f = g and PSPATH(u) <<2 PSPATH(v)) where $u=f(u_1,..,u_n)$ and $v=g(v_1,..,v_m)$

It can be proved that <ps satisfies the same properties as PSO; the next example shows that <ps is also easy to use . Moreover, the precedence required to orient a rule can be easily computed.

Example 2-16: Let us consider the rewriting system :

(1)	not(not(x))	----->	x
(2)	not(x or y)	----->	not(x) and not(y)
(3)	not(x and y)	----->	not(x) or not(y)
(4)	x and(y or z)	----->	(x and y) or (x and z)
(5)	(y or z)and x	----->	(y and x) or (z and x)

An empty precedence is enough to orient (1), because of the subterm property of <ps. To orient (2) we need to have :

{not(x)and not(y),not(x),x} <<j { not(x or y) , x or y ,x}

But : not(x) <j not(x or y)

Hence (2) is oriented with <ps iff : (and < not) or (and < or)

By exchanging the symbols 'and' and 'or' we get the condition for (3):

(or < not) or (or < and)

In order to have (4) directed with <ps , we need to have :

{(x and y) or (x and z),x and y,x} <<j {x and(y or z),x}

But : (x and y) <j (x and (y or z))

To bound (x and y) or (x and z) for <j , the necessary and sufficient condition is : or < and

Then the other paths of the right-hand side of (4) are bounded too .

Let us finally summarize the conditions :

or < and < not

III-RDO REVISITED

1-DEFINITION OF RDO (see[2][3])

$T(F,X,\square)$ is the set of terms with at most one terminal occurrence of $\square$, where $\square$ is a symbol not in F that can be viewed as the empty term. If X is empty, we denote this set as $T(F,\square)$. If u and v belong to N+ then u/v is the word w∈N+ such that vw=u. t/u is the subterm of t at the occurrence u . t[u←t'] is the term obtained by replacing t/u by t' in t . If t belongs to $T(F,X,\square)$ $|t|=|\{u \in occ(t);t(u)\neq\square \text{ and } t(u)\notin X\}|$. A path p of a term t is an occurrence such that ar(t(p))=0. Let p be a path of t, u a strict prefix of p, i the integer such ui is a prefix of p ; ui is denoted by suc(u,p).

Definition 3-1: elementary decomposition

Given $t \in T(F,\square)$, p a path of t, u a prefix of p, the elementary decomposition $d_u^p(t)$ of t in u along the path p is :

if $t(u)=\Box$ then ø else the quadruple:

$$\langle t(u), d^{p/suc(u,p)}(t/suc(u,p)), TT, d^{u}(t[u\leftarrow\Box])\rangle$$

where $d^{p}(t)$ is the decomposition of t along the path p, that is the set

$$\{d^{p}_{u}(t);\ u \text{ is a prefix of } p\ \}$$

TT is the multiset $\{t/uj\ ; 1\leq j\leq ar(t(u)), uj \neq suc(u,p)\}$

We define also the multiset $d(t) = \{d^{p}(t)\ ;\ p \text{ is a path of } t\}$

Remark: the term $t[u\leftarrow\Box]$ is called the "context" of t in u. TT is called the "followers part".

Definition 3-2: RDO

Given a partial ordering on F, we define the recursive decomposition ordering in the following way : s <rdo t iff $d(s) \ll* \ll* d(t)$, where $\ll* \ll*$ stands for the multiset of multiset ordering extending <* and:

$$d^{p}_{u}(s)=\langle f, d^{p/suc(u,p)}(s'), SS, d^{u}(s'')\rangle <* \ d^{q}_{v}(t)=\langle g, d^{q/suc(v,q)}(t'), TT, d^{v}(t'')\rangle$$

iff in a lexicographical way

dec1: $f < g$

dec2: $d^{p/suc(u,p)}(s') \ll* \ d^{q/suc(v,q)}(t')$

dec3: SS <<rdo TT

dec4: $d^{u}(s'') \ll* \ d^{v}(t'')$

2-REMOVING THE CONTEXT FROM THE DEFINITION OF RDO .

2-1-AN EXAMPLE.

Suppose we want to show :

```
s =  f        <rdo       t =  g      with the precedence f < g
     |                        |
     h                        h
    / \                      / \
   a   b                    a   b
```

To get $d^{11}_{11}(s) \ll* \ d^{11}_{11}(t)$ we have to prove :

$d^{11}_{11}(s) <* \ d^{11}_{11}(t)$ with dec4

and $d^{11}_{1}(s) <* \ d^{11}_{1}(t)$ with dec4

But this computation is useless, because the last inequality is, in fact, a consequence of the previous one. Indeed :

```
d^1( f ) <<* d^1( g )   =>   d^11 ( f  ) <<* d^11 ( g  )
     |            |                  |                |
     □            □                  h                h
                                    / \              / \
                                   □   b            □   b
```

In the following, we give a new (equivalent) definition of RDO that gets rid of this redundancy, by eliminating the contexts in decompositions. Clearly, terms can be reconstructed from their decompositions with contexts, but without context as well. As a consequence, contexts are not really needed, as we show next.

2-2-DEFINITION OF RD ALIAS "SIMPLIFIED RDO".

Definition 3-3: simple decomposition

Given $t \in T(F)$, p a path of t, u a prefix of p, the simple decomposition $D_u^p(t)$ of t in u along the path p is the triple $< g , a, TT >$ where

$g = t(u)$

$a = D^{p/suc(u,p)}(t/suc(u,p))$

TT is the multiset $\{t/uj \ ; \ 1 \leqq j \leqq ar(t(u)) \ , \ uj \neq suc(u,p)\}$

and the simple decomposition of t along the path p is the set

$D^p(t) = \{ D_u^p(t) \ ; \ u \text{ prefix of } p\}$

Let us define as well the multiset : $D(t) = \{ D^p(t) \ ; \ p \text{ path of } t\}$

Definition 3-4: RD

The simplified recursive decomposition ordering is defined as it follows:

$s <rd\ t$ iff $D(s) \ll\!\bigcirc \ll\!\bigcirc D(t)$

with $D_u^p(s) = <f,a,SS> \ <\!\bigcirc \ D_v^q(t) = <g,b,TT>$ iff lexicographically

DEC1 : $f < g$
DEC2 : $a \ll\!\bigcirc b$
DEC3 : $SS \ll rd \ TT$

Remark 3-5: A small d is used to denote elementary decompositions, while a capital D is used to denote simple decompositions.

2-3-RDO AND RD ARE EQUIVALENT .

If we need the context when comparing two paths p and q, using the RDO, this implies that the two paths end by the same sub-sequence of sub-terms. Therefore, the last simple decompositions encountered on p are equal to the last simple decompositions of q . Hence, we do not need them when comparing p and q with RD, unlike RDO. This is the key of our proof that RDO = RD. We state the previous remark more formally in the next lemma :

Lemma 3-6:

Let p a path of s, q a path of t. We suppose that $D_u^p(s) = D_v^q(t)$ where u and v are prefixes of p and q , respectively . Then :
$D^p(s) \ll\!\bigcirc\ D^q(t)$ iff $D^u(s[u\leftarrow\square]) \ll\!\bigcirc\ D^v(t[v\leftarrow\square])$

We can now state the main result :

Theorem 3-7:

Given p and q, two paths of s and t respectively, we have :
$d^p(s) \ll\!* \ d^q(t)$ iff $D^p(s) \ll\!\bigcirc\ D^q(t)$

Sketch of the proof : by induction on $|s|+|t|$;

First case : the paths p and q end by the same sub-sequence of subterms. So, we can simplify p and q by their common suffix and we are brought back to compare two paths u and v of $s[u\leftarrow\square]$ and $t[v\leftarrow\square]$ respectively with u and v prefix of p and q respectively. This is done by the induction hypothesis.

Second case : p and q have not the same tail. Hence, we never need contexts when comparing the elementary decompositions of p with those of q. There-fore, we could as well perform the comparison with simple decompositions .

The last theorem yields immediately :

Corollary 3-8:

s <rdo t   iff   s <rd t

When comparing two terms with RDO, we just need to compare the maximal decompositions of each term: this is the called "++ strategy " in [2]. This is not possible with RD. However, Pierre Lescanne, who implemented both of them in his REVE system, noticed that, even with the ++strategy, RDO appeared to be less efficient than RD, in most of the cases.

3-IMPROVING THE RDO

Example 3-9: Given the terms :

```
s =  *                    and      t = *
    / \                               / | \
   z    *                           z  -  -
       / \                             |  |
      x   y                            x  y
```

with the precedence * < - , we can show that s <rdo t is false . It is sufficient to prove that we have not d^1(s) <<* d^1(t) .

```
But   d^1(s) = { <*,z, * , □> }    d^1(t) = { <*,z, { -, - }, □ > }
                      / \                           |  |
                     x   y                          x  y
```

```
and  {  *  }  <<rdo   { - , - }  is false
       / \              |   |
      x   y             x   y
```

However we have :

```
   d( * )    <<* <<*   d (-) +  d (-)
     / \                  |        |
    x   y                 x        y
```

On the other hand, we could verify : s <pso t and s<ps t, so we have another counterexample showing that PSO is not included in RDO.

RDO fails to order s and t because it requires paths to be gathered in the "follower" part of decompositions, so neither -x, nor -y can bound x*y and they cannot help each other to do that. More generally, if SS and TT are two multisets of terms, then:

```
SS <<rdo TT  implies  Σ   d(r)   <<* <<* Σ    d(q)
                      r∈SS               q∈TT
```

but the converse is false. So, if the last condition is taken instead of dec3 in the definition of RDO the comparison should be more sucessful.

The previous example suggested us an easy way to improve RDO. Instead of comparing the multisets of subterms that constitute the third part of decompositions, also called "the followers", we compare the multiset sums of the paths of these subterms, without taking into account the original subterm they belong to.

In the following, we shall extend RD in that direction. However, the same could be done with RDO itself.

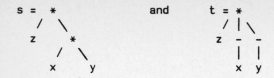

Definition 3-10: IRD

We define on T(F) the improved RD in the following way :

$s <_{ird}\ t \quad \text{iff} \quad D(s) \ll_{\bullet} \ll_{\bullet} D(t)$ where :

$D^{p}_{u}(s)=\langle f,a,SS\rangle \ <_{\bullet}\ D^{q}_{v}(t)=\langle g,b,TT\rangle$ iff in a lexicographical way :

DEC1: $f < g$

DEC2: $a \ll_{\bullet} b$

DEC3 bis: $\sum_{r\in SS} D(r) \ll_{\bullet} \ll_{\bullet} \sum_{q\in TT} D(q)$

Now, with this slight change in the definition of RD, we get in the example 3-9: s <ird t, and we can prove straightforward that RDO is strictly included in IRD :

Theorem 3-11:

s <rdo t => s <ird t

In [6], another ordering is described, and the authors give the following example of two terms that can be compared with their ordering, but where RDO does not apply. This example is quite similar to example 3-9 :

s = h(a(z),g(a(a(x)),x),g(b(b(y)),y))
t = h(a(z),g(a(x),b(y)),g(a(x),b(y))

and we may prove, as in 3-9 : t <ird s .

As a matter of fact, it will be shown in the next section that IRD and KAPUR-NARENDRAN-SIVAKUMAR ordering (KNS in short) are the same ordering. Now, if we compute the complexity of comparing two terms s and t using IRD, by the method described in [6], we get an upper bound $O(|s|^4 * |t|^4)$. With the path ordering of [6], the upper bound is $O(|s|^5 * |t|^5)$. This is not surprising, since this last ordering uses contexts .

4-IRD AND KNS ARE EQUIVALENT.

We proceed as follows :

A) We give an alternative definition of KNS, which we think is simpler and more efficient.

B) We show that IRD and KNS are equivalent.

A) alternative definition of KNS ordering.

In this subsection, the notations and the definitions are taken from [6]. Let P1=<k1,T1>.<k2,T2>....<km,Tm> and P2=<h1,S1>....<hn,Sn> be two paths of subterms. We suppose, for simplicity, that no variable is involved. KNS ordering is denoted by <T, and the path comparison is performed as follows:

P2 <p P1 iff for all <hj,Sj> in P2 there exists <ki,Ti> in P1 such that :
  a. hj < ki or
  b. hj = ki and

     1. RC(<hj,Sj>,P2) <p RC(<ki,Ti>,P1) or
     2. RC(<hj,Sj>,P2) == RC(<ki,Ti>,P1) and Sj <T Ti or
     3. RC(<hj,Sj>,P2) == RC(<ki,Ti>,P1) and Sj = Ti and
       LC(<hj,Sj>,P2) <p LC(<ki,Ti>,P1)

Now, let us have a closer look at condition 3. This condition plays the role of "context comparison" within RDO. If P1 and P2 have no common suffix, then we never have to use the test b.3. We can always reduce the situation, to the previous one, thanks to the next result, that states a converse of lemma 5 of [6] :

Lemma 3-12 :

Let P1,P2,P3,P4,P5 be paths such that P4==P1.P3 and P5==P2.P3. Then:
  P5 <p P4   iff P2 <p P1 .

This leads to a more efficient definition of <p and KNS ordering:

Proposition 3-13 :

Let P1' and P2' be the paths we get from P1 and P2 by deleting their common suffix. Then P2 <p P1 iff for all <hj,Sj> in P2' there exists <ki,Ti> in P1' such that a. or b.1. or b.2. is true.

We are now ready to prove :

B) IRD and KNS are equivalent.

It is sufficient to prove that the path comparisons using <<● or <p always yield the same result :

Proposition 3-14 :

Let P and Q be two paths of s and t, respectively. Then: P <p Q   iff D^P (s) <<● D^q (t)

Proof : (by induction on $|s|+|t|$) assume P <p Q , and let P' and Q' be the paths we get by deleting the common suffix of P and Q. Let <hj,Sj> be in P', with u such that Sj=s/u. We suppose that <ki,Ti> in Q' take care of <hj,Sj>, and v is such that Ti = t/v. Let us show that D^p_u(s) <● D^q_v(t). The only non trivial case to consider is b.3, that is : hj = ki and RC(<hj,Sj>,P) == RC(<ki,Ti>,Q) and Sj <T Ti. We have by definition of <T :

MP(Sj) <<p MP(Ti). The concerned paths of this last inequality belong to smaller terms. Therefore, we can apply the induction hypothesis :

$$\sum_{a \in MP(Sj)} D(a) \ll_{\bullet} \ll_{\bullet} \sum_{b \in MP(Ti)} D(b)$$

The relation above is nothing else but DEC3 bis.

A similar argument proves the converse.

CONCLUSION.

PSO and RDO have many common features: both of them work on paths of subterms, and improve RPO; furthermore, PSO could be easily expressed in terms of decompositions. They essentially differ when comparing subterms with same roots: PSO splits the paths and compares in parallel all paths of subterms issued from the root; on the contrary, RDO goes on with the same path and checks the other paths later on. In other words, PSO works breadth first, and RDO works depth first. This is why these two orderings do not always give the same result. But, we have been able to improve RDO by incorporating some ideas of PSO. We can sum up our results in the following diagram :

$$\text{PSO} \supset \text{RPO} \subset \text{RDO} \overset{\text{see[2]}}{=} \text{RD} \subset \text{IRD} = \text{KNS}$$

An interesting feature of RD is its conceptual simplicity, that makes modifications easier. In particular, we can incorporate status "a la KAMIN et LEVY" in RD by comparing decompositions in a lexicographic way. This was not easy with RDO [7]. Besides symbols with lexicographical status, we may have symbols with "depth-first" status or "breadth-first" status. So, according to the choice of the status of the fonction symbols, we can make RD more or less similar either to RDO or to PSO. This cannot be detailed here by lack of space, but may be found in [8].

Acknowledgement . I would like to thank Pierre Lescanne for his helpful suggestions, and Jieh Hsiang, Jean-Pierre Jouannaud, Emmanuel Kounalis, Alain Quere and Jean-Luc Remy for reading the manuscript.

REFERENCES

[1] Plaisted D. A recursively defined ordering for proving termination of term rewriting systems. University of Illinois sept.78 UIUCDCS_R_78_943

[2] Jouannaud J-P, Lescanne P., Reinig F. Recursive decomposition ordering Formal description of programming concepts Bjorner D. North Holland 1983

[3] Lescanne P. Some properties of decomposition orderings,a simplification ordering to prove termination of rewriting systems. RAIRO Informatique theorique.No 4_82

[4] Jouannaud J-P., Lescanne P. On multiset orderings. Information Processing Letters No 15_82 pp57-63

[5] Dershowitz N. Ordering for term rewriting systems Proc. 20th Symposium on foundations of computer science 1979.

[6] Kapur D.,Narendran P.,Sivakumar G. A path ordering for proving termination of Term Rewriting Systems To appear in CAAP '85

[7] Lescanne P. Uniform termination of term rewriting systems - Recursive decomposition ordering with status. CAAP '84.

[8] Rusinowitch M. Extension de la notion de status dans les ordres de decomposition. Internal report. CRIN 85.

ASSOCIATIVE PATH ORDERINGS *

Leo Bachmair
Department of Computer Science
University of Illinois at Urbana-Champaign, U.S.A.

David A. Plaisted
Department of Computer Science
University of North Carolina at Chapel Hill, U.S.A.

Abstract. In this paper we introduce a new class of orderings - *associative path orderings* - for proving *termination* of *associative commutative term rewriting systems.* These orderings are based on the concept of *simplification orderings* and extend the well-known *recursive path orderings* to E-congruence classes, where E is an equational theory consisting of associativity and commutativity axioms. The associative path ordering is similar to another termination ordering for proving AC termination, described in Dershowitz, et al. (83), which is also based on the idea of *transforming terms.* Our ordering is conceptually simpler, however, since any term is transformed into a single term, whereas in Dershowitz, et al. (83) the transform of a term is a multiset of terms. More important yet, we show how to lift our ordering to non-ground terms, which is essential for applications of the Knuth-Bendix completion method but was not possible with the previous ordering.

Associative path orderings require less expertise than polynomial orderings. They are applicable to term rewriting systems for which a *precedence ordering* on the set of operator symbols can be defined that satisfies a certain condition, the *associative pair condition.* The precedence ordering can often be derived from the structure of the reduction rules. We include termination proofs for various term rewriting systems (for rings, boolean algebra, etc.) and, in addition, point out ways of dealing with equational theories for which the associative pair condition does not hold.

1. Introduction

We assume that the reader is familiar with the basic concepts concerning reduction relations and term rewriting systems. We briefly summarize the most important notions below. For a more thorough discussion of term rewriting systems see Huet and Oppen (80) and Huet (80).

---

* This research was supported in part by the National Science Foundation under grant MCS 83-07755.

A *signature* or *arity function* is a function $a:F\to \mathbf{N}$ ($\mathbf{N}$ is the set of non-negative integers). F is called the set of *function* or *operator symbols*. The set of *ground terms* $T(F)$ (abbreviated by G) is defined as being the smallest set such that $f(t_1, \ldots, t_n)\in T(F)$ if $f\in F$, $a(f)=n$, and $t_1, \cdots, t_n\in T(F)$. We will assume that F is finite and G is non-empty. Let V be a (denumerable) set disjoint from F. Elements of V are called *variables* and denoted $x,y,z, \cdots$. The set $T(F\cup V)$, where variables are considered as constants, will be abbreviated by T. Elements of T are called *terms* and denoted $s,t, \cdots$. For any term t, $V(t)$ denotes the set of variables occurring in t. The (top-level) *operator symbol* $fs(t)$ of a term $t=f(t_1, \ldots, t_n)$ is f.

A *substitution* is a mapping σ from $T(F,V)$ into itself. We will only consider substitutions for which $\sigma(x)=x$ for almost all $x\in V$. $D(\sigma)$ denotes the set $\{x : \sigma(x)\neq x\}$. A substitution σ is completely determined by specifying its values for all $x\in D(\sigma)$. It is called *ground* if and only if $\sigma(x)$ is a ground term, for all $x\in D(\sigma)$. We will informally use sequences of integers, *occurrences*, to characterize access paths in a term. For example, the set of occurrences of $t=0+I(x+y)$ is the set $\{\Lambda,1,2,2.1,2.1.1,2.1.2\}$. The subterm $t/2.1$ of t at occurrence 2.1 is the term $x+y$. Let s and s' be terms and let u be an occurrence of s. Then $s[u\leftarrow s']$ denotes the result of *replacing* the subterm of s at occurrence u by s'. For example, $t[2.1\leftarrow 0]$ is the term $0+I(0)$.

An *equational theory* is a set $E\subset T\times T$. The equation (s,t) is written $s=t$ and the congruence relation generated by E is denoted by $=_E$. A *term rewriting system* (TRS) is a finite set $R=\{(l_i,r_i) : l_i,r_i\in T,\ V(r_i)\subset V(l_i)\}$. The pair (l_i,r_i) is called *rewrite* or *reduction rule* and is written $l_i\to r_i$. The *reduction relation* $\to_R$ on T is defined as follows: $s\to_R t$ if and only if there exist an occurrence u of s, a substitution σ, and a reduction rule $l\to r$ in R, such that $s/u=\sigma(l)$ and $t=s[u\leftarrow\sigma(r)]$. Occasionally we will abbreviate $\to_R$ by $\to$. The symbols $\to^+$, $\to^*$ and $\leftrightarrow$ denote the transitive, transitive-reflexive, and symmetric closure of $\to$, respectively.

Two essential properties of term rewriting systems are *termination* and *confluence*. A TRS R *terminates* (or is *noetherian*) if there is no infinite sequence of terms $t_1 \to_R t_2 \to_R t_3 \to_R \cdots$. R terminates if and only if $\to_R^+$ is a well-founded (strict) partial ordering on T. A TRS R is called *confluent* if, for any terms s, t, and t', with $s\to_R^* t$ and $s\to_R^* t'$, there is a term s', such that $t\to_R^* s'$ and $t'\to_R^* s'$. A term t is *irreducible* or in *normal form* if and only if there is no term t' such that $t\to_R t'$. If t' is irreducible and $t\to^* t'$, then t' is called a *R-normal form of t*. In a confluent and noetherian (*canonical*) TRS every term has a unique normal form and the equivalence of two terms can be decided by comparing their respective normal forms. Knuth and Bendix (70) developed a criterion for checking confluence of a given TRS R that is based on the fact that the confluence test can be localized and restricted to so-called critical pairs. They also showed how a non-confluent TRS may be made into a confluent one by adding appropriate rules to it. This completion method, as well as the confluence test, work for noetherian term rewriting systems. Techniques for proving termination are therefore essential for practical applications of the Knuth-Bendix method.

Most techniques for proving termination of a TRS are based on the concept of simplification orderings. A relation $\to$ on G is *monotonic* (or has the *replacement property*) if

$t \to t'$ implies $f(\cdots t \cdots) \to f(\cdots t' \cdots)$, for all terms t, t', $f(\cdots t \cdots)$, $f(\cdots t' \cdots)$ in G. A partial ordering $>$ on G is called a ***simplification ordering*** if it is monotonic and has the following *subterm property:* $f(\cdots t \cdots) > t$, for all terms t and $f(\cdots t \cdots)$. In a simplification ordering 'syntactically simpler' terms are smaller. That is, if a term t is homeomorphically embedded in a term s, then $s > t$, for any simplification ordering $>$. We need the following result on simplification orderings.

THEOREM 1. (Dershowitz (79)). *A TRS R terminates if there exists a simplification ordering $>$ on G such that $\sigma(l) > \sigma(r)$, for all reduction rules $l \to r \in R$ and for every ground substitution σ with $V(l) \subset D(\sigma)$.*

An important class of simplification orderings are recursive path orderings, which extend a given partial ordering $>$, also called a *precedence ordering*, on the set of operator symbols F to the set of terms G.

DEFINITION 1. Let $>$ be a partial ordering on F. The *recursive path ordering* $>_{rpo}$ on G corresponding to $>$ is defined recursively as follows:

$$s = f(s_1, \cdots, s_m) >_{rpo} t = g(t_1, \cdots, t_n)$$

if and only if

(a) $f = g$ and $\{s_1, \cdots, s_m\} \gg_{rpo} \{t_1, \cdots, t_n\}$, or

(b) $f > g$ and $s >_{rpo} t_i$, for all i, $1 \le i \le n$, or

(c) $f \not\geq g$ and $s_i \gtrsim_{rpo} t$, for some i, $1 \le i \le m$.

Here $\gg_{rpo}$ is the extension of $>_{rpo}$ to multisets and $s \gtrsim_{rpo} t$ means $s >_{rpo} t$ or $s \sim t$, where the *permutation equivalence* $\sim$ is defined by

$s = f(s_1, \ldots, s_n) \sim t = f(t_1, \ldots, t_n)$ if and only if, for some permutation π, $s_i \sim t_{\pi(i)}$, for all i, $1 \le i \le n$.

For a detailed discussion of termination orderings see Dershowitz (82) and Huet and Oppen (80). In the following sections we extend these techniques for proving termination of a TRS and introduce orderings for proving termination of a reduction relation modulo a set of equations.

2. Equational term rewriting systems

A basic idea underlying the concept of rewriting systems is that of reducing a given term to a simpler one. An equation is converted into a directed rewriting rule in such a way that the right-hand side of the rule is 'simpler' than the left-hand side. However, there are equations where left-hand side and right-hand side are intrinsically incomparable. For example, using the commutativity axiom $x + y = y + x$ as a directed rewriting rule results in a non-terminating TRS. One way to handle theories that contain such equations is to extend the notion of rewriting and to allow reductions modulo a set of equations. Extensions of the classical Knuth-Bendix completion method are described in Lankford and Ballantyne (77), Peterson and Stickel (81), Huet (80), and Jouannaud and Kirchner (84). These methods are based on complete unification algorithms for the equational theory E.

A given equational theory A can often be partitioned into two sets R and E, where E is a set of equations and R can be regarded as a set of directed rewrite rules. Such a tuple (R,E) is called an *equational term rewriting system* (ETRS).

DEFINITION 2. The reduction relation $\rightarrow_{R/E}$ on T corresponding to (R,E) is defined as follows: $s \rightarrow_{R/E} t$ (*s reduces to t relative to R and E*) if and only if there are terms s' and t' in T such that $s =_E s' \rightarrow_R t' =_E t$.

DEFINITION 3. R is called *E-terminating* if and only if there is no infinite sequence of terms $t_1 \rightarrow_{R/E} t_2 \rightarrow_{R/E} t_3 \rightarrow_{R/E} \cdots$.

Note that R is E-terminating if and only if $\rightarrow^+_{R/E}$ is a well-founded ordering on T. The following termination theorem holds:

THEOREM 2. *An ETRS (R,E) terminates if there is a simplification ordering* $>$ *on G such that* $s \rightarrow_{R/E} t$ *implies* $s > t$, *for all ground terms s and t.*

Proof. The proof for this theorem is based on the same idea as the proof for Theorem 1. □

The theorem quantifies over all possible reductions $s \rightarrow_{R/E} t$ on ground terms. This requirement can be refined. We say that a (binary) relation $\rightarrow$ on T is *E-compatible* if and only if $s =_E s' \rightarrow t' =_E t$ implies $s \rightarrow t$. If $>$ is an E-compatible ordering, then $>$ contains $\rightarrow^+_{R/E}$ if and only if it contains $\rightarrow^+_R$. To see this assume that $>$ contains $\rightarrow^+_R$, i.e. $u \rightarrow_R v$ implies $u > v$, for all terms u and v. Let s, s', t and t' be such that $s =_E s' \rightarrow_R t' =_E t$. Then $s' > t'$ and therefore, since $>$ is E-compatible, also $s > t$. Thus $>$ contains $\rightarrow^+_{R/E}$. This suggests the following theorem, which is an extension of Theorem 1 to equational term rewriting systems:

THEOREM 3. *An ETRS (R,E) terminates if there exists an E-compatible simplification ordering* $>$ *on G such that* $\sigma(l) > \sigma(r)$, *for every rule* $l \rightarrow r$ *of R and every ground substitution* σ *with* $V(l) \subset D(\sigma)$.

Proof. Let $>$ be an E-compatible simplification ordering satisfying the stated requirement. By Theorem 2 and the remarks above it suffices to show that $s \rightarrow_R t$ implies $s > t$, for all ground terms s and t. But this can be proved easily under the given assumptions. □

Our approach to the problem of E-termination is based on Theorem 3. We propose to construct E-compatible simplification orderings by extending well-known orderings like the recursive path ordering using the idea of transforming terms. That is, terms are first appropriately transformed and then compared using some ordering for proving termination of R. A different approach to the problem of E-termination, based on the following theorem, has been suggested by Jouannaud and Munoz (84).

THEOREM 4. (Munoz (83)). *Let (R,E) be an ETRS and let* $\rightarrow$ *be a reduction relation with* $\rightarrow_R \subset \rightarrow \subset \rightarrow_{R/E}$. *If* $\rightarrow$ *terminates and is E-commuting then R is E-terminating.*

A reduction relation $\to$ is *E-commuting* if and only if for all terms s, s' and t with $s' =_E s \to^+ t$, there exists a term t' such that $s' \to^+ t' =_E t$. If a reduction relation is not E-commuting it can sometimes be extended to an E-commuting relation by adding appropriate rules to R. This process is similar to the completion process for non-confluent TRSs and need not always terminate. The termination property of the extended (E-commuting) set of rules can be proved using existing methods for proving termination of $\to$ Candidates for $\to$ are $\to_R$ and $\to_{R,E}$. Simplification orderings may be used for proving termination of $\to_R$. The reduction relation $\to_{R,E}$ is defined as follows: $s \to_{R,E} t$ if and only if there exist an occurrence u of s, a rule $l \to r$ in R, and a substitution σ, such that s/u is not a variable, $s/u =_E \sigma(l)$ and $t = s[u \leftarrow \sigma(r)]$. Note that $\to_{R,E}$ is different from $\to_{R/E}$, since $\to_{R,E}$ allows E-equality to be applied only to the subterm at occurrence u, whereas $\to_{R/E}$ allows unrestricted E-equality steps. Consequently it should be simpler to prove termination of $\to_{R,E}$ than of $\to_{R/E}$. However, at the present time no specific orderings are known for proving termination of $\to_{R,E}$. Of course, if E is an associative-commutative theory, the associative path orderings we will describe below can be used for that purpose.

3. Associative-commutative term rewriting systems

We will now give a formal definition of associative-commutative rewriting systems and introduce a formalism for representing associative-commutative terms. A *commutative law* is an equation of the form $f(x,y)=f(y,x)$, for some function symbol f. An *associative law* is an equation of the form $f(x,f(y,z))=f(f(x,y),z)$ or $f(f(x,y),z)=f(x,f(y,z))$. An equational theory E is called an *associative commutative (AC) theory* if every equation in E is either an associative or commutative law. An ETRS (R,E) is called an *AC rewriting system* if E is an AC theory. Let (R,E) be an AC rewriting system. F_A and F_C denote the set of *associative* and *commutative operators*, respectively. $F_{AC} := F_A \cap F_C$ is called the set of *associative-commutative* (AC) operators. A term $f(t_1, \ldots, t_n)$, where f is an AC operator, is called an *AC term.*

Given a set of operator symbols F, a *varyadic signature* (over F) is a function $a:F \to 2^{\mathbf{N}}$, where $2^{\mathbf{N}}$ is the set of all subsets of $\mathbf{N}$. This basically means that we allow operators with variable arity. For example, if $a(f)=\{2,3\}$ then both $f(a,b)$ and $f(a,b,c)$ are syntactically correct terms. More precisely, the set $TV(F)$ of *varyadic terms* is defined as being the smallest set such that $f(t_1, \ldots, t_n)$ is in $TV(F)$ if $f \in F$, $n \in a(f)$ and $t_1, \ldots, t_n \in TV(F)$. The set $TV(F \cup V)$ of varyadic terms containing variables, where V is disjoint from F and variables are considered as constants, is denoted by $TV(F,V)$. Let now a be an (ordinary) signature with set of function symbols F and let E be an AC theory over T. The varyadic signature a' corresponding to a is defined as follows: $a'(f):=\{a(f)\}$ if $f \notin F_A$, and $a(f):=\mathbf{N}-\{0\}$, otherwise. That is, associative operators may take any positive number of arguments, whereas non-associative operators have fixed arity. Associative path orderings are based on transforms that map terms over an ordinary signature a into terms over the corresponding varyadic signature a'.

AC terms are conveniently represented as flattened terms, i.e. terms that have no nested occurrences of associative operators. If a term s is flattened, then there must be no subterm t of s such that $fs(t)=f \in F_A$ and t contains a top-level subterm t' with $fs(t')=f$.

DEFINITION 4. The *flattening* operation $\bar{\ }$ on varyadic terms is defined as follows. Let $t=f(t_1, \cdots, t_n)$ be a term. Then

(F1) $\bar{t} := t$ if t is a constant or variable;

(F2) $\bar{t} := f(\bar{t_1}, \ldots, \bar{t_n})$ if $f \notin F_A$ or if $fs(t_i) \neq f$, for all i, $1 \leq i \leq n$;

(F3) $\bar{t} := t'$, where t' results from t by replacing t_i by $\bar{t_i}$, if $fs(t_i) \neq f$, and replacing t_i by $t_{i1}, \ldots, t_{\epsilon_i}$, if $\bar{t_i}=f(t_{i1}, \ldots, t_{\epsilon_i})$, otherwise.

We call $\bar{t}$ the *flattened version* of t. For example, if f is an associative operator and t is the term $f(a,f(b,f(c,d)))$, then $\bar{t}$ is the term $f(a,b,c,d)$. If N is a multiset of terms $\{t_1, \ldots, t_n\}$, then $\bar{N}$ denotes the multiset $\{\bar{t_1}, \cdots, \bar{t_n}\}$.

Whenever two terms s and t are equal under associativity and commutativity then their flattened versions are equal up to permutation, i.e. $\bar{s} \sim \bar{t}$. We may therefore use a *multiset notation* to denote AC terms. That is, we will use an expression $\tilde{f}(N)$, where f is a commutative operator and N is a multiset of terms $\{t_1, \cdots, t_n\}$, to denote a term $t=f(t_1, \cdots, t_n)$. Also, given multisets $N_1, \ldots, N_k$, we will write $f(N_1, \ldots, N_k)$ to denote the multiset $\{f(t_1, \ldots, t_k) : t_i \in N_i, \text{ for } 1 \leq i \leq k\}$.

EXAMPLE 1. $\tilde{f}(\{a,b,c,d\})$ denotes the term $f(a,b,c,d)$, whereas $f(\{a,b\},\{c,d\})$ denotes the multiset $\{f(a,c),f(b,c),f(a,d),f(b,d)\}$. Frequently, we will delete brackets of singleton multisets and write, for example, $f(\{a,b\},c)$ instead of $f(\{a,b\},\{c\})$. Suppose that $g(N)$ is a multiset of flattened terms, then flattening $f(f(a,b),\tilde{f}(g(N)))$ yields $\tilde{f}(\{a,b\} \cup g(N))$.

4. Associative path orderings

Let (R,E) be an AC rewriting system. In order to simplify the presentation we will assume from now on that every associative operator is also commutative and every commutative operator is associative, i.e. $F_{AC}=F_A=F_C$. The results below can easily be adapted to the case where F also contains functions that are associative but not commutative. The following example illustrates a basic problem with extending recursive path orderings to congruence classes of terms.

EXAMPLE 2. Suppose we apply the recursive path ordering to flattened terms. Let $*$ and $+$ be AC operators with $* > +$. Certainly, $a*b >_{rpo} a+b$. Then, $(a*b)*c >_{rpo} (a+b)*c$, $\overline{(a*b)*c} = *(a,b,c)$, and $\overline{(a+b)*c} = (a+b)*c$. However, $*(a,b,c) >_{rpo} (a+b)*c$ is false. Thus this ordering is not monotonic.

Associative path orderings are based on recursive path orderings, but instead of simply comparing the flattened versions of terms in the recursive path ordering, terms are transformed before they are compared. The transform we use may be viewed as a sequence of reduction steps with respect to some set of reduction rules that depend on the given precedence ordering. We have to impose some conditions on the precedence ordering, however, in order to ensure that this proposed ordering, which consists of comparing the transformed versions of terms in the recursive path ordering, in fact defines a simplification ordering.

DEFINITION 5. A precedence ordering $>_F$ on F satisfies the *associative pair condition* if and only if the set F_{AC} can be partitioned into two disjoint sets $\{f_1, \cdots ,f_p\}$ and $\{g_1, \cdots ,g_q\}$ such that $p \geq q$ and

(a) for all i, $1 \leq i \leq p$, f_i is minimal in F, and
(b) for all i, $1 \leq i \leq q$, $g_i >_F f_i$, and
(c) for all i, $1 \leq i \leq q$, g_i is minimal in $F-\{f_i\}$.

This condition precludes, for instance, a precedence ordering $>$ with $* > +$ and $* > \oplus$, where $*, +$ and $\oplus$ are AC operators.

DEFINITION 6. Let $>_F$ be a partial ordering on F that satisfies the associative pair condition. Then we define the *associative path ordering* $>_{apo}$ on G corresponding to $>_F$ as follows:

$s >_{apo} t$ if and only if $M(s) >_{rpo} M(t)$ or $M(s) = M(t)$ and $s > t$,

where $>$ is an admissible ordering and the *transform* $M(t)$ of a term $t = f(t_1, \cdots ,t_n)$ is defined by

$$M(t) := M_2(M_1(\bar{t})), \text{ where}$$
$$M_1(t) := \overline{f(M(t_1), \cdots ,M(t_n))} \text{ and}$$
$$M_2(t) := \overline{\tilde{f}_i(g_i(\cdots N_1 \cdots N_k \cdots))},$$
$$\text{if } t = g_i(\cdots \tilde{f}_i(N_1) \cdots \tilde{f}_i(N_k) \cdots), \text{ where } k \geq 1; \text{ and } t \text{ otherwise.}$$

An ordering $>$ is called *admissible* if it is monotonic and E-compatible and if there is no infinite sequence $t_1 > t_2 > t_3 > \cdots$ such that $M(t_1) = M(t_2) = M(t_3) = \cdots$.

EXAMPLE 3. The *size* $|t|$ of a term t is the number of operator symbols and variables in t (counting symbols with their multiplicity). For instance, if $s' = x*(y+z)$ and $t' = (x*y)+(x*z)$ then $|s'| = 5$ and $|t'| = 7$. Let $>$ be the ordering defined by $s > t$ if and only if $|s| \prec |t|$ and no variable appears more often in s than in t. Here $\prec$ is the natural order on integers. The ordering $>$ is monotonic and E-compatible. Furthermore, since $|t| \prec |M(t)|$, there can be no infinite sequence $t_1 > t_2 > \cdots$ such that $M(t_1) = M(t_2) = \cdots$. This ordering is therefore admissible and may be used for comparing terms with the same transform.

EXAMPLE 4. Let $s = (a*b)*c$ and $t = (a+b)*c$, where $*$ and $+$ are AC operators with $* > +$. Then $s >_{apo} t$ since $M(s) = *(a,b,c) >_{rpo} (a*b)+(a*c) = M(t)$. Thus transforming terms solves the problem we had in Example 2.

The associative pair condition guarantees that the transform M is well-defined and that the associative path ordering is in fact a simplification ordering. M_2 corresponds to the A-transform in Plaisted (84). As can be seen from the example above, transforming a term basically consists of multiplying out the g_i, distributing them over the f_i. In fact, we may characterize the transform M using a reduction relation in the following way. Let D be the set of all distributivity rules of the form $g(f(x,y),z) \rightarrow f(g(x,z),g(y,z))$ or $g(x,f(y,z)) \rightarrow f(g(x,y),g(x,z))$, where f and g are AC operators with $g >_F f$. If the precedence ordering $>_F$ satisfies the associative pair condition, then D is E-terminating and the normal form t' of a term t is unique up to associativity and commutativity. Furthermore, $M(t) \sim \overline{t'}$, where t' is a D-normal form of t. Comparing two terms in the associative path ordering may therefore be viewed as first reducing both terms to normal form (applying the distributivity rules in D) and then comparing the flattened normal forms in the recursive path ordering.

Several properties of the transform M may readily be observed.

LEMMA 1. (T1) If $s =_E t$ then $M(s) \sim M(t)$.
(T2) $M(f(t_1, \cdots, t_n)) = f(M(t_1), \cdots, M(t_n))$ if $f \notin F_{AC}$.
(T3) $M(f(t_1, \cdots, t_n)) = \overline{f(M(t_1), \cdots, M(t_n))}$ if $f \neq g_i$.

We may state now our main results on associative path orderings.

LEMMA 2. Any associative path ordering $>_{apo}$ is E-compatible.

Proof. If $s' =_E s >_{apo} t =_E t'$, then $M(s') = M(s)$ and $M(t') = M(t)$. Therefore, either $M(s') >_{rpo} M(t')$ or $M(s') = M(t')$ and, since $>'$ is E-compatible, $s' >' t'$. In either case $s' >_{apo} t'$. □

THEOREM 5. *Any associative path ordering is a simplification ordering.*

Proof. Proving that an associative path ordering is a partial ordering poses no problem. For the proof of the subterm and replacement properties several cases have to be distinguished depending on the different possible outcomes of transforming terms. A detailed proof is given in Bachmair (84). □

Theorems 3 and 5 and Lemma 2 yield the following termination theorem:

THEOREM 6. *An AC rewriting system (R,E) terminates if there exists an associative path ordering $>_{apo}$ on G such that $\sigma(l) >_{apo} \sigma(r)$, for each rule $l \rightarrow r$ of R and every ground substitution σ with $V(l) \subset D(\sigma)$.*

We will next give a method for comparing terms with variables in the associative path ordering. When applying Theorem 6 we have to compare, for given terms s and t, $\sigma(s)$ and $\sigma(t)$, for every ground substitution σ whose domain contains all variables in s and t. We will generalize the associative path ordering in such a way that only a finite number of the potentially infinitely many ground substitutions σ have to be checked.

In the recursive path ordering terms that contain variables are compared by replacing every variable x by a new constant c_x. The corresponding method for associative path orderings is more complicated since the result of transforming a term may depend on the particular substitution that is applied to the term. For instance, given a term $g(x,c)$, where c is a constant, we may substitute $f(c,c)$ for x to obtain $g(f(c,c),c)$, a term that can be transformed to $f(g(c,c),g(c,c))$ (assuming f and g are AC operators with $f < g$). However, substituting c for x results in $g(c,c)$, a term to which the transform is not applicable. We have to consider both cases when comparing $g(x,c)$ with some other term. In general, we say that a variable x has a *critical occurrence* for an AC operator f_i in a term s if s contains a subterm s' of the form $g_i(x,t)$ or $g_i(t,x)$, where $fs(t) \neq f_i$. If a variable x has a critical occurrence in s, then the result of transforming $\sigma(s)$ depends on the value of $\sigma(x)$ as we have seen in the example above. Note that a variable may have critical occurrences for more than one AC operator.

Let s and t be terms with $V(t) \subset V(s)$ and let $\Sigma(s)$ denote the set of all ground substitutions σ with $V(s) \subset D(\sigma)$. Furthermore, for every variable x in s, let $C(s,x)$ denote the set consisting of c_x and, in addition to c_x, of all expressions $f_i(c_x,d_x)$, such that x has a critical occurrence for f_i in s. Finally, let $\Lambda(s)$ denote the set of all substitutions σ such that $\sigma(x) \in C(s,x)$, if $x \in V(s)$, and $\sigma(x)=x$, otherwise. We define the mapping L from $\Sigma(s)$ to $\Lambda(s)$ by

$$\sigma_L(x)=f_i(c_x,d_x), \text{ if } fs(\sigma(x))=f_i \text{ and } x \text{ has a critical occurrence for } f_i \text{ in } s,$$
$$\sigma_L(x)=c_x, \text{ otherwise.}$$

The connection between σ and σ_L is as follows: $M(\sigma_L(s)) >_{rpo} M(\sigma_L(t))$ implies $M(\sigma(s)) >_{rpo} M(\sigma(t))$. Therefore we essentially have to consider only the finitely many substitutions in $\Lambda(s)$ when comparing s and t. We have to take care, however, of the case of comparing terms that have the same transform. Such terms are compared in the associative path ordering with respect to a given admissible ordering $>$. We require that the ordering $>$ can be extended to non-ground terms and that $M(s)=M(t)$ and $s>t$ imply $\sigma(s)>\sigma(t)$, for every ground substitution σ. The ordering given in Example 3, for instance, satisfies these requirements. Now, in order to prove $\sigma(s) >_{apo} \sigma(t)$, for all substitutions σ in $\Sigma(s)$, we only have to show $\sigma_L(s) >_{apo} \sigma_L(t)$, for all substitutions σ_L in $\Lambda(s)$. Let us summarize the considerations above.

DEFINITION 7. The *generalized associative path ordering* $>_{gapo}$ on T is defined by $s >_{gapo} t$ if and only if $\sigma_L(s) >_{apo} \sigma_L(t)$ for all substitutions $\sigma_L \in \Lambda(s)$.

THEOREM 7. *Let (R,E) be an AC rewriting system. Then* $l >_{gapo} r$ *implies* $\sigma(l) >_{apo} \sigma(r)$, *for each rule* $l \to r$ *in R and every ground substitution* σ *with* $V(l) \subset D(\sigma)$.

We may improve the efficiency of the lifting process by replacing x by $f_i(S_x)$ instead of $f_i(c_x,d_x)$, where the symbolic multiset S_x represents $\{c_x,d_x\}$. The transform may be applied directly to the shorter expressions containing $f_i(S_x)$ by treating S_x as a constant. Furthermore, if $C(s,x)$ contains any expression $f_i(c_x,d_x)$ we need not consider substitutions σ_L with $\sigma_L(x)=c_x$ because systematically replacing c_x by $f_i(c_x,d_x)$ (or by $f_i(S_x)$) in s and t does not change the result of comparing s and t. This may considerably reduce the size of $\Lambda(s)$. The newly introduced constant symbols c_x are unrelated to anything else with respect to the ordering $>$ on function symbols. However, if there is some constant c which is minimal among all constants we may assume $c_x \geq c$.

EXAMPLE 5. Let $*$ and $+$ be AC operators with $*>+$. Suppose s is $x*y$ and t is $x+y$. Since both x and y have critical occurrences for $*$ in s we replace them by c_x+d_x and c_y+d_y, respectively, and obtain $s'=(c_x+d_x)*(c_y+d_y)$ and $t'=(c_x+d_x)+(c_y+d_y)$. Now, $M(s')=+(c_x*c_y, c_x*d_y, d_x*c_y, d_x*d_y)$ and $M(t')=+(c_x,d_x,c_y,d_y)$. Since $M(s') >_{rpo} M(t')$ we may conclude $s >_{gapo} t$.

EXAMPLE 6. Consider the two terms $s=x*(y+z)$ and $t=x*y+x*z$. Since no variable has a critical occurrence in s we may replace every variable by a new constant. Both terms have the same transform, but we may compare them with respect to the ordering given in Example 3 to obtain $s >_{gapo} t$.

Theorems 6 and 7 provide the basis for proving termination of AC rewriting systems: given an ETRS (R,E), construct a precedence ordering $>_F$ such that $l >_{gapo} r$ for every reduction rule $l \to r$ in R. In the next section we will demonstrate this technique with several examples.

5. Examples

EXAMPLE 7. *Boolean algebra.* The following canonical ETRS for Boolean algebra is taken from Hsiang (83). R contains the following rules:

(R1) $x+0 \to x$
(R2) $x*0 \to 0$
(R3) $x*1 \to x$
(R4) $x*x \to x$
(R5) $(x+y)*z \to x*z+y*z$
(R6) $x+x \to 0$

E consists of the associativity and commutativity laws for $*$ and $+$. 0 and 1 are constants, they stand for *FALSE* and *TRUE*, respectively. The AC operators $*$ and $+$ stand for *AND* and *EXCLUSIVE-OR*, respectively. For constructing a precedence ordering we only have to consider the reduction rules (R5) and (R6) since all other rules may be ordered correctly using the subterm property. For rule (R5) we need to know $* >_F +$, see Example 6; for rule (R6) we need to know that 0 is a minimal constant, thus $1 >_F 0$. The resulting precedence ordering $>_F$ satisfies the associative pair condition, thus we may conclude from Theorem 7 that (R,E) terminates.

EXAMPLE 8. The following example is taken from Huet (80). F consists of operators $0,1,e,+,*$, where 0 and 1 are constants, e is unary, and $+$ and $*$ are binary. E contains the equations

$x+y=y+x$,
$(x+y)+z=x+(y+z)$,
$x*y=y*x$,
$(x*y)*z=x*(y*z)$.

R consist of the following rules:

(R1) $x+0 \to x$
(R2) $x*1 \to x$

(R3) $e(0) \to 1$

(R4) $e(x+y) \to e(x) * e(y)$

(R5) $(x+y) * z \to x * z + y * z$

We may use the associative path ordering corresponding to the following precedence ordering to prove termination of (R,E): $e >_F * >_F +$ and $e >_F 1$. A different termination proof, based on extending the set of reduction rules rather than on transforms, is given by Jouannaud and Munoz (84). They have to design a rather complex ad-hoc ordering for proving termination of $\to_{R',E}$, where R' is a certain extension of R.

EXAMPLE 9. *Rings.* The following example is taken from Hullot (80). R consists of the rules

(R1) $x+0 \to x$

(R2) $x+I(x) \to 0$

(R3) $I(0) \to 0$

(R4) $I(I(x)) \to x$

(R5) $I(x+y) \to I(x)+I(y)$

(R6) $x*(y+z) \to (x*y)+(x*z)$

(R7) $(x+y)*z \to (x*z)+(y*z)$

(R8) $x*0 \to 0$

(R9) $0*x \to 0$

(R10) $x*I(y) \to I(x*y)$

(R11) $I(x)*y \to I(x*y)$

(R,E) is a canonical ETRS for rings, with E consisting of the associativity and commutativity law for $+$. An appropriate precedence ordering is the following: $* >_F I >_F +$. For comparison, consider the following polynomial interpretation that can also be used for proving termination of (R,E):

$\tau(0)=2,$

$\tau(-)=\lambda x. 2\times(x+1),$

$\tau(+)=\lambda x,y. x+y+5,$

$\tau(*)=\lambda x,y. x\times y+1.$

It clearly requires more expertise to find an appropriate polynomial interpretation than to find a suitable precedence ordering $>_F$.

EXAMPLE 10. The following canonical ETRS (R,E) for *associative commutative rings* with unit is also taken from Hullot (80). E consists of the associativity and commutativity laws for $+$ and $*$. R consists of the following rules:

(R1) $x+0 \to x$

(R2) $x+I(x) \to 0$

(R3) $I(0) \to 0$

(R4) $I(I(x)) \to x$

(R5) $I(x+y) \to I(x)+I(y)$
(R6) $x^*(y+z) \to (x^*y)+(x^*z)$
(R7) $x^*0 \to 0$
(R8) $x^*I(y) \to I(x^*y)$
(R9) $x^*1 \to x$

We cannot use the ordering $>_F$ given above, since now both + and * are AC operators, and therefore the associative pair condition is not satisfied anymore. We introduce a different canonical ETRS for the same structure using a new constant c that represents $I(1)$. R' consists of the following rules:

(R0) $I(x) \to c^*x$
(R1) $x+0 \to x$
(R2') $x+(c^*x) \to 0$
(R2'') $1+c \to 0$
(R4') $c^*c \to 1$
(R6) $x^*(y+z) \to (x^*y)+(x^*z)$
(R7) $x^*0 \to 0$
(R9) $x^*1 \to x$

Termination of (R',E) can be proved using the associative path ordering corresponding to the ordering $>_F$ on F, with $I >_F * >_F +$, $I >_F c >_F 0$, and $c >_F 1$.

EXAMPLE 11. Let us consider the standard confluent equational term rewriting system R for associative-commutative rings again. We cannot use an associative path ordering since the AC operator * has to be greater than both I and +, which violates the associative path condition. One way to deal with this situation is to consider the operators I and + as being equivalent. That is, we preprocess R by introducing a new operator f that replaces both I and +. Let R' denote the resulting rewriting system and let t' denote the term resulting from t by replacing all occurrences of I and + by f. Then, assuming f is an AC operator with E' being the corresponding equational theory, $s \sim_E t$ implies $s' \sim_{E'} t'$ and $s \to_R t$ implies $s' \to_{R'} t'$. Therefore, for any infinite sequence of terms $t_1 \to_{R/E} t_2 \to_{R/E} t_3 \cdots$ there is an infinite sequence of terms $t'_1 \to_{R'/E'} t'_2 \to_{R'/E'} t'_3 \cdots$. Thus E'-termination of R' implies E-termination of R. For our example we get the following set of rules R':

(R1') $f(x,0) \to x$,
(R2') $f(x,f(x)) \to 0$,
(R3') $f(0) \to 0$,
(R4') $f(f(x)) \to x$,
(R5') $f(f(x,y)) \to f(f(x),f(y))$,
(R6') $x^*f(y,z) \to f(x^*y,x^*z)$,
(R7') $x^*0 \to 0$,
(R8') $x^*f(y) \to f(x^*y)$,
(R9') $x^*1 \to x$.

Rules (R1'), (R3'), (R4'), (R7') and (R9') can be ordered correctly by the subterm property, (R2') if 0 is minimal among all constants, that is, if $1 >_F 0$. For the remaining three rules we need $* >_F f$. The two terms in each of these three rules are transformed into the same term. We will specifiy an appropriate admissible ordering $>$ in which to compare these terms. Rules (R5') and (R6') may be ordered by inverse of size. For rule (R8') we have to refine this ordering, since both terms are of the same size. We lexicographically use another associative path ordering, this one corresponding to a precedence ordering $>'$ with $f >' *$, to order this rule correctly. In summary, the admissible ordering $>$ that we use, lexicographically compares two given terms first by inverse of size (as defined in Example 3), and, if the terms are of the same size, then with respect to an associative path ordering corresponding to $f >' *$. The precedence ordering $>_F$ satisfies the associative pair condition. We may conclude that R'/E' and therefore R/E are terminating.

6. Conclusions

We have introduced a class of termination orderings for associative commutative term rewriting systems, called associative path orderings, that are based on the idea of transforming terms. Associative path orderings extend the well-known recursive path orderings and provide a conceptually simpler alternative to polynomial interpretations. They may be applied in any context in which a precedence ordering that satisfies a certain condition, the associative pair condition, can be specified. We have shown how to compare non-ground terms in this ordering and have demonstrated the usefulness of the ordering with a number of examples. In addition, we pointed out ways to deal with situations where the associative pair condition is too restrictive. We believe that the associative pair condition may be relaxed in such a way that the method can be applied to a wider range of problems and have undertaken research in that direction. The idea of using transforms may also be used for proving E-termination when E is not an AC theory.

Acknowledgements. We would like to thank Nachum Dershowitz for his valuable comments.

References

L. Bachmair, Termination orderings for associative commutative rewriting systems, Report UIUCDCS-R-84-1179, Dept. of Computer Science, Univ. of Illinois at Urbana-Champaign, December 1984.

N. Dershowitz, A note on simplification orderings. *Information Processing Letters 9* (1979), 212-215.

N. Dershowitz, Orderings for term-rewriting systems, *Theoretical Computer Science 17* (1982), 279-301.

N. Dershowitz, J. Hsiang, N.A. Josephson and D.A. Plaisted, Associative-commutative rewriting. *Proc. 8th IJCAI,* Karlsruhe, 1983, 990-994.

J. Hsiang, *Topics in automated theorem proving and program generation,* Ph. D. thesis, Univ. of Illinois at Urbana-Champaign, 1983.

G. Huet, Confluent reductions: abstract properties and applications to term rewriting systems. *J. ACM 27* (1980), 797-821.

G. Huet and D.C. Oppen, Equations and rewrite rules: a survey. *Formal languages: Perspectives and Open Problems* (R. Book, ed.), New York: Academic Press, 1980, 349-405.

J.-M. Hullot, A catalogue of canonical term rewriting systems, Technical Report CSL-113, SRI International, Menlo Park, Calif., April 1980.

J.-P. Jouannaud and H. Kirchner, Completion of a set of rules modulo a set of equations, *11th Ann. ACM Symp. on Principles of Programming Languages,* Salt Lake City, Utah, 1984, 83-92.

J.-P. Jouannaud and M. Munoz, Termination of a set of rules modulo a set of equations, *Proc. 7th Int. Conf. on Automated Deduction* (R. Shostak, ed.). Lecture Notes in Comp. Scie. 170, Berlin: Springer Verlag, 1984, 175-193.

D. Knuth and P. Bendix, Simple word problems in universal algebras. *Computational Problems in Abstract Algebra* (J. Leech, ed.), Pergamon Press, 1970, 263-297.

D. Lankford and A. Ballantyne, Decision procedures for simple equational theories with associative commutative axioms: complete sets of associative commutative reductions. Technical Report, Univ. of Texas at Austin, Dept. of Math. and Comp. Scie., 1977.

M. Munoz, *Probleme de terminaison finie des systemes de reecriture equationnels.* Ph. D. thesis, Universite Nancy 1, 1983.

G.E. Peterson and M.E. Stickel, Complete sets of reductions for some equational theories, *J. ACM 28* (1981), 233-264.

D.A. Plaisted, An associative path ordering, *Proc. NSF Workshop on the Rewrite Rule Laboratory,* Report 84GEN008, General Electric, Schenectady, New York, April 1984, 123-136.

A Procedure for Automatically Proving the Termination of a Set of Rewrite Rules

David Detlefs and Randy Forgaard
MIT Laboratory for Computer Science

1 Introduction

In this paper, we present an algorithm that can automatically prove the termination of many sets of rewrite rules. Previous techniques for proving termination of sets of rewrite rules have either required user help in guiding the proof, or have been too restrictive to be generally applicable. Besides being interesting in its own right, a procedure that proves termination automatically is an important step towards the construction of a procedure that automatically produces a convergent set of rewrite rules from a set of equations.

It is not possible to decide whether an arbitrary set of rewrite rules is terminating. Nevertheless, we are often interested in trying to prove that a particular set of rewrite rules, $\mathcal{R}$, terminates, because

- Termination allows one to decide whether $\mathcal{R}$ is confluent.
- If $\mathcal{R}$ is confluent, termination allows one to decide the equational theory of the rewrite rules.
- If $\mathcal{R}$ is not confluent, termination allows the use of the Knuth-Bendix completion procedure to help achieve confluence.

A standard method for showing termination uses a simplification ordering [Dershowitz 82] on terms, $\succ$. A proof that $\mathcal{R}$ terminates consists of showing that every rewrite rule, $\lambda \rightarrow \rho$, in $\mathcal{R}$ is ordered under $\succ$. Thus, the problem of ensuring that $\mathcal{R}$ terminates reduces to the problem of choosing an appropriate simplification ordering. In this paper, we present an algorithm that will either construct an ordering $\succ$ that proves the termination of $\mathcal{R}$, or terminate in failure. In section 5.1 we show that our procedure is as "powerful" as a large class of other termination

This research was supported by the National Science Foundation under Grant MCS-8119846-A01 and by Office of Naval Research Contract N00014-83-K-012 with DARPA funding.

Authors' address: MIT Laboratory for Compute Science, 545 Technology Square, Cambridge, MA 02139.

proof methods. The procedure is implemented in the REVE 2 [Forgaard 84] rewrite-rule based theorem prover. Our experience with it indicates that it is sufficiently general and efficient to be effective in a wide variety of practical applications.

Section 2 presents the overall algorithm, using a successive-refinement approach. Section 3 presents the "higher-order ordering" we use. Section 4 describes a procedure that computes "minimal extenders" for a given rewrite rule. Finally, section 5 relates our ordering to other termination orderings, and discusses our experience with the implementation.

2 Approach to the Problem

We can characterize one class of commonly-used methods of proving termination (including RPO [Dershowitz 82], RPOS [Kamin 80], RDO [Jouannaud 82], and RDOS [Lescanne 84]), as *higher-order orderings.* A higher-order ordering is a function, $\mathcal{H}$, which maps sets of rules, $\mathcal{R}$, into another function, $\mathcal{O}$, called an *orderal*. An orderal maps *registries*, *r*, into ordering relations, $\succ$, on terms. For example, the RPO higher-order ordering, when applied to a particular set of rewrite rules, $\mathcal{R}$, produces an RPO orderal. An RPO orderal is applied to a registry that consists of a *precedence*, a quasi ordering on the operator symbols that appear in $\mathcal{R}$. The RPO orderal uses the information in the registry to order terms. An ordering, such as RPO, that stores information about operators in a registry, and uses that information to order terms, is known as a *registered ordering.* All the orderings cited above are registered orderings, though they store different information in their registries. (The "polynomial" orderings [Lankford 75a, Lankford 79, Lankford 75b] are examples of orderings that are not registered orderings.) For registered orderings, the problem of finding an ordering that proves the termination of a set of rules $\mathcal{R}$ reduces to the problem of finding a *terminating registry, r*, such that $\succ \; = [\mathcal{H}(\mathcal{R})](r)$ proves their termination.

2.1 Exhaustive Search Methods

One way of finding a terminating registry is exhaustive search. As long as we have an $\mathcal{H}$ such that for all finite set of rules $\mathcal{R}$, $\mathcal{H}(\mathcal{R})$ has a finite domain, then we can simply test all the registries, *r*, in that domain to see if any are terminating registries. The problem with this approach, of course, is that it is disastrously inefficient. All the higher-order orderings that we have looked at have the property that the number of registries that must be examined in such an exhaustive search grows as an exponential function of the number of operators in the rule set $\mathcal{R}$.

Clearly, some method of pruning the search is needed. One easy modification would be to start with a set of all the candidate registries, and to proceed rule by rule, throwing away any registries that did not order a particular rule. When the last rule had been processed, the remaining registries would be the complete set of registries that order $\mathcal{R}$. Unfortunately, this algorithm is still too inefficient for practical use. The problem lies with the great number of registries in the domain of $\mathcal{O}$. Consider a typical higher-order ordering, such as RPOS or RDOS (which use the same registry types.) For a rule set, $\mathcal{R}$, with only five different operators, there are 15,000 registries in the domain of $\mathcal{H}(\mathcal{R})$.

2.2 Minimal-Extenders-Based Search Methods

To make our procedure more efficient, we modify it so that it examines only a small subset of the domain of $\mathcal{H}(\mathcal{R})$. To do this, we need to assume the existence of a function which computes *minimal extenders.*

To define the concept of minimal extenders, we first define the concept of an *extension relation.*

Definition 1. A relation, $\stackrel{ex}{\succeq}$, is an *extension relation for a higher-order ordering* $\mathcal{H}$ if and only if $\forall\ \mathcal{R}$: Set[rule],

(1) $\stackrel{ex}{\succeq}$ is a non-empty quasi ordering over the domain of $\mathcal{H}(\mathcal{R})$, with a unique least element called the *empty registry* (denoted $r\!\downarrow$), and

(2) $\mathcal{O} = \mathcal{H}(\mathcal{R})$ has the property
$\forall\ \lambda \rightarrow \rho \in \mathcal{R}, r_1, r_2 \in domain(\mathcal{O}), [r_2 \stackrel{ex}{\succeq} r_1 \Rightarrow (\lambda\ \mathcal{O}(r_1)\ \rho \Rightarrow \lambda\ \mathcal{O}(r_2)\ \rho)]$

If $\stackrel{ex}{\succeq}$ is an extension relation, then $\stackrel{ex}{\succ}$, or *strict extension,* is the strict partial ordering induced by $\stackrel{ex}{\succeq}$.

If an extension relation, $\stackrel{ex}{\succeq}$, exists for a higher-order ordering, $\mathcal{H}$, $\mathcal{H}$ is said to be *monotonic in its registry with respect to* $\stackrel{ex}{\succeq}$. Informally, monotonicity states that if two terms are ordered under a registry r_1, then they are ordered under any registry r_2 that is an extension of r_1.

We can now define the "minimal extenders" function. We assume that the higher-order ordering $\mathcal{H}$ is monotonic in its registry with respect to the extension relation $\stackrel{ex}{\succeq}$. If $\lambda \rightarrow \rho$ is a rule in a rule set $\mathcal{R}$, and r is a registry in the domain of $\mathcal{O} = \mathcal{H}(\mathcal{R})$, then the set of minimal extenders of a registry r and a rule $\lambda \rightarrow \rho$ with respect to $\stackrel{ex}{\succeq}$ is defined by the specification

function MinimalExtenders (r, $\lambda \rightarrow \rho$, $\mathcal{O}$, $\stackrel{ex}{\succeq}$) **returns** (*ms:* Set[registry])

Let R be the set of extensions of r that order $\lambda \rightarrow \rho$.
$R := \{r' \text{: registry} \mid r' \stackrel{ex}{\succeq} r \wedge \lambda\ \mathcal{O}(r')\ \rho\}$

Let ms be the set of minimal elements of R.
$ms := \{r' \in R \mid \neg \exists r_2 \in R \text{ s.t. } r' \stackrel{ex}{\succ} r_2\}$

If it is possible to effectively compute MinimalExtenders(r, $\lambda \rightarrow \rho$, $\mathcal{O}$, $\stackrel{ex}{\succeq}$), then we can find the set of all minimal registries that order a set of rules, $\mathcal{R}$. Let $\mathcal{O} = \mathcal{H}(\mathcal{R})$. Initialize a set of registries, *rs,* to contain only the empty registry, $r\downarrow$. Then proceed rule by rule. For each rule, $\lambda \rightarrow \rho$, initialize an empty set of registries, *rs2.* Then, for each registry, r, in the old set, *rs*, we add the registries in MinimalExtenders(r, $\lambda \rightarrow \rho$, $\mathcal{O}$, $\stackrel{ex}{\succeq}$) to the new set, *rs2.* When all the registries in *rs* have been processed, set *rs* to be *rs2,* and go on to the next rule. This procedure maintains the loop invariant that after each rule has been processed, *rs* contains the complete set of minimal registries that order all the rules considered so far. When the last rule has been processed, *rs* will contain the complete set of minimal registries that order $\mathcal{R}$.

The above procedure can be viewed as a breadth-first search that locates all the minimal registries that order a rule set. In practical applications, it is seldom necessary, or even desirable, to compute all the terminating registries. Usually, all that is required is that one be computed, if it exists. If we want to identify a single terminating registry, a depth-first search is more efficient.

A depth-first version of the search procedure starts with the empty registry and the first rule, and computes the set of extensions of that registry that order the rule. It then picks one of these extensions, and proceeds recursively with this extension and the next rule. When no rules are left, the terminating registry is returned. If a call is made where there are no extensions to the given registry that order the rule, *failure* is reported to the parent invocation, which then tries the next member of its set of extensions. If all members of this set are tried without success, then the *failure* signal is propogated upward. This version of automatic ordering procedure is implemented in REVE 2.3.

3 EPOS: A New Higher-Order Ordering

In this section we describe a new higher-order ordering, EPOS, that has the features we identified in the previous section. It is parameterized over a registry type where the "is-an-extension-of" relation, $\stackrel{ex}{\succeq}$, has a natural meaning, and it is monotonic in its registry with respect to that relation. Further, it is possible to write an efficient algorithm to compute "MinimalExtenders" with respect to it. We will first describe the aspects of previous orderings that made them unsuitable for our purposes, and then describe how we modified one of them so that it fit the requirements described in section 2. See [Forgaard 84] for a more formal definition of EPOS. Section 4 will describe the algorithm that computes "MinimalExtenders" for EPOS.

EPOS is based very closely on RPOS [Kamin 80], which, in turn, was an extension of RPO [Dershowitz 82]. RPO, as discussed previously, is a registered ordering, where the registry contains a quasi ordering on operator symbols called the precedence. RPOS is similar to RPO, differing only when it compares two terms whose top operators are equivalent in the precedence. In this case, it refers to a part of the registry called the "status map," which maps each operator to a "status.[1]" This status information tells the ordering how to proceed in such a case. Three status map values are used in RPOS. The *multiset* status, Ⓜ, indicates that the argument lists of the terms being compared should be treated as multisets, i.e., their order is irrelevant. The two *lexicographic* statuses, Ⓛ *(left-to-right)*, and Ⓡ *(right-to-left,)* indicate that the arguments should be compared by forming sequences of terms by taking the arguments in forward and reverse order, respectively, and then lexicographically comparing these sequences.

The addition of this finer-grained information to the registry enables RPOS to order rule sets that RPO cannot, such as sets containing associative rules. The higher-order orderings RDO and RDOS [Jouannaud 82, Lescanne 84] bear a relationship similar to that of RPO and RPOS.

The problem with RPOS (and RDOS), for our purposes, is that the addition of the status map makes it difficult to find a "natural" extension relation on registries. RPOS is monotonic with

---

[1]Kamin & Lévy did not use a formal notion of status map. Our use of status is adapted from Lescanne's REVE 1 and from [Lescanne 84].

respect to the precedence relation: adding another edge to the precedence graph will not invalidate the ordering of any previous rules. The status map is another matter: any change to the status map may cause a previously ordered rule to be invalidated. Of course, we could still define an "unnatural" extension relation $\succeq^{ex}$ based solely on the precedence part of the registry. This would be "unnatural" in the sense that no two registries with different status maps would be comparable under this relation. In our algorithm, this would imply that the "MinimalExtenders" procedure would have to return very large sets of registries, since almost all registries would be minimal. Calculations show that the loss of efficiency would be severe enough to make the algorithm impractical.

Our solution to this problem was to modify RPOS, producing a higher-order ordering which we call EPOS. Our first modification was to change the status map so that we can find a natural extension relation, $\succeq^{ex}$, and to define EPOS in such a way that it is monotonic in its registry with respect to $\succeq^{ex}$. To accomplish this, we add another status value to the range of the status map.

To the three status map values of RPOS, we add an *undefined* status, which we write as Ⓤ. In the empty registry, $r\downarrow$, all operators have *undefined* status. We then define an extension relation for status maps as follows: a status map ψ_2 is an extension of another status map ψ_1 if and only if

$$\forall f : (\psi_1(f) \neq \text{Ⓤ} \Rightarrow (\psi_2(f) = \psi_1(f)).$$

That is, a status map may be extended by changing the mapping of an operator from Ⓤ to some non-Ⓤ value, but, once changed, it may not be changed again. Having defined extension relations for the components of a registry, we can combine them to form an extension relation on registries. We write a registry, r, as a pair, $\langle\pi,\psi\rangle$, of a precedence, π, and a status map, ψ, and say that if $r_1 = \langle\pi_1,\psi_1\rangle$ and $r_2 = \langle\pi_2,\psi_2\rangle$, $r_2 \succeq^{ex} r_1$ if and only if π_2 is an extension of π_1 and ψ_2 is an extension of ψ_1.

It remains to define EPOS to handle the extra status value and make it monotonic in its registry with respect to this extension relation. Whenever we come to a point in EPOS where we we are comparing two terms whose root operators are equivalent in the precedence, we use the statuses of their root operators, as in RPOS. If we find that one or both of those operators has the status Ⓤ, we construct the set of all non-Ⓤ status assignments to those operators such that the statuses of the two root operators are *compatible*. *Compatible* is a reflexive, symmetric relation on statuses; Ⓜ is compatible only with Ⓜ, and a lexicographic status is compatible only with another lexicographic status. To be orderable in EPOS, the terms must be orderable under all these non-Ⓤ compatible status assignments. For instance, if the root operators are f and g, and $\psi(f) = \psi(g) =$ Ⓤ, then the two terms must be ordered under each of the status assignments below.

{$\psi(f) =$ Ⓜ, $\psi(g) =$ Ⓜ}
{$\psi(f) =$ Ⓛ, $\psi(g) =$ Ⓛ}
{$\psi(f) =$ Ⓛ, $\psi(g) =$ Ⓡ}
{$\psi(f) =$ Ⓡ, $\psi(g) =$ Ⓛ}
{$\psi(f) =$ Ⓡ, $\psi(g) =$ Ⓡ}

If $\psi(f) =$ Ⓛ and $\psi(g) =$ Ⓤ, we need only ensure that the terms are ordered under the extensions {$\psi(g) =$ Ⓛ} and {$\psi(g) =$ Ⓡ}.

In designing EPOS, we made one other modification to RPOS. In examining our algorithms for finding terminating registries, we observed that it is desirable whenever possible to avoid unnecessarily restrictive registry choices. The addition of of the Ⓤ status was one result of this observation: why should we choose one of Ⓜ, Ⓛ, or Ⓡ when any one of them will order the current rule? In the same vein, we observed that it is often the case that RPOS often requires one to make a precedence decision too early, by requiring that operators f and g be related by $f > g$ or $f = g$, when either choice would order the terms in question. To avoid this, we modified the precedence used by EPOS so that operators can be related by a greater-than-or-equal-to relation, $f \succeq g$. If we encounter two operators related this way in EPOS, we must ensure that the terms are ordered under both the $>$ and $=$ assumptions for those operators, just as when we encountered a Ⓤ status we had to ensure that the terms were orderable under all the statuses represented by the Ⓤ. A registry in which $f \succeq g$ can be extended either by making $f > g$ or $f = g$. The addition of the $\succeq$ relationship often allows "MinimalExtenders" to return a smaller set of registries, thus cutting down on the search space.

4 Computing Minimal Extenders for EPOS

In the above section, we have met half of the requirements we put on our higher-order ordering in section 2. EPOS is monotonic in its registry with respect to a natural extension relation. The other requirement is that we be able to efficiently compute the "MinimalExtenders" function. This section describes, at a high level, an algorithm that performs this computation. See [Forgaard 84] for a more formal and detailed description.

The computation of minimal extenders has been often seen as an intractable problem. Indeed, the method for computing minimal extenders that we present here has worst-case exponential behavior. However, for typical examples, we have found that our algorithm usually requires no more than a few seconds per equation.

A basic assumption of our algorithm is that we have AND and OR operations on *suggestions* and *suggestion sets.* A *suggestion* is a description of a set of modifications that can be made to a registry. Two suggestions for modifying a registry are *inconsistent* if, when they are applied to that registry either 1) create a precedence cycle, or 2) change the status of an operator whose status was Ⓜ, Ⓛ, or Ⓡ. If two suggestions are consistent, ANDing them yields the singleton suggestion set containing the suggestion that is the combination of the two. ANDing inconsistent suggestions yields the empty suggestion set. ORing suggestions merely returns a suggestion set containing both suggestions. The AND of two suggestion sets is computed by constructing the cartesian product of the two sets, and then taking union of all the the suggestion ANDs of these pairs of suggestions. ORing suggestion sets is merely set union.

Our algorithm is dependant on the structure of EPOS. In EPOS, as in RPOS, the basic procedure in comparing two terms $s = f(s_1, ..., s_m)$ and $t = g(t_1, ..., t_n)$ is to compare f and g in the precedence, and, depending on the result, to make recursive calls to EPOS on appropriate subterms. Our strategy is to assume that when these recursive calls cannot order their arguments, they return sets of minimal suggestions that cause them to be orderable. Our problem is to combine these suggestions into minimal suggestions for the terms as a whole. Note that the MinimalExtenders algorithm is *one-way:* we are only computing suggestions that make the left-hand side of a rule greater than the right.

Suggestions originate when, in the original invocation, or in a recursive call on subterms, EPOS does not find enough information present in the registry about the root operators of its argument terms to permit the terms to be compared. In this case, we construct a set of *hypotheses:* suggestions that realize every possible extension to the current registry that can be made involving only f and g. For instance, if the root operators f and g are unrelated in the precedence, we would construct the hypotheses $\{f > g\}$ and $\{f = g\}$. We also construct an empty suggestion set, $\mathcal{S}$. For each hypothesis, we make a copy of the current registry, and modify it according to the hypothesis. We then make a recursive call to EPOS with the new registry and the old terms. If EPOS now has enough information to order the terms, then the hypothesis is ORed into $\mathcal{S}$. The recursive call to EPOS may return further suggestions, in which case we AND the singleton suggestion set consisting of the hypothesis with these new suggestions, and OR the result into $\mathcal{S}$. When all the hypotheses have been considered, $\mathcal{S}$ is returned.

5 Other Issues

5.1 The "Power" of EPOS as Compared to Other Higher-Order Orderings

The "power" of a higher-order ordering is usually discussed in terms of the sets of rules that particular instantiations can order. For instance, RDOS is more powerful than RPOS because, for any registry, the set of rules that RPOS can order with that registry is contained in the set of rules that RDOS can order with the same registry, and, for some registry, this containment is strict. For the same reasons, COS [Plaisted 84, Forgaard 84] is more powerful than RDOS. Under this definition of power, EPOS is equivalent to RPOS, and is thus less powerful than either RDOS or COS [Lescanne 84, Forgaard 84].

One might wonder why we chose to base our work on the least powerful of these orderings. It would be possible to make modifications to, say, RDOS that would make it monotonic in the status, and write a similar "MinimalExtenders" procedure. However, we will show that there is a relevant definition of power under which all the orderings mentioned above are equivalent, and then explain the engineering decisions that led us to choose RPOS.

Let us define the relation $\succeq^{rs}$, read *at least as rule-set-powerful*, on higher-order orderings.

Definition 2. $\mathcal{H}_1 \succeq^{rs} \mathcal{H}_2$ if and only if

$\forall\, \mathcal{R}$: Set[rule] [$\exists\, r_1$ s.t. [$\mathcal{H}_1(\mathcal{R})$]($r_1$) orders $\mathcal{R} \Rightarrow \exists\, r_2$ s.t. [$\mathcal{H}_2(\mathcal{R})$]($r_2$) orders $\mathcal{R}$]

This relation defines a partial order on higher-order orderings. Let us call $\simeq^{rs}$, read *rule-set equivalent*, the equivalence relation induced by this partial order.

We say that a registry, r, is *total* for an ordering, $\mathcal{H}$, and a rule set, $\mathcal{R}$, when there are no strict extensions to r in the domain of $\mathcal{H}(\mathcal{R})$. Instantiations of the higher-order orderings EPOS, RPOS, RDOS, and COS for the same rule set yield orderals with the same domain. When these orderals are applied to a total registry, they yield exactly the same ordering on terms. That is, they are equally powerful in the original sense under a total registry [Forgaard 84]. Every registry that is not total has a total extension, so the existence of a registry that orders a set of rules implies the existence of a total registry that orders them. To see that this implies that EPOS, RPOS, RDOS, and COS are rule-set equivalent, we merely observe that if, for any of them, a given registry orders a set of rules, then there exists a total extension of that registry under which all of them order the set of rules.

With this consideration in mind, we observe that RPOS is the least powerful of the higher-order orderings mentioned because, in some sense, it is the least complicated. This makes the engineering of a "MinimalExtenders" procedure easier for it than for some of the others. Comparisons with "MinimalExtenders" procedures for other higher-order orderings should be possible soon; Lescanne is developing a new implementation of RDOS which generates minimal extenders.

5.2 Experience with EPOS

EPOS, and the automatic termination proof procedure, are implemented in REVE 2.3. An example of the use of the automatic ordering procedure follows.

The example is a rewriting system for group theory with right division, and is taken from [Lescanne 83]. An abridged and annotated script of the automatic proof of termination is given.

```
User equations:

 1.    (e / x) == i(x)
 2.    (x / x) == e
 3.    (x / (y / z)) == ((x / i(z)) / y)
 4.    ((x / y) / i(y)) == x
 5.    ((x / i(y)) / y) == x
 6.    i(e) == e
 7.    i(i(x)) == x
 8.    i((x / y)) == (y / x)
 9.    (x * y) == (x / i(y))
10.    (x / e) == x
```

Equation 1 is not orderable, but there are three suggestions: 1) / > i, 2) / = i and /(M), and 3) / = i and /(R). The first is accepted.

```
Accepted precedence suggestion:
    / > i

Ordered the equation:
    (e / x) == i(x)
    into the rewrite rule:
    (e / x) -> i(x)
Accepted precedence suggestion:
    / >= e

Ordered the equation:
    (x / x) == e
    into the rewrite rule:
    (x / x) -> e

Accepted precedence suggestion:
    /(R)

Ordered the equation:
    (x / (y / z)) == ((x / i(z)) / y)
    into the rewrite rule:
    (x / (y / z)) -> ((x / i(z)) / y)

Ordered the equation:
    ((x / y) / i(y)) == x
    into the rewrite rule:
    ((x / y) / i(y)) -> x

Ordered the equation:
    ((x / i(y)) / y) == x
    into the rewrite rule:
    ((x / i(y)) / y) -> x

Ordered the equation:
    i(e) == e
    into the rewrite rule:
    i(e) -> e

Ordered the equation:
    i(i(x)) == x
    into the rewrite rule:
    i(i(x)) -> x
```

At this point, an equation is encountered for which there are no extensions. The program must backtrack to the last point where a registry extension was made.

```
Couldn't order the equation

i((x / y)) == (y / x)
```

```
so backtracking automatic termination proof.

Reconsidering registry extension choice for the equation:

(x / (y / z)) == ((x / i(z)) / y)
```

There was only one suggestion for this equation, and it has already been tried. Therefore, the program must backtrack further. Eventually, we backtrack all the way to equation 1, indicating that no extension to the registry formed by accepting the first suggestion can order all the rules. Therefore the second suggestion is tried.

```
Reconsidering registry extension choice for the equation:

(e / x) == i(x)

Accepted precedence suggestion:
    / = i     /(M)

Ordered the equation:
    (e / x) == i(x)
    into the rewrite rule:
    (e / x) -> i(x)

Accepted precedence suggestion:
    / >= e

Ordered the equation:
    (x / x) == e
    into the rewrite rule:
    (x / x) -> e
```

This path, too, comes to an equation with no extenders.

```
Couldn't order the equation

(x / (y / z)) == ((x / i(z)) / y)

so backtracking automatic termination proof.

Reconsidering registry extension choice for the equation:

(x / x) == e

Couldn't order the equation

(x / x) == e

so backtracking automatic termination proof.
```

Backtracking again brings us to equation 1, where we accept the third and last suggestion. This brings success.

```
Reconsidering registry extension choice for the equation:

(e / x) == i(x)

Accepted precedence suggestion:
    / = i     /(R)

Ordered the equation:
    (e / x) == i(x)
    into the rewrite rule:
    (e / x) -> i(x)

Accepted precedence suggestion:
```

```
    / >= e

Ordered the equation:
    (x / x) == e
    into the rewrite rule:
    (x / x) -> e

Ordered the equation:
    (x / (y / z)) == ((x / i(z)) / y)
    into the rewrite rule:
    (x / (y / z)) -> ((x / i(z)) / y)

•
•
•

Accepted precedence suggestion:
    * > /

Ordered the equation:
    (x * y) == (x / i(y))
    into the rewrite rule:
    (x * y) -> (x / i(y))

Ordered the equation:
    (x / e) == x
    into the rewrite rule:
    (x / e) -> x

No user equations.

No critical pair equations.

Rewrite rules:

  1.   (e / x) -> i(x)
  2.   (x / x) -> e
  3.   (x / (y / z)) -> ((x / i(z)) / y)
  4.   ((x / y) / i(y)) -> x
  5.   ((x / i(y)) / y) -> x
  6.   i(e) -> e
  7.   i(i(x)) -> x
  8.   i((x / y)) -> (y / x)
  9.   (x * y) -> (x / i(y))
 10.   (x / e) -> x

Your system is terminating!
```

The final terminating registry is as follows: ("/(R)" indicates a right-to-left status for "/," and "/" and "i" are members of the same equivalence class.)

```
-> oper

Operator precedence:

* > { /, i, e }
{ /(R), i } >= { e } > { }
e > { }
```

This example took 8.3 seconds of VAX 750 CPU time, 15 seconds elapsed time, to run.

The above example requires that / = i to order the rule set. This is actually quite rare; almost all rule sets encountered in practice can be ordered by registries in which the precedence is a strict partial order. If we take advantage of this fact, we can save significant effort. When we don't include equality suggestions in the set of minimal extenders, there are many fewer extenders, and it takes less time to compute them. REVE 2.3 includes an implementation of EPOS which does not make equivalence suggestions. To contrast the performance difference between the two versions, we ran the automatic ordering procedure on an axiomitization of the "set" data type. Using EPOS with equivalence suggestions took 97.6 seconds of CPU time, while EPOS without equivalence suggestions used only 10.6 seconds.

5.3 Using EPOS in the Knuth-Bendix Completion Procedure

We have presented EPOS and its associated "MinimalExtenders" algorithm in the context of automatically proving the termination of an existing set of rewrite rules. A common use of termination proof methods is in the Knuth-Bendix completion procedure. Fortunately, the features of EPOS that made it useful in the first context also make it useful in the context of Knuth-Bendix.

The importance of the concepts of "incrementality" and "monotonicity," the ability of a higher-order ordering to dynamically suggest that new information be added to the registry to order a new equation while maintaining the integrity of the proof of termination of the already-ordered rules, was first recognized by Lescanne and Jouannoud, and realized in RDO [Jouannaud 82]. Their algorithm, which was used in REVE 1, greatly simplified the construction of a termination proof during the Knuth-Bendix completion procedure. RDOS [Lescanne 84], which was used in REVE 2, had the same properties, and was able to order more rule sets. However, both required some degree of expertise, since their implementations provided only a very simple form of precedence and status suggestions. With our method, whenever an unorderable equation is found, the user is presented with the complete set of minimal extensions to the registry that will order the equation. On a practical level, this greatly simplifies the process for the user: instead of having have some kind of intuition about the operators, he or she merely has to choose one of a set of possibilities.

When a procedure is very simple, the natural question is to ask whether it can be automated. The answer is that the termination proof part of the completion procedure may be, but the automation of the entire Knuth-Bendix process is still an unsolved problem. The difficulty is that equations are dynamically added in Knuth-Bendix, so the process may never terminate. It would certainly be possible to invent a scheme for the termination proof which would generate minimal extenders, pick one, and recurse, backing up the entire process when it becomes impossible to extend the registry to order an equation. The unsolved parts of designing an automatic Knuth Bendix procedure involve such considerations as generating heuristics to tell when a path is diverging, handling "incompatible" equations [Forgaard 84], deciding what kind of data structures to use to save the process state when backtracking is done, and others. We suspect that as such procedures are developed, the use of orderings that allow the computation of minimal extenders will play a large part in their termination proof mechanisms.

References

[Dershowitz 82] N. Dershowitz, "Orderings for Term-Rewriting Systems," in *Theoretical Computer Science, Vol. 17*, North-Holland, 1982, pp. 279-301. Preliminary version in *Proc. 20th IEEE Symp. on Foundations of Computer Science*, San Juan, Puerto Rico, October 1979, pp. 123-131.

[Forgaard 84] R. Forgaard, "A Program for Generating and Analyzing Term Rewriting Systems," Master's Thesis, MIT Lab. for Computer Science, September 1984.

[Jouannaud 82] J.-P. Jouannaud, P. Lescanne, and F. Reinig, "Recursive Decomposition Ordering," *Proc. 2nd IFIP Workshop on Formal Description of Programming Concepts*, Garmisch-Partenkirchen, W. Germany, June 1982. Also in "Recursive Decomposition Ordering and Multiset Orderings," Technical Memo TM-219, MIT Lab. for Computer Science, June 1982.

[Kamin 80] S. Kamin and J.-J. Lévy, "Attempts for Generalising the Recursive Path Orderings," Dept. of Computer Science, Univ. of Illinois, Urbana-Champaign, February 1980. Unpublished manuscript.

[Lankford 75a] D. S. Lankford, "Canonical Algebraic Simplification in Computational Logic," Technical Report ATP-25, Automatic Theorem Proving Project, Univ. of Texas, Austin, May 1975.

[Lankford 75b] D. S. Lankford, "Canonical Inference," Technical Report ATP-32, Mathematics Dept., Univ. of Texas, Austin, December 1975.

[Lankford 79] D. S. Lankford, "On Proving Term Rewriting Systems are Noetherian," Technical Report MTP-3, Mathematics Dept., Louisiana Tech. Univ., May 1979.

[Lescanne 83] P. Lescanne, "Computer Experiments with the REVE Term Rewriting System Generator," *Proc. 10th ACM Symp. on Principles of Programming Languages*, Austin, TX, January 1983, pp. 99-108.

[Lescanne 84] P. Lescanne, "Uniform Termination of Term Rewriting Systems: Recursive Decomposition Ordering with Status," *Proc. of 6th Colloq. on Trees in Algebra and Programming*, Bordeaux, France, Cambridge Univ. Press, March 1984. Also as "How to Prove Termination? An Approach to the Implementation of a new Recursive Decomposition Ordering," *Proc. of an NSF Workshop on the Rewrite Rule Laboratory, Sept. 6-9, 1983*, General Electric Corporate Research and Development Report No. 84GEN008, Schenectady, NY, April 1984, pp. 109-121.

[Plaisted 84] D. A. Plaisted, private communication, January 1984.

PETRIREVE : PROVING PETRI NET PROPERTIES WITH REWRITING SYSTEMS

C. CHOPPY, C. JOHNEN
Laboratoire de Recherche en Informatique
Université de Paris-Sud
Bâtiment 490
91405 Orsay - Cedex, FRANCE

ABSTRACT

We present here an approach using rewriting systems for analysing and proving properties on Petri nets. This approach is implemented in the system PETRIREVE. By establishing a link between the graphic Petri net design and simulation system PETRIPOTE and the term rewriting system generator REVE, PETRIREVE provides an environment for the design and verification of Petri nets. Representing Petri nets by rewriting systems allows easy and direct proofs of the behaviour correctness of the net to be carried out, without having to build the marking graph or to search for net invariants.

I - INTRODUCTION

Petri nets were developped in order to modelize concepts of asynchronous and concurrent processes. Petri nets are widely used : their formalism is simple and allows a number of properties to be modelized. Various proof techniques are available to check these properties [Bra 83]. The design and verification of Petri nets require an integrated and highly interactive environment ; such an environment should comprise a graphic editor and tools for checking the behaviour of the net and its structural properties. **PETRIREVE** provides such an environment by establishing a link between a graphic system for Petri net design and simulation, **PETRIPOTE** [Bea 83], and the rewriting "laboratory" **REVE** [Les 83, FG 84]. PETRIREVE builds a set of equations that corresponds to a net designed under PETRIPOTE. Thanks to an appropriate ordering on places computed by PETRIREVE, orienting the set of equations into rewrite rules is in accordance with the transition firing. The completion algorithm transforms this system into a simpler representation of the net (thus easier to analyse). The operation correctness and structural properties of the net can be checked in different ways : some properties of the net (boundedness, confluence) are related to the properties of the rewriting system ; other properties can be checked by adding the corresponding equation to the rewriting system, in particular, invariance, reachability of a marking, proper termination, and quasi-liveness.

We shall briefly sketch the properties one wants to prove for Petri nets, before describing our approach to representing the behaviour of a Petri net with a rewriting system ; we then address the meaning of the rules generated by REVE on the representing system w.r.t. the behaviour of the net and of the completed resulting system (that represents a simpler net). Finally, we present the correctness proofs which can thus be carried out directly using the ordering provided by REVE and the completion algorithm.

II - PETRI NETS

II.1 - *Specification* and *design of Petri nets*

Among the various tools allowing the representation of concurrent processes, Petri nets can be distinguished by their wide use, and the practical and theoretical results they yield. A Petri net is defined as a tuple (P, T, Pre, Post), P being a set of *places*, T a set of *transitions*, Pre and Post being the *towards* and *forwards incidence functions* (integer functions defined over the cartesian product of places and transitions). The behaviour of a net is specified by the following rule : a transition t is *firable* if and only if, for all places p, the number of tokens is greater than Pre(p, t). When a transition t is fired, for all places p, the number of tokens is decreased by Pre(p, t) and increased by Post(p, t). This rule specifies how firing transitions modifies the marking, i.e. how a new marking can be reached from a previous one.

A nice aspect of Petri nets is that they can be represented *graphically* and that one can visualize the states reached during an execution. For this purpose, we used the PETRIPOTE system [Bea 83] which is a graphic tool for the design and simulation of Petri nets, developed on a PERQ workstation. This system is highly interactive : the user works on the graphic picture of the net, and all commands modify the picture in real-time. Places are represented by circles, transitions by squares, towards and forwards incidence functions by arrows. The available commands allow the user to create, move, turn, copy and delete places, transitions, arrows (with capacities if needed), and selected parts of a net. The resulting net can be stored and plotted ; the behaviour of the net can be simulated graphically.

II.2 - *Properties ensuring behaviour correctness of Petri nets*

Petri nets make up a precise enough model to accurately describe mechanisms such as the basic conflicts between different actions (represented by the transitions) in a system of concurrent processes. Moreover, Petri nets give an overall view of the system allowing the control of the correctness of the information exchange :

• Properties such as the *coherence* of exchanged informations can be checked. Since the tokens represent the resources, place invariants can be examined. *Invariance* means that there exists a weighting on the places such that the weighted sum of the markings of every place is constant. *Boundedness* implies that the number of resources is finite, therefore the number of messages does not grow infinitely.

• Other properties express that the information may actually be exchanged. The reachability of some specific markings (final states, reception states, ...) expresses that specific states of the process may occur. Some properties guarantee the executability of actions, i.e. the possibility of firing transitions : for instance, quasi-liveness ensures that, for a given marking, the transition is firable in a finite time.

Various approaches are available to attempt to check some of these properties. A straightforward way of examining the behaviour of a *marked* Petri net is to build the

marking graph : if this graph is finite then some properties such as ***lack of deadlock***, ***net persistency*** (no transition conflicts) can be checked. However, since this graph depends on the initial marking, no structural property can be inferred from it.
Techniques related to linear algebra allow net invariants (which are structural properties) to be found ; these techniques are used to compute linear equations linking the place token numbers, from which specific properties of the net can be inferred ; however, these equations do not always allow deadlocks to be inferred [MR 80].
Using these techniques may be time and space consuming when the nets become large ; this complexity may be reduced by carrying out transformations on the net that preserve its essential properties, thus allowing a simpler and equivalent representation of the net to be analysed [Ber 83].
Algebraic techniques have been investigated for expressing communicating processes [Jul 81, JP 81, Oue 84] and proving the correctness of programs w.r.t. their specifications. [Ber 81, Ber 82, STE 82] use algebraic techniques for specifying and proving some properties of communication protocols with the AFFIRM system ; their approach is oriented towards problems related to communication protocols, and, using the AFFIRM system [Ger 80], they make explicit use of induction.
We investigate, here, properties of Petri nets that may be checked using the net behaviour representation by a term rewriting system.

III - PETRIREVE : "NETS MEET REWRITES"

III.1 - *Representing Petri net behaviour by means of term rewriting systems*

The problem here is to define a way of representing the behaviour of a net by means of a rewriting system ; in addition, since this rewriting system is to be used for proof purposes with a Knuth-Bendix completion algorithm, it should be noetherian and confluent.
The functioning of a net can be described as the repetition of two steps : the first step is the search for a firable transition ; the second step is the firing of this transition. Deadlock occurs if no transition is firable. If, for a given marking, several transitions are firable, only one of them will be fired. The final result may depend on the transition chosen since a Petri net can be non deterministic. This functioning will be expressed by the rewriting of a term representing a state (i.e. a marking or a

set of markings) of the net. For a given Petri net, we define an operator ***state*** with as many integer arguments as the number of places in the net : each argument corresponds to a place p_i, and its value vp_i is the number of tokens in that place (0 and s are respectively the zero constant and the successor function of the integers). The rewriting rules represent the firing of the transitions : the left-hand side of a rule expresses the marking for which the transition is firable, the right-hand side the corresponding marking after firing the transition.

If no transition is firable, the net has reached a deadlock ; this is expressed by a rule :

state (arg1, arg2, ...) --> deadlock (arg1, arg2, ...).

The left-hand side term represents a state where no transition can be fired ; this rule expresses that the right-hand side term cannot be further rewritten using the transition rules.

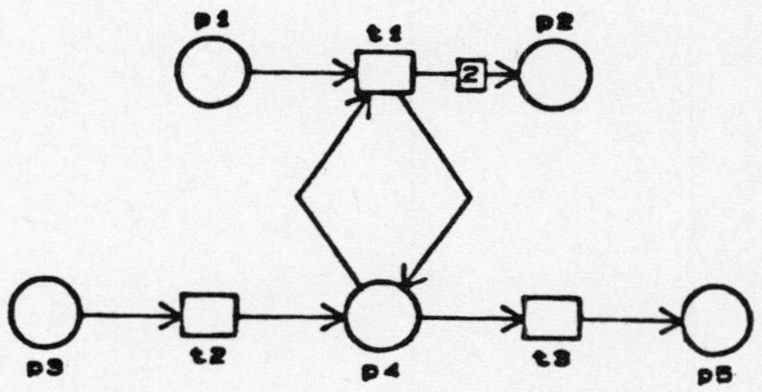

figure 1 : doubling net

For instance, the Petri net in figure 1 represents a process that multiplies by two an integer given as an input. The place p1 contains the integer to be doubled, p2 contains the result, p3 marks the start of the process and p5 the end of the process, p4 indicates that the process has begun but has not ended. Transition t1 realizes the doubling, t2 starts the process, t3 stops it. The rule :

state(s(vp1),vp3,s(vp4),vp5,vp2) --> state(p1,vp3,s(vp4),vp5,s(s(vp2)))

expresses the firing of transition t1 : its left-hand side corresponds to the conditions required for the firing of t1, i.e. p1 and p4 should have at least one token ; its right-hand side expresses that after t1 is fired, p1 lost a token, and p2 gained two. The rule :

state (vp1,s(vp3),vp4,vp5,vp2) --> state (vp1,vp3,s(vp4),vp5,vp2)

expresses the firing of transition t2. The rule :

state (vp1,vp3,s(vp4),vp5,vp2) --> state (vp1,vp3,vp4,s(vp5),vp2)

expresses the firing of transition t3.

Markings that yield deadlocks also have to be searched for. A sufficient (and necessary) condition for both t1 and t3 not to be firable is that p4 has no token ; moreover, t2 is not firable, if and only if, p3 has no token ; the following rule expresses that the net has reached a state that is a deadlock :

state (vp1,0,0,vp5,vp2) --> deadlock (vp1,0,0,vp5,vp2).

Such a set of rules corresponding to the behaviour of a net is automatically build by PETRIREVE : starting from the internal representation of the net provided by PETRIPOTE, PETRIREVE looks for each transition incidence function, and for all the possible deadlocks, and expresses them as rules. These rules are transmitted to REVE as a set of equations.

As shown in the above example, the order of the arguments (corresponding to the number of tokens in each place) does not simply follow the naming of the places : PETRIREVE provides an ordering of the arguments such that the resulting system is finitely terminating when possible (we will discuss the problem of representing cycles in paragraph IV.1) ; this ordering also has to take into account the orientation induced by the net behaviour when a transition is fired.

III.2 - *An ordering problem*

REVE [Les 83, FG 84] is a term rewriting system generator which builds confluent and uniformly terminating term rewriting systems from sets of equations, and proves theorems in equational theories, making use of the Knuth-Bendix completion algorithm. It uses the (incremental) recursive decomposition ordering with status [JLR 82, Les 84] to prove that the rewriting system terminates.

The ordering provided by REVE gives (by default) a multiset status to operators. In our case, the multiset status is not appropriate and would seldom lead to a finitely terminating system ; for instance, in the doubling net of figure 1, the only equation that could be oriented is the one corresponding to transition t1 :

state(s(vp1),vp3,vp2,s(vp4),vp2) <-- state(vp1,vp3,s(vp4),vp5,s(s(vp2)))

(and this would reverse the firing of the transition), the other equations could not be oriented.

In fact, since all the arguments have the same weight, this orientation would depend globally on the number of tokens lost or gained by the places, and would not correspond to the firing of the transition.
This problem is solved (i) by using the *left-to-right* status, and (ii) by an appropriate ordering of the arguments of *state*, i.e. an ordering ensuring that the left-hand side has more weight than the right-hand side.
The left-to-right status gives more weight to a subterm further to the left (than to one further to the right), for instance :

state (vp1,vp3,s(vp4),vp5,vp2) > state (vp1,vp3,vp4,s(vp5),vp2) .

Since firing a transition takes tokens from places and distributes them to places, an appropriate ordering of the arguments of *state* should verify the following conditions :
- places that never lose tokens are furthest to the right
- places that lose tokens are to the left ; and there should be at least one place that loses tokens (with its corresponding argument) more to the left that any place where the number of tokens is increased.

There are cases where it is not possible to find an ordering that would be appropriate for all the equations. This may be the case when there are non constant cycles in the net : equations have then to be manually oriented and termination is no longer guaranteed.

III.3 - *An ordering algorithm*

An algorithm that orders the place arguments of *state* so that a maximum of net equations are properly oriented by REVE, is integrated in PETRIREVE [Joh 84]. Whenever the conditions given above may be satisfied, this algorithm will construct an approriate ordering for the *state* arguments.
For each transition t two sets of places are constructed : the set IN(t) of places gaining tokens, and the set OUT(t) of places losing tokens. One of the arguments, belonging to IN(t), must be strictly greater (w.r.t. the order) than members of OUT(t). In order to complete this ordering, we take its transitive closure : if a transition t2 is firable after a transition t1, then OUT(t1) will include OUT(t2). However, f a place belongs both to IN(t) and to OUT(t), it cannot be used to establish an ordering w.r.t. members of OUT(t), therefore the algorithm removes it from IN(t). If

this leads to an empty IN(t) (in particular, this may be the case when there are cycles in the net), there is no ordering that verifies the conditions given in III.2 ; the algorithm will not consider the corresponding transition in order to construct, nevertheless, an ordering with the remaining ones ; however, the resulting ordering will not ensure finite termination. If the IN(t)s have a single element, the ordering is straightforward. If they have more than one element, finding the appropriate ordering will be performed using backtracking (reducing IN(t)s to one element).

To find an ordering for the places of the doubling net (see figure 1), PETRIREVE produces the inequalities :

$$\{p1\} > \{p2\}, \quad \{p3\} > \{p4\} \quad \text{and} \quad \{p4\} > \{p5\}.$$

Taking the transitive closure, the second inequality becomes : {p3} > every {p4, p5}. No place belongs to both an IN(t) and an OUT(t), therefore no exclusion is necessary. PETRIREVE uses backtracking to find a possible ordering : p1, p3, p4, p5 and p2.

Once an ordering on the places is found, PETRIREVE builds the set of equations corresponding to the firing of transitions and to reaching deadlock states. It then calls REVE with these net equations : REVE first orients them, then computes critical pairs.

IV - CRITICAL PAIRS, NON DETERMINISM AND CYCLES

IV.1 - *Non determinism, cycles*

In this section, we address the meaning, w.r.t. the net behaviour, of the critical pairs generated by REVE. A critical pair expresses that, for a given marking, two transitions are firable, in other words, that there is a conflict between these two transitions. If a critical pair is generated by REVE, then the corresponding Petri net is non deterministic.

The first example is the doubling net, where transitions t1 and t3 are conflicting. The rules generated in this case show that there is a reachable deadlock where the doubling is not achieved and that priorities should be introduced in order to express the intended behaviour correctly (cf. IV.2).

A second example is a net admitting a *constant cycle* - i.e., for every marking where a cycle transition is firable, there exists a non empty firable transition sequence and this firing does not modify the current marking. An equation representing a transition of the cycle will be removed since it reduces to syntactical equality (this is a consequence of the fact that a transition sequence does not modify the current marking). Some rules generated by critical pairs correspond to firing transition sequences.

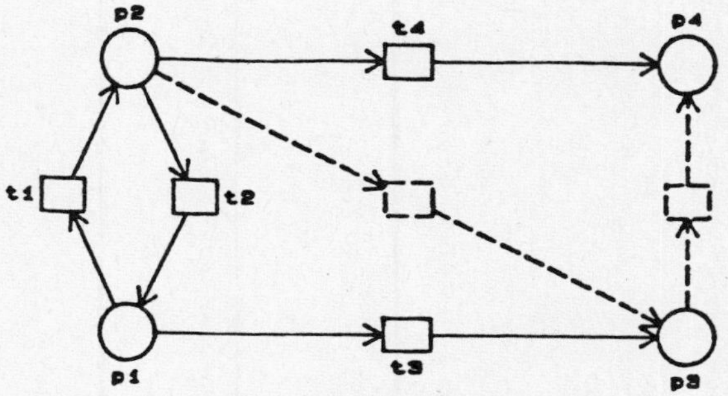

figure 2

The Petri net of figure 2 has a constant cycle : if t1 (resp t2) is firable then the sequence of transition t1, t2 (resp t2, t1) is firable. Moreover the firing of this sequence does not change the current marking. Any place ordering seems to prevent the automatic orientation of the equations. As described in III.3, the PETRIREVE ordering algorithm provides, nevertheless, an ordering. Here it is p1, p2, p3, p4. The rule corresponding to the transition t1 is :

state(s(vp1),vp2,vp3,vp4) —> state(vp1,s(vp2),vp3,vp4) .

The rule corresponding to the transition t2 is :

state(vp1,s(vp2),vp3,vp4) —> state(s(vp1),vp2,vp3,vp4) .

The rule corresponding to the transition t3 is :

state(s(vp1),vp2,vp3,vp4) —> state(vp1,vp2,s(vp3),vp4) .

The rule corresponding to the transition t4 is :

state(vp1,s(vp2),vp3,vp4) —> state(vp1,vp2,vp3,s(vp4)) .

The rule corresponding to a deadlock reached in p3 is :

state(0,0,vp3,vp4) --> deadlock (0,0,vp3,vp4).

During the completion, the equation corresponding to t2 will become an equation between two identical terms, therefore it will no longer appear in the rewriting system. Thus, the rewriting system corresponding to this Petri net is finitely the generated rules may express a transition sequence (when there is a constant cycle in the net), or a conflict between two states that may be either a deadlock or a state within a cycle (figure 3). In the latter case, since places that never lose tokens correspond to rightmost arguments, the rewriting rule is oriented from the cycle to the deadlock (the reverse would lead to an infinite generation of rules). The reductions performed by REVE on the rewriting system lead to a simpler representation of the Petri net to be analysed.

IV.2 - *Representing priority nets*

As mentioned in the previous paragraph, in the example of the critical pair generated in the doubling net, some conflicts between transitions express a contradiction between the behaviour of the net and its intended behaviour. These conflicts may be solved by attributing priorities to transitions, thus building a ***priority net***.

The doubling net of figure 1, presents a conflict between transitions t1 and t3. The Knuth-Bendix completion of the set of equations representing the doubling net generates critical pairs, among which :

deadlock (s(vp1),0,0,s(vp5),vp2) --> deadlock (vp1,0,0,s(vp5),s(s(vp2)))

which expresses a conflict between two possible deadlocks. In fact, in the first one, the doubling is not achieved (s(vp1)). The end of the process (i.e. firing of t3) should not be notified before the doubling is achieved. Therefore, the conflict between t1 and t3 is contradictory to the intended behaviour of the net. What is actually wanted is that transition t1 have priority over transition t3.

PETRIREVE provides the opportunity to deal with priority nets : the user can specify priorities for transitions, and the set of rules will be computed according to these priorities.

Priorities are translated in the rules by expressing that a non priority transition is firable only when priority ones are not firable. Places p are *determinant* for a transition t if their number of tokens allows the transition to be fired (i.e. in the towards transition function, Pre(p, t) > 0). To inhibit a transition t, it is sufficient that the number of tokens of a determinant place be less than Pre(p, t), there are therefore several ways (as many as the sum, let us call it N(t), of determinant places Pre(p,t)) of inhibiting a transition. To express that a transition is firable only when priority ones are not firable, one has to look for all the markings (as many as the product of the N(t)s) that inhibit the priority transitions to the exclusion of those markings that would inhibit both priority and non priority transitions. When a place is determinant for several priority transitions, only one of them has to be taken into account (since the others would lead to redundant rules).

Returning to our doubling net example, in order to ensure a proper behaviour of the net, transition t1 should have priority over t3. The determinant places for t1 are p1 and p4 ; since p4 is also determinant for t3, it will not be considered ; in this case :

state (0,vp3,s(vp4),vp5,vp2) -> state (0,vp3,vp4,s(vp5),vp2)

is the only one rule constructed for the firing of t3.

V - RESULTS ON NET BEHAVIOURS

V.1 - *Correctness proofs*

A way of representing a net behaviour by means of a rewriting system has now been established, and in the last section we addressed the meaning, w.r.t. the net, of critical pairs generated by REVE on this system. We now present the behaviour correctness (cf. II.3) proofs that can directly be carried out in this way.

The properties of the net are related to the properties of the rewriting system. **Boundedness** is related to *finite termination* : if the rewriting system is finitely terminating then the Petri net is *bounded*, if it is not finitely terminating then, either the net is *unbounded*, or there are **non-constant cycles** in the net.
Confluency is related to the nature of the generated rules. If any generated rule expresses the firing of a transition or of a sequence of transitions, then the Petri net is confluent (when, for a given marking, several transitions are firable, the choice of a transition does not affect the result). If this is not the case, the net is not confluent.

Invariance is proved by adding the appropriate equation to the system if the completion ends in success. For instance, it is possible to prove that the doubling net terminating. Only the equation associated with t2 could destroy the finite termination of the rewriting system. A rewriting rule is generated that expresses a conflict between t1 and t3 :

state(vp1,s(vp2),vp3,vp4) --> state(vp1,vp2,s(vp3),vp4)

This rule corresponds to firing the transition sequence : t2, t3 (see the dashed line between p2 and p3 on figure 2). A second rule is generated by the previous one and t4 rule :

state(vp1,vp2,s(vp3),vp4) --> state(vp1,vp2,vp3,s(vp4))

(see the dashed line between p3 and p4 on figure 2). which leads, together with the deadlock rule, to the rule :

deadlock (0,0,s(vp3),vp4) --> deadlock (0,0,vp3,s(vp4))

that expresses that the two deadlocks can be reached from a (same) given initial marking. Through right-hand side reduction, this leads to the rewriting system :

state(0,0,vp3,vp4) --> deadlock (0,0,vp3,vp4)
state(s(vp1),vp2,vp3,vp4) --> state(vp1,vp2,vp3,s(vp4))
state(vp1,s(vp2),vp3,vp4) --> state(vp1,vp2,vp3,s(vp4))
state(vp1,vp2,s(vp3),vp4) --> state(vp1,vp2,vp3,s(vp4))
deadlock (0,0,s(vp3),vp4) --> deadlock (0,0,vp3,s(vp4))

The resulting net is a simpler representation of the net and may be analysed more easily. It shows of the conflict between the two deadlocks and the deadlock reachability.

In conclusion, critical pairs express that, through a transition conflict, two markings are reachable from a (same) given marking ; various cases may be distinguished :

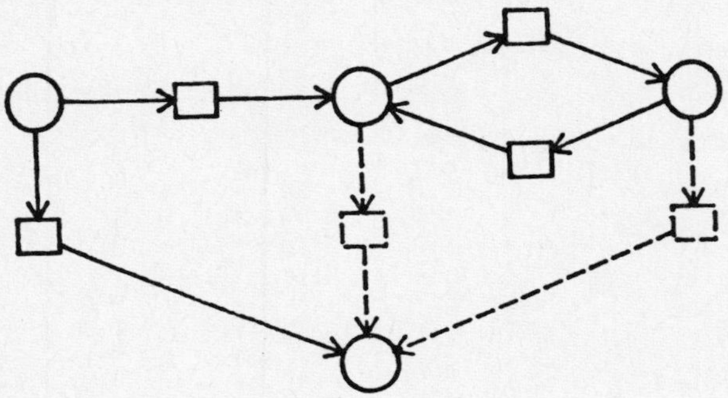

figure 3

The dashed lines represent the rules generated by the completion procedure.

(figure 1), has the invariant (vp1 * 2) + vp2 by adding the equation :

inv (state (vp1, vp3, vp4, vp5, vp2)) == add (mult (vp1,2),vp2)

to the doubling net completed system.

The **reachability** of a given marking is shown by adding the (ground term) equation : initial marking == final marking to the system. If the completion is a mere rewriting from the initial marking to the final one, reachability is proven.
In particular, **proper termination** is defined w.r.t. initial and final markings and means that (i) the net is convergent and (ii) the final marking is reachable from the initial one ; this property can be proved with the rewriting system (convergence of the system together with proof of reachability).
Quasi-liveness of a transition is proved when a marking, that allows the firing of this transition, can be reached from the given initial marking.

If the rewriting system is convergent, then one can prove theorems in the induction theory ; for instance, one can prove (by adding a single equation) that, for some pattern of markings, a final pattern of marking can be reached.

V.2 - *Applications other types of nets*

Some extensions of Petri nets can be dealt with within this framework :
• in paragraph IV.2, the representation for **priority nets** integrated in PETRIREVE is presented ; this representation can be extended in a straightforward way to **nets with inhibitory arcs** (where firing a transition may be forbidden when some places are not empty).
• **Capacity nets** (that allow a maximum number of tokens to some places to be set) may be represented as well, but the number of equations per transition is a function of the capacity of the out places and of the towards and forwards incidence functions; it is more advisable to represent the equivalent Petri net : each place has to be doubled, but there is only one equation per transition.
• Representing **coloured nets** seems more difficult : they allow for different classes of tokens ; the corresponding Petri net could be used, but coloured nets have such an abbreviation power that, in general, completion would take very long to achieve without them.

VI - CONCLUSION

By establishing a link between the graphic system for Petri net design and simulation PETRIPOTE and the term rewriting system generator REVE, PETRIREVE provides an environment for design and verification of Petri nets. Representing Petri nets by rewriting systems allows direct and easy proofs for showing that a marking is reachable, for finding structural properties of a net (such as being bounded, confluent, presenting a constant cycle, etc.) without having to build the marking graph or to search for net invariants.
PETRIREVE builds a set of equations that corresponds to a net designed under PETRIPOTE. Thanks to an appropriate ordering on places computed by PETRIREVE, orienting the set of equations into rewrite rules is in accordance with the transition firing. The completion algorithm transforms this system into a simpler and equivalent representation of the net (thus easier to analyse). The operation correctness and structural properties of the net can be checked in different ways : some properties of the net (boundedness, confluence) are related to properties of the rewriting system ; other properties can be checked by adding the corresponding equation to the rewriting system, in particular, invariance, reachability of a marking, proper termination and quasi-liveness.
PETRIREVE provides a rewriting system representation for priority nets as well. This representation can be extended to nets with inhibitory arcs and to capacity nets.

PETRIREVE is realized in PASCAL on a VAX-UNIX with a connection to a PERQ-POS.

VII - ACKNOWLEDGEMENTS

Special thanks are due to *Gérard Berthelot* for many helpful suggestions and discussions concerning this work We thank *Michel Bidoit* for fruitful discussions, and detailed comments on earlier versions of this paper. We also thank *Michel Beaudouin-Lafon* and *Solange Karsenty* for their help in creating the interface between our system and PETRIPOTE.

VIII - REFERENCES

[Bea 83] Beaudouin-Lafon M., "Petripote : a graphic system for Petri-nets design and simulation", Proc 4th European Workshop on Applications and Theory of Petri Nets, Toulouse, France, 1983, pp. 20-30

[Ber 83] Berthelot G., "Transformations of Petri net", Proc. 5th European Workshop on Application and Theory of Petri nets, Arhus University, Denmark, 1984.

[Ber 81] Berthomieu B., "Algebraic Specification of Communication Protocols". Research Report ISI//RR-81-98.

[Ber 82] Berthomieu B., "Techniques algébriques pour la spécification et vérification de protocoles de communication", 1er Colloque AFCET de Génie Logiciel, Paris, 1982.

[Bra 83] Brams G.W, "Réseau de Petri théorie et pratique", Paris, Masson, 1983.

[FG 84] Forgaard R., Guttag J.V., "REVE : a term rewriting system generator with failure-resistant Knuth-Bendix", Proc. of an NSF Workshop on the rewrite rule laboratory, Sep 1983, J. V. Guttag, D. Kapur and D.R. Musser eds., Report no 84GEN008, Avril 1984, General Electric.

[Ger 80] Gerhardt S. et al., "An overview of AFFIRM : a specification and verification system", Proc IFIP, Australia, 1980.

[HH 80] Huet G., Hullot J-M., "Proofs induction in equational theories with constructors", Proc 21 st Symp. on Foundations of Computer Science, Los Angeles, October 1980, pp 96-107.

[HH 81] Huet G., Hullot J-M., "A complete proof of correctness of the KNUTH-BENDIX completion algorithm", Journal of Computer and System Science 23(1):11-21, August 1981.

[HO 80] Huet G., Oppen D.G., "Equations and rewrite Rules A SURVEY", in "Formal Language Theory : Pespectives and open Problems", New-York, ed R.Book, Academic Press, 1980, pp 349-405.

[Joh 84] Johnen C., "PETRIREVE : Parallélisme et systèmes de réécritures", D.E.A. Report, L.R.I., Orsay, September 1984.

[Jul 81] Julliand J., "Expression des communications entre processus d'un programme parallèle par des types abstraits", Thèse, Besançon, 1981.

[JP 82] Julliand J., Perrin G.R., "Construction de programmes parallèles et spécification des communications par des types abstraits", AFCET group meeting GROPLAN, Auron, France, 1981.

[JLR 82] Jouannaud J.P., Lescanne P., Reinig F., "Recursive decomposition ordering", Conf. on Formal Description of Programming Concepts, Garmish, 1982.

[Les 83] Lescanne P., "Computer experiments with the REVE term rewriting system generator", Proc 10th Symp. on Principle of Programming Languages, Association for Computing Machinery, Austin TX, USA, 1983, pp. 99-108.

[Les 84] Lescanne P., "Uniform termination of term rewriting systems : recursive decomposition with status", Proc CAAP, Bordeaux, France, Cambridge University Press, 1984.

[MR 80] Memmi G., Roucairol G., "Linear algebra in the net theory", Proc. of Advanced Course on General Net Theory of Processes and Systems, W. Brauer ed., Springer Verlag L.N.C.S 1984.

[Oue 84] Ouerghi M.S., "Sémantique algébrique d'un langage de programmation supportant le concept de processus communicants", Thèse de 3ème cycle, Nancy, 1984.

[Rei 81] Reinig F., "Les ordres de décomposition: un outil incrémental pour prouver la terminaison finie de systèmes de réécriture de termes", Thèse de 3ème cycle, France, Nancy, CRIN, 81-R-040, Oct 1981.

[STE 82] Sunshine C.A., Thompson D.H., Erickson R.W., Gerhardt S.L., Schwabe D., "Specification and verification of communication protocols in AFFIRM using state transition models", IEEE Trans. on Software Engineering, vol SE-8, no 5, Sep 1982.

FAIRNESS IN TERM REWRITING SYSTEMS

by

Sara Porat and Nissim Francez

Computer Science Dept.

Technion, Haifa, Israel

Abstract: The notion of ***fair derivation*** in a term-rewriting system is introduced, whereby every rewrite rule ***enabled infinitely often*** along a derivation is infinitely-often applied. A term-rewriting system is ***fairly-terminating*** iff all its fair derivations are finite. The paper presents the following question: ***is it decidable, for an arbitrary ground term rewriting system, whether it fairly terminates or not***? A positive answer is given for several subcases. The general case remains open.

1. Introduction

In this paper we introduce the notion of ***fairness*** to the context of ***term rewriting systems*** (TRS). Fairness is traditionally studied in the context of programming languages for nondeterminism and concurrency. In this context, most of the interesting problems turn to be highly undecidable [HA 84]. By shifting the discussion to more abstract models of computation, some insight may be gained in the decidable cases. Previous results [PFMZ 82, PF 84] were obtained in the area of context-free grammars, providing an exact characterization of ***fair termination*** in that model. By passing to the richer model of TRS, a more interesting notion of ***enabledness*** arises, with some interesting consequences with respect to fairness. The ultimate goal of this study is to characterize the boarder line between the decidable cases of fair termination and the undecidable ones. As *ground* TRS are known to have a decidable termination property, this model is a natural candidate for being in that boarder line. In particular since for the "next" powerful model, that of *linear* TRS [GKM 83], termination is undecidable. In this paper we provide a partial resolution of this issue by showing that for some special cases of the ground TRS fair termination is also decidable. In particular, the case of *non-globally-finite* TRS for which the rewrite rules are not necessarily length-increasing is still open.

A useful property of ordinary termination decision procedures for TRS, namely, the ability to reduce the general question to that of derivations starting with the l.h.s of a rule [DE 81], is preserved here also.

2. Basic Definitions and Notations

In this section we introduce the basic definitions regarding fairness in the context of TRS and state the basic problem.

Definition: A *Term Rewriting System* (TRS) $S = (F,X,R)$ consists of:

F: a finite set of symbols called ***function symbols***.

X: an infinite set of *variables*.

R: a finite set of *Rewrite Rules* (RR) of the form $l \rightarrow r$, where l and r are *terms* over (F,X).

In case $X = \phi$ we say that S is ***ground***.

[]

Note that all function symbols have variable arity.

We assume that RRs are always well formed in that the collection of variables in r is contained in that of l. We use the standard definitions of *subterm* and *substitution*. We use τ to range over terms (written in prefix notation) and σ to range over substitutions.

Definition:

1) An RR $l \rightarrow r$ is ***enabled*** in a term τ iff there exist a subterm τ' of τ and a substitution σ such that $\tau' = l\sigma$.

2) A term τ' is ***enabled*** in a term τ iff τ' is a subterm of τ and there exist an RR $l \rightarrow r$ and a substitution σ such that $\tau' = l\sigma$.

[]

Definition: $\tau \rightarrow \bar{\tau}$ iff there is an RR $l \rightarrow r$ enabled in τ and $\bar{\tau}$ is obtained by replacing an occurrence of the subterm $l\sigma$ in τ by the term $r\sigma$. (In this case we say that $\bar{\tau}$ is obtained by *applying* the rule $l \rightarrow r$ on τ.)

[]

Definition: An *S-derivation* is a (finite or infinite) sequence

$d = < \tau_1 \rightarrow \cdots \rightarrow \tau_i \rightarrow \cdots >$

[]

Definition: A TRS S is *terminating* iff it does not admit any *infinite* S-derivation.

[]

Remark: It is known [HL 78] that termination is an undecidable property for general TRS. On the other hand termination is decidable for *ground* TRS [HL 78, DE 81, DT 84].

We now come to the new notions related to fairness. The nondeterminism displayed by a TRS is two folded. Both the choice of the rule to be applied (from the enabled RRs) and the choice of the subterm to be replaced (from the enabled subterms) are made nondeterministically. We consider here one aspect of this nondeterminism only.

Definition: An S-derivation d is *rule fair* (abbreviated to *fair*) iff it is finite, or it is infinite and every RR enabled infinitely often along d is also infinitely often applied along d.

[]

The concept of rule fair, as defined here, is similar to the definition of a *strongly fair* computation in [F 85], in contrast with the definition of an *unconditionally fair* computation in [F 85] (or an *impartial* computation in [LPS 81]); within an infinite unconditionally-fair computation *every* direction (in our context *every* rule) is applied infinitely often. In order to clarify this point, let's consider the following example.

Example:
Let

$R = \{a \rightarrow f(a), b \rightarrow c\}.$

The infinite derivation

$d = < a \rightarrow f(a) \rightarrow f(f(a)) \rightarrow \ldots >$

is fair as the first rule is infinitely often applied and the second one is never enabled.

[]

The dual definition of *subterm fairness* of a derivation seems to be less natural. First note that the set of all enabled terms can be infinite in contrast to the finite set of enabled rules. Though we are not going to consider here subterm fairness, the following examples will point out the difference between the two notions of fairness and the problem in defining subterm-fairness.

Examples:

1) $R = \{a \rightarrow f(a), a \rightarrow b\}.$

The infinite derivation

$d = < a \rightarrow f(a) \rightarrow f(f(a)) \rightarrow f(f(f(a))) \rightarrow \cdots >$

is not rule-fair (the second rule is never applied, though enabled in every term along the derivation). Since in every term along d only one subterm is enabled, in every possible definition of subterm-fairness this derivation will be subterm-fair.

2) $R = \{a \rightarrow g(a, g(a, a)), g(x, y) \rightarrow b\}.$

The infinite derivation

$d = < a \rightarrow g(a, g(a, a)) \rightarrow g(a, b) \rightarrow$

$$\to g(g(a,g(a,a)),b) \to g(g(a,b),b) \to$$

$$\to g(g(g(a,g(a,b)),b),b) \to g(g(g(a,b),b),b) \to \cdots >.$$

is rule-fair (both rules are infinitely often enabled). Along the derivation, different subterms of the form $g(x, y)$ are enabled, but the second rule is applied by replacing those occurrences (subterms) so that the new term will have at least one a as a subterm (so, the derivation can continue). It seems there is some sort of unfairness that depends on the ***structure*** of the subterm.

[]

Definition: A TRS S is ***fairly terminating*** iff it does not admit infinite fair derivations, i.e. its only fair derivations are the trivially-fair ones, the finite ones.

[]

Clearly, as general TRS are known to be as powerful as Turing machines, it follows [HA 84] that their fair termination is highly undecidable.

Following are examples of a non fairly-terminating TRS and of a fairly-terminating one.

Example: (a non fairly-terminating TRS)
Let

$$R = \{f(a,b,x) \to f(x,x,b),\ b \to a\}.$$

The infinite derivation

$$d = < f(a,b,b) \to f(b,b,b) \to f(a,b,b) \to f(b,b,b) \to \cdots >$$

is fair as both rules of R are applied infinitely often.

[]

Example: (a fairly terminating TRS)
Let

$$R = \{f(x,x) \to f(a,b),\ b \to a,\ b \to c\}.$$

It is possible to prove the fair termination of this TRS by the methods discussed in the sequel. Intuitively, after some finite number of applications of the third rule (in independent subterms) all the rules become disabled.

[]

The central issue addressed in this paper is the decidability of the problem of fair termination of ***ground*** TRS. As we mentioned, ground TRS gave rise to several decidable properties, e.g. confluence, global finiteness and acyclicity (and hence, termination) [DT 84] , etc. Thus, it seems interesting to find out whether fair termination is still in the same class.

In the next section, we show that it suffices to consider derivations starting in a l.h.s of an RR in order to characterize the presence of fair derivations. In the following section this characterization is used to obtain partial results regarding the central problem.

3. Fair derivations in ground TRS

We start with some observations about the derivations in ground TRS. First we present the notation for describing ***positions*** within terms, needed in order to refer in some unique way to subterms. We take as positions finite doted lists of natural numbers, i.e. expressions of the form $n_1.n_2. \cdots .n_k$ for some $k \geq 0$. In case $k = 0$, we use the notation λ for the empty sequence. The position u defines, for each term τ, the subterm τ/u in the following way:

1) $\tau/\lambda = \tau$.
2) If $\tau/u = f(\tau_1, \cdots, \tau_n)$, then for every $j, 1 \le j \le n$, $\tau/u.j = \tau_j$.

Consider a derivation

$$d = <\tau_1 \to \cdots >$$

and let u_i^d be the position of the subterm of τ_i replaced in the i'th step. Let

$$U^d = \{u_i^d \mid i \ge 1\}$$

namely, the set of positions of replacements along d. Clearly, $U^d \ne \phi$. We omit the superscript d when clear from context. Let $U_{\min}^d$ be the subset of *minimal* positions in U (these having no proper prefix in U).

Example: Consider a ground TRS with the only rule $a \to f(a)$ and the infinite derivation

$$f(a) \to f(f(a)) \to \cdots \to f^i(a) \to \cdots$$

Here $U = \{1, 1.1, 1.1.1, \cdots\}$ and $U_{\min} = \{1\}$

[]

$U_{\min}$ is always a finite set with cardinality depending on τ_1.

A special kind of derivations, described next, plays an important role in the sequel, in that it allows the restriction to derivations starting in l.h.s of RRs.

An S-derivation is called *major* if for some i, $i \ge 1$, $\tau_i = l$ and $\tau_{i+1} = r$ where $l \to r$ is the rule applied at that stage. In other words, the whole term is replaced at some stage of a major derivation.

Consider an S-derivation d, where $|U_{\min}| = m$.
The m *induced major derivations* are obtained from d as follows:

If $U_{\min} = \{\lambda\}$ then d itself is an induced major derivation. Otherwise, let $U_{\min} = \{w_1, \cdots, w_m\}$. The i'th induced derivation starts from a term τ_1/w_i. Consider a step $\tau_i \to \tau_{i+1}$ in d. There is some position $w_j \in U_{\min}$ which is the prefix of u_i in $U_{\min}$. That step induces a step in the induced derivation starting in τ_1/w_j. The same rule is applied but this time attributed to position v, where $u_i = w_j.v$. From the construction it follows that each of these induced derivations is also major.

We now relativize fairness to subsets of rules.

Definition: For $R' \subseteq R$, an infinite S-derivation d is $R'-fair$ if every RR in R' is infinitely-often applied if infinitely-often enabled along d.

[]

Let k_τ be the number of arguments of the outermost function symbol of τ ($k_\tau > 0$ in case $\tau = f(\tau^1, \cdots, \tau^{k_\tau})$, for some $f \in F$).

Theorem: (general restriction)

There is an infinite fair S-derivation iff there are $m \le |R|$ infinite S-derivations $d_1, \cdots, d_m$ each starting in a l.h.s of some RR, and for every RR $l \to r$, if it is only finitely often applied along every d_i, then it is also only finitely often enabled along every d_i.

Proof:

(if) Assume such m infinite derivations. Note that each d_i is R_i-fair, for some cover $\{R_i \mid 1 \le i \le m\}$ of R. For $m = 1$ the claim is trivial. Thus assume $m > 1$. As each given derivation is fair w.r.t some subset of rules, we construct an interleaving of the given derivations which is fair w.r.t R itself. The given derivations are all the induced major derivations of that interleaving. Let $k = \max_{l \to r \in RR} k_l$, f - some function symbol, l_0 - a l.h.s. of some rule that is applied infinitely often along some d_i.

The interleaved derivation d starts with the following term τ, which embeds as arguments of f the initial terms of the m given derivations.

$$\tau = \begin{cases} f(\tau_1, \tau_2, \cdots, \tau_m) & m > k \\ f(\tau_1, \tau_2, \cdots, \tau_m, \underbrace{l_0, \cdots, l_0}_{k-m+1 \text{ times}}) & m \le k \end{cases}$$

where $\tau_j, 1 \le j \le m$ is the first term of the given d_j.

The intuitive description of the interleaving is as follows. It consists of segments of length m, in which one step is taken from each d_i and arranged in a round robin. The first segment consists of all the corresponding first steps in the given derivations, and, in general, the n'th segment consists of the corresponding n'th steps of the given derivations. The structure of τ is exactly the one needed to support such an interleaved derivation.

Thus, in the j'th step in the i'th segment, the rule applied is the one applied in the i'th step of d_j. The corresponding position is $j.u_i^{d_j}$.

Every RR that is enabled infinitely often along d is infinitely often enabled along some d_i. (The structure of τ prevents the case in which a rule is enabled infinitely often along d, but only finitely often along every d_i.) So, by the given assumption, there is some d_j where this rule is infinitely often applied. So, the resulting derivation d is R-fair.

(only-if)

Assume an infinite fair S-derivation d is given. Consider its induced major derivations.

For every $RR \in R$ that is infinitely often applied along d, there is an induced major derivation d_{RR} where this rule is infinitely often applied. So, we match an infinite induced major derivation of d to every such RR, and we get a set of $m \le |R|$ infinite derivations. Every such derivation d_{RR} defines an infinite derivation d'_{RR} (actually, a tail of it) that starts from a l.h.s. of some rule. For every rule, if it is finitely often applied along every d'_{RR}, then by the construction of the matching, this rule is finitely often applied along d. So, by the fairness assumption, it is also finitely often enabled along every d'_{RR}. To see this, note that if a rule is enabled on a term along an induced derivation, it is enabled on the corresponding superterm along the original derivation. Hence, the resulting set satisfies the desired condition.

[]

Remark : Assume there is a set of $m \le |R|$ infinite S-derivations $d_1, \cdots, d_m$ each starting in a l.h.s. of some RR. Each d_i is $R_i$$-fair$, for some cover $\{R_i \mid 1 \le i \le m\}$ of R. Such a set does not imply the existence of an infinite fair S-derivation. Consider the following counter example:

R :: 1) $a \to f(a)$

2) $g(a,b) \to c$

3) $a \to g(a,b)$

The infinite derivation

$$d_1 = < a \to f(a) \to f(f(a)) \to \ldots >$$

is $\{1,2\}$-fair, and the infinite derivation

$d_2 = < a \to g(a,b) \to g(g(a,b),b) \to \dots >$

is {3}-fair. One can prove that the given TRS is fairly-terminating.

The results of this theorem do not apply to any subset of terms over F. For example, if the subset restrict a function symbol to a fixed arity (in which case $f(\tau_1, \tau_2, \cdots, \tau_n)$ is a term only if f is of arity n), the theorem is no more true. This point will be discussed in the last section.

4. Decidability of fair termination of ground TRS

As mentioned in the introduction, we do not have yet a positive settlement of the decidability problem of fair termination of ground TRS in the general case. However, from the theorem in the previous section, a positive settlement of some special cases is obtained.

Definition: A TRS is *globally finite* iff for every term τ, the set of terms $\{\tau' \mid \tau \xrightarrow{*} \tau'\}$ is finite.

[]

We use GFGTRS for globally finite ground TRS.

Remark: The property of global finiteness is decidable for ground TRS [DT 84].

Theorem: (decidability of fair termination for GFGTRS)

It is decidable whether an arbitrary GFGTRS S is fairly terminating.

Proof:

Consider some fixed enumeration of the RRs in R,

$l_i \to r_i, \; i = 1, \cdots, n.$

We associate with S a directed graph $G_S = (V_S, E_S)$. Both the nodes and the edges are labeled. The nodes in V_S are terms. Each node is labeled by the set (of indices) of the rules enabled on that term. There is an edge in E_S from τ_1 to τ_2 labeled i if $\tau_1 \to \tau_2$ by applying the i'th rule. The set of nodes of G_S is constructed iteratively.

First, $\{l_i \mid 1 \le i \le n\}$ is included in V_S. At each step of the iteration, add to the current V_S the set $V' = \{\tau' \mid \tau'' \to \tau', \tau'' \in V_S\}$. By the global finiteness, this iteration eventually stops, and the graph obtained is finite.

There is a directed cycle in G_S iff there is an infinite S-derivation starting from a l.h.s of some RR.

A cycle is called R'*-fair* iff for every $RR = l_i \to r_i \in R'$: if there is a node v on the cycle labeled by an index set containing i, then there is an edge e on the cycle labeled by i. In other words, every RR enabled on the cycle is applied along the cycle.

A cycle in G_S defines an S-derivation d that starts from a l.h.s. of some rule, and for every j so that j is contained in an index set labeling some node in the cycle, $l_j \to r_j$ is infinitely often enabled along d; and for every j so that j is labeling some edge in the cycle, $l_j \to r_j$ is infinitely often applied along d.

An infinite S-derivation d starting in a l.h.s. of some rule defines a cycle in G_S, and for every j so that $l_j \to r_j$ is infinitely often enabled along d there is a node labeled by an index set containing j in the cycle; and for every j so that $l_j \to r_j$ is infinitely often applied along d there is an edge labeled by j in the cycle.

By the general restriction theorem S is not fairly terminating iff there are $m \leq n$ cycles, and for every $RR = l_i \to r_i \in R$, if in every cycle there is no edge labeled by i, then in every cycle there is no node labeled by an index set containing i.

The presence of the required cycles is decidable by simple graph-theoretic considerations.

[]

We now present some examples to the constructions discussed above.

Examples:

1) R:: 1) $a \to b$

2) $b \to a$

3) $a \to c$

The graph G_S is shown in figure 1. In G_S there is only one cycle in which no edge is labeled by 3, but there is a node labeled by $\{1,3\}$. So, by the decidability theorem for GFGTRS this system is fairly terminating.

2) R:: 1) $f(a) \to f(c)$

2) $h(f(c)) \to h(f(a))$

3) $a \to b$

4) $g(f(b)) \to g(f(a))$

The graph G_S is shown in figure 2. In the graph G_S of this example there are two cycles. For every i, $1 \leq i \leq 4$, there is an edge in some cycle labeled by i. By the decidability theorem for GFGTRS the system is not fairly terminating.

3)

In this example, we show the insufficiency of the procedure described in the proof of the decidability theorem in case there is no global finiteness. In such a case, the graph G_S is infinite (see figure 3) and infinite fair derivation does not imply the presence of a cover by a finite number of partially-fair cycles. The rules in this example are:

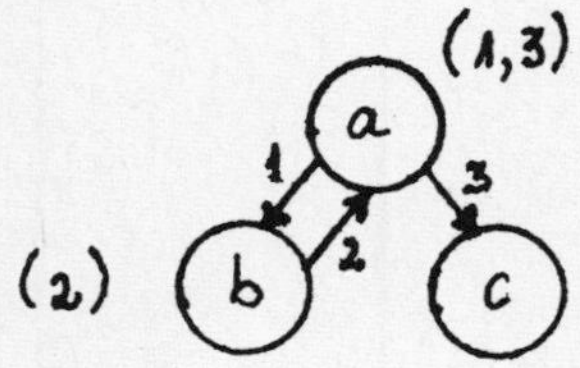

Figure 1: the graph of a fairly terminating GFGTRS

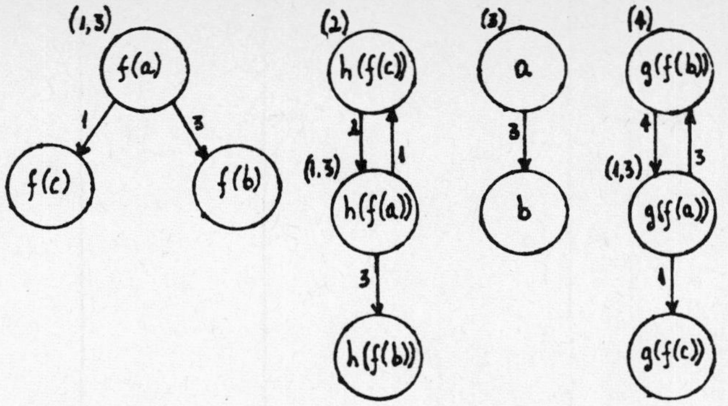

Figure 2: disjoint partially-fair cycles covering R

R:: 1) $a \to f(a)$

2) $a \to b$

3) $b \to a$

The system is obviously not fairly terminating. There are infinitely many cycles in the graph. In every cycle there is no edge labeled by 1, but there is a node labeled by {1,2}.

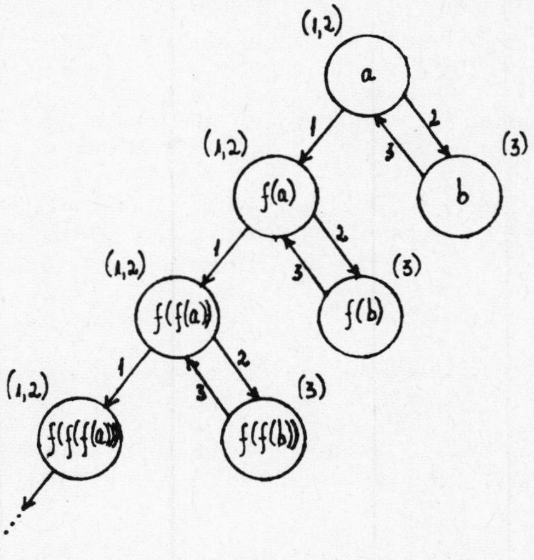

Figure 3: a graph for a non globally finite TRS

[]

Definition: The *depth* $dep(\tau)$ of a ground term τ is defined by

1) $dep(f) = 1$, for some $f \in F$

2) $dep(f(\tau_1, \cdots, \tau_n) = \max_i dep(\tau_i) + 1$.

[]

We use UN-TRS (unary/nullary TRS) for TRS in which $k_l \leq 1$ and $k_r \leq 1$ for every $l \to r \in RR$.

Definition: A ground TRS is called *(length−)increasing* iff each rule $l \to r$ satisfies $dep(l) \leq dep(r)$.

[]

Theorem: (decidability of fair termination of increasing UN-TRS)

It is decidable whether an increasing UN-TRS is fairly terminating.

Proof:

Let the RRs be numbered by $1, \cdots, n$. Let $m = \max_i dep(l_i)$. The set $T_m = \{\tau \mid dep(\tau) \leq m\}$ is finite. We again consider a labeled graph $G_S = (V_S, E_S)$ in order to characterize the behaviour of S. The set of nodes is $V_S \subseteq T_m$. A node $\tau \in T_m$ is labeled by an index set I, the set of indices of all RRs enabled on τ.

The intuitive idea behind the construction of G_S is that an S-derivation $\tau_1 \to \tau_2 \to \cdots$ satisfies $dep(\tau_i) \leq dep(\tau_{i+1})$ for all $i \geq 1$. Thus, in a term of depth greater than m, only the subterm of depth not greater than m need to be considered as subterms of greater depth may never become enabled.

Define a *transition function* δ: $T_m \times R \to T_m$.
Consider $\tau \in T_m$ and $\tau \xrightarrow{i} \tau'$.
If $\tau' \in T_m$ then $\delta(\tau, i) = \tau'$.
If $\tau' \notin T_m$ then $\delta(\tau, i) = \tau''$, the subterm of τ' the depth of which is exactly m.
There is an edge in E_S from τ_1 to τ_2 labeled by i if $\delta(\tau_1, i) = \tau_2$.
Again, the set of nodes V_S is constructed iteratively. First, $\{ l_i \mid 1 \leq i \leq n \}$ is included in V_S. At each step of the iteration, add to the current V_S the set $V' = \{ \tau' \mid \delta(\tau'', i) = \tau', \tau'' \in V_S, 1 \leq i \leq n \}$. By the finiteness of T_m, this iteration eventually stops.

Every cycle in this graph defines an infinite derivation and vice versa. The presence of an infinite fair derivation in the TRS depends on the presence of the appropriate cycles like in the proof of the theorem for GFGTRS.

[]

We now come back to the TRS in example 3, which is not fairly terminating but could not be shown as such by the GFGTRS decidability theorem.

Example: Here $m = 1$, $T_m = \{a, b\}$. The graph is shown in figure 4. Since this graph contains an R-fair cycle, the system is not fairly terminating.

[]

We cannot simply apply the procedure described in the last proof to decide whether an arbitrary increasing TRS is fairly terminating.

Example:
Let

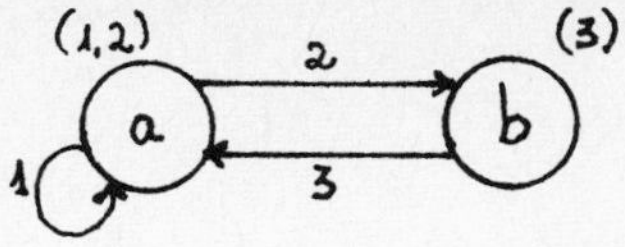

Figure 4: the deciding graph for example 3

$R = \{ a \to f(a, a),\ a \to b \}$.

In a term of depth greater than 1, only subterms of depth 1 need to be considered, but there is no bound for the number of such subterms.

[]

5. Fixed arity

In this section we assume that every function symbol f has a fixed arity ar_f .
We use F-TRS for TRS that satisfies this assumption.

Theorem: (restriction for unary/nullary functions in F-TRS)

If for every $f \in F$, $ar_f \leq 1$ then:
there is an infinite fair S-derivation iff there is an infinite fair S-derivation starting in a l.h.s of some RR.

The proof is very similar to that of the general restriction theorem, so it is omitted.

[]

In case there is $f \in F$ with $ar_f > 1$, the situation is quite different. Suppose there are $m \leq |R|$ infinite derivations, each starting in a l.h.s. of a rule, and for every $RR = l \to r$, if it is only finitely often applied along every given derivation, then it is also only finitely often enabled along every given derivation. The existence of such derivations does not necessarily imply the existence of an infinite fair derivation.

Example: Consider again the TRS $S = (F, \phi, R)$ the graph of which is described in figure 2.
Let

$$F' = \{a, b, c, h, f, g, f'\}$$

where

$$ar_a = ar_b = ar_c = 0,\quad ar_h = ar_f = ar_g = 1,\quad ar_{f'} = 2.$$

Let $R \subseteq R'$, and for every two terms τ and τ' that are nodes in G_S $f'(\tau, \tau') \to a \in R'$.

One can prove that the F-system $S' = (F', \phi, R')$ is fairly terminating though we have the two cycles in the graph $G_{S'}$ as in G_S, defining two derivations satisfying the desired condition.

[]

By adding a nullary function symbol f_0 to the set F we can achieve again the sufficiency of the condition.

Theorem: (general restriction for F-TRS)

Let $S = (F, \phi, R)$ and $S' = (F \cup \{f_0\}, \phi, R)$ where $f_0 \notin F$ and $ar_{f_0} = 0$.
If there is $f \in F$ with $ar_f > 1$ then:
there is an infinite fair S'-derivation iff there are $m \leq |R|$ infinite S-derivations $d_1, \cdots, d_m$ each starting in a l.h.s of some RR, and for every RR $l \to r$, if it is only finitely often applied along every d_i, then it is also only finitely often enabled along every d_i.

Proof:

(if) For $m = 1$ the claim is trivial. Thus assume $m > 1$. As in the general restriction theorem, we construct an interleaving of the given derivations. The interleaved derivation d starts now with the term τ, which embeds as arguments of f at various depths the initial terms of the m given derivations. As $ar_f > 2$ is possible, the positions of the arguments from the third onwards are padded with the new term f_0. We use the abbreviation $T_0(b)$ for

$f_0, \cdots, f_0$

$ar_f - b$ times, $b \in \{1, 2\}$.

$$\tau = \underbrace{f(f(\cdots}_{m \text{ times}} f(\tau_1, T_0(1)), \tau_2, T_0(2)), \cdots), \tau_m, T_0(2))$$

where $\tau_j, 1 \leq j \leq m$ is the first term of the given d_j.
We abbreviate the position $\underbrace{1. \cdots .1}_{k \text{ times}}$ as 1^k.

Again, the interleaved derivation consists of segments of length m. In the j'th step in the i'th segment, the rule applied is the one applied in the i'th step of d_j, but now the corresponding position is

$$\begin{cases} 1^m.u_i^{d_1} & j = 1 \\ 1^{m-j}.2.u_i^{d_j} & j > 1 \end{cases}$$

The function symbol f_0 acts as a filler so, again, every RR that is enabled infinitely often along d is infinitely often enabled along some d_i. Thus, the resulting derivation d is R-fair.

(only-if)
The set of m infinite derivations constructed exactly as in the (only-if) proof of the general restriction theorem consists of S-derivations and satisfies the desired condition.

[]

Remark: All the decidability theorems stated above can be easily modified to apply also to TRS containing a ground r.h.s and, possibly, variables in the l.h.s . The construction of the deciding graphs will start from the r_is instead of the l_is.

Acknowledgment: Conversations with Nachum Dershowitz were helpful. The part of the second author was partially supported by the fund for the promotion of research, the Technion.

References:

[DE 81] N. Dershowitz: "Termination of linear rewriting systems", proc. 8th ICALP symp. Acre, Israel, July 1981. In: LNCS 115 (O.Kariv, S.Even - eds.), Springer 1981.

[DT 84] N. Dauchet, S. Tison: "Decidability of confluence for ground term rewriting systems", (undated manuscript), Lille university.

[F 85] N. Francez: **"Fairness"**, to appear in Texts and monographs in comp. sci., Springer Verlag, 1985.

[GKM 83] J. Guttag, D. Kapur, D. R. Musser: "On proving uniform termination and restricted termination of rewriting systems", SIAM J. of Computing, 12, 1, 1983.

[HA 84] D. Harel: "A general result about infinite trees and its applications", proc. 16th ACM-STOC, Washington D.C , May 1984.

[HL 78] G. Huet, D. S. Lankford: "On the uniform halting problem for term rewriting systems", TR 283, INRIA 1978.

[LPS 81] D. Lehmann, A. Pnueli, J. Stavi: "Impartiality, justice and fairness: the ethics of concurrent termination", proc. 8th ICALP symp. Acre, Israel, July 1981. In: LNCS 115 (O. Kariv, S. Even - eds.), Springer 1981.

[PF 84] S. Porat, N. Francez: "Fairness in context-free grammars under canonical derivations" proc. STACS, Saarbrucken, January 1985. (Also: TR 340, comp. sci. dept., Technion, 1984).

[PFMZ 82] S. Porat, N. Francez, S. Moran, S. Zaks: "Fair derivation in context-free grammars", Information and Control 55, 1982.

Two Results in Term Rewriting Theorem Proving[1]

Jieh Hsiang

Department of Computer Science
State University of New York at Stony Brook
Stony Brook, NY 11794

Abstract

Two results are presented in this paper. (1) We extend the term rewriting approach to first order theorem proving, as described in [HsD83], to the theory of first order predicate calculus with equality. Consequently, we have showed that the term rewriting method can be as powerful as paramodulation and resolution combined. Possible improvements of efficiency are also discussed.

(2) In [KaN84], Kapur & Narendran proposed a method similar to [HsD83]. Motivated by the Kapur-Narendran method, we introduce a notion of splitting for theorem proving in first order predicate calculus. The splitting strategy provides a better utilization of the reduction mechanism of term rewriting systems than the N-strategy in [HsD83], although it generates more critical pairs. Comparisons and the relation between the splitting strategy, Kapur-Narendran method, and the N-strategy are also given.

We conjecture that our way of dealing with first order theories with full equality can be extended to the splitting and the Kapur-Narendran methods as well.

Due to the lack of space, we only give a sketch of the proofs of the completeness of the two theorem proving methods. They will be provided in detail in a longer version of the paper.

1. Introduction

We assume that the reader is familiar with the notion of term rewriting systems as described in [HuO80]. In this section we briefly describe the preliminaries in the term rewriting approach to first order theorem proving.

Different from other theorem proving methods, the term rewriting approach represents Boolean formulas as terms in the Boolean ring form (i.e. with the logical operators AND and EXCLUSIVE-OR). Such a representation yields a unique normal form for every formula in propositional calculus ([HsD83]). To avoid repetition of previous results, we shall simply mention here that the normal form of a logical formula is a polynomial with +-nilpotence and *-idempotence assumed (i.e. $x+x=0$ and $x*x=x$). For example, the normal form of $P(x)*P(x)+P(x)+Q(y)*R(x,y)*1+P(x)*0+1$ is $Q(y)R(x,y)+1$, with the connective * ignored to improve readability. Other Boolean connectives can be converted into the Boolean ring form using the rules:

---

[1] Research supported in part by the NSF grant DCS-8401624

$x \supset y \rightarrow xy+x+1$
$x \vee y \rightarrow xy+x+y$
$x \equiv y \rightarrow x+y+1$
$\neg x \rightarrow x+1$

where 1 stands for true and 0 for false. We call the normal form corresponding to a (skolemized) first order formula a Boolean term. Note that under this convention, all Boolean terms are irreducible with respect to the canonical system of Boolean algebra (in the form of Boolean ring).

1.1. Unification of Boolean terms

The unification problem with Boolean terms is more complicated than first order unification, since Boolean terms involve the operators * and +, which are AC. In [HsD83] we showed that for our theorem proving purposes, the only unification which we need to deal with are those between terms which are conjunctions of atomic formulas. As a convention, we call such a Boolean term (a conjunction of atomic formulas) an N-term. Even though * is AC, unification between N-terms is considerably simpler than AC unification. It is because in Boolean terms, (1) the only variables involved in the unification are the variables in the predicates and these variables are not operands of the AC-operator *, and (2) there is no repetition of identical formulas (by the idempotence of *). Therefore the unification problem becomes merely finding out different ways of unifying atomic formulas in two sets of atomic formulas. A specialized unification algorithm (called BN-unification) which utilizes these facts is given in [HsD83]. A similar algorithm which provides a more intuitive interpretation of this unification process is given in [KaN84]. We now briefly describe the unification process of N-terms.

> Two N-terms s and t are P-unifiable under σ if σ is a most general unifier such that sσ=tσ upon permutation.

For example, P(fx)P(y) and P(z)P(fw) are P-unifiable, under two independent most general unifiers {x←w,y←z} and {y←fw,z←fx}.

In theorem proving applications, we usually only require parts of two N-terms unifying with each other. This notion is captured in [KaN84] as follows:

> Definition Given two N-terms s and t, if there exist (nontrivial) subterms u_1 and u_2 of s and t such that $s=u_1s_1$, $t=u_2t_1$, and u_1 and u_2 are P-unifiable under σ, then $(s_1t)\sigma$ is an overlap of s and t.

The above overlap can also be written as $(s_1u_1t_1)\sigma$, or $(st_1)\sigma$, or simply $(st)\sigma$, since their normal forms are all identical. For simplicity of notation, u_1 stands for any combination of any part of subterms of s (as long as it is not empty), it does not have to be an initial segment of s. As an example, P(a)P(x)Q(x) and P(b)P(y) have the following overlaps:

First term	Second term	unifier	overlap
<u>P(a)P(x)</u>Q(x)	<u>P(b)P(y)</u>	{x←b, y←a}	P(a)P(b)Q(b)
P(a)<u>P(x)</u>Q(x)	<u>P(b)</u>P(y)	{x←b}	P(a)P(b)P(y)Q(b)
P(a)<u>P(x)</u>Q(x)	P(b)<u>P(y)</u>	{y←x}	P(a)P(b)P(x)Q(x)
<u>P(a)</u>P(x)Q(x)	P(b)<u>P(y)</u>	{y←a}	P(a)P(b)P(x)Q(x)

The underlined parts in the above table are the subterms which are unified against each other.

1.2. N-Strategy and the KN method -- An Overview

The N-strategy ([HsD83]) and the KN-method ([KaN84]) are two of the attempts to use Boolean ring and term rewriting for first order theorem proving. The basic approach of these methods is to treat Boolean formulas as Boolean rules, apply certain superposition inferences to produce new rules from them and certain reduction inference to simplify the Boolean terms using these Boolean rules, and continue this process until the contradictory rule $1 \rightarrow 0$ is generated.

The most fundamental difference between the two is that the N-strategy yields confluence only on 1 and 0, which is exactly what refutational theorem proving requires, while the KN-method yields a general confluence result. On the technical side, the major difference between the two are the orderings which the two methods employ for ordering Boolean equations into rules. The N-strategy uses a very simplistic ordering, allowing only 0 or 1 on the right hand sides of rules. The KN-method, which is nonclausal, allows more effective orderings which put larger parts of the Boolean terms on the right hand side. While more details about these orderings will be given later, we now simply assume that there is a noetherian ordering for orienting Boolean equations into Boolean rules. (Note that in our application domain, this can always be done.) As a consequence of the different formations of rules, each of the two methods has a difference deduction (superposition) inference and a different notion of reduction.

In the KN-method, four types of superpositions are needed ([KaN84]). Three of them are special inference rules for dealing with axioms of Boolean algebra. The more basic superposition process is the following:

Definition Given two Boolean rules $us+\alpha_1 \rightarrow \beta_1$ and $vt+\alpha_2 \rightarrow \beta_2$, if u and v are P-unifiable under an mgu σ, then

$$<[(\alpha_1+\beta_1)t]\sigma,\ [(\alpha_2+\beta_2)s]\sigma>$$

is an O-critical pair.[2]

An O-critical pair is divergent if the irreducible form of $[(\alpha_1+\beta_1)t]\sigma+[(\alpha_2+\beta_2)s]\sigma$ is not 0. In the above definition, u, v, s, and t are N-terms, and α_i and β_i can be any Boolean term. For convenience we choose the first N-terms in the rules for overlaping, in general they can be any of the N-terms on the left hand sides. The same applies to the other superposition processes in this paper. Note that in their definition, the subterms used for unification (.i.e. u and v) can both be the trivial term 1. An O-critical pair $<\alpha, \beta>$ is not converted into a rule by orienting the two Boolean terms in one direction or another. Instead, it is treated as an equation $\alpha+\beta=0$ and rearranged into a rule by distributing the terms over the two sides of = according to the employed ordering. Therefore when a critical pair $<\alpha, \beta>$ is converted into a rule, part of β may end up on the left hand side and vice versa. The reason that such rearrangements can be done is due to the nilpotence of +.

---

[2] O stands for overlap.

The reduction relation in the KN-method is defined with distributivity assumed. To be more precise, a Boolean rule $\alpha \rightarrow \beta$ can reduce a Boolean term γ if $\gamma = l\rho + \lambda$ for some N-term l, Boolean terms ρ and λ, and there is some unifier (matcher) σ such that $\rho = \alpha\sigma$. We call such a reduction relation the distributive reduction. Note that this type of reductions involves pattern matching with both operators $*$ and $+$ since α can be any Boolean term. For example, the rule $P(x)+Q(y) \rightarrow R(x)$ can simplify $R(b)P(a)+R(b)Q(b)$ to $R(b)R(a)$ since the term can be factored into $R(b)(P(a)+Q(b))$, and the second factor matches with $P(x)+Q(y)$.

In the N-strategy, which is clausal, Boolean rules are represented as $\alpha \rightarrow \delta$ where α is a Boolean term and δ is either 0 or 1. As a convention, from now on we reserve the Greek letter δ to represent either 0 or 1. The N-strategy allows a more restrictive type of superpositions.

Definition A Boolean rule $l \rightarrow 0$ is an N-rule if l is an N-term.
Given two Boolean rules

(1) $l \rightarrow 0$, which is an N-rule, and

(2) $t_1+t_2+\ldots+t_n \rightarrow \delta$,

if $l=l_1l_2$ and l has an overlap $(l_2t_1)\sigma$ with t_1, then

$$\langle (l_2t_2+\ldots+l_2t_n+l_2\delta)\sigma, 0 \rangle$$

is an N-critical pair of the two rules. An N-critical pair is divergent if the irreducible form of $(l_2t_2+\ldots+l_2t_n+l_2\delta)\sigma$ is not 0.

From the above definition, the N-strategy does not find critical pairs among arbitrary rules, but only between an N-rule and another rule. This eliminates a majority of the possible superpositions. The reduction inference in the N-strategy is also simpler: we allow a rule to be used for reduction only when it is of the form $l \rightarrow \delta$ where l is an N-term. Therefore the operator $+$ needs not be considered during simplification, neither is the distributivity axiom used. Further comparison of the KN-method and the N-strategy will be given later.

2. A Complete method for First Order Predicate Calculus with Equality

In this section we extend the first order term rewriting theorem proving to first order predicate calculus with equality. The method we show here is clausal and is based on the N-strategy.

As described in [HsJ83], clauses are transformed into Boolean ring form as follows:

Given a clause $C=P_1 \vee \ldots \vee P_k$ where P_i's are literals, define

$$r(C) = \begin{cases} 1 & \text{if } C \text{ is empty} \\ P+1 & \text{if } C \text{ is } P \\ P & \text{if } C \text{ is } \neg P \\ r(P_1)*r(P_2 \vee \ldots \vee P_k) & \text{otherwise} \end{cases}$$

The logical meaning of $r(C)=0$ is $C=1$. Note that the literal P can also be an equality. In order to separate the = of the first order theory from the = of Boolean equations, we represent the former as ==. For example,

```
f(x,y)==if (x==y) then g(x,y)
                  else g(x,x)
```

is represented as two rules:

$(x{==}y)(f(x,y){==}g(x,y))+(x{==}y)\rightarrow 0$ (from $(x{==}y)\supset f(x,y){==}g(x,y)$) r1
$(x{==}y)(f(x,y){==}g(x,x))+(f(x,y){==}g(x,x))+(x{==}y)\rightarrow 1$ (from $(x\neq y)\supset f(x,y){==}g(x,x)$) r2

We also emphasize that the predicate == is assumed to be commutative.

In the following section we present the deduction inference (as superposition processes) in our strategy.

2.1. EN-Superposition

The first superposition process has the same effect as the resolution inference in resolution type methods. Similar to the superposition process used in the N-strategy, we restrict the form of superposition so that the number of superpositions needed is reduced as much as possible.

It is easy to see that when a clause C is transformed into a rule, every negative literals in C appear in every N-terms of r(C). For example, $\neg P(x)\vee\neg Q(x)\vee R(y)\vee(s{==}t)$ becomes the rule $P(x)Q(x)R(y)(s{==}t)+P(x)Q(x)R(y)+P(x)Q(x)(s{==}t)+P(x)Q(x)\rightarrow 0$; and $\neg P(x)\vee\neg Q(x)$ becomes $P(x)Q(x)\rightarrow 0$. The second example also shows that if all literals in C are negative, then the corresponding rule of C is an N-rule. We call an N-subterm a <u>factor</u> of a Boolean rule if it appears in every maximal N-term of the rule. For instance, the largest factor of the first example is P(x)Q(x), and that of the second is also P(x)Q(x). In general, if a Boolean rule is transformed directly from a clause, then the conjunction of its negative literals will be its largest factor. In the following discussion we sometimes need to emphasize a factor in a Boolean term. For convenience, we do so by presenting a rule as $t\alpha+\beta\rightarrow 0$, where t is an N-term, β is the part of the Boolean term which does not contain t as a factor, and α is the rest of the Boolean term with t factored out. The δ, which is the right hand side of the rule, is also included in β for simplicity. Before introducing the EN-superposition process, we need a few more definitions.

<u>Definition</u> A clause C is an <u>EN-clause</u> if the only positive literals (if any) in C are equalities.

For instance, $\neg P(x)\vee\neg Q(x)\vee(s{==}t)$ is an EN-clause, so is $\neg P(x)\vee(u\neq v)\vee(s{==}t)$. Note that $(u\neq v)$ is considered as $\neg(u{==}v)$, a negative literal.

<u>Definition</u> A Boolean rule $\alpha\rightarrow 0$ is an <u>EN-rule</u> if α has a factor l such that $\alpha=l\beta$, and β is a Boolean term with only the == predicate symbol.

For example, the above two clauses are converted into EN-rules $P(x)Q(x)(s{==}t)+P(x)Q(x)\rightarrow 0$ and $P(x)(u{==}v)(s{==}t)+P(x)(u{==}v)\rightarrow 0$, or equivalently, $P(x)Q(x)((s{==}t)+1)\rightarrow 0$ and $P(x)(u{==}v)((s{==}t)+1)\rightarrow 0$. It is easy to see that an EN-clause will be transformed into an EN-rule.

The first superposition process which we introduce is restricted to between an EN-rule and another rule.

<u>Definition</u> Given an EN-rule $l\alpha\rightarrow 0$ where l is the maximal factor, and another rule $t\beta+\gamma\rightarrow 0$. If $l=l_1l_2$ and l has an overlap $(l_2t)\sigma$ with t, then

$$\langle l_2\alpha\gamma,0\rangle$$

is an <u>EN-critical pair</u>.

An EN-critical pair is divergent if the irreducible form of $l_2\alpha\gamma$ is not 0. A divergent critical pair is converted into a Boolean rule the way an N-critical pair is, by putting 1 to the right hand side if it is a subterm. This process of finding EN-critical pairs is called the EN-superposition process.

Note that N-rules are also EN-rules (where the maximal factor is the entire term). And EN-superposition is the same as N-superposition if an N-rule, instead of an EN-rule, is used in the EN-superposition process.

2.1.1. Interpreting the EN-superposition

We call a resolution an EN-resolution if one of the parent clauses is an EN-clause. Similar to the N-superposition which simulates the all-negative resolution, EN-superposition simulates EN-resolution. It is straightforward to see how such a simulation can be done. We will not show the detail here.

2.2. P-Superposition

It is easy to see that every Boolean rule of the form $P_1 \ldots P_n \rightarrow 1$ is logically equivalent to the rules $P_1 \rightarrow 1$, $P_2 \rightarrow 1$, ... and $P_n \rightarrow 1$. Therefore whenever a critical pair $\langle P_1 \ldots P_n, 1\rangle$ is generated, it is always converted into rules $P_1 \rightarrow 1$ through $P_n \rightarrow 1$. We call these rules (of the form $P \rightarrow 1$) P-rules, where P is an atomic formula. P-rules are also used in a superposition process, which we call P-superposition.

Definition: Given a P-rule $P \rightarrow 1$ and a rule $\alpha[L] \rightarrow \delta$, where L is an atom in the Boolean term α, if there is an mgu σ such that $P\sigma = L\sigma$, then

$$\langle (\alpha[1])\sigma,\ \delta\rangle$$

is a P-critical pair of the two rules, where $\alpha[1]$ is α with all occurrences of L replaced by 1.

A P-critical pair $\langle t, \delta\rangle$ is divergent if the irreducible form of $t+\delta$ is not 0. Although the P-superposition process is not needed for the completeness of the N-strategy, it is crucial when equality exists in the language. It is because equality assumes the reflexive axiom:

$$(x{=}{=}x) \rightarrow 1,$$

which is a P-rule. As a special case of P-superposition with the reflexive axiom, we have:

Given a Boolean rule $\alpha[(t{=}{=}s)] \rightarrow \delta$ where $(t{=}{=}s)$ is a subterm of α, if $s\sigma = t\sigma$ for some mgu σ, then $\langle (\alpha[1])\sigma,\ \delta\rangle$ is a P-critical pair.

In other words, if the two sides of an equality in a rule unify with each other, then a new rule will be generated with the proper instantiation of variables and with that equality replaced by 1.

2.3. Merge Superposition

The next superposition process simulates factoring in resolution. Its necessity was first pointed out in [Pau84] and [KaN84].

Definition Given a Boolean rule $t_1 + \ldots + t_n \rightarrow \delta$, where $n \geq 1$. If there are atomic formulas L_1 and L_2, and an mgu σ such that $t_1 = L_1 L_2 s$ and $L_1\sigma = L_2\sigma$, then $\langle (t_1 + \ldots + t_n)\sigma, \delta\rangle$ is an M-critical pair.

It is not hard to see how factoring can be simulated using the merge superposition. This superposition process is also needed in the N-strategy.

2.4. Para-Superposition

Although the N-strategy has been extended to include domain theories with equational axioms assumed ([HsD83]), it still cannot handle equalities in non-unit clauses. Attempts of incorporating non-unit equalities into the term rewriting framework have been done mainly in the form of conditional term rewriting (e.g. [BDJ79], [Lan79], [Rem83], [Kap83], [BeK82]), however none of the approaches is complete for the full first order theory with equality. For instance, the example given in the previous section will usually be presented in these methods as:

$(x{==}y) \supset f(x,y) \rightarrow g(x,y)$ s1
$(x \neq y) \supset f(x,y) \rightarrow g(x,x)$ s2

with the parts before $\supset$ as the conditions for the rewrites to apply. The problem with such approaches is that they cannot perform substitution within the equalities in the conditions and, consequently, cannot prove properties which require such substitutions. As an example, none of the aforementioned methods can prove $f(a,b)=g(a,a)$, where a and b are two uninterpreted constants. It is because in the case where a=b and s1 applies, f(a,b) can only be rewritten to g(a,b) but not to g(a,a) unless the substitution of $b \rightarrow a$ is somehow done.

In order to perform substitution within the equalities themselves, we introduce a superposition called para-superposition. In the following discussion we sometimes factor out an atomic formula in (part of) a Boolean rule. As before, we present such a Boolean rule as $L\alpha+\beta \rightarrow 0$. We also use $\alpha[r]$ to indicate that r is a nonvariable subterm of α.

Definition: Given two rules
(1) $\alpha_1[r] \rightarrow \delta$
(2) $(t{==}s)\alpha_2+\beta_2 \rightarrow 0$,
if there is an mgu σ such that $t\sigma=r\sigma$, then

$$<((\alpha_1[s]+\delta)\beta_2)\sigma,\ 0>$$

is a para-critical pair between the two rules. We also say that it is a para-critical pair from para-superposing rule (2) into rule (1).

Note that since == is commutative, the above para-superposition can also be performed on the right hand side of the equality (s, in this case). However in some cases when t and s can be oriented under certain ordering, only one way substitution needs be performed. (Detail will be given later.) Also note that since we restrict the subterm r in $\alpha[r]$ to be a nonvariable subterm, the usual no paramodulation into a variable restriction in some paramodulation strategies is implicitly imposed. The most important feature of the above definition is that none of the N-terms in rule (2) which contains the subterm (t==s) needs be kept in the para-critical pair. Also, if β_2 of the second rule in the definition is 0, then there is no divergent para-critical pair.

2.4.1. Soundness and Completeness of Para-Superposition

The soundness of para-superposition can be seen from the following derivation of logical equivalences. The soundness of EN-superposition can be done in a similar way. Since substitution is sound, without loss of generality, we shall assume that the two rules are

$\alpha_1[t] \rightarrow \delta$
$(t{==}s)\alpha_2+\beta_2 \rightarrow 0$

to eliminate the unifier σ. The two rules mean the logical equivalences:

(1) $\alpha_1[t] = \delta$, and

(2) $(t{==}s)\alpha_2 = \beta_2$.

Consequently we have:

(3) $\alpha_1[t](t{==}s)\alpha_2 = \alpha_1[s](t{==}s)\alpha_2$

This is true since the implicit multiplication means logical conjunction and the equality between Boolean terms means logical equivalence. By applying (1) and (2) on the left hand side of (3), we have

(4) $\alpha_1[t](t{==}s)\alpha_2 = \delta\beta_2$.

The right hand side of (3), after applying (2), yields

(5) $\alpha_1[s](t{==}s)\alpha_2 = \alpha_1[s]\beta_2$.

Equations (3), (4) and (5) establish $\alpha_1[s]\beta_2 = \delta\beta_2$, or, equivalently, $(\alpha_1[s]+\delta)\beta_2 = 0$.

A remark about inequality should be made here. In the Boolean ring form, an inequality $t \neq s$ is treated as $(t{==}s)+1$, whose first subterm is regarded just as an equality in the corresponding Boolean rule. Therefore it is possible to para-superpose an equality in a rule which is actually an inequality in the original context. Firstly, the above soundness proof still applies in this case, since no assumption of the original context of the equality used in para-superposition was necessary. Therefore the cost of para-superposing an "inequality" is only efficiency, not soundness. Secondly, note that when transforming a clause with an inequality $t \neq s$ into a Boolean rule, the corresponding equality $t{==}s$ must appear in every N-subterm of the transformed Boolean term. In other words, the atom $(t{==}s)$ will be a factor for the entire Boolean rule, therefore by definition no divergent para-critical pair will be generated.

A simple case analysis can be used to show that paramodulation (without paramodulating into a variable) can be simulated by para-superposition. We shall skip the detail here.

2.4.2. Uni-Directional Para-Superposition

The para-superposition procedure, if applied fully, requires both sides of an equality (==) in a Boolean rule be para-superposed whenever possible. This can be very inefficient in general. Therefore it is important to find criteria under which para-superposition can be restricted to uni-directional only.

A special type of rules which can be used for para-superposition is the unit equations

$$(t{==}s) \rightarrow 1.$$

In certain more restricted theories, if $t>s$ for some well-founded ordering, the rule can be treated as $t \rightarrow s$ and only t needs be used for para-superposition. Such rules are regular rewrite rules and can be used for rewriting instances of t to s accordingly but not the other way around. We call these rules obtained from orienting unit equalities the <u>domain rules</u>. The most obvious examples of such restricted theories are the equational theories on which the original Knuth-Bendix procedure is applicable. As another example, in [HsD83] we showed that if all the equalities in the input formulas are unit equalities, and if they are all orientable into domain rules under a well-founded partial ordering, then they can be treated as rewrite rules. Actually in this case, the N-strategy with uni-directional para-superposition yield a complete strategy (called the RN-strategy in [HsD83]).

We now try to extend this result to non-unit and unorientable equalities. Our method is very similar to Peterson's method in [Pet83]. First assume that there is a simplification ordering $>_G$ on the Herbrand universe which is order isomorphic to ω. Let $>$ be the extension of $>_G$ to the extended Herbrand universe (i.e. domain terms with variables, not just ground terms) such that $t>s$ if and only if $t\sigma >_G s\sigma$ for every ground instantiation σ. Note that $>$ is now a (partial) well-founded simplification ordering. With such an ordering, we can impose the following uni-directional restrictions on para-superposition:

(I) A unit-equation rule $t{==}s \rightarrow 1$ such that $t>s$ can be treated as a domain rule $t \rightarrow s$.

(II) When performing para-superposition with a rule $(t{==}s)\alpha_2+\beta_2 \rightarrow 0$, $s\sigma$ can be used to replace $t\sigma$ only when $s\sigma \not> t\sigma$.

Non-orientable unit equations are a special case of restriction (II) (with $\alpha_2=\beta_2=1$). Also, if $t>s$ in a non-unit equational rule $(t{==}s)\alpha_2+\beta_2 \rightarrow 0$, then we can (implicitly) treat the rule as $(t \rightarrow s)\alpha_2+\beta_2 \rightarrow 0$, although the subterm $t \rightarrow s$ cannot be used as a domain rule for simplification purposes.

As yet another remark, although the notation $\rightarrow$ is used for both Boolean rules and domain rules, the meanings it represent in the two are not the same. The rewriting relation obtained from a domain rule $t \rightarrow s$ is not the same as the rewriting relation of a Boolean rule $\alpha \rightarrow \delta$. While the Boolean rule denotes the logical equivalence of α and δ, the logical equivalence of a domain rule $t \rightarrow s$ is really $(t{==}s)=1$, not $t=s$. The significance of this is that a domain rule $t \rightarrow s$ can still be para-superposed into by another Boolean rule. For example, given a domain rule $t[u] \rightarrow s$ and a Boolean rule $(u{==}r)\alpha+\beta \rightarrow 0$ where $u>r$, $<((t[r]{==}s)+1)\beta, 0>$ is a legitimate para-critical pair from the Boolean rule into the domain rule.

2.5. Simplification

Simplification in our strategy is similar to the N-strategy. That is, only N-rules, P-rules, and the domain rules are used for simplification.

2.6. A Complete Strategy

Our complete strategy for first order predicate calculus with equality is essentially the Knuth-Bendix completion procedure which generates EN, P, Merge, and para-superpositions. Further restriction of generating uni-directional para-superpositions instead of para-superpositions is also imposed provided that the ordering used for ordering domain terms is a simplification ordering which is order isomorphic to ω on the Herbrand universe.

Theorem Given a set of first order clauses S, S is E-unsatisfiable if and only if $1 \rightarrow 0$ can be generated from $R \cup \{(x{==}x) \rightarrow 1\}$ using the above strategy, where R is the set of Boolean rules converted from S.

A sketch of the proof is given in the appendix. A complete proof will be given in a longer paper. The proof is very similar to the one in [Pet83]. Similar to [Pet83], we do not need the functional reflexive axioms. The major difference (improvement) of our proof is the additional restriction of generating

[3] Simplification orderings are defined in [Der82].

only the EN-critical pairs as opposed to general resolution.

2.7. Examples and Discussion

The strategy is not yet implemented. In the following we give a couple of simple examples.

Example 1 The first example is taken from [BDJ79], which contains some famous "counterexamples" to various appoaches to conditional term rewriting.

$$f(x,y)==\text{if } (x==y) \text{ then } g(x,y) \text{ else } g(x,x)$$

Show that $\forall x,y(f(x,y)==g(x,x))$.

The four input rules are

$(x==x)\rightarrow 1$ r0

$(x==y)(f(x,y)==g(x,y))+(x==y)\rightarrow 0$ r1

$(x==y)(f(x,y)==g(x,x))+(f(x,y)==g(x,x))+(x==y)\rightarrow 1$ r2

$(f(a,b)==g(a,a))\rightarrow 0$ r3

By the EN-superposition, r2 and r3 produces an EN-critical pair $\langle (a==b),1\rangle$ which becomes a domain rule:

$b\rightarrow a.$ r4

R4 simplifies r3 to

$(f(a,a)==g(a,a))\rightarrow 0.$ r5

R5 and r1, using EN-superposition again, generates a EN-critical pair $\langle (a==a),0\rangle$ which simplifies to $\langle 1,0\rangle$, the contradiction. The same effect can be obtained by para-superposing r1 into r5, which produces the para-critical pair $\langle (g(a,a)==g(a,a))(a==a),0\rangle$. Note that all the applications of EN-superposition above are actually N-superpositions.

All the other examples in [BDJ79] can be proved in a similar fashion.

Example 2 This example is from [ChL73].

$(x==x)\rightarrow 1$		c0
$Q(c)(c==d)+Q(c)\rightarrow 0$	$(\neg Q(c)\vee(c==d))$	c1
$Q(c)(g(c)==g(d))\rightarrow 0$	$(\neg Q(c)\vee(g(c)\neq g(d)))$	c2
$Q(c)(a==b)+Q(c)+(a==b)\rightarrow 1$	$(Q(c)\vee(a==b))$	c3
$Q(c)(g(a)==g(b))+(g(a)==g(b))\rightarrow 0$	$(Q(c)\vee(g(a)\neq g(b)))$	c4

We may assume that in the simplification ordering, d>c>b>a. Para-superposing c1 into c2, we get a para-critical pair $\langle Q(c)(g(c)==g(c))Q(c),0\rangle$, which becomes a rule:

$Q(c)\rightarrow 0$ c5

C5 immediately deletes every N-term in the rule base which contains Q(c). This includes eliminating c1 and c2, and replacing c3 and c4 by

$b\rightarrow a$ c6

$(g(a)==g(b))\rightarrow 0$ c7

C6 reduces c7 to $(g(a)==g(a))\rightarrow 0$ which, with c0, gives us the contradiction.

We do not intend to claim any significant gain of efficiency of our method over other methods for first order theory with equality (such as demodulation and the modification method). Perhaps only a good implementation with fast results can be the final judgement. For an implementation of a term rewriting based theorem prover for first order logic with equality, we suggest that other methods (such as the E-Knuth Bendix procedure [JoK84], the conditional methods by [Rem83], [Lan79]) be incorporated for solving special cases which can be efficiently done using those methods.

3. The Splitting Strategy

We now depart ourselves from equalities and concentrate on "pure" first order predicate calculus. In this section we introduce a notion call splitting, and show how to use it to achieve more reduction power in first order term rewriting theorem proving.

3.1. Motivation

By moving Boolean terms to the right hand sides of rules, the KN-method provides much better utilization of reduction than the N-strategy. However, the tradeoff for this reduction power are a more complicated superposition process and the need of performing reductions with the incorporation of distributivity. Neither can they employ restrictions such as superposing only on the N-rules.

Although the KN-method moves terms to the right hand sides, there may still be rules with more than one head terms on the left hand sides. Such rules constitute one major source of complexity. It is because (1) the O-superposition process is performed between pairs of terms of the two left hand sides, therefore among two rules each with n and m head terms, there are nm potential pairings. (2) The existence of multiple headterms also results in the need of distributive reduction. Such a reduction process is complicated since it involves both operators + and *. If there is only one head term on the left hand side of a rule, then reduction using that rule will never involve distributivity. Splitting is a technique which tries to put even more Boolean terms to the right hand sides so that the number of rules with multiple head terms is reduced to minimum and only with a fixed format. By doing so, a more natural notion of superpositions (simply from taking the overlaps of the left hand sides and reduce accordingly) can be used, and the notion of reduction is also simpler.

3.2. Ordering Boolean Terms

The first goal in our method is to provide an ordering for the set of Boolean terms so that Boolean rules can have as many subterms on the right hand side as possible and still preserve the noetherian property. Similar to [KaN84], we build such an ordering in an incremental way: first find a well-founded ordering for the atomic formulas, then extend it to the N-terms, then to all the Boolean terms. Finally, a Boolean equation $s_1+\ldots+s_n=0$ is ordered into a rule under this ordering $>$ following the guideline that the left hand side of the rule should be the least maximum. In other words, it should be oriented into a rule $s_{i_1}+\ldots+s_{i_m} \rightarrow s_{i_{m+1}}+\ldots+s_{i_n}$ such that $s_{i_1}+\ldots+s_{i_m} > s_{i_{m+1}}+\ldots+s_{i_n}$, and for every $k<m$ and indices $j_1, \ldots, j_k$, $s_{j_1}+\ldots+s_{j_k} \not> s_{j_{k+1}}+\ldots+s_{j_n}$. Following Buchberger's convention ([Buc76]), when a Boolean equation is oriented into a rule $\alpha \rightarrow \beta$, α is the head and β the rest. A Boolean rule is called a mono-rule if its head is an

N-term.

Without loss of generality, we assume that there is a well-founded total ordering $>_P$ on the set of predicate symbols and a well-founded total ordering on the set of function (including 0-ary) symbols. This assumption is reasonable since there are at most countably many predicate and function symbols. We extend the second ordering to a well-founded ordering on the extended Herbrand universe (e.g. the recursive path ordering [Der82]) and denote it by $<_F$. The two orderings combined is extended to the set of atomic formulas:

<u>Definition</u> Given two atomic formulas $s=P(s_1, \ldots, s_n)$ and $t=Q(t_1, \ldots, t_m)$, define $<_A$ to be: $s<_A t$ if
(1) $P<_P Q$ or
(2) $P=Q$ and $\{s_1, \ldots, s_n\} <<_F \{t_1, \ldots, t_m\}$ where $<<_F$ is the multiset ordering of $<_F$.

The multiset ordering in (2) of the above definition can also be replaced by a lexicographic ordering.

The distinctive character of this ordering is that two terms may be comparable even if they contain different variables. For example, if $P<_P Q$, then $P(x)<_A Q(y)$! In fact, if $P<_P Q$, then $P(s)<_A Q(t)$ for every atomic formulas of the form $Q(t)$ and $P(s)$. In general such an ordering of terms will cause infinite descending chains, but it does not happen in our case. It is because the set of predicate symbols is disjoint from the extended Herbrand universe. Thus, the variable y in Q(y) will never be substituted by any term which contains P. This kind of property can also be utilized for obtaining termination orderings for term rewriting systems of many-sorted algebra.

To extend $<_A$ to N-terms we use, once again, the multiset ordering:

<u>Definition</u> Given two (sorted) N-terms $s=s_1 \ldots s_n$ and $t=t_1 \ldots t_m$,
define $<_N$ as: $s<_N t$ if $\{s_1, \ldots, s_n\} <<_A \{t_1, \ldots, t_m\}$.

Finally, we generalize $<_N$ to a well-founded partial ordering $<_B$ on the set of Boolean terms.

<u>Definition</u> Given two Boolean terms $s=s_1+\ldots+s_n$ and $t=t_1+\ldots+t_m$ where s_1 through t_m are N-terms,
define $<_B$ as: $s<_B t$ if $\{s_1, \ldots, s_n\} <<_N \{t_1, \ldots, t_m\}$.

The essential idea behind the above ordering is to compare two Boolean terms by their sets of maximal incomparable (under $<_N$) N-terms.

<u>Theorem</u> $<_A$, $<_N$, and $<_B$ defined above are well-founded partial orderings on their respective domains.

The proofs for all three are easy.

<u>Corollary</u> If two N-terms are not comparable under $<_N$, then they must have the same numbers of the same predicate symbols.

This corollary is trivially true but useful, since it shows that incomparable N-terms must look much alike. The converse of the corollary is not true.

As mentioned before, a Boolean equation $s_1+\ldots+s_n=0$ should be arranged so that the left hand side is the "minimal maximum". By the above corollary, the minimal maximum subterm of a Boolean term is the sum of the "largest" N-terms and they have identical numbers of occurrences of the same predicates. For example, the Boolean equation

$$P(x)Q(x)+P(b)Q(a)+P(x)+R(h(x),z)+R(g(y),z)+1=0$$

where $P>_p Q>_p R$ will be oriented as

$$P(x)Q(x)+P(b)Q(a)\rightarrow P(x)+R(h(x),z)+R(g(y),z)+1$$

since P(x)Q(x) and P(b)Q(a) are incomparable and both are larger than the rest of the Boolean term. The same equation should be ordered as

$$R(h(x),z)+R(g(y),z)\rightarrow P(x)Q(x)+P(b)Q(a)+P(x)+1$$

if the ordering of the predicates is $R>_p Q>_p P$.

3.3. The Splitting Procedure

The ordering above leaves as many N-terms at the right hand sides of rules as possible. However, there still can be multiple N-terms as the head of a rule. Also, it does not seem likely that any ordering will ever produce nothing but mono-rules since terms such as R(h(x),z) and R(g(y),z) are inherently incomparable.

Let us revisit the example in the previous section:

$$R(h(x),z)+R(g(y),z)\rightarrow P(x)Q(x)+P(b)Q(a)+P(x)+1.$$

Recall that the logical meaning of the rule is

$$\forall x,y,z(R(h(x),z)+R(g(y),z) \equiv P(x)Q(x)+P(b)Q(a)+P(x)+1).$$

By the nature of Boolean ring, it is also equivalent to

$$\forall x,y,z(R(h(x),z)+P(x)Q(x)+P(x) \equiv R(g(y),z)+P(b)Q(a)+1).$$

Since the variable y does not appear on the left hand side, the truth value of R(g(y),z)+P(a,b)Q(a)+1 is a constant with respect to y. By the same token, the truth value of the left hand side, R(h(x),z)+P(x)Q(x)+P(x), is also a constant with respect to x. This means we can create a new predicate T, with variables only those involved in both sides of the equation, such that

$$R(h(x),z)+P(x)Q(x)+P(x) \equiv T(z) \equiv R(g(y),z)+P(b)Q(a)+1.$$

Therefore the above equation can be split into two:

$$R(h(x),z)+P(x)Q(x)+P(x) \equiv T(z),$$

$$R(g(y),z)+P(b)Q(a)+1 \equiv T(z).$$

By treating the new predicate as smaller than any other existing predicate, the two equations become two mono-rules:

$$R(h(x),z)\rightarrow P(x)Q(x)+P(x)+T(z),$$

$$R(g(y),z)\rightarrow P(b)Q(a)+1+T(z).$$

We now define this splitting procedure formally. First we use $v(\alpha)$ for the set of variables in α. Suppose we have a rule

$$\alpha_1+\ldots+\alpha_n\rightarrow\beta$$

where α_i's are N-terms. Separate β into two parts β_1 and β_2 (one or both parts may be 0), and let

$$V=(v(\alpha_1)\cup\ldots\cup v(\alpha_{\lfloor n/2\rfloor})\cup v(\beta_1)) \cap (v(\alpha_{\lfloor n/2\rfloor+1})\cup\ldots\cup v(\alpha_n)\cup v(\beta_2)).$$

If $V=\{x_1, \ldots, x_k\}$, then the above rule is split into

$$\alpha_1+\ldots+\alpha_{\lfloor n/2\rfloor}\rightarrow\beta_1+T(x_1, \ldots, x_k)$$

and

$$\alpha_{\lfloor n/2\rfloor+1}+\ldots+\alpha_n\rightarrow\beta_2+T(x_1, \ldots, x_k).$$

We do this recursively, each time creating a new predicate symbol which does not yet exist, until all rules become mono-rules. There is only one case where we do not split further, it will be discussed in the next subsection. We also assume that each newly created predicate symbol is smaller than the rest of the predicates in the existing rules. To ensure that the created predicates have as few arguments as possible, we always split the α's and β's in a way that yields the smallest number of variables in V.

Another way of splitting is to partition away the α's one at the time (i.e. split $\alpha_1+\ldots+\alpha_n$ into α_1 and $\alpha_2+\ldots+\alpha_n$) instead of from the middle. When one of the α_i's is more general than others (such as α_1 is $R(x,y)$), such a splitting produces faster reductions and is more efficient. However in the worst case it can produce n-1 new predicates instead of log(n) as before.

The idea of introducing a new function/predicate symbol to resolve unresolvable critical pairs was first suggested by Knuth-Bendix ([KnB70]). It was used successfully in the term rewriting environment REVE [Les83]. Our use of this technique is a little different, however, since we rearrange the positions of the Boolean terms. Neither is our technique meant for ordering unresolvable critical pairs since every Boolean equation is orderable under $>_B$.

3.3.1. Permutative Rules

Although splitting can be applied to all Boolean equations and create nothing but mono-rules, there is a special case which we do not split and keep rules with multiple head terms. The reason for doing so is to prevent the splitting procedure from going indefinitely. A typical example is the rule:

$$P(x,y)+P(y,x)\rightarrow 0.$$

If splitting is applied, the two new rules will be

$$P(x,y)\rightarrow T(x,y)$$

$$P(y,x)\rightarrow T(y,x)$$

which will create yet another Boolean equation $T(x,y)+T(y,x)=0$ and cause a loop.

To prevent this from happening, we give the following restriction during splitting. First we call an atomic formula <u>strictly linear</u> if (1) it has no function symbols in its argument, and (2) every variable appears only once. For example, $P(x,y,z)$ is a strictly linear term but $P(x,f(y),z)$ is not. Neither is $P(x,x,y)$ or $P(a,x,y)$. Intuitively, loops might occur if the Boolean equation to be split has a strictly linear atomic formula as an N-subterm, and splitting produces a new predicate with the same number of variables as that atom. To be more precise, we do the following when splitting: First we check if the Boolean equation has a strictly linear formula as an N-subterm, if not, then we split. Otherwise, we check if, for a strictly linear formula L in the equation, splitting can produce a new predicate with less number of variables than that in L. If so, we split; otherwise we don't. For example, we perform splitting on P(x,y)+P(y,z)=0, but not on P(x,y)+P(y,x)=0, nor on P(x,y)+P(y,f(z))+P(z,f(x))=0. It is because in the latter two cases, splitting can only produce new predicates with two variables, the same as the number of variables in P(x,y).

Definition A Boolean equation is permutative if it is of the form $P(\mathbf{t}_1)+\ldots+P(\mathbf{t}_k)=\alpha$ where one of $P(\mathbf{t}_i)$'s is a strictly linear atomic formula, and $P(\mathbf{t}_1)+\ldots+P(\mathbf{t}_k)>_B\alpha$.

For convenience, we use **t**, a list of terms, to represent the arguments of P. It is easy to see that all the Boolean equations which cannot be split are permutative equations, although the converse is not true. An unsplittable permutative Boolean equation $P(\mathbf{t}_1)+\ldots+P(\mathbf{t}_k)=\alpha$ is converted into a permutative rule $P(\mathbf{t}_1)+\ldots+P(\mathbf{t}_k)\rightarrow\alpha$ instead of being split into mono-rules.

The format of the permutative rules is very restricted. And as we shall see later, superpositions involving them can be defined in a fairly simple way.

3.4. The Superposition Processes

The superposition procedure for the splitting strategy is more complicated than the N-strategy since the formalism is more flexible and superpositions need be performed on all rules, not just a selected few. However, the concept behind these superposition processes is not hard to understand since most of the rules are mono-rules, and critical pairs among them can be produced by simply taking overlaps of the only N-terms on the left hand sides.

In order to deal with the permutative rules effectively, we separate the superposition processes for the permutative rules from those for the mono-rules. In the following discussion, all divergent critical pairs are converted into rules according to the ordering and the splitting procedure described above. (Therefore one divergent critical pair may produce several rules.)

3.4.1. Single Overlap Superposition

Recall the definition of overlaps in section 1, we define the superposition from taking an overlap from the heads of two mono-rules as follows:

Definition: Given two mono-rules $su\rightarrow\alpha$ and $tv\rightarrow\beta$ where u and v are two N-subterms of the heads and are P-unifiable under σ, then

$$\langle(\alpha t)\sigma,\ (\beta s)\sigma\rangle$$

is an S-critical pair of the two rules.

"S" stands for a critical pair generated from a "Single" overlap $(sut)\sigma$. This superposition process is the most basic process in our strategy. Comparing to the O-superposition process in [KaN84], where critical pairs are also taken from overlaps, S-superposition is more intuitive since it is defined on mono-rules which have only one head term.

3.4.2. Merge Superposition

The second kind of superposition simulates the idempotence property of * (x*x=x). It is similar to the merge superposition given before.

<u>Definition</u> Given a mono-rule $L_1L_2t \rightarrow \alpha$ where L_1 and L_2 are two arbitrary atomic formulas in the head. If $L_1\sigma = L_2\sigma$ for some mgu σ, then

$$\langle (L_1t)\sigma,\ \alpha\sigma \rangle$$

is an <u>M-critical pair</u>.

Intuitively, the merge superposition can be thought of as taking a simple overlap between $L_1L_2t \rightarrow \alpha$ and the idempotence rule $x*x \rightarrow x$ in the canonical system for Boolean algebra.

3.4.3. Idempotence Superposition

The next superposition process is another inference mechanism for resolving potential superpositions caused by the idempotence rule.

<u>Definition</u> Given a mono-rule $Lt \rightarrow \alpha$ where L is an arbitrary atomic formula in the head term. Then

$$\langle L\alpha,\ \alpha \rangle$$

is an <u>I-critical pair</u>.

The I-critical pair is generated from taking a single overlap LLt of Lt and $x*x$ of the idempotence rule, then reduce the overlap to $L\alpha$ and Lt (which gets further reduced to α) accordingly. The potential inefficiency caused by the idempotence superposition mechanism is remarkable, since it applies to every atomic formula in every rule.

We would like to mention that none of the examples that we tried (by hand) actually needs this type of superposition to produce a proof, therefore we are not sure whether it is actually needed for the completeness of the theorem proving strategy. However, we should also remark that this mechanism is needed to obtain a confluent system with the axioms of Boolean ring assumed. As an example, consider a system of one rule:

$$PQ \rightarrow R$$

where P, Q, and R are predicates. Neither of the first two superposition processes will generate any critical pair. However, the system cannot deduce PR=R, which is a valid equation since PPQ can be reduced to both R (by merging P and P then reduce) and PR. Therefore this one-rule system is not confluent. Using the idempotence superposition, we can produce two more rules: $PR \rightarrow R$ and $QR \rightarrow R$. These three rules form a confluent system.[4]

3.4.4. Permutative Superpositions

Three types of superpositions are needed to deal with permutative rules, one between a permutative rule and another rule, one deals with idempotence of $*$, and one with the nilpotence of $+$.

---

[4]The same example also applies to the Kapur-Narendran method.

Definition Given a permutative rule

(1) $P(\mathbf{t}_1)+\ldots+P(\mathbf{t}_k)\rightarrow\alpha$ and another rule

(2) $\beta[P(\mathbf{s})]\rightarrow\gamma$.

If $\mathbf{s}\sigma=\mathbf{t}_1\sigma$ for some mgu σ, then

$$<(\beta[P(\mathbf{t}_2)+\ldots+P(\mathbf{t}_k)+\alpha])\sigma,\ \gamma\sigma>$$

is a PR-critical pair.

The term $\beta[P(\mathbf{s})]$ means that $P(\mathbf{s})$ is a subterm of β.

The next superposition process is similar to the idempotence superposition given above.

Definition Given a permutative rule $P(\mathbf{t}_1)+\ldots+P(\mathbf{t}_k)\rightarrow\alpha$. Then

$$<P(\mathbf{t}_1)+P(\mathbf{t}_1)P(\mathbf{t}_2)+\ldots+P(\mathbf{t}_1)P(\mathbf{t}_k),P(\mathbf{t}_1)\alpha>$$

is a PI-critical pair.

The last superposition deals with the nilpotence ($x+x\rightarrow 0$) property.

Definition Given a permutative rule $P(\mathbf{t}_1)+\ldots+P(\mathbf{t}_k)\rightarrow\alpha$ If $P(\mathbf{t}_1)\sigma=P(\mathbf{t}_2)\sigma$ where σ is an mgu, then

$$<(P(\mathbf{t}_3)+\ldots+P(\mathbf{t}_k))\sigma,\ \alpha\sigma>$$

is a PN-critical pair.

3.5. Simplification

Although the KN-method yields more reductions than the N-strategy, it also needs the stronger distributive reduction. The reduction relation in the splitting strategy, on the other hand, needs distributivity only nominally. Therefore its reduction process is easier to understand and to implement.

It is easy to see how mono-rules are used for reduction. It is done exactly the same way as in the N-strategy, by pattern matching which involves only the operator $*$. Since the operator + never appears on the left hand side of a mono-rule, nothing which concerns + needs be done. The permutative rules do involve +, therefore distributivity needs be considered. Fortunately, the permutative rules have a very restrictive format. To be more specific, a permutative rule $P(\mathbf{t}_1)+\ldots+P(\mathbf{t}_k)\rightarrow\alpha$ can reduce a term β only when β has a subterm γ which can be factored into $l(P(\mathbf{s}_1)+\ldots+P(\mathbf{s}_k))$ for some N-term l, and there is some matcher σ such that $\mathbf{s}_i=\mathbf{t}_i\sigma$ for all i. This is much easier to do than the general distributive reduction.

3.6. A Complete Strategy using Splitting

The first order theorem proving strategy with splitting (called the splitting strategy) is essentially the Knuth-Bendix completion procedure which generates single overlap, merge, idempotence, and the permutative superpositions, and uses the splitting procedure to convert divergent critical pairs and Boolean equations into Boolean rules. Also, the simplification process is as described above. This strategy is complete for first order predicate calculus, that is, a given set of

Boolean equations is inconsistent if and only if the splitting strategy can produce a critical pair <1,0>.

Due to the lack of space, we will only outline the proof of completeness of the splitting strategy here. Since the splitting strategy is essentially a modification of the KN-method, we also prove the completeness of the splitting strategy based on the completeness of the KN-method. This is done by showing that the splitting strategy has the same reduction power as the KN-method. To be more specific, we show that if a Boolean term can be reduced to 0 using the KN-method, then it can also be reduced to 0 in the splitting strategy. As a direct consequence, if the starting first order formula is inconsistent, then the KN-method will eventually reduce 1 to 0, and so will the splitting strategy.

To do so, we need to show the following three things:

(1) Any reduction that can be performed by a rule in KN-method (distributive reduction in particular) can be performed by some corresponding rules in the splitting strategy.

(2) each new = between two Boolean terms established from performing superposition in the KN-method can be established from the splitting strategy.

(3) When a critical pair in KN-method is converted to a Boolean rule, the reductions that can be performed by the new Boolean rule can be performed by the splitting strategy as well.

The possibility of introducing an infinite descending chain of new predicate symbols during splitting is avoided by the use of the permutative rules.

4. Discussion

The splitting method grows out of an attempt to understand (and simplify) the KN-method. In addition to the 0-superposition given in the first section, the KN-method also needs more general versions (in the sense of having rules with more than one N-terms as the heads) of the merge and idempotence superpositions, as well as a superposition process for the nilpotence of +.

It is interesting to compare the splitting strategy and the KN-method with the N-strategy. The N-strategy uses a simplistic termination ordering which requires every Boolean term except 0 and 1 be put on the left hand side. It also requires the input to be in clausal form. Consequently, it yields much less reduction of terms and cannot fully utilize the nice notion of simplification which is the forte of the term rewriting methods. On the other hand, such a sacrifice enables us to obtain a method which yields only the confluence of 0 and 1, not general confluence as in the other methods. As shown before, for such a weak confluence property, only the N-superpositions and the merge superpositions are needed. Thus, comparing to the superposition processes of the KN-method and splitting, the N-strategy produces much less superpositions. Note that the weak confluence property of the N-strategy does not hamper its completeness as a theorem proving method. Quite on the contrary, refutational theorem proving requires exactly the confluence of 0 and 1, and nothing more.

An obvious nonclausal strategy that arises naturally from this Boolean ring based term rewriting approach to first order theorem proving is to choose a better termination ordering (thus, more reduction power) and use the AC-Knuth-Bendix procedure ([PeS81]) on the set of rules and the canonical system for Boolean algebra (BA). In addition to the problem with providing a general confluence, such a method is also inefficient due to the complexity involved in AC-unification and superpositions with BA. Therefore it becomes important to analyze the procedure and eliminate as much redundancy as possible.

The KN-method (and the splitting strategy as well) provides such a better ordering and tries to resolve the complexity which comes with the AC-Knuth-Bendix. While the approach described in [KaN84] is algebraic (based on the Grobner basis algorithm in [Buc76]), we now try to interpret their method from a term rewriting viewpoint. Similar to the N-strategy, they also utilize the nice property of Boolean terms (such as predicate symbols do not unify with each other and the idempotence of *) to simulate AC-unification. Their simulation is more complicated than the N- and splitting strategies, however, since they need to deal with both AC-operators * and +. Such a simulation lead to the introduction of the O-superpositions (which is essentially an extended version of the single overlap superposition in the splitting strategy). However, since the heads of Boolean rules in their method may contain more than one N-term, the quotients from the overlaps (s and t) need be distributed over the rest of the N-terms in the head of the other rule. This further complication is eliminated in the splitting strategy by the splitting procedure.

To resolve the potential superpositions caused by BA, the rules in BA are examined and additional superposition procedures are designed to simulate possible superpositions. While three of the six rules in BA will not produce any divergent critical pairs, the idempotence rule is handled, in [KaN84], partly by the extended merge superposition and partly by the extended idempotence superposition. As a side effect, the idempotence superposition has also partially taken care of the distributivity rule. (The distributivity rule is handled by the combination of the idempotence superposition, the O-superposition, and the distributive reduction.) The nilpotence rule of + is handled by introducing a nilpotence superposition. In the splitting strategy, the nilpotence rule is resolved mostly by the splitting procedure. The problem caused by the distributive law is also reduced considerably in the splitting strategy since most of the rules are mono-rules and the rest are permutations.

We now give an example, which will hopefully illustrate some differences between the KN-method and the splitting strategy. Also, we use our termination ordering instead of theirs, since ours provides more reductions. Suppose we have two rules

$$P(x)+P(y)+P(z)+P(w)\rightarrow 0,$$
$$P(x)Q(x)+P(y)Q(y)+P(z)Q(z)+P(w)Q(w)\rightarrow 0.$$

The splitting strategy will split the heads of the two rules respectively and eventually produce:

$P(x)\rightarrow T_2$ s1

$T_2Q(x)\rightarrow T_1$ s2

where T_1 and T_2 are predicates generated by the splitting. (T_1 and T_2 contain no free variable since no common variables appears during the splitting.) The idempotence superposition process, if used, will generate three more rules:

$T_2P(x)\rightarrow T_2$ (Idem. from s1) s3

$T_1Q(x)\rightarrow T_1$ (Idem. from s2) s4

$T_1T_2 \rightarrow T_1$ (Idem .from s2) s5

The KN-method, on the other hand, will first use the nilpotence superposition to cancel parts of the heads and simplify the two rules to:

$P(x)Q(x)+P(y)Q(y) \rightarrow 0$ k0
$P(x)+P(y) \rightarrow 0.$ k1

By taking an overlap superposition on the first two N-terms of the two heads, we get the following rule k2 which eliminates k0:

$P(x)Q(z)+P(y)Q(y) \rightarrow 0$ k2.

Unfortunately, the idempotence superposition process generates more rules:

$P(x)P(y) \rightarrow P(x)$ (Idem. from k1) k3
$P(x)P(y)Q(y) \rightarrow P(x)Q(z)$ (Idem. from k2) k4
$P(y)Q(y)Q(z) \rightarrow P(x)Q(z)$ (Idem. from k2) k5
$P(x)Q(y)+P(x)Q(z) \rightarrow 0$ (from k3 and k4) k6
$P(x)Q(z)Q(w) \rightarrow P(u)Q(z)$ (from k4 and k5) k7

...

There are some more rules that can be generated, we did not enumerate them all.

As can be seen from the above example, the idempotence superposition process is the major cause of inefficiency in both the KN-method and the splitting strategy. The latter salvages the problem somewhat by splitting the rules into smaller segments, although the potential problem persists. Note that this problem does not exist at all in the N-strategy.

As mentioned before, none of the examples which we tried actually used the idempotence superposition to find a proof. Therefore we feel that, for the first order theorem proving purposes, the idempotence superposition may not be needed for the completeness of the splitting strategy. We think it is also true for the KN-method. Note that such improvements are possible since the idempotence superpositions might only have to do with the general confluence, but not the confluence of 0 and 1. We are investigating ways of trimming down the superpositions in these methods to yield, similar to the N-strategy, only the confluence of 0 and 1.

4.1.1. Extending the Splitting Strategy to Include Equality

It is not hard to see how the para-superposition inference can be done in the formalism of the KN-method or the splitting strategy. By replacing the EN-superposition with the 0 or S superpsition, plus the other special superpsitions mentioned before, we should be able to achieve several nonclausal theorem proving methods for first order theory with equality. Note that permutation will not produce a problem for equality since equality is assumed to be commutative. The potential inefficiency of para-superposing into an inequality can be resolved somewhat by employing a method of polarity by [Mur82]. However, we have not yet found a proof for the completeness of these methods.

Acknowledgement

Discussions with Nachum Dershowitz, Deepak Kapur, David Plaisted, and Michael Rusinowitch have helped clearing some subtle points in the methods. I also thank Jean-Luc Remy for helping me collecting thoughts in the early stage of this research. The final draft of the paper is done when the author is visiting the University of Nancy, France, under the sponsorship of CNRS, France.

References

[BeK82] J. A. Bergstra and J. W. Klop, Conditional Rewrite Rules: Confluency and Termination, IW 198/82, SMC, Amsterdam, 1982.

[BDJ79] D. Brand, J. A. Darringer and W. H. Joyner, Completeness of Conditional Reductions, Proc. 4th Conference on Automated Deduction, , 1979, 36-42.

[Buc76] B. Buchberger, A Theoretical Basis for the Reduction of Polynomials to Canonical Forms, ACM-SIGSAM Bulletin, , August, 1976, 19-29.

[ChL73] C. L. Chang and C. T. Lee, Symbolic Logic and Mechanical Theorem Proving, Academic Press, 1973.

[Der82] N. Dershowitz, Orderings for Term Rewriting Systems, J.TCS 17, 3 (1982), 279-301.

[HsJ83] J. Hsiang and N. A. Josephson, TeRSe: A Term Rewriting Theorem Prover, The Rewrite Rule Laboratory Workshop, Schenectady, NY 12345, September 1983.

[HsD83] J. Hsiang and N. Dershowitz, Rewrite Methods for Clausal and Nonclausal Theorem Proving, Proc. 10th ICALP, , July 1983, 331-346.

[HuO80] G. Huet and D. C. Oppen, Equations and Rewrite Rules: A Survey, in Formal Languages: Perspectives and Open Problems, R. Book (ed.), Academic Press, 1980.

[Hue81] G. Huet, A Complete Proof of Correctness of Knuth-Bendix Completion Algorithm, J. Computer and System Sciences 23, (1981), 11-21.

[JoK84] J. Jouannaud and H. Kirchner, Completion of a Set of Rules Modulo a Set of Equations, 11th Symposium on Principles of Programming Languages, Salt Lake City, Utah, January, 1984.

[Kap83] S. Kaplan, Conditional Rewrite Rules, Report No 150, CNRS, France, December, 1983.

[KaN84] D. Kapur and P. Narendran, An Equational Approach to Theorem Proving in First-Order Predicate Calculus, Unpiblished manuscript, GE Research Lab, April 1984.

[KnB70] D. E. Knuth and P. B. Bendix, Simple Word Problems in Universal Algebras, in Computational Algebra, J. Leach (ed.), Pergamon Press, 1970, 263-297.

[Lan79] D. S. Lankford, Some New Approaches to the Theory and Application of Conditional Term Rewriting Systems, Report, Louisiana Tech Univ., 1979.

[Les83] P. Lescanne, Computer Experiments with the REVE Term Rewriting System Generator, 10th ACM Symp. on Prin. of Programming Languages, , 1983.

[Mur82] N. Murray, Completely Non-Clausal Theorem Proving, Artificial Intelligence 18, (1982), 67-85.

[Pau84] E. Paul, A New Interpretation of the Resolution Principle, 7th Conf. on Automated Deduction, Nappa Valley, CA, May, 1984, 333-355.

[PeS81] G. E. Peterson and M. E. Stickel, Complete Sets of Reductions for Some Equational Theories, J. ACM 28, (1981), 233-264.

[Pet83] G. E. Peterson, A Technique for Establishing Completeness Results in Theorem Proving with Equality, SIAM J. of Computing 12, 1 (1983), 82-100.

[Rem83] J. L. Remy, Conditional Term rewriting System for Abstract Data Types, Submitted for Publication, University of Nancy, France, June 1983.

Appendix

We now sketch the proof of completeness of the theorem proving stratgy for first order predicate calculus with equality. Due to the lack of space, we assume that the readers are familiar with Peterson's proof of completeness of paramodulation and resolution as given in [Pet83]. We only give here the parts which are different from Peterson's. The complete proof will be given elsewhere.

Peterson's proof is based on a modified notion of semantic tree. He first assume that there is a simplification ordering on the set of atomic formulas. The ordering is also order isomorphic to ω on the Herbrand universe. This condition is important for, among other things, performing induction on the tree. The semantic tree which Peterson uses is different from the usual semantic tree in that (1) it is a fixed semantic tree, that is, the order of which the ground atomic formulas labels the arcs is the same as the ordering for the Herbrand universe. (2) Each node N may have one or two children according to the following rule: Say the next ground literals for N are B_k and $\neg B_k$, first, if B_k is an identity s==s, then N has just one child, labeled s==s; if B_k is not reducible with respect to the equalities in the partial interpretation from the root to N (called I_N), then N has two children, labeled B_k and $\neg B_k$; if B_k can be reduced to some literal C using an equality in I_N, then N has one child either B_k or $\neg B_k$, depending on whether C is a positive or negative literal. As a convention, if a node has two children, we always label the one on the left positive and the one on the right negative. Peterson calls an internal node N a reduction node if (1) the arc above it is labeled by an equality s==t and (2) N has a sibling node. Each failure node N is marked with a minimal (w.r.t. I_N reducibility and the ordering for the Herbrand universe) ground clause C_N which falsifies I_N. A failure node N is called an R-failure node if C_N is I_N-irreducible. Otherwise it is called a P-failure node. A resolution inference node is a node whose children (or child) are all R-failure nodes. A paramodulation inference node is a P-failure node N such that the siblings of all its reduction ancestor nodes are R-failure nodes.

Peterson showed, by traversing the tree in a particular way, that in a closed semantic tree there has to be at least one resolution inference node or one paramodulation inference node. And in either case, the semantic tree can be "shrunk" either by resolution or by paramodulation.

The major difference between our strategy and Peterson's method is that Peterson imposes no restriction on the type of resolutions while we allow only EN-resolutions (EN-superpositions). Most of the lemmas in Peterson's proof still hold in our proof. However, in order to deal with this restriction of inference, we need to traverse the closed semantic tree in a different way. For simplicity of notation, we still present the rest of the proof in terms of clauses and resolutions (instead of Boolean rules and superpositions). This will not alter the proof much since there is a correspondence between factoring and merge superposition, and between EN-resolution and EN-superposition. We first give some definitions: An internal node N is an <u>R-reduction node</u> (<u>labeled by</u> Ps) if it has two children Ps and ¬Ps, where P is a predicate other than ==, and Ps is marked by a failure node. An internal node N is a <u>P-reduction node</u> (<u>labeled by</u> s==t) if it has two children s==t and s≠t, and s≠t is marked by a failure node. We traverse the closed semantic tree in the following way:

R = **P** = Φ;
Start from the root, go down the arcs until reach a failure node:
If the node N

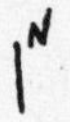

(1) has one child, go down.

(2) is an R-reduction node labeled by Ps, then choose the right path, and **R**:=**R**∪{C}, where C marks the failure node of the other child (i.e. for the arc Ps).

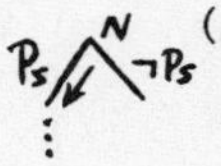

(3) is not an R-reduction node and the right arc is labeled by Ps, then choose the left path.

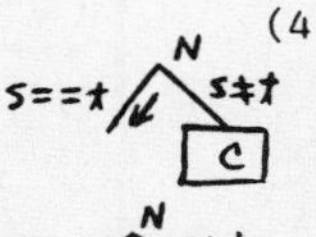

(4) is a P-reduction node labeled by s==t, then choose the left path, and **P**:=**P**∪{C}, where C marks the falure node of the other child (i.e. for the arc s≠t).

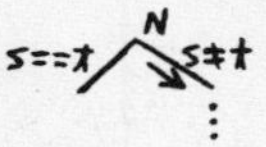

(5) is otherwise, then choose the right path.

Put the final failure node in **R**.

The proof path may end with one of the following:

(1) A fork

(2) A

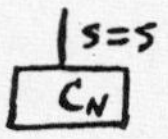

where C_N is I_N-irreducible

(3) A

where C_N is I_N-reducible.

Case (2) is trivial, and the semantic tree can be shrunk by performing resolution between the lifted clause of C_N and x==x (or, correspondingly, P-superposition on the lifted clause of C_N and x==x→0).

<u>Lemma 1</u> If there is a P-failure node in **P**∪**R**, then there is a paramodulation inference node in **P**∪**R**.

<u>Proof</u> We do the following: Go down from the root along the proof path obtained from the above algorithm until meet the **first** P-failure node N in **P**∪**R** (recall that a node N is a P-failure node if C_N is I_N-reducible). Then N is a paramodulation inference node since, by the construction of the proof path, the sibling of any reduction ancestor node of N has to be a failure node. And since N is the first P-failure node, these previous ones must be R-failure nodes.

Corollary 1 If the above algorithm end with case (3), then there exists a paramodulation inference node in **PUR**.

The corollary is obviously true since case (3) implies that the algorithm ends with a P-failure node, and therefore has at least one P-failure node.

If there is a paramodulation inference node, then Theorem 7 of Peterson's proof can be used to shrink the tree. Therefore from now on we may assume that all nodes in **PUR** are R-failure nodes (i.e. they are I_N-irreducible with respect to the respective N), and the traversing algorithm ends with a fork (Case 1).

Let L and $\neg L$ be the literals labeling the arcs of the last fork before the algorithm stops, and C_1 and C_2 mark their corresponding (failure) nodes.

Proposition

(1)

$\neg L \varepsilon C_1$ and $L \varepsilon C_2$.

(2)

For any $C \varepsilon \mathbf{R}$ other than C_2, the only positive literals other than equalities that can appear in C are those labeling the arcs of the R-reduction nodes above C.

The propositions are true by the construction of the proof path.

Now there are two cases to be considered.

Case 1: C_1 is an EN-clause. Then EN-resolution can be performed between C_1 and C_2 on the literal L. And the closed semantic tree will be shrunk consequently. By using the resolution lifting lemma (and factoring), this can be lifted to non ground case. Note that the resolution lifting lemma can be used here because both C_1 and C_2 are irreducible (R-failure nodes).

Case 2: C_1 is not an EN-clause. That is, there may be some non-equality positive literal Ps in C_1. In this case, we use the following way to produce an EN-clause C'_1 to replace C_1. Then we can apply the argument in Case 1 to shrink the tree.

We first enumerate all the clauses in **R** by the order of their generation. (Recall that all these clauses are R-failure nodes.) Let D be the first R-failure node in the enumeration that contains a non-equality positive literal, say Ps. Then any clause in **R** that appears before D must be an EN-clause. Since $Ps \varepsilon D$, by the construction of the proof path, there is an R-reduction node above D labeled by Ps. Let C be the clause which marks the arc Ps, then by definition $C \varepsilon \mathbf{R}$, $\neg Ps \varepsilon C$, and C is an EN-clause. By performing EN-resolution between C and D on the literal Ps, a new clause will be produced which does not contain Ps. The same procedure can be repeated until all non-equality positive literals in D are eliminated, and an EN-clause D' will be produced which can be used to replace D.

By repeating the above procedure to all the non EN-clauses in **R** (except C_2), eventually all of them (including C_1) will be replaced by EN-clauses. Then by Case 1, we can successfully shrink the tree. Note that we do not need to worry that the literal $\neg L$ will disappear from C'_1, since L does not appear in any of the previous nodes in **R**.

HANDLING FUNCTION DEFINITIONS THROUGH INNERMOST SUPERPOSITION AND REWRITING

Laurent Fribourg

L.I.T.P.- 2, Place Jussieu 75005 Paris - France

Abstract

This paper presents the operating principles of SLOG, a logic interpreter of equational clauses (Horn clauses where the only predicate is '='). SLOG is based on an oriented form of paramodulation called superposition. Superposition is a complete inference rule for first-order logic with equality. SLOG uses only a strong restriction of superposition (innermost superposition) which is still complete for a large class of programs. Besides superposition, SLOG uses rewriting which provides eager evaluation and handling of negative knowledge. Rewriting combined with superposition improves terminability and control of equational logic programs.

1. Introduction

In [13], we have described the operational semantics of a logic programming language with equality. The language is made of equational clauses, i.e. Horn clauses where the only predicate is equality. The other predicates Q are viewed as boolean functions and are written Q=*true*. A program is a finite set of equational clauses. The computation process is not based on resolution as in Prolog, but on clausal superposition. Clausal superposition is an oriented form of replacement of an equal by an equal. As such, it is far more time and space consuming than resolution, since unification applies not only to the goal literals but to all the subterms of these literals. To be competitive with Prolog, an interpreter of equational clauses must then incorporate important strategy refinements.

In this paper, we present the operating principles of SLOG, an efficient implemented interpreter of the equational clauses language. SLOG is based on a strong restriction of superposition, called innermost superposition, which applies only if the matched subterm contains itself no matchable proper subterm. SLOG solves a goal formula, following a linear strategy. For each subgoal, innermost superposition is performed at only one selected subterm occurrence.

The procedure is not complete in general. However, we give sufficient conditions on programs, often satisfied in practice, which ensure completeness.

In addition to the equational clauses, a specific set of rewrite rules will be included within each program. Rewrite rules are inductive consequences of the program. The superposition process is then followed by a rewriting process which simplifies subgoal formulas and thus reduces the store memory space.

Furthermore, rewrite rules allow the statement of negative information. These negative statements, together with the built-in strategies, allow the treatment of logic programming non-termination problems in a natural, declarative way.

2. Superposition logic programs

Originally, superposition is an operation used in the Knuth-Bendix completion procedure, which applies to two oriented equations (rewrite rules) [22]. The *clausal superposition* is an extension of superposition to conditional equations and can be used as a computation rule [13]. Clausal superposition is decomposed into two parts:

definite-superposition and *goal-superposition*. In the equational case, goal-superposition can be viewed as the *narrowing* inference rule (see [12] [18] [24] [34]). The computational use of narrowing and its links with Prolog have been independently investigated in [9] [11] [15] (see also [8] [35] for a simulation of narrowing by resolution over decomposed expressions).
In this paper, we pursue the approach developed in [13]. In this section, we recall some basic definitions of [13] and further introduce optimized strategies.

2.1 Equational clauses
In [13], we have proposed a formalism of so-called (Horn) equational clauses, which are (Horn) clauses, where the only predicate symbol is '='. Originally, the functional signature Σ was unsorted. Following [15], we extend our definitions to the case of a many-sorted signature. One has a set of sorts and a set Σ of function symbols, called *signature*. Each function symbol has a *rank*, denoted $s_1 \times \ldots \times s_k \to s$, consisting of the string $s_1 \ldots s_k$ of the argument-sorts followed by the value-sort s.

definition
An *equational clause* is a first-order logic (with equality) formula of the form $L_1=R_1,\ldots,L_m=R_m$ <- $M_1=N_1,\ldots,M_n=N_n$,
where L_i and R_i (resp. M_j and N_j) are terms of same sort, for all $1 \le i \le m$ (resp. $1 \le j \le n$).

We have the distinguished sort *boolean*, and distinguished constants *true* and *false* of sort *boolean*. Throughout the paper, $bool_i$ denotes a term which is either *true* or *false*. The expressions 'boolean term' and 'boolean function' stand for 'term of sort *boolean*' and 'function symbol of value-sort *boolean*' respectively.
In the formalism of equational clauses, predicates Q (distinct from '=') are viewed as boolean functions : an atom $Q(M_1,\ldots,M_k)$ is written $Q(M_1,\ldots,M_k)=$*true*, whereas $\sim Q(M_1,\ldots,M_k)$ is written $Q(M_1,\ldots,M_k)=$*false*.

definition
A *boolean-body equational clause* C is an equational clause of the form $L_1=R_1,\ldots,L_m=R_m$ <- $Q_1=bool_1,\ldots,Q_n=bool_n$,
where R_i is a term (for all $1 \le i \le n$), Q_j is a boolean term, and $bool_j$ is either *true* or *false* (for all $1 \le j \le n$).
The L_i's, R_i's and Q_j's are respectively called the *definite left-hand sides*, *definite right-hand sides* and *condition-terms* of C.

In the following, for convenience sake, we consider only boolean-body equational clauses. Such a restriction does not reduce the expressive power of the language. Actually, in order to express as a condition literal that two terms M and N of sort s (distinct from *true* and *false*) are equal, we use a new equality symbol E_s for each sort s, and write $E_s(M,N)=$*true*. We show in § 2.2.3 that such a formalism does not reduce the deduction power of the interpreter.

definition
A *goal boolean-body equational clause* is a boolean-body equational clause of the form <- $Q_1=bool_1,\ldots,Q_n=bool_n$.

definition
A *definite boolean-body clause* C is a boolean-body equational clause of the form :
L=R <- $Q_1=bool_1,\ldots,Q_n=bool_n$.
A variable which belongs to a condition-term or right-hand side of C, but not to the

left-hand side is called an *extra-variable* of C.

definition

A *boolean-body equational program* P is a finite set of boolean-body equational definite clauses.

Henceforth, the terms 'clause' and 'program' are respectively used instead of 'boolean-body equational clause' and 'boolean-body equational program'.

2.2 Inference rules

2.2.1 Strict goal-superposition

In this paper, we focus on a special case of clausal superposition, called *strict goal superposition*.

definition

Let G be the goal <- $Q_1=bool_1,...,Q_n=bool_n$, and let C be the definite clause $L=R$ <- $Q'_1=bool'_1,...,Q'_m=bool'_m$ of a program P.

Then G' is a *strict goal-superposant* of C into G at occurrence o ,using the most general unifier (mgu) σ ,iff

Q_1 has a non-variable subterm M at occurrence o unifiable with L, by mgu σ ($M\sigma = L\sigma$) and G' is the goal :

<-$(Q'_1=bool'_1,...,Q'_m=bool'_m,Q_1[o\leftarrow R]=bool_1,Q_2=bool_2,...,Q_n=bool_n)\sigma$.

The literal $Q_1=bool_1$ of G is the *superposed literal*, and the literal $Q_1\sigma[o\leftarrow R]=bool_1$ of G' is the *superposant literal*.

Remarks

1. The difference between general and strict goal-superposition is that, in strict goal-superposition, the replaced term M cannot be a variable.
2. With respect to the definition given in [13], the superposant literal $Q_1[o\leftarrow R]$ is no longer the leftmost literal of the new goal, but comes after the C body literals. This modification has been introduced for sake of computation efficiency. Actually, in the superposition definition, the order of the superposant literals are significant only because the superposed literal is assigned to be leftmost. This assignation corresponds to Prolog strategy with respect to general SLD-strategy. An SLD-like strategy selecting an arbitrary literal for superposition, instead of the leftmost one, would not change the completeness results given hereafter.

2.2.2 Trivial removal

definition

The *trivial removal* is the inference rule which removes all trivial equation of the form *true=true* or *false=false* from all goal.

Given a goal G, the goal G' obtained from G by trivial removal, is called the *minimal form* of G.

This inference rule is systematically performed. When trivial removal follows a superposition of a clause C into G, it simulates the process of resolution of C against G.

example

C: member(x, y.L)=*true* <- member(x, L)=*true*   G: <- member(2, 1.L)=*true*

The superposition of C into G gives <- (member(2, L)=*true*, *true*=*true*) and then by trivial removal, <- member(2, L)=*true* .

2.2.3 Reflecting

In [13], we introduced an additional rule called reflecting which consists of removing from a goal G the leftmost literal M=N if M and N were unifiable. In our framework, there are two cases depending on whether or not M and N are distinct from *true* and *false*. If both M and N are distinct from *true* and *false*, then M=N is written E_s(M,N)=*true*; then reflecting is simulated by superposition of the clause E_s(x,x)=*true* <- into G, which gives *true*=*true*, and by trivial removal. If one of the terms M and N is *true* or *false*, then reflecting applies if one of these terms, say M, is a variable and N is *true* or *false*. Stricly speaking, we should keep the reflecting rule to treat this case. Actually, in the following, such a case never happens because, we assume that:

1) definite clauses contain no boolean extra-variable,
2) the initial goal G contains no boolean variable.

It is then easy to see that goal-superposants derived from G cannot contain any boolean variable.

Thus, in our framework, we can get rid of the reflecting rule without loss of deduction power, provided the incorporation of the clauses $E_s(x,x)$=*true* <- into the programs. This incorporation is implicit in the following.

2.3 Superposition completeness results

In [13], we stated the completeness of goal-superposition with definite-superposition. However, the completeness result of strict superposition (no superposition into variables) was only conjectured.

The completeness of strict-goal superposition (without definite superposition) has been recently proved by Hussmann in the case where *P*, viewed as a conditional rewriting system, is *confluent* and sought answer-substitutions are under *normal form* [19] (see also [36] for a full discussion in the unit case).

To attempt to make a program *P* confluent, we can use a conditional Knuth-Bendix algorithm which add conditional critical pairs by means of *strict definite superposition* (see [21]). We then retrieve the original strategy of (strict) superposition described in [13]. An interesting alternative to deal with the *P*-confluency problem (and more generally with automated deduction) consists in using the original Knuth-Bendix algorithm following a positive unit strategy, rather than superposition input strategy (see [27]).

Unfortunately, the brute force of (strict) goal-superposition often leads to unacceptable overcomputation. As an illutration, let us consider the following program P_{NL} inspired from a Prolog program for Natural Language (see [29]).

noun(x,"MAN(x)")=man <- ; 'man' is the noun associated with the predicate MAN
noun(x,"WOMAN(x)")=woman <- ; 'woman' is the noun associated with the predicate WOMAN
propernoun("JOHN")=John <- ; 'john' is the propernoun associated with the constant JOHN
tv(x,y,"LOVES(x,y)")=loves <- ; 'loves' is the transitive verb associated with the predicate LOVES
intv(x,"LIVES(x)")=lives <- ; 'lives' is the intransitive verb associated with the predicate LIVES
det(x,P1,P2,"all x / P1 ==> P2")=every <- ; 'every' is the determinant associated with the expression "all / "

```
det(x,P1,P2,"exists x / P1 & P2")=a <-        ; 'a' is the determinant associated with
                                                the expression "exists / "
np(x,P1,P).L=det(x,P1,P2,P).noun(x,P2).L <-   ; the composition of a determinant
                                                with a noun is a noun-phrase
np(x,P,P).L=propernoun(x).L <-                ; a propernoun is a noun-phrase
vp(x,P).L=tv(x,y,P1).np(y,P1,P).L <-          ; the composition of a transitive verb
                                                with a noun-phrase is a verb-phrase
vp(x,P).L=intv(x,P).L <-                      ; an intransitive verb is a verb-phrase
s(P).L=np(x,P1,P).vp(x,P1).L <-               ; the composition of a noun-phrase
                                                with a verb-phrase is a sentence
```

Consider the goal G_{NL}: <- *E*(s(z).[],every.man.loves.a.woman.[])=*true*. With brute goal-superposition strategy, the same answer {z := "all x/ MAN(x) ==> exists y/ WOMAN(y) & LOVES(x,y)"} is generated 896 times.

Remark

Because of the equational formalism, the program P_{NL} straightaway has the structure of Definite Clause Grammars, and does not need any transformation preprocessing as in Prolog (see [29]).

In the following section, we define restrictive strategies for applying goal-superposition.

2.4 Innermost strategies

In keeping with [17], we assume the signature Σ to be partitioned as a set *C* of elements called *constructors* and a set *D* of elements called *defined operators*.
GC is the set of ground terms formed solely from constructors, and *GCV* is the set of terms formed solely from constructors and variables.
The constants *true* and *false* are the only terms of value-sort *boolean* in *GC*.
A *GC*-substitution (resp. *GCV*-substitution) is a substitution $\{x_j := M_j\}$, where the M_j's are member of *GC* (resp. *GCV*).

definitions

A term M is *innermost* iff M is of the form $f(M_1,\dots,M_k)$, where f is a defined operator and all the M_i's are only formed of constructors and variables.
A program *P* is *lhs-innermost* iff all the left-hand sides of the *P*-clauses are innermost terms.

An *innermost occurrence* of a goal G is the occurrence of an innermost term in G.
An *innermost superposition* is a strict-goal superposition at an innermost occurrence.
Innermost superposition yields *innermost superposants*.
Given an innermost occurrence o in a goal G, the *innermost superposition class* of G in *P* at occurrence o is the set of all the (innermost) superposants of the *P* clauses into G at occurrence o.

example: sum, product and less-than-or-equal functions on natural numbers

C	0:	$\rightarrow$ *integer*
	s:	*integer* $\rightarrow$ *integer*
	true:	$\rightarrow$ *boolean*
	false:	$\rightarrow$ *boolean*
D	+:	*integer* $\times$ *integer* $\rightarrow$ *integer*
	$*$:	*integer* $\times$ *integer* $\rightarrow$ *integer*
	le:	*integer* $\times$ *integer* $\rightarrow$ *boolean*

P	x*0=0 <-	x+0=x <-	le(0,x)=*true* <-
	x*s(y)=x*y+x <-	x+s(y)=s(x+y) <-	le(s(x),s(y))=le(x,y) <-

Consider the goal G: <- le(w+(x+y),y*x+z)=*true*. There are two innermost superposition classes of *P* in G; the first one corresponds to the subterm x+y, the second one to the subterm y*x.
The first class is {<- le(w+x,0*x+z)=*true*, <- le(w+s(x+y'),s(y')*x+z)=*true* }
The second class is {<- le(w+(0+y),0+z)=*true*, <- le(w+(s(x')+y),(y*x'+y)+z))=*true*}.

An *innermost-occurrence selection rule* is a function φ from the set of terms to the set of occurrences such that the value of the function for a term M is always an innermost occurrence, called the *φ-occurrence* (the *leftmost-innermost* rule is the rule which selects the leftmost innermost occurrence of M).
This function extends to the set of goals in the following way:
for any goal G: <- M_1=*$bool_1$*, ... , M_n=*$bool_n$*, φ(G) is $\varphi(M_1)$.
The innermost superposition class of G at occurrence φ(G) is called the φ-class.
An innermost superposition (resp. innermost superposant) into a goal G at occurrence φ(G) is called a φ-superposition (resp. φ-superposant) of G.

definition

An **S**-derivation of G' from *P* ∪ {G} via φ consists of a finite sequence $G_0, G_1, \ldots, G_n$ of goals and a sequence $\sigma_1, \sigma_2, \ldots, \sigma_n$ of mgu's such that :

1) G_0 is the minimal form of G, and G_n is G'
2) for all i, $1 \le i \le n$, G_i is the minimal form of the φ-superposant of a *P*-clause into G_{i-1}.

Compared with the superposition procedure described in [13] , **S**-derivation introduces two restrictions :

1. *Linear strategy* : for all i $(1 \le i \le n)$, G_i is derived from G_{i-1},
2. *One-innermost class restriction* : only the φ-class of superposition is generated.

The first restriction is natural, as far as no definite-superposition is performed. Our interest in the second restriction originates from a complete narrowing restriction described in [14]. We subsequently learned that a similar restriction had been investigated in [8]. The results of the two following sections can be viewed as an extension of the completeness results of [8] to the general case of conditional equational theories. The innermost restriction is also used in [25], but the completeness question is not examined.

definitions

An **S**-refutation of *P* ∪ {G} is an **S**-derivation of the empty clause from *P* ∪ {G}.
An **S**-computed answer of *P* ∪ {G} is the substitution obtained by restricting the composition of $\sigma_1\sigma_2\ldots\sigma_n$ to the variables of G, where $\sigma_1, \sigma_2, \ldots, \sigma_n$ is the mgu sequence of the substitutions used in an **S**-refutation of *P* ∪ {G}.

Since general superposition (as well as trivial removal) is sound, the **S**-derivation is sound, we have:

Theorem 1 (soundness)

Let *P* be a program, G: <- M_1=*$bool_1$*,...,M_n=*$bool_n$* a goal, and ν an **S**-computed answer of *P* ∪ {G}. Then, for all i $(1 \le i \le n)$, $P \models_E M_i\nu$=*$bool_i$* .

3. Completeness of φ-superposition

In the case where P is made of unconditional equations, we have shown that innermost superposition (actually unconditional goal-superposition followed by normalization, i.e. narrowing) is complete under certain hypotheses [14]. This basically requires the fact that P is a canonical rewriting system and that all ground innermost term is reducible. We now extend the completeness results in the framework of logic programs.

3.1 Background

Let us recall some definitions of Conditional Rewriting (full definitions are given in [20]; note however that, as in [19], the constraints of [20] over the right-hand side and conditions variables are removed).

Let P be a program. We use the notation -->_P for the *reduction* via P. The *rewriting* relation via P, denoted *-->_P, is the reflexive-transitive closure of -->_P.

The *reduction* relation via P, is the finest relation closed by substitution and replacement, and containing the set of directed equations $L\sigma=R\sigma$, where $L=R$ <- $Q_1=bool_1$, ..., $Q_n=bool_n$ is a P-clause, and $Q_i\sigma \text{ *-->}_P\, bool_i$ $(1 \le i \le n)$.

P is *ground-confluent* iff for all ground terms M_1, M_2 and M_3, $M_1 \text{ *-->}_P M_2$ and $M_1 \text{ *-->}_P M_3$ implies there is some M_4 such that $M_2 \text{ *-->}_P M_4$ and $M_3 \text{ *-->}_P M_4$.

M is *P-reducible* if $M \text{ -->}_P N$, for some term N; otherwise, M is *P-irreducible* or in *P-normal form*. M is a *rewrite-form* of N via P iff $M \text{ *-->}_P N$. N is a *P-normal form* of M iff $M \text{ *-->}_P N$ and N is in P-normal form.

P is *ground-noetherian* (resp. noetherian) iff for no ground term M (resp. no term M) is there an infinite chain of reductions issuing from M. In a ground-noetherian program P, any ground term M has a (not necessarily unique) normal form, denoted M↓. Given a substitution σ: $\{x_j := M_j\}$, the P-normal form of σ, denoted $\sigma\downarrow$, is the substitution $\{x_j := M_j\downarrow\}$. Given a goal G <- $Q_1=bool_1,\dots,Q_n=bool_n$, the *P-normal form* of G, denoted G↓, is the goal <- $Q_1\downarrow=bool_1,\dots,Q_n\downarrow=bool_n$.

P is *ground-canonical* iff P is ground-confluent and ground-noetherian.

The expression ' $P \models_E C$ ' will be used to indicate that C is a logical consequence of P and the equality axioms.

In a ground-confluent program P, we have, for all ground terms M and N:

$P \models_E M=N$ iff $M \text{ *-->}_P K$ and $N \text{ *-->}_P K$, for some ground term K (*property 3.1.1*).

We introduce the following notion of *innermost reduction*.

We use the notation -i->_P for the innermost reduction via P. The *innermost rewriting* via P, denoted *-i->_P, is the reflexive-transitive closure of -i->_P.

The *innermost-reduction* relation associated with P, is the finest relation closed by *GCV*-substitution and replacement, and containing the set of directed equations $L\sigma=R\sigma$, where σ is a *GCV*-substitution and L=R is the head of a P-clause L=R <- $Q_1=bool_1$, ..., $Q_n=bool_n$ such that $Q_i\sigma \text{ *-i->}_P\, bool_i$ (for all $1 \le i \le n$).

An innermost-normal form of a term M via P is a term N issued from M by innermost-rewriting such that no innermost-reduction applies.

We call *φ-reduction* an innermost reduction which replaces a subterm located at a φ-occurrence.

3.2 Properties of lhs-innermost programs

In the following, we assume that programs P are lhs-innermost. We have then the easy properties:

property 3.2.1: any term of *GC* is P-irreducible.

property 3.2.2: any computed answer is a *GCV*-substitution.

Let us introduce the following mapping CS_P of Herbrand interpretations (i.e. set of ground equations, in our case):

$CS_P(J) = \{ L\sigma=R\sigma \in B(P) /$ ($L=R$ <- $Q_1=bool_1,\ldots,Q_q=bool_q$) is a *P*-clause,
σ is a *GC*-substitution such that $Q_i\sigma$ $*\text{-->}_J$ $bool_i$, for any i ($1 \leq i \leq q$) $\}$

As usual, the mapping CS_P^n is defined by : $CS_P^0(J) = J$, $CS_P^{n+1}(J) = CS_P(CS_P^n(J))$
We shall use CS^n for $CS_P^n(\phi)$, and *CW* for $\cup_{i=0}^{\infty} CS_P^i(\phi)$.
Since L is innermost and σ is a *GC*-substitution, the left-hand sides $L\sigma$ of CS^n are innermost-terms.
Consider the set P_{GC} of all the *GC*-instances of the *P*-clauses. By the least-fixpoint theory, it can be seen that, for any ground terms M and N, M $*\text{-->}_{CW}$ N iff M $*\text{-->}_{P_{GC}}$ N (for detailed proofs of similar equivalences in the general reduction framework, see [20] [32]). Furthermore, it can be easily seen that M $*\text{-->}_{P_{GC}}$ N iff M $*\text{-i->}_P$ N. So we have:

property 3.2.3: For all ground terms M and N, M $*\text{-i->}_P$ N iff M $*\text{-->}_{CW}$ N .

3.3 Completeness study

Given an lhs-innermost program *P* and a goal G, we are interested, in our approach, by finding not all the answers for G, but only the answers made of constructors (actually, by property 3.2.2, all **S**-computed answer is a *GCV*-substitution). In the following, we deal with the problem of *GC-completeness*.

definition

Let *P* be a (lhs-innermost) program and G: <- $M_1=bool_1$, ... , $M_n=bool_n$ a goal.
S-derivation is *GC-complete* for $P \cup \{G\}$ iff:
for any *GC*-substitution ϑ such that $P \models_E M_i\vartheta=bool_i$ (for all i, $1 \leq i \leq n$), there is an **S**-computed answer ν of $P \cup \{G\}$ and a substitution ρ such that $\nu\rho$ is ϑ.
S-derivation is *GC-complete* for *P* iff **S**-derivation is *GC*-complete for $P \cup \{G\}$, for any goal G.

The following lemma states that in a sequence of innermost-reductions, the order of reductions is irrelevant and then can follow the φ-rule.

lemma 3.3.1

Let M be a ground term and N a ground term of *GC*. Then M $*\text{-->}_{CS^n}$ N iff there is a sequence of φ-reductions from M to N via CS^n.

Proof: (<=) trivial.
(=>) Let us prove that, if there exists a sequence of p reductions from M to N via CS^n,then there exists a sequence of φ-reductions from M to N. The proof is by induction on p.
Base case (p=0): trivial.
Suppose the result holds for q ($0 \leq q \leq p-1$).
Consider a sequence of p reductions $\rho_1,\ldots,\rho_p$ via CS^n from M to N; let $M_1,\ldots,M_p$ be the successive intermediate rewrite-forms (M_p is N), and let T be the subterm of M at occurrence φ(M). Since the rewriting is innermost, the term T remains within the successive rewrite-forms M_i until the step r where T itself is reduced (such a reduction

ultimately occurs, since the final form contains no defined operator). Clearly, the reduction ρ_r is independent from the sequence $\rho_1,\ldots,\rho_{r-1}$, and $\rho_r\rho_1,\ldots,\rho_{r-1}$ is still a reduction sequence from M to M_r. Let M'_1 be the term obtained from M by the φ-reduction ρ_r. M'_1 is rewritten into N via the sequence $\rho_1\ldots\rho_{r-1}\rho_{r+1}\ldots\rho_p$ of p-1 reductions, so, by induction hypothesis, there is a sequence S of φ-reductions from M'_1 to N. By combining ρ_r with S, we obtain the desired φ-reductions sequence from M to N. ▪

lemma 3.3.2 (ground completeness)

Let *P* be an lhs-innermost program, G': <- $M'_1=bool'_1$, ..., $M'_p=bool'_p$ a ground goal, and φ' an innermost-occurrence selection rule.
If, for all i ($1\le i\le p$), M'_i *-i->$_P$ $bool'_i$, then there is an S-refutation via φ' of G' and a set of *GC*-instances of *P*-clauses.

Proof: Let us suppose that M'_i *-i->$_P$ $bool'_i$, for all $1\le i\le p$; then M'_i *-->$_{CW}$ $bool'_i$ (by property 3.2.3). Hence there exists an integer n such that M'_i *-->$_{CS^n}$ $bool'_i$. So, by lemma 3.3.1, there is a sequence S'_i of φ-reductions via CS^n from M'_i to $bool'_i$. Let us prove that there exists an S-refutation of G' and *GC*-instances of *P*-clauses. The proof is by induction on n.
Base case (n=0): M'_i and $bool_i$ are identical ($1\le i\le p$), so there is an S-refutation of G' by trivial removal.
Suppose that the result holds for n-1.
If M'_1 is $bool'_1$ (case I), then by trivial removal, we obtain the goal G' - $\{M'_1=bool'_1\}$. Otherwise (case II), consider the sequence $\{M'_{1,1},\ldots,M'_{1,q}\}$ of the rewrite-forms of M'_1 ($M'_{1,q}$ is $bool'_1$). M'_1 is φ'-reducible via CS^n into $M'_{1,1}$; so there is a subterm T' of M'_1 at occurrence o, a clause C: L=R <- $Q_1=bool_1$, ... , $Q_r=bool_r$ and a *GC*-substitution σ such that o is $\varphi'(M'_1)$, T' is $L\sigma$, $M'_1[o\leftarrow R\sigma]$ is $M'_{1,1}$ and $Q_i\sigma$ *-->$_{CS^{n-1}}$ $bool_i$. Hence there is a φ'-superposant G'_1 of $C\sigma$ into G' such that G'_1 is <- $Q_1\sigma=bool_1$, ... , $Q_r\sigma=bool_r$, $M'_{1,1}=bool'_1$, ... , $M'_p=bool'_p$. Let us consider the subgoal G'': <- $Q_1\sigma=bool_1$, ..., $Q_r\sigma=bool_r$. For all i ($1\le i\le r$),$Q_i\sigma$ *-->$_{CS^{n-1}}$ $bool_i$. Hence, by induction hypothesis, there is an S-refutation Δ of H'' and *GC*-instances of *P*. The φ'-superposition of the *GC*-instance $C\sigma$ into G' followed by the S-refutation Δ of H'' gives an S-derivation of G'_1: <- $M'_{1,1}=bool'_1$, ... , $M'_p=bool'_p$. As this process is iterated, we successively produce ground clauses G'_i whose leftmost literal left-hand side $M'_{1,i}$ are intermediate steps in the production of the normal form $bool'_1$. The process stops at the step q where the leftmost literal of G'_q is the irreducible trivial equation $bool'_1=bool'_1$. Then, trivial removal gives the goal G' - $\{M'_1=bool'_1\}$.
Thus, in all cases, G' - $\{M'_1=bool'_1\}$ is derived. If p = 1, then the empty clause has been generated. Otherwise, the whole process continue, and the literals of G' are one-by-one eliminated until the empty clause is produced. ▪

lemma 3.3.3 (lifting)

Let *P* be an lhs-innermost program, G a goal and φ an innermost-occurrence selection rule. Let G' be an instance of G under a *GC*-substitution ϑ, and C' an instance of a *P*-clause C under a *GC*-substitution σ.
Let φ' be an innermost-occurrence selection defined on goals *GC*-instances by:
$\varphi'(H\eta) = \varphi(H)$, for all goal H and all *GC*-substitution η.
Then, for all φ'-superposant G'_1 of C' into G' using mgu τ, there exists a goal G_1 and a *GC*-substitution ϑ_1 such that G_1 is a φ-superposant of C into G, G'_1 is $G_1\vartheta_1$, and ϑ is $\tau\vartheta_1$.

Proof: G is of the form <- M_1=*bool'*$_1$, ... , M_p=*bool'*$_p$, and C is of the form L=R <- Q_1=*bool*$_1$, ... , Q_r=*bool*$_r$. Since G'_1 is a φ'-superposant of C' into G', there is a subterm T' of $M_1\vartheta$ at occurrence o, such that o is $\varphi'(M_1\vartheta)$, T' is $L\sigma$, and G'_1 is <- $Q_1\sigma$=*bool*$_1$, ..., $Q_r\sigma$=*bool*$_r$, $M_1\vartheta[o\leftarrow R\sigma]$=*bool'*$_1$, ... , $M_p\vartheta$=*bool'*$_p$. Now, T' is the ϑ-instance of a subterm T of M at occurrence o. So we have $T\vartheta = L\sigma$; therefore, T and L are unifiable with mgu $\tau \cup \lambda$, and there is a substitution η such that $\vartheta = \tau\eta$ and $\sigma = \lambda\eta$; since ϑ and σ are *GC*-substitutions, η is also a *GC*-substitution. Since the ϑ-instance of T is the term $L\sigma$ whose head symbol is a defined function, and since ϑ is a *GC*-substitution, the term T cannot be a variable. Furthermore, $\varphi(G)$ is o (by definition of φ'). Hence, there is a φ-superposition of C into G, yielding G_1: <- $Q_1\lambda$=*bool'*$_1$,..., $Q_r\lambda$=*bool'*$_r$, $M_1\tau[o\leftarrow R\lambda]$=*bool*$_1$,...,$M_p\tau$=*bool*$_p$. We have: $G_1\eta = G'_1$, and $\vartheta = \tau\eta$. So η is the expected *GC*-substitution ϑ_1. ▪

Theorem 2

Let *P* be an lhs-innermost program, G: <- M_1=*bool*$_1$, ..., M_p=*bool*$_p$ a goal, and ϑ a *GC*-substitution such that $M_i\vartheta$ *-i->$_P$ *bool*$_i$, for all i (1≤i≤p). Then there is an **S**-computed answer ν of $P \cup \{G\}$, and a substitution ρ such that $\nu\rho$ is ϑ.

Proof: from lemma 3.3.2, there is a ground **S**-derivation $\{G'_1,...,G'_n\}$ of successive rewrite-forms G'_i of G' (G'_n is the empty clause). Now, by applying repeatedly the lifting lemma 3.3.3, we see that all G'_i is a *GC*-instance under substitution ϑ_i of the φ-superposant G_i. Besides, the mgu τ_i (restricted to the variables of G_{i-1}) used in the φ-superposition from G_{i-1} to G_i is such that $\tau_i\vartheta_i$ is ϑ_{i-1} (ϑ_0 denoting ϑ); so $\tau_1...\tau_i\vartheta_i$ is ϑ. Also, whenever G'_i has a trivial equation *bool=bool*, the corresponding literal in G_i must have the form N=*bool*, where N has *bool* as a ϑ_i-instance. Now, N cannot be a variable (see § 2.2.3), and then must be *bool*. Conversely, it is obvious that any equation in G'_i corresponding to a trivial equation in G_i, is trivial. Thus trivial removal always applies simultaneously to G_i and G'_i. The empty clauses G_n and G'_n are simultaneously generated at a step n, and we have: $\tau_1...\tau_n\vartheta_n = \vartheta$. Now, the restriction of $\tau_1...\tau_n$ to the variables of G is the computed answer ν. Therefore, the restriction of ϑ to the variables of G is the expected substitution ρ. ▪

Remark

The program P_{NL} and the goal G_{NL} of §2.3 satisfy theorem 2 hypotheses (provided an appropriate partition of Σ into *C* and *D*). So **S**-derivation gives the expected answer {z := "all x/ MAN(x) ==> exists y/ WOMAN(y) & LOVES(x,y)"}; this answer is generated only once.

definitions

Let *P* be a program and G: <- M_1=*bool*$_1$, ... , M_n=*bool*$_n$ a goal.

P is *innermost-normalizing* for G iff, for all *GC*-substitution ϑ such that $M_i\vartheta$ *-->$_P$ *bool*$_i$ (for all i, 1≤i≤n), $M_i\vartheta$ *-i->$_P$ *bool*$_i$ (for all i, 1≤i≤n).

A program *P* is *well-innermost-reducing* iff, for all ground boolean term M such that M *-->$_P$ *bool*, M *-i->$_P$ *bool*.

In the following, we assume that programs *P*, are not only lhs-innermost but also ground-confluent. (for general confluency sufficient conditions, see [3] [20] [28] [32]; for ground-confluency criteria, see [21] [33]). From property 3.2.1, it easily follows there is no equations between constructors in the theory defined by an lhs-innermost ground-confluent program, i.e., for any ground terms M and N of *GC*, $P \models_E$ M=N iff M and

N are identical. Therefore, by property 3.1.1, we have, for all ground term M: $P \models_E$ M=***bool*** iff M $*\!\!\dashrightarrow_P$ ***bool***. Then, by theorem 2, it easily follows:

Theorem 3

Let *P* be an lhs-innermost ground-confluent program.
S-derivation is *GC*-complete for *P* ∪ {G} iff *P* is innermost-normalizing for G.
S-derivation is *GC*-complete for *P* iff *P* is well-innermost-reducing.

4. Completeness sufficient criteria

Given an lhs-innermost ground-confluent program *P* and a goal G, the problem of **S**-derivation completeness for *P* (resp. for *P* ∪ {G}) is thus equivalent to the problem of knowing whether or not *P* is well-innermost-reducing (resp. innermost-normalizing for G). We claim that, in practice, many programs are lhs-innermost and ground-confluent, or can be transformed into equivalent programs which fullfill these hypotheses. However, programs may not be well-innermost-reducing because function definitions are "incomplete". For instance, consider two defined functions f and g, two constructors 0 and 1, a program *P*: {f(x)=0 <- , g(0)=1 <-} and the goal G: <-*E*(f(g(1)),0)=***true***. There is no **S**-refutation of *P* ∪ {G}, because g is not defined for 1.
We now give sufficient conditions for a ground-canonical program *P* to be well-innermost-reducing. Note that, in case *P* being ground-canonical, *P* is well-innermost-reducing iff, for all ground boolean (distinct from ***bool***) term such that M $*\!\!\dashrightarrow_P$ ***bool***, M is innermost-reducible (i.e. M $\text{-i-}\!\!>_P$ N, for some N).
Given a boolean defined operator f and a program *P*, we say that f is ***non-defined on false*** in *P* iff there is no k-tuple of terms $<M_1,...,M_k>$ such that $P \models_E f(M_1,...,M_k)=$***false***; we say that f is ***first-order*** iff f has no argument of sort ***boolean***.

proposition 4.1

Let *P* be an lhs-innermost ground-canonical program.
P is well-innermost-reducing if one of the following conditions is fulfilled:
(1) all boolean ground term M reducible via *P* is innermost-reducible via *P*
(2) all ground innermost term M is reducible via *P*.
(3) all ground non-boolean innermost term M is reducible via *P*, and all boolean function is first-order and non-defined on ***false*** in *P*.
(4) all boolean ground term M (distinct from ***true***) whose normal form via *P* is ***true***, is innermost-reducible via *P*, and all boolean function is non-defined on ***false*** in *P*.

In practice, many programs are written in keeping with (3) (e.g., see the example of § 2.4). The conditions on boolean functions are in keeping with Prolog predicate definitions by means of Horn clauses. The condition on non-boolean defined functions is the natural adaptation to our framework of a sufficient criterion for the Huet-Hullot principle of definition (see [17], § 2)).

5. Superposition with Rewriting

5.1 Rewriting via inductive consequences

Suppose that *P* is not only ground-confluent but also ground-noetherian (hence ground-canonical). The construction used in the proof of theorem 2, can then be viewed as a process for producing clauses G'_i which are instances of G and are also intermediate steps in the production of G'↓. Now, in the construction, the derivation of G'↓ can be hastened by incorporating a process for rewriting the superposant G_i, at each step i.
From now on, we consider not only definite clauses used in superposition, but also definite clauses used in rewriting. An obvious means to to maintain soundness is to

take a set of logical consequences of P for R. More generally, we can incorporate into R, any clause C which is an inductive consequence of P, in the following sense:

definition

C is an *inductive consequence* of P iff, for any *GC*-substitution σ: $P \models_E C\sigma$.

example: sum on natural numbers

P:	x+0=x <-	R:	x+0=x <-
	x+s(y)=s(x+y) <-		x+s(y)=s(x+y) <-
			0+x=x <-
			s(x)+y=s(x+y) <-

definition

An *SLOG program* Q is a pair $<P,R>$, where P and R are programs such that R is made only of inductive consequences of P.

P and R will be respectively referred to as the *definition program* and the *rewrite system* of Q.

We assume given a rewriting process Π_R associated with R, which maps any goal G:<- $M_1=bool_1,\ldots,M_n=bool_n$, into a goal G':<- $M'_1=bool_1,\ldots,M'_n=bool_n$, such that $M_i \overset{*}{\longrightarrow}_R M'_i$, for all i ($1 \leq i \leq n$). G' is called the Π_R-form of G.
The definition of S-derivation is then extended as follows:

definition

Let Q:$<P,R>$ be an SLOG-program.

An S-derivation of G' from $P \cup \{G\}$ via φ consists of a finite sequence $G_0,G_1,\ldots,G_n$ of goals and a sequence $\sigma_1,\sigma_2,\ldots,\sigma_n$ of mgu's such that :

1) G_0 is the minimal form of the Π_R-form of G, and G_n is G'

2) for all i, $1 \leq i \leq n$, G_i is the minimal form of the Π_R-form of a φ-superposant of a P-clause into G_{i-1}.

Note that Rewriting affects all the literals of the goal and is not necessarily innermost, whereas Superposition only applies to the leftmost literal and is innermost.

The soundness theorem 1 becomes:

Theorem 4 (soundness)

Let Q:$<P,R>$ be an SLOG-program, G: <- $M_1=bool_1,\ldots,M_n=bool_n$ a goal, and ν an S-computed answer of $Q \cup \{G\}$.

Then, for any *GC*-substitution ρ and any i ($1 \leq i \leq n$), $P \models_E M_i\nu\rho=bool_i$.

Given an SLOG-program Q:$<P,R>$ and a goal G, we say that S-derivation is *GC-complete* for Q (resp. for $Q \cup \{G\}$) iff it is *GC*-complete for P (resp. *GC*-complete for $P \cup \{G\}$).

In the following, we consider SLOG-programs Q:$<P,R>$ such that P is lhs-innermost and ground-canonical, and $P \cup R$ is noetherian (for sufficient criteria for the noetherian property, see [10] [23]). We have the new lifting lemma:

lemma 5.1

Let Q:$<P,R>$ be an SLOG-program, such that P is lhs-innermost,ground-canonical and well-innermost-reducing, and $P \cup R$ is noetherian.

Let G: <- $M_1=\textit{bool'}_1,\ldots,M_n=\textit{bool'}_n$ be a goal. Let ϑ be a *GC*-substitution such that $M_i\vartheta$ *-i->$_P$ *bool'*$_i$, for all i ($1\le i\le n$). Let G' be the ground instance of G under ϑ, and H the Π_R-form of G.

There exists a clause H'': <- $N''_1=\textit{bool'}_1,\ldots,N''_n=\textit{bool'}_n$ such that:

a) H'' is a ground instance of H under a *GC*-substitution,

b) H'' is a rewrite-form of G' via $P \cup R$,

c) N''_i *-i->$_P$ *bool'*$_i$, for all i ($1\le i\le n$).

Proof: Since G' is an instance of G, all the reductions via *R* which take G to H apply to G' and give a rewritten clause H' which is an instance of H under a substitution, say σ. Let H'' be the instance of H under the $P\cup R$-normal substitution $\sigma\downarrow$ of σ. It can be seen that H'' is also the result of applying a finite sequence of reductions to H' via $P\cup R$, and as such can be thought as a further rewrite-form of G' via $P\cup R$, which proves b). N''_i is obtained from M'_i through rewriting via $P\cup R$ ($1\le i\le n$). Since *bool'*$_i$ is obtained from M'_i through rewriting via *P*, we have, for all i: $P\cup R \models_E N''_i=\textit{bool'}_i$. Since *R* is a set of inductive consequences of *P*, we have: $P \models_E N''_i=\textit{bool'}_i$. Since *P* is ground-confluent, we have: N''_i *-->$_P$ *bool'*$_i$; hence, since *P* is well-innermost-reducing, N''_i *-i->$_P$ *bool'*$_i$, for all i ($1\le i\le n$), which proves c) . Furthermore, $\sigma\downarrow$ is a *GC*-substitution (otherwise, there would be a condition-term N''_j of H'' containing a *P*-irreducible innermost term T and the innermost-normal form via *P*, *bool'*$_j$, would still contain T as a subterm). This proves a).

By combining the constructions used in the proofs of theorem 2 and lemma 5.1, and by ground-confluency, we have:

Theorem 5

Let *Q*:<*P*,*R*> be an SLOG-program such that *P* is lhs-innermost, ground canonical and well-innermost-reducing, and $P\cup R$ is noetherian.
Then **S**-derivation (with rewriting) is *GC*-complete for *Q*.

5.2 Rewriting via CWA-valid clauses

In logic data bases and classic logic programming, negative information can be derived from positive information, using the so-called principle of Closed World Assumption (see [31]). We are going to formalize such a notion in our framework.

definition

A ***boolean clause*** is a clause of the form C: L=R <- $Q_1=\textit{bool}_1,\ldots,Q_n=\textit{bool}_n$, where L and R are boolean terms.

definition

Given a program *Q*: <*P*,*R*>, a boolean clause C: $f(M_1,\ldots,M_k)$=R <- $Q_1=\textit{bool}_1,\ldots, Q_n=\textit{bool}_n$ satisfies the *Closed World Assumption* for *Q* (or is *CWA-valid* for *Q*) iff f is non-defined on *false* in *P*, and either:

1. R is *false*, and for any *GC*-substitution σ,
$\sim(Q \models_E (f(M_1\sigma,\ldots,M_k\sigma)=\textit{true} \leftarrow Q_1\sigma=\textit{bool}_1,\ldots, Q_n\sigma=\textit{bool}_n))$, or
2. R is neither *true* nor *false*, and for any *GC*-substitution σ,
$Q \models_E (f(M_1\sigma,\ldots,M_k\sigma)=\textit{true} \leftarrow R\sigma=\textit{true}, Q_1\sigma=\textit{bool}_1,\ldots, Q_n\sigma=\textit{bool}_n)$ and
$Q \models_E (R\sigma=\textit{true} \leftarrow f(M_1\sigma,\ldots,M_k\sigma)=\textit{true}, Q_1\sigma=\textit{bool}_1,\ldots,Q_n\sigma=\textit{bool}_n)$.

From now on, given an SLOG-program *Q*:<*P*,*R*>, the rewrite part *R* may contain not only inductive consequences of *P*, but also CWA-valid clauses.
The Completeness Theorem 5 still holds (proof is unchanged). The Soundness Theorem 4

is modified as follows:

Theorem 6 (soundness)

Let Q:<P,R> be an SLOG-program, G: <- M_1=*bool*$_1$,...,M_n=*bool*$_n$ a goal, and ν an S-computed answer of $Q\cup\{G\}$. Then, for any *GC*-substitution ρ and any i ($1\leq i\leq n$),

- $P \models_E M_i\nu\rho$=*true*, if *bool*$_i$ is *true*.
- ~($P \models_E M_i\nu\rho$=*true*), if *bool*$_i$ is *false*.

6. Applications of Rewriting

The purpose of incorporating Rewriting into S-derivation is two-fold: it is first used to implement eager evaluation, and, second as a means of detecting failure.

Rewriting provides eager evaluation by performing several (not necessarily innermost) superpositions in one step. In contrast with Superposition, Rewriting replaces goals by their Π_R-forms and does not store the intermediate rewrite-forms, thus gaining memory space and reducing the search tree.

Rewriting is a means of detecting failure since any rewriting of a subgoal M=*true* (resp. M=*false*) as the contradictory literal *false=true* (resp. *true=false*) leads to rejection of the whole goal. Actually, in pure S-derivation, the goal will be rejected only if the contradictory subgoal is the leftmost one (in that case, no further superposition applies). In order to systematically perform rejection, we extend the definition of the minimal form as follows:

definition

The *minimal form* of a goal G is either:

- *true=false*, if G contains an equation *true=false* or *false=true*, or
- the goal obtained from G by trivial removal, otherwise.

Clearly, the Soundness theorem 6 and Completeness theorem 5 are unchanged.

Failure detection is useful for treating non-termination cases. As pointed out in [13], equational programs may infinitely loop, even if their counterparts in Prolog terminate (see the sum example, § 2.3 [13]). The essential reason is that Prolog assumes that two non-unifiable terms, such as 0 and s(x+y), are unequal, whereas the superposition process may apply (using x+0=x <-, for instance) and attempt to yield two unifiable terms. A natural remedy consists of adding negative information, such as the CWA-valid clause C: E_{int}(0,s(x))=*false* <-, in the rewrite system of the program. Rewriting a goal G then replaces a literal such as E_{int}(0,s(x+y))=*true* by *false=true*, which leads to failure. More generally, consider the set *CR* of the following clauses:

$E_s(c(x_1,\ldots,x_k),d(y_1,\ldots,y_l))$=*false* <- ,

for each k-ary constructor c (of value-sort *s*) and each *l*-ary constructor d (of value-sort *s*) distinct from c,

$E_s(c(x),c(y))=E_{s1}(x,y)$ <-

for each 1-ary constructor c of rank $s1 \rightarrow s$.

$E_s(c(x_1,\ldots,x_k),c(y_1,\ldots,y_k))$=ANDk$(E_{s1}(x_1,y_1),\ldots,E_{sk}(x_k,y_k))$ <- ,

for each k-ary constructor c ($k\geq 2$) of rank $s1 \times\ldots\times sk \rightarrow s$

where the ANDn's are operators of rank *bool* ×...× *bool* → *bool* which are themselves defined by:

ANDn$(x_1,\ldots,x_{i-1},$*true*$,x_{i+1},\ldots,x_n)$=ANDn-1$(x_1,\ldots,x_{i-1},x_{i+1},\ldots,x_n)$ <- , for all integer n>2 and all i, $1 \le i \le n$

AND2(*true*,x)=x <-
AND2(x,*true*)=x <-
ANDn($x_1,\ldots,x_{i-1}$,*false*,$x_{i+1},\ldots,x_n$)=*false* <- ,

for all integer n>1 and all i, $1 \le i \le n$

In the following, we assume that ANDn clauses are included in the the definition program and rewrite system of all SLOG-programs. Suppose now that *CR* is included in the rewrite system of an SLOG-program <*P*,*R*>. It can be seen that *CR* satisfies the CWA-principle provided that, for any sort s, E_s(x,x)=*true* <- is the only clause in *P* whose left-hand side begins by E_s. Furthermore, rewriting via *CR* simulates the application of two inference rules which are useful for failure detection: ***rejection*** and ***decomposition***. The rejection rule rejects any goal containing an equation of the form $E_s(c(M_1,\ldots,M_k),d(N_1,\ldots,N_l))$=*true*, where c and d are distinct constructors; the decomposition rule decomposes any subgoal $E_s(c(M_1,\ldots,M_k),c(N_1,\ldots,N_k))$=*true* into $E_{s1}(M_1,N_1)$=*true*,...,$E_{sk}(M_k,N_k)$=*true*, where c is a constructor . Rejection and decomposition are derived from rules introduced by Huet and Hullot in their modified Knuth-Bendix algorithm [17] (decomposition is also implemented in PROLOG II, under the name of *splitting* [7]).

These inference rules allow treatment not only of some looping cases inherent in SLOG (infinite failure superposition branch), but also of some looping cases inherent in Prolog (infinite failure resolution branch). For example, let us consider the append3 problem given in [26]. The classical relation append is defined by the Prolog program:

```
append([], X, X) <-
append(X.Y, Z, X.W) <- append(Y, Z, W)
```

The goal <- append(1.V, W, X), append(X, Y, 2.Z)
leads to an infinite loop, whatever the order of literals and clauses.

Consider now the problem in SLOG. The constructors are the natural numbers and the operator '.' , the only defined operator is append, and the program <*P*,*R*> is defined by:

P: append([], X)=X <-
append(X.Y, Z)=X.append(Y, Z) <-

R: append([], X)=X <-
append(X.Y, Z)=X.append(Y, Z) <-

The goal <- E_{list}(append(append(1.V, W), Y), 2.Z)=*true* is rewritten via *R* as the goal <- E_{list}(1.(append(append(V, W), Y), 2.Z)=*true* which is decomposed into <- E_{int}(1,2)=*true*, E_{list}(append(append(V, W),Y), Z)=*true*, then rejected. Note that rewriting via *R* performs an eager evaluation which is essential to the failure detection.

The set *CR* is a particular case of negative knowledge. In [2], it is shown that negative knowledge generally improves the terminability of programs. This negative knowledge is handled naturally through Rewriting. As an illustration, let us consider the following Prolog program *Above* borrowed from [2]:

```
on(a,b) <-
on(b.c) <-
above(X,Y) <- on(X,Y).
above(X,Y) <- above(X,Z), on(Z,Y).
```

The goals <- above(a,a) and <- above(c,a) lead to an infinite loop. As pointed out in [2], the negative knowledge
{ ~above(X,X) <-, ~above(X,Y) <- above(Y,X) } can stop the execution of such infinite loops. However, this requires first the automatic creation by the system of a query ~A whenever a query A exists, and second the parallel resolution of both queries. A similar effect can be obtained by ordinary **S**-derivation, just by means of priority of Rewriting over Superposition. Let us consider the definition program *P* associated with *Above* and the following CWA-compatible rewrite systems *R1* and *R2*:

P: on(a,b)=*true* <-
on(b.c)=*true* <-
above(X,Y)=*true* <- on(X,Y)=*true*
above(X,Y)=*true* <- above(X,Z)=*true*, on(Z,Y)=*true*

R1: on(a,b)=*true* <-
on(b.c)=*true* <-
above(X,X)=*false* <-

R2: on(a,b)=*true* <-
on(b.c)=*true* <-
above(X,Y)=*true* <- on(X,Y)=*true*
above(X,Y)=*true* <- above(X,Z)=*true*,. on(Z,Y)=*true*.
above(X,X)=*false* <-
above(X,Y)=*false* <- above(Y,X)=*true*

P is lhs-innermost and ground-canonical, *R1* (resp. *R2*) satisfies the CWA-principle, and *P*∪*R1* (resp. *P*∪*R2*) is noetherian. Furthermore, we have: above(a,a) *-->$_{R1}$ *false* (resp. above(c,a) *-->$_{R2}$ *false*). Therefore, given a procedure Π_{R1} (resp. Π_{R2}) computing the *R1*-normal forms (resp. *R2*-normal forms) of goals, **S**-derivation using Π_{R1} (resp. Π_{R2}) transforms the goal <- above(a,a)=*true* (resp. <- above(c,a)=*true*) into <- *false*=*true*, then stops.
Unfortunately, besides pattern matching, procedure Π_{R2} requires an additional mechanism because, in the *R2*-clause: above(X,Y)=*true*<-above(X,Z)=*true*,on(Z,Y)=*true* , the variable Z is an extra-variable. Even if *R*-clauses contain no extra-variable and *R* is a canonical system, the *R*-normal form of a term may be not computable in case *R* contains a non-unit clause (see [20]). In contrast, let us recall that, when *R* is a purely equational canonical system, any sequence of reductions yields the normal form. This illustrates the gap between purely equational and conditional Rewriting. So far, in SLOG, we have chosen to implement purely equational Rewriting only. Note however that Prolog clauses P <- $Q_1,\ldots,Q_n$ are often iff-clauses and can be converted into unit equations of the form P=ANDn($Q_1,\ldots,Q_n$)<- (such a transformation is given in the sorting program, below). Note also that, to take advantage of the Rewriting failure detection, we only need a procedure Π_R detecting boolean terms whose normal forms are *false*; Π_R may stop rewriting a goal condition-term when it turns out that the current rewrite-form cannot be rewritten into *false*. The ***head normalization*** procedure (see [1]) is an example of such a rewriting process.

Rewriting allows treatment not only of Prolog non-termination problems but also of more general control problems. Such problems are often met in Prolog when solving a "Generate and Test" goal. Such a goal has the form <- P(x),Q(x), where P generates solutions and Q tests whether the solution is acceptable.
Generally, the rough Prolog implementation is inefficient, because of its leftmost literal strategy. Indeed, in the resolution process of P, at a step n the vector of variables, x,

may be bound in such a way that the final solution of P will not be able to satisfy the Test predicate Q. Prolog will produce the complete solution for P before rejecting it, whereas failure can be immediately detected by solving Q at step n+1. This optimized strategy is traditionally implemented by attaching some inhibition-activation control instructions to the predicate P and Q. A similar effect is produced in SLOG , here again simply by means of priority of rewriting over superposition, and without extra control-information. In SLOG, the goal is of the form <- P(x)=*true*,Q(x)=*true*. After each superposition step, the new binding of x is tested by the Rewriting process. If the rewriting of Q gives *false*, then the whole goal is rewritten as *false*=*true*, which leads to immediate failure. If the rewriting of Q as *false* does not occur during the building of the solution of P, then it must still be checked that Q(x) can be transformed into *true* for the generated instance of x.

For example, consider a naive formulation of the sorting problem in Prolog :

```
    sort(L,M) <- permutation(L, M), ordered(M)   ,
```

where:

```
    permutation([], []) <-
    permutation(a.L, u.M) <- delete(u, a.L, N),permutation(N,M)
    ordered([]) <-
    ordered(a.[]) <-
    ordered(a.b.L) <- le(a,b),ordered(b.L)
    delete(u, u.L, L) <-
    delete(u, v.L, v.M) <- delete(u, L, M)
```

This Prolog program requires control optimizations in order to stop the permutation process after the generation of two consecutive elements a and b such that b < a (see [30]).

In contrast, in SLOG, consider the goal <- permutation(L, M)=*true*, ordered(M)=*true* and the program <*P*,*R*> defined by:

```
P:  permutation([], [])=true <-
    permutation(a.L, u.M)=true <- delete(u, a.L, N)=true,
                                      permutation(N, M)=true
    ordered([])=true <-
    ordered(a.[])=true <-
    ordered(a.b.L)=AND2(le(a,b), ordered(L)) <-
    delete(u, u.L, L)=true <-
    delete(u, v.L, v.M)=true <- delete(u, L, M)=true
    le(0,x)=true <-
    le(s(x),s(y))=le(x,y) <-

R:  ordered(a.b.L)=AND2(le(a,b), ordered(b.L)) <-
    le(s(x),s(y))=le(x,y) <-
    le(s(x),0)=false <-
```

The computation optimization is automatically performed by the SLOG interpreter without control instructions: as soon as computation binds M to a.b.N, the term ordered(M) is rewritten as AND2(le(a,b),ordered(b.N)) which is itself rewritten as false if b < a.

The classical 8-queens problem (roughly stated by
<- permutation(1.2.3.4.5.6.7.8.[],L),safe(L)) can be treated as well.

Thus, rewrite systems turn out to be a powerful and declarative manner to get rid of infinite loops and perform control.

7. Equations between constructors

Up to now, we we have not handled *equations between constructors*, i.e. definite clauses whose left-hand and right-hand sides contain only constructors and variables. We now extend the SLOG-program definition as follows: An SLOG-program **P** is a triple $<P,E_C,R>$, where E_C is a set of equations with constructors and R is a set of inductive consequences of $P \cup E_C$. Besides φ-superposition with the P-clauses, we allow superposition of the E_C-clauses onto the arguments of the term located at the φ-occurrence. Given two occurrences o_1 and o_2 of two terms M_1 and M_2, we say that $o_1 < o_2$ iff M_2 is a strict subterm of M_1 (for a formal definition of the preorder < over occurrences, see [16]). The definition of **S**-derivation is extended as follows:

definition

Let **P**:$<P,E_C,R>$ be an SLOG-program. An **S**-derivation of G' from **P** ∪ {G} via φ consists of a finite sequence $G_0,G_1,\ldots,G_n$ of goals and a sequence $\sigma_1,\sigma_2,\ldots,\sigma_n$ of mgu's such that :

1) G_0 is the minimal form of the Π_R-form of G ,and G_n is G'
2) for all i ,$1 \leq i \leq n$, G_i is either:
   - the minimal form of the Π_R-form of a strict goal-superposant of a P-clause into G_{i-1} at the occurrence $\varphi(G_{i-1})$, or
   - the minimal form of the Π_R-form of a strict goal-superposant of an E_C-clause into G_{i-1}, at an occurrence o greater than $\varphi(G_{i-1})$ (w.r.t. <).

The definition of **S**-derivation *GC*-completeness (see § 3.3) is naturally extended by replacing P by $P \cup E_C$ and *GC*-substitution by $P \cup E_C$-normal *GC*-substitution. The sufficient criteria of completeness of § 4 can be adapted to deal with E_C. For example, adaptation of criterion (2) gives: **S**-derivation is *GC*-complete for P if P is lhs-innermost, $P \cup E_C$ is ground-canonical, $P \cup E_C \cup R$ is noetherian, and for all ground innermost term $f(N_1,\ldots,N_k)$, where the N_i's are in $P \cup E_C$-normal form, $f(N_1,\ldots,N_k)$ is $P \cup E_C$-reducible.
Such conditions are satisfied by the program $<P,E_C,R>$ defining less-than-equal-to over integers, where C is {0,s,p,*true*,*false*}, D is {le}, and:

P:	le(0,0)=*true* <-	E_C:	s(p(x))=x <-
	le(0,p(0))=*false* <-		p(s(x))=x <-
	le(0,s(x))=*true* <- le(0,x)=*true*		
	le(0,p(x))=*false* <- le(0,x)=*false*	*R*:	s(p(x))=x <-
	le(s(x),y)=le(x,p(y)) <-		p(s(x))=x <-
	le(p(x),y)=le(x,s(y)) <-		

For a statement of the confluency and noetherian property, see [21].

8. Implementation

The SLOG interpreter program is written in LISP and runs on VAX/UNIX at the Laboratoires de Marcoussis.
The innermost selection rule φ selects the leftmost innermost subterm in G. Candidate definite clauses for φ-superposition are tried in their order in the definition program. The general strategy is depth-first.
Rewriting is implemented for unit definite clauses only (unconditional Rewriting) and transforms all the goal equations to their head normal form. The decomposition and rejection inference rules are implemented as additional built-in procedures.
A number of classical Prolog programs which pose problems with respect to control,

negation and equality have been converted into SLOG and successfully run. We are currently experimenting with using SLOG for prototyping and testing (see [5] [6]).

9. Conclusion

SLOG inherits its clear functional syntax from Horn Equational Clauses. It also inherits its deductive power from superposition-based theorem provers.
A refined strategy of clausal superposition together with Rewriting has been implemented and greatly increases the interpreter efficiency. Completeness is still maintained for a large class of programs.
Furthermore, these built-in strategies allow us to treat negation and control problems in a powerful, declarative manner.
SLOG will hopefully be an efficient Logic Programming tool, with little need for extra control instructions. Another potential application of SLOG is automatic program verification, since the built-in innermost superposition and rewriting procedures can be used to construct inductive proofs (see [14][4]).

Acknowledgements:
I would like to thank Drew Adams, Jean Faget and Anne Mauboussin for numerous fruitful discussions, Stephane Kaplan and Laurent Kott for their valuable comments on the paper and Rene Velly for carefully reading an earlier draft.

References

[1] Abramson,H., " A Prological Definition of HASL, a Purely Functional Language with Unification Based Conditional Binding Expressions" New Generation Computing 2:1, pp. 3-35, 1984.

[2] Aida,H., Tanaka,H. & Moto-oka,T., "A Prolog Extension for Handling Negative Knowledge", New Generation Computing 1:1, pp. 87-91, 1983.

[3] Bergstra,J & Klop,J., "Conditional Rewrite Rules: Confluency and Termination" Research Report IW 198/82, Mathematical Centre, Amsterdam, 1982.

[4] Bidoit,M. & Choquer,M.A., "Preuves de Formules Conditionnelles par Recurrence", Proc. AFCET IA, Grenoble, Nov. 1985.

[5] Bouge,L., Choquet,N., Fribourg,L. & Gaudel, M.C.G., "Application of Prolog to Test Sets Generation from Algebraic Specifications", Coll. on Software Engineering, LNCS 186, pp.261-275, March 1985.

[6] Choquet,N., Fribourg,L. & Mauboussin A., "Runnable Protocol Specifications using the logic interpreter SLOG", 5th IFIP Workshop on Protocol Specification, Verification and Testing, Toulouse-Moissac, June 1985.

[7] Colmerauer,A., "Prolog and Infinite Trees", in *Logic Programming*, K.L. Clark and S.A. Tarnlund (Eds.), Academic Press, 1982.

[8] Deransart,P., "An Operational Algebraic Semantics of PROLOG programs", Proc. Programmation en Logique, Perros-Guirec, CNET-Lannion, March 1983.

[9] Dershowitz,N. & Josephson N.A., "Logic Programming by Completion" 2nd International Logic Programming Conference, Upsala, pp. 313-320, 1984.

[10] Dershowitz,N., "Orderings for Term-Rewriting Systems", TCS 17:3, pp.279-301, 1982.

[11] Durand,J., "LOGRE: un Prototype de Systeme de Programmation en Logique Utilisant des Techniques de Reecriture", These 3eme cycle, U. of Nancy, 1984.

[12] Fay,M., "First-Order Unification in an Equational Theory" Proc. 4th Workshop on Automated Deduction, pp. 161-167, Feb. 1979.

[13] Fribourg,L., "Oriented Equational Clauses as a Programming Language", J. Logic Programming 1:2, pp. 165-177, August 1984.

[14] Fribourg,L., "A Narrowing Procedure for Theories with Constructors", 7th Intl. Conf. on Automated Deduction, LNCS 170, pp. 259-281 ,1984.

[15] Goguen,J.A. & Meseguer J., "Equality,Types,Modules and Generics for Logic Programming", J. Logic Programming 1:2, pp. 179-210, August 1984.

[16] Huet,G., "Confluent Reductions: Abstract Properties and Applications to Term Rewriting Systems", J.ACM 27:4, pp. 797-821, Oct. 1980.

[17] Huet,G. & Hullot,J.M., "Proofs by Induction in Equational Theories with Constructors", 21st FOCS, pp. 96-107, 1980.

[18] Hullot,J.M., "Canonical Forms and Unification" 5th Intl. Conf. on Automated Deduction, LNCS 87, pp. 318-334, 1980.

[19] Hussmann,H., "Unification in Conditional-Equational Theories" Technical Report MIP-8502, U. Passau, January 85. Short version in: Proc. EUROCAL 85 Conf., Linz.

[20] Kaplan,S., "Conditional Rewrite Rules", TCS 33, pp. 175-193, 1984.

[21] Kaplan,S., "Fair Conditional Term Rewriting Systems: Unification, Termination and Confluence", Technical Report 194, U. Orsay, November 1984.

[22] Knuth,D.E. & Bendix P.B., "Simple Word Problems in Universal Algebras", in *Computational Problems in Abstract Algebra*, J. Leech (Ed.), Pergamon Press, New York, pp. 263-297, 1970.

[23] Jouannaud,J.P., Lescanne,P. & Reinig,F. "Recursive Decomposition Ordering", in *IFIP Working Conf. on Formal Description of Programming Concepts II*, North-Holland, D. Bjorner (Ed.), 1983.

[24] Lankford,D.S., "Canonical Inference", Technical Report ATP-32, Dept of Mathematics, U. of Texas, 1975.

[25] Malachi,Y., Manna,Z. & Waldinger,R.J., "TABLOG: the Deductive Tableau Programming Language", ACM Lisp and Functional Programming Conf., pp. 323-330, 1984.

[26] Naish,L., "Automating Control for Logic Programs" Technical Report 83/6, Dept of Computer Science, U. Melbourne, 1984.

[27] Paul,E., "On Solving the Equality Problem in Theories Defined by Horn Clauses" EUROCAL Conf., Linz, 1985 (to appear in LNCS).

[28] Pletat,U., Engels,G., Ehrich,H.D., "Operational Semantics of Algebraic Specifications with Conditional Equations", Proc. 7th CAAP Conf., Lille,France, 1982.

[29] Pereira,F.C.N., Warren,H.D., "Definite Clause Grammars for Language Analysis a Survey of the Formalism and a Comparison with Augmented Transition Networks", Artificial Intelligence **13**, pp. 231-278, 1980.

[30] Pereira,L.M., "Logic Control with Logic", 1st Intl. Logic Programming Conf., pp. 9-18, Marseille, 1982.

[31] Reiter,R., "On Closed World Data Bases", in *Logic and Databases*, H. Gallaire and J. Minker (Eds.), Plenum Press, New York, pp. 55-76, 1980.

[32] Remy,J.L., "Etude des Systemes de Reecriture Conditionnels et Application aux Types Abstraits Algebriques" Doctoral Thesis, I.N.P.L., Nancy, France, 1982.

[33] Remy,J.L., Zang,H., "REVEUR4: A System to Proceed Experiments on Conditional Term Rewriting Systems", Proc. of 2th ECAI Conf., Pisa, 1984.

[34] Slagle,J.R., "Automated Theorem Proving for Theories with Simplifiers, Commutativity and Associativity", J.ACM 21:4, pp. 622-642, Oct. 1974.

[35] Tamaki,H., "Semantics of a Logic Programming Language with a Reducibility Predicate", IEEE Intl. Symp. on Logic Programming, Atlantic City, pp. 259-264, Feb. 1984.

[36] You,J.H., "On the Completeness of First-Order Unification in Equational Theories", unpublished manuscript, 1985.

AN IDEAL-THEORETIC APPROACH TO WORD PROBLEMS AND UNIFICATION PROBLEMS OVER FINITELY PRESENTED COMMUTATIVE ALGEBRAS

Abdelilah Kandri–Rody[†]
Department des Mathematiques
Faculte des Sciences
University Cadi Ayyad
Marrakech, Morocco

Deepak Kapur[*] and Paliath Narendran
Computer Science Branch
Corporate Research and Development
General Electric Company
Schenectady, New York

ABSTRACT

A new approach based on computing the Gröbner basis of polynomial ideals is developed for solving word problems and unification problems for finitely presented commutative algebras. This approach is simpler and more efficient than the approaches based on generalizations of the Knuth-Bendix completion procedure to handle associative and commutative operators. It is shown that (i) the word problem over a finitely presented commutative ring with unity is equivalent to the polynomial equivalence problem modulo a polynomial ideal over the integers, (ii) the unification problem for linear forms is decidable for finitely presented commutative rings with unity, (iii) the word problem and unification problem for finitely presented boolean polynomial rings are co-NP-complete and co-NP-hard respectively, and (iv) the set of all unifiers of two forms over a finitely presented abelian group can be computed in polynomial time. Examples and results of algorithms based on the Gröbner basis computation are also reported.

Key Words: Word Problem, Unification Problem, Finitely Presented Algebras, Commutative Algebras, Gröbner Basis, Polynomial Ideals, Term Rewriting, Knuth-Bendix Completion Procedure.

---

† This work was done when Kandri-Rody was a graduate student at Rensselaer Polytechnic Institute, Troy, NY.

* Partially supported by the National Science Foundation grant MCS-82-11621.

AN IDEAL-THEORETIC APPROACH TO WORD PROBLEMS AND UNIFICATION PROBLEMS OVER FINITELY PRESENTED COMMUTATIVE ALGEBRAS

1. INTRODUCTION

We present a new approach for developing decision procedures for word problems and unification problems for finitely presented commutative algebraic structures. The approach is based on the Gröbner basis computation developed for polynomial ideals over the ring of integers in [10,12] and is simpler and more efficient for implementation than the approaches based on generalizations of the Knuth-Bendix completion procedure to handle associative and commutative (AC) operators developed in [16,23]. For related approaches for computing a Gröbner basis of a polynomial ideal over the integers, also see [4,20,24,28].

The results reported in this paper are:

1. the word problem over a finitely presented commutative ring with unity is equivalent to the polynomial equivalence problem modulo an ideal over $Z[X_1,...,X_n]$,
2. the unification problem over a finitely presented commutative ring with unity is the same as finding whether a polynomial has a solution modulo an ideal over $Z[X_1,...,X_n]$. The unification problem is undecidable as Hilbert's 10th problem is a special case of the unification problem over a free commutative ring with unity,
3. the unification problem over a finitely presented commutative ring with unity is decidable if we restrict ourselves to linear forms,
4. the word problem over a finitely presented boolean (polynomial) ring is co-NP-complete,
5. the unification problem over the boolean ring is NP-complete whereas the unification problem over a finitely presented boolean (polynomial) ring is co-NP-hard,
6. computing a reduced Gröbner basis over linear polynomials is essentially the same as computing the Hermite normal form of an integral matrix, which implies that the uniform word problem for finitely presented abelian groups can be solved in polynomial time, and
7. the set of all unifiers of two forms of a finitely presented abelian group can be computed in polynomial time.

The Gröbner basis approach has been implemented to solve uniform word problems over finitely presented commutative semi-groups, abelian groups, commutative rings with unity, boolean rings etc.. In fact, the same algorithm solves the uniform word problem for finitely presented abelian semi-groups and commutative rings with unity; for solving word problems over finitely presented boolean rings, this algorithm is modified to include, in the presentations, the relation $a * a = a$ for each generator a, as well as $1 + 1 = 0$. For finitely presented abelian groups, the algorithm for commutative ring is slightly modified so that it does not assume the existence of the multiplication operation of a commutative ring. We also discuss the relation between the Gröbner basis computation and unification (of elementary terms) over finitely presented abelian groups.

For approaches to solve word problems and unification problems based on extensions of the Knuth-Bendix completion procedure for handling AC-operators, see [2,17,18,19,21].

In the next section, we define the word problem and unification problem over finitely presented algebras to avoid any possible confusion due to the terminology used in the paper. Section 3 is a background material on rewriting systems, polynomial ideals and Gröbner basis. Section 4 is a discussion of word problems and unification problems over finitely presented commutative rings with unity; we also establish a relationship between polynomial rings over integers and commutative rings freely generated by a finite set of generators, by showing how each generator serves the role of an indeterminate. Section 5 discusses these problems over finitely presented boolean rings. Section 6 considers these problems over finitely presented abelian groups. In Section 7, we discuss word problems over finitely presented commutative semi-groups.

2. FINITELY PRESENTED ALGEBRAS, WORD PROBLEM, UNIFICATION PROBLEM

Consider a variety (or family) of algebraic structures defined by a collection of axioms, in particular equations (or identities). For example,

$$x + -x = 0$$

$$x + y = y + x$$

$$x + (y + z) = (x + y) + z$$

$$x + 0 = x$$

defines a variety of abelian groups.

A *word problem on a variety* V is to decide, given two words w_1 and w_2 constructed from (first-order) variables and operators of the variety, whether w_1 and w_2 are equivalent in the variety. This problem is commonly known as the *identity problem*; however, in this paper we have chosen to follow the terminology of [15].

The *unification problem (on elementary terms) on a variety* V is to determine, given two words w_1 and w_2 constructed from variables and operators of the variety, whether there exists a substitution σ for variables such that $\sigma(w_1)$ and $\sigma(w_2)$ are equivalent in the variety.

If we allow other uninterpreted function symbols (different from the operators of the variety) also for building words, then we refer to those word (unification) problems as *general* word (unification) problems.

An algebra A in a variety V is *finitely presented* if and only if there exists a finite set of generators $\{a_1, ..., a_n\}$ and a finite set of equations $\{e_{11} = e_{21}, \cdots, e_{1k} = e_{2k}\}$, relating words constructed using these generators and operators of the variety, which define A. Generators and defining equations relating these generators constitute a ***finite presentation*** P of A.

The ***word problem*** over an algebra A of variety V with a finite presentation P is to determine, given two words w_1 and w_2 constructed using the generators in P and the operators of V, whether w_1 and w_2 are equivalent in A.

The ***uniform word problem over a variety*** V is to determine, given a finite presentation P of an algebra A of variety V and two words w_1 and w_2 of the finitely presented algebra specified by P, whether w_1 and w_2 are equivalent in A.

The ***unification problem (on elementary terms) on an algebra*** A ***of variety*** V with a finite presentation P is to determine, given two words w_1 and w_2 constructed from variables, generators of A and operators of variety V, whether there exists a substitution σ for variables such that $\sigma(w_1)$ and $\sigma(w_2)$ are equivalent in A. The unification problem is also often called the ***word equation problem.***

3. BACKGROUND

3.1 Rewrite Relations

Most of this will be familiar to the reader who has some familiarity with the literature on term rewriting systems [9].

Let $\rightarrow$ be a binary relation on a set S, called a ***rewriting relation.*** The reflexive, transitive closure of a rewrite relation $\rightarrow$ is denoted by $\rightarrow^*$, is referred to as ***reduction.*** An element p in S is said to be ***in normal form*** if and only if there is no q such that $p \rightarrow q$. If $p \rightarrow^* q$ and q is in normal form, then q is said to be a ***normal form*** of p.

A rewrite relation $\rightarrow$ is said to be ***finitely terminating*** or ***Noetherian*** if and only if there cannot be any infinite sequence of the form $a_1 \rightarrow a_2 \rightarrow a_3 \rightarrow \cdots$. The relation $\rightarrow$ is

— ***confluent*** if and only if for all p, q, r such that $p \rightarrow^* q$ and $p \rightarrow^* r$ there exists s such that $q \rightarrow^* s$ and $r \rightarrow^* s$.

— ***locally confluent*** if and only if for all p, q, r such that $p \rightarrow q$ and $p \rightarrow r$ there exists s such that $q \rightarrow^* s$ and $r \rightarrow^* s$.

It can be shown, fairly easily, that if $\rightarrow$ is both Noetherian and locally confluent then it is confluent. A rewrite relation $\rightarrow$ that is both noetherian and confluent is said to be ***canonical.***

3.2 POLYNOMIAL IDEALS

Let $R[X_1, ..., X_n]$ be the ring of polynomials with indeterminates $X_1, ..., X_n$ over R, where R is a commutative ring with unity. Let us assume a total ordering on indeterminates, in particular, without any loss of generality, $X_1 < X_2 < \cdots < X_n$. A ***term*** is any power product $\prod_{i=1}^{n} X_i^{k_i}$, where $k_i \geq 0$; the ***degree*** of a term is $\sum_{i=1}^{n} k_i$. A ***monomial*** is a term (or power product) multiplied by a nonzero coefficient from R. A ***polynomial*** is a sum of monomials.

We can define a well-founded total ordering on terms in many ways. In this paper, we use the degree and lexicographic ordering. Terms $t_1 = \prod_1^n x_i^{k_i} < t_2 = \prod_1^n x_i^{j_i}$ if and only if (1) the degree of $t_1 <$ the degree of t_2, or (2) the degree of $t_1 =$ degree of t_2 and there exists an $i \geq 1$, such that $k_i < j_i$ and for each $1 \leq i' < i$, $k_{i'} = j_{i'}$.

When R is Z, then monomials are ordered using their terms and coefficients. We say that an integer c is *less than* another integer c', written as $c \ll c'$, if and only if $|c| < |c'|$ or ($|c| = |c'|$, c is positive and c' is negative); $|c|$ stands for the absolute value of c. Thus, $0 \ll 1 \ll -1 \ll 2 \ll -2 \ll \cdots$ The ordering $\ll$ on Z is total and well-founded. Given two monomials $m_1 = c_1 t_1$ and $m_2 = c_2 t_2$, $m_1 \ll m_2$ if and only if $t_1 < t_2$, or ($t_1 = t_2$ and $c_1 \ll c_2$). It is easy to see that the ordering $\ll$ on monomials is total and well-founded.

Consider a polynomial $p = m + r$ such that the term of the monomial m is greater than those within r; then m is called the ***head-monomial*** of p, the term of m is called the ***head-term*** of p, the coefficient of m is called the ***head-coefficient*** of p and r is called the ***reductum*** of p. The ordering $\ll$ on monomials can be used to define a ordering $\ll$ on polynomials as: polynomials $p_1 \ll p_2$ if and only if either (1) $m_1 \ll m_2$, or (2) $m_1 = m_2$ and $r_1 \ll r_2$, where m_i and r_i are, respectively, the head-monomial and reductum of p_i, $i = 1, 2$. It is easy to see that the ordering $\ll$ on polynomials in $Z[X_1, ..., X_n]$ is total and well-founded.

Given a set B of polynomials, the ***ideal*** I generated by B is the set of all polynomials which can be expressed as a linear combination of the elements in the basis. That is,

$$I = \{ p \mid p = \sum a_i b_i \}$$

where a_i is any polynomial and b_i is an element of B. This is often expressed in this paper as $I = (b_1, \cdots, b_k)$. (Note the distinction between the use of braces and that of parentheses; $\{b_1, \cdots, b_k\}$ stands for a ***set*** of polynomials whereas $(b_1, \cdots, b_k)$ denotes the ***ideal*** generated by them.) An ideal is said to be ***trivial*** if and only if it is the entire ring, and ***non-trivial*** otherwise. If R is a Noetherian ring, then by Hilbert's theorem [27], every ideal of $R[X_1,...,X_n]$ is finitely generated. All of the rings that are considered in this paper are Noetherian.

Let I be an ideal over $R[X_1,...,X_n]$ specified by a finite basis $B = \{b_1,...,b_k\}$. The ***ideal membership problem*** is to determine, given a polynomial p and a basis B, whether p is in the ideal I generated by B. The ***polynomial equivalence problem modulo an ideal*** is to determine, given two polynomials p and q and a basis $B = \{b_1, ..., b_k\}$, whether there exist polynomials q_i such that

$$p = q + \sum_i q_i b_i$$

The polynomial equivalence problem can be reduced to the ideal membership problem by asking whether $p - q$ is in the ideal $I = (b_1, ..., b_k)$.

The ***triviality problem*** is to determine, given a set B of polynomials, whether the ideal generated by B is trivial.

A polynomial p has a solution in R if and only if there exist elements of R such that when these are substituted for indeterminates in p, p evaluates to 0.

Let a *form* be defined as a polynomial which besides using indeterminates, also involves (first-order) variables. An *equation* $t_1 = t_2$, where t_1 and t_2 are forms, has *a solution modulo an ideal* I if and only if there exist polynomials which can be substituted for variables in t_1 and t_2 such that the polynomials q_1 and q_2 obtained after this substitution are equivalent modulo I.

3.3 Grobner Bases

A basis B is called a *Gröbner basis* for an ideal I if for any polynomial q, no matter how q is reduced using polynomials in B, the result is always the same, i.e., it is unique [3,5]. An equivalent definition is that for any polynomial p in I, p reduces to 0 using the polynomials in B. To precisely define a Gröbner basis of an ideal over $Z[X_1,...,X_n]$, it is necessary to define how polynomials are used as rewrite rules, or, in other words, how a polynomial reduces another polynomial. We give below some definitions; an interested reader may wish to consult [10,11,12] for more details.

Consider a polynomial $P = m_1 + r_1$ where m_1 and r_1 are, respectively, the head-monomial and reductum of P. Let $m_1 = c_1 t_1$, where c_1 and t_1 are respectively the head-coefficient and head-term of m_1. Then the rewrite rule corresponding to P is: $c_1 t_1 \rightarrow - r_1$. In case the head-coefficient c_1 of P is negative, P is multiplied by -1 and the result is used as a rewrite rule. For example, the rewrite rule corresponding to $2X_1^2 X_2 - X_2$ is $2X_1^2 X_2 \rightarrow X_2$. A rule $L \rightarrow R$, where $L = c_1 t_1$ and $c_1 > 0$ rewrites a monomial $c\ t$ to $(c - \epsilon c_1) t + \epsilon \sigma R$ where $\epsilon = 1$ if $c > 0$, $\epsilon = -1$ if $c < 0$, if and only if (1) there exists a term σ such that $t = \sigma t_1$ and (2) either $c > (c_1 / 2)$ or $c < -(c_1 - 1)/2$. If $-(c_1 - 1)/2 \leq c \leq (c_1 / 2)$ or there does not exist any σ such that $t = \sigma t_1$, then the monomial $c\ t$ cannot be rewritten.

A polynomial Q is rewritten to Q' using the rule $L \rightarrow R$ if and only if (1) $Q = Q_1 + c\ t$ and $c\ t$ is the largest monomial in Q that can be rewritten using the rule, and (2) $Q' = Q_1 + (c - \epsilon c_1) t + \epsilon \sigma R$, where $\epsilon = 1$ if $c > 0$ and $\epsilon = -1$ otherwise. If there is no monomial in Q which can be rewritten using the rule, then Q is in *normal form* with respect to the rule. For example, using the rule $2X_1^2 X_2 \rightarrow X_2$, the polynomial

$$4X_1^3 X_2 + 5X_1 X_2^2 - 3X_1^2 X_2 \rightarrow 2X_1^3 X_2 + X_1 X_2 + 5X_1 X_2^2 - 3X_1^2 X_2$$

$$\rightarrow 2X_1 X_2 + 5X_1 X_2^2 - 3X_1^2 X_2.$$

The result can be further reduced as the monomial $-3X_1^2 X_2$ is reducible:

$$2X_1 X_2 + 5X_1 X_2^2 - 3X_1^2 X_2 \rightarrow 2X_1 X_2 + 5X_1 X_2^2 - X_1^2 X_2 - X_2$$

$$\rightarrow 2X_1 X_2 + 5X_1 X_2^2 + X_1^2 X_2 - 2X_2.$$

We assume that after rewriting by a polynomial, indeterminates in terms are ordered using the prespecified ordering on indeterminates, monomials whose terms (power products) are equal are combined, and terms with zero coefficients are omitted.[1]

Let $T = \{L_1 \rightarrow R_1, ..., L_k \rightarrow R_k\}$ be the set of rules corresponding to a basis $B = \{b_1, \cdots, b_k\}$ of an ideal I such that $L_i \rightarrow R_i$ is the rule corresponding to b_i. Let $\rightarrow$ denote the rewriting relation defined by T, i.e., a polynomial $Q \rightarrow Q'$ if and only if Q rewrites to Q' using some rule $L_i \rightarrow R_i$ in T. It is easy to see (using the ordering defined on polynomials earlier) that $\rightarrow$ is Noetherian.

A basis B is a *Gröbner basis* if and only if the rewriting relation $\rightarrow$ defined by B is canonical.

In [10], we discuss an algorithm for generating the Gröbner basis of a polynomial ideal over $Z[X_1,...,X_n]$. (See [4] for a similar algorithm independently developed by Buchberger.) The algorithm is similar to the Knuth-Bendix completion procedure. It accepts a finite basis of an ideal and an ordering on indeterminates and generates a Gröbner basis for the ideal generated by the input basis which is unique upto the ordering on the indeterminates. In [12], we have generalized this algorithm so that it works on polynomial rings over an arbitrary Euclidean ring.

The ideal membership problem (and hence the polynomial equivalence problem modulo an ideal) can be easily solved using the Gröbner basis of an ideal. To check whether a polynomial p is in an ideal I generated by a basis B or not, generate the Gröbner basis GB of I from B using some ordering on indeterminates; then reduce p using GB; if the result is 0, then p is in I and otherwise it is not in I. Thus to test for equivalence of p and q, it is enough to reduce p and q using GB and check whether their normal forms are the same or not. Note that this is similar to proving that an equation is in an equational theory by generating a canonical system for the equational theory.

Our approach for solving word problems and unification problems over commutative algebras uses the above results about polynomial ideals and their Gröbner bases. In the next section, we establish a relationship between polynomial rings over integers and commutative rings freely generated by a finite set of generators, by showing how each generator serves the role of an indeterminate.

4. COMMUTATIVE RINGS WITH UNITY

The word problem or the identity problem over a free commutative ring with unity is known to be decidable; see [16,23] for a canonical term rewriting system which can be used to

1. We could as well have defined the rewriting relation induced by a polynomial using a division algorithm on integer coefficients that produces the least remainder; an interested reader may wish to refer to [12] for such a definition of the rewriting relation induced by a polynomial. We have used the definition given in [10] which uses repeated subtraction on integer coefficients as this definition is simpler to understand.

generate canonical forms of words, thus giving us a decision procedure for the word problem.[2] The unification problem over a free commutative ring is discussed later after we establish the relationship between a free commutative ring generated by a finite set of generators and the polynomial ring over the integers.

4.1 Word Problem over Finitely Presented Commutative Rings with Unity

Let A be a finitely presented ring with generators $a_1, \ldots, a_n$ and the relators (or relations) $e_{11} = e_{21}, \ldots, e_{1k} = e_{2k}$. As said above, each of e_{ij} is a word constructed from $a_1, \ldots, a_n$ and the ring operations. Assuming some ordering on the a_i's, say $a_1 < \cdots < a_n$, we can transform each $e_{1j} - e_{2j}$ into its canonical sum-of-products form, say p_j, which is a polynomial in $Z[a_1,\ldots,a_n]$.

Theorem 1: The word problem over a finitely presented ring with generators $a_1, \cdots, a_n$ and relators $e_{1i} = e_{2i}$, for $1 \leq i \leq k$ is the same as the polynomial equivalence problem modulo the ideal I specified by the basis $\{p_1, \cdots, p_k\}$ in $Z[a_1,\ldots,a_n]$, where p_i is the canonical sum of products form of $e_{1i} - e_{2i}$.

Proof: The polynomial equivalence problem modulo an ideal I is to check, given two polynomial r and s, whether there exist some polynomials q_i such that $r = s + \sum q_i\, p_i$. This reduces to asking whether the words r and s are equivalent in the equational theory of $p_i = 0$, which is also the equational theory of $e_{1i} = e_{2i}$.

If two words w_1 and w_2 are equivalent with respect to relators $e_{1i} = e_{2i}$, then there exists a sequence of steps involving replacement of e_{1i} by e_{2i} or vice versa, using which w_1 can be transformed to w_2. Using induction on the number of such steps, it can be shown that $w_1 = w_2 + \sum q_i\, (e_{1i} - e_{2i})$. Hence the result. *Q.E.D.*

So, the algorithm for computing the Gröbner basis of a ideal over a polynomial ring of integers discussed in [10] can be used to solve the uniform word problem over a finitely presented commutative ring with unity. (Because of the Hilbert basis theorem [27], the algorithm in [10] is guaranteed to terminate with the Gröbner basis of the ideal specified by the input.) From the presentation of the ring, we can generate its Gröbner basis assuming some total ordering on indeterminates, then compute the normal forms of the words under consideration with respect to this basis and check whether the two normal forms are the same. The Gröbner basis is the canonical basis of the finitely presented commutative ring which is isomorphic to $Z[a_1,\ldots,a_n]/I$. The Gröbner basis algorithm can also be used for solving the uniform word problem over finitely presented commutative rings with unity of any charcteristic; to a presentation of such a ring, we add the relation $m = 0$, where m is the characteristic of the ring, and then apply the Gröbner basis algorithm. Later, we discuss finitely presented boolean rings which are of characteristic 2.

As noted in [10], the ordering on indeterminates considerably affects the performance of the algorithm. We give below some examples run using this algorithm which has been implemented on a VAX/780 in ALDES and Franz Lisp and on the Symbolics 3600 in Zetalisp.

2. Henceforth, by a commutative ring, we shall mean a commutative ring with unity.

Example 1: Consider the commutative ring generated by generators X, Y, W with the following presentation:

(1) $-W + X\ Y^2 + 4\ X^2 + 1 = 0$

(2) $Y^2\ W + 2X + 1 = 0$

(3) $-X^2\ W + Y^2 + X = 0.$

The canonical basis for the commutative ring using the ordering $X < Y < W$ is

(1) $W^2 - W - 4\ Y^2 + 2\ X^2 - 3\ X = 0$

(2) $-W + X\ Y^2 + 4\ X^2 + 1 = 0$

(3) $X^2\ W - Y^2 - X = 0$

(4) $Y^2\ W + 2\ X + 1 = 0$

(5) $-3\ X\ W - Y^2 + 2\ X^4 + 13\ X^3 + X - 1 = 0$

(6) $W + Y^4 + 2\ X^3 - 3\ X^2 - 1 = 0$

Example 2: The presentation is

(1) $2\ X^2\ Y^3\ W^5 + 5\ X\ Y^2 + X\ W - 6\ Y = 0$

(2) $X^2 + 2\ X + 1 = 0$

(3) $X^2\ Y^2 - 1 = 0$

(4) $8\ X\ Y\ W - 8 = 0$

(5) $6\ X + 3\ Y + 2\ W = 0$

The canonical basis of the above presentation generated using the ordering $X < Y < W$ turns out to be $1 = 0$. Thus the ideal is trivial as all words in the ring are equivalent to each other.

Example 3: Consider the presentation [21]

(1) $Y^6 + X^4\ Y^4 - X^2\ Y^4 - Y^4 - X^4\ Y^2 + 2\ X^2\ Y^2 + X^6 - X^4 = 0$

(2) $2\ X^3\ Y^4 - X\ Y^4 - 2\ X^3\ Y^2 + 2X\ Y^2 + 3\ X^5 - 2\ X^3 = 0$

(3) $3\ Y^5 + 2\ X^4\ Y^3 - 2\ X^2\ Y^3 - 2\ Y^3 - X^4\ Y + 2\ X^2\ Y = 0$

The canonical basis obtained using the ordering $X < Y$ is:

(1) $4\ Y^4 + 4\ X^4\ Y^2 - 8\ X^2\ Y^2 - 4\ X^6 + 4\ X^4 = 0$

(2) $X^2\ Y^4 + 2\ Y^4 + 2\ X^4\ Y^2 - 6\ X^2\ Y^2 - 3\ X^6 + 4\ X^4 = 0$

(3) $4\ X\ Y^5 - 8\ X\ Y^3 - 4\ X^5\ Y + 8\ X^3\ Y = 0$

(4) $Y^6 + X^4 Y^2 - 2X^2 Y^2 - 2X^6 + 2X^4 = 0$

(5) $-X Y^4 + 2X^3 Y^2 + 2X Y^2 + 2X^7 - X^5 - 2X^3 = 0$

(6) $2Y^5 + 4X^2 Y^3 - 4Y^3 + 4X^6 Y - 6X^4 Y + 4X^2 Y = 0$

(7) $3Y^5 + 2X^4 Y^3 - 2X^2 Y^3 - 2Y^3 - X^4 Y + 2X^2 Y = 0$

(8) $3Y^4 + 2X^6 Y^2 + 2X^4 Y^2 - 2X^2 Y^2 + X^8 - 2X^6 - X^4 = 0$

(9) $2X^5 Y^2 + 2X Y^2 + X^9 - 2X^3 = 0$

(10) $4X^2 Y^3 - 2Y^3 + X^8 Y + 2X^6 Y - 4X^4 Y + 2X^2 Y = 0$

4.2 The Unification Problem

Theorem 2: The unification problem for terms t_1 and t_2 involving variables over a finitely presented commutative ring A generated by $a_1, ..., a_n$, and relators $e_{1i} = e_{2i}$, $1 \leq i \leq k$, is the same as finding whether $t_1 = t_2$ have a solution modulo $I = (p_1, \cdots, p_k)$ in $Z[a_1,...,a_n]$, where p_i is the canonical sum of products form of $e_{1i} - e_{2i}$.

Proof: Follows from Theorem 1 in the previous section. *Q.E.D.*

Theorem 3: Hilbert's 10th problem is a special case of the unification problem over free commutative rings with unity.

Proof: Integers can be simulated within a free commutative ring with unity with no generators at all. For example, we can simulate any positive integer k as the summation of 1 repeated k times, and any negative integer $-k$, where k is positive, as the summation of -1 k times. If the indeterminates in an instance of Hilbert's 10th problem are replaced by variables, then the problem of unifying the resulting term with zero in the free commutative ring is the same as finding an integer solution of the original polynomial. The term can be unified with 0 if and only if its polynomial has an integer solution. *Q.E.D.*

The above theorem shows that the unification problem over a free commutative ring is undecidable since Hilbert's 10th problem is undecidable. In the next section we show that a restricted case of this problem - where the polynomials under consideration are *linear* over the variables - is decidable.

4.2.1 Linear Forms

By a *linear form* we mean an expression of the form $p_1 y_1 + p_2 y_2 + \cdots + p_m y_m + q$ where $p_1, \ldots, p_m, q$ are polynomials belonging to $R[X_1, \cdots, X_n]$ and $y_1, \ldots, y_m$ are variables. (Non-linear forms can be similarly defined.) A linear form $p_1 y_1 + p_2 y_2 + \cdots + p_m y_m + q$ has *a solution modulo an ideal I* (over $R[X_1, \cdots, X_n]$) if and only if there exist polynomials $r_1, \ldots, r_m$ such that $p_1 r_1 + p_2 r_2 + \cdots + p_m r_m + q$ belongs to I. The unification problem of linear forms is equivalent to a linear form having a solution.

Lemma 1: Let $L = p_1 y_1 + p_2 y_2 + \cdots + p_m y_m + q$ be a linear form and $I = (f_1, \ldots, f_r)$ be an ideal over $R[X_1, \cdots, X_n]$. Then L has a solution modulo I if and only if q belongs to the ideal $J = (f_1, \ldots, f_r, p_1, \ldots, p_m)$.

Proof: "If part": Since q belongs to J, $q = \sum d_i f_i + \sum b_j p_j$ which implies that L has a solution modulo I. In particular, the $-b_j$'s are the solutions.

"Only if part": If L has a solution modulo I, say $y_j = b_j$ for all j, then $\sum b_j p_j + q =_I 0$ which means that q belongs to the ideal J.

Corollary 1: The following problem is decidable:

Instance: A linear form L, a set $\{X_1, \cdots, X_n\}$ of indeterminates and a polynomial ideal I over $Z[X_1, \cdots, X_n]$.

Question: Does L have a solution modulo I ?

However the general problem (of solving non-linear forms) can be shown to be undecidable, again by reducing Hilbert's 10th problem to it.

4.3 Boolean Rings

A *boolean ring* $B = (\{0, 1\}, +, *)$ is a commutative ring where the multiplicative identity 1 has the property $1 + 1 = 0$. In other words, 1 is its own inverse. An alternate way of viewing the boolean ring is in terms of propositional calculus, whereby + stands for '*exclusive-or*' and * for '$\wedge$'. A *boolean ring of polynomials* is any ring of polynomials with coefficients from B with the additional property that $X * X = X$ for every indeterminate X ("the idempotence law"). The reader can now easily see that this implies $p * p = p$ for every polynomial p in the ring. Thus only *flat* polynomials, i.e. those in which the degree of an indeterminate in a term is always either 0 or 1, need be considered; for instance, $X^3 + Y$ is equivalent to $X + Y$ which is flat. Throughout the rest of this section we denote a boolean ring of polynomials with indeterminates $X_1, \ldots, X_n$ by $B[X_1, \cdots, X_n]$ (even though this abuses the notation).

The above notion of "boolean ring of polynomials" enables us to express the entire propositional calculus in terms of polynomials, since the operators '*exclusive-or*' and '$\wedge$' are enough to express any propositional formula. (See [8] for methods for converting formulae in terms of '$\wedge$', '$\vee$' and '$\neg$' into the above-mentioned polynomial form.) This enables us to show [1,10,14] that theorem-proving in propositional calculus can be reduced to testing whether a polynomial ideal over $B[X_1, \cdots, X_n]$ is *trivial*. This "ideal-theoretic" approach to theorem-proving has been extended to first-order logic with a few modifications [14].

Theorem 4: Given a set of polynomials S over a boolean polynomial ring, the problem of determining, whether $1 \in (S)$ is co-NP-complete.

Consider a set of boolean polynomials S and polynomials p and q. Let I be the ideal generated by S. Clearly, $p \underset{I}{=} q$ if and only if $p - q \in I$ if and only if $(p - q)^n \in I$ for some n. Now it is not hard to show by an argument similar to that used in the proof of Hilbert's Nullstellensatz in [27] that $(p - q)^n \in I$ for some n if and only if $(S, (p - q) * Y + 1)$, where Y is a new indeterminate, contains 1; if $p - q$ is not in I, then there exists an assignment of Y such that the polynomial $(p - q) * Y + 1$ has a zero common with I. All this leads us to

Theorem 5: The word problem for finitely presented boolean polynomial rings is co-NP-complete.

On the other hand,

Theorem 6: The unification problem over the boolean ring B is NP-complete.

The unification problem over the boolean ring B turns out to be the same as the satisfiability problem. Since the word problem for finitely presented boolean (polynomial) rings is a special case of the unification problem over finitely presented boolean (polynomial) rings, we also have

Theorem 7: The unification problem over finitely presented boolean (polynomial) rings is co-NP-hard.

Note that the unification problem is clearly decidable, since the number of flat boolean polynomials over a finite set of indeterminates is finite. It can also be viewed as a special case of the validity problem for quantified boolean formulae; let $A = \{a_1, \ldots, a_n\}$ be a set of indeterminates, $P = \{p_1 = 0, \ldots, p_k = 0\}$ be a presentation, $V = \{y_1, \ldots, y_m\}$ be a set of variables and e and f be two forms built from A and V that have to be unified. We can assume without loss of generality that $f = 0$. Now it can be shown that e and 0 are unifiable if and only if the formula $\forall a_1 \cdots \forall a_n \exists y_1 \cdots \exists y_m : P \Rightarrow (e = 0)$ is valid, where a_i and y_j range over boolean values; thus the problem is complete for the class Π_2^P in the polynomial hierarchy. (See [7], Section 7.2, for the definitions and further details on the polynomial hierarchy.)

5. Finitely Presented Abelian Groups

5.1 Word Problem

Let G be an abelian group with the set of generators $A = \{a_1, \ldots, a_n\}$, operator + and a finite set of relations F. Each relation in F can be viewed as an equation of the form $c_1 * a_1 + \cdots + c_n * a_n = 0$ where the c_i's are integers. (The notation $c * a_i$, where c is an integer, denotes $a_i + \cdots + a_i$ ($|c|$ times) if c is positive and $-a_i + \cdots + -a_i$ ($|c|$ times) if c is negative.) In other words, each relation in F is a linear polynomial from $Z[a_1, \cdots, a_n]$ with a constant term of 0.

Treating every presentation F as a set of integral polynomials clearly enables us to solve the uniform word problem in the obvious fashion; all that we have to do is to compute the corresponding Gröbner basis. But since every term in a finitely generated abelian group can be represented by a linear integral polynomial, we need to make use of only the linear polynomials in these Gröbner bases. Thus what we have to compute is not the entire Gröbner basis but a modified Gröbner basis, called the *Gröbner basis for Abelian Groups* (referred to as "AG-Gröbner basis" hereafter), that can be obtained by deleting all the non-linear polynomials from the actual one.

The above-mentioned approach for computing AG-Gröbner bases is clearly inefficient. A better way would be to avoid the generation of non-linear polynomials altogether during the computation. Such an algorithm can be obtained by a slight modification of the algorithm in [10]. A brief description of the algorithm is given below.

Let $\{a_1, \ldots, a_n\}$ be the set of generators and $F = \{e_1 = 0, \ldots, e_k = 0\}$ be the set of equations under consideration. The algorithm assumes a total ordering $>$ on generators. Consider the indeterminate highest in the ordering and not considered so far, say a_i. Take the extended gcd of its non-zero coefficients, say $c(1,i)$, ..., $c(k,i)$, in all equations in the set F in which a_i appears. Let the extended gcd give the result $(d, m_1, \cdots, m_k)$, i.e., $d = m_1 c(1,i) + \cdots + m_k c(k,i)$. Then $m_1 e_1 + \cdots + m_k e_k = 0$ is the equation for a_i which is included in the canonical basis. Substitute for $d\ a_i$ in all equations in F; this reduction would get rid of a_i in the new equations that we get. Obviously, if the coefficient of a_i is 1 (or -1) in some equation e_j, then e_j can be included in the basis straightaway. (We do not have to compute the extended gcd.)

Repeat the above process until all equations are taken care of or all generators are taken care of.

Definition: Let M be an integer matrix. M is said to be ***upper triangular*** if and only if the following conditions hold: (a) $M_{ij} = 0$ for all $0 < j < i$. (b) $M_{ii} \neq 0$ for all i.

Let $G = \{p_1, \ldots, p_k\}$ be a set of linear polynomials over $Z[a_1, \cdots, a_n]$ such that

$$G = C * [a_1, \cdots, a_n]^T$$

where C is an $k \times n$ matrix. (Thus the p_i's have no constant terms.)

A rule in a Gröbner basis is ***redundant*** if and only if its left-hand side can be reduced using other rules.

Lemma 2: G is an AG-Gröbner basis with respect to the total ordering $>$ with no redundant rules if and only if C is in upper triangular form.

Proof: "If part": Consider the linear polynomials generated from $C * [a_1, \cdots, a_n]^T$. Since the left-hand side of the rule corresponding to every polynomial thus obtained is a linear term, i.e., term of degree 1, and each left-hand side involves a distinct indeterminate, all critical pairs are trivial, or, in other words, they do not generate a linear polynomial as a new rule. So, the basis is an AG-Gröbner basis and no rule is redundant because none of the left-hand sides can be simplified using other rules; however the right-hand side of a rule could be reduced.

"Only if part": If G is an AG-Gröbner basis with no redundant rules, then every left-hand side has a distinct indeterminate and every right-hand side involves indeterminates lower than the indeterminate on the left-hand side. Thus its polynomials can be put into a upper triangular form using the ordering on indeterminates. *Q.E.D.*

Let L be a set of linear polynomials over $Z[a_1, \cdots, a_n]$ with no constant terms and let D be an integral matrix such that $L = D * [a_1, \cdots, a_n]^T$. By the above lemma, computing the AG-Gröbner basis of L is nothing but converting D into upper triangular form. The algorithms presented in [13] (see also [6]) for constructing Hermite Normal Forms of integral matrices enable us to accomplish this in polynomial time. Thus, we have:

Theorem 8: The uniform word problem for finitely presented abelian groups can be solved in polynomial time.

The following examples are taken from [21]; the results were obtained by running the AG-Gröbner basis algorithm discussed above.

Example 4: The presentation is

$$B - 2E + 3C + 9A - 3D + 8F + 5G = 0$$
$$-B + 6H + 2E + 7A + 8D + 5F + 2G = 0$$
$$-2B + 4H + 2E + 4C + 5A - D + 6F + 6G = 0$$
$$7B + H - 3E + 6C + 4A + 9D + 7F = 0$$
$$2B - 2H + E - C + 9A + 3D + 4F - 3G = 0$$
$$-3B + 7H + 8E + 5C + 9A + 8F + G = 0$$
$$3B + 5H + 5E - C - 2A + 3D + F + 9G = 0$$
$$-H + 2E - 2C - 2A + 8D + 3F + 7G = 0$$

Using the total ordering $B > H > E > C > A > D > F > G$ on indeterminates, we obtain the following canonical basis is:

$$B + 5770416G = 0$$
$$H + 4512026G = 0$$
$$E + 5472958G = 0$$
$$C + 652996G = 0$$
$$A + 5267750G = 0$$
$$D + 6568077G = 0$$
$$F + 4856406G = 0$$
$$6634025G = 0$$

Example 5: The presentation is:

$$3F + 6E + 8C - 2B - 3A = 0$$
$$-F + 7E + D + 9C - 3B - 3A = 0$$
$$8F + 5E + 6D - 2C - B + 7A = 0$$
$$-2F + E + 4C + 2B + 6A = 0$$
$$6F + 7E + 2D + 5C - B + 3A = 0$$
$$2F + 7E + 3D + 8C + 4B + 9A = 0$$

If we use the total ordering $F > E > D > C > B > A$ on generators, the canonical basis is

$F + B + 728A = 0$
$E + 2B + 1090A = 0$
$D + 4B + 1435A = 0$
$C + 4B + 548A = 0$
$7B + 161A = 0$
$1498A = 0$

5.2 Unification Problem over Finitely Presented Abelian Groups

Lemma 3: The unification problem is decidable for finitely presented abelian groups.

Proof: Let G be an abelian group with the set of generators A $= \{a_1, \ldots, a_n\}$, operator + and a presentation F, where each relation in F is represented as a linear polynomial from $Z[a_1, \cdots, a_n]$ with a constant term of 0.

Let V $= \{y_1, \cdots, y_m\}$ be a set of variables and e_1 and e_2 be two forms involving variables from V. Forms e_1 and e_2 can be thought of as linear polynomials over $V \cup A$ with integer coefficients. Let $e = e_1 - e_2$.

Claim 1: Let $L = \{p_1, \ldots, p_m\}$ be a set of linear polynomials in $Z[a_1, \cdots, a_n]$ with the following property: every p_i in L is either a constant (i.e., an integer) or has no constant term at all. Let I be the ideal generated by L and let p be a linear polynomial in $Z[a_1, \cdots, a_n]$. Then $p \in I$ if and only if there exist $q_1, \ldots, q_m$ such that
(a) $p = p_1 q_1 + \cdots + p_m q_m$ and
(b) $p_i q_i$ is linear for all i, $1 \leq i \leq m$.

Proof: ($\Leftarrow$): Trivial.

($\Rightarrow$): We can assume, without loss of generality, that $L = \{p_1, \ldots, p_m, c\}$ where the p_i's are linear polynomials with no constant term and c is an integer. $p \in I$ implies that there exist polynomials $q_1, \ldots, q_m, r$ such that

$$p = p_1 q_1 + \cdots + p_m q_m + rc .$$

Assume $p \neq 0$, since the result trivially holds true for 0. The following possibilities have to be considered now:

(a) At least one of the q_i's has a constant term.

(b) r has linear terms (i.e., monomials of degree 1) or constant terms.

It should be obvious that either (a) or (b) should hold, because p would not be linear otherwise.

Let us first consider the case when (a) holds. Let $q_j = q_j' + d_j$ for some j, $1 \leq j \leq m$ such that q_j' has no constant term. Then $p' = p - d_j p_j$ is a linear polynomial and

$$p' = p_1 q_1 + \cdots + p_j q_j' + \cdots + p_m q_m + rc .$$

Consider (b), i.e., let $r = r' + w$ where w is a linear polynomial and r' has no linear terms. Now $p'' = p - cw$ is a linear polynomial and

$$p'' = p_1 q_1 + \cdots + p_m q_m + r' c .$$

Since the above steps can be repeated, the claim is proved. *Q.E.D.*

Claim 2: e_1 is unifiable with e_2 modulo G if and only if e, considered as a linear form over $Z[a_1, \cdots, a_n]$, has a solution modulo the ideal generated by F.

Proof: The 'only if' part is trivial. To prove the 'if' part, first observe that $e = d_1 y_1 + d_2 y_2 + \cdots + d_m y_m + q$ for some d_i $(1 \leq i \leq m)$ and q, where the d_i's are integers and q is a linear polynomial in $Z[a_1, \cdots, a_n]$. By Lemma 1, e has a solution if and only if q belongs to the ideal $J = (F, d_1, \ldots, d_m)$ and now Claim 1 enables us to complete the proof. *Q.E.D.*

Lemma 4: Let I be an ideal over $Z[a_1, \cdots, a_n]$ and $GB = \{p_1, \ldots, p_m\}$ be its Gröbner basis with respect to the degree + lexicographic ordering. Then, for all polynomials p in $Z[a_1, \cdots, a_n]$, $p \in I$ if and only if there exist polynomials $q_1, \ldots, q_m$ such that
(a) $p = p_1 q_1 + \cdots + p_m q_m$ and
(b) degree($p_i q_i$) $\leq$ degree(p) for all i, $1 \leq i \leq m$.

Proof: Obvious from the way rewriting with respect to a polynomial is defined and the property that $p \in I$ if and only if $p \rightarrow^* 0$, where $\rightarrow$ is the rewriting relation induced by GB, since GB is a Gröbner basis of I. *Q.E.D.*

Corollary 2: Let I and GB be as in Lemma 4 and let GB consist only of non-constant polynomials. Then, for a linear polynomial p in $Z[a_1, \cdots, a_n]$, $p \in I$ if and only if there exist integers $c_1, \ldots, c_m$ such that $p = p_1 c_1 + \cdots + p_m c_m$, where p_i are linear polynomials in GB.

The above corollary enables us to exhibit yet another decision procedure for the unification problem for finitely presented abelian groups. As in the previous section, let AG be an abelian group with the set of generators $A = \{a_1, \ldots, a_n\}$, operator + and a finite set of relations F. The presentation F consists of linear polynomials $c_{i,1} * a_1 + \cdots + c_{i,n} * a_n = 0$ for $1 \leq i \leq k = |F|$, where the $c_{i,j}$'s are integers. We can also assume, without loss of generality, that F is an AG-Gröbner basis. Let $V = \{y_1, \cdots, y_m\}$ be a set of variables and e_1 and e_2 be two expressions involving variables from V. Forms e_1 and e_2 can be thought of as linear polynomials over $V \cup A$ with integer coefficients. Let $e = e_1 - e_2 = d_1 y_1 + d_2 y_2 + \cdots + d_m y_m + q$ for some d_i $(1 \leq i \leq m)$ and q, where the d_i's are integers and q is a linear polynomial in $Z[a_1, \cdots, a_n]$. Let G be the $k \times n$ matrix $[c_{i,j}]$. Thus $F = G * [a_1, \cdots, a_n]^T$.

Our aim is to find solutions to the y_i's in terms of linear expressions over $a_1, \cdots, a_n$. Let $|y_i|_{a_j}$ stand for the coefficient of a_j in the expression for y_i. Thus

$$y_i = \sum_{j=1}^{n} |y_i|_{a_j} * a_j$$

Let $q = Q_1 a_1 + \cdots + Q_n a_n$. By Corollary 2, every linear polynomial in the ideal generated by F is the sum of *integral multiples* of polynomials in F. This enables us to write equations of the form

$$d_1 \mid y_1 \mid_{a_1} + \cdots + d_m \mid y_m \mid_{a_1} + Q_1 = K_1 c_{1,1} + K_2 c_{2,1} + \cdots + K_k c_{k,1}$$

where the $\mid y_j \mid_{a1}$'s and the K_i's are variables ranging over the integers. We get n such equations, since we have to account for the sums of coefficients corresponding to every generator a_i. Note that the linear polynomials appearing on the right-hand sides of the equations can also be expressed as $G^T * [K_1, \cdots, K_n]^T$.

A succinct representation of all possible solutions to a set of linear diophantine equations with integer coefficients can be obtained in polynomial time [6,13]. Together with the results in the previous section, this gives us the following theorem:

Theorem 9: The following problem can be solved in polynomial time:

> **Instance**: An abelian group AG with a set of generators A and a presentation F, and two linear expressions e_1 and e_2 involving A and a set of variables V.
>
> **Problem**: Find the set of all unifiers of e_1 and e_2. (In other words, find the set of all substitutions θ to the variables that occur in e_1 and e_2 such that $\theta(e_1) = \theta(e_2)$.)

6. Finitely Presented Commutative Semigroups

A finitely presented commutative semigroup can be presented as a set of equations of the form $t_1 = t_2$, where t_1 and t_2 are terms in $Z[a_1, \cdots, a_n]$ (we are using $*$ as the binary operation of a commutative semigroup). Thus it follows that the uniform word problem over a finitely presented commutative semigroup can be solved as a special case of the uniform word problem over commutative rings with unity; we merely restrict our attention to polynomials of the form $t_1 - t_2$. The computation steps turn out to be the same as those in [2].

The following examples of finitely presented commutative semigroups are taken from [2] and run using our algorithm for commutative rings with unity.

Example 6:

$B\ A^2 = C$
$C\ B = C^2$
$C^2\ B\ A = C\ A$

Assuming the ordering $A > B > C$ on generators, we get the canonical basis

$C\ B = C^2$
$C\ A^2 = C^3$
$B\ A^2 = C$
$C^4 = C^2$
$C^3\ A = C\ A$

Example 7:

$$
\begin{aligned}
D^3 C^5 B^4 A^2 &= D^2 C^2 B^3 A \\
D^4 C^3 B A^8 &= D^2 C^4 B^8 A \\
D^2 C^2 B^2 A^2 &= D C^2 \\
C^3 B^8 A &= D^3 B^2 \\
D^7 A^7 &= C^8
\end{aligned}
$$

Let $A < B < C < D$ be the ordering on the generators. Our program generated a canonical basis different from the one reported in [2]; our result is given below:

$$
\begin{aligned}
D^2 C^2 &= D C^2 \\
D C^3 &= D C^2 \\
D C^2 B &= D C^2 \\
D C^2 A &= D C^2 \\
D^4 B^2 &= D C^2 \\
C^{10} &= D C^2 \\
C^8 B^2 &= D C^2 \\
C^3 B^8 A &= D^3 B^2 \\
D^7 A^7 &= C^8
\end{aligned}
$$

Later, we discovered that indeed the basis reported by Lankford and Ballantyne is not a canonical basis because, by their basis, the word $A^2 B^2 C^5 D^2$ has two distinct normal forms - $C^5 D$ and $A B C^2 D$. The presence of a bug in their implementation was later confirmed by Lankford in personal communication.

7. REFERENCES

[1] Agnarsson, S., Kandri-Rody, A., Kapur, D., Narendran, P., and Saunders, B.D., "The Complexity of Testing whether a Polynomial Ideal is Nontrivial," Proceedings of the *Third MACSYMA User's Conference*, Schenectady, NY, July, 1984, pp. 452-458.

[2] Ballantyne, A.M., and Lankford, D.S., "New Decision Algorithms for Finitely Presented Commutative Semigroups," *Computer and Mathematics with Applications* Vol. 7 pp. 159-165, 1981.

[3] Buchberger, B., *An Algorithm for Finding a Basis for the Residue Class Ring of a Zero-Dimensional Polynomial Ideal* (in German), Ph.D. Thesis, Univ. of Innsbruck, Austria, Math., Inst., 1965.

[4] Buchberger, B., "A Critical-Pair/Completion Algorithm in Reduction Rings," *Proc. Logic and Machines: Decision Problems and Complexity*, (eds. by E. Borger, G. Hasenjaeger, D. Rodding), Springer LNCS 171, pp 137-161, 1984.

[5] Buchberger, B., and Loos, R., "Algebraic Simplification," in *Computer Algebra: Symbolic and Algebraic Computation* (Eds. B. Buchberger, G.E. Collins and R. Loos), Computing Suppl. 4 (1982), Springer Verlag, New York, pp. 11-43.

[6] Chou, T.J., and Collins, G.E., "Algorithms for the Solutions of Systems of Linear Diophantine Equations," *Siam J. Comput.* 11 (1982), pp. 687-708.

[7] Garey, M.R. and Johnson, D.S., *Computers and Intractability*, W.H. Freeman, 1979.

[8] Hsiang, J., *Topics in Theorem Proving and Program Synthesis,* Ph.D. Thesis, University of Illinois, Urbana-Champagne, July 1983.

[9] Huet, G., "Confluent Reductions: Abstract Properties and Applications to Term Rewriting Systems," *JACM,* Vol. 27, No. 4, October 1980, pp. 797-821. on Automata, Languages, and Programming (1983), Spain.

[10] Kandri-Rody, A., and Kapur, D., "Computing the Gröbner Basis of a Polynomial Ideal over Integers," Proceedings of the *Third MACSYMA Users' Conference*, Schenectady, NY, July 1984, pp. 436-451.

[11] Kandri-Rody, A., and Kapur, D., "Algorithms for Computing the Gröbner Bases of Polynomial Ideals over Various Euclidean Rings," Proceedings of the *EUROSAM, '84*, Cambridge, England, July 1984.

[12] Kandri-Rody, A., and Kapur, D., "An Algorithm for Computing the Gröbner Basis of a Polynomial Ideal over a Euclidean Ring," General Electric Corporate Research and Development Report 84CRD045, April, 1984; Revised, December, 1984.

[13] Kannan, R., and Bachem, A., "Polynomial Algorithms for Computing the Smith and Hermite Normal Forms of an Integer Matrix," *Siam J. Comput.* 8 (1979), pp. 499-507.

[14] Kapur, D., and Narendran, P., "An Equational Approach to Theorem Proving in First-Order Predicate Calculus," to appear in the *Proc. of the IJCAI-85*, Los Angeles, August, 1985.

[15] Knuth, D.E. and Bendix, P.B., "Simple Word Problems in Universal Algebras," in *Computational Problems in Abstract Algebras.* (Ed. J. Leech), Pergamon Press, 1970, pp. 263-297.

[16] Lankford, D.S., and Ballantyne, A.M., "Decision Procedures for Simple Equational Theories with Commutative-Associative Axioms: Complete Sets of Commutative-Associative Reductions," Automatic Theorem Proving Project, Dept. of Math. and Computer Science, University of Texas, Austin, TX 78712, Report ATP-39, August 1977.

[17] Lankford, D.S., Butler, G., and Brady, B., "Abelian Group Unification Algorithms for Elementary Terms," *Proceedings of a NSF Workshop on the Rewrite Rule Laboratory,* September 6-9, 1983, General Electric Report, April, 1984.

[18] Lankford, D.S., Butler, G., and Ballantyne, A.M., "A Progress Report on New Decision Algorithms for Finitely Presented Abelian Groups," *7th Conference on Automated Deduction*, Springer Verlag LNCS 170 (ed. R.E. Shostak), NAPA Valley, Calif., May, 1984, pp. 128-141.

[19] Lankford, D.S, and Butler, G., "On the Foundations of Applied Equational Logic," *Talk Given at General Electric Research and Development Center*, Schenectady, NY, Feb., 1984.

[20] Lauer, M., "Canonical Representatives for Residue Classes of a Polynomial Ideal," *SYMSAC* 1976, pp. 339-345.

[21] Le Chenadec, P., "Canonical Forms in Finitely Presented Algebras," *7th International Conf. on Automated Deduction*, Springer Verlag LNCS 170 (ed. R.E. Shostak), Napa Valley, Calif, May, 1984, pp. 142-165.

[22] Matijasevitch, J., "Enumerable Sets are Diophantine," *Dokl. Akad. Nauk. SSSR* 191 (1970), pp. 279-282.

[23] Peterson, G.L., and Stickel, M.E., "Complete Sets of Reductions for Some Equational Theories," *JACM* 28 (1981), pp. 233-264.

[24] Schaller, S., *Algorithmic Aspects of Polynomial Residue Class Rings*, Ph.D. Thesis, Computer Science Tech. Report 370, University of Wisconsin, Madison, 1979.

[25] Stickel, M.E., "A Unification Algorithm for Associative-Commutative Functions," *JACM* 28 (1980), pp. 423-434.

[26] Szmielew, W., "Elementary Properties of Abelian Groups," *Fund. Math.* XLI (1954), pp. 203-271.

[27] van der Waerden, B.L., *Modern Algebra*, Vols. I and II, Fredrick Ungar Publishing Co., New York, 1966.

[28] Zacharias, G., *Generalized Grobner Bases in Commutative Polynomial Rings*, Bachelor Thesis, Lab. for Computer Science, MIT, 1978.

Combining Unification Algorithms for Confined Regular Equational Theories

Kathy Yelick

Laboratory for Computer Science
Massachusetts Institute of Technology

Abstract: This paper presents a method for combining equational unification algorithms to handle terms containing "mixed" sets of function symbols. For example, given one algorithm for unifying associative-commutative operators, and another for unifying commutative operators, our algorithm provides a method for unifying terms containing both kinds of operators. We restrict our attention to a class of equational theories which we call confined regular theories. The algorithm is proven to terminate with a complete and correct set of E-unifiers. An implementation has been done as part of a larger system for reasoning about equational theories.

1. Background

Given two terms containing function symbols and variables, the classical unification problem is to find a uniform replacement of terms for the variables that makes the two terms equal. Equational unification extends the classical problem to solving equations in an equational theory. That is, given a set of equational axioms, find a substitution for the variables in two terms that makes them provably equal from the set of axioms.

Unification was first described by Herbrand in 1930, and was first put to practical use by Robinson as a basic step in *resolution* [Robinson 65], an inference rule used as a complete proof system for first order predicate calculus. Because of its power, resolution is often used as the basis for automatic theorem provers and is also exploited in implementing the logic programming language, PROLOG [Kowalski 74]. Unification is a basic step in completion algorithms for *term rewriting systems*, [Knuth 70, Forgaard 84a]. Term rewriting systems, like resolution, can be used as a basis for automatic theorem provers [Huet 82, Kapur 84, Goguen 80, Hsiang 83], checking formal specifications [Goguen 79, Kownacki 84], and interpreting logic programming languages [Dershowitz 83a, Fribourg 84]. Unification is also used in type inference algorithms for languages such as ML [Milner 78], in which polymorphic typing is used as a compromise between strictly typed and typeless languages.

Until recently, most applications made use only of classical unification; however, the need for equational unification is clear. For example, a PROLOG clause stating the commutativity of a user defined function will cause the program to loop. Similarly, a commutative axiom in a term rewriting system cannot be oriented into a rewrite rule without losing the termination property of the system. In both cases, a solution is to "build in" commutativity into the system, i.e., in the unification process, so the axiom is not explicitly needed. *Equational term rewriting systems* are described in [Peterson 81, Jouannaud 84, Dershowitz 83b, Kirchner 84a]. A further review of areas in which equational unification may be useful is given in [Siekman 84].

This research was supported by the National Science Foundation under Grant MCS-8119846-A01 and by Office of Naval Research Contract N00014-83-K-012 with DARPA funding.

Author's address: MIT Laboratory for Computer Science, 545 Technology Square, Cambridge, MA 02139.

For each equational theory of interest, a unification algorithm must be discovered and implemented, and with some notable exceptions (see Section 6), this process is not automatic. In fact, given two algorithms for different equational theories, the problem of combining the unification algorithms is non-trivial. It is this problem which is studied and partially solved here. This paper provides an algorithm for combining equational unification algorithms for a restricted class of equational theories.

The remainder of this paper is divided into six main sections: In Section 2, we present some definitions, including a more formal definition of equational unification. Section 3 discusses our generalization of the problem, and the basic assumptions of our approach. Section 3.3 describes some simplifying restrictions and discusses the motivation behind the restrictions. Our unification procedure is given in Section 4.1, along with an example in Section 4.2. [Yelick 85] presents a proof of correctness for the algorithm; the main ideas behind the theorems are stated without proof in Section 5. Finally, a short survey of related work can be found in Section 6 and a summary of our conclusions in Section 7.

2. Definitions

The following definitions are consistent with the definitions of [Fages 84] and [Huet 80]. We begin with basic definitions of terms and functions on terms. Section 2.2 describes equational theories, incorporating both algebraic and proof theoretic notions. The central problem of this work, equational unification, is defined in Section 2.3.

2.1. First Order Terms and Substitutions

Let V be a countable set of variables and F be a family of function symbols with associated arity such that V and F are disjoint. We recursively define the set of terms, T(F, V), where each term is either a variable or a function symbol of arity n followed by n terms. We assume the sets V and F to be fixed and, thus, use T in place of T(F, V). Function symbols of arity zero, called *constants*, will be denoted by the letters a, b, c, d, to be distinguished from variables, denoted by the letters u, v, w, x, y, z. Terms formed from function symbols alone, T(F), are called *ground terms* and are denoted **G**.

Given a term, t, let $\mathcal{V}(t)$ be the set of variables in t and $\mathcal{F}(t)$ be the set of function symbols in t. The root symbol of the tree representation of a term, t, will be denoted *t.root*—*t.root* is a variable if t is a variable, and a function symbol if t is not a variable.

A *substitution* is a mapping from variables to terms, extended to an endomorphism (a homomorphism from a set to itself) on terms. A substitution will be denoted by a set of variable-term pairs, $\{v_1 \leftarrow t_1, v_2 \leftarrow t_2, \ldots\}$, where all variables outside the set are implicitly mapped to themselves. The empty substitution, i.e., the mapping in which each variable is mapped to itself, will be written ι. The universe of substitutions will be denoted S. We define the *domain*, $\mathcal{D}$, of a substitution, σ, as follows: $\mathcal{D}(\sigma) = \{v \mid \sigma v \neq v\}$. In addition, we define the range, $\mathcal{R}$, as $\mathcal{R}(\sigma) = \bigcup_{v \in \mathcal{D}(\sigma)} \{\sigma v\}$, and the range variables, $\mathcal{I}$, as $\mathcal{I}(\sigma) = \bigcup_{t \in \mathcal{R}(\sigma)} \mathcal{V}(t)$.

A term, t, is said to be *an instance of* a term, s, if and only if there exists a substitution, σ such that $t = \sigma s$. When the domain of σ is restricted to the variables in $\mathcal{V}(s)$, σ is unique and is called the *match* of t by s.

Substitutions may be *composed* using functional composition, i.e., for any term, t, $(\sigma_1 \circ \sigma_2)\, t = \sigma_1(\sigma_2 t)$. A substitution, σ_1, is *more general than* another, σ_2, if and only if there exists a third substitution, τ, such that $\sigma_2 = \tau \circ \sigma_1$. We denote this partial ordering by $\sigma_1 \leq \sigma_2$.

2.2. Equational Theories

An equation is a pair of terms, $t = s$. A *congruence* relation is an equivalence relation, $\sim$, which is additionally closed under *replacement of equals*, i.e., $t_1 \sim s_1, \ldots, t_n \sim s_n \Rightarrow f(t_1, \ldots, t_n) \sim f(s_1, \ldots, s_n)$ for all $f \in F$ of arity n. Given a set of equations, E, the *equational theory presented by* E is the set of equations, E*, formed by the finest congruence over T that contains E and is closed over instantiation. In other words, E* is exactly the set of equations derivable from E by a finite proof, using reflexivity, symmetry, transitivity, replacement of equals, and instantiation as inference rules. We will consistently use E and E*, respectively, as a set of axioms and the equational theory presented by those axioms. The congruence relation on terms may be written $t \underset{E}{=} s$, when $t = s$ is an element of E*.

An *algebra*, $\mathcal{A}$, is a pair $(\tilde{A}, \tilde{F})$, where $\tilde{A}$ is a set of elements called the *carrier* of $\mathcal{A}$ and $\tilde{F}$ is a set function symbols, each mapping $\tilde{A}^n$ to $\tilde{A}$ for some arity, n. A mapping, μ, from V to $\mathcal{A}$, (i.e., to the carrier of $\mathcal{A}$) extended as a homomorphism from T to $\mathcal{A}$, is called an $\mathcal{A}$-assignment. For example, in the *term algebra*, $\mathcal{T} = (T(F, V), \tilde{F})$, the carrier is the set of terms and $\tilde{F}$ contains term constructors, one for each function symbol in F. The identity map is an example of a $\mathcal{T}$-assignment.

If $\mu t = \mu s$ for all $\mathcal{A}$-assignments, μ, then $\mathcal{A}$ is called a *model* of the equation $t = s$, and $t = s$ is said to be *valid* in $\mathcal{A}$; we denote this condition by $\mathcal{A} \models t = s$. We extend $\models$ to a set of equations by: $\mathcal{A} \models$ E if and only if $t = s \in E \Rightarrow \mathcal{A} \models t = s$. Given a set of equations, E, we denote the class of all models of E by $\mathcal{M}$(E). Birkhoff showed that the syntactic definition of equational theory given above is equivalent to defining an equational theory semantically as the set of equations valid in all models of E, E* = *Eq* $\mathcal{M}$(E) [Birkhoff 35, Grätzer 78].

The congruence relation on terms in an equational theory is extended to substitutions by $\sigma_1 \underset{E}{=} \sigma_2$ if and only if $\forall \nu \in V\, (\sigma_1 \nu \underset{E}{=} \sigma_2 \nu)$. In many cases we are interested only in the effect of a substitution on a particular set of variables, V. We augment our definition as follows: $\sigma_1 \overset{V}{\underset{E}{=}} \sigma_2$ if and only if $\forall \nu \in V\, (\sigma_1 \nu \underset{E}{=} \sigma_2 \nu)$. Furthermore, we say that σ_1 is *more general than* σ_2 *modulo E over V*, written $\sigma_1 \overset{V}{\underset{E}{\leq}} \sigma_2$, if and only if

$$\exists\, \tau \text{ such that } \tau \circ \sigma_1 \overset{V}{\underset{E}{=}} \sigma_2.$$

The congruence relation defined by $\sigma_1 \overset{V}{\underset{E}{\leq}} \sigma_2$ and $\sigma_2 \overset{V}{\underset{E}{\leq}} \sigma_1$ will be denoted $\sigma_1 \overset{V}{\underset{E}{\equiv}} \sigma_2$.

If there exists a non-trivial model of E, i.e., a model $\mathcal{A} = (\tilde{A}, \tilde{F})$ such that $\mathcal{A} \models$E and $|\tilde{A}| > 1$, then the theory presented by E is said to be *strictly consistent*. Syntactically, an equational theory has only the trivial model if and only if $x \underset{E}{=} y$, since any equation is a substitution instance of this one. The unification problem in an inconsistent theory is always trivial. By assumption, we will work with only strictly consistent equational theories.

2.3. Equational Unification

The equational unification problem is to solve an equation of the form $t = s$ in the quotient algebra, $\mathcal{T}/\underset{E}{=}$, whose carrier is the set of congruence classes of terms defined by E.

Definition. Let t and s be terms and E be a set of equations. A substitution, σ, is said to be an *E-unifier* of t and s if and only if:

$$\sigma t \underset{E}{=} \sigma s.$$

Let U_E denote the set of all E-unifiers of terms t and s, i.e., $U_E(t, s) = \{\sigma \in S \mid \sigma t \underset{E}{=} \sigma s\}$. In general, U_E is infinite; we represent it by a *complete set of unifiers*, CSU_E, from which set the U_E can exactly be generated by considering all instances of each substitution in the CSU_E. If every element of a CSU_E is necessary for completeness, it is called a *minimal complete set of unifiers*, written μCSU_E.

Definition. If $V = \mathcal{V}(t) \cup \mathcal{V}(s)$ then Σ is a μCSU_E of t and s if and only if:

(1) *Consistency:* Σ contains no non-unifying substitutions.

$$\Sigma \subseteq U_E$$

(2) *Completeness:* Σ generates all unifiers.

$$\forall \sigma \in U_E(t, s)\ \exists\, \sigma' \in \Sigma \quad \sigma' \overset{V}{\underset{E}{\leq}} \sigma$$

(3) *Minimality:* No substitution in Σ is redundant.

$$\forall \sigma, \sigma' \in \Sigma \quad \sigma \overset{V}{\underset{E}{\not\leq}} \sigma'$$

When it exists, a μCSU_E is unique up to $\overset{V}{\underset{E}{\equiv}}$ [Fages 84]. The size of the μCSU_E is bounded for certain values of E. If $E = \emptyset$, there is always a singular μCSU_E for any two unifiable terms. If E contains only the associative and commutative axioms (the AC theory) then the μCSU_E is always finite. If E contains only the associative axiom, then there are some pairs of terms for which the μCSU_E is infinite. If there is a finite CSU_E then a μCSU_E exists and can be found by filtering out non-minimal unifiers through matching. In general, though, the properties of minimality and completeness may conflict, so that no μCSU_E exists [Fages 83].

If whenever a unification procedure terminates it generates a consistent and complete set of unifiers, the procedure is said to be *partially correct*. If in addition the procedure always terminates, it is said to be *totally correct*.

In many cases, it will be necessary for a unification algorithm to use more variables in the range of the unifiers than occur in the terms being unified. Because unification procedures are often used within larger systems containing variables of their own, it is useful to require an additional property. A set of unifiers, Σ, of t and s is said to be *protective*, if, given a finite set of variables, W, such that $\mathcal{V}(t) \cup \mathcal{V}(s) \subseteq W$:

$$\forall \sigma \in \Sigma \quad (\mathcal{D}(\sigma) \subseteq V) \text{ and } (W \cap \mathcal{I}(\sigma) = \emptyset).$$

Without loss of generality, we will require protection of all unification algorithms, both for the pragmatic reason above and for the technical reason that it makes unifiers idempotent, (i.e., $\mathcal{D}(\sigma) \cap \mathcal{I}(\sigma) = \emptyset \Rightarrow \sigma \circ \sigma = \sigma$) which will be used in the proofs.

3. A Generalized Approach

Much of the work to date in equational unification has been theoretically motivated--deciding whether there exists a unification algorithm for a particular equational theory and what form the algorithm takes. Much of the the work has involved simplifying assumptions on the structure of terms, i.e., algorithms are usually developed to handle terms whose operator sets all belong to a single set of axioms. The disadvantage to this approach is that each time a new axiom is added to theory, a unification algorithm must be found and implemented for the entire set of axioms. If we were given a term containing the function symbols + and ★, and we know that + is associative and commutative and ★ is commutative, it was not sufficient to have two E-unification algorithms, one for the AC theory and one for the commutative theory, we needed an algorithm defined specifically for the theory combining associativity and commutativity for + with commutativity for ★.

Our approach is generalized in the following sense: Given a unification algorithm for E_1, and a unification algorithm for E_2, we can, in some cases, automatically generate an algorithm for the combined theory of E_1 and E_2. In the previous example, this would mean automatic generation of the unification algorithm for the term containing + and ★, given the two algorithms for AC and commutative unification.

3.1. Partitioning Equational Theories

This section describes our way of dividing the problem of unification modulo E by partitioning the set of equations, E, according to the distribution of function symbols in E.

Our procedure is recursive; a top-level procedure performs the steps in unification that are common to all equational theories and then calls an appropriate equational unification algorithm. Each E-unification algorithm is implemented to perform unification in a single equational theory, making no assumptions about the properties of the operators in the subterms, but recursively calling the top-level general unification procedure to unify subterms. The algorithms are assumed totally correct, but minimality is not required because it is difficult to guarantee without the costly filtering process, and because it is usually not necessary in applications of E-unification.

Our first underlying assumption is that the sets of operators handled by different unification algorithms are disjoint. If we consider only sets of axioms having pairwise disjoint operator sets, then each operator will be contained in exactly one set of axioms, and thus only one unification algorithm will need to know about the equational properties of that symbol. Formally, we define a partitioning on the axioms presenting E^* by:

Definition. Let $\pi = \{E_1, E_2, \ldots, E_n\}$, where each E_i is a set of equations. π is a *partitioned presentation* of an equational theory E^* if and only if:

(1) $\mathcal{F}(E_i) \cap \mathcal{F}(E_j) = \emptyset,\ \forall\, i \neq j \leq n$

(2) $\bigcup_{i \leq n} E_i$ is a presentation of E^*, and

(3) $\emptyset \in \pi$.

Each of the E_i's presents a theory, E^*_i, called a *sub-theory* of E^*. The empty set of equations in (3) represents the empty equational theory, which is a sub-theory of any theory. Semantically, the meaning of the combination of these sub-theories is the intersection of their models, i.e., $\mathcal{M}(E) = \bigcap_{i \leq n} \mathcal{M}(E_i)$.

The partition on equations, π, naturally defines an equivalence relation on function symbols. $f_1 =_\pi f_2$ if and only if either:

(1) There exists $E_i \in \pi$ such that $f_1 \in \mathcal{F}(E_i)$ and $f_2 \in \mathcal{F}(E_i)$.

(2) Or, for all $E_i \in \pi$, $f_1 \notin \mathcal{F}(E_i)$ and $f_2 \notin \mathcal{F}(E_i)$.

The equivalence class of symbols containing f will be denoted $[f]$, e.g., if one of the sub-theories is the AC theory for + where + has an identity constant, 0, then $[+] = \{+, 0\}$. Any function that does not appear in any of the E_i's is called *uninterpreted*.

This equivalence relation on function symbols will provide a convenient way of naming unification algorithms of sub-theories. We will refer the the set of function symbols in E_i as the set of *constrained* function symbols for the theory E^*_i; if $E_i = \emptyset$ then its set of constrained symbols will be all the uninterpreted symbols. The unification algorithm corresponding to the theory in which f is constrained will be denoted E[f]_*unify*.

An example should help clarify our definitions. Let E be presented by the axioms in figure 3-1, and let F be the set $\{+, *, a, \bullet, \star, b, f, g\}$. $\pi = \{E_1, E_2, E_3, E_4, E_5\}$ is a partitioned presentation of E.

$\pi = \{E_1, E_2, E_3, E_4, E_5\}$

E_1: $x + y = y + x$
$(x + y) + z = x + (y + x)$

E_2: $x * y = y * x$
$(x * y) * z = x * (y * z)$
$a * a = a$

E_3: $x \bullet y = y \bullet x$
$(x \bullet y) \bullet z = x \bullet (y \bullet z)$

E_4: $x \star y = y \star x$

E_5: $\emptyset$

Classes of F: $\{F_1, F_2, F_3, F_4, F_5\}$

$F_1 = \mathcal{F}(E_1) = \{+\}$

$F_2 = \mathcal{F}(E_2) = \{*, a\}$

$F_3 = \mathcal{F}(E_3) = \{\bullet\}$

$F_4 = \mathcal{F}(E_3) = \{\star\}$

$F_5 = \{b, f, g\}$

Figure 3-1: A Partitioned Presentation

There is a final technicality to clarify before beginning the discussion of our procedure. Although we speak of an E-unification algorithm for a particular equational theory, each algorithm is really for an isomorphism class of equational theories. For example, if both + and • are AC, as in figure 3-1, we can use the same algorithm for unifying a pair of terms containing + or a pair of terms containing •. The two equational theories, + AC and • AC, are not equal theories, but the isomorphism is so natural that we would normally consider them to be the same. A difficulty arises when the two theories are combined, i.e., when terms to be unified contain more than one operator with the same equational properties. To resolve this issue, each E-unification algorithm is parameterized over the set of names of constrained symbols. In this example, AC-unification for + and AC-unification for • are both instances of the same E-unification algorithm. For the purpose of this discussion, we will assume a different unification procedure exists for each instance of a theory, although in the implementation we do not duplicate the actual code.

3.2. Some Basic Functions

Our procedure begins by transforming the input terms into simpler terms containing only operators from a subset of the axioms, a subset for which there is a known E-unification algorithm. The information lost in the transformation is saved in the form of a substitution. This substitution is combined, through E-unification of substitutions, with each sub theory unifier of the transformed terms. Section 3.2.1 describes this transformation process on terms and Section 3.2.2 describes a procedure for unifying substitutions.

3.2.1. Homogeneous Terms

A term, t, is called *homogeneous* with respect to a set of function symbols, F, if and only if $\mathcal{F}(t) \subseteq$ F. *Homog* converts an inhomogeneous term (i.e., a term containing operators that are not in F) into a homogeneous term. The basic operation of *Homog* is to replace all maximal subterms whose top function symbol is outside F with a new variable.

Definition. Let F be a set of function symbols and t be a term, then *Homog*(t, F) is defined as:

(1) If t is a variable, then *Homog*(t, F) $= t$.

(2) If $t = f(t_1,...,t_n)$ and $f \in$ F, then *Homog*(t, F) $= f($*Homog*$(t_1$, F$),...,$*Homog*$(t_n$, F$))$.

(3) If $t = f(t_1,...,t_n)$ and $f \notin$ F, then *Homog*(t, F) $= v$, where v is a new variable.

Homog(t, F) is unique for t, up to names of the new variables. Technically, we should be more precise about the new variables that are used, for example, in (2) we assume any new variables in *Homog*(t_i, F) are disjoint from both the old variables in t_j and new ones In *Homog*(t_j, F), for $i \neq j$. To assure the property of protection on our procedure, these new variables must also be disjoint from the set of protected variables.

Taking F = $\{a, *\}$ and v_1, v_2, v_3 to be new variables, we have the following values for *Homog*:

$$Homog(x * (a + y), F) = x * v_1$$
$$Homog(x * (a * b), F) = x * (a * v_2)$$
$$Homog(x + y, F) = v_3.$$

In our procedure we will homogenize a term with respect to some equivalence class of F as defined by π, namely the equivalence class of the head symbol. We will therefore use $\hat{t}$ to denote *Homog*(t, [$t.root$]).

To take a homogeneous term back to the term from which it was formed, we find a *preserving substitution.* If t' is a homogeneous form of t, then notice that t is an instance of t' and we can therefore find the match of t for t'. We will denote the match, in this case called a preserving substitution, by $\mathcal{P}(t, t')$. $\mathcal{P}(t, t')$ maps each new variable in t' to the term it replaced in t.

3.2.2. Unification of Substitutions

Definition. Given a set of equations, E, a substitution, σ, is said to *E-unify* two substitutions, φ_1 and φ_2 if and only if:

$$\sigma \circ \varphi_1 \underset{E}{=} \sigma \circ \varphi_2.$$

We need an effective procedure, call it *map_unify*, for finding unifiers of two substitutions, φ_1, φ_2. In looking for a unifier of two substitutions, as in testing for equality of substitutions, we restrict ourselves to the domain of the substitutions, $V = \mathfrak{D}(\varphi_1) \cup \mathfrak{D}(\varphi_2)$. A *corresponding pair of terms* is defined to be a pair, $\langle t_1, t_2 \rangle$, where $t_1 = \varphi_1 v$ and $t_2 = \varphi_2 v$ for some $v \in V$. We unify each corresponding pair of terms in substitutions sequentially, accumulating the unifiers, and applying the results to remaining pairs; the end result is be a set of unifiers of the substitutions. If any corresponding pair is not unifiable, then the substitution are not unifiable. The following routine, *map_unify*, which assumes the existence of our main procedure, the *CR-unify* procedure for terms (presented in Section 4.1), performs the desired function. The assumption is necessary here because the two procedures, *map_unify* and *CR-unify*, are mutually recursive.

```
map_unify = proc (φ1, φ2:subst) returns(Σ:subst_set)
    Σ0 := {ι}
    i := 0
    for v ∈ 𝔇(φ1)∪𝔇(φ2) do
        i := i + 1
        Σi := {τi∘σi-1 | σi-1∈Σi-1 & τi∈CR-unify(σi-1φ1v, σi-1φ2v)}
        end
    return(Σi)
    end map_unify
```

Figure 3-2: Procedure *map_unify*, for Unification of Substitutions

---

3.3. A Restriction

CR-unify terminates for all equational theories, and all the substitutions are indeed unifiers. However, it is complete for a restricted class of equational theories which we called *confined regular* theories. (See [Yelick 85] for a discussion of the difficulties of removing the restriction.)

An equation, $t = s$, where either t or s is a variable and the other term is a non-variable, is called a *non-confining* equation. A set of equations containing no non-confining equations is called *confined*. The problem caused by non-confining equations is that a single congruence class of terms in the theory may contain terms with root symbols from more than one equivalence class of F. An example of an non-confined theory is the theory of idempotence. Let E be the theory presented by $\pi = \{\{x \cdot x = x\}, \emptyset\}$, and let f be a function symbol in F. The equation $f(x) \cdot f(x) \underset{E}{=} f(x)$ is in E, even though $\cdot$ and f are in different equivalence classes of F. The problem caused by having roots in different equivalence classes will be apparent in the description of *CR-unify* (Figure 4-1), where we begin the unification process by unifying in the sub-theory of the roots. We can restrict the class of equational theories to confined theories by restricting the the axioms to confined sets [Yelick 85].

Lemma 1 shows that in confined theories there are no equations whose right and left root symbols are constrained by different sub-theories. If this lemma were not true, case (4) of *CR-unify* could not unconditionally return the empty set of unifiers.

Lemma 1. If t and s are non-variable terms such that $t \underset{E}{=} s$, then $t.root =_{\pi} s.root$.

Proof: By induction on the length of proof that $t \underset{E}{=} s$ [Yelick 85].

Our algorithm is not complete for all confined theories. A further restriction on the theory, which is sufficient for completeness of the algorithm, is reqularity of the theories; a theory is *regular* if and only if for all equations in the theory, $t \underset{E}{=} s$, $\mathcal{V}(t) = \mathcal{V}(s)$. The restriction to regular theories, like the restriction on confined theories, is syntactically checkable, i.e., the theory is regular if and only if every presentation is regular [Yelick 85]. The lemma on regularity that is used in the proof of correctness is too technical for the current discussion, but intuitively, non-regular theories may allow a variable to be unified with a inhomogeneous term containing the variable.

4. The *CR-unify* Procedure

The main procedure, a procedure for generalized equational unification of terms, is presented below. We follow the description of the procedure with an example. The basic assumptions are summarized here. E^* is a strictly consistent confined regular equational theory, with a fixed partitioned presentation, $\{E_1, \ldots, E_n\}$. For each E_i, there is a known unification algorithm that returns a CSU_{E_i}, given any two terms that are homogeneous in $\mathcal{F}(E_i)$.

4.1. Procedure Description

The *CR-unify* procedure is given in Figure 4-1. If t and s are both variables, then they are unifiable by $\{t \leftarrow s\}$. If t is a variable and s is not, then *variable_unify* is called. If t and s are both non-variables with root symbols from different equivalence classes of F, then any substitution instance of t and s will also have root symbols with this property. By Lemma 1, no such equation can be in E, so t and s are not unifiable.

If both t and s are non-variables with root symbols in the same equivalence class, then we form homogeneous terms, $\hat{t}$ and $\hat{s}$, and find the preserving substitution, $\mathcal{P}(t, \hat{t}) \cup \mathcal{P}(s, \hat{s})$. The union of these substitutions is well-defined because the domain of each substitution contains only new variables from *Homog*(t) and *Homog*(s), and these two variable sets are assumed to be disjoint. The set of sub-theory unifiers, P, is found by unifying homogeneous terms in the appropriate sub-theory, and the preserving substitution is combined with each $\rho \in P$ by unification of substitutions. If t and s are not E-unifiable, then Σ, the final set of unifiers, is empty.

```
CR-unify = proc (t, s: term) returns (subst_set)
    case
        is_variable(t) and is_variable(s) ⇒                     % case 1
            return({{t←s}})
        is_variable(t) and ~is_variable(s) ⇒                    % case 2
            return(variable_unify(t, s))
        is_variable(s) and ~is_variable(t) ⇒                    % case 3
            return(variable_unify(s, t))
        t.root ≠_π s.root ⇒                                     % case 4
            return (∅)
        t.root =_π s.root ⇒                                     % case 5
                γ := 𝒫(t, t̂) ∪ 𝒫(s, ŝ)
                Γ := E[t.root]_unify (t̂, ŝ)
                Σ := ∪_{ρ∈Γ} map_unify(ρ, γ)
                return(Σ)
        end
    end CR-unify

variable_unify = proc (v: variable, s: term) returns (subst_set)
    γ := 𝒫(s, ŝ)
    case
        v ∉ 𝒱(s) ⇒                                              % case A
            return ({{v ← s}})
        v ∈ 𝒱(s) & v ∉ ℐ(γ) ⇒                                   % case B
            Γ := E[s.root]_unify (v, ŝ)
            Σ := ∪_{ρ∈Γ} map_unify(ρ, γ)
            return(Σ)
        v ∈ 𝒱(s) & v ∈ ℐ(γ) ⇒                                   % case C
            return(∅)
        end
    end variable_unify
```

Figure 4-1: The *CR-unify* Procedure for Equational Unification

If one term is a variable, and one a non-variable, then *variable_unify* is called and we have the following cases. If v does not occur in s (case A), then the terms are unifiable by the substitution, $\{v \leftarrow s\}$. The case where v occurs in s but not in $\mathcal{I}(\gamma)$, i.e., v occurs only in the homogeneous part of s (case B), is similar to case 5 of *CR-unify*. If either v occurs in both s and $\mathcal{I}(\gamma)$ (case C), the algorithm simply returns the empty set.

4.2. An Example

This example shows unification in the equational theory, E, as presented in Figure 3-1. Let the inputs be terms, $t = b + (x * y)$ and $s = a + z$. Both are non-variable terms and the sub-theory of the root operator (+ in both cases), is presented by E_1. Case 5 of *CR-unify* is the appropriate case. Following this branch, we compute the homogeneous terms, $t' = v_1 + v_2$ and $s' = v_3 + z$, with respect to F_1, and the combined preserving substitution, $\gamma = \{v_1 \leftarrow b, v_2 \leftarrow x * y, v_3 \leftarrow a\}$.

The homogeneous terms are unified in the sub-theory of E_1, the AC theory for +. E_1-unifying t' and s' results in a complete set of AC-unifiers. This set will contain two unifiers that are within $\overset{V}{\underset{E}{\equiv}}$ of:

$$\rho_1 = \{v_3 \leftarrow v_1, z \leftarrow v_2\}$$
$$\rho_2 = \{v_3 \leftarrow v_2, z \leftarrow v_1\}.$$

We proceed by calling *map_unify* with ρ_1 and γ. (Both ρ_1 and ρ_2 will be considered eventually, and the choice of which unifier to look at first is arbitrary.) No unifiers are found using ρ_1 because we are forced to unify a from F_2 with b from F_5.

We call *map_unify* again, this time with ρ_2 and γ. *Map_unify* proceeds until it is necessary to unify $x * y$, with a. The terms are E_2-unifiable with the single most general unifier, $\{x \leftarrow a, y \leftarrow a\}$. Using this E_2-unifier, the single element of Σ is the substitution $\{z \leftarrow b, v_1 \leftarrow b, v_2 \leftarrow a * a, x \leftarrow a, y \leftarrow a\}$. We can check our result by applying the substitution to the original terms, t and s and testing for equality modulo E.

$$b + (a * a) \underset{E}{=} a + b$$

5. Proof of Correctness

In this section we present an overview of the proofs given in [Yelick 85]. They are divided into two main pieces: a proof of partial correctness and a proof of termination. The proofs are too long to present in full detail here; instead, we opt for a less precise and more intuitive argument of correctness. Some details of the *CR-unify* procedure, such as generation and protection of new variables and order of recursive calls, have also been left out of this description.

5.1. Consistency and Completeness

The proof of partial correctness of *CR-unify* is by induction on the depth of recursion. The main lemmas needed for the proofs of consistency and completeness are used to show that the diagram of Figure 5-1 is correct. There are two levels of detail at which the diagram should be viewed. Consider first only the mappings, i.e., the labels on edges; note that the right and left halves are mirror images; each shows that $\sigma \circ \rho \underset{E}{=} \sigma \circ \gamma$. Now consider the labels on vertices, $\hat{t}$ and $\hat{s}$ are homogeneous terms and t and s are some possibly inhomogeneous instances of these terms, ρ is an E_i-unifier of $\hat{t}$ and $\hat{s}$, and σ is an E-unifier of t and s.

The consistency argument says roughly that if γ is the preserving substitution, then for any sub-theory unifier of the homogeneous terms, ρ, all E-unifiers of ρ and γ are E-unifiers of t and s. The completeness argument says roughly that for any E-unifier, σ, there exists some sub-theory unifier, ρ, of the homogeneous terms, such

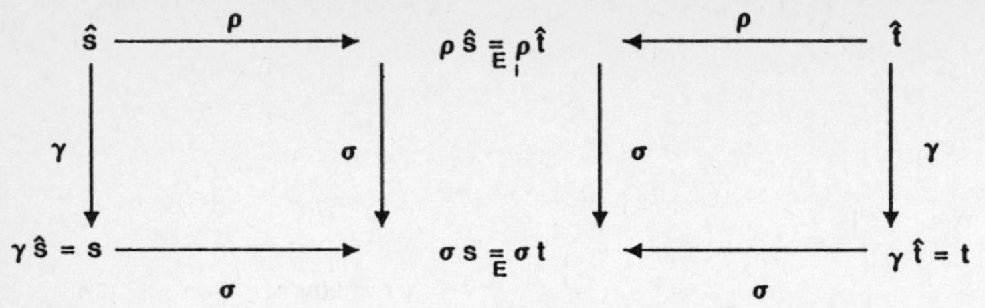

Figure 5-1: Diagram Exemplifying Correctness Properties

that σ is an E-unifier of ρ and γ. The actual lemmas used in the induction proofs of consistency and completeness, are stated in Lemmas 2 and 3, respectively.

Lemma 2. Let t and s be homogeneous terms in F, the set of constrained symbols for some sub-theory, E_i^* of E^*. Let ρ, γ, and σ be substitutions:

$$(\rho t \underset{E_i}{=} \rho s) \ \& \ (\sigma \circ \rho \underset{E}{=} \sigma \circ \gamma) \quad \Rightarrow \quad \sigma(\gamma t) \underset{E}{=} \sigma(\gamma \rho).$$

Proof: See [Yelick 85].

Lemma 3. Let t and s be non-variable terms such that *t.root* and *s.root* are constrained by E_i, a sub-theory of E^* and let σ be a substitution. If E^* is confined, then:

$$\sigma t \underset{E}{=} \sigma s \quad \Rightarrow \quad \exists\, \rho \text{ such that } \rho \hat{t} \underset{E_i}{=} \rho \hat{s}.$$

Proof: See [Yelick 85].

The proof of the Lemma 2 is quite straightforward, while the proof of Lemma 3 is by construction of ρ and involves more technical detail.

The partial correctness of *CR-unify* can be stated by the following two theorems, both proven by induction on the depth of recursion.

Theorem I. Given two terms, t and s, if *CR-unify*(t, s) terminates are returns the substitution σ, then:

$$\sigma t \underset{E}{=} \sigma s.$$

Proof: By induction on the depth of recursion [Yelick 85].

Theorem II. Let E^* be a confined regular equational theory, t and s be terms, and V be set of variables such that $V = \mathcal{V}(t) \cup \mathcal{V}(s)$. If $\sigma t \underset{E}{=} \sigma s$, then if *CR-unify*$(t, s)$ terminates, it will return some substitition σ' such that:

$$\sigma' \overset{V}{\underset{E}{\leq}} \sigma.$$

Proof: By induction on the depth of recursion [Yelick 85].

5.2. Termination

If recursive calls from *CR-unify* were made only to subterms of the original inputs, then termination would be obvious. However, at each iteration within *map_unify*, the substitution accumulated thus far is applied to the next corresponding pair of terms, so the terms of a recursive call are not necessarily subterms of the inputs, and may actually be larger than the inputs. We define a noetherian ordering, i.e., a partial order with no infinite decreasing chains, on pairs of terms. This ordering is proven to be strictly decreasing with each level of recursion for the *CR-unify* procedure. The termination proof and noetherian ordering are generalizations of Fages' proof of termination and ordering for AC-unification [Fages 84]. The following theorem can be stated for *CR-unify*.

Theorem III. Given terms t and s, *CR-unify*(t, s) will terminate.

Proof: By noetherian induction on t and s [Yelick 85].

6. Related Work

There are currently known complete E-unification algorithms for commutative operators [Livesey 76], AC operators, [Livesey 76], [Fages 84], [Ballantyne 81], signed trees [Kirchner 81], and abelian group operators [Lankford 84] (termination in the general case still an open problem). The AC algorithm has been extended to handle operators that are also idempotent, ACI, or have a unit element, ACU, [Livesey 76], or both, ACUI, [Fages 84]. A procedure for enumerating unifiers of an associative operator is described in [Plotkin 72]. These algorithms are all theory-specific, the equational theory is built into the algorithm rather than being a parameter to the algorithm.

The unification procedures based on *narrowing* [Slagle 74] are of a more automatic nature. For equational theories representable by a convergent term rewriting system there is an algorithm to automatically generate a unification procedure [Fay 79]. [Hullot 80] gives sufficient conditions for termination of the narrowing procedure, along with some improvements, and [Jouannaud 83] generalizes this work to equational term rewriting systems.

[Kirchner 84b] gives a general algorithm for the *decomposable theories*, theories in which a natural decomposition process occurs during unification. For example, if f is a symbol that does not appear at the root of either side of any equations in E, then the problem of E-unifying terms of the form $f\ (s_1,...,s_n)$ and $f\ (t_1,...,t_n)$, modulo E, is proven equivalent to unifying all pairs s_i, t_i, $1 \leq i \leq n$.

Nelson and Oppen provide an algorithm for cooperating decision procedures for predicate calculus theories [Nelson 79], much in the same way we provide an algorithm for cooperating unification procedures for equational theories. A similarity between the structure of the two algorithms is apparent when unification is considered in the Martelli and Montanari style of propagating equalities [Martelli 82]. [Shostak 84] improves on the algorithm of [Nelson 79] by localizing the shared information more effectively, thereby improving the algorithms efficiency and extendibility.

7. Conclusions and Future Work

We define a new generalized approach to equational unification by examining the conditions under which a set of E-unification algorithms can be combined to yield a single unification procedure for the combined equational theory. We present an algorithm for combined equational unification and prove it is consistent and terminating for all equational theories, and that it is complete for the confined regular theories.

A consequence of our method and the proofs is that any confined regular equational theory with a known E-unification algorithm for homogeneous terms, (also known as the *variable-only case for* E) can be automatically extended to the general case, i.e., the case where terms may contain uninterpreted function symbols or more than one instance of operators with E's properties. The proof of termination, correctness and completeness of such a generalization is an instance of our proof.

A preliminary implementation has been made as part of the REVE term rewriting system generator [Lescanne 83, Forgaard 84b, Kirchner 84c]. The implementation supports the modified *CR-unify* algorithm and allows for simple modular extension to new sub-theories, as their unification algorithms are implemented. In the current version, the unification algorithms for the AC and empty theories have been implemented. The implementation of the REVE system, including our unification algorithm, was done in CLU [Liskov 81].

The most pressing problem left open in this work, is to remove the restriction that equational theories be confined and regular.

References

[Ballantyne 81] A. M. Ballantyne and D. S. Lankford, "New Decision Algorithms for Finitely Presented Commutative Semigroups," in *Computers & Mathematics with Applications, Vol. 7*, Pergamon Press Ltd., 1981, pp. 159-165.

[Birkhoff 35] G. Birkhoff, "On the Structure of Abstract Algebras," *Proc. Cambridge Phil. Soc., Vol. 31*, 1935, pp. 433-454.

[Dershowitz 83a] N. Dershowitz, "Computing with Rewrite Systems," Technical Report ATR-83(8478)-1, Aerospace Corp., El Segundo, CA, January 1983.

[Dershowitz 83b] N. Dershowitz, N. A. Josephson, J. Hsiang, and D. Plaisted, "Associative-Commutative Rewriting," *8th IJCAI, Karlsruhe, West Germany*, 1983.

[Fages 83] F. Fages and G. Huet, "Complete Sets of Unifiers and Matchers in Equational Theories," *Trees in Algebra and Programming*, CAAP '83, Proceedings of the 8th Colloquium, L'Aquila, Italy, Lecture Notes in Computer Science, Springer-Verlag, March 1983, pp. 205-220.

[Fages 84] F. Fages, "Associative-Commutative Unification," *Proc. 7th CADE, Napa Valley*, Springer-Verlag, 1984, pp. 194-208.

[Fay 79] M. Fay, "First-order Unification in an Equational Theory," *Proc. 4th Workshop on Automated Deduction*, Austin, TX, February 1979, pp. 161-167.

[Forgaard 84a] R. Forgaard and J. V. Guttag, "REVE: A Term Rewriting System Generator with Failure-Resistant Knuth-Bendix," *Proc. of an NSF Workshop on the Rewrite Rule Laboratory, Sept. 6-9, 1983*, General Electric Corporate Research and Development Report No. 84GEN008, Schenectady, NY, April 1984, pp. 5-31.

[Forgaard 84b] R. Forgaard, "A Program for Generating and Analyzing Term Rewriting Systems," Master's Thesis, MIT Lab. for Computer Science, 1984.

[Fribourg 84] L. Fribourg, "Oriented Equational Clauses as a Programming Language," *ICALP*, 1984.

[Goguen 79] J. A. Goguen and J. J. Tardo, "An Introduction to OBJ: A Language for Writing and Testing Formal Algebraic Program Specifications," *Proc. Specification of Reliable Software*, Institute of Electrical and Electronics Engineers, April 1979, pp. 170-189.

[Goguen 80] J. A. Goguen, "How to Prove Algebraic Inductive Hypotheses Without Induction, With Applications to the Correctness of Data Type Implementation," *Lecture Notes in Computer Science, Vol. 87: Proc. 5th Conf. on Automated Deduction*, Les Arcs, France, Springer-Verlag, New York, July 1980, pp. 356-373.

[Grätzer 78] G. Grätzer, *Universal Algebra*, Springer-Verlag, 1969, 1978.

[Hsiang 83] J. Hsiang and N. Dershowitz, "Rewrite Methods for Clausal and Non-Clausal Theorem Proving," *Proc. 10th EATCS Intl. Colloq. on Automata, Languages, and Programming*, Barcelona, 1983, pp. 331-346.

[Huet 80] G. Huet and D. C. Oppen, "Equations and Rewrite Rules: A Survey," in R. Book (Ed.), *Formal Language Theory: Perspectives and Open Problems*, Academic Press, New York, 1980, pp. 349-405.

[Huet 82] G. Huet and J. M. Hullot, "Proofs by Induction in Equational Theories with Constructors," *Journal of the ACM* **25**, pp. 239-266, 1982.

[Hullot 80] J. M. Hullot, "Canonical Forms and Unification," *Lecture Notes in Computer Science, Vol. 87: Proc. 5th Conf. on Automated Deduction*, Les Arcs, France, Springer-Verlag, New York, July 1980, pp. 318-334.

[Jouannaud 83] J.-P. Jouannaud, C. Kirchner, and H. Kirchner, "Incremental Construction of Unification Algorithms in Equational Theories," *Proc. 10th EATCS Intl. Colloq. on Automata, Languages, and Programming*, Barcelona, 1983, pp. 361-373.

[Jouannaud 84] J. P. Jouannaud and H. Kirchner, "Completion of a Set of Rules Modulo a Set of Equations," Technical Note, SRI Intl. Computer Science Laboratory, Menlo Park, CA, April 1984.

[Kapur 84] D. Kapur and D. R. Musser, "Proof by Consistency," *Proc. of an NSF Workshop on the Rewrite Rule Laboratory, Sept. 6-9, 1983*, General Electric Corporate Research and Development Report No. 84GEN008, Schenectady, NY, April 1984, pp. 245-267.

[Kirchner 81] C. Kirchner and H. Kirchner, "Solving Equations in the Signed Trees Theory," Technical Report 81-R-056, Centre de Recherche en Informatique de Nancy, UER de Mathematiques, Universite de Nancy I, 54037 Nancy Cedex, 1981.

[Kirchner 84a] H. Kirchner, "A General Inductive Completion Algorithm and Application to Abstract Data Types," *Proc. 7th CADE, Napa Valley, CA*, Springer-Verlag, 1984, pp. 282-302.

[Kirchner 84b] C. Kirchner, "A New Equational Unification Method: A Generalisation of Martelli-Montanari's Algorithm," *CADE*, 1984.

[Kirchner 84c] C. Kirchner and H. Kirchner, private communication, 1984.

[Knuth 70] D. E. Knuth and P. B. Bendix, "Simple Word Problems in Universal Algebras," in J. Leech (Ed.), *Computational Problems in Abstract Algebra*, Pergamon, Oxford, 1970, pp. 263-297.

[Kowalski 74] R. A. Kowalski, "Predicate Logic as a Programming Language," *Proc. IFIP-74 Congress*, North-Holland, 1974, pp. 569-574.

[Kownacki 84] R. W. Kownacki, "Semantic Checking of Formal Specifications," Master's Thesis, MIT Lab. for Computer Science, June 1984.

[Lankford 84] D. Lankford, G. Butler, and B. Brady, "Abelian Group Unification Algorithms for Elementary Terms," *Proc. of an NSF Workshop on the Rewrite Rule Laboratory, Sept. 6-9, 1983*, General Electric Corporate Research and Development Report No. 84GEN008, Schenectady, NY, April 1984, pp. 301-318.

[Lescanne 83] P. Lescanne, "Computer Experiments with the REVE Term Rewriting System Generator," *Proc. 10th ACM Symp. on Principles of Programming Languages*, Austin, TX, January 1983, pp. 99-108.

[Liskov 81] B. Liskov, R. Atkinson, T. Bloom, E. Moss, J. C. Schaffert, R. Scheifler, A. Snyder, *Lecture Notes in Computer Science, Vol. 114: CLU Reference Manual*, Springer-Verlag, New York, 1981.

[Livesey 76] M. Livesey and J. Siekmann, "Unification of A + C Terms (Bags) and A + C + I Terms (Sets)," Technical Report Interner Bericht Nr. 3/76, Institut für Informatik I, Universität Karlsruhe, 1976.

[Martelli 82] A. Martelli and U. Montanari, "An Efficient Unification Algorithm," *ACM Transactions on Programming Languages and Systems* 4(2):258-282, April 1982.

[Milner 78] R. Milner, "A Theory of Polymorphism in Programming," *Journal of Computer and System Sciences* **17**, pp. 348-375, 1978.

[Nelson 79] G. Nelson and D. Oppen, "Simplification by Cooperating Decision Procedures," *ACM Transactions on Programming Languages and Systems* **1**(2):245-257, Oct 1979.

[Peterson 81] G. E. Peterson and M. E. Stickel, "Complete Sets of Reductions for Some Equational Theories," *Journal of the ACM* **28**(2):233-264, April 1981.

[Plotkin 72] G. D. Plotkin, "Building-in Equational Theories," in *Machine Intelligence, Vol. 7*, Halsted Press, 1972, pp. 73-90.

[Robinson 65] J. A. Robinson, "A Machine-Oriented Logic Based on the Resolution Principle," *Journal of the ACM* **12**(1):23-41, January 1965.

[Shostak 84] R. E. Shostak, "Deciding Combinations of Theories," *Journal of the ACM* **31**(1):1-12, January 1984.

[Siekman 84] J. Siekman, "Universal Unification," *Proc. 7th CADE, NAPA Valley, CA*, Springer-Verlag, 1984, pp. 1-42.

[Slagle 74] J. R. Slagle, "Automated Theorem-Proving for Theories with Simplifiers, Commmutativity and Associativity," *JACM* **21**(4):622-642, October 1974.

[Yelick 85] K. A. Yelick, "A Generalized Approach to Equational Unification," Master's Thesis, MIT Lab. for Computer Science, 1985. (To appear.)

An Algebraic Approach to Unification Under Associativity and Commutativity

Albrecht Fortenbacher

Universität Karlsruhe, Institut für Informatik
D-7500 Karlsruhe, FRG

IBM Thomas J. Watson Research Center
Yorktown Heights, N.Y. 10598, USA

Introduction

Term rewriting systems are unable to handle mathematical theories with associativity and commutativity in the ordinary way. The usual approach of ordering the equations and using them as rewrite rules does not work. A rule of the form $x \cdot y \rightarrow y \cdot x$ will make such a system non Noetherian. One possible solution to this problem is to build associativity and commutativity into the matching and unification algorithms.

Siekmann and Livesey *[SL76]*, and Stickel *[St81]* independently presented algorithms to unify two terms with an associative and commutative operator. Both algorithms flatten terms and regard the argument lists as Abelian strings (multisets) thus transferring a unification problem in the free algebra into a problem in an Abelian monoid. The algorithms differ in the way in which they find mappings which equate strings.

Siekmann and Livesey restrict themselves to strings over variables and constants. This allows them to derive a system of diophantine equations and use the solutions to generate the set of unifiers directly.

Their algorithm is very efficient, but does not seem to be applicable to terms of a more general form, such as terms containing more than one operator.

Stickel uses a "variable abstraction", which reduces the set of equations to a singleton. With every mapping derived from the solutions to this equation he gets a set of pairs of terms to which the algorithm is applied recursively. If this fails, the mapping has to be disregarded. More efficient versions of this "pure" algorithm are used in systems for data type completion *[KB70,Hl80]*.

The following work describes and formalizes the connections between solutions of a diophantine equation and a unifier for a pair of terms. An algorithm directed by this information selects only a few combinations of solutions which are expected to gain a unifier, and reduces the number of recursive unification calls rapidly.

The reader is assumed to be familiar with the basics of Σ-algebras and term rewriting systems. Given a signature Σ and a set of variables V, the free algebra $T(\Sigma \cup V)$ is the algebra of all terms over Σ and V. A substitution is a Σ-endormorphism on $T(\Sigma \cup V)$. And given a set of equations, E, the set of all associative and commutative operators (ac-operators) Σ_{ac} consists of all $\bullet \in \Sigma$ with both $(x \bullet y = y \bullet x) \in E$ and $(x \bullet (y \bullet z) = (x \bullet y) \bullet z) \in E$. For details, see the survey by Huet and Oppen *[HO80]*.

1. An Algebraic Problem

In this section we solve a unification problem in an Abelian monoid. Let h_1 and h_2 be two elements of an Abelian monoid $(H, \bullet)$ with identity ε and $h_1, h_2 \in H - \{\varepsilon\}$, and regard "=" as the finest congruence relation defined by associativity and commutativity of "$\bullet$". The problem we solve is that of finding a "$\bullet$"-endomorphism Φ with $\Phi(h_1) = \Phi(h_2)$.

Terminology

We "normalize" h_1 and h_2 by removing common arguments and grouping the remaining ones:

$$\left.\begin{aligned} h_1 &= a_1^{p_1} \bullet \cdots \bullet a_m^{p_m} \\ h_2 &= a_{m+1}^{p_{m+1}} \bullet \cdots \bullet a_n^{p_n} \end{aligned}\right\} \quad \text{with } a_i \in H - \{\varepsilon\}\ , p_i \geq 1 \text{ and } a_i \neq a_j \text{ for } i \neq j$$

Now all a_i are pairwise distinct, and no a_i can be represented as $b_1 \bullet b_2$ with $b_1, b_2 \in H - \{\varepsilon\}$.

Definition

For h_1, h_2 as above we define:

- a diophantine equation E_{h_1, h_2} : $\sum_{i=1}^{m} p_i x_i - \sum_{i=m+1}^{n} p_i x_i = 0$
- S_{h_1, h_2} : $\{s \in N^n \mid s \text{ is a nonnegative solution for } E_{h_1, h_2}\}$
- B_{h_1, h_2}: $\{s \in S_{h_1, h_2} \mid s \text{ is a basic solution for } E_{h_1, h_2}\}$
  (a solution is ***basic*** if it is neither trivial nor the sum of two nontrivial solutions)

These definitions enable us now to construct an endomorphism Φ under which h_1 and h_2 are equated.

The method is as follows:

(1) Choose $s_1, \ldots, s_r \in S_{h_1, h_2}$ and $k_1, \ldots, k_r \in H - \{\varepsilon\}$ with $r \geq 1$.
(Let s_j be $(s_{j1}, \ldots, s_{jn})$ for $1 \leq j \leq r$.)

(2) Define Φ on $a_1, \ldots, a_n$:
$\Phi(a_i) \rightarrow k_1^{s_{1i}} \bullet \cdots \bullet k_r^{s_{ri}}$ for $1 \leq i \leq n$ ■

Lemma

$\Phi(h_1) = \Phi(h_2)$

Proof

- $\Phi(h_1)$ and $\Phi(h_2)$ can be represented as $k_1^{m_1} \bullet \cdots \bullet k_r^{m_r}$ and $k_1^{n_1} \bullet \cdots \bullet k_r^{n_r}$ where all k_j are pairwise distinct (see the definition of Φ in step (2))

- It remains to prove: $\forall\ 1 \le j \le r \quad [m_j = n_j]$
  This follows from $m_j = \sum_{i=1}^{m} p_i s_{ji}$, $n_j = \sum_{i=m+1}^{n} p_i s_{ji}$ and $(s_{j1}, \ldots, s_{jn})$ is a solution for E_{h_1, h_2} ■

Example 1

Let $(H, \bullet)$ be an Abelian monoid and $H - \{\varepsilon\}$ the closure of $T(\Sigma \cup V)$ under $\bullet$
$t_1 = x \bullet a \bullet x \bullet a$ and $t_2 = g(y) \bullet g(a) \bullet z \bullet z$

We can find a "$\bullet$"-endomorphism Φ as follows :

- compute normal forms $h_1 = x^2 \bullet a^2$ and $h_2 = g(y) \bullet g(a) \bullet z^2$
- compute the equation E_{h_1, h_2} : $2x_1 + 2x_2 - x_3 - x_4 - 2x_5 = 0$
- choose two solutions $s_1 = (10110)$, $s_2 = (11002) \in S_{h_1, h_2}$ and $k_1, k_2 \in T(\Sigma \cup V)$
- define Φ on x , a , $g(y)$, $g(a)$, z :
  $\Phi(x) = k_1 \bullet k_2$, $\Phi(a) = k_2$, $\Phi(g(y)) = k_1$, $\Phi(g(a)) = k_1$, $\Phi(z) = k_2^2$

$\Phi(h_1) = k_1^2 \bullet k_2^4 = \Phi(h_2)$ ■

2. Endomorphism vs. Substitution

The next goal is to connect the notions of endomorphism and substitution. More precicely, we want to construct an endomorphism Φ , as shown in section 1, and decide whether it "behaves" like a substitution.

Terminology

Starting with this section, we shall use the following notation:

- o $H - \{\varepsilon\} = T(\Sigma \cup V)$
- o $f \in \Sigma_{ac}$
- o $t_1 \bullet t_2 = f(t_1, t_2)$ for $t_1, t_2 \in T(\Sigma \cup V)$
- o $\left\{ \begin{array}{l} h_1 = a_1^{p_1} \bullet \cdots \bullet a_m^{p_m} \\ h_2 = a_{m+1}^{p_{m+1}} \bullet \cdots \bullet a_n^{p_n} \end{array} \right\}$ as in section 1
- o an endomorphism Φ with $\Phi(h_1) = \Phi(h_2)$
- o a set of solutions $\{s_1, \ldots, s_r\}$, $s_j \in S_{h_1, h_2}$

In this section we want to see whether a "f"-endomorphism Φ , which equates h_1 and h_2, can be regarded as a Σ-endomorphism, i.e. a morphism with respect to all operators. If so, Φ corresponds to a substitution φ. To determine this we must address two questions:

- o Does there exist a φ with $\Phi(a_i) = \varphi(a_i)$ for all a_i ?

- o If yes, how can such a φ be constructed using $s_1, \ldots, s_r \in S_{h_1, h_2}$?

Definition

Associated with each solution $s_j \in S_{h_1, h_2}$, we define the following quantities:

$$Q_j = \{1 \le i \le n \mid s_{ji} \ge 1, a_i \notin V\}$$

$$q_j = \begin{cases} a_{\min Q_j} & \text{if } Q_j \neq \{\} \\ z_j & \text{otherwise} \end{cases} \qquad \text{for } 1 \le j \le r$$

where z_j is a newly generated variable

Given an endomorphism Φ constructed via the method of the previous section, and a substitution φ satisfying

$$\forall\, 1 \le i \le n \;\left[\, \Phi(a_i) = k_1^{s_{1i}} \bullet \cdots \bullet k_r^{s_{ri}} \right] \tag{1}$$

$$\forall\, 1 \le i \le n \;[\, \Phi(a_i) = \varphi(a_i)\,] \tag{2}$$

three direct consequences arise from [1] and [2]:

$$\forall\, 1 \le i \le n \;\left[\sum_{j=1}^{r} s_{ji} \ge 1 \right] \tag{3}$$

$$\forall\, 1 \le i \le n \;\left[a_i \notin V \Rightarrow \sum_{j=1}^{r} s_{ji} = 1 \right] \tag{4}$$

$$\forall\, 1 \le i_1, i_2 \le n\,,\; 1 \le j \le r \;\left[\; i_1, i_2 \in Q_j \Rightarrow \exists \text{ substitution } \sigma \;[\; \sigma(a_{i_1}) = \sigma(a_{i_2}) \;]\right] \tag{5}$$

Remark

The substitution σ is called a ***unifier*** for $\{h_1, h_2\}$.

Proof of [3]

Assume the contrary. Then there exists an i with $\Phi(a_i) = \varepsilon$, but a substitution φ cannot be ε for any $t \in T(\Sigma \cup V)$ ■

Proof of [4]

Assume there is an i with $\sum_{j=1}^{r} s_{ji} \geq 2$ and $a_i \notin V$.

Then there exist terms t_1, t_2 so that $\Phi(a_i) = t_1 \bullet t_2 = f(t_1, t_2)$. From the normalization of h_1 and h_2, a_i cannot be of the form $t_1{}' \bullet t_2{}'$. However this contradicts [1], because φ, as a substitution, preserves the term structure ■

Proof of [5]

Assume $i_1, i_2 \in Q_{j_0}$ and $a_{i_1}, a_{i_2} \notin V$.

[4] => $\sum_{j=1}^{r} s_{ji_1} = s_{j_0 i_1} = 1$ and $\sum_{j=1}^{r} s_{ji_2} = s_{j_0 i_2} = 1$

[1] => $\Phi(a_{i_1}) = k_{j_0}$ and $\Phi(a_{i_2}) = k_{j_0}$

[2] => $\varphi(a_{i_1}) = \varphi(a_{i_2})$ ■

The conditions [3] – [5] are necessary but not sufficient for the existence of a φ. We now present an algorithm which constructs φ :

(1) Let $\begin{cases} \vartheta = \{a_i \leftarrow q_1^{s_{1i}} \bullet \cdots q_r^{s_{ri}} \mid a_i \in V\} \\ \sigma \text{ be the fixed point of } \vartheta \text{ (if one exists)} \end{cases}$

This means that if we can find an n, such that $\vartheta^n = \vartheta^{n+1}$, then $\sigma = \vartheta^n$.

(2) Find a substitution τ which unifies $\{\sigma(a_i) \mid i \in Q_j\}$ for all $1 \leq j \leq r$

(3) Let $\varphi = \tau\sigma$ (if τ and σ exist) ■

Example 2

Let $h_1 = x^2 \bullet a^2$, $h_2 = g(y) \bullet g(a) \bullet z^2$, $s_1 = (10110)$ and $s_2 = (11002)$, as in example 1. Then we construct $Q_1 = \{ 3 , 4 \}$, $q_1 = g(y)$, $Q_2 = \{ 2 \}$ and $q_2 = a$. Obviously, s_1 and s_2 satisfy [3] – [5]. We construct $\sigma = \vartheta = \{ x \leftarrow g(y) \bullet a , z \leftarrow a^2 \}$. Then τ has to unify $\{ a \}$ and $\{ g(y) , g(a) \}$. Finally, we get $\varphi = \{ x \leftarrow g(a) \bullet a , y \leftarrow a , z \leftarrow a^2 \}$, with $\varphi(h_1) = g(a)^2 \bullet a^4 = \varphi(h_2)$ ■

Lemma

If the values k_j in [1] are defined as $k_j = \varphi(q_j)$ for $1 \leq j \leq r$, then [2] holds.

Proof

Letting $a_i \in V$,

$$\varphi(a_i) = \tau\sigma(a_i) = \tau((\sigma(q_1))^{s_{1i}} \bullet \cdots \bullet (\sigma(q_r))^{s_{ri}}) \quad (\sigma \text{ is a fixed point of } \vartheta)$$
$$= (\tau\sigma(q_1))^{s_{1i}} \bullet \cdots \bullet (\tau\sigma(q_r))^{s_{ri}} = k_1^{s_{1i}} \bullet \cdots \bullet k_r^{s_{ri}} = \Phi(a_i)$$

Letting $a_i \notin V$, there exists exactly one $1 \leq j \leq r$ with $s_{ji} = 1$

$$\tau \text{ unifies } \{\sigma(a_i) \mid i \in Q_j\} \Rightarrow \varphi \text{ unifies } \{a_i \mid i \in Q_j\} \quad (\varphi = \tau\sigma)$$

$$\Rightarrow \varphi(a_i) = \varphi(q_j) = k_j = \Phi(a_i)$$ ■

Corrollary

The substitution φ is a unifier for h_1 and h_2.

3. A Minimal and Complete Set of Unifiers

Definition

We use the following definitions (with some minor simplifications) from the survey by Huet and Oppen *[HO80]*.

- idempotent substitutions:
  ϑ is ***idempotent*** if and only if $\forall\, v \in V\ [\ \vartheta(v) = \vartheta\vartheta(v)\ ]$

- a ***subsumption preorder*** , $\leq$, on substitutions:
  $\vartheta_1 \leq \vartheta_2$ if and only if $\exists\, \lambda\ \ \forall\, v \in X\ \left[\ \vartheta_2(v) = \lambda\vartheta_1(v)\ \right]$
  where $X = \{v \in V \mid v \text{ occurs in } h_1 \text{ or } h_2\}$

- a ***minimal complete set of unifiers*** Θ for h_1 and h_2 :
  $\forall\, \varphi \in \Theta\ \left[\ \varphi(h_1) = \varphi(h_2) \text{ and } \varphi \text{ is idempotent}\ \right]$
  $\psi(h_1) = \psi(h_2) \Rightarrow\ \exists\, \varphi \in \Theta\ [\ \varphi \leq \psi\ ]$ (completeness)
  $\forall\, \varphi_1, \varphi_2 \in \Theta\ [\ \varphi_1 \leq \varphi_2 \Rightarrow\ \varphi_1 = \varphi_2\ ]$ (minimality)

In this section we present an algorithm to construct a minimal complete set of unifiers, and prove its correctness.

Algorithm

$$\Theta \leftarrow UNIFY(h_1, h_2)$$

UNIFY creates a set Θ of idempotent substitutions

(1) Compute B_{h_1, h_2}, then regard all subsets B of B_{h_1, h_2}, for which [3] – [5] are true.

(2) Let $B = \{b_1, \dots, b_r\}$ and $b_j = (b_{j1}, \dots, b_{jn})$ for $1 \le j \le r$, and let

$I = \{1 \le i \le n \mid a_i \in V\}$. ($I$ describes the set of all variable arguments.)

Define Q_j and q_j as

$$Q_j = \{1 \le i \le n \mid b_{ji} = 1, i \notin I\}$$

$$q_j = \begin{cases} a_{\min Q_j} \text{ if } Q_j \neq \{\} \\ z_j \text{ (a new variable) otherwise} \end{cases}$$

for $1 \le j \le r$.

(3) Construct $\vartheta^{(i)} = \{ a_i \leftarrow q_1^{b_{1i}} \bullet \cdots \bullet q_r^{b_{ri}} \}$ for $i \in I$, and define ϑ as the union of all $\vartheta^{(i)}$.

A fixed point of ϑ exists if and only if the following sequence $i_1, \dots, i_d$ exists with

- $I = \{i_1, \dots, i_d\}$
- $\forall\, 1 \le e \le d$ $\left[\text{ none of the variables } a_{i_e}, a_{i_{e+1}}, \dots, a_{i_d} \text{ occurs in } \vartheta^{(i_e)}(a_{i_e}) \right]$

Then $\sigma = \vartheta^{(i_1)} \dots \vartheta^{(i_d)}$ is this fixpoint.

(4) Extend the Robinson unification [*Ro*65] by *UNIFY* for ac-terms and compute a minimal complete set of unifiers Θ' for all sets $\{\sigma(a_i) \mid i \in Q_j\}$.

(5) For all $\tau \in \Theta'$ add to Θ. ■

Example 3

Given $h_1 = x^2 \bullet a^2$ and $h_2 = g(y) \bullet g(a) \bullet z^2$ as in the previous examples. We compute eight basic solutions: $b_1 = (10110)$, $b_2 = (10200)$, $b_3 = (10020)$, $b_4 = (10001)$, $b_5 = (01110)$, $b_6 = (01200)$, $b_7 = (01020)$ and $b_8 = (01001)$. The substitutions b_2, b_3, b_6 and b_7 cannot be part of any combination of basic solutions, because this would violate [4]. Furthermore, b_5 violates [5]. So only $\{b_1, b_8\}$ and $\{b_1, b_4, b_8\}$ satisfy [3] - [5]. Note that of the 256 possible sets of basic solutions, there are 161 satisfying [3], of which 3 satisfy [4], and only 2 of which satisfy [5]. The minimal complete set of unifiers for h_1 and h_2 is shown in the appendix ■

Theorem

$UNIFY(h_1, h_2)$ is a minimal complete set of unifiers for h_1 and h_2.

First we have to prove that *UNIFY* terminates for any h_1 and h_2. The fundamental ordering we use was introduced in *[Fa83]*, where Fages gives a very detailled proof for the Stickel algorithm.

Definition

- A subterm t' of term t is a ***proper subterm*** if and only if:
  $$[\, t' = g(t_1', t_2') \text{ and } t = g(t_1, t_2) \,] \Rightarrow g \notin \Sigma_{ac}$$
  By ***Subt***(t) we denote the set of all proper subterms of t.
  Example: $g(x_1, x_2)$ is not a proper subterm of $g(g(x_1, x_2), x_3)$ if $g \in \Sigma_{ac}$

- Let t be a term and T_0 a set of terms.
  Op$(t,T_0) = \{g \in \Sigma \mid$ the function symbol g occurs with argument t in an element of $T_0\}$
  Example: $Op(x,\{f(g(x,y),x)\}) = \{f, g\}$

- We define the ***weight*** of a set of terms T as the pair (α, β) where
  $\alpha = \#\{x \in V \mid Op(x,T) \geq 2\}$
  $\beta = \#\{t \mid t \in Subt(t_0) \text{ for any } t_0 \in T\}$
  Example: the weight of $\{f(x), g(f(y),x)\} = (1,5)$

- let T_1 and T_2 be sets of terms with weight (α_1, β_1) and (α_2, β_2)
  $(\alpha_1, \beta_1) < (\alpha_2, \beta_2)$ if and only if $\alpha_1 < \alpha_2$ or $(\alpha_1 = \alpha_2$ and $\beta_1 < \beta_2)$
  This defines a Noetherian ordering on all sets of terms.

Lemma

UNIFY terminates for any h_1 and h_2.

Proof

We have to prove that the weight of the arguments decreases with every recursive call of *UNIFY.*

This can be done in three steps:

(1) To prove: weight of $\{\sigma(h_1), \sigma(h_2)\} \leq$ weight of $\{h_1, h_2\}$

It is sufficient to show that no $\vartheta^{(i)}$, $i \in I$, increases the weight

- a_i occurs under at least two function symbols

  $\Rightarrow$ α decreases, because $\vartheta^{(i)}$ replaces a_i

- a_i occurs only under f

  $\Rightarrow$ $\vartheta^{(i)}(a_i)$ cannot be a proper subterm

  $\Rightarrow$ α and β do not increase

(2) To prove: weight of $\{\sigma(a_i) \mid i \in Q_j\} <$ weight of $\{\sigma(h_1), \sigma(h_2)\}$

for all $1 \leq j \leq r$ with $\#Q_j \geq 2$

this holds, because β decreases:

every $Subt(\sigma(a_i))$ is a subset of $\big(Subt(\sigma(h_1)) \cup Subt(\sigma(h_2)) - \{\sigma(h_1), \sigma(h_2)\} \big)$

(3) Robinson unification does not create new subterms and thus increase the weight ■

Remark

Implicitly, all the following proofs are inductions over the weight of the arguments to *UNIFY.*

Lemma (correctness)

All substitutions $\varphi \in UNIFY(h_1, h_2)$ are unifiers for h_1 and h_2.

Proof

This follows from the proof in section 2 ■

Remark

We can regard every unfier ψ for h_1 and h_2 as an endomorphism on $(H, \bullet)$.

ψ defines $b_1, \dots, b_r \in B_{h_1, h_2}$ and $k_1, \dots, k_r \in T(\Sigma \cup V)$ with

$$\forall\, 1 \le i \le n \left[\psi(a_i) = k_1^{b_{1i}} \bullet \cdots \bullet k_r^{b_{ri}} \right]$$

Every $\varphi \in$ *UNIFY*(h_1, h_2) defines exactly those basic solutions which are used by *UNIFY* to compute φ.

Lemma (completeness)

UNIFY(h_1, h_2) is a complete set of unifiers for h_1 and h_2.

Proof

Let ψ be a unifier for h_1 and h_2 which defines $b_1, \dots, b_r$ and $k_1, \dots, k_r$. We shall show that, using $b_1, \dots, b_r$, *UNIFY* computes a substitution φ with $\varphi \le \psi$. Since ψ is a unifier for h_1 and h_2, [3] – [5] hold for $b_1, \dots, b_r$. If we define $\lambda = \{ q_j \leftarrow k_j \mid q_j \in V \}$, then $\forall\, 1 \le j \le r$ $\left[\psi\lambda(q_j) = k_j \right]$. The existence of $\{i_1, \dots, i_d\}$ in step (3) of *UNIFY* is guaranteed by ψ.

First we prove $\psi\lambda\sigma(a_{i_e}) = \psi(a_{i_e})$ for $1 \le e \le d$

$e = 1$:

$$\psi\lambda\sigma(a_{i_1}) = \psi\lambda(q_1^{b_{1i_1}} \bullet \cdots \bullet q_1^{b_{ri_1}}) = k_1^{b_{1i_1}} \bullet \cdots \bullet k_1^{b_{ri_1}} = \psi(a_{i_1})$$

$2 \le e \le d$:

$$\psi\lambda\sigma(a_{i_e}) = \psi\lambda\vartheta^{(i_1)} \dots \vartheta^{(i_e)}(a_{i_e}) = \psi\lambda\vartheta^{(i_1)} \dots \vartheta^{(i_e-1)}(q_1^{b_{1ie}} \bullet \cdots \bullet q_r^{b_{rie}})$$
$$= (\psi\lambda\sigma(q_1))^{b_{1ie}} \bullet \cdots \bullet (\psi\lambda\sigma(q_1))^{b_{rie}} = (\psi\lambda(q_1))^{b_{1ie}} \bullet \cdots \bullet (\psi\lambda(q_r))^{b_{rie}} = k_1^{b_{1ie}} \bullet \cdots \bullet k_r^{b_{rie}} = \psi(a_{i_e})$$

This follows by induction over e, because $\vartheta^{(i_e)}$ does not contain any $v \in \{a_{i_e}, a_{i_{e+1}}, \dots, a_{i_d}\}$

Now we know $\sigma \le \psi$ and that ψ is a unifier for all $Q_j' = \{\sigma(a_i) \mid i \in Q_j\}$. *UNIFY* computes a complete set of unifiers for these Q_j', and a φ with $\varphi \le \psi$. The completeness is proven by induction over the weight ∎

Lemma (minimality)

$UNIFY(h_1, h_2)$ is minimal.

Proof

Assume $\varphi_1, \varphi_2 \in UNIFY(h_1, h_2)$ with $\varphi_1 \leq \varphi_2$.

$\exists\, \lambda$ with $\lambda\varphi_1 = \varphi_2$ and $\forall\, i \in I\ \lambda(a_i) = a_i$, since φ_1 is idempotent

$\Rightarrow$ φ_1 and φ_2 define the same basic solutions $b_1, \ldots, b_r$

φ_1 and φ_2 are both computed using $b_1, \ldots, b_r \in B_{h_1, h_2}$

$\Rightarrow$ $\sigma_1 = \sigma_2$ $\Rightarrow$ $\tau_1 \leq \tau_2$ (σ_i is the substitution which is used for computing φ_i)

Assume $\tau_1 \neq \tau_2$ $\Rightarrow$ $\exists\ 1 \leq j \leq r, i_1, i_2 \in Q_j$ with $UNIFY(\sigma(a_{i_1}), \sigma(a_{i_2}))$ is not minimal.

This is a contradiction to our induction assumption over the weight ■

4. An Efficient Algorithm

Our next goal is to find an efficient implementation for *UNIFY*. Huet *[Hu78]* shows how to compute the finite set of basic solutions. But how can we find all subsets thereof which can be used to compute a unifier?

All subsets deserving attention must at least satisfy [3] and [4]. Additionally they should not violate [5]. This leads to the following procedure:

(1) Eliminate every basic solution which cannot be a member of any subset. This is the case if $b_{ji} \geq 2$ for an $a_i \notin V$, which violates [4], or if the set $\{a_i \mid i \in Q_j\}$ is not unifyable ([5]).

(2) Unify the set $\{a_i \mid i \in Q_j\}$ for every basic solution b_j. This obviates the need for performing these unifications for every subset containing b_j .

(3) With regard to (1) and (2) find all subsets which satisfy [3] and [4].

The pure Stickel algorithm looks for all subsets with [3], whereas Hullot's more efficient implementation *[Hl79]* uses [3] and [4].

Now we are looking for a reasonable realisation of (1) and (2). There are three possibilities:

P1: Use the Robinson unification algorithm *[Ro65]* to make a plausibility check: Disregard all pairs with the same ac-operator and look for a "disagreement pair" that has two different operators. Unification is impossible if such a disagreement pair exists.

P2: Unify $\{a_i \mid i \in Q_j\}$ by the Robinson algorithm. Pairs with the same ac-operator are postponed. This computes a substitution and a set of unsolved unification problems for every b_j. Hullot *[Hl79]* uses a similiar technique when he regards subsets of solutions.

P3: Compute a minimal complete set of unifiers for every $\{a_i \mid i \in Q_j\}$.

Time comparision

Efficiency grows from P1 to P3. This has two reasons: every basic solution which can be disregarded makes the number of subsets shrink, and common computations are done only once. If two basic solutions are combined which try to substitute the same variable x by two different terms t_1 and t_2, then t_1 and t_2 have to be unified.

Space comparision

Obviously space efficiency worstens from P1 to P3.

Robinson proved that a single substitution can be realized by updating pointers *[Ro71, Ku82]*. This means, that P2 needs hardly more space than P1, but is much more time efficient. Thus P2 turns out to be the best solution.

Appendix A. Unification in SAC-2

The following is the image of a computer session run on an IBM 3081 under CMS at the IBM Watson Research Center, Yorktown Heights. The algorithm, which is written in ALDES *[Lo76]*, uses the computer algebra system SAC-2 *[Co80]* as well as a package for data type completion *[Ku82]*. For more information see *[Fo83]*.

```
THE FOLLOWING DATA TYPE WAS READ

   TYPE T.
   CONSTS  A,B,C - T
   VARS  W,X,Y,Z - T
   OPS  F(T,T) - T . G(T) - T . +(T,T) - T
   AC  F , +
   END

UNIFICATION OF     F(A,X)     AND     F(B,Y)
      Y - F(A,V1) , X - F(B,V1)
      Y - A , X - B
IN 5 MS

UNIFICATION OF     +(X,X)     AND     +(Y,Z)
      Z - +(V3,V3,V2) , Y - +(V2,V1,V1) , X - +(V3,V2,V1)
      Y - +(Z,V1,V1) , X - +(Z,V1)
      Z - +(V3,V3) , Y - +(V1,V1) , X - +(V3,V1)
      Z - +(V3,V3,Y) , X - +(V3,Y)
      Z - X , Y - X
IN 12 MS

UNIFICATION OF     F(X,X,Y,A,C)     AND     F(B,B,Z,C)
      Z - F(A,V2,X,X) , Y - F(V2,B,B)
      Z - F(A,X,X) , Y - F(B,B)
      Z - F(A,Y,V1,V1) , X - F(B,V1)
      Z - F(A,Y) , X - B
IN 12 MS

UNIFICATION OF     F(+(X,A),+(Y,A),C,C)     AND     F(+(Z,Z,Z),W)
      W - F(+(X,A),C,C) , Z - +(A,V1) , Y - +(A,A,V1,V1,V1)
** 1934 CELLS, 7 MS.
      W - F(+(X,A),C,C) , Z - A , Y - +(A,A)
      W - F(+(Y,A),C,C) , Z - +(A,V2) , X - +(A,A,V2,V2,V2)
      W - F(+(Y,A),C,C) , Z - A , X - +(A,A)
IN 30 MS

UNIFICATION OF     F(+(X,A),+(Y,A),+(Z,A))     AND     F(+(W,W,W),Z,Z)
      W - +(A,V1) , Z - +(+(A,V1,V1,V1),A) , Y - +(A,V1,V1,V1) , X - +(A,V1,V1,V1)
      W - A , Z - +(A,A) , Y - A , X - A
IN 19 MS

UNIFICATION OF     F(X,A,X,A)     AND     F(G(A),G(Y),Z,Z)
      Z - F(A,V1) , Y - A , X - F(V1,G(A))
      Z - A , Y - A , X - G(A)
IN 9 MS
```

```
32 SYMBOLS AND 84 PROPERTIES.
1 GARBAGE COLLECTIONS, 1934 CELLS RECLAIMED, IN 7 MS.
268 CELLS IN AVAIL, 2500 CELLS IN SPACE.
TOTAL TIME 190 MS.
```

Reference

[Co80] **Collins, G.E.** *ALDES and SAC-2 Now Available* SIGSAM Bulletin 10/2, 1980.

[Fa83] **Fages, F.** *Associative-Commutative Unification* Preliminary Draft, INRIA, 1983.

[Fo83] **Fortenbacher, A.** *Algebraische Unifikation* Diplomarbeit, Institut für Informatik, Universität Karlsruhe, 1983.

[Hl79] **Hullot, J.M.** *Associative-Commutative Pattern Matching* Fifth Internation Joint Conference on Artificial Intelligence, Tokyo, 1979.

[Hl80] **Hullot, J.M.** *A catalogue of Canonical Term Rewriting Systems* Techn. Report CSL-113, SRI International, 1980.

[HO80] **Huet, G.,Oppen, D.C.** *Equations and Rewrite Rules: a Survey.* In *Formal Languages: Perspectives and Open Problems.*, Ed. Book, R., Academic Press, 1980.

[Hu78] **Huet, G.** *An Algorithm to Generate the Basis of Solutions to Homogeneous Linear Diophantine Equations* Inf. Process. Lett. 7/3, 1978.

[KB70] **Knuth, D.E., Bendix, P.B.** *Simple Word Problems in Universal Algebras* In *Computational Problems in Abstract Algebra*, Ed. Leech, Pergamon Press, Oxford, 1970.

[Ku82] **Küchlin, W.W.** *An Implementation and Investigation of the Knuth-Bendix Completion Procedure* Interner Bericht, Institut für Informatik, Universität Karlsruhe, 1982.

[Lo76] **Loos, R.G.K.** *The Algorithm Description Language ALDES (Report)* SIGSAM Bulletin 10/1, 1976.

[Ro65] **Robinson, J.A.** *A Machine-Oriented Logic Based on the Resolution Principle* JACM 12, 1965.

[Ro71] **Robinson, J.A.** *Computational Logic. The Unification Computation.* In *Machine Intelligence 6*, Eds. Michie, Meltzer, Edinburgh University Press, 1971.

[SL76] **Siekmann, J., Livesey, M.** *Unification of A+C-Terms (Bags) and A+C+I-Terms (Sets)* Interner Bericht 3/76, Institut für Informatik, Universität Karlsruhe 1976.

[St81] **Stickel, M.E.** *A Unification Algorithm for Associative-Commutative Functions* JACM 28, 1981.

UNIFICATION PROBLEMS WITH ONE-SIDED DISTRIBUTIVITY

Stefan Arnborg and Erik Tidén
Royal Institute of Technology
Department of Numerical Analysis and Computing Science
S-100 44 Stockholm 70
SWEDEN

Abstract

We show that unification in the equational theory defined by the one-sided distributivity law $x \times (y+z) = x \times y + x \times z$ is decidable and that unification is undecidable if the laws of associativity $x + (y+z) = (x+y)+z$ and unit element $1 \times x = x \times 1 = x$ are added. Unification under one-sided distributivity with unit element is shown to be as hard as Markov's problem, whereas unification under two-sided distributivity, with or without unit element, is $\mathcal{NP}$-hard. A quadratic time unification algorithm for one-sided distributivity, which may prove interesting since available universal unification procedures fail to provide a decision procedure for this theory, is outlined. The study of these problems is motivated by possible applications in circuit synthesis and by the need for gaining insight in the problem of combining theories with overlapping sets of operator symbols.

1. Introduction.

Unification in equationally defined theories has a large number of applications (Siekmann [10]) and is also a fairly difficult problem in the sense that relatively few standard techniques are known and these do not seem to cover most cases. An important problem of a general nature is to characterize the unification properties of a combination of theories in terms of properties of the constituent theories. In our case this problem occurred in an investigation of circuit synthesis from specifications given as equations in a process algebra. A number of such algebras which are, at least partly, equationally defined have been suggested, see, e.g., Bergstra and Klop [1]. They have a fairly large number of function symbols interrelated by common types of permutative axioms as well as idempotency and unit element laws. Particularly, some of these theories have only one-sided distributivity for some function symbol pairs.

An ideal probing ground for investigating unification in combinations of theories is given by the lattice of equational theories below Peano arithmetic. Our interest has been in particular to develop a unification algorithm for one-sided distributivity and to investigate the complexity of unification in theories which have unit element laws.

Unification under one-sided distributivity has a theoretical interest of its own. It is one of the few well-known simple axioms for which no unification algorithm has been reported. Another interesting aspect of unification under one-sided distributivity is that, although there is an efficient algorithm, the known universal unification algorithms fail to provide a decision algorithm.

We shall be concerned with the following axioms and their combinations:

$$A: \quad x + (y + z) = (x + y) + z$$
$$D_l: \quad x \times (y + z) = x \times y + x \times z$$
$$D_r: \quad (x + y) \times z = x \times z + y \times z$$
$$U: \quad x \times 1 = 1 \times x = x$$
$$\Phi: \quad \text{(no axiom)}$$

As can be seen above, we use the infix representation with standard priority rules instead of the usual prefix notation. Otherwise we use standard notation, see, e.g., Huet and Oppen [5]. Letters r, s, t denote terms, u a string of integers used as a pointer to a subexpression t/u of a term t, and v, w, x, y, z denote variables. $s =_T t$ denotes, depending on the context, an equation or an identity. In the first case we are normally looking for a 'solution' σ such that $\sigma(s) =_T \sigma(t)$ is an identity. (Sometimes the notation $< s, t >_T$ is used for equations).

2. Decidability of unification under D_l and under U.

In the following study of one-sided distributivity we consider left distributivity, defined by the axiom D_l above. (Needless to say, all results carry over to right distributivity.)

The theory of left distributivity is known to be a *permutative* theory, and to have a unitary unification problem, i.e., if two terms are unifiable they have a most general unifier (Szabó [11]). Here, a *permutative* theory T is a theory such that for all terms t, the congruence class $\{s \mid s =_T t\}$ is finite. The axiom D_l can be oriented in both ways, giving two confluent, Nœtherian term rewriting systems and two associated canonical forms for terms.

The Fay-Hullot universal unification procedure based on narrowing [6] can be made very efficient in the term rewriting system were factors are 'multiplied in' as far as possible ($\{x \times (y + z) \to x \times y + x \times z\}$). This is because there need be no search involved in the narrowing process: If one of the terms has multiplication where the other has a plus sign, the multiplication sign is changed to a plus sign by exactly one narrowing substitution and this substitution must be part of the unifying substitution if there is one. However, this is not enough to provide a terminating algorithm, and we have not succeeded in finding a complete set of stopping rules, thus turning the semi-decision procedure into a decision procedure. Instead, we build a unification algorithm on principles similar to schemes developed, e.g., by Huet [4] and Martelli and Montanari [9].

The idea is to 'decompose' equations into sets of smaller equations, as in the following lemma, which shows how equations between terms with the same top symbol can be decomposed.

Lemma 1: Equation $s_1 \times s_2 =_{D_l} t_1 \times t_2$ or $s_1 + s_2 =_{D_l} t_1 + t_2$ is equivalent to the set $\{s_1 =_{D_l} s_2, \quad t_1 =_{D_l} t_2\}$.

Proof: Let $\downarrow_\times$ be the canonical form associated with the term rewriting system $\{x \times (y + z) \to x \times y + x \times z\}$. We have

$$\sigma(s_1 + s_2) =_{D_l} \sigma(t_1 + t_2) \Longleftrightarrow \sigma(s_1 + s_2) \downarrow_\times = \sigma(t_1 + t_2) \downarrow_\times$$
$$\Longleftrightarrow \sigma(s_1) \downarrow_\times + \sigma(s_2) \downarrow_\times = \sigma(t_1) \downarrow_\times + \sigma(t_2) \downarrow_\times$$
$$\Longleftrightarrow (\sigma(s_1) =_{D_l} \sigma(t_1) \wedge \sigma(s_2) =_{D_l} \sigma(t_2)),$$

from which the second case follows. The first case follows similarly from using the canonical form $\downarrow_+$ associated with the term rewriting system $\{x \times y + x \times z \rightarrow x \times (y+z)\}$. ∎

Here, and in the following, we mean by equivalence of sets, or *systems*, of equations that they can replace each other in the context of a larger system of equations, and the solutions of the larger systems are essentially the same. When new variables are introduced they must, of course, be new in the whole system and not only in the subset that is replaced.

Kirchner [7] has constructed an elegant universal unification procedure based on Martelli and Montanari's technique, for a class of equational theories. However, Kirchner's procedure is not applicable to left distributivity. Despite Lemma 1, in Kirchner's terminology, left distributivity is not a decomposable theory. This is so essentially because equations between terms with different top symbols have non-trivial solutions. It is not trivial to extend Kirchner's procedure to handle this case. Furthermore, the main difficulty in developing an algorithm for left distributivity is to detect the cases where a decomposition process fails to terminate. The algorithm we have developed suggests an area for research into extending the applicability of Kirchner's procedure.

We describe our algorithm for terms without constants (0-ary function symbols). Constants are easily taken care of by stopping with failure as soon as a constant becomes equated with a different constant, a sum or a product. We first show that the 'occurs check' of ordinary (empty theory) unification can be applied in unification of terms in permutative theories. Then we show how a system of equations in D_l of maximal term depth δ can be modified into an equivalent system of maximum term depth $\max(2, \delta - 1)$, which process can be iterated until the maximal depth is 2. Ultimately, a system where each equation has one (left-hand) side of depth 1 (i.e., a variable) and one (right-hand side) of depth 2 (i.e., a sum or product of two variables) is obtained. We then reduce the sizes of blocks with common left-hand side to at most two equations, a sum, a product, or a sum and a product. Finally, blocks of size two are eliminated by equating the right-hand sides and removing the sum. Unfortunately, this may generate new blocks of size two. We derive two acyclicity tests, one based on the generalized occurs check and one tailored to D_l which together are shown adequate, i.e., in every infinite chain of eliminations of a block of size 2 in our system, one of these two conditions will ultimately occur, and none of these conditions can arise in a system with a finite solution.

Lemma 2: Terms s and t are not unifiable in any permutative theory T if $t/u =_T s$ and $u \neq \Lambda$, i.e., if one of the terms is T-equal to a proper subterm of the other.

Proof: If there were a unifying substitution σ of such terms s, t, we would have $\sigma(t) =_T \sigma(s)$ and $\sigma(t)/u =_T \sigma(s)$ from which we can derive

$$\sigma(t)[u \leftarrow \sigma(t)] =_T \sigma(s)$$

$$\sigma(t)[u \leftarrow (\sigma(t)[u \leftarrow \sigma(t)])\,] =_T \sigma(s)$$

$$\sigma(t)[u \leftarrow (\sigma(t)[u \leftarrow (\sigma(t)[u \leftarrow \sigma(t)])\,])\,] =_T \sigma(s),$$

and an infinite sequence of terms equivalent to $\sigma(s)$ in T, which by definition can not be the case in a permutative theory. ∎

Lemma 3: Equation $s_1 \times s_2 =_{D_l} t_1 + t_2$ is equivalent to the set $\{v_1 =_{D_l} s_1, \quad v_2 + v_3 =_{D_l} s_2, \quad v_1 \times v_2 =_{D_l} t_1, \quad v_1 \times v_3 =_{D_l} t_2\}$, where v_1, v_2, v_3 are new variables.■

Lemma 4: Equation $x =_{D_l} t_1 \circ t_2$ is equivalent to the set $\{x =_{D_l} v_1 \circ v_2, \quad v_1 =_{D_l} t_1, \quad v_2 =_{D_l} t_2\}$, where v_1, v_2 are new variables and $\circ$ is $+$ or $\times$. ■

Lemma 5: The set $\{x =_{D_l} y \circ z, \quad x =_{D_l} v \circ w\}$ is equivalent to $\{x =_{D_l} y \circ z, \quad y =_{D_l} v, \quad z =_{D_l} w\}$, where $\circ$ is $+$ or $\times$. ■

If an equation $v_1 =_{D_l} v_2$ is generated, it can be removed after a systematic replacement of v_1 by v_2 in the other equations. The substitution must also be saved for later use if the unifier is desired after its existence has been assured. It follows from Lemmas 1, 3–5 that any unification problem in D_l is equivalent to a system of equations where the left-hand side of each equation is a variable and the right-hand side is a sum or product of two variables, and where no variable occurs as left hand side in more than two equations (the right hand sides are a sum, a product, or a sum and a product). A system of this type will be called a *simple system*. We now introduce a transformation of simple systems to simple systems which does not increase the number of sums in the system:

Lemma 6: The set $\{x =_{D_l} y \times z, \quad x =_{D_l} w + v\}$ is equivalent to $\{x =_{D_l} y \times z, \quad z =_{D_l} v_1 + v_2, \quad w =_{D_l} y \times v_1, \quad v =_{D_l} y \times v_2\}$, where v_1 and v_2 are new variables.■

The transformation indicated in Lemma 6 followed by a number of applications of Lemma 5 takes a simple system to another simple system in a finite number of steps. We introduce the relation M so that $\Sigma_1 M \Sigma_2$ holds when Σ_1 can be transformed in this way to Σ_2. Starting with a simple system Σ_1 one can repeatedly apply the transformation, and so compute a sequence Σ_i, $i = 1, 2, \ldots$, such that $\Sigma_i \, M \, \Sigma_{i+1}$. Unfortunately, as the following example shows, this process does not terminate for all input systems: Applying the transformation once to the set:

$$\{x =_{D_l} y \times z, \quad x =_{D_l} w + z\},$$

gives the set:

$$\{x =_{D_l} y \times z, \quad z =_{D_l} v_1 + v_2, \quad w =_{D_l} y \times v_1, \quad z =_{D_l} y \times v_2\}.$$

In the latter set, the equations for z have precisely the same form as the equations for x have in the input set, so the process will not terminate. When the process terminates, however, we have a solution to the original unification problem *iff* there is no cycle in the way the left-hand side variables depend on each other (Lemma 2). We now associate two directed graphs to a simple system and show that no solution exists if any one of them is cyclic:

The *dependency graph* $\mathcal{D}(\Sigma)$ of a simple system Σ is an edge colored directed multi-graph. It has as vertices the variables of Σ. For equation $x =_{D_l} y + z$ in Σ it has an l_+-colored edge (x, y)

and an r_+-colored edge (x, z). An equation $x =_{D_l} y \times z$ similarly generates two edges with colors $l_\times$ and $r_\times$.

The ***sum propagation graph*** $\mathcal{P}(\Sigma)$ of a simple system Σ is a directed simple graph. It has as vertices the equivalence classes of the symmetric, reflexive, and transitive closure of the relation defined by $r_\times$-colored edges in $\mathcal{D}(\Sigma)$. It has an edge (v, w) *iff* there is an edge in $\mathcal{D}(\Sigma)$ from a vertex in v to a vertex in w with color l_+ or r_+.

Lemma 7: A simple system Σ has no solution if either of $\mathcal{D}(\Sigma)$ or $\mathcal{P}(\Sigma)$ is cyclic.

Proof: The first part follows from Lemma 2. Assume $\mathcal{D}(\Sigma)$ acyclic and that $\mathcal{P}(\Sigma)$ has the cycle $(v_1, \ldots, v_n)$. This cycle will remain when Σ is transformed by the M transformation. The $r_\times$-colored edges of $\mathcal{D}(\Sigma)$, when acyclic, define a unique lowest element $\check{v}_i$ in each v_i (remember that the v_i are variable sets) which is the source of no $r_\times$-colored edge. For some v_i, an r_+- or l_+-colored edge corresponding to an edge of the cycle will not have source $\check{v}_i$, or the dependency graph is cyclic. We can thus apply transformation M to Σ once. By repeating the argument we see that either Σ is equivalent to a system with cyclic dependency graph or Σ is equivalent to each element in a sequence of simple systems with an unbounded number of variables, in which some variable is dependent on an unbounded number of new variables. Since the size of the value for a variable in a solution to a simple system is not less than the number of variables it depends on, there can in no case be a finite solution to Σ. ∎

Lemma 8: In every infinite sequence Σ_i, $i = 1 \ldots \omega$, such that $\Sigma_i \, M \, \Sigma_{i+1}$, one of the following conditions will occur after a finite number of steps:

(i) $\mathcal{D}(\Sigma_i)$ is cyclic;

(ii) $\mathcal{P}(\Sigma_i)$ is cyclic.

Proof: Assume that neither of the two conditions is met in a sequence Σ_i, $i = 1, 2, \ldots$. We shall show that this implies that the sequence is finite. Since $\mathcal{D}(\Sigma_i)$ is acyclic, the $r_\times$- colored edges define a chain with a lowest element $\check{v}$ on the variables in every vertex v of $\mathcal{P}(\Sigma_i)$. Applying the M transformation to a variable in a vertex v can extend this chain in another vertex v' only if there is an edge (v, v') in $\mathcal{P}(\Sigma_i)$. Since $\mathcal{P}(\Sigma_i)$ remains acyclic, the chains defined by the $r_\times$-colored edges therefore reach a maximal length after a finite number of steps. Furthermore, every application of the M transformation to a variable in a vertex v of $\mathcal{P}(\Sigma_i)$ 'moves' the sources of an l_+-colored and an r_+-colored edge closer to the unique lowest element $\check{v}$ in v, and since there is a non-increasing number of sums in a system, every l_+- and r_+-colored edge will have source $\check{v}$ for some v after a finite number of steps. When this has occurred, the transformation no longer applies, so the sequence is finite. ∎

From Lemmas 7 and 8 we immediately have:

Theorem 9: D_l has a decidable unification problem. ∎

The dependency and sum propagation graphs can be checked for acyclicity using an on-line transitive closure algorithm using, e.g., Tarjan's efficient disjoint union algorithm for merging vertices in the graphs [12], since edges of the two graphs do not have to be deleted. After a simple system has been obtained, the number of steps required is bounded by the number of $+$-symbols in the system times the number of $\times$-symbols in the system. This gives a quadratic performance in terms of the actual solution size for a solvable system. It is also not difficult to show that the running time, with suitable data structures, is quadratic in the size of the input terms.

The theory U is still decidable although considerably harder. It has a finitary unification problem, as shown below. Without constants, the decision problem is trivial, since if there is a unifying substitution there will also be a unifier where all variables are set to 1. If we allow constants, or if we ask for unifyability under the restriction that a designated variable is not set to 1, we have a more difficult problem:

Theorem 10: Unification under U is $\mathcal{NP}$-hard and the decision problem is $\mathcal{NP}$-complete.

Proof: (membership in $\mathcal{NP}$): For a unification problem in n variables, form the 2^n unification problems where a subset of the variables are constrained to 1 (and the remaining ones to non-1). Each such system is decidable by unification in Φ, and in linear time. (hardness for $\mathcal{NP}$): We shall use a transformation from "ONE-IN-THREE 3-SATISFIABILITY", an $\mathcal{NP}$-complete problem [3]. An instance of this problem is a set of k clauses $\{C_1, C_2, \ldots, C_k\}$, each of which is the disjunction of three non-negated literals. The question is: Is there a satisfying truth assignment for the conjunction of the clauses which assigns **true** to exactly one literal in each clause? Construct a unification problem in U with two constants, a and b, as follows: One term s is a right-bracketed product of k a's and k b's : $a \times (b \times (a \times (b \times \ldots (a \times b) \ldots)))$. The other term t is a product of k terms $t_1, \ldots, t_k$ and k b's: $t_1 \times (b \times (t_2 \times (b \times \ldots (t_k \times b) \ldots)))$, where each subterm t_i is an arbitrarily nested product of three variables representing the literals in C_i. A satisfying truth assignment corresponds to a solution to the equation $s =_U t$, where a is substituted for the '**true**' variables and 1 is substituted for the others. Conversely, it is easily seen that every solution of the equation must have this form, and the corresponding truth assignment satisfies the conjunction of the clauses. Note, finally, that the proof can be carried out even if there is only one constant, a, by replacing b with $(a \times a)$ everywhere in the construction. ∎

3. Complexity of unification in combined theories with D_l.

We denote combinations of theories by a string of the letters denoting their axioms. Thus, e.g., D_lU denotes the theory defined by the axioms D_l and U. D denotes D_lD_r.

Let $\# : \mathcal{T} \to \mathcal{N}$ be a function from terms to positive integers defined recursively as follows:

$$\#(s \times t) = \#(s)\#(t)$$
$$\#(s + t) = \#(s) + \#(t)$$
$$\#(x) = 1$$

Lemma 11: If T is consistent with Peano arithmetic, then $s =_T t$ implies $\#(s) = \#(t)$. ∎

A unification problem Σ' in D_l can thus be translated directly to a Diophantine system Σ such that Σ' has a solution only if Σ has a solution in positive integers (because no term t has $\#(t) = 0$). Likewise, an arbitrary Diophantine system Σ can be translated to a unification problem Σ'. An integer constant c in Σ will be coded as some c-fold sum of terms without $+$ symbols in Σ'.

Deciding solvability of a Diophantine system in positive integers is the famous tenth problem of Hilbert. It was shown undecidable by Matiyasevich, see, e.g., Davis [2]. Since we have just showed unification in D_l decidable, solvability of a Diophantine system Σ cannot be equivalent to solvability of the corresponding system Σ'. However, we can obtain undecidable unification problems by suitably strengthening the theory D_l with axioms imposing equivalence (with respect to solvability) between Σ and a suitably choosen Σ', while preserving the property expressed by Lemma 11:

Theorem 12: (Szabó [11]) Unification under DA is undecidable.

Proof: In the sum of products representation of an arbitrary Diophantine system Σ, let n be the highest degree of a term. Remove all non-unit coefficients by moving negative terms to the other side of the equality sign and expanding non-unit coefficients as sums (e.g., $2xy$ is changed to $xy + xy$). A term of degree m is multiplied $n - m$ times from the left with some constant a. Translate to a system in DA by choosing some right-bracketed product for each term (e.g., the term xy of degree 2 in a system of degree 5 is translated to $a \times (a \times (a \times (x \times y)))$ in Σ'). Solvability of Σ is now equivalent to solvability of Σ'. ∎

Theorem 13: Unification under D_lAU is undecidable.

Proof: Remove negative coefficients in an arbitrary Diophantine system Σ by moving negative terms to the other side of the equality sign. Then replace each constant c by $1+1+\cdots$ (c times), and regard the result as a system Σ' in D_lAU. If a variable x has the value n in a solution to Σ it has the value $1+1+\cdots$ (n times) in Σ'. ∎

Theorem 14: Every theory T satisfying $DA \subset T$ or $D_lAU \subset T$ and consistent with Peano arithmetic has an undecidable unification problem. ∎

The part of Theorem 14 that concerns DA is due to Szabó [11].

This technique does not work for the theories D_lU, D_lA, DU or D. There is a possibility that these theories have a unification problem of the same nature as A (this problem is also known as *string unification* or *Markov's problem*), for which only a decision procedure is known which is apparently not elementary [8]. From a practical point of view there is little difference between an undecidable and a non-elementary problem, and in both cases algorithms must be tailored to the types of problem instances occurring in the application.

Theorem 15: Markov's problem is polynomial time reducible to unification in D_lA and to unification in D_lU.

Proof: The result for D_lA is immediate. For D_lU, consider terms consisting exclusively of the symbols $+$ and 1, '1-sums' for short. Some 1-sums p have the property that they are not equal to any product of two other 1-sums except the products $1 \times p$ and $p \times 1$ (e.g., the right-bracketed sum $1 + (1 + (1 + \ldots (k$ times) has this property for any k). We call such 1-sums prime 1-sums. It is not difficult to show that multiplication of 1-sums is associative in D_lU. Furthermore, it is possible to show that every 1-sum has a unique 'factorization' into a product of prime 1-sums. By coding every constant in Markov's problem as a unique prime 1-sum and using $\times$ as the associative operator one can therefore construct a unification problem in D_lU for every instance of Markov's problem, and this unification problem has a solution *iff* the instance of Markov's problem has a solution. ∎

Theorem 16: Unification under DU and under D is (at least) $\mathcal{NP}$-hard.

Proof: Almost the same transformation from "ONE-IN-THREE 3-SATISFIABILITY" that was used to show that unification under U is $\mathcal{NP}$-hard shows that the unification problem of DU is $\mathcal{NP}$-hard. The only difference is that the use of the constant b should be removed by replacing the 'construction' $x \times (b \times y)$ by $x + y$ everywhere. The transformation has to be changed to show $\mathcal{NP}$-hardness for D-unification. The right-hand side of the unification problem will have exactly the same form as for DU, but the constant left-hand side will be:

$$
\begin{aligned}
&(a \times (a \times a) + a \times (a \times a)) + \\
&((a \times (a \times a) + a \times (a \times a)) + \\
&\qquad \ldots (k \quad \text{times}))
\end{aligned}
$$

(remember that k is the number of clauses), where a is some constant. A satisfying truth assignment corresponds to a solution of the unification problem in which $(a + a)$ is substituted for the '**true**' variables and a is substituted for the others. Conversely, every solution of the unification problem must have this form, and thus correspond to a satisfying truth assignment. ∎

The above is of course a rather modest result considering that the main question is whether or not these theories are decidable.

4. Conclusions.

The combinations of the axioms we considered are shown as a lattice structure in Figure 1, where we also indicate the decidability status of each combination. The most important results in the figure were obtained by Makanin [8] for associativity and Szabó [11] for DA. Szabó [11] and Siekmann [10] mention unification under D as an important open problem. Our result for D_l may have been expected, but the proof was more difficult to find than we expected. The result for D_lAU shows that neither D nor DA can be a unique simplest theory for which the unification problem is undecidable.

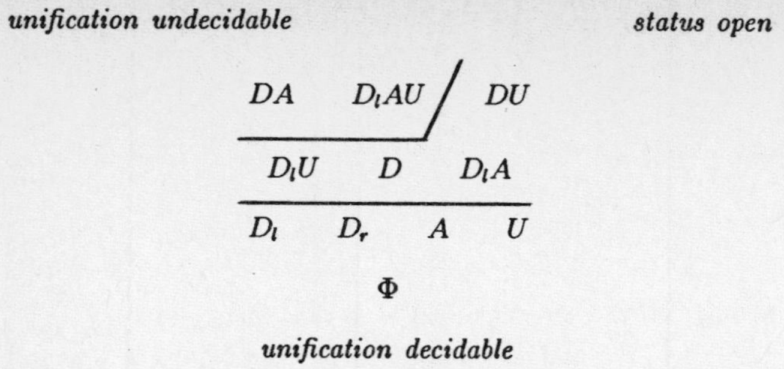

Fig. 1: Decidability status for combinations of D_l, D_r, A, U.

References

1. Bergstra, J.A. and Klop, J.W.: The Algebra of Recursively defined Processes and the Algebra of Regular Processes, *ICALP 84, LNCS 172, 82–94*, Springer, 1984.
2. Davis, M.: Hilberts tenth problem is unsolvable, *Amer. Math. Monthly , vol 80,* 1973.
3. Garey, M.R. and Johnson, D.S.: Computers and Intractability, W.H. Freeman and Company, 1979.
4. Huet, G.: Résolution d'équations dans des langages d'ordre $1, 2, \ldots, \omega$. *Thèse de doctorat d'état, Université Paris VII,* 1976.
5. Huet, G. and Oppen, D.C.: Equations and Rewrite Rules: A Survey, in *Formal Languages: Perspectives and Open Problems*, Ed. R. Book, Academic Press, 1980.
6. Hullot, J.M.: Canonical Forms and Unification, *Proc. 5th Workshop on Automated Deduction, LNCS 87, 318–334*, Springer, 1980.
7. Kirchner, C.: A New Equational Unification Method: A Generalisation of Martelli-Montanari's Algorithm, *7th Int. Conf. on Automated Deduction, LNCS 170, 224–247,* Springer, 1984.
8. Makanin, G.S.: The Problem of Solvability of Equations in a Free Semigroup, *Soviet Akad., Nauk SSSR, Tom 233, no 2,* 1977.
9. Martelli, A. and Montanari, U.: An Efficient Unification Algorithm, *ACM Trans. Programming Languages and Systems 4(2), 258–282,* 1982.
10. Siekmann, J.: Universal Unification, *7th Int. Conf. on Automated Deduction, LNCS 170, 1–42,* Springer, 1984.
11. Szabó, P.: Unifikationstheorie erster Ordnung. *Thesis, Univ. Karlsruhe,* 1982.
12. Tarjan, R.E.: Efficiency of a Good but not Linear Set Union Algorithm, *JACM 22(2), 215–225.*

Acknowledgements

We would like to thank our colleague Wojciech Janczewski for explaining the work of Makanin [8] to us.

This research was partly supported by the Swedish Board for Technical Development (STU).

FAST MANY-TO-ONE MATCHING ALGORITHMS

Paul Walton Purdom, Jr.
Indiana University
Bloomington, IN 47405

and

Cynthia A. Brown
Northeastern University
Boston, Massachusetts 02115

Matching is a fundamental operation in any system that uses rewriting. In most applications it is necessary to match a single subject against many patterns, in an attempt to find subexpressions of the subject that are matched by some pattern. In this paper we describe a many-to-one, bottom-up matching algorithm. The algorithm takes advantage of common subexpressions in the patterns to reduce the amount of work needed to match the entire set of patterns against the subject.

The algorithm uses a compact data structure called a ***compressed dag*** to represent the set of patterns. All the variables are represented by a single pattern node. Variable usages are disambiguated by a ***variable map*** within the pattern nodes. Two expressions that differ only in the names of their variables are represented by the same node in the compressed dag. A single compressed dag contains all the patterns in the system.

The matching proceeds bottom-up from the leaves of the subject and set of patterns to the roots. The subject keeps track of the variable bindings needed to perform the match. A hashing method is used to speedily retrieve specific nodes of the compressed dag.

The algorithm has been implemented as a part of a Knuth-Bendix completion procedure. In comparison with the standard matching algorithm previously used, the new algorithm reduced the number of calls to the basic match routine to about 1/5 of their former number. It promises to be an effective tool in producing more efficient rewriting systems.

Introduction

A ***matching*** of a term p to a term s is an assignment of values to the variables of p that makes it equal to s. Matching is a necessary preliminary step in applying a rewrite rule to an expression, and as such it is a fundamental operation in any system that uses rewriting.

In a typical rewrite system, an expression (the ***subject***) must be simplified by applying any rule from a set of rewrite rules whose left side (the *pattern*) matches any of the subject's subexpressions. Thus, each subexpression of the subject must be tested against the entire set of patterns until a match is found. Using the traditional dag (directed acyclic graph) algorithm, the time for this process is at best proportional to the number of patterns times the size of the subject; at worst, it is proportional to the size of the subject times the size of the set of patterns. (The size of an expression is the number of nodes in its dag representation.) The idea of a many-to-one matching algorithm is to represent the patterns in such a way that much of the work involved in a repetitious application of ordinary matching can be avoided.

A thorough study of linear pattern matching on trees was done by Hoffmann and O'Donnell [HOD82], who developed fast bottom-up algorithms for many-to-one matching using linear patterns. (A linear expression is one in which each variable occurs only once.) In this paper we build on their ideas to develop a fast algorithm for arbitrary many-to-one matching. The algorithm makes use of a highly compact representation of the set of patterns which we call a *compressed dag*. It was designed to be used in the context of the Knuth-Bendix completion procedure [KB70], and therefore allows for dynamic updating of the pattern representation. Matching consumes a major portion of the time in a typical run of the Knuth-Bendix procedure (in our measurements it was applied ten times as much as unification and was by far the most frequently used basic operation), so an improvement in the efficiency of matching should lead to a major speed-up of the Knuth-Bendix procedure. Similar gains can be expected for other systems that make heavy use of many-to-one matching.

The Compressed Dag

We begin by describing the data structures used by the algorithm. The fundamental structure is the *compressed dag* used to represent the set of patterns. A dag is typically used to represent an expression that may contain common subexpressions. Each unique subexpression is represented by exactly one node in the dag; if two expressions use the same subexpression, they both point to that node. An expression in which all subexpressions are unique would be represented by a dag which was a tree. Figure 1 shows the dag for the expression $X * Y + X * Z$ (where X, Y, and Z are variables).

An ordinary dag contains a distinct leaf node for each *distinct* variable in the expression it represents. The compressed dag contains a *single* node representing any variable. The difference between a dag and a compressed dag is therefore in the representation of subexpressions that differ only in the names of their variables. In a dag, these subexpressions have distinct nodes; in a compressed dag, they are represented by the same node. One problem remains: keeping track of the use of variables.

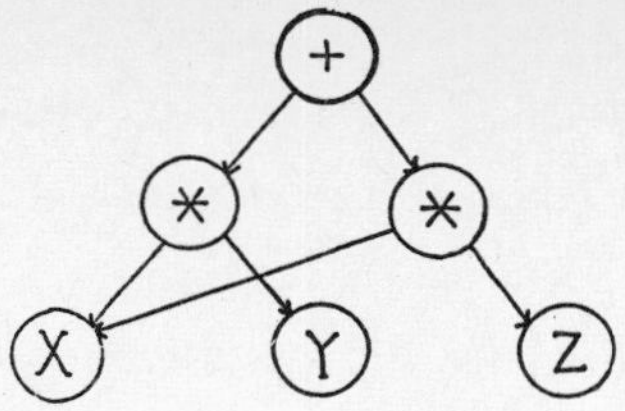

Figure 1. A dag for the expression $X * Y + X * Z$

Figure 2. A compressed dag for the expression of Figure 1.

Variable names are not of any particular significance in themselves; they are simply indicators for where the same quantity must be substituted uniformly in the expression. Therefore, the information that must be given when the variable nodes are combined has to do with where and how a variable is used repeatedly. In the compressed dag, the variables of each node (i.e., the variables used in the expression represented by the node) are renamed using unique names of the form $V_1, V_2, \ldots, V_n$ from left to right in order of first occurrence. For each node, the *variable map* records how the variables of the subnodes are identified with variables of the node.

Conceptually, the variable map may be thought of as an uneven array, with a row for each child of the current node. Each row has a number of positions equal to the number of distinct variables in the corresponding child. The entries in the row tell which variable in the current node is associated with each variable in the child.

For example, consider Figure 2, which shows the compressed dag for the expression $X * Y + X * Z$. There are three distinct variables in this expression, so renaming gives $V_1 = X, V_2 = Y$, and $V_3 = Z$. The two main subexpressions, $X * Y$ and $X * Z$, are the same except for variable names, as they are represented by the same node, which stands for the expression $V_1' * V_2'$. The variable map for the main expression is shown as a small rectangle to the right of the node. The first row corresponds to $V_1 * V_2$ (i.e., to $X * Y$). Its first position contains a 1, showing V_1' is mapped to V_1; its second position contains a 2, showing V_2' is mapped to V_2. The second row of the variable map corresponds to $V_1 * V_3$ ($X * Z$). Its first position contains a 1, showing that V_1' maps to V_1; its second position is a 3, showing that V_2' maps to V_3.

The variable map for the node $V_1' * V_2'$ is very simple. Each child is just a variable, so the rows contain only one position. The child in each case is the unique variable node. The 1 in the first row shows that the first variable is V_1', while the 2 in the second row shows that the second variable is V_2'. (The expression $X * X$ would have a separate node in this compressed dag.

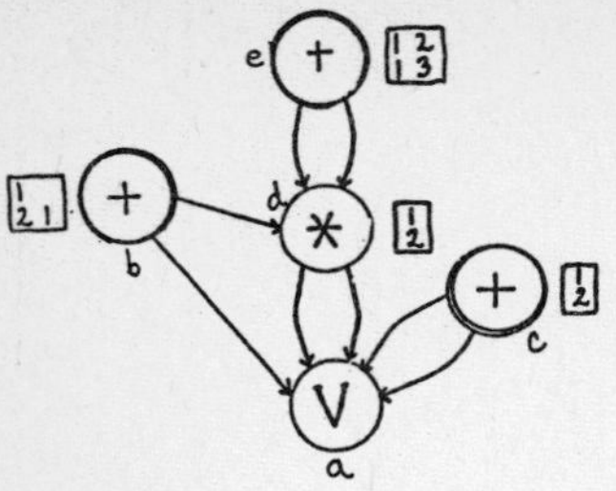

Figure 3. A compressed dag for the patterns $X*Y+X*Z$, $X+Y*X$, and $X+Y$.

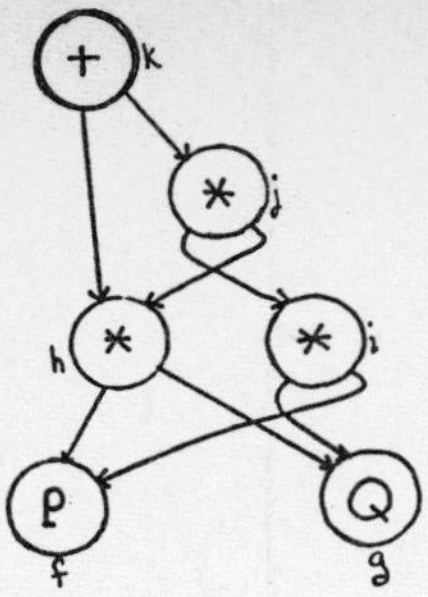

Figure 4. A dag for the expression $P*Q+(Q*P)*(P*Q)$.

Its variable map would have two rows, each containing a 1.) Using the compressed dag and the variable maps, it is easy to construct an expression identical to the original expression except for variable names.

So far we have described the compressed dag for a single expression. In the many-to-one matching algorithm, *all* the patterns are represented using a single compressed dag with multiple roots, one for each pattern. Figure 3 shows the compressed dag for the set of patterns $X*Y+X*Z$, $X+Y*X$, and $X+Y$. Each node in the compressed dag has been given a letter name, for ease of reference later.

The Matching Algorithm

The purpose of the matching algorithm is to find subexpressions of the subject that are matched by a pattern, and to keep track of the bindings of variables in the pattern necessary to obtain the match. The basic idea, which we adopted from [HOD82], is to use a bottom-up approach. In this section we give a high-level description of the matching algorithm; some implementation details are left for the following section.

Unlike the set of patterns, the subject is represented as an ordinary dag. Matching begins at the leaves of the subject. If any pattern contains a variable, then the set of patterns has a variable node, which matches any node in the subject. In addition, any constant node in the subject is matched by the corresponding constant node in the set of patterns, if it exists. Each node in the subject keeps a list of the pattern nodes that match it, together with the variable bindings needed to perform the match. These bindings map each variable in the pattern node to a node in the subject. For example, if there is a variable node in the set of patterns, then each node in the subject records that it is matched by the variable node, and that a binding of the variable is the subject node itself.

After all the children of a subject node have been matched, we attempt to match the node itself. Taking the operator of the node and the first child, we check to see whether there is a match for them in the set of patterns: a pattern node that matches the first child and has a parent with the correct operator as its value. The following steps have to be repeated for each such match. The first step is to record the variable bindings for the parent pattern node that are implied by the match of the first child, using the variable map. We then check for a match of the second child of the pattern node against the second child of the subject that is consistent with the variable bindings already established. That is, we use the variable map to ensure that variables of the pattern node that occur in both children have been bound to the same subject node in both children during the bottom-up match. Subsequent children are checked in the same way as the second one. If a node and all its children are matched, then the complete match is successful and is recorded in the subject node. Matching a subject node with the root of a pattern signals an opportunity to apply a rewriting rule.

As an example, consider the patterns of Figure 3 and the subject $P*Q+(Q*P)*(P*Q)$, whose dag is shown in Figure 4. Proceeding from the leaves upward, both node f (which represents expression P) and node g (representing Q) are matched by the variable node (node a) in the set of patterns. Nodes h (representing $P*Q$) and i (representing $Q*P$) are matched by the variable node and by node d (representing $V_{d1}*V_{d2}$) in the set of patterns. Node h matches d with V_{d1} set to f and V_{d2} set to g; i matches d with V_{d1} set to g and V_{d2} set to f.

Now consider node j (representing $(Q*P)*(P*Q)$). Each of its children has two matches, one to the variable and one to d. However, node d has no parent whose operator is a $*$, so the only match (besides the match to the variable) is to d again, with V_{d1} set to i and V_{d2} set to h.

Now we are ready to match k, the main node of the subject. Its operator is $+$, so we must look for $+$ nodes in the set of patterns whose first child has been matched against the first child of k. There are three such nodes, b, e, and c. For each of these nodes in turn, we consider whether the match of its first child against h is compatible with a match of the second child against j.

The first child of b (b represents the expression $V_{b1}+V_{b2}*V_{b1}$) is the variable node. It matches h using V_a set to h. Thus we must have V_{b1} set to h, by the variable map. To extend this match of k and its first child to include the second child (j), we must find a match to j by the second child of b that is compatible with setting V_{b1} to h. This requires matching d to j with V_{d2} set to h, since the variable map for b tells us that the first variable of the node (i.e., V_{b1}) is identified with the second variable of its second child (i.e., V_{d2}). Looking at the matches for j, the match to the variable can be disregarded because it matches j with a rather than with d, but the match

Subject Node	Pattern Node	Variable Assignments
f	a	$V_a = f$.
g	a	$V_a = g$.
h	a d	$V_a = h$. $V_{d1} = f,\ V_{d2} = g$.
i	a d	$V_a = i$. $V_{d1} = g,\ V_{d2} = f$.
j	a d	$V_a = j$. $V_{d1} = i,\ V_{d2} = h$.
k	a b c	$V_a = k$. $V_{b1} = h,\ V_{b2} = i$. $V_{c1} = h,\ V_{c2} = j$.

TABLE 1. Summary of matches of Figure 4 against Figure 3.

to d matches the correct node and also agrees on the value for V_{b1}. This match also sets V_{d1} to i, which implies that V_{b2} is set to i. We thus have a complete match of b to k, with V_{b1} set to h and V_{b2} set to i.

The second pattern node to consider is e. We have a match for its first child, d, to h, with V_{d1} set to f and V_{d2} set to g. By the variable map, this requires setting V_{e1} to f and V_{e2} to g. To extend the match, we must find a match to j by the second child of e that agrees with these settings of the variables. One of the matches of j is to a; the second one is to d, but it requires setting V_{e1} to h, so our partial match of e to k cannot be extended.

The third + node in the pattern is c (representing $V_{c1} + V_{c2}$). We match the first child of c (the variable) with V_a set to h, requiring that V_{c1} be set to h, and the second child (also the variable) with V_a set to j, requiring that V_{c2} be j. This gives another complete match.

Table 1 summarizes the results of this example, showing all the matches for each node in Figure 4 against the set of patterns in Figure 3.

Implementation Considerations

In the previous section we described the basic concept of the matching algorithm; in this section we explain some modifications that lead to a more efficient implementation. In doing the bottom up match it is important to be able to quickly locate parent nodes on the basis of their children and their operator. There are several good approaches to this problem; the one we have investigated uses hashing and a modified version of the compressed dag data structure.

We first describe the modified data structure. Each parent node in the original compressed dag is broken up into n *partial parent* nodes, where n is the number of children of the original

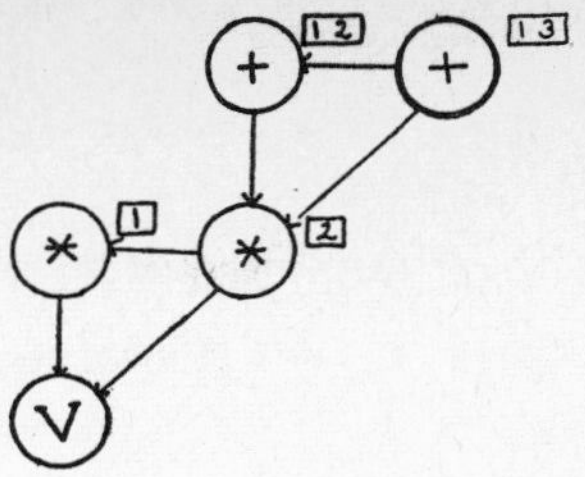

Figure 5. The curried version of the dag of Figure 2.

node. Each of the nodes contains the operator and two pointers: one to its child and one to the previous node in the series (the previous node pointer is **nil** in the partial parent of the first child). As in our earlier dags, there is a unique node for a given set of pointers and variable map, so expressions with the same operator and first few operands share their first few nodes. We call this data structure a *curried dag*, since the transformation is reminiscent of the process of currying a lambda expression. Figure 5 shows the curried dag for the dag of Figure 2.

The curried dag is used in combination with a hash table. The hash table is built bottom-up, just as the set of patterns is. There is an entry in the hash table for the variable node and for each constant. There is also an entry for each set of non-leaf nodes that differ only in their variable maps; it is hashed to using the value of its operator, its current child pointer, and its previous node pointer. These sets nearly always have one element.

To match a nonleaf node, we check for matches for its first child. For each such match, we look in the hash table for the list of nodes having the correct operator, the pattern that matched the first child of the subject node as its child, and a **nil** previous node pointer. For each node on the list, its variable map is used to establish an appropriate set of variable bindings; we then continue by looking at the matches for the second child of the subject. For each such match, we attempt to find a list of nodes in the hash table that has the matching pattern node as its current child, the main operator of the subject node as its operator, and the node that matched the first child and the main operator as its previous node. If such a list is found, we check each element's variable bindings to see whether it can be used to extend a previous partial match. We continue in the same way until a complete match (or matches) is found. The list of matches for a node usually contains just one or two elements; it contains at least one if there is a variable node, since the variable node matches everything.

The use of curried dags helps to reduce the number of inquiries to the hash table. If nodes were stored in the hash table according to the main operator and all the children, then for a subject with an n-ary operator, each of whose operands had been matched in k ways, it would require n^k inquiries to determine which combinations were present. With a curried dag, some possible values for low-numbered children will usually be eliminated. If a total of k possible matches survive at each stage, then $k + (n-1)k^2$ inquiries will be needed altogether. If all the operators are unary or binary, then there is no advantage to using a curried dag.

An alternate approach is to have each pattern node contain pointers to those nodes for which it is the first child. To make access more rapid, the pointers can be stored in lists according to the main operator of the parent, and the lists can be indexed by the operators. Partial parents of n children would require a list of pointers to the appropriate partial parents of $n+1$ children. The trade-off between the two approaches depends on the nature of the patterns and on the average number of matches. If there tend to be a small number of successors (nodes with one more child) for each partial parent, the alternate method works well, while if there tend to be a small number of matches for each child, then the main method works well.

Because of the way the variable maps are constructed, each variable of the first child of a node is mapped to the variable in the parent with the same number. This means that a parent node need not include a variable map for its first child. Significant time can also be saved by giving special treatment to matches with the variable node.

Performance

The goal in developing the many-to-one bottom-up matching algorithm was to make matching time proportional to the size of the subject, and independent of the number or size of the patterns. We know of no way to achieve such good performance in the worst case, so we need to consider our algorithm's typical behavior.

In Hoffman and O'Donnell's bottom-up method, [HOD82], extensive preprocessing of the patterns is used to produce a table that drives the matching phase. Given the sets of patterns matched by the left child and right child of a node, the table precomputes the set of patterns that can be matched by the node itself. Provided the table fits in memory, the matching is guaranteed to run in a time that is linear in the size of the subject. In the worst case, the size of the table can be exponential in the size of the patterns. Hoffmann and O'Donnell identified interesting sets of patterns on which the table size is guaranteed to be reasonably small.

We have taken a somewhat different approach to this problem. Our preprocessing phase (which builds the curried dag and the hash table) is linear in the size of the patterns. For our intended applications it is also important to be able to change the set of patterns dynamically at a moderate cost, and our method achieves that goal. Instead of precomputing the set of possible matches for a given set of matches on the children, we keep lists of matches on the children and

Example	Standard	New	Other
group	4055	885	887
central groupoid	87145	4828	11737

TABLE 2. Matches on newly proposed rules by standard and new matching algorithms while processing examples from [KB70]. The Other column shows the matches of old rules against new rules; both programs used the standard algorithm for these.

explore each list as it arises. As long as the lists stay reasonably small, this does not waste a significant amount of time, and it uses much less space than the other approach.

We implemented the matching algorithm as part of a Knuth-Bendix completion program. The program is written in WEB, the Pascal programming system created by Knuth [Kn84]. The new algorithm replaces a straightforward top-down one-rule-at-a-time matching algorithm. We ran a number of examples using both the new and the old algorithms. Table 2 summarizes the results of these tests on two important examples from [KB70]: the first group theory example (Example 1) and the second central groupoid example (Example 16 with four axioms). The Standard column of the Table gives the number of matches done on newly-proposed rules by the standard top-down matching algorithm. The New column gives the corresponding number for the new algorithm. Both programs used the standard method when testing old rules using a new rule as a pattern; the number of such matches is shown in the Other column. The programs were almost identical except for the matching algorithm that was used.

Table 2 shows the promise of the new matching algorithm. It greatly reduces the number of of matching operations required in the Knuth-Bendix procedure, and should also lead to a smaller running time. In the present implementation, both methods run at about the same speed (1.5 seconds for the standard method versus 1.8 seconds for the new on the group theory example; 15.0 seconds for the standard versus 12.8 seconds for the new on the central groupoid.) This implementation does not take full advantage of the new method, since it must keep a representation of each rule in both compressed and uncompressed form, leading to considerable extra overhead.

The Knuth-Bendix procedure does three kinds of processing that involve pattern-matching and its variants: matching a subject against many patterns, in an attempt to simplify it; matching a single pattern against many subjects, when trying to see if a new rule can be used to simplify any of the existing rules; and unification. Moreover, rules are used both as patterns and as subjects. At present the patterns in our algorithm are represented as a compressed dag, while the subject is an ordinary dag; this requires that the rules be stored in both forms by the system. It is desirable to find algorithms for the two types of pattern matching and for unification which use compressed dags as the only structure for storing terms. There appears to be no real difficulty in doing this. The current approach was selected because it is a little simpler.

The troubling aspect of our measurements is that the running time of our new algorithm did not improve rapidly with problem size. There are two reasons for this. First, with the new algorithm, matching was no longer taking much of the time, while the overhead of maintaining two data structures was. This overhead will disappear once algorithms that need a single data structure are programmed. Second, the average number of matches per node is large enough that algorithms that depend quadratically on the average number of matches are slower than one would like. (For the central groupoid example, 5 matches per node was common.) We plan, therefore, to also carefully investigate the alternate algorithm of the previous section, since its time increases linearly with the average number of matches per node.

Extensions

Extensions of the Knuth-Bendix procedure that use associative and commutative (ac) unification and matching [St81] promise to extend its usefulness to a wide class of equational systems. The matching algorithm was designed so that it would be straightforward to extend it to do ac matching.

While matching takes up the major portion of the Knuth-Bendix procedure's time, unification is also a significant factor in the running time. There is a need for many-to-one unification in the Knuth-Bendix procedure. It is possible to adapt existing unification algorithms to run on compressed dags. However, these existing algorithms proceed in a top-down manner and so would get no advantage from the special properties of the compressed dag. It is an interesting question as to whether an efficient bottom-up unification algorithm can be developed.

References

[HOD82] Christoph M. Hoffmann and Michael J. O'Donnell, *Pattern Matching in Trees*, JACM **29** (1982) pp. 68-95.

[KB70] Donald E. Knuth and Peter B. Bendix, *Simple Word Problems in Universal Algebras*, in *Computational Problems in Universal Algebra* (edited by John Leech), Pergamon (1970) pp. 263–297.

[Kn84] Donald E. Knuth, *Literate Programming*, The Computer Journal **27** (1984) pp 97–111.

[St81] Mark E. Stickel, *A Unification Algorithm for Associative-Commutative Functions*, J. ACM **28** (1981) pp 423–434.

COMPLEXITY OF MATCHING PROBLEMS

Dan Benanav*, Deepak Kapur*, Paliath Narendran

Corporate Research and Development
General Electric Company
Schenectady, NY

ABSTRACT

We show that the associative-commutative matching problem is NP-complete; more precisely, the matching problem for terms in which some function symbols are uninterpreted and others are both associative and commutative, is NP-complete. It turns out that the similar problems of associative-matching and commutative-matching are also NP-complete. However, if every variable appears at most once in a term being matched, then the associative-commutative matching problem is shown to have an upper-bound of $O(|s| * |t|^3)$, where $|s|$ and $|t|$ are respectively the sizes of the pattern s and the subject t.

Key Words: Matching, Associative, Associative-Commutative, Commutative, NP-Completeness.

---

* Partially supported by the National Science Foundation grant MCS-82-11621.

COMPLEXITY OF MATCHING PROBLEMS

1. INTRODUCTION

Associative-commutative matching and unification algorithms play an important role in automated reasoning, program verification, specification analysis, etc., when certain operators under consideration have the associative-commutative properties. To our knowledge, Plotkin [12] was the first one to have studied an approach for handling such specialized operators by integrating them into unification algorithms; since then, methods have been suggested for handling such operators using the paramodulation and narrowing techniques in resolution proof systems [7,9,13] and by extending the Knuth-Bendix completion procedure for generating canonical term rewriting systems [8,11]. In these applications, associative-commutative matching is extensively performed and from various computer implementations of these applications, especially those based on rewriting techniques, it is clear that the performance of associative-commutative matching algorithms dominates the overall performance [2,5].

We show that the associative-commutative matching problem is NP-complete; this result is an indication why a general associative-matching algorithm is not likely to perform well. We show that in fact, commutative-matching as well as associative-matching are also NP-complete. However, for a restricted version of associative-commutative matching, where every variable in a term being matched has a unique occurrence, the problem is shown to have an upper bound of $O(|s| * |t|^3)$, where $|s|$ and $|t|$ are respectively the sizes of the pattern s and the subject t.

The constructions employed in showing these NP-completeness results are related. The 3SAT problem (satisfiability problem for the case when every clause has 3 literals) is reduced to each of these problems. There appear to be three steps in the construction: (i) simulating boolean values 'true' and 'false' using ground terms, (ii) constructing terms from a 3SAT formula in such a way that (a) variables of the formula can get either of the boolean values, and (b) there is a match if and only if that match, when suitably interpreted, is a satisfying assignment for the formula, and (iii) extra variables are used to match the subterms that are 'left over', namely those not used for matching variables in the formula.

In the next section, we give basic definitions. In Section 3, various problems referred to in the paper are defined. Section 4 shows that associative-commutative matching problem is NP-complete. In Section 5, we show that if every variable in a term being matched appears uniquely, then the associative-commutative matching problem has a polynomial upper-bound. The NP-completeness of the associative-matching problem and the commutative-matching problem are proved respectively in Sections 6 and 7.

2. Definitions

Let F be a finite set of function symbols of fixed arity and X be a denumerable set of variables. By $T(F, X)$ we denote the set of all possible terms that can be constructed using F and X. For a term t, $Var(t)$ denotes the set of all variables that occur in t. For example, $Var(f(x, y, g(y))) = \{x, y\}$. The *size* of a term s is the number of occurrences of function and variable symbols in s and is denoted by $|s|$.

A function f is *associative* if and only if it satisfies the following axiom:

$$f(f(x, y), z) = f(x, f(y, z)). \qquad \text{(A)}$$

A function f is *commutative* if and only if it satisfies

$$f(x, y) = f(y, x). \qquad \text{(C)}$$

We often refer to a function that is both associative and commutative as an 'ac-operator'.

A term t that involves associative function symbols is often represented in 'flattened' form. For example, if f is associative, then $f(a, f(b, c))$ is represented as $f(a\ b\ c)$. (In other words, f is treated as a varyadic symbol.) Flattening a term with respect to a function f can be done as follows: first represent a term in right-associative form. Such a term will be of the form $f(t_1, f(t_2, \cdots, f(t_{n-1}, t_n) \cdots)$ where $t_1, t_2, \ldots, t_n$ do not start with f. Then we simply represent the term as $f(t_1, t_2, \cdots, t_n)$. It can be easily shown that flattening a term can be done in linear time with respect to the size of the term.

A *substitution* is a mapping θ from variables names to terms such that $\theta(v) = v$ for all but a finite number of variables symbols. It can be denoted by an expression of the form $\{v_1 \leftarrow t_1, \cdots, v_k \leftarrow t_k\}$, where the $k \geq 0$ variable symbols $v_1, \cdots, v_k$ are distinct. (The case $k = 0$ is the identity substitution.) By the size of a substitution θ denoted in this way we shall mean $k + \sum_{i=1}^{k} |t_i|$. We shall denote the size of θ by $|\theta|$. The domain of a substitution θ is extended to the set of all terms by inductively defining $\theta(f(t_1, \cdots, t_n))$ to be $f(\theta(t_1), \cdots, \theta(t_n))$.

A substitution θ is said to *match* a term s with a term t if and only if $t = \theta(s)$. In this case, s is often called the *pattern* and t the *subject.*

Two terms s and t are said to be *associative-commutative equivalent*, expressed as $s \underset{ac}{=} t$, if and only if they are equivalent under the equational theory of the axioms (A) and (C). For example, if f is associative and commutative, then $f(f(a, b), c) \underset{ac}{=} f(c, f(b, a))$. We similarly define associative equivalence ($\underset{A}{=}$) and commutative equivalence ($\underset{C}{=}$).

3. Problem Definitions

The following is a list of problems that will be referred to in this paper.

1. **Associative-Commutative Equivalence** (referred to as **ACEQ**)

   Instance: A set of variable symbols V, a set of function symbols F some of which may be associative and commutative, and terms t_1, t_2 from $T(F,V)$.

   Question: Is $t_1 \underset{ac}{=} t_2$?

2. **Associative-Commutative Matching** (referred to as **ACM**)

   Instance: A set of variable symbols V, a set of function symbols F some of which may be associative and commutative, and terms t_1, t_2 from $T(F,V)$.

   Question: Does there exist a θ such that $\theta(t_1) \underset{ac}{=} t_2$?

3. **Distinct-Occurrences ACM** (referred to as **DO-ACM**)

   Instance: A set of variable symbols V, a set of function symbols F, some of which may be associative and commutative, two terms t_1, t_2 from $T(F,V)$ where every variable in t_1 occurs only once. (In other words, $v \in \text{vars}(t_1) \Rightarrow$ #occurrences of v in $t_1 = 1$).

   Question: Does there exist a θ such that $\theta(t_1) \underset{ac}{=} t_2$?

4. **Monotone 3SAT** (referred to as **Mono-3SAT**)

   Instance: A set of variables $U = \{z_1, z_2, \dots, z_m\}$, a set of clauses $C = \{c_1, c_2, \dots, c_n\}$ where each clause is a set of literals, each literal is z_i or $\overline{z_i}$ for

   $1 \leq i \leq m$ and each clause satisfies the following:
   1) For all i such that $1 \leq i \leq n$ $|c_i| = 3$.
   2) (For all literals l, $l \in c_i \Rightarrow l = z_j$ for some j (i.e., l is positive)) or (For all l, $l \in c_i \Rightarrow l = \overline{z_j}$ for some j (i.e., l is negative).

   Question: Does there exist a truth assignment I: $U \rightarrow \{1,0\}$ such that C is satisfiable ?

   This problem is known to be an NP-complete problem [1].

Definition: Given I: $U \rightarrow \{1,0\}$ and clause c then $Image(c, I) = \{(1,n),(0,m)\}$ where n = # of true literals in c and m = # of false literals in c under the mapping I.

For example if $c = \{z_1, z_2, \overline{z_3}\}$ and $I(z_1) = 1$, $I(z_2) = 0$, $I(z_3) = 1$, then $Image(c, I) = \{(1,1), (0,2)\}$.

4. Associative-Commutative Matching is NP-Complete

Theorem 1: ACM is NP complete.

Proof: It is easy to show that ACM $\in$ NP. Let t_1, t_2 be terms and θ be a substitution such that $\theta(t_1) \underset{ac}{=} t_2$. Clearly the size of θ cannot be greater than $(|t_2| + |t_1|)$. Thus given two terms t_1 and t_2 as input, we merely have to

(a) choose θ such that $|\theta| \le (|t_1| + |t_2|)$,

(b) apply θ to t_1 to get a new term t_1', and

(c) check whether $t_1' \underset{ac}{=} t_2$.

Step (b) can obviously be done in polynomial time. Step (c) can also be done in polynomial time since ACEQ $\in$ P as will be shown later in the paper.

To show that ACM is NP-complete we will show that Mono-3SAT is polynomially transformable to ACM.

Suppose that we are given an instance of the Mono-3SAT problem with $U = \{z_1, z_2, \ldots, z_m\}$ and $C = \{c_1, c_2, \ldots, c_n\}$. Let f be an ac-operator, g an operator of arity n that is neither commutative nor associative and let 1 and 0 be nullary operators (constants).

Let $U' = \{u_{11}, u_{12}, \ldots, u_{n1}, u_{n2}\}$ be a set of variables with $U \cap U' = \emptyset$. Let $V = U \cup U'$ and $F = \{f, g, 1, 0\}$. We can show that two terms t_1 and t_2 over F and V can be constructed in polynomial time with respect to the input in such a way that C is satisfiable if and only if there exists a θ such that $\theta(t_1) \underset{ac}{=} t_2$.

First let H: Clauses $\rightarrow$ Terms be defined as follows:

$$H(c_i) = f\,(z_1\ z_2\ z_3\ u_{i1}\ u_{i2}) \text{ if } c_i = \{z_1, z_2, z_3\} \text{ or if } c_i = \{\overline{z_1}, \overline{z_2}, \overline{z_3}\}$$

and let G : Clauses $\rightarrow$ Terms be defined as:

$$G(c_i) = f\,(1\ 1\ 1\ 0\ 0) \text{ if } c_i = \{z_1, z_2, z_3\}$$
$$= f\,(0\ 0\ 0\ 1\ 1) \text{ if } c_i = \{\overline{z_1}, \overline{z_2}, \overline{z_3}\}$$

For example if $c_2 = \{p, q, r\}$ then $H(c_2) = f\,(p\ q\ r\ u_{21}\ u_{22})$ and $G(c_2) = f\,(1\ 1\ 1\ 0\ 0)$.
Now let $t_1 = g\,(s_1\ s_2\ \cdots\ s_n)$ where $s_i = H(c_i)$ and
$t_2 = g\,(s_1'\ s_2'\ \cdots\ s_n')$ where $s_i' = G(c_i)$.
It is obvious that these terms can be constructed in polynomial time with respect to the input.

Now suppose there exists a θ such that $\theta(t_1) \underset{ac}{=} t_2$. Let $I: U \rightarrow \{1,0\}$ be defined by $I(v) = \theta(v)$. Since g is neither commutative nor associative, it must be true that for all i $\theta(s_i) \underset{ac}{=} s_i'$. Suppose $c_i = \{z_1, z_2, z_3\}$. Then by construction $s_i = f\,(z_1\ z_2\ z_3\ u_{i1}\ u_{i2})$ and

$s_i' \;=f\,(1\,1\,1\,0\,0)$ and so $\theta(f\,(z_1\,z_2\,z_3\,u_{i1}\,u_{i2})) \underset{ac}{=} f\,(1\,1\,1\,0\,0)$. Observe that this can be true if and only if 3 and only 3 of the variables in $\{z_1, z_2, z_3, u_{i1}, u_{i2}\}$ map to 1 under the substitution θ. Since at most both of the variables u_{i1} and u_{i2} map to 1 under θ it must be the case that either z_1, z_2 or z_3 map to 1 under θ. Therefore clause c_i is satisfied under I. Likewise if $c_i = \{\overline{z_1}, \overline{z_2}, \overline{z_3}\}$ then $\theta(f\,(z_1\,z_2\,z_3\,u_{i1}\,u_{i2})) \underset{ac}{=} f\,(0\,0\,0\,1\,1)$ and either z_1, z_2 or z_3 map to 0 under θ and thus either $\overline{z_1}$, $\overline{z_2}$, or $\overline{z_3}$ map to 1 under θ. It is clear that C is satisfied under the mapping I since $I = \theta$ and every clause is satisfied under I.

Now suppose that C is satisfiable. Let $I\colon U \rightarrow \{1,0\}$ be a truth assignment satisfying C. We will construct a substitution θ such that $\theta(t_1) \underset{ac}{=} t_2$.

Partition C into the following classes.

$$\begin{aligned}
P_1 &= \{c_i \mid c_i \text{ is positive and Image}(c_i, I) = \{(1,1),(0,2)\}\\
P_2 &= \{c_i \mid c_i \text{ is positive and Image}(c_i, I) = \{(1,2),(0,1)\}\\
P_3 &= \{c_i \mid c_i \text{ is positive and Image}(c_i, I) = \{(1,3),(0,0)\}\\
N_1 &= \{c_i \mid c_i \text{ is negative and Image}(c_i, I) = \{(0,1),(1,2)\}\\
N_2 &= \{c_i \mid c_i \text{ is negative and Image}(c_i, I) = \{(0,2),(1,1)\}\\
N_3 &= \{c_i \mid c_i \text{ is negative and Image}(c_i, I) = \{(0,3),(1,0)\}
\end{aligned}$$

Define $\theta(v) = I(v)$ for $v \in U$

$\theta(u_{i1}) = 1$ if $c_i \in P_1 \cup P_2 \cup N_2 \cup N_3$

$\theta(u_{i1}) = 0$ if $c_i \in P_3 \cup N_1$

$\theta(u_{i2}) = 1$ if $c_i \in P_1 \cup N_3$ and

$\theta(u_{i2}) = 0$ if $c_i \in P_2 \cup P_3 \cup N_1 \cup N_2$.

Now it is an easy matter to check that for $c_i \in P_1 \cup P_2 \cup P_3$ that

$$\theta(s_i) = \theta(H(c_i)) \underset{ac}{=} f\,(1\,1\,1\,0\,0) = G(c_i) = s_i'$$

and that for $c_i \in N_1 \cup N_2 \cup N_3$

$$\theta(s_i) = \theta(H(c_i)) \underset{ac}{=} f\,(0\,0\,0\,1\,1) = G(c_i) = s_i' \,.$$

Thus, for all i, $\theta(s_i) \underset{ac}{=} s_i'$ and $\theta(g\,(s_1\,s_2\,\cdots\,s_n)) \underset{ac}{=} g\,(s_1'\,\,s_2'\,\,\cdots\,\,s_n')$. *Q.E.D.*

The above construction also shows that the problem remains NP-complete even if there is only one ac-operator and at least three operators that are neither commutative nor associative.[1]

---

* The NP-completeness of associative-commutative matching was also shown independently by Ashok Chandra and Paris Kanellakis [4] by reducing the bin-packing problem to it.

Since associative-commutative matching is a special case of associative-commutative unification as pointed out by Peterson and Stickel [11], associative-commutative unification is at least NP-hard. However, it will be interesting to develop a complexity bound for associative-commutative unification.

5. Restricted Associative-Commutative Matching

In this section, we show that a restricted associative-commutative matching problem, namely DO-ACM, can be done in polynomial time. The idea behind the algorithm is this: if two terms, say t_1 and t_2, having no variable at all in common can be matched with s_1 and s_2 respectively, then a substitution can be found that does both matches "simultaneously." This substitution is merely the **union** of the two former substitutions since no conflicts are possible.

Thus to match two flattened terms $t = f\,(t_1\, t_2 \;\cdots\; t_n)$ and $s = f\,(s_1\, s_2 \;\cdots\; s_n)$ all that we have to do is this: for each t_i, find an s_j that it can be matched with, making sure that no two t_i's are matched with the same s_j. In other words, what we need is a **bijection** π from $\{1,n\}$ onto $\{1,n\}$ such that t_i can be matched with $s_{\pi(i)}$. This can be found recursively by the following steps:

a. For every t_i find all s_j's that it can be matched with. This can be done by an exhaustive search.

b. Form an n-by-n undirected bipartite graph G with nodes corresponding to each t_i and s_j such that there is an edge between nodes t_i and s_j if and only if t_i can be matched with s_j.

c. Check to see if there is a matching of size n.

The following example will illustrate this: let $t = f\,(g\,(x\;\; a)\; g\,(b\;\; b\;\; y))$ and $s = f\,(g\,(a\;\; b\;\; b)\; g\,(a\;\; a))$. We get the graph G (see Figure 1)

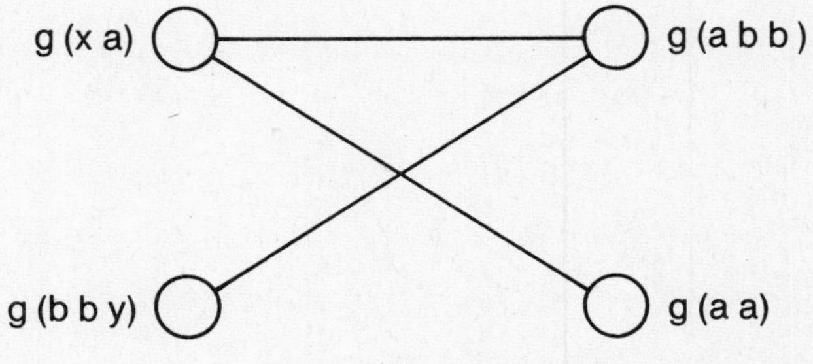

Figure 1.

and the maximum matching (of size 2) is the one that matches $g\,(x\;\; a)$ with $g\,(a\;\; a)$ and $g\,(b\;\; b\;\; y)$ with $g\,(a\;\; b\;\; b)$. Thus the substitution is $\{x \leftarrow a,\, y \leftarrow b\}$.

We now give a formal proof of the method discussed above and show that it can be performed in polynomial time.

Theorem 2: DO-ACM can be solved in polynomial time.

Proof: To prove this we first need the following two theorems.

Theorem 2.1: Let $t = f\,(t_1\, t_2\, \cdots\, t_n)$ and $s = f\,(s_1\, s_2\, \cdots\, s_n)$ be two flattened terms, where t_i are non-variables. Then if there exists a one to one function π:$\{1,n\} \rightarrow \{1,n\}$ and a substitution ψ such that $\psi(t_i) \underset{ac}{=} s_{\pi(i)}$ then $\psi(t) \underset{ac}{=} s$.

Theorem 2.2: Let $t = f\,(t_1\, t_2\, \cdots\, t_n)$, $s = f\,(s_{n+1}\, \cdots\, s_{n+m})$, where f is an ac-operator and further let $Var(t) \cap Var(s) = \emptyset$ and #occurrences of v in $t = 1$ for all v in $Var(t)$. Let $G = <V, U, E>$ be the bipartite graph with

$V = \{i \mid i \leq n$ and t_i not a variable$\}$

$\overline{V} = \{1, 2, \ldots, n\} - V$

$U = \{n+1, \ldots, n+m\}$ and

$E = \{\, \{i,j\} \mid i \in V$ and $j \in U$ and there exists θ such that $\theta(t_i) \underset{ac}{=} s_j\}$.

Then the following holds: There exists ψ such that $\psi(t) \underset{ac}{=} s$ if and only if

(1) There exists maximum matching M of G with $|M| = |V|$

(2) $n \leq m$ and

(3) $m > n \Rightarrow \overline{V} \neq \emptyset$.

We will prove only (1), (2), (3) $\Rightarrow$ there exists ψ such that $\psi(t) \underset{ac}{=} s$ and leave it to the reader to prove the opposite direction. Suppose that (1), (2) and (3) hold. Since $|M| = |V|$, and M is a matching then for each $i \in V$ there is one and only one $\{i,j\} \in M$. For each i let θ_i be a substitution such that $\theta(t_i) \underset{ac}{=} s_j$ where $\{i,j\}$ is an edge in M. By definition of E we know that at least one such θ_i exists. Let ψ' be the substitution defined by $\psi' = \bigcup_{i \in V} \theta_i$. Note that ψ' is well-defined since the variables in t_i and t_j are always distinct for $i \neq j$.

Now suppose that $\overline{V} = \emptyset$. Then $m \leq n$ by (3). Thus $m \leq n$ and $m \geq n$ (by condition (2)) and thus $n = m$. The mapping π defined by $\pi(i) = j$ if $\{i,j\} \in M$ defines a one to one function from V onto U. To see this suppose that $\pi(i) = \pi(i')$. Then $\{i,\pi(i)\} \in M$ and $\{i',\pi(i')\} \in M$ by definition of π. Now if $i \neq i'$ then $\{i,\pi(i)\}$ and $\{i',\pi(i')\}$ would be distinct edges in M with a common element, namely $\pi(i)$ and $\pi(i')$. However since M is a matching this cannot be the case and thus $i = i'$. Also π satisfies $\theta_i(t_i) = s_{\pi(i)}$ and since

$\theta_i(t_i) = \psi'(t_i)$, by definition of ψ', then $\psi'(t_i) = s_{\pi(i)}$. Thus by Theorem 2.1, $\psi'(t) \underset{ac}{=} s$.

Suppose that $\overline{V} \neq \emptyset$ and is given by $\overline{V} = \{n_1, n_2, \cdots, n_k\}$. Also let U' be defined by $U' = \{j \mid j \in U$ and for all i, $i \in V \Rightarrow \{i,j\} \in M\}$
$= \{m_1, m_2, \cdots, m_p\}$. Let ψ be the substitution defined as follows:

$$\psi(v) = s_{m_i} \text{ for } v = t_{n_i}, \ i \in \{1, \ldots, k-1\},$$

$$\psi(v) = f\,(s_{m_{k+1}} \ldots s_{m_p}) \quad \text{for } v = t_{n_k},$$

$\psi(v) = \psi'(v)$ otherwise.

It is left to the reader to check that $\psi(t) \underset{ac}{=} s$. *Q.E.D.*

Given two terms $t = f\,(t_1 t_2 \cdots t_n)$, $s = f\,(s_{n+1} \cdots s_{n+m})$ as in theorem 2.2 and the graph $G = \langle V, U, E \rangle$ we can find a maximum matching M of G in $O(|V|, |E|)$ or in $O(m^3)$ since $|V| \leq n \leq m$ and $|E| \leq n \cdot m \leq m^2$ [10]. Obviously conditions 2 and 3 can be checked in linear time. Thus given the graph V we can determine if there exists a θ such that $\theta(t) \underset{ac}{=} s$ in $O(m^3)$ time.

In order to determine the graph V and to determine whether a suitable substitution exists we can write a recursive algorithm that first attempts to find the set of edges in E by calling itself with inputs t_i and s_j for each i and j. Let $Tm(|t|, |s|)$ be the time taken by this algorithm. Clearly,

$$Tm(|t|, |s|) \leq \left[\sum_{j=n+1}^{n+m} \sum_{i=1}^{n} Tm(|t_i|, |s_j|)\right] + k \cdot m^3 \text{ for some } k.$$

This algorithm will terminate eventually since we will only have to check conditions (2) and (3). Now we will show that $Tm(|t|, |s|) \leq k \cdot |t| \cdot |s|^3$ by induction, assuming $Tm(|t_i|, |s_j|) \leq k \cdot |t_i| \cdot |s_j|^3$ as follows:

$$\left[\sum_{j=n+1}^{n+m} \sum_{i=1}^{n} Tm(|t_i|, |s_j|)\right] + k \cdot m^3 \leq \left[\sum_{j=n+1}^{n+m} \sum_{i=1}^{n} k \cdot |t_i| \cdot |s_j|^3\right] + k \cdot m^3$$

$$\leq k \cdot \left[\sum_{i=1}^{n} |t_i|\right] \cdot \left[\sum_{j=n+1}^{n+m} |s_j|^3\right] + k \cdot m^3 \leq k \cdot \left[\sum_{i=1}^{n} |t_i|\right] \cdot \left[\sum_{j=n+1}^{n+m} |s_j|\right]^3 + k \cdot m^3$$

$$\leq k \cdot \left[\sum_{i=1}^{n} |t_i| \cdot |s|^3\right] + k \cdot |s|^3 \leq k \cdot |s|^3 \cdot (1 + \sum_{i=1}^{n} |t_i|)$$

$$\leq k \cdot |s|^3 \cdot |t|.$$

The case when the top-level function symbol of t and s is neither commutative nor associative is trivial. This completes the proof. *Q.E.D.*

Corollary 2: ACEQ can be done in polynomial time.

Proof: This is easy to see since ACEQ is equivalent to DO-ACM if we consider all the variables in the two terms to be constants. *Q.E.D.*

We conjecture that the associative-commutative matching problem remains in polynomial time as long as it is possible to put a bound on the number of times every variable can occur in a term being matched. Since in practice, one hardly sees a variable occurring more than 2 or 3 times, it may in fact be possible to develop an efficient associative-commutative matching algorithm for such practical cases. This is the strategy we have adopted in the implementation of such algorithms in RRL [5].

6. Associative Matching (AM)

Instance: A set of function symbols F some of which may be associative, a set of variables V and two terms t_1, t_2 from $T(F,V)$.

Question: Does there exists a θ such that $\theta(t_1) \underset{A}{=} t_2$?

Theorem: AM is NP-complete.

Sketch of the proof: It is easy to see that AM is in NP. The construction employed in showing that AM is NP-hard is given below.

Let $C = \{c_1, c_2, \cdots c_m\}$ be an instance of 3SAT over the boolean variables $x_1, \ldots, x_n$. Take $F = \{f, a, h\}$ where f is an associative function symbol, a is a nullary (constant) symbol and h is an $(n+m)$-ary function symbol.

Let $V = \{x_1, \ldots, x_n\} \cup \{y_1, \ldots, y_n\} \cup \{u_1, \ldots, u_m\}$, where each y_i acts the role of $\overline{x_i}$ and the u_i's are dummy symbols. The truth and falsity of a boolean variable x_i is simulated by the conditions $x_i = a$ and $x_i = f(a,a)$ respectively.

Define, for $1 \leq i \leq n$,

$$s_i = f(x, y) \text{ and}$$
$$t_i = f(a, f(a,a)) = f(a \ a \ a).$$

(Note that if s_i has to be matched with t_i, either x_i or y_i must be made equal to a and not both.) For each clause c_j, we do the following: let x_1, x_2 and x_3 be the variables in c_j. Then we set

$$p_j = f(z_1 \ z_2 \ z_3 \ u_j) \text{ and}$$
$$q_j = f(a \ a \ a \ a \ a \ a).$$

where $z_i = x_i$ if the literal x_i appears in c_j and $z_i = y_i$ if the literal $\overline{x_i}$ appears in c_j, for $i = 1,2,3$. Here again, note that to match p_j with q_j at least one of the z_i's must be set equal to a.

Finally set $s = h(s_i, \ldots, s_n, p_i, \ldots, p_m)$ and $t = h(t_i, \ldots, t_n, q_i, \ldots, q_m)$. The reader can easily verify that s can be associative-matched with t if and only if C is satisfiable. *Q.E.D.*

Thus the problem remains NP-complete even if there is only one associative operator and at least two non-associative operators. The result also implies that the associative unification problem is at least NP-hard. Related results are claimed in [3].

7. Commutative matching (CM)

Instance: A set of function symbols F some of which may be commutative, a set of variables V and two terms t_1, t_2 from $T(F,V)$.

Question: Does there exists a θ such that $\theta(t_1) \underset{C}{=} t_2$?

Theorem: CM is NP-complete.

Sketch of the proof: The construction is as follows:

Let $C = \{c_1, c_2, \cdots c_m\}$ be an instance of 3SAT over the boolean variables $x_1, \ldots, x_n$. Take $F = \{f, g, a, h, 0, 1\}$ where f is a binary commutative function symbol, g is a ternary function symbol, a, 0 and 1 are nullary (constant) symbols and h is an m-ary function symbol.

Let $V = \{x_1, \ldots, x_n\} \cup \{u_{ij} \mid 1 \leq i \leq m, 1 \leq j \leq 3\}$. The truth and falsity of a boolean variable x_i is simulated by the conditions $x_i = 1$ and $x_i = 0$ respectively.

For each clause c_j, we do the following: let x_1, x_2 and x_3 be the variables in c_j. There are exactly 7 sets of truth-value-assignments that make the clause c_j true. Let $q_1, \ldots, q_7$ be 7 (distinct) terms that 'represent' these assignments; for $i = 1, \ldots, 7$, define $q_i = g(b_1, b_2, b_3)$ where $b_i \in \{1,0\}$ and the assignment (b_1, b_2, b_3) satisfies c_j. Let

$$s_j = f(f(f(g(x_1, x_2, x_3), u_{j1}), u_{j2}), u_{j3}) \text{ and}$$
$$t_j = f(f(f(q_1, q_2), f(q_3, q_4)), f(f(q_5, q_6), f(q_7, a))).$$

(See Figure 2)

Finally define $s = h(s_1, \cdots, s_m)$ and $t = h(t_1, \cdots, t_m)$. It can be shown that s can be commutative-matched with t if and only if C is satisfiable. *Q.E.D.*

As in the case of the two previous NP-completeness results this proof also shows that CM remains NP-complete even if there is only one commutative operator and at least five non-commutative operators. The result is also interesting in another respect. The commutative unification problem is known to be NP-complete (see p. 252 in [1] where this result is attribut-

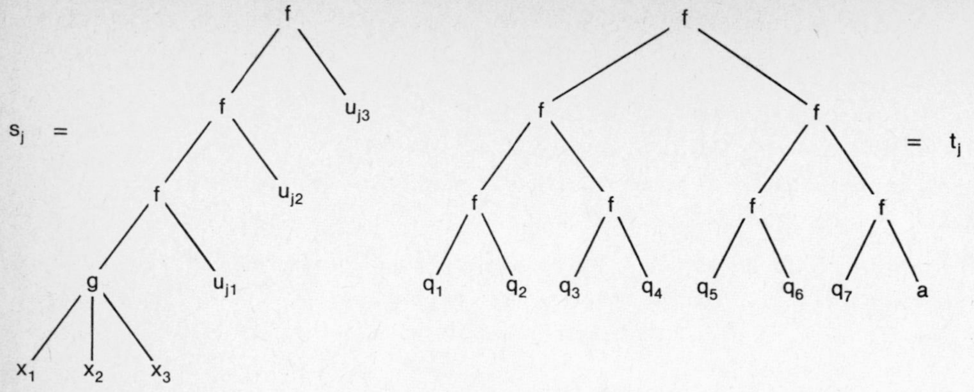

Figure 2.

ed to Ravi Sethi). For commutative operators, the matching problem and unification problem thus surprisingly turn out to be of the same complexity. This is similar to the case of unification and matching problems over a free theory where the complexity is linear for both problems. This leads us to conjecture that associative-commutative unification is also NP-complete.

ACKNOWLEDGEMENT: The NP-completeness of associative-commutative matching problem (ACM) was established during the course of discussions with Snorri Agnarrson who contributed ideas for simplifying the proof.

8. REFERENCES

[1] Garey, M.R. and Johnson, D.S., *Computers and Intractability*, W.H. Freeman, 1979.

[2] Hullot, J.M., "Associative-Commutative Pattern Matching," *Fifth International Joint Conference on Artificial Intelligence*, Tokyo, Japan, 1979.

[3] Iwama, K., "On Equations Including String Variables," *Proc. 23rd Ann. Symp. on Foundations of Computer Science*, 1982, pp. 226-235.

[4] Kanellakis, P., private communication.

[5] Kapur, D. and Sivakumar, G., "Architecture of and Experiments with RRL, a Rewrite Rule Laboratory," *Proceedings of a NSF Workshop on the Rewrite Rule Laboratory*, September 6-9, 1983, General Electric CRD Report, 84GEN004, April, 1984, pp. 33-56.

[6] Knuth, D.E. and Bendix, P.B., "Simple Word Problems in Universal Algebras," in *Computational Problems in Abstract Algebras* (ed. J. Leech), Pergamon Press, 1970, pp. 263-297.

[7] Lankford, D.S., "Canonical Inference," Report ATP-32 Dept. of Mathematics and Computer Sciences, Univ. of Texas, Austin, TX (1975).

[8] Lankford, D.S., and Ballantyne A.M., "Decision Procedures for Simple Equational Theories with Commutative-Associative Axioms: Complete Sets of Commutative-Associative Reductions," Memo ATP-39, Dept. of Mathematics and Computer Sciences, Univ. of Texas, Austin, TX (1977).

[9] Lankford, D.S., and Ballantyne, A.M., "The Refutation Completeness of Blocked Permutative Narrowing and Resolution," *Fourth Conference on Automated Deduction*, 1979.

[10] Papadimitriou, C.H., and Steiglitz, K., *Combinatorial Optimization: Algorithms and Complexity*, Prentice-Hall, 1982.

[11] Peterson, G.E., and Stickel, M.E., "Complete Sets of Reductions for Some Equational Theories," Journal of the ACM, Vol. 28, No. 2, pp. 233-264.

[12] Plotkin, G., "Building in Equational Theories," *Machine Intelligence* 7 (eds. Meltzer and Michie), pp. 73-90.

[13] Slagle, J., "Automated Theorem Proving with Simplifiers, Commutativity and Associativity," *JACM* Vol. 21, 1974, pp. 622-642.

[14] Stickel, M.E., "A Unification Algorithm for Associative-Commutative Functions," *JACM* 28 (1980), pp. 423-434.

THE SET OF UNIFIERS IN TYPED λ-CALCULUS AS REGULAR EXPRESSION

Marek Zaionc
Institute of Computer Science
Jagiellonian University
Kopernika 27, 31-501 Kraków, Poland

1. Introduction

The main problem for mechanization of the theorem proving in the typed λ-calculus is the problem of determining whether two terms of a fixed type with free variables have the common instance. This unification problem is undecidable for orders≥2 (see Huet(1973) and Goldfarb(1981)). The Huet(1975) paper contains the description of semi-decision algorithm which in the case of success, returns a substitution called the most general unifier. This algorithm produces the matching tree, in which the most general unifiers are represented by the final branches. The most interesting is the case when the matching tree is infinite and consists of infinite number of most general unifiers. I have noticed that some infinite matching trees have an interesting property: for every infinite branch there is a node which occurs earlier in this tree. It means that there are some fragments which repeated in this tree.

In this paper I consider some class of unification problems. For the fixed problem from this class the set of unifiers can be represented by the regular expression built up on the basis of finite alphabet. This alphabet consists of symbols called elementary substitutions. Every word is interpreted as a composition of the elementary substitutions.

2. Typed λ-calculus

Our language is derived from the Church's simple theory of types. Every term possesses a unique type which indicates its position in a functional hierarchy. The language is defined as the βη typed λ-calculus. The nonstandard notation of application $T(S_1,\dots,S_n)$ instead of $(\dots(TS_1)S_2)\dots S_n)$ is used. The equivalent notation of types such as $t_1,\dots,t_n \rightarrow 0$ instead of

$t_1 \to (t_2 \to \ldots \to (t_n \to 0)\ldots)$ is more convenient for terms which are written always in the long-normal form.

The set of types is introduced as follows: 0 is a type and if $t_1,\ldots,t_n$ are types then $t_1,\ldots,t_n \to 0$ is a type. If t' is a type and t is type of the form $t_1,\ldots,t_n \to 0$ then by $t' \to t$ we mean the type $t',t_1,\ldots,t_n \to 0$. If t is the type of the form $t_1,\ldots,t_n \to 0$ then t_i is called a component of t and is denoted as t[i]. By $t[i_1,\ldots,i_k]$ we denote $t[i_1]\ldots[i_k]$. For any type t we define rank(t) and arg(t). If t=0 then rank(t)=arg(t)=0. If $t=t[1],\ldots,t[n] \to 0$ then arg(t)=n and rank(t)=max(rank(t[i]))+1. Type t is called regular if rank(t)≤ 3 and for every i if $1 \leq i \leq arg(t)$ then $arg(t[i]) \leq 1$.

For any type t a denumerable set of variables V(t) is given. Any variable of type t is the term of type t. If T is a term of type $t_1,\ldots,t_n \to 0$ and $T_1,\ldots,T_s$ $(s \leq n)$ are terms of types $t_1, \ldots, t_s$ respectively then $T(T_1,\ldots,T_s)$ is a term of type $t_{s+1},\ldots,t_n \to 0$. If T is a term of type t and $x_1,\ldots,x_s$ are variables of types $t_1,\ldots,t_s$ respectively then $\lambda x_1 \ldots x_s . T$ is a term of type $t_1 \to ..(t_s \to t)..)$ If T is a term of type t we write $T \in t$. If T is a term and x is a variable of the same type as a term S then T[x/S] denotes the substitution of the term S for each free occurrence of x in T. The axioms of equality between terms have the form of α,β,η conversions (see Friedman(1975)) with two added equations:

$$\lambda x_1 \ldots x_k . \lambda x_{k+1} \ldots x_n . T = \lambda x_1 \ldots x_n . T \qquad \text{for } k<n$$
$$(T(T_1,\ldots,T_k))(T_{k+1},\ldots,T_n) = T(T_1,\ldots,T_n) \qquad \text{for } k<n$$

By the Cl(t) we mean the set of all closed terms (without free variables) of type t. If Y is a set of variables then Cl(t,Y) is the set of all terms of type t with only free variables from Y. Obviously $Cl(t,\emptyset) = Cl(t)$. Term T is in the long normal form if

$$T = \lambda x_1 \ldots x_n . y(T_1,\ldots,T_k)$$

where y is an x_i for $i \leq n$ or y is a free variable, T_j for $j \leq k$ are in the long normal form and term $y(T_1,\ldots,T_k)$ is a term of type 0.

3. Term grammars

Let NT be a finite set of variables (the elements of NT correspond to nonterminal elements in the classical grammars). A production is a pair (y,T) denoted also by $y \Rightarrow T$ where y and T has the common type t and T Cl(t,NT). A grammar is a finite set of productions. The relation $y \overset{*}{\Rightarrow} T$ in grammar G is defined inductively:

if $y \Rightarrow T \in G$ then $y \overset{*}{\Rightarrow} T$ holds if $y \overset{*}{\Longrightarrow} T$ and $z \overset{*}{\Longrightarrow} S$ hold then $y \overset{*}{\Longrightarrow} T[z//S]$ holds

where the term $T[z//S]$ denotes the substitution of one occurrence of z by the term S in T. By L(G,y) we mean the set of all closed terms which are generated from y by the grammar G i.e. if $y \in t$ then

$$L(G,y) = \{T \in Cl(t) : y \overset{*}{\Longrightarrow} T\}$$

If $y \overset{*}{\Longrightarrow} T$ and $z \overset{*}{\Longrightarrow} S$ hold then relation $y \overset{*}{\Longrightarrow} T[z/S]$ holds. Grammar G is called regular if on the right side of every production a non-terminal variable occurs not more than once.

Example 1

Let t be a following regular type $(0,0 \to 0) \to 0,0 \to 0$. The grammar which generates all closed terms of type t is following:

$y \Longrightarrow \lambda pa.a$ [a]
$y \Longrightarrow \lambda pa.p(\lambda bc.y(p,a))$ [b]
$y \Longrightarrow \lambda pa.p(\lambda bc.y(p,b))$ [c]
$y \Longrightarrow \lambda pa.p(\lambda bc.y(p,c))$ [d]

Closed term $\lambda px_1.p(\lambda x_2x_3.p(\lambda x_4x_5.p(\lambda x_6x_7.x_4)))$ can be obtained by means of productions b c b a as well as c c b a or d c b a.

Theorem 1

For every regular type there exists a regular grammar which generates all closed terms of this type.

Proof. Let type t be regular and have the form $t[1],\ldots,t[n] \to 0$. If $rank(t[i])=0$ then $t[i]=0$. If $rank(t[i])=1$ then $t[i]=(0 \to 0)$. If $rank(t[i])=2$ then $t[i]=(0,\ldots,0 \to 0) \to 0$.

Case 1. If there is $i \leq n$ such that $rank(t[i])=0$. Set NT is defined as $\{y\}$ where $y \in t$ and grammar consists of following productions:

$y \Longrightarrow \lambda x_1 \ldots x_n . x_i$ $[a_i]$
for every i such that $t[i]=0$

$y \Longrightarrow \lambda x_1 \ldots x_n . x_i(y(x_1,\ldots,x_n))$ $[b_i]$
for every i such that $t[i]=(0 \text{-- } 0)$

$y \Longrightarrow \lambda x_1 \ldots x_n . x_i(\lambda z_1 \ldots z_p . y(x_1,\ldots,x_n))$ $[c_i]$
for every i such that $rank(t[i])=2$ where $p=arg(t[i,1])$

$y \Longrightarrow \lambda x_1 \ldots x_n . x_i(\lambda z_1 \ldots z_p . y(x_1,\ldots,x_{j-1},z_r,x_{j+1},\ldots,x_n))$ $[\bar{c}_i^r]$
for every i and for every r such that $rank(t[i,1])=2$ and $r \leq arg(t[i,1])$ where $p=arg(t[i,1])$ and j is the greatest index such that $t[j]=0$

If such a case the constructed grammar consists of $n+\sum_{i \in t_1} arg(t[i,1])$ productions, where t_2 denots the subset of the interval $\{1,\ldots,arg(t)\}$ defined as:

$t_2 = \{i \leq arg(t): rank(t[i])=2\}$

Case 2. If for every $i \leq n$ $rank(t[i])=1$ or $rank(t[i])=2$. Set NT is defined as $\{y_1, y_2\}$ where $y_1 \in t$ and $y_2 \in t' = t[1], \ldots, t[n], 0 \to 0$. The type t' satisfies Case 1. For the type t' is constructed a grammar which generates all closed terms of the type t' with y_2 as a nonterminal variable. Such a grammar is extended by following productions:

$y_1 \Rightarrow \lambda x_1 \ldots x_n . x_i(y_1(x_1, \ldots, x_n))$
for every i such that $t[i]=(0 \to 0)$
$y_1 \Rightarrow \lambda x_1 \ldots x_n . x_i(\lambda z_1 \ldots z_p . y_2(x_1, \ldots, x_n, z_r))$
for every i and for every r such that $rank(t[i])=2$
and $r \leq arg(t[i,1])=p$

In such a case the constructed grammar consists of

$$2n+2\sum_{i \in t_2} arg(t[i,1]) - |t_2| + 1$$

productions.

Correctnes of constructing the grammar (only for the first case). Without a loss of generality we can assume that $rank(t[i])=2$ for $1 \leq i \leq n$, $rank(t[i])=1$ for $n+1 \leq i \leq n+k$ and $rank(t[i])=0$ for $n+k+1 \leq i \leq n+k+s$. Any closed long normal form term of type t is

$$M = \lambda z_1 .. z_n u_1 .. u_k x_1 .. x_s . U_0 z_{r_0}(\lambda x_{s+1} \ldots x_{s+p_0} . U_1 z_{r_1}(\ldots \ldots$$
$$\ldots . U_c z_{r_c}(\lambda x_{s+p_{c-1}+1} \ldots x_{s+p_c} . U_{c+1}(x_L) \ldots \ldots)$$

where $c \in N$, $r_i \in \{1, \ldots, n\}$ for $0 \leq i \leq c$, $p_i = \sum_{j=0}^{i} arg(t[r_j, 1])$ for $0 \leq i \leq c$. U_i is a word on $u_1, \ldots, u_k$ associated to the right for $0 \leq i \leq c+1$. Number L belongs to interval $\{1, \ldots, s+p_c\}$. Let us assume that the number of letters which occur in the U_i is $q_i \in N$.

$$U_i = u_{m_{i,1}} \ldots u_{m_{i,q_i}}$$

where $m_{i,j} \in \{1, \ldots, k\}$ for $0 \leq i \leq c+1$ and $1 \leq j \leq q_i$. If $1 \leq L \leq s$ then the term M is obtained as a result of the application of the following productions:

$$b_{m_{0,1}}, \ldots, b_{m_{0,q_0}}, c_{r_0}, b_{m_{1,1}}, \ldots, b_{m_{1,q_1}}, \ldots \ldots, b_{m_{c,1}}, \ldots, b_{m_{c,q_c}},$$
$$c_{r_c}, b_{m_{c+1,1}}, \ldots, b_{m_{c+1,q_{c+1}}}, a_L$$

Let us assume that $s < L$. v is defined as a positive number such that $\sum_{w=0}^{v-1} arg(t[r_w, 1]) < L$ and $\sum_{w=0}^{v} arg(t[r_w, 1]) \geq L$. Term M is obtained in this case as a result of the applications of the same productions as in the previous case without v-th occurrence of c_{r_v} which is replaced by $\bar{c}^e_{r_v}$ where $e=L-\sum_{w\geq 0}^{v-1}arg(t[r_w,1])$, and without the last production a_L, which is replaced by a_{n+k+s}.

Theorem 2

Let t be a regular type and $C_1,\ldots,C_n$ are constants of types $t_1,\ldots,t_n$ respectively, where every t_i is a component of some regular type. There exists a regular grammar G which produces all closed terms built up by means of constants $C_1,\ldots,C_n$.

Proof. Type t' defined as $t_1,\ldots,t_n \rightarrow t$ is regular. Let G' be a regular grammar which produces closed term of type t' (see theorem 1) Grammar G is obtained from G' by following replacement of productions if $y' \Rightarrow T \in G'$ then $y \Rightarrow T(C_1,\ldots,C_n) \in G$ where $y' \in t'$ and $y \in t$.

4. Infinite trees

Infinite trees have been thoroughly studied by Courcelle (see Courcelle(1983)). We adopt several Courcelle results to investigate the properties of some class of Huet matching trees.

Σ-tree over a finite alphabet Σ is understood as a prefix-closed subset of Σ^* (i.e. if $\alpha\beta \in T$ then $\alpha \in T$). If $\alpha \in T$ then T/α denotes a subtree of T issued from node α (i.e. the tree $T' = \{\beta \in \Sigma^* : \alpha\beta \in T\}$). Any prefix-closed subset of T/α is called a subtree of T. The depth of a node α is defined as a number of letters in word α and is denoted by dep(α). The nodes in tree T are ordered in the natural way (i.e. $\alpha \leq \beta$ iff $\exists \gamma \in \Sigma^* : \alpha\gamma = \beta$). The node α is terminal iff there is no β such that $\alpha < \beta$. The language of all terminal elements in T is denoted by L(T). The path $P \subset T$ is a finite or infinite sequence of nodes $(\alpha_0, \alpha_1, \ldots)$ such that $\alpha_0 = \Lambda$ and for every $i > 1$ $\alpha_i = \alpha_{i-1}\beta$ for some $\beta \in \Sigma$. We say that a node $\alpha \in T$ satisfies the condition $\emptyset$ in the tree T iff there is a node $\beta \in T$ such that $dep(\beta) < dep(\alpha)$ and $T/\alpha = T/\beta$. The tree is called regular iff for every infinite path $P \subset T$ there is a node $\alpha \in P$ which satisfies the condition $\emptyset$ in T. This definition is equivalent to Courcelle regular tree definition (see Courcelle(1983) p 126) according to which tree T is regular iff the set $\{T/\alpha : \alpha \in T\}$ is finite. The skeleton of the tree T is understood as a subtree T' of T such that

$$T' = \{\alpha \in T : \forall \beta \in T \text{ if } \beta < \alpha \text{ then } \beta \text{ does not satisfy } \emptyset \text{ in } T\}$$

Several properties of regular tree hold:

Lemma 1

The skeleton of regular tree is finite.

Lemma 2

For every infinite path P of regular tree there exists such a node $\alpha \in P$ that there is a node $\beta \in P$ such that $\beta < \alpha$ and $T/\alpha = T/\beta$.

Lemma 3

For every regular tree T there exists a regular expression R over the alphabet Σ such that R describes language $\mathbf{L}(T)$. Such a regular expression will be denoted by R(T) and can be found as a solution of a system of linear language equations.

5. Unification problems

A finite grammar $\{x_1 \Rightarrow T_1, \ldots, x_n \Rightarrow T_n\}$ we call substitution if every variable $x_1, \ldots, x_n$ is different. By Λ we understand the empty substitution (identity). Let $s = \{x_1 \Rightarrow T_1, \ldots, x_n \Rightarrow T_n\}$ and $s' = \{y_1 \Rightarrow S_1, \ldots, y_k \Rightarrow S_k\}$ be substitutions. By ss' we understand a substitution $\{x_1 \Rightarrow T_1[y_1/S_1, \ldots, y_k/S_k], \ldots, x_n \Rightarrow T_n[y_1/S_1, \ldots, y_k/S_k]\}$. Let X and Y be sets of substitutions. By XY we understand the set $\{ss' : s \in X,\ s' \in Y\}$. We define X^i inductively as $X^0 = \{\Lambda\}$ and $X^{i+1} = XX^i$ and $X^* = \bigcup_{i=0}^{\infty} X^i$. Let T be a term and s be a substitution, by sT we understand the term $T[x_1/T_1, \ldots, x_n/T_n]$. Let T,T' be terms of type t. Unification problem is following: decide if there exists a substitution s such that sT=sT'. Such a substitution s is called a unifier. The unifier s is more general than unifier s' if there is a non-identity substitution s'' so that ss''=s'. Unifier s is most general if for every unifier s', s' is not more general than s. By $[T_1 ; T_2]$ we understand the set of all most general unifiers for the terms T_1 and T_2. We assume that the reader is familiar with the Huet(1975) and Pietrzykowski(1973) papers. The Huet paper contains the description of algorithm which builds the matching tree. The nodes of this tree are unification problems. The arcs are labelled by substitutions. The node $[T_1 ; T_2]$ is connected with node $[S_1 ; S_2]$ by arc labelled by substitution s iff $sT_1 = S_1$ and $sT_2 = S_2$. It means that the unification problem $[T_1 ; T_2]$ can be reduced to the problem $[S_1 ; S_2]$. Problem $[T_1 ; T_2]$ is empty if $T_1 = T_2$ and is marked by (S). The most interesting is the case when matching tree is infinite and includes an infinite number of most general unifiers. We will investigate the skeleton of the matching tree in the case when the number of atomic substitutions labelling the arcs is finite. The construction of the matching tree is given in the Huet(1975) paper. In the present paper I consider such unification problems that the number of elementary substitutions in a potentially infinite tree is finite. Problem $[T_1 ; T_2]$ is regular iff

1° if a variable x occurs free in the term T_1 or T_2 then the type of x is regular (see the definition in section 2)

2° if a constant C occurs in T_1 or T_2 then the type of C is a component of some regular type

For every free variable of the regular type there is a finite grammar generating all closed terms of this type (see theorems 1,2). The names of all the productions in such grammars we call an alphabet. Let Σ be such an finite alphabet. Every word from Σ^* can be interpreted as a substitution. This interpretation is defined in the following way: if "a" is a name of a production α then $I(a)=\alpha$, if $a\in\Sigma$ and $w\in\Sigma^*$ then $I(aw)=I(a)\circ I(w)$ where $\circ$ is a composition of substitutions. In the fixed unification problem we look for such words $w\in\Sigma^*$ that I(w) is a unifier.

Let the problem $[T_1 ; T_2]$ be regular, and Σ be a finite alphabet of productions. For the Huet matching tree H the tree H' is defined as follows: tree H' is obtained from H by cutting of all such nodes which do not belong to any infinite path and all its terminal descendants are marked by F.

$$H'=\{w\in H: w\in P \text{ for some infinite path } P \text{ or there exists } w'\in H \; w\leq w' \text{ and } w' \text{ is marked by } S\}$$

For the matching tree for the regular problem $[T_1 ; T_2]$ there exists the Σ-tree which is defined as follows:

$$T^{(H)}=\{v\in\Sigma^* : \text{the problem } [I(v)T_1 ; I(v)T_2] \text{ is a node of tree } H'\}$$

Lemma 4

Let H be the matching tree for the problem $[T_1 ; T_2]$. If $v\in L(T^{(H)})$ then I(v) is a most general unifier for the problem $[T_1 ; T_2]$.

Proof. If $v\in L(T^{(H)})$ then the problem $[I(v)T_1 ; I(v)T_2]$ is terminal in the matching tree H and is marked by S. Therefore I(v) is a most general unifier.

Example 2

Let us consider the regular unification problem $[g(\lambda x.x) ; B(A)]$ The free variable is g of the type $(0\rightarrow 0)\rightarrow 0$. The constants A and B has the types 0 and $(0\rightarrow 0)$ respectively. The grammar generating all closed terms of the type $(0\rightarrow 0)\rightarrow 0$ is following (see theorem 2)

$g\Longrightarrow \lambda u.A$ [a]

$g\Longrightarrow \lambda u.B(g(u))$ [b]

$g\Longrightarrow \lambda u.u(g(u))$ [c]

The alphabet is $\Sigma=\{a,b,c\}$. The skeleton of the matching tree is following:

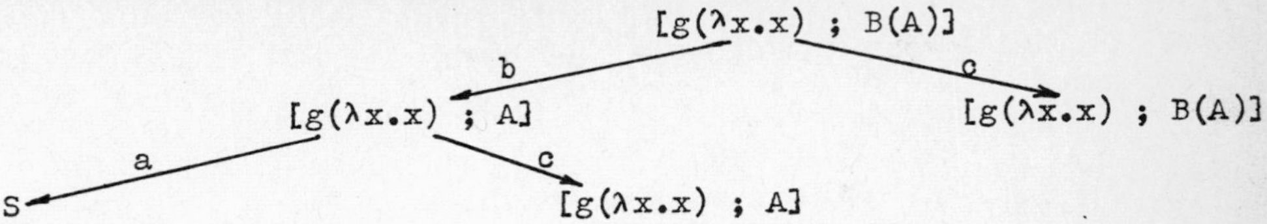

Applying the production c to the main problem we obtain the same problem. The similar situation is with the problem $[g(\lambda x.x) ; A]$ and production c. Let X be a set of words over alphabet Σ which are interpreted as the most general unifiers for the problem $[g(\lambda x.x) ; B(A)]$. Let Y be a set of words for the problem $[g(\lambda x.x) ; A]$. The system of two linear language equations is satisfied: $X=cX \cup bY$, $Y=a \cup cY$. The solutions are $Y=c^*a$, $X=c^*bc^*a$. Interpretation of any word of regular expression X is the most general unifier of the main problem. The word $c^m bc^n a$ is interpreted as the following unifier:

$$g \Rightarrow \lambda u.\underbrace{u(u\ldots u}_{m\text{-times}}(B(\underbrace{u\ldots u}_{n\text{-times}}(A)\ldots)$$

6. Approximation of the set of most general unifiers by the regular expressions

Let H be an infinite matching tree for regular problem $[T_1;T_2]$. $L(T^{(H)})$ is a language consisting of all the words which are interpreted as most general unifiers. We will describe the algorithm for the construction of the regular expression approaches for the language $L(T^{(H)})$. To every $n \in N$ we will assign a regular expression $R(n)$. By $T_n^{(H)}$ we understand the following subtree of $T^{(H)}$.

$$T_n^{(H)}=\{w \in T^{(H)}:\ dep(w) \leq n \text{ and } \exists w' \ T^{(H)} \ dep(w') \leq n \text{ and } w < w' \text{ and } (w' \text{ is terminal in } T^{(H)} \text{ or } w' \text{ satisfies } \emptyset \text{ in } T^{(H)})\}$$

By $T^{(H)}(n)$ we understand the following subtree of the tree $T^{(H)}$.

$$T^{(H)}(n)=\{w \in T^{(H)}:\ \exists w' \in T_n^{(H)} \quad T^{(H)}/w = T^{(H)}/w'$$

Lemma 5

The tree $T^{(H)}(n)$ is regular.

Proof. Let P be an infinite path in the tree $T^{(H)}(n)$. There exists $w \in P$ such that $n < dep(w)$. If $w \in T^{(H)}(n)$ then there exists $w' \in T_n^{(H)}$ such that $T^{(H)}/w = T^{(H)}/w'$ so $dep(w') \leq n$. Then $dep(w') < dep(w)$. Therefore w satisfies the condition $\emptyset$.

The regular expression $R(n)$ is defined as the regular expression which describes the language $L(T^{(H)}(n))$ (see lemma 3)

Lemma 6

For every tree $T^{(H)}$ the following condition is true:

$\forall\, i \in N \quad R(i) \subset R(i+1)$

Proof. It is easy to notice that $T^{(H)}(i)$ is a subtree of $T^{(H)}(i+1)$.

Lemma 7

For every tree $T^{(H)}$ $R(i) \subset L(T^{(H)})$.

Proof. The tree $T^{(H)}(i)$ is a subtree of the tree $T^{(H)}$.

Theorem 3

Let $[T_1 \; ; \; T_2]$ be a regular unification problem. For every most general unifier $s \in [T_1 \; ; \; T_2]$ there is $n \in N$ and a word w such that $w \in R(n)$ and $I(w)=s$.

Proof. From the completeness of the Huet method we know that the unifier s is to be found in the matching tree for the problem $[T_1 \; ; \; T_2]$. From theorems 1 and 2 we know that there exists a finite grammar which generates all terms of such types, which are the types of all the free variables from the problem $[T_1 \; ; \; T_2]$. Let Σ be an alphabet which consists of all the names of productions of this grammar. There is a word $w \in \Sigma^*$ such that $I(w)=s$. The n is a dep(w).

Example 3

Let us consider the unification problem $[f(\lambda u.u(g(u)),A) \; ; \; A]$. The types of the variables f and g are $((0 \rightarrow 0) \rightarrow 0), 0 \rightarrow 0$ and $(0 \rightarrow 0) \rightarrow 0$ respectively. The grammar generating all closed terms of such types is following:

$f \Longrightarrow \lambda kx.x$	[a]
$f \Longrightarrow \lambda kx.k(\lambda y.f(k,x))$	[b]
$f \Longrightarrow \lambda kx.k(\lambda y.f(k,y))$	[c]
$f \Longrightarrow \lambda kx.A$	[d]
$g \Longrightarrow \lambda u.u(g(u))$	[p]
$g \Longrightarrow \lambda u.A$	[r]

Let us mark by P,Q,R the following unification problems:

$P=[f(\lambda u.u(g(u)),A) \; ; \; A]$

$Q=[f(\lambda u.u(g(u)),g(\lambda y.f(\lambda v.v(g(v)),y))) \; ; \; A]$

$R=[g(\lambda y.y) \; ; \; A]$

The matching tree cut at the depth 1 is following:

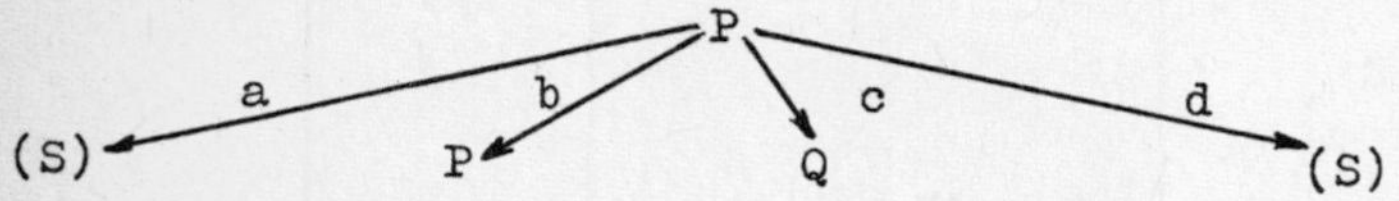

Let $X \subset \Sigma^*$ be defined as $L(T^{(H)}(1))$. Set X describes the matching tree cut at the depth 1 with dropped node Q and arc labelled by c.

The equation is $X=(a\cup d)\cup bX$. Then $X=b^*(a\cup d)$. Therefore $R(1)=b^*(a\cup d)$. The matching tree cut at the depth 2 is obtained by following extension.

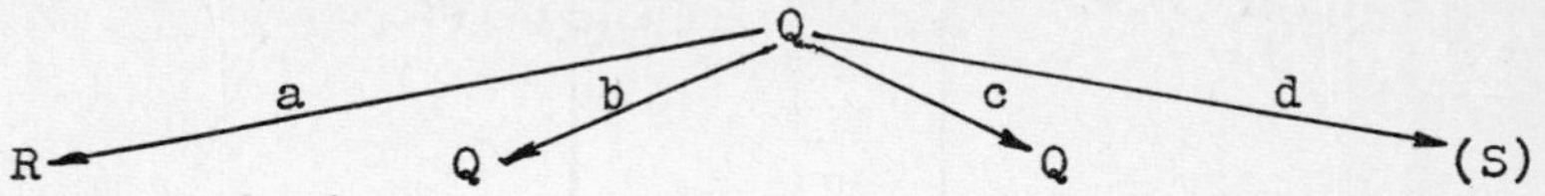

Let $X\subset\Sigma^*$ is defined as $L(T^{(H)}(2))$, and Y is $L(T^{(H)}(2)/c)$. Y describe the tree issued from node Q cut at the depth 2 with dropped node R and arc labelled by a. The equations are following $X=(a\cup d)\cup bX\cup cY$, $Y=d\cup(b\cup c)Y$. Then $Y=(b\cup c)^*d$, $X=b^*(a\cup d\cup c(b\cup c)^*d)$. Therefore $R(2)=R(1)\cup b^*c(b\cup c)^*d$. The matching tree cut at the depth 3 is obtained by following extension.

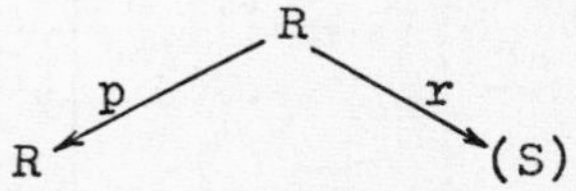

Let X is defined as $L(T^{(H)}(3))$ and Y is $L(T^{(H)}(3)/c)$ and Z is $L(T^{(H)}(3)/ca)$. Z describe the tree issued from the node R. The equations are following $X=(a\cup d)\cup bX\cup cY$, $Y=d\cup(b\cup c)Y\cup aZ$, $Z=r\cup pZ$. Then $Z=p^*r$, $Y=(b\cup c)^*(d\cup ap^*r)$, $X=b^*((a\cup d)\cup c(b\cup c)^*(d\cup ap^*r))$. Therefore $R(3)=R(2)\cup b^*c(b\cup c)^*ap^*r$. The tree $T^{(H)}$ is regular and $T^{(H)}=T^{(H)}(3)$. We find the sets of substitutions as an interpretation of the regular expressions. Regular expression R(1) is interpreted as the set of unifiers which are of the form:

$f\Longrightarrow \lambda kx_0.k(\lambda x_1.k\ldots k(\lambda x_n.x_0)\ldots)$ for the component b^*a
$f\Longrightarrow \lambda kx_0.k(\lambda x_1.k\ldots k(\lambda x_n.A)\ldots)$ for the component b^*d

Regular expression $R(2)=R(1)\cup b^*c(b\cup c)^*d$. The additional segment $b^*c(b\cup c)^*d$ is interpreted as the following set of unifiers:

$$f\Longrightarrow \lambda kx_0.k(\lambda x_1.k\ldots k(\lambda x_n.A)\ldots)$$

This set is identical with interpretation of the expression b^*d. In my paper Zaionc(1984) I have proved the theorem about ambiguity of the regular grammars. The regular expression $R(3) = R(2)\cup b^*c(b\cup c)^*ap^*r$. The additional segment $b^*c(b\cup c)^*ap^*r$ is interpreted as the set of unifiers which are of the form:

$$f\Longrightarrow \lambda kx_0.k(\lambda x_1.k\ldots k(\lambda x_n.x_i)\ldots)$$
$$g\Longrightarrow \lambda u.u(u(\ldots u(A)\ldots)$$

for $i\leq n$.

References

Courcelle, B.(1983). Fundamental properties of infinite trees. Theoretical Computer Science 25, 95-169.

Goldfarb,W.(1981). The undecidability of the second-order unification problem. Theoretical Computer Science 13, 225-230.

Friedman,H.(1975). Equality between functions. Lecture Notes in Mathematics vol. 453, 22-37.

Huet,G.(1973). The undecidability of unification in third order logic. Information and Control 22(3), 257-267.

Huet,G.(1975). A unification algorithm for typed λ-calculus. Theoretical Computer Science 1, 27-58.

Pietrzykowski,T.(1973). A complete mechanization of second-order type theory. Journal of the ACM 20(2), 333-365.

Zaionc,M.(1984). Gramatyki termów w λ-rachunku z typami. Ph.D Thesis Computer Science Department, University of Warsaw (in Polish).

Equational Systems for Category Theory and Intuitionistic Logic

Gérard Huet

INRIA
BP 105
78150 LE-CHESNAY
FRANCE

This paper did not arrive in time.